the STYLE SOURCEBOOK

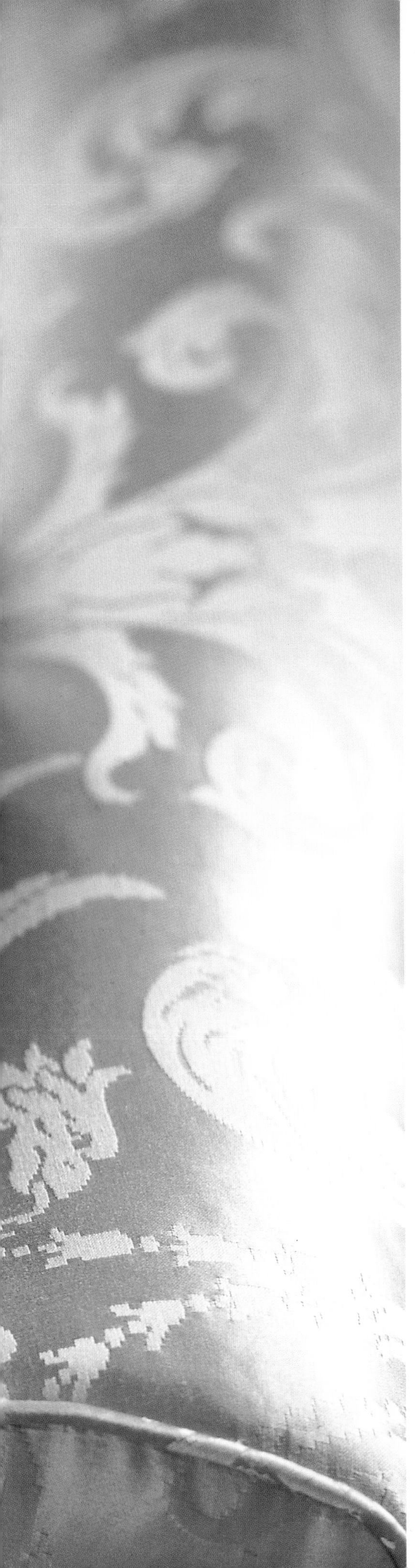

the STYLE SOURCEBOOK

JUDITH MILLER

STEWART, TABORI & CHANG
NEW YORK

Published in 1998 and distributed in the U.S. by
Stewart, Tabori & Chang,
a division of U.S. Media Holdings, Inc.
115 West 18th Street, New York, NY 10011

Chief Contributor John Wainwright
Contributors Chris Blanchett, Penny McGuire, Olga Moyle
Consultants Jill Draper, David Gunton, Tessa Smith-Agassi, Michael Szell, Christine Woods
Senior Editor Penelope Cream
Senior Art Editor Emma Boys
Editor Julia North
American Editors Arlene Sobel, Melanie Falick
Designer Kenny Grant
Editorial Assistants Patrick Evans, Anna Nicholas
Design Assistant Estelle Bayllis
Production Controllers Rachel Staveley, Kate Thomas
Picture Researchers Sally Claxton, Lois Charlton
Executive Editor Judith More
Executive Art Editor Janis Utton
Special Photography Steve Tanner
Special Location Photography James Merrell

First published in Great Britain in 1998 by
Mitchell Beazley, an imprint of Reed Consumer Books Limited,
Michelin House, 81 Fulham Road, London SW3 6RB
also Auckland and Melbourne, Australia

Distributed in Canada by
General Publishing Company Ltd.
30 Lesmill Road
Don Mills, Ontario, M3B 2T6, Canada

Distributed in all territories except for the UK, British Commonwealth, and Japan by
Grantham Book Services Ltd.
Isaac Newton Way, Alma Park Industrial Estate
Grantham, Lincolnshire, NG31 9SD, England

Library of Congress Cataloging-In-Publication Data

Miller, Judith
The style sourcebook : the definitive illustrated directory of fabrics, paints, wallpapers, tiles, flooring / Judith Miller
p. cm.
Includes index.
ISBN 1-55670-631-6
1. Decoration and ornament—United States—Directories. 2. Decoration and ornament—Information services—United States—Directories. I. Title.

NK1705.M56. 1998
745.4'029'473—dc21 97-41166
CIP

Printed by Toppan Printing Co. Ltd. in China
10 9 8 7 6 5 4 3 2 1

Contents

Foreword 6

Using *The Style Sourcebook* 8

Style Guide **10**
- Medieval to pre-16th century 12
- 16th & 17th centuries 14
- Early 18th century 18
- Late 18th century 22
- Early 19th century 28
- Mid-19th century 36
- Late 19th century 42
- Early 20th century 48
- Late 20th century 52

Fabrics **56**
- Plains 58
- Patterned Pile 66
- Damask & Brocade 72
- Tapestry 82
- Motifs 88
- Florals 106
- Pictorials 124
- Overall Pattern 142
- Geometrics 156
- Lace & Sheers 174
- Braids & Trimmings 184

Wallpapers **196**
- Plains 198
- Motifs 206
- Florals 222
- Pictorials 238
- Overall Pattern 250
- Geometrics 264

Paints & Finishes **278**
- Paints 280
- Specialist Paints & Waxes 290
- Wood Finishes 294

Tiles **298**
- Plains 300
- Motifs 306
- Florals 316
- Pictorials 326
- Overall Pattern 334
- Geometrics 340

Flooring **348**
- Wooden Flooring 350
- Matting 358
- Carpets 362
- Sheet Flooring 376

Glossary 385

Directory 388

Index 396

Acknowledgments 402

Foreword

Since the end of the Second World War, there has been an enormous growth of interest in interior decoration. The restoration and opening up of many historically important houses has introduced a wider public to the finest examples of the art. Indeed, what in previous centuries was largely the preserve of a wealthy minority has probably become the one art form practiced by almost everyone. Fueling this has been the publication of books and magazines, and, more recently, television programs illustrating both historical and contemporary interiors, and, above all, demonstrating the tremendous decorative potential of all of our homes.

Fortunately, exploiting this potential has become much easier and more affordable as designers and manufacturers have responded to our enthusiasm by producing the essential decorative media in ever more extensive ranges of historical and contemporary patterns and colors. Having spent much of the last 20 years combining writing books and presenting television programs on interior decoration with the practicalities of restoring and redecorating houses, I have come to appreciate fully the considerable diversity of fabrics, wallpapers, paints, tiles, and floor coverings that are now available. What I have found lacking, however, is a comprehensive guide that locates particular materials, motifs, patterns, and colors within specific historical periods. This is an omission I believe we have remedied with the publication of *The Style Sourcebook*, which encompasses–through myriad samples–fashionable decorations from the Middle Ages to the present day. I believe that you will find this book informative, inspirational, user-friendly, and, above all, an invaluable guide when choosing decorative schemes for your period or modern home, regardless of whether your personal preferences are historical or contemporary.

Judith Miller

Using *The Style Sourcebook*

KEY TO SYMBOLS

Application and usage symbols complete the caption information for each sample. Different types of material may feature different symbols, for example, certain usages would apply to tiles but not to wallpapers. Usages and applications are only recommendations –feel free to experiment: fabrics, for example, could be used in a variety of situations and locations.

- T Only available through the trade
- Suitable for windows
- Suitable for bedcovers
- LC Suitable for loose (slip)covers
- Suitable for upholstery
- W Suitable for walls
- C Suitable for ceilings
- F Suitable for floors
- Suitable for woodwork
- Suitable for stonework
- Suitable for metalwork
- Suitable for plasterwork
- S Suitable for plastic
- Suitable for glass
- Suitable for work surfaces
- Suitable for exterior use
- Special application
- Special treatment required
- Stain resistant
- Antislip
- Hand-blocked or hand-printed
- Available in other sizes

Over two thousand samples, from the widest range of international designs, provide inspiration for selecting the ingredients for any interior scheme, from medieval to modern. The Style Guide presents a historical overview of interior design and major stylistic developments, while the chapters that follow contain hundreds of samples of every style, color, and pattern, divided into the main design types, such as florals, geometrics, and motifs. Each design type or material is further categorized by period, ranging from medieval to late 20th century, allowing you to select your favorite designs and colors, item by item and era by era.

Useful Features

Various easy-to-use design features on every page make the information in *The Style Sourcebook* highly accessible. Color-coded bands, each indicating a particular century, are on the edge of every page to allow you to turn instantly to a specific era. The same color is used in the border of the special feature boxes, linking them to their most relevant period.

Each sample is accompanied by a detailed caption listing all the information needed for ordering, such as name, code number (if applicable), and the color shown. Sizes, repeat, and composition are also indicated, together with any relevant symbols for usage, special applications, and other information (*see* Key to Symbols, left).

Further Information

The samples in the book have been obtained from a wide variety of international manufacturers and suppliers, whose details are listed in the Directory of Suppliers (*see* page 388). The Glossary provides further information about the technical, artistic, and historical terms mentioned the book.

STYLE AND DATE HEADING
Every spread of samples is identified by the type of design and the date of the decorative style. A detailed introduction provides an overview of the era.

DESIGN OVERVIEW
Each design type is discussed with reference to its specific use in interior decoration, and is illustrated with color examples of room settings and furniture.

KEY DESIGNS
The most significant designs are highlighted and their historical, cultural, and artistic importance is discussed.

COLOR BANDS
Easily identifiable color bands represent the different historical periods, allowing designs of a particular era to be found quickly across all chapters.

CAPTIONS
Every sample illustrated has a detailed caption that provides all the information necessary for ordering the featured design and color required.

SCALE BAR
A scale bar beneath the sample indicates the size at which it is reproduced. The largest samples are actual size, while the smallest are at 25 percent of their full size.

BOX FEATURE
Important historical or technical topics are discussed in detail in a separate box. The box is color coded according to the appropriate corresponding date.

The Samples

FABRICS

Jack Lenor Larsen/Solace 8590/93
Color **coral** Alternative colors **available**
Composition **52% viscose, 48% polyester**
Width **51in/130cm** Repeat **13in/33cm**
Price ★★★★★

Price Guide	per yard/meter
$1.00-34.00	★
$35.00-84.00	★★
$85.00-169.00	★★★
$170.00–224.00	★★★★
$225.00+	★★★★★

The samples shown in the Fabrics section (*see* pages 56-195) are categorized by design or pattern type and historical period. The composition of each fabric is shown by fiber type and expressed in terms of percentages.

The price of each fabric is given by the yard/meter; this may vary slightly depending on where and when it is bought. Suggested uses and any special features are indicated at the end of each caption.

Also included in the Fabrics section are the Braids & Trimmings pages. Described here are the different types of braids, ribbons, fringes, and tassels.

TILES

Original Style/Rose & Trellis 6970A Color **multi** Alternative colors **not available**
Composition **ceramic** Size **6 x 6 x ¼in/ 15 x 15cm x 7mm** Price ★ [W]

Price Guide	per tile/set
$1.00-9.00	★
$10.00–19.00	★★
$20.00–34.00	★★★
$35.00–59.00	★★★★
$60.00+	★★★★★

The measurements given for the samples in the Tiles section (*see* pages 298-347) = the longest side x the shortest side(s) x the thickness. This is not an indication of which way up a tile should be used–some tile designs can be placed horizontally, vertically, or even diagonally.

Prices are given for each tile, or, where the design consists of a number of tiles, for the price of the total set or panel. The tiles are shown without scale bars, and each tile is shown in its entirety. Some tiles are available in a variety of sizes and this is indicated by the symbol ⊞.

WALLPAPERS

Bradbury & Bradbury/Glasgow Panel
Color **natural** Alternative colors **available**
Width **27in/68.5cm** Length **2½yd/2m**
Repeat **–** Price ★

Price Guide	per yard/meter
$1.00-9.00	★
$10.00–19.00	★★
$20.00–34.00	★★★
$35.00–59.00	★★★★
$60.00+	★★★★★

The Wallpapers section (*see* pages 196-277) is divided by design type and then by historical period. Full-size wallpapers as well as borders and friezes are illustrated, and the latter can be combined with plainer designs.

Prices for wallpapers are shown by the yard/meter, and the symbol ♣ indicates those that are hand-blocked or hand-printed–these are generally more expensive than the machine-printed designs.

Certain wallpapers need painting or finishing after hanging, and this requirement is also indicated by the relevant caption symbol.

FLOORING

Fired Earth/Rousham Diagonal RDN
Color **natural** Alternative colors **not available** Composition **100% inland grass** Width **4½yd/4m** Repeat **–**
Price ★ ⊞

Price Guide	per square yard/meter
$1.00-34.00	★
$35.00-84.00	★★
$85.00-169.00	★★★
$170.00–224.00	★★★★
$225.00+	★★★★★

The Flooring section (see pages 348-383) is divided first into the type of flooring material–wood, matting, carpet, and sheet flooring–and then into different historical periods. Certain types of flooring were available earlier than others, and this is reflected in the era divisions.

Prices in this section are given per square yard/meter (except in the case of some of the borders, which are sold by the linear yard/meter, so check with the supplier before ordering). Inlaid wooden flooring is often made up on commission to fit the area required, so is priced according to space and type.

PAINTS & FINISHES

Liberon Waxes Color **gilt cream chantilly**
Composition and finish *spirit-based:* **satin sheen** Price ★★★★

Price Guide	per gallon/liter
$1.00-9.00	★
$10.00–19.00	★★
$20.00–49.00	★★★
$50.00+	★★★★

The divisions within the Paints & Finishes section (*see* pages 278-297) concentrate on the application material, such as regular paints, specialist paints, and wood finishes, which is then categorized by date where applicable.

Prices for the samples in this section are per gallon/liter; however, certain finishes are only needed in tiny amounts (such as gilt waxes) and so may be supplied in smaller quantities.

The composition and finish of each paint is given; many colors are available in a variety of finishes, each suitable for a different use.

USING THE SCALE BAR

Most of the samples in the book, apart from those such as tiles and paints that may vary in size or are not measured by area, have a scale bar beneath them. This scale bar has four divisions that are shaded according to the relative size of the sample shown, in proportion to its actual size.

A single shaded division indicates that the sample is illustrated at a quarter (or 25 percent) of its full size; two shaded divisions mean that the sample is at half (or 50 percent) its actual size; three shaded divisions indicate that the sample is at three-quarters of its actual size (or 75 percent), while a completely shaded bar means that the sample is shown at actual size (100 percent).

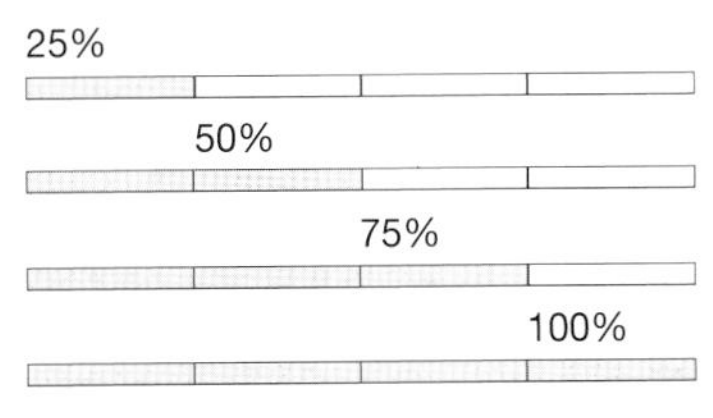

Style Guide

Medieval to pre-16th Century

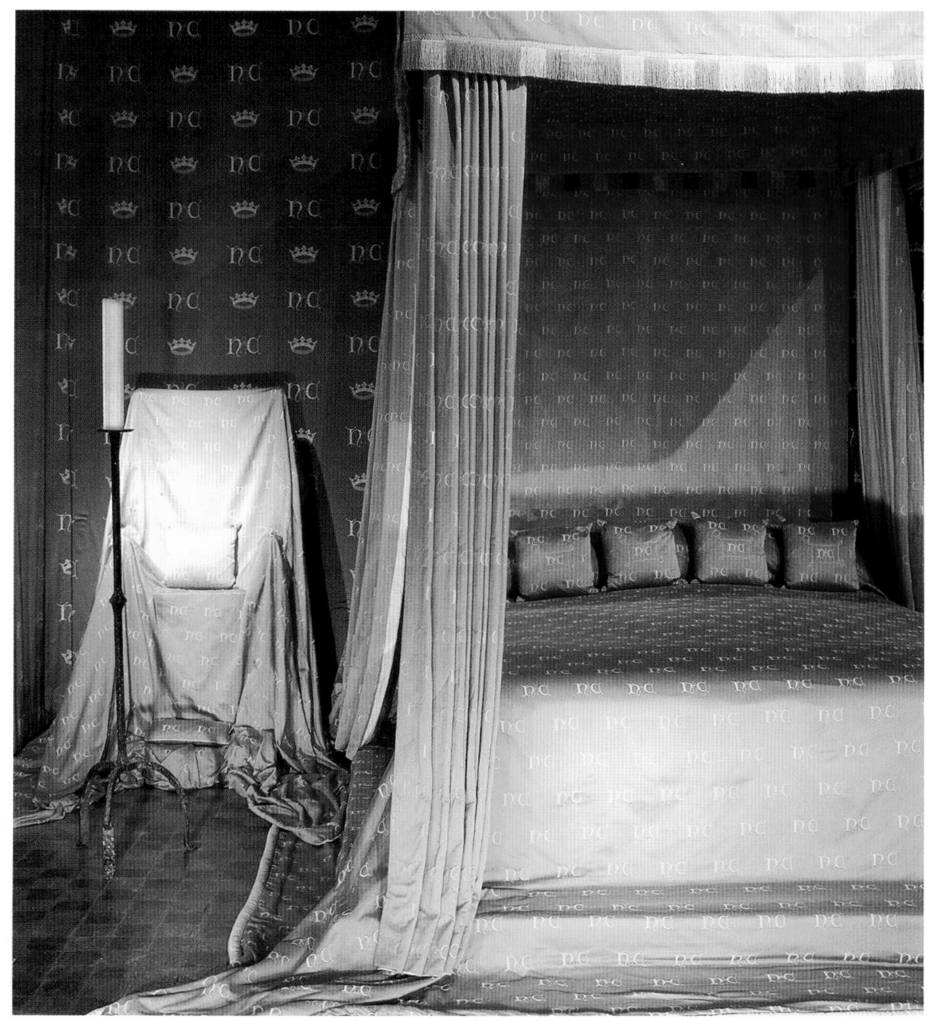

ABOVE & RIGHT Monogrammed silk bed- and wall-hangings, and a matching handwoven rug and chair throw, furnish this medieval-style bedroom at Leeds Castle in Kent, England. Before the 18th century, monograms were the preserve of the aristocracy, and were used to denote ownership or patronage. The colors used here are typical of grand Medieval and early Renaissance interiors.

LEFT Limewashed walls and monogrammed silk hangings provide the background for a military-style, sheer-draped tented bathtub at Leeds Castle. The woven rush matting provides a near-authentic substitute for the loose rushes that were often laid over wooden floorboards before the 17th century.

During the Middle Ages, interior decoration was the preserve of the seignorial classes. They alone had the money and time to devote to this domestic endeavor. What is now described as Medieval style was confined to their stone-built or timbered castles and manor houses.

Medieval interiors were sparsely furnished, so the architectural shell played a major role in the decorative scheme. The first and lower floors had brick, flagstone, or tiled flooring, and the upper floors had oak or elm floorboards. Ceilings were often coffered, and the stone walls left exposed or covered with coarse plaster–the latter was lime-washed and often painted with stenciled motifs. The wooden studs and braces of timbered walls were exposed and the wattle-and-daub panels in between were limewashed and sometimes stenciled. Battened plank doors were set under arches as were most mullion windows.

Furniture was mostly oak, elm, or chestnut. Tables were wooden boards supported on trestles; seating largely consisted of benches and stools; and beds were simple pallets or canopied four-posters. Soft furnishings included silk, woolen, and tapestry bed- and wall-hangings, embroidered quilts, floor cushions, and rush and straw matting floor coverings, and, in the grandest households, Oriental carpets that were used as table coverings.

Throughout the Middle Ages, the decorative motifs that adorned furniture, woodwork, tiles, and textiles were derived from three vocabularies of ornament: Romanesque, Gothic, and Heraldic. The Romanesque combined Classical Roman, Oriental, pagan, and Christian motifs, and included chevrons, foliage, people, and beasts. Gothic ornament included architectural elements such as lancets, foils, and tracery, as well as flora and fauna and human figures. Heraldic decoration consisted of motifs and emblems such as cyphers, the "Tree of Life," and human and animal figures.

16th & 17th Centuries

The increasing prosperity beyond the nobility to the rapidly expanding merchant classes of Europe and the newly established American colonies in the 16th and 17th centuries was reflected in an ever-increasing emphasis on domestic comfort. Stylistically, the most significant development was the widespread adoption of classical (mainly Roman) forms of ornament. Originating in Renaissance Italy, the Classical style was often loosely interpreted in Europe (and later America) via engraved treatises and pattern books. Classical ornament was sometimes combined with Medieval–especially Gothic and Heraldic–types during the 16th century, but it virtually supplanted them in the elaborate Baroque interiors of the 17th century. Oriental styles of decoration became popular in the late 17th century as the trading links with China and India strengthened.

Architecturally, the 16th century saw the incorporation of geometrically patterned marble and elaborate marquetry and parquetry flooring on the first floor of grander houses, but bricks, tiles, flagstones, and wooden floorboards were still in widespread use. In most houses, ceilings still consisted of exposed beams and joists, filled in with limewashed plaster panels. Limewashed and coarse-plastered stone walls were still much in evidence, as was exposed studwork in timbered houses. However, there was a much greater use of wainscoting throughout the period, either full height or to frieze or dado level. Carved or applied decoration was highly fashionable, with linenfold patterns, arabesques, strapwork, and roundels being especially favored. Paneling made from hardwoods was invariably untreated, stained, or limed; softwood paneling (particularly prevalent in America) was either flat-painted, or, especially in the 17th century, grained in imitation of expensive hardwoods.

ABOVE The hangings and draperies on this 16th-century bed at Parham House in Sussex, England, include flame stitch-patterned drapes (ca. 1615) on the posts, and an embroidered coverlet, back panel, canopy, and valance hand-stitched (ca. 1585) by Mary, Queen of Scots.

RIGHT This wall at St Mary's in Sussex, England, features wood-grained, *trompe l'oeil* arcading, executed by a Flemish painter-stainer for the visit of Queen Elizabeth I of England in 1585.

FAR RIGHT Set against limed oak doors and paneling, the 17th-century furniture at Parham House includes an armchair upholstered with Flemish needlework. The pictorial covering features designs typical of the period.

ELIZABETH OF FRANCE

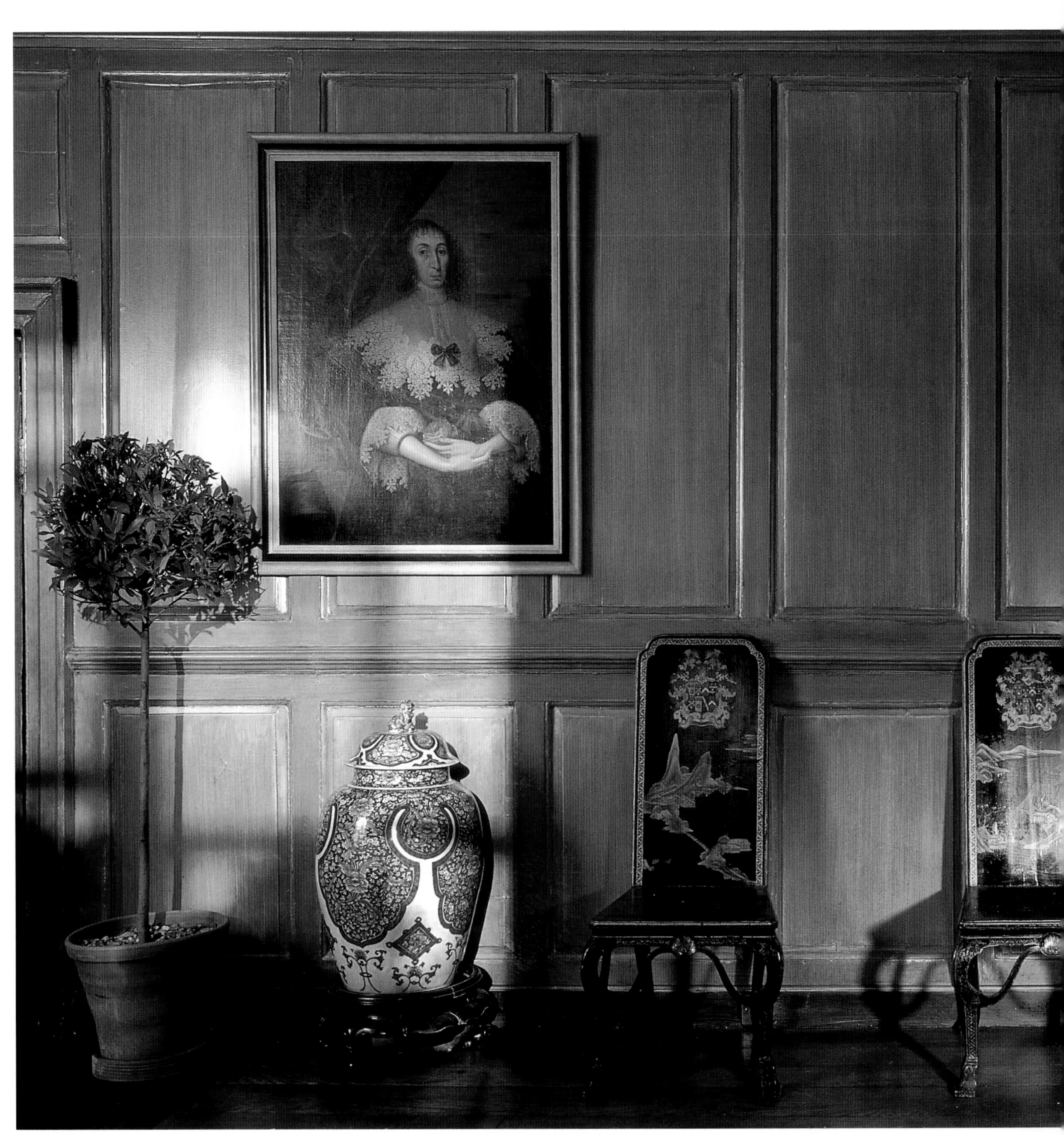

By the late 16th century transomed windows had become as common as medieval mullions, with diagonally arranged quarries being superseded during the 17th century by larger, rectangular panes.

The most significant development in furniture design was the introduction of upholstery, mostly in the form of back stools and armchairs covered in turkeywork, leather, velvet, or tapestry. Such fabrics, together with elaborate crewelwork, damasks, lace, and, in the late 17th century, imported chintzes, were also in widespread use as bed- and wall-hangings. Although rush matting was the main form of floor covering, Oriental carpets began to appear on floors in the late 17th century, having previously been confined to table coverings.

ABOVE Upholstered seating first appeared in Europe in the 1620s. The favored fabrics of the period included leather, velvet, and, as here, flame stitch-patterned tapestry.

LEFT Pale burgundy-painted wall-paneling and stained and polished wooden floor-boards provide the foil for the gilt and ebony framed portraits, *chinoiserie* lacquered chairs, and Chinese vases that are shown here.

Early 18th Century

ABOVE Pale colors, such as straw and pearl gray, were popular in the first half of the 18th century. In this New York apartment they provide an understated background for a symmetrical display of botanical watercolors and Queen Anne walnut furniture.

LEFT Rococo elements in this early 18th-century English interior include silk *chinoiserie* upholstery, a swagged nut garland, scallop-shell candle shields, and classical carvings on the furniture and woodwork.

Two very distinct styles of architecture and decoration dominated the first half of the 18th century. The first, Palladianism, was derived from the writings and engravings of the 16th-century Italian architect Andrea Palladio, and was especially popular in Britain, and, from the 1740s, in America. Classical Roman in origin, the style in its purest form was characterized by bold, austere, and, in the grandest houses, large architectural elements, such as Venetian windows. It was also notable for its harmony of proportion and detail. Floorboards were bare wood, augmented with sisal matting or Oriental or turkeywork carpets, and ceilings were plain-plastered or compartmentalized with plaster moldings. Walls were either fully paneled and flat-painted (often in gray and green), or wood-grained, or plastered, with the latter covered either in silk hangings or hand-painted wallpaper, providing the background for paintings, prints, or engravings. Furniture, much of it solid or veneered walnut, was generally sparse. Typical pieces included bureau-bookcases, tripod tables, upholstered armchairs, and occasional and dining chairs. The seating was often upholstered in a fabric that coordinated with the window treatment.

In continental Europe, the austerity of Palladian Classicism was superseded in the 1720s by the second distinctive style, Rococo, a lighter, exotic, even frivolous style that first appeared in informal buildings such as tea pavilions. It was characterized by the use of *rocaille*, *chinoiserie*, *singeries*, and Turkish and Indian figures, combined with flowers and foliage, and with light scrollwork and diaper patterns. In England, Rococo, which extended to architectural fixtures and fittings, furniture, fabrics, and wallpapers, was combined with Gothick style, a romanticized revival of certain elements of Gothic style, such as ogee arches and quatrefoils. However, neither pure Rococo, nor Rococo-Gothick, made an impact in America.

ABOVE The window and bed draperies in a bedroom at the Château de Morsan in France are embellished with patterns and motifs inspired by Indian styles of ornament. The walls are hand-painted with delftware-style designs.

RIGHT This painted Rococo settee with its ornate *rocaille*- and scrolled-leaf carvings has a buttoned velvet squab and is flanked by pairs of topiary sentinels and Kang Hsi vases. The classical window treatment is typical of early to mid-18th-century reception rooms, and incorporates swagged pull-up sheers, pleated and tied-back yellow silk drapes, and a swagged-and-tailed pelmet embellished with bullion fringing, tassels, and fabric rosettes. The plain paneled walls are painted a light yellow, a fashionable color of this era.

Late 18th Century

ABOVE The most striking feature of this late 18th-century-style New York apartment is the brightly colored wallpaper. Exotic blooms, birds, and insects characterize *chinoiserie* papers of this period.

LEFT Classical Roman motifs embellish the gilded architectural fixtures and fittings and furniture in the French Empire-style faux marble-walled Grand Salon at the Château de Compiègne.

RIGHT The bare pine floorboards, gray-white walls divided with cobalt blue stripes, furniture, and striped bed- and window-hangings, epitomize late 18th-century Swedish style.

While *chinoiserie* and Gothick remained much in evidence during the second half of the 18th century, especially in Britain, the predominant style of ornament and decoration during this period was Neoclassicism. It emerged in Europe in the 1750s as a reaction to the flamboyant and often frivolous Rococo style, and reached America in the 1780s. In many respects it can be seen as a natural development of early 18th-century Palladianism. Like Palladian style, Neoclassicism drew inspiration from Classical Roman architecture, but unlike Palladianism it also encompassed Ancient Greek ornament. Neoclassicism was based on direct observations of Roman and Greek architecture and ornament, made possible by a series of archaeological excavations, notably in Rome, Pompeii, and Herculaneum, and the subsequent publication of the illustrated accounts and pattern books of influential architects and designers, such as Robert and James Adam, who visited these sites.

Neoclassical interiors were characterized by an elegance and lightness of style, and a general preference for linear decoration, in marked contrast to the heavier, sculptural qualities of Palladian interiors. For example, plain butt-jointed wooden floorboards, which had been in widespread use in the upper stories of houses for centuries, were now used at first floor level. When made from finely figured hardwoods, they were often stained and polished and left uncovered; when made of softwoods (such as pine or fir) they were invariably covered with pile carpet which, in the grandest of houses, came from the factories at Savonnerie or Aubusson in France, or Wilton in England. Ceilings were usually plain-painted plaster, augmented with simple cornice moldings. However, the grandest featured Neoclassical motifs on painted and gilded plaster panels. Most walls were divided by a dado rail, and either flat-painted or covered with intricately

The Great Eighteenth-Century Exhibition
LOVERS
THE EIGHTEE

ENTURY

patterned papers also displaying Neoclassical imagery. Engravings or prints, as well as traditional gilt-framed portrait and landscape paintings, were hung on the walls.

The lightness and delicacy of ornament that characterized Neoclassicism was mirrored in the furniture of the period–the leading designers of which were Sheraton and Hepplewhite in Britain. The most fashionable pieces were veneered in satinwood and the most decorative were embellished with painted swags of flowers, ornamental bows, and cupids and other mythological or pastoral scenes set in panels. Pieces were usually made from solid or veneered mahogany.

The influence of Neoclassicism also spread to 18th-century soft furnishings. Swagged-and-tailed drapes were a common window treatment, while Neoclassical motifs and patterns were featured on both window- and bed-hangings, and on upholstered furniture whenever plain fabrics were not used. However, the most striking characteristic of the soft furnishings of the period was the eschewing of lavish, heavy fabrics, such as tapestries and woolen velvets, in favor of lightweight silks, printed cottons, and sheers.

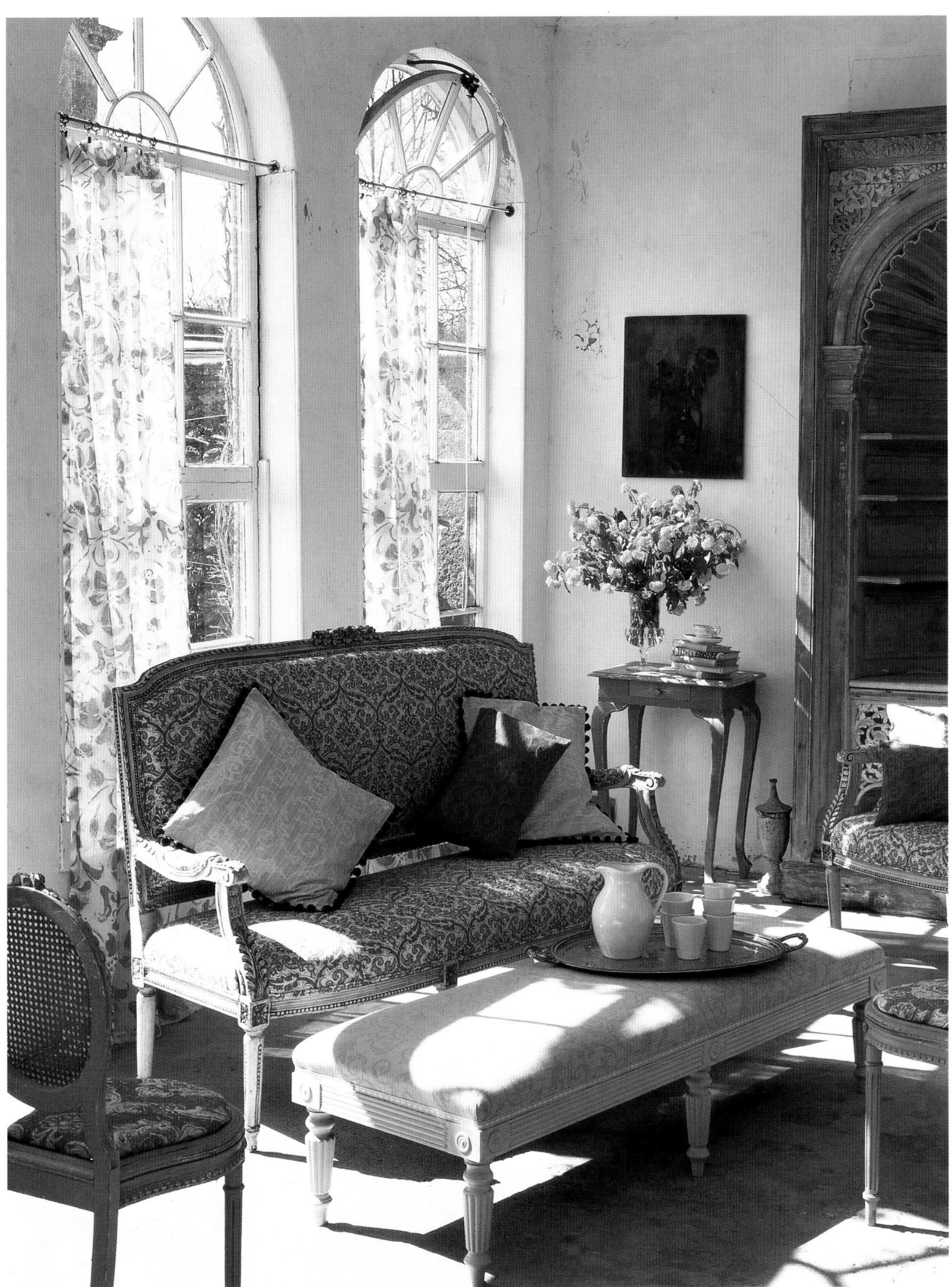

FAR LEFT Floral-patterned tiles were often used in late 18th-century chimney-pieces, and usually either matched or echoed the floral designs found on upholstery and textile hangings.

CENTER LEFT Chinese and European styles of ornament are reproduced in the upholstery and wallpaper in this reconstruction of a late 18th-century French interior. Flowers, birds, and animals, set against a vivid yellow background, were highly fashionable at this time.

LEFT The curtains and upholstery fabrics in this late 18th-century drawing room are embellished with plant-form imagery typical of the period. While the top covers on the painted and gilded chairs and settee show intricate and stylized floral and vegetal patterns, the curtains display naturalistic floral forms that were fashionable from the late 1760s onwards.

PREVIOUS PAGES This late 18th-century Rococo-style French bedroom has been reconstructed in a New York apartment. The pale green walls and ceiling provide a complementary background for a display of engraved fashion plates (published during the reign of Louis XVI of France) and embroidered silk panels. The tasseled draperies on the *lit à la polonaise* (a Polish-style bed named after Louis IV of France's queen who was Polish) are striped and floral Belgian cotton, taken from a documentary design, and are color coordinated with the walls and the floral-patterned table covering.

Early 19th Century

ABOVE Striped fabrics, often embellished with trailing flowers or floral repeats, were the height of fashion in Neoclassical American, English, and, as here, French interiors during the early 19th century.

RIGHT & LEFT These two early 19th-century interiors at the Jumel Mansion in New York are decorated and furnished in Empire style. Both feature Neoclassical wallpapers, applied to make a tripartite division of the walls. The daybed and *lit-en-bateau* (a boatlike bed) are both decorated with Classical and Egyptian motifs.

During the early 19th century, interior decoration was still essentially Neoclassical. However, the predominant styles of the period–Empire and Regency–contrasted with the often intricate detailing of late 18th-century Neoclassicism in their employment of purer, simpler classical forms. They drew inspiration from not only Ancient Roman and Greek ornament, but also, in celebration of Napoleon's conquests, ancient Egyptian and contemporary military motifs.

Empire style originated in France during the late 1790s in the post-Revolutionary restorations of French palaces. The basic architectural style of these palaces was Classical, and mostly derived from Imperial Roman examples rather than Greek. Typical motifs applied to architectural fixtures and fittings, furniture, and drapery included laurel wreaths, medallions, and imperial eagles, as well as birds and animals such as swans and lions.

At the beginning of the 19th century, Empire style swept across most of Europe, followed by America. From ca. 1820, regional variations of note included the gradual transformation of American Empire style into Greek Revival, in which motifs and imagery of Roman origin were supplanted by those of Greek derivation; English Regency style, which had much in common with French Empire style, but drew more heavily on Greek ornament; and Biedermeier, a simpler, more functional version of French Empire style that became fashionable in Austria and Germany.

Key elements of these early 19th-century Neoclassical styles included an increased use of wall-to-wall cut-pile or Brussels-weave carpets. In most houses, ceilings were generally lower than before, and made of plain plaster, and embellished with a central medallion or garland from which hung a chandelier. In larger houses, walls were often divided into frieze, field, and dado; in smaller ones the frieze was often omitted in favor of a simple cornice.

Fashionable wall coverings included flat paint, textiles, and wallpapers (mainly pictorial). Swagged-and-tailed or festooned draperies were also popular, and were usually tied back to flank embroidered lace under-curtains or plain silk shades. Favored fabrics for draperies included lightweight silks and floral-patterned chintzes, while damasks and reps proved popular for upholstered seating. Painted faux finishes–marbles, porphyries, bronzes, and wood grains–were also much in evidence.

Neoclassical furniture was mainly made from mahogany, maple, and rosewood. Popular table styles included sofa, Pembroke, Loo, and combined work-and-games tables; bowfronted sideboards and *chiffoniers*; saber-leg chairs; and *lits-en-bateau* and chaises longues. A new development was the groupings of chairs and tables in reception rooms to facilitate conversation.

ABOVE Redecorated in its original color scheme of mauve and yellow, this bedroom in an early 19th-century New York mansion on the Hudson River features a Federal four-poster bed with a tented-and-swagged silk canopy.

RIGHT A collection of Duncan Phyfe furniture stands on a handwoven, wall-to-wall Savonnerie carpet. The Neoclassical furnishings are enhanced by faux marble paneling on the walls.

PREVIOUS PAGES This Welsh interior features a velvet-upholstered chaise longue and a priceless French Aubusson carpet.

FOLLOWING PAGES Vivid yellow walls, drapes, and upholstery provide a strong color contrast to mahogany and ebony furniture in this early 19th-century American reception room.

EAST

Mid-19th Century

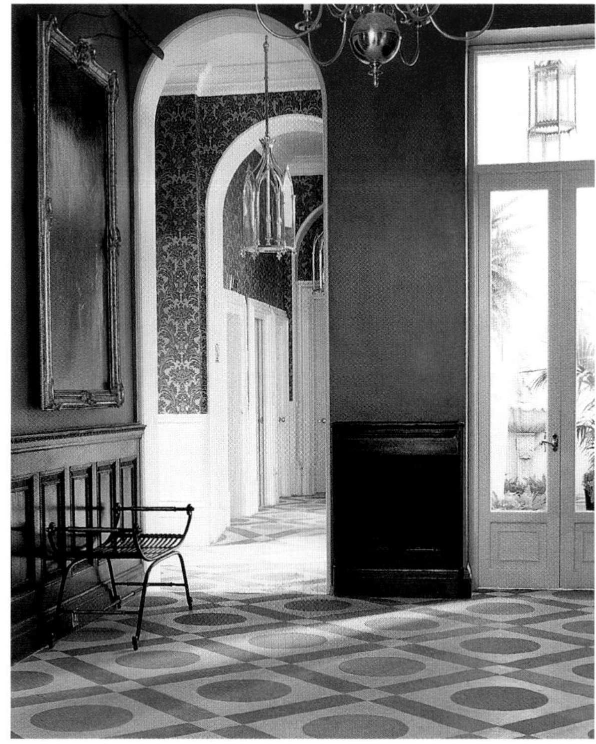

ABOVE The smoking room at Cedar Grove, a mid-19th-century American mansion, features a pair of deep red, gold-fringed velvet drapes with elaborate swagged-and-tailed valances. The carpet is also red and gold–a popular color combination in mid-Victorian interiors.

LEFT Eclectic groupings of red-and-yellow damask and striped plush upholstered chairs were often found in mid- and late Victorian interiors. However, the dominant feature of this English Gothic Revival room is the magnificent chimney-piece with its gilded wood-and-plaster moldings.

RIGHT Ceramic tiles and marble slabs were often employed as floor coverings in the entrance areas and first floor hallways of Victorian houses. Geometric patterns were fashionable during the mid-19th century.

During the middle of the 19th century, an eclectic mix of decorative styles was in fashion on both sides of the Atlantic, the majority of which were revivals (often loosely interpreted) of popular styles from previous centuries. They included a Renaissance Revival, based on the 16th-century use of classical (mainly Roman) forms and relics of Medieval Gothic style; a Baroque Revival (known as Second Empire style in France), which followed the Renaissance Revival and employed classical architectural detailing, imagery, and motifs that were very similar to those employed in the original Baroque style of the 17th century; a Rococo Revival, derived from the flamboyant 18th-century French Rococo, especially favored in boudoirs, bedrooms, and ladies' drawing rooms; and a Greek Revival, a strand of early 19th-century Neoclassicism particularly fashionable in America and Britain. There was also a Gothic Revival which, unlike the romanticized Gothick style of the late 18th century, was characterized by historically accurate recreations of Medieval Gothic styles of ornament. In addition to these historic revivals, styles appeared that included motifs and imagery derived from Chinese, Persian, Indian, and Arabic ornament, and from primitive African and South American art. These were brought about through increased trade, and the travels of architects and ornamentists such as Owen Jones, whose *Grammar of Ornament* (1856) was highly influential.

Although the range of revival or historical styles was extensive, and different styles were often employed in different rooms in the same house, most mid-19th-century interiors incorporated a number of common decorative elements. For example, in grander houses, marble slabs or tiles were used on the floors of entrance areas, while in less affluent dwellings simulations of these in linoleum provided a cheaper alternative. However, in most rooms, wooden floorboards were

RIGHT Large-scale panoramic or scenic papers were very popular in grander houses in the United States during the middle of the 19th century. Most of them were designed in France by companies such as Zuber, and they were exported in great numbers after the fall of Napoleon in 1815. This example shows a sight-seeing tour on a steamboat around the base of Niagara Falls.

LEFT The parlor of the 19th-century Monmouth Mansion in Natchez, Mississippi, is furnished with mid-19th-century mahogany furniture. This armchair, like the rest of the suite, is upholstered with a pale blue silk damask that is patterned with vases, urns, and plant forms derived from Classical Greco-Roman ornament. The drapes behind are made from the same fabric and secured with rope-and-tassel tiebacks.

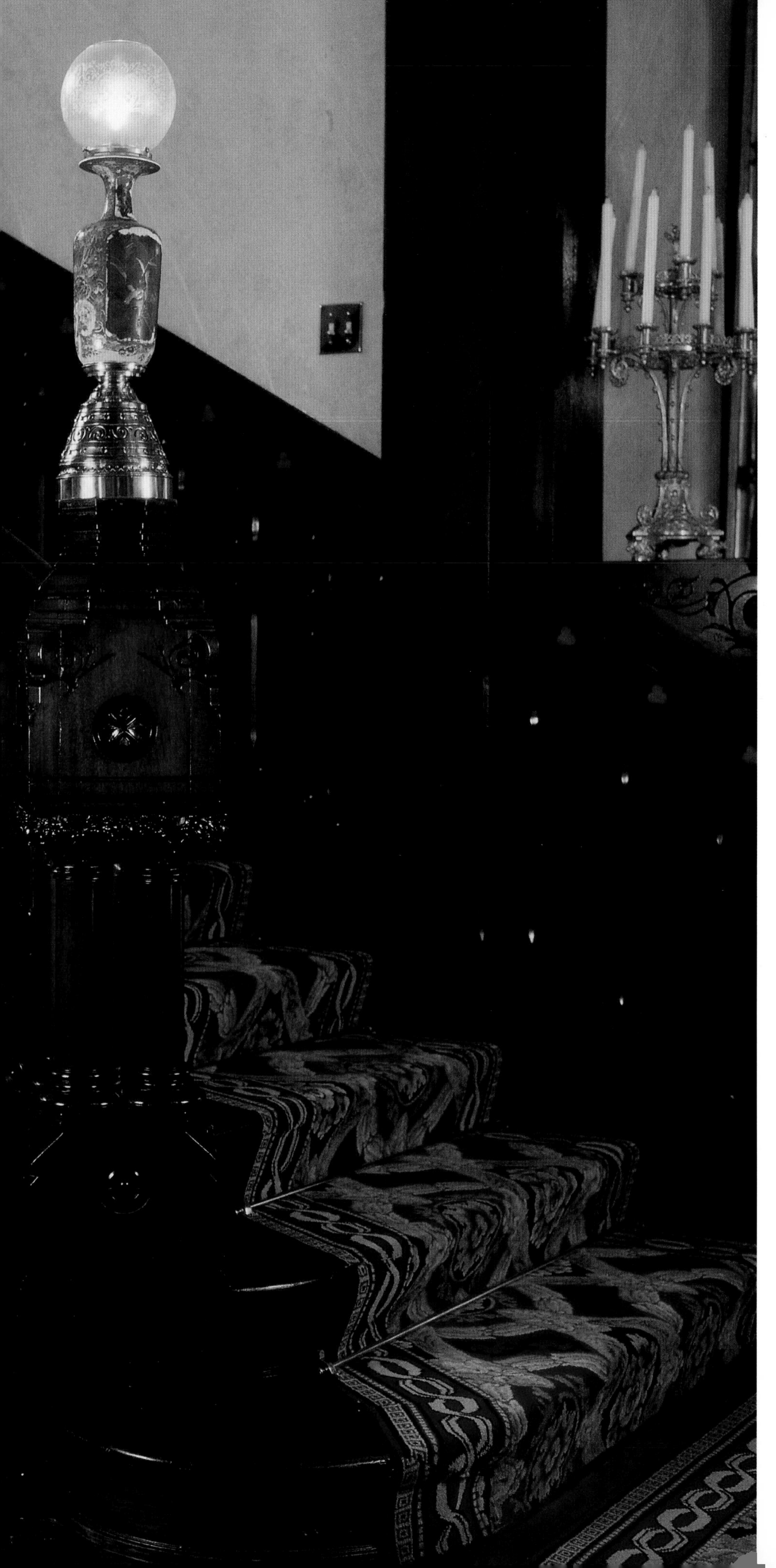

the norm; these were covered with either a centrally placed, patterned carpet or floorcloth, and the borders were stained and polished, stenciled, flat-painted, or laid as parquet. Plaster moldings (cornices and central medallions), often highly elaborate, also came back into fashion, and while many were flat-painted in a single color, others were vibrantly polychromatic.

After ca. 1860, most walls were divided into the classic division of frieze, field, and dado. Silk hangings remained a fashionable, if expensive, choice in affluent households, and flat-painting (often augmented with repeat stencil motifs at dado- and picture-rail height) was also employed. However, wallpaper was the principal form of covering following the development of mass production printing techniques, which made it affordable for the rapidly expanding middle classes.

Faux marble and wood-grained finishes were also much in evidence on doors and other woodwork, and on softwood chimneypieces–the latter a more economical substitute for those made of marble, granite, cast iron, and hardwoods such as mahogany. Solid and veneered hardwood furniture was also produced in great quantities during this period to complement the numerous historical styles. However, the most characteristic pieces were the large number of upholstered chairs, settees, and sofas, which were mostly sumptuously stuffed, often deep-buttoned, and augmented with cushions. The fashion for heavy fabrics was extended to the elaborate, layered window treatments of the period, with lined damask, velvet (or plush), and rep much in evidence, topped by large pelmets and drawn or tied back over lace or muslin insertions (either plain or intricately patterned). There was also a profusion of paintings, prints, and collections of decorative artifacts, the latter displayed on mantelshelves and in glass-fronted cabinets or built-in open shelving.

ABOVE This New York interior bears all the hallmarks of the mid-19th-century American Gothic Revival–subdued lighting, rows of gilt-framed paintings hung against a diaper-pattern wallpaper, and American Gothic Revival furniture.

LEFT Standing on a tiled floor in the hall of a *manoir* near Bordeaux, France, this mid-19th-century mahogany French armchair retains its original floral-pattern, cut-velvet upholstery.

FAR LEFT Most stair runners in mid-19th-century American houses displayed either stylized or naturalistic floral patterns set within borders that featured repeated geometric motifs.

Late 19th Century

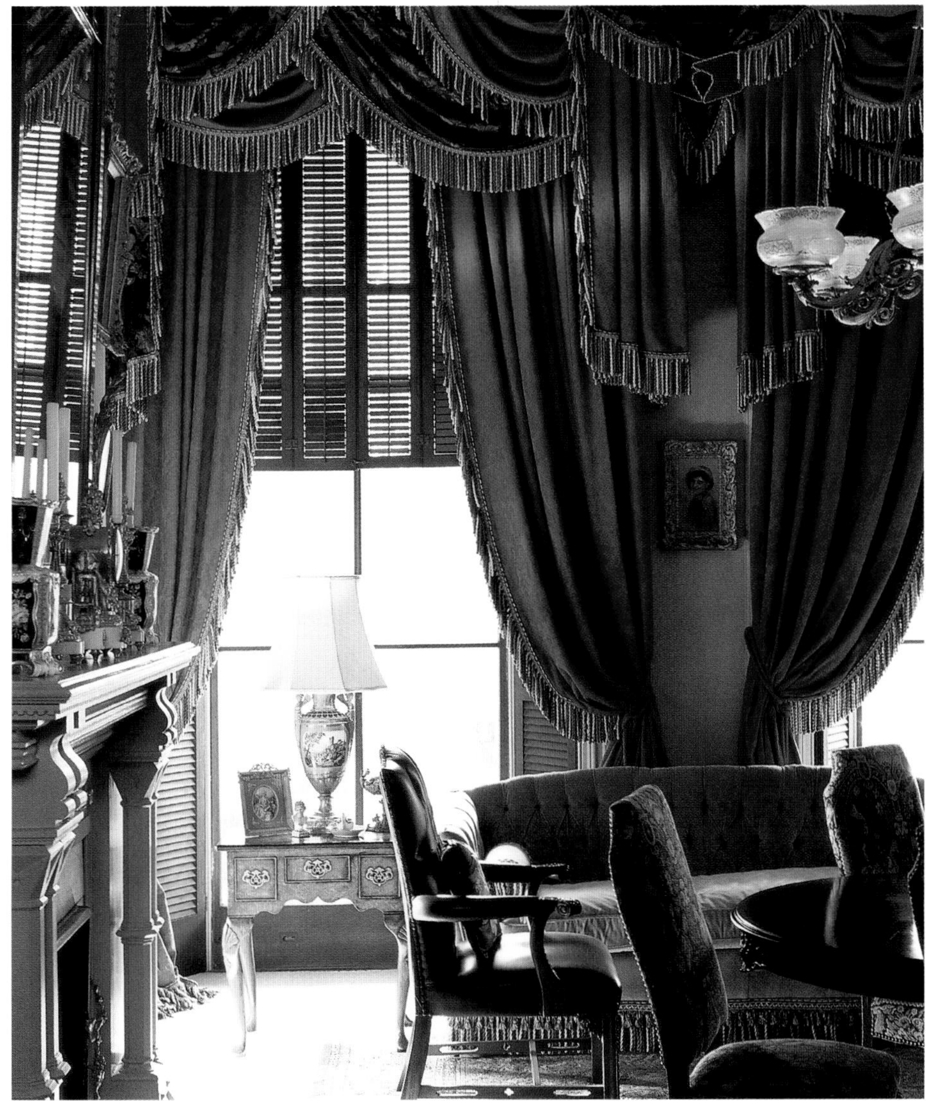

During the last three decades of the 19th century, the fashion for employing different historical or period-revival styles in different rooms of the same house was still prevalent on both sides of the Atlantic. It was not unusual to find a Medieval dining room, a Louis XIV drawing room, a Rococo parlor, a Gothic library, and a Moresque boudoir under the same roof. However, in the late 1860s a reaction to this eclecticism began to emerge among leading artists and designers such as William Morris and Charles Eastlake. They wanted not only to reintroduce a more coherent decorative style, but also to reduce the characteristic clutter of Victorian interiors and reestablish the aesthetic and constructional qualities of preindustrial, hand-crafted furnishings in the wake of the plethora of poorly designed, factory-made goods that were available.

The two closely related styles at the forefront of this reaction to eclecticism were the Aesthetic and the Arts and Crafts Movements. Both were primarily styles of decoration dependent almost entirely for effect upon color and pattern, rather than on a particular architectural style. They were successfully applied to houses as architecturally diverse as 15th- or 16th-century stone-built or timbered manor houses, 18th-century town houses, and 19th-century row houses.

The motifs and imagery that appeared on Aesthetic and Arts and Crafts wallpapers, tiles, furniture, soft furnishings, and artifacts were derived from Classical, Medieval (Gothic), Renaissance, and Chinese and Japanese vocabularies of ornament, with Oriental artifacts and motifs being especially favored by Aesthetic Movement designers. Apart from tasteful design and good craftsmanship, key elements in Aesthetic and Arts and Crafts schemes included a tripartite division of the walls into frieze, field, and dado using three interrelated but distinct wallpaper patterns; color coordination of overmantels to match either the walls or furniture;

ABOVE Swagged, bullion-fringed, silk damask drapes hang in the living room at the Calhoun Mansion (built in the 1870s) in Charleston, S.C.

RIGHT A silk canopy, lace hangings, and a lace bedspread furnish this rosewood and walnut half-tester bed in the Garth Woodside Mansion in Hannibal, Missouri.

LEFT This window treatment at the Calhoun Mansion features watered silk drapes secured with bullion-fringed tiebacks. It has an elaborate pelmet swagged with matching silk. The deep-buttoned chairs are typical of late Victorian interiors.

ROSE
The
Wilderness
shall
as the
ROSE

ROSE
The
wilderness
shall
as the

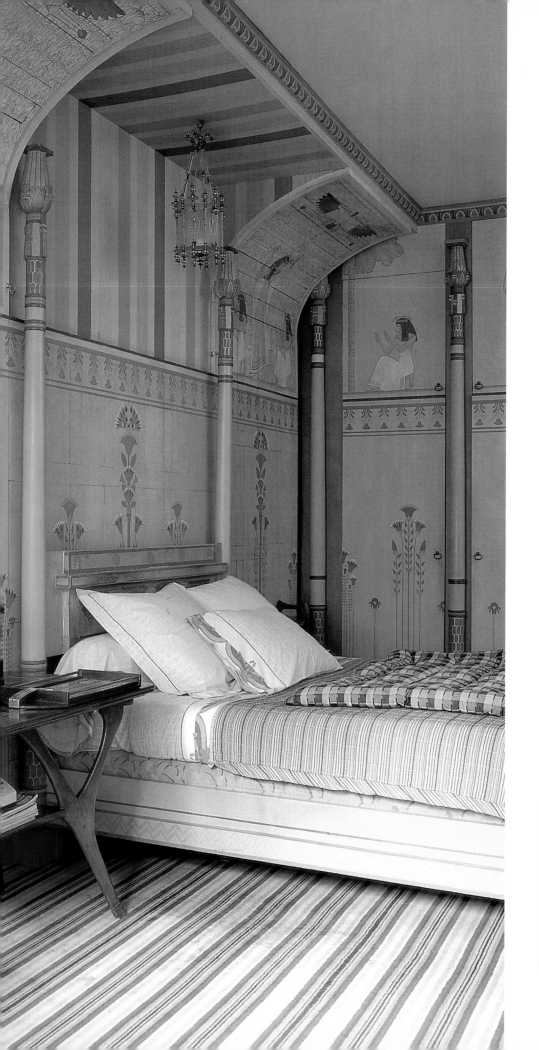

stained or flat-painted woodwork that acted as a foil for brightly colored, vegetable- and mineral-dyed papers and fabrics; Oriental rugs and carpets, or rush matting, laid over bare wooden floorboards; and groupings of furniture, pictures, and ornaments.

In the 1890s, Art Nouveau emerged in Europe and Britain. Peaking in popularity around the turn of the century, and generally out of favor by 1910, it took two distinct stylistic paths: one based on austerely elegant, elongated rectilinear forms and tight, precise floral ornament and the other composed of wild, flowing curvilinear elements characterized by restless whiplash lines. Design elements included the use of deep friezes and fields and a revival of stenciled decoration. "Greenery-yallery" colors such as olive and sage green and mustard were employed, as were browns, lilacs, violets, and muted purples. Stylized vegetal and bird motifs (especially peacocks) were popular, and there was a preference for artifacts such as ceramics and metalwares over pictures. Window treatments were simple, with curtains either abandoned altogether, or having plain or muted patterns.

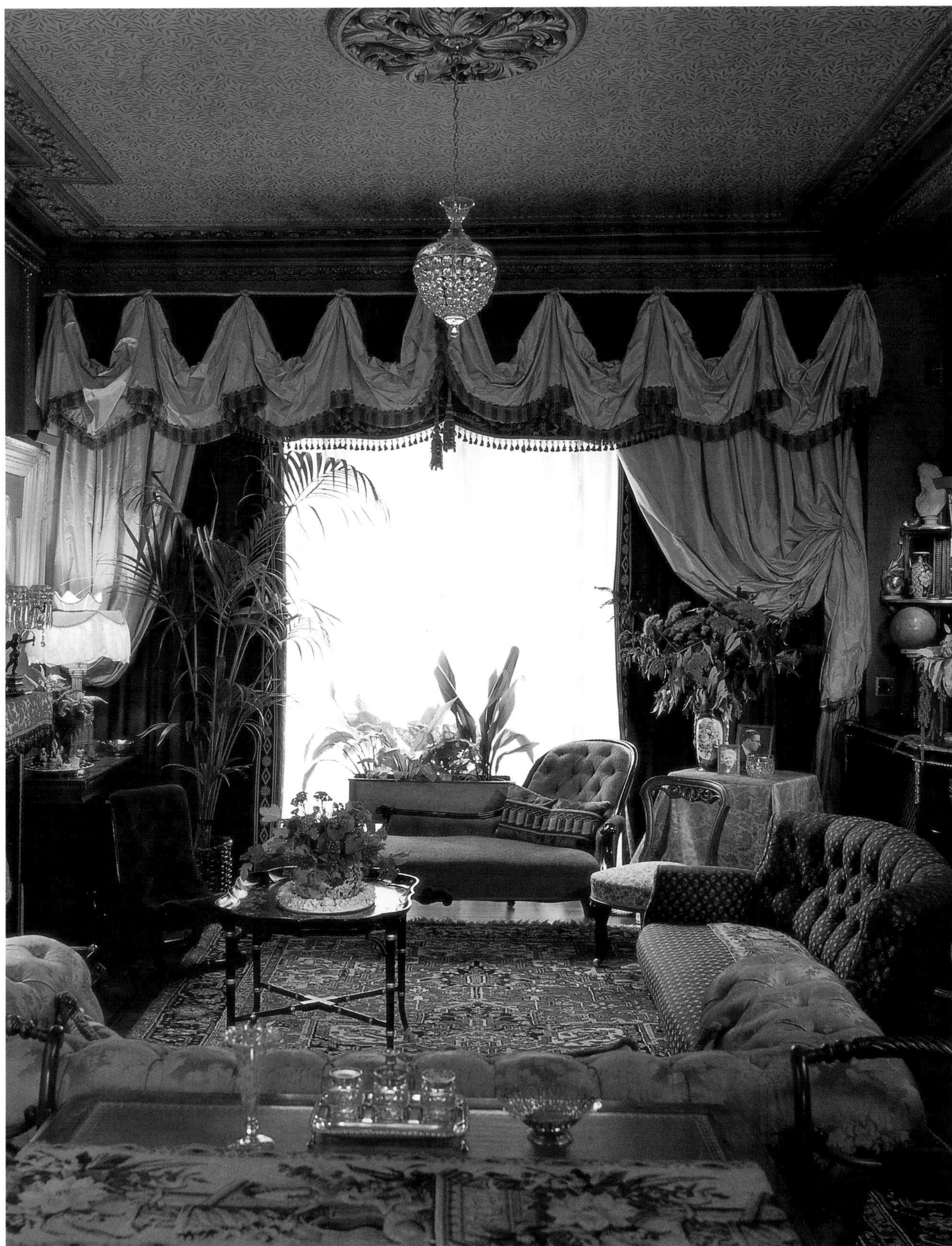

LEFT The eclectic nature of many Victorian interiors is evident here. Classical influence shows in the window treatment and plaster moldings; Egyptian motifs can be seen on the canvas-work panel; the pile-woven rug is Middle Eastern; the upholstery is 19th-century European in style; and the willow pattern on the ceiling paper is derived from Japanese ornament.

CENTER LEFT This armchair is covered with a printed paisley pattern fabric that was very popular in late 19th-century interiors. The design is based on pinecones and small incidental motifs found on Indian fabrics. The leopard-spot pillow cover is a typical example of the exotic faux animal-skin fabrics favored at this time.

FAR LEFT The late 19th-century fascination with Oriental ornament is shown in Françoise Lafon's Egyptian-style bedroom. The striped wallpaper and flat-weave carpet are inspired by patterns found on Egyptian textiles. The sand yellow and pale blue and green color scheme is also quintessentially Egyptian–the green being *eau de nil* (Nile water pale green).

PREVIOUS PAGES The Arts and Crafts Movement was as influential in America in the late 19th century as it was in England, its country of origin. The oak furniture and wall-paneling in this American interior are representative of the style. The wallpaper frieze illustrates the extent to which medieval styles of decoration were rekindled in Arts and Crafts designs.

Early 20th Century

ABOVE This Art Deco living room is in the Geffrye Museum in London, England. Period features include an abstract-patterned carpet, geometrically patterned upholstered furniture, and an asymmetrical, mottled-tile fireplace.

LEFT Chocolate brown, black, cream, and yellow are recurring colors in Art Deco interiors. The zebra-skin rug laid over a complementary colored carpet is also typical of the style.

A number of revivalist styles were fashionable in the early 20th century on both sides of the Atlantic. However, the two styles that dominated the period were Art Deco and Modernism.

The term Art Deco was first coined in 1925, and used to describe the displays at the *Exposition Internationale des Arts Décoratifs et Industriels Modernes*. The style was derived from elements in the work of the Deutscher Werkbund and the Wiener Werkstätte, from the early 20th-century art movements of Cubism, Expressionism, Futurism, and Fauvism, and from African and native South American art. Before the mid-1920s, Art Deco was characterized by the use of rounded and romantic motifs such as garlands and rosebuds. However, during the late 1920s and 1930s these were superseded by abstract and geometric motifs, Egyptian imagery, South American stepped shapes, sun motifs, and motifs suggesting speed and dynamism. The key elements of the style included clean lines and smooth planes in walls, ceilings, floors, and woodwork; contrasting colored walls and woodwork; textiles with geometric or bold floral patterns; plump, upholstered sofas and armchairs and other furniture that was often veneered with exotic woods, or lacquered in black, scarlet, or pale yellow and embellished with *chinoiserie* motifs.

Underpinning Modernist styles of architecture and decoration, which were avidly adopted on both sides of the Atlantic between the First and Second World Wars, was a desire to render the home, in the words of architect and designer Le Corbusier, a "machine for living in." In practice, this involved shunning unnecessary ornament and highlighting the industrial origins of modern building materials, furniture, and textiles. Elements included the use of chrome and glass furniture and fittings; pale walls and ceilings; abstract- or geometric-patterned curtains and carpets, often laid over parquet flooring; and the minimum of displayed artifacts.

RIGHT Traditional striped and floral patterns remained fashionable for the first half of the 20th century. In this bedroom they are combined in a paper that displays broad blue-and-white stripes embellished with naturalistic bouquets (some depicted in Classical Greco-Roman vases) inspired by 18th-century decoration.

LEFT Light color schemes were very much in vogue during the first half of the 20th century. Here, the mint green-painted walls and ceiling provide an unobtrusive and complementary background for the furnishings. Oriental influence is evident in the display cabinet, table covering, and in the stylized plant forms on the rug. African ornament is represented in the faux leopard-skin lampshades, and in the Egyptian motifs on the upholstered chair by the fireplace. The latter is also embellished with Neoclassical floral motifs.

Late 20th Century

Two broad, discernible trends were apparent in decorative styles after the end of the Second World War: one retrospective, the other futuristic. In the former category were a range of historical or revival styles that either replicated or adapted the original. These were evidence of a nostalgia for previous lifestyles, psychologically fueled by a rejection of the unremitting rationality and the minimal use of color and pattern of Modernism, and by understandable apprehensions about the dawn of the new millennium. Specific examples in Britain and Europe included an Art Nouveau Revival during the 1960s and an Art Deco Revival in the 1970s and 1980s. Meanwhile, in America, 18th-century Colonial and late 18th- and 19th-century Federal styles proved especially fashionable. Less specific examples included the "English country house" look, based on the comfortable, chintz-covered rural interiors of the 19th and early 20th centuries, but now applied to both urban and rural houses; and a general revival of medieval and 16th- and 17th-century classical motifs and imagery, particularly on fabrics. Successful recreations of traditional decorative

ABOVE Minimalism, which was inspired by traditional Japanese interiors, was in vogue in the West during the late 20th century. Featured were clean lines of furniture and an uncluttered style of the rooms.

RIGHT This Provençal sitting room, with its yellow-painted, rough-plastered walls, rush seating, and earth-colored upholstery, conveys a sophisticated view of rural calm and simplicity.

LEFT The walls of Charles Jencks's 1980s Post-Modernist London residence are painted with colors and stenciled with small motifs that are symbolic of the four seasons. Both the fireplace and mantelshelf columns are faux marble.

styles were made much easier once the manufacturers of fabrics, paints, wallpapers, and fixtures and fittings responded to popular demand by producing substantial ranges of highly authentic period reproductions.

In contrast to this trend, many architects, designers, and manufacturers enthusiastically embraced new materials and different kinds of motifs and imagery to create innovative decorative styles. For example, motifs and patterns for fabrics and wallpapers began to be based on contemporary fine (Pop and Op) art as well as on microphotographic images of cellular structures, such as insulin and myoglobin. New synthetic fibers, plastics, and alloys all started to be employed in the manufacture of textiles, wallpapers, and furniture.

The late 20th century also witnessed the strikingly decorative recoloring and patterning of previously plain, unornamented, Modernist architectural shells with Gothic or Classical Revival, or ethnic fabrics, furniture, and architectural fixtures and fittings.

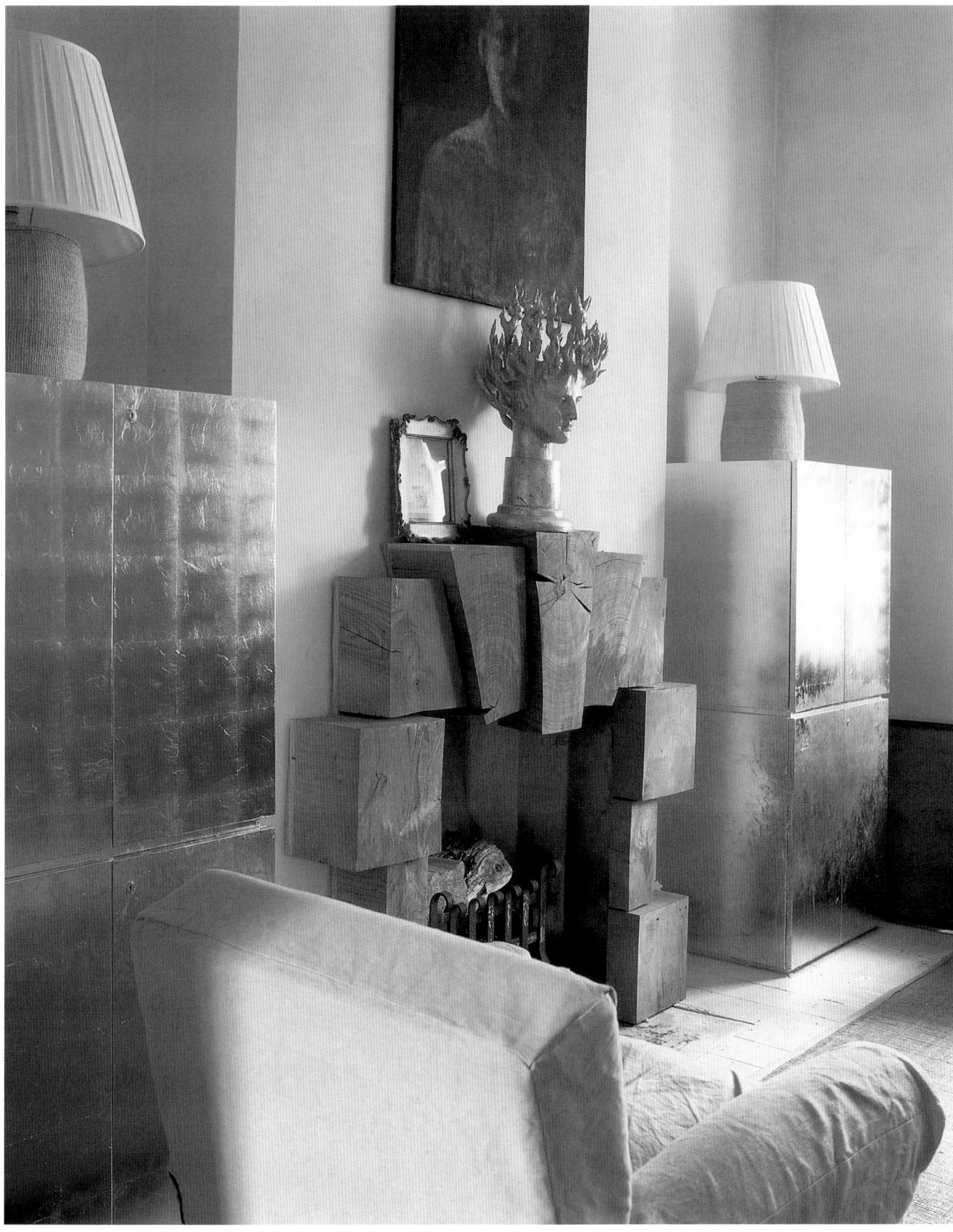

LEFT Colors, textures, and geometric forms, rather than applied patterns, lie at the heart of this late 20th-century decorative scheme. The most striking features of the room include a stone-block fireplace and a pair of cabinets finished with gold leaf. These have been set against an unobtrusive background of mottled green and yellow walls.

CENTER LEFT Pale color schemes incorporating plain or delicate floral-patterned fabrics were a fashionable treatment for bedrooms for much of the 20th century, especially starting in the 1980s.

FAR LEFT During the latter years of the 20th century, some fabric manufacturers, such as Liberty, took traditional patterns and motifs and represented them in exciting new colors. The leaf and sprig motifs on the upholstered chairs boast hot pink and yellow grounds, a theme taken up in the bold, floral-striped curtains and in the coordinated floral-check runner on the table.

Fabrics

Plain Fabrics

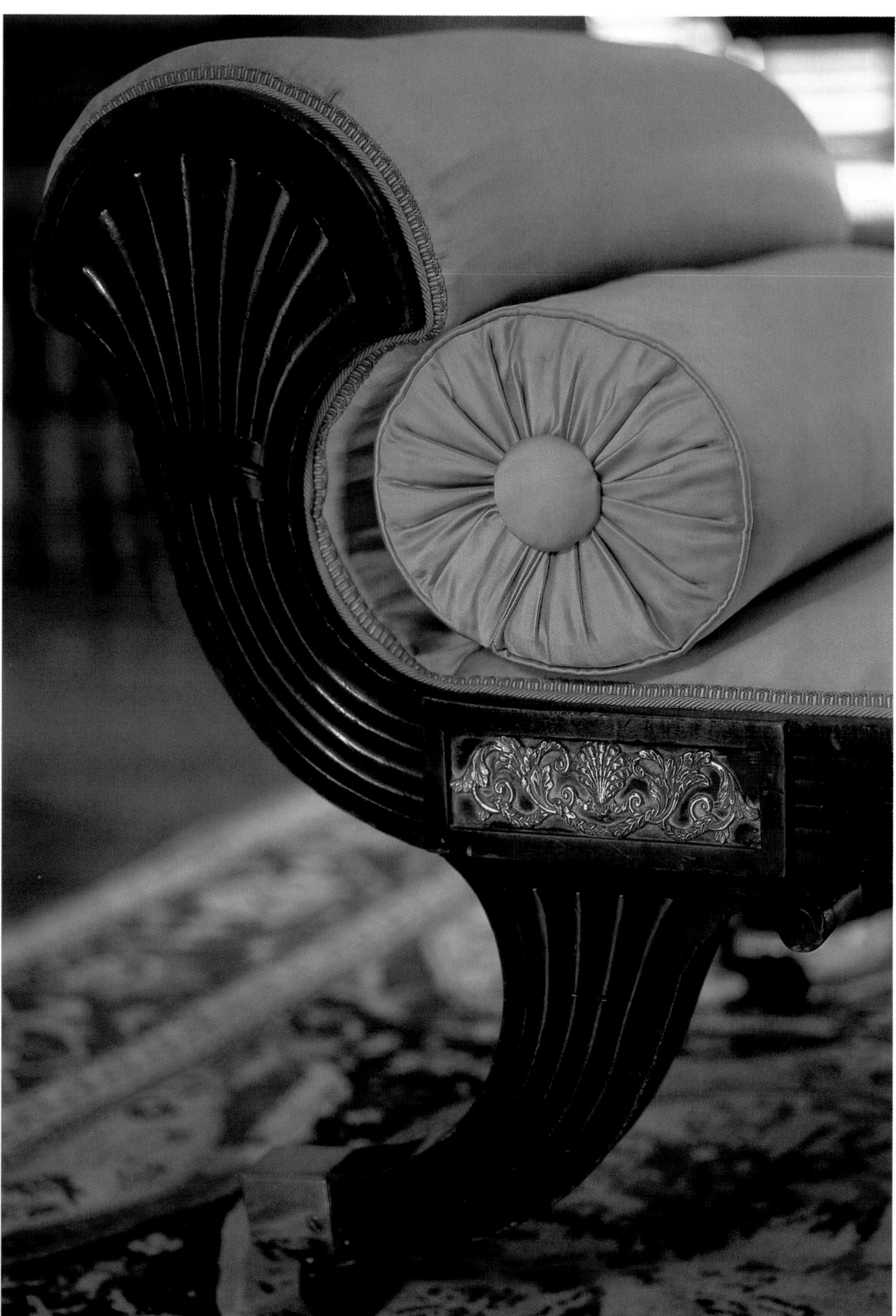

Single-color cloths that are not embellished with woven or printed patterns are known collectively as "plains." Their appeal resides in their color or texture or a combination of both. Plains include taffetas, canvas, cambric, calico, and tweeds that have a plain ("tabby") weave of uniform warp and weft threads passing alternately over and under one another. However, many other fabrics traditionally ascribed to the plains category belie the description "plain" in one of three ways.

First, many plains are self-patterned by variations in their weave; these include seersuckers, in which alternate bands of tight and slack warps create a puckered effect; ribbed fabrics, such as poplin and rep, which have thick and thin yarns; and zigzag herringbones. Second, many neutral-colored fabrics, such as slubby silks and noiles, display more than one color as a result of the presence of naturally occurring specks in the fibers. And third, some plains, such as silk moirés, are dyed one color, but they show variations in tone as a result of "hot-pressing" during manufacture.

LEFT A detail of an Empire-style mahogany daybed, made ca.1815 in New York for the Nathaniel Russell House in South Carolina. The bed and its matching bolster are upholstered with a plain yellow silk top cover that complements the carved and gilded panels featuring scrolling foliage and shell motifs along the sides of the bed.

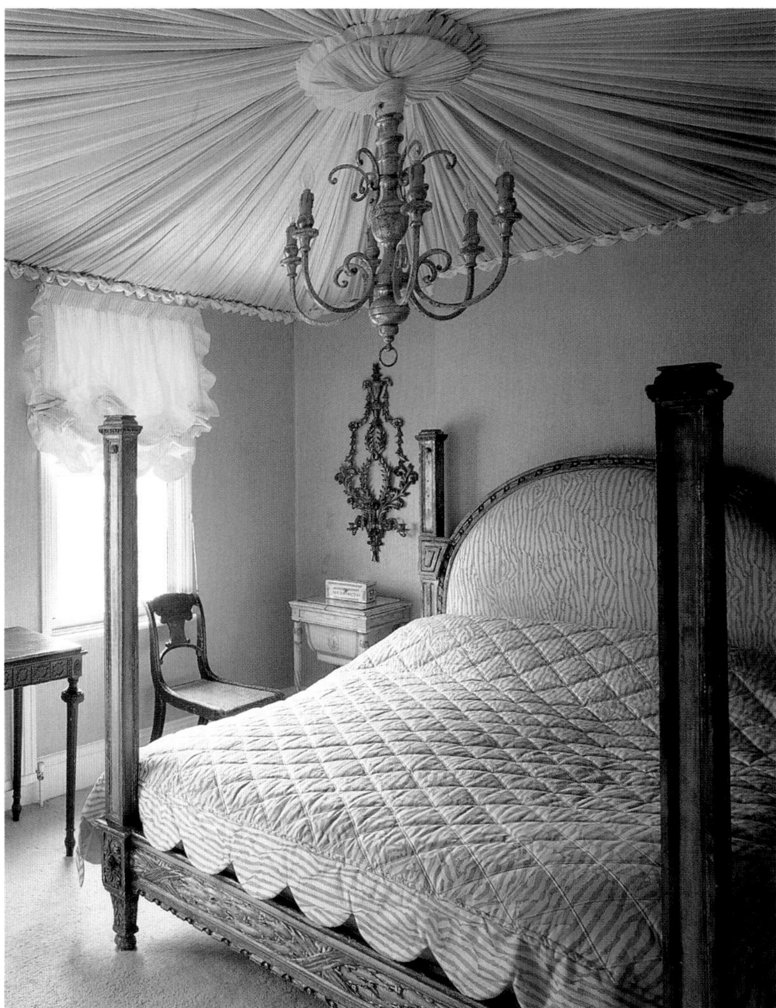

ABOVE Tented ceilings were particularly fashionable in France and England in the early 19th century. They have their origins in the military camps and tournaments of the Middle Ages, and were revived during the Napoleonic wars. The ruched yellow silk example shown here is in a 20th-century recreation of a Regency bedroom.

COTTON DUCK

Although most fabrics are used for the same purpose today as they were in the past, some are now employed in ways in which they were never originally intended. For example, cotton duck (the name is derived from the glazed surface, which sheds water) is a strong, thick cloth that is finer than canvas. During the 19th century it was made of linen and was used to make sails, tents, cooks' aprons, and physicians' coats. Today, however, it is often made up into durable slipcovers for chairs and couches.

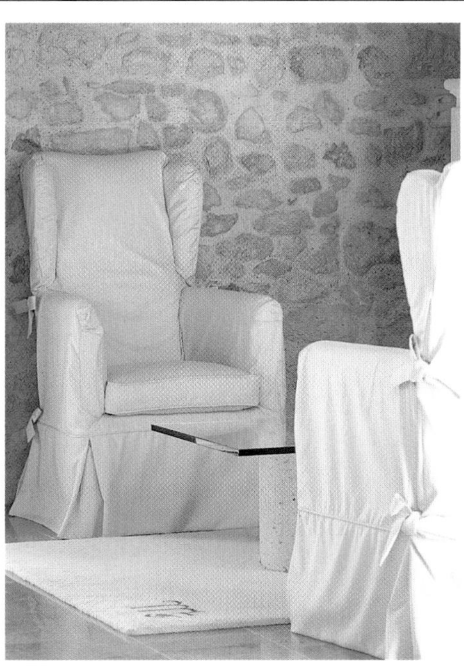

KEY DESIGNS

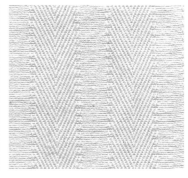

1 Plain-woven fabrics have been made from durable coarse and fine linen since the Middle Ages. Slight stiffness and ease of creasing has made linen weaves better suited to upholstery than to draping.

2 Plain or neutral-colored herringbones are subtly self-patterned. Usually made from cotton or linen, they have become increasingly fashionable for upholstery and hangings during the 20th century.

3 Plain-colored pile fabrics, such as cut or uncut velvets and velours, have been favored since the Renaissance, and were especially used for upholstered furniture in mid-19th century interiors.

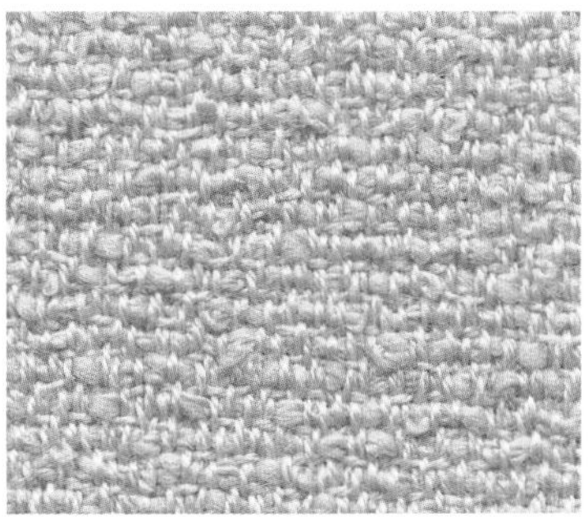

4 Many plains are employed for their texture as much as for their color. The coarseness of texture is determined by the nature of the weave and the thickness of the yarn(s), in this case wool.

5 Fine, plain-weave cottons are suitable for monochromatic dyeing, both vegetable and synthetic. As they drape well they are often employed for window- and bed-hangings and slipcovers.

6 Plain-weave silks are also ideal for monochromatic dyeing, and display pure, saturated colors that have been exploited by interior designers from the Renaissance to the present day.

1 **De Le Cuona Designs/Utility Oak** Color **green** Alternative colors **available** Composition **100% linen** Width **57½in/146cm** Repeat – Price ★★

2 **Ian Mankin/Striped Jacquard** Color **natural** Alternative colors **available** Composition **100% cotton** Width **54in/137cm** Repeat – Price ★ LC

3 **Jab/Maharadscha** Color **red** Alternative colors **available** Composition **100% silk** Width **48in/122cm** Repeat – Price ★★

4 **Jab/Atlantic** Color **yellow** Alternative colors **available** Composition **99% wool, 1% nylon** Width **51in/130cm** Repeat – Price ★★★

5 **Pippa & Hale/Minena Arcadia** Color **blue** Alternative colors **available** Composition **100% cotton** Width **54in/137cm** Repeat – Price ★

6 **Seamoor Fabrics/Kaleidoscope** Color **crushed rose** Alternative colors **available** Composition **100% cotton** Width **48in/122cm** Repeat – Price ★

Plains

Some plain, neutral-colored furnishing fabrics are produced by tinting the fibers from which they are made with pale dyes (either vegetable or synthetic). Other "neutrals," such as cambric, are bleached to whiten the fibers. However, many of the "neutrals" considered fashionable in this and previous centuries rely for color on the natural pigmentation of their fiber(s). Notable examples of these fabrics include: unbleached calico, which is a creamy color relieved by small brown flecks of cottonseed that remain in the cotton yarn; brown Holland, which is an unbleached, closely woven, pale brown linen popular for window blinds during the 18th and 19th centuries; black and white horsehair fabrics, which is woven from unadulterated horsehair of those colors and favored for upholstery since the 18th century; neutral-colored slub silks and noiles, which display the grainy brown specks inherent in natural silk; and Tussah silk, produced from cocoons spun by wild silkworms, which produce a textured, pale brown yarn.

1

2

1 Ian Sanderson/Donovan Color **natural** Alternative colors **available** Composition **65% cotton, 35% linen** Width **54in/137cm** Repeat – Price ★★

2 Ian Sanderson/Crushed linen Color **natural** Alternative colors **available** Composition **100% linen** Width **59in/150cm** Repeat – Price ★★

3 Jab/Atlantic 1-1002-177 Color **cream** Alternative colors **not available** Composition **99% wool, 1% nylon** Width **51in/130cm** Repeat – Price ★★★

4 De Le Cuona Designs/ Herringbone Natural LL103212 Color **natural** Alternative colors **available** Composition **100% linen** Width **45in/114cm** Repeat – Price ★★

5 Ian Sanderson/Sophia Color **creme** Alternative colors **available** Composition **83% viscose, 17% cotton** Width **55in/140cm** Repeat – Price ★★

4

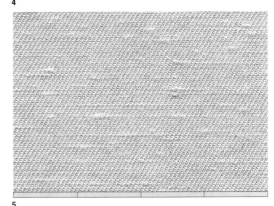

5

3

6

6 Monkwell/Brushed Ooti 05401 Color **Arabia** Alternative colors **available** Composition **100% cotton** Width **54in/137cm** Repeat – Price ★★

7 De Le Cuona Designs/ Fine Brown Glazed LL 10 3224 Color **brown** Alternative colors **available** Composition **100% linen** Width **45in/114cm** Repeat – Price ★★

8 Jab/Murano 1-6050-122 Color **gold** Alternative colors **available** Composition **54% viscose, 46% cotton** Width **51in/130cm** Repeat – Price ★★

HORSEHAIR FABRIC

Woven from the horse mane and tail hairs on a silk, cotton, linen, or wool warp, horsehair fabric has been used for upholstery since the early 18th century, most notably on Hepplewhite and Chippendale chairs. Favored colors of this fabric have included black, green, gray, gold, red, and ivory.

John Boyd Textiles/Ricana RI/620/6 Color **ivory** Alternative colors **available** Composition **68% horsehair, 32% cotton** Width **22in/56cm** Repeat – Price ★★★

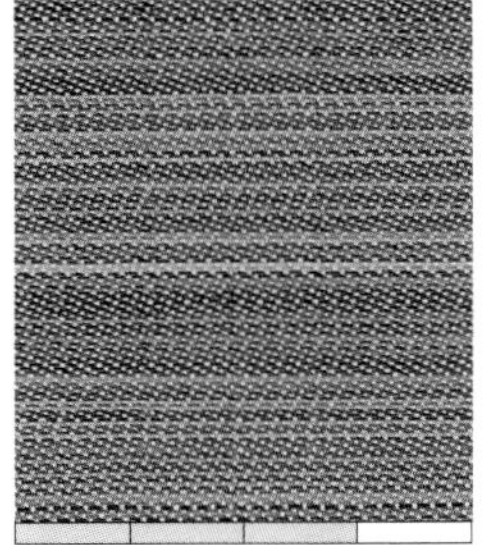

John Boyd Textiles/Criollo CR/227 Color **light gray** Alternative colors **available** Composition **68% horsehair, 32% cotton** Width **25½in/65cm** Repeat – Price ★★★

7

8

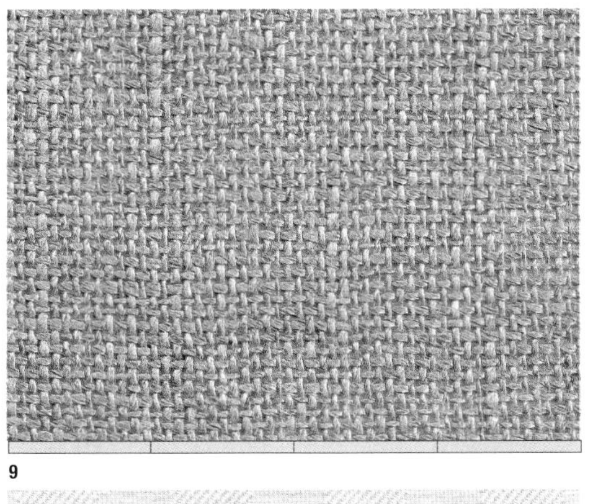

9

9 De Le Cuona Designs/Heavy Natural LL 10 3 Color **natural** Alternative colors **available** Composition **100% linen** Width **45in/114cm** Repeat **–** Price ★★

10

10 Ian Mankin/Pavilion Color **natural** Alternative colors **available** Composition **100% cotton** Width **54in/137cm** Repeat **¾in/2cm** Price ★

11 Hodsoll McKenzie/Plain Rep 356/101-106 Color **natural** Alternative colors **available** Composition **76% cotton, 24% silk** Width **50in/127cm** Repeat **–** Price ★★★

12 Brunschwig & Fils/Brendan Woven Texture 801700 Color **02** Alternative colors **available** Composition **100% cotton** Width **54in/137cm** Repeat **3½in/9cm** Price ★★★★

13 Marvic Textiles/Misa Moiré Plain 6565 Color **daisy** Alternative colors **available** Composition **52% linen, 48% viscose** Width **55in/140cm** Repeat **–** Price ★★

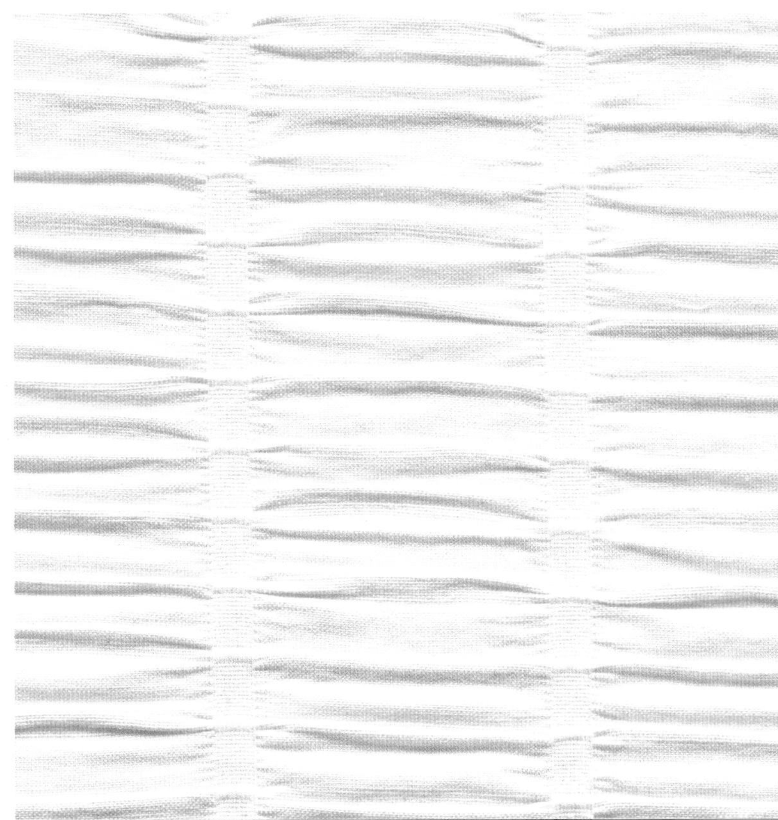

14

11

14 Ian Sanderson/Dunbar Color **ecru** Alternative colors **available** Composition **100% cotton** Width **59in/150cm** Repeat **–** Price ★★

15 De Le Cuona Designs/Delicate Cream LL 10 3200 Color **cream** Alternative colors **available** Composition **100% linen** Width **45in/114cm** Repeat **–** Price ★★

16 Ian Mankin/Pacific Plain Color **spice** Alternative colors **available** Composition **100% cotton** Width **54in/137cm** Repeat **–** Price ★

17 Jab/Girasole 1-2039-145 Color **145** Alternative colors **available** Composition **100% cotton** Width **55in/140cm** Repeat **–** Price ★★★

18 Baumann Fabrics/Fortuna COL 211 Color **1** Alternative colors **not available** Composition **100% cotton** Width **63in/160cm** Repeat **15¾in/40cm** Price ★★★★

19 Marvic Textiles/Moiré Celeste 47 Color **primula** Alternative colors **available** Composition **54% viscose, 28% cotton, 18% linen** Width **53½in/136cm** Repeat **–** Price ★★

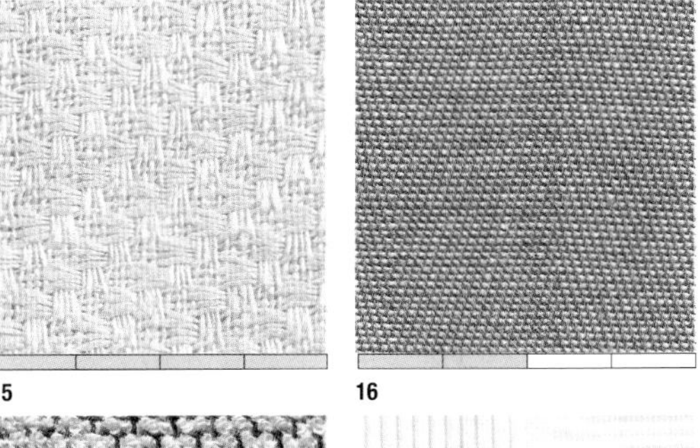

15 16

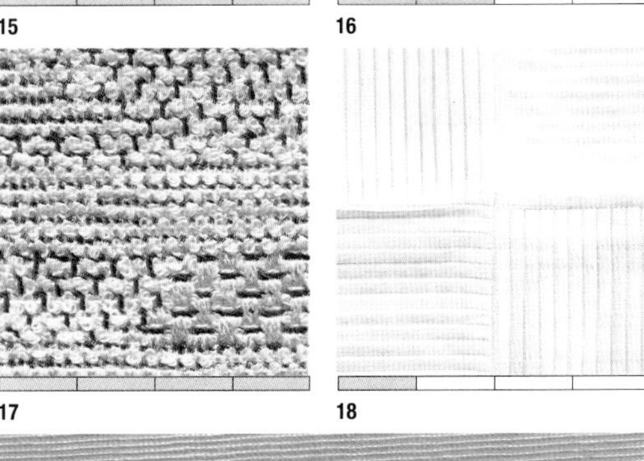

17 18

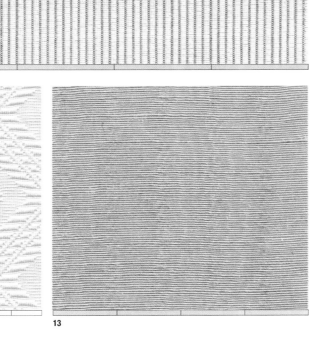

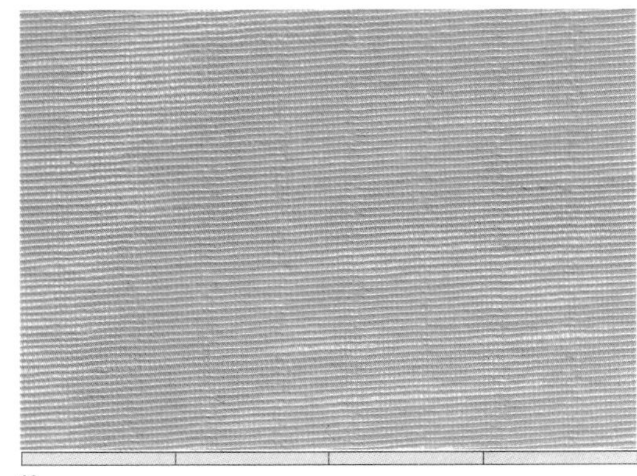

19

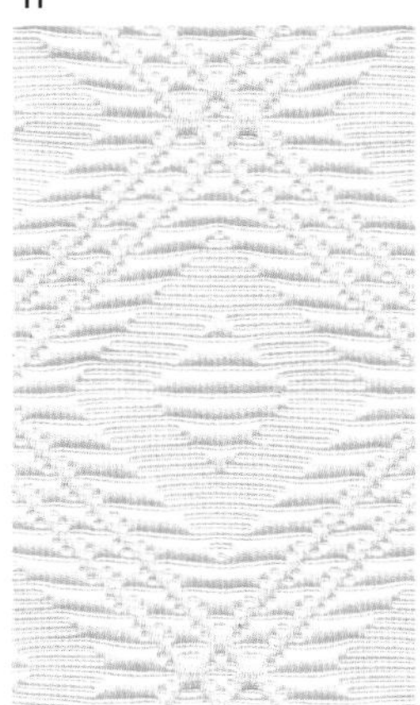

12

13

Plains

Plain fabrics rely heavily on both their color and texture for decorative effect. The appearance of any particular color is affected by a number of factors, including the texture of the fabric and the nature of the weave to the angle and intensity of natural or artificial light to which the fabric is exposed. In other words, the same color dye will look markedly different on a ribbed wool or worsted rep (a closely woven ribbed fabric) than it will on a smooth satin-weave silk. However, the appearance of color goes beyond the physical properties of the fibers to which the color is applied and the environmental conditions under which the fabrics are used and displayed. The nature of the pigments used also contributes to the appearance of a plain fabric. For example, in the mid-19th century, synthetic aniline dyes were developed by extracting benzine oil from coal tar and combining it with acids. The result was a wide range of new, vibrantly colored pigments that appeared gradually from the 1850s to the 1880s. Notable among them were "mauveine," magenta, various purple-blues and greens, Manchester brown and yellow, Congo blue, and a synthetic substitute for indigo.

Osborne & Little/Ghillie Wool F12411 Color **02** Alternative colors **available** Composition **92% wool, 8% nylon** Width **55in/140cm** Repeat – Price ★★

Zimmer & Rohde/Option 1910 Color **162** Alternative colors **available** Composition **52% cotton, 48% polyester** Width **55in/140cm** Repeat – Price ★★★

Abbott & Boyd/Albarracin 9740-0 Color **cream** Alternative colors **available** Composition **70% cotton, 28% viscose, 2% polyester** Width **54¼in/138cm** Repeat – Price ★★★

Monkwell/Plain 5446 Color **811** Alternative colors **available** Composition **91% cotton, 9% modacrylic** Width **47in/120cm** Repeat – Price ★

Olicana/Yachting Cotton Color **red rag** Alternative colors **available** Composition **100% cotton** Width **54in/137cm** Repeat – Price ★ [W]

Jab/Maharadscha 6943-211 Color **orange** Alternative colors **available** Composition **100% silk** Width **48in/122cm** Repeat – Price ★★

Scalamandré/Adriatic Antique Taffeta 5870-028 Color **maize** Alternative colors **available** Composition **100% silk** Width **55⅞in/142cm** Repeat – Price ★★★ [T]

Zimmer & Rohde/Priya 6989-226 Color **tan** Alternative colors **available** Composition **100% silk** Width **47in/120cm** Repeat – Price ★★★

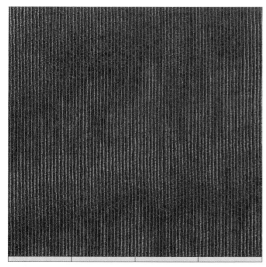

Osborne & Little/Nomad Plain Moiré F1281/02 Color **02** Alternative colors **available** Composition **36% viscose, 32% wool, 16% cotton, 16% polyamide** Width **55in/140cm** Repeat – Price ★★★

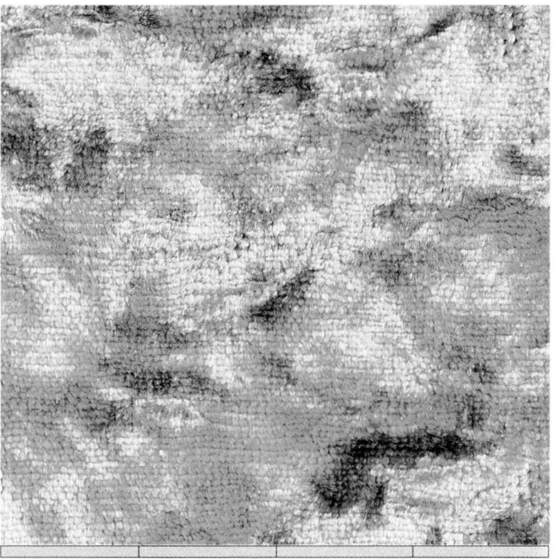

Abbott & Boyd/Traviata Color **05** Alternative colors **available** Composition **77% viscose, 23% polyamide** Width **55in/140cm** Repeat – Price ★★★★

Percheron/Velour Verdi 2245-6 Color **red** Alternative colors **available** Composition **58% linen, 42% cotton** Width **51in/130cm** Repeat – Price ★★★★★

Donghia/Piega 0488/9325 Color **18** Alternative colors **available** Composition **55% cotton, 23% polyester, 13% polyacrylic, 9% viscose** Width **52in/133cm** Repeat – Price ★★★★

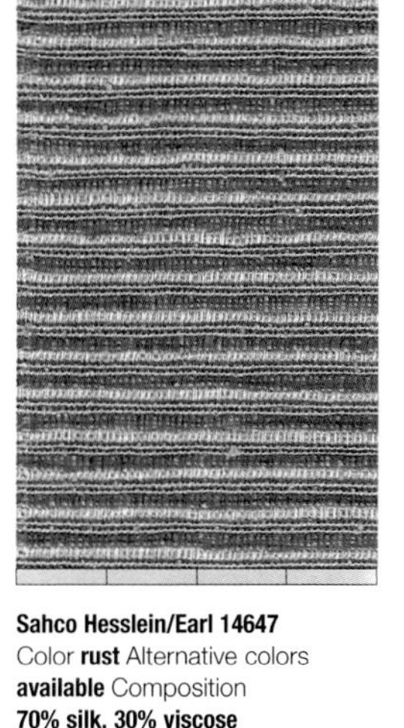

Sahco Hesslein/Earl 14647 Color **rust** Alternative colors **available** Composition **70% silk, 30% viscose** Width **55in/140cm** Repeat – Price ★★★

Ian Sanderson/Sophia Color **sungold** Alternative colors **available** Composition **83% viscose, 17% cotton** Width **55in/140cm** Repeat – Price ★★

Jab/Tosca 1-6048 Color **449** Alternative colors **available** Composition **100% silk** Width **55in/140cm** Repeat – Price ★★★

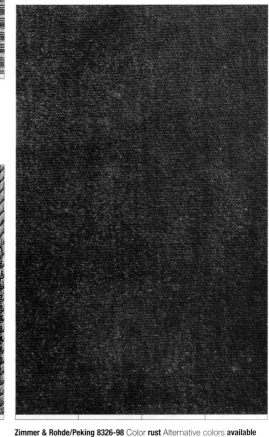

Zimmer & Rohde/Peking 8326-98 Color **rust** Alternative colors **available** Composition **50% silk, 25% cotton, 25% polyester** Width **55in/140cm** Repeat – Price ★★★★★

Plains

Synthetic dyes and colors were first introduced in the 1850s and continued to be developed and used during the 20th century. However, many believed that they never matched the chromatic intensity and purity of color obtained from traditional vegetable dyes–a contemporary view that echoed William Morris's original reaction to the artificiality and "garishness" of the aniline dyes of the 19th century and his advocacy of a return to the use of vegetable and mineral dyes.

There is no doubt that, when it comes to color, new technology and increased industrialization do not automatically equate to better quality. Indeed, the brilliance, intensity, subtle variation, and diversity of hue of vegetable dyes used from the Middle Ages to the mid-19th century (and enjoying a revival today) will probably never be matched synthetically. For example, during the 17th century, "drugs" from the Orient and the Americas, such as saffron, indigo, quercitron, and brazilwood, were employed to produce a vast spectrum of tints, including greens as diverse as parakeet, emerald, carnation, duck,and moss, in addition to a palette of 12 different shades of blue and *caca d'oie* (goose excrement).

6

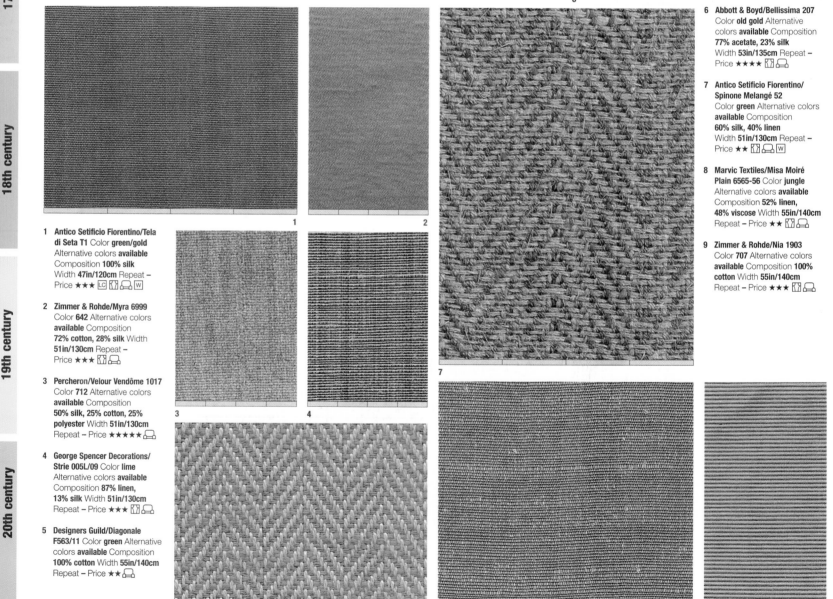

1

2

7

1 **Antico Setificio Fiorentino/Tela di Seta T1** Color **green/gold** Alternative colors **available** Composition **100% silk** Width **47in/120cm** Repeat **–** Price ★★★ LC W

2 **Zimmer & Rohde/Myra 6999** Color **642** Alternative colors **available** Composition **72% cotton, 28% silk** Width **51in/130cm** Repeat **–** Price ★★★

3 **Percheron/Velour Vendôme 1017** Color **712** Alternative colors **available** Composition **50% silk, 25% cotton, 25% polyester** Width **51in/130cm** Repeat **–** Price ★★★★★

4 **George Spencer Decorations/ Strie 005L/09** Color **lime** Alternative colors **available** Composition **87% linen, 13% silk** Width **51in/130cm** Repeat **–** Price ★★★

5 **Designers Guild/Diagonale F563/11** Color **green** Alternative colors **available** Composition **100% cotton** Width **55in/140cm** Repeat **–** Price ★★

3

4

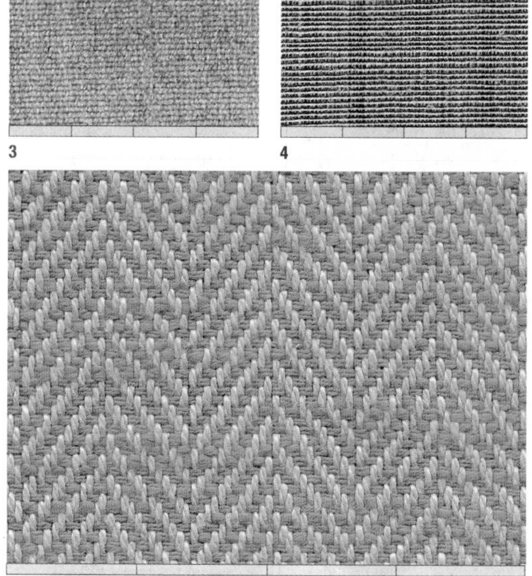

5

8

9

6 **Abbott & Boyd/Bellissima 207** Color **old gold** Alternative colors **available** Composition **77% acetate, 23% silk** Width **53in/135cm** Repeat **–** Price ★★★★

7 **Antico Setificio Fiorentino/ Spinone Melangé 52** Color **green** Alternative colors **available** Composition **60% silk, 40% linen** Width **51in/130cm** Repeat **–** Price ★★ W

8 **Marvic Textiles/Misa Moiré Plain 6565-56** Color **jungle** Alternative colors **available** Composition **52% linen, 48% viscose** Width **55in/140cm** Repeat **–** Price ★★

9 **Zimmer & Rohde/Nia 1903** Color **707** Alternative colors **available** Composition **100% cotton** Width **55in/140cm** Repeat **–** Price ★★★

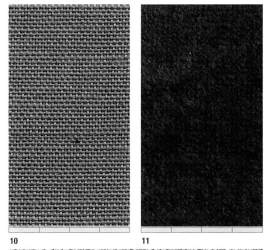

10

11

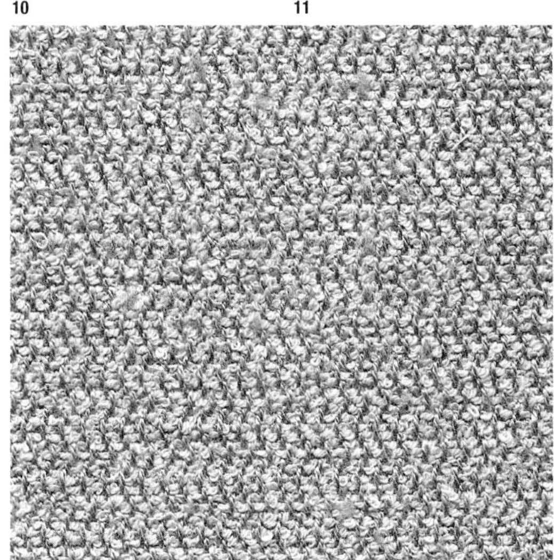

12

10 Today Interiors/L'Orient FR2263 Color **blue** Alternative colors **available** Composition **63% linen, 28% cotton, 9% nylon** Width **54in/137cm** Repeat **–** Price ★★

11 Jab/Syit 1-6002 Color **255** Alternative colors **available** Composition **100% cotton** Width **55in/140cm** Repeat **–** Price ★★★

12 Zimmer & Rohde/Corela 1913 Color **663** Alternative colors **available** Composition **57% cotton, 43% viscose** Width **55in/140cm** Repeat **–** Price ★★

13 Pippa & Hale/Minena Arcadia MIF 090 Color **blueberry** Alternative colors **available** Composition **100% cotton** Width **54in/137cm** Repeat **–** Price ★

14 Olicana/Calypso Color **paradisian pink** Alternative colors **available** Composition **100% cotton** Width **57in/145cm** Repeat **–** Price ★★ W

15 Nice Irma's/Blackberry Color **blackberry** Alternative colors **available** Composition **100% cotton** Width **48in/122cm** Repeat **–** Price ★ LC

16 Zimmer & Rohde/Idris 6991-556 Color **blue** Alternative colors **available** Composition **100% silk** Width **53in/135cm** Repeat **–** Price ★★★

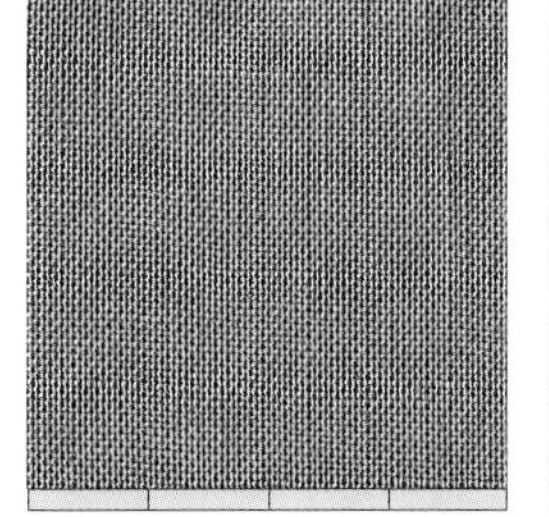

13

14

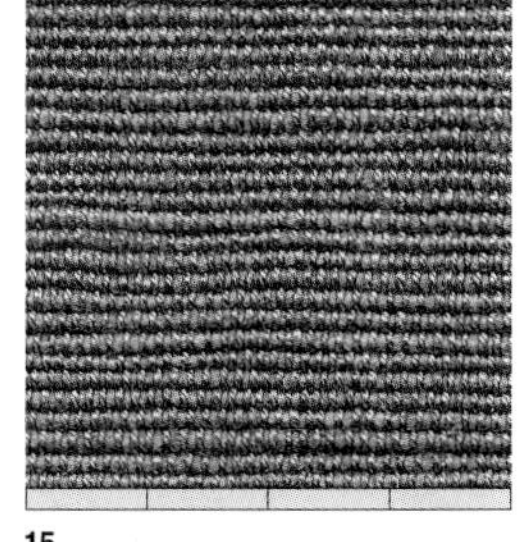

15

16

MOIRÉS

Fashionable since the early 18th century, moirés are ribbed fabrics onto which clouded or watered (wavelike) effects are imposed by passing them between heavy iron or copper rollers. Traditionally, the fabric is left dry while subjected to intense, uneven pressure from the rollers. However, liquid and heat can also be applied for the same effect. Most moirés are heavy silk, but some are wool or worsted. In the 20th century, moirés were often made from rayon or were a mixture of cotton and viscose.

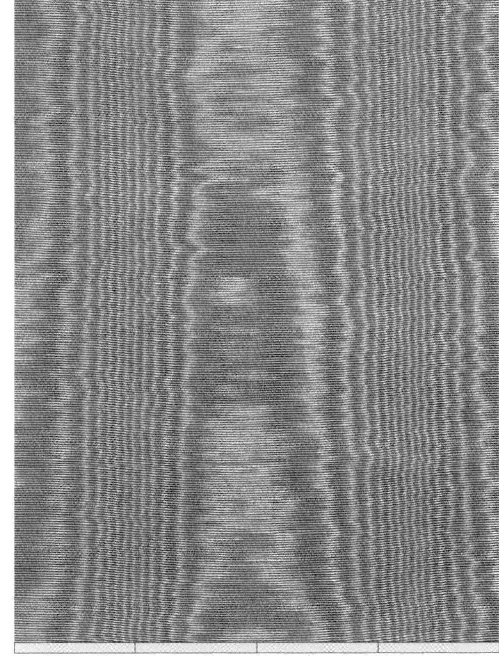

Marvic Textiles/Marvic Moiré 45-27 Color **leman** Alternative colors **available** Composition **58% cotton, 42% viscose** Width **53½in/136cm** Repeat **–** Price ★★ W

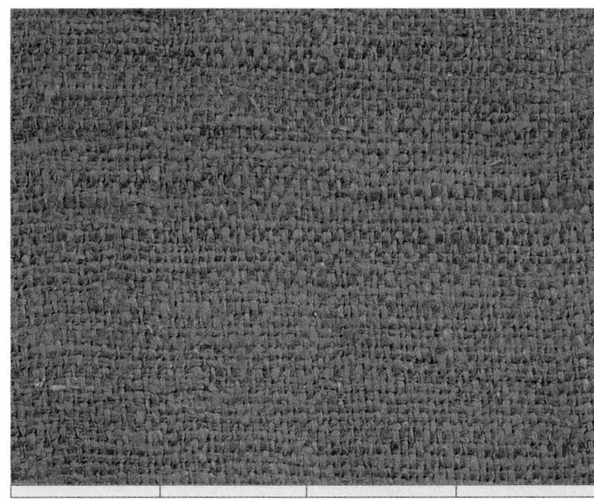

17

17 Designers Guild/Laelia F568/01 Color **blue** Alternative colors **available** Composition **100% cotton** Width **54in/137cm** Repeat **–** Price ★★

18 Jab/Maharadscha 6943-252 Color **silver** Alternative colors **available** Composition **100% silk** Width **48in/122cm** Repeat **–** Price ★★

19 Jab/Artus 1-6047-581 Color **aqua** Alternative colors **available** Composition **70% cotton, 30% polyester** Width **55in/140cm** Repeat **–** Price ★★

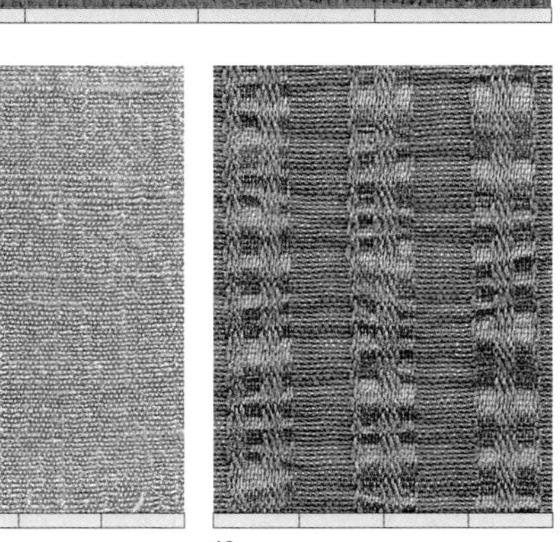

18

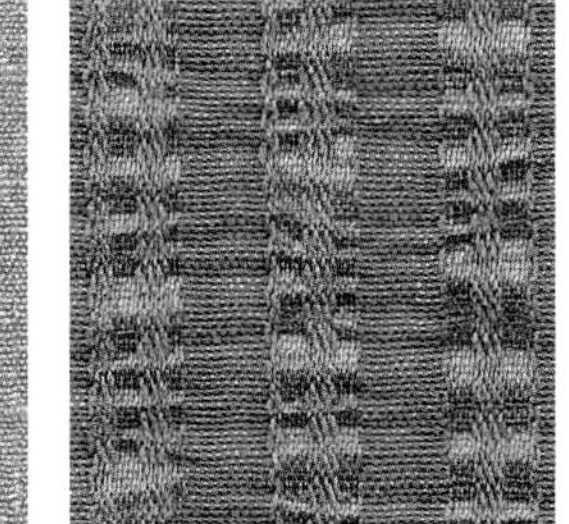

19

Patterned Pile

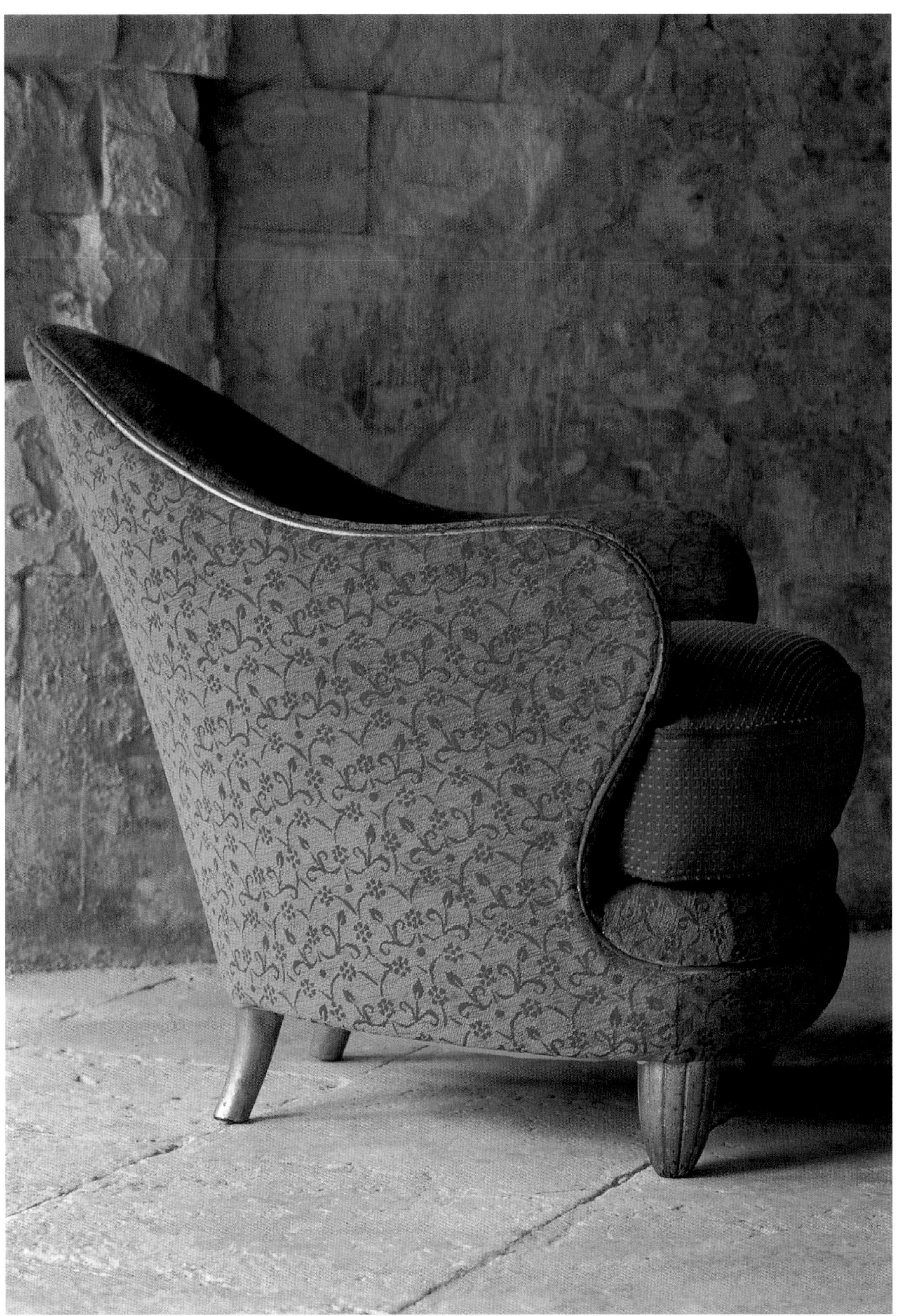

Traditionally woven from silk, mohair, wool, worsted, or cotton, pile fabrics have been produced for drapery since the Middle Ages and for upholstery since the 17th century. The best-known are Genoa, Utrecht, and *gaufrage* velvets. Related types include moquette ("mock velvet"); chenille ("poor man's velvet"); plush (a wool velvet); Manchester velvet (a cotton variety); velour (cotton); and corduroy (also cotton). All are distinguished by their raised pile, which consists of rows of loops woven into a simple ground weave. The loops can be cut, which gives them a furlike texture, or left uncut. The direction of the pile, and the angle at which light strikes it, determine the density and sheen of the colors, which can vary from dark matte to bright and shimmering. Patterns are created during weaving, or stamped on afterward with a metal plate or cylinder. If the pattern is woven leaving areas of ground weave exposed, the fabric is referred to as "voided"; alternatively, if the ground is completely covered with patterned pile, the fabric is described as "solid."

LEFT This 1930s tub chair has been reupholstered in two jacquard *strié* chenilles from Osborne & Little's "Elgin" collection. The chair frame is covered with a thick-textured chenille displaying an overall-repeat pattern of trailing foliage and daisies, while the top cover on the cushion is a thinner-textured chenille with a checkerboard pattern incorporating raised dots.

ABOVE This 19th-century painted chair from France has been reupholstered with a flamboyant cut-pile velvet. The naturalistic red-and-green flower-and-leaf pattern is well defined by a contrasting pale yellow ground weave. The back of the chair nestles into a pair of heavy yellow silk damask curtains.

SELF-PATTERNS

When recreating this typical mid-19th century interior, Swiss designer Christophe Gollut used a voided, cut-pile velvet to upholster the mahogany seating. With the ground weave exposed, a voided pattern will allow the manufacturer to produce a self-colored pattern in the pile, thereby creating a damask effect (*see* pages 72-81) and giving the pattern increased texture and definition.

KEY DESIGNS

1 Genoa velvets were first made in Italy during the 15th century, and are characterized by bold, multicolored floral-patterned piles, in this case red and gold on a plain green ground.

2 Stylized foliage is among the most traditional of pile fabric patterns. This fabric has a woven pile, but *gaufrage* (stamped) foliage patterns have also proved popular since the 16th century.

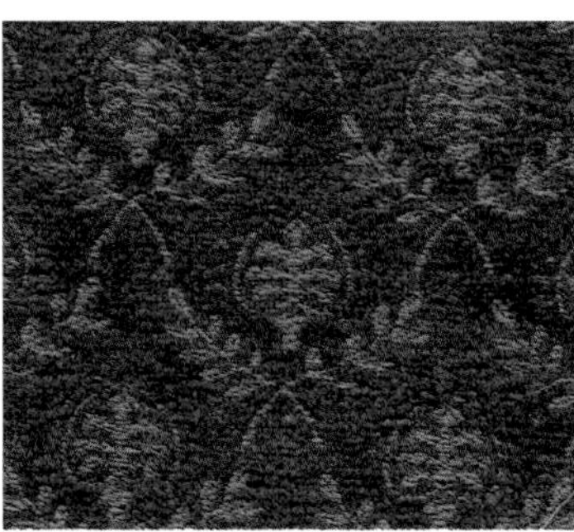

3 Overall-pattern repeats of small motifs, such as the plant forms on this Empire-style chenille, became easier to produce following the invention of the dobby loom in 1824.

4 Pomegranate motifs set in formalized vegetal patterns were derived from Oriental and classical ornament. They have appeared on pile fabrics since the Renaissance.

5 Inspired by military bunting, striped velvets were very fashionable in the late 18th and early 19th centuries. This example features a cut, blue-stripe pile on a sage green ground.

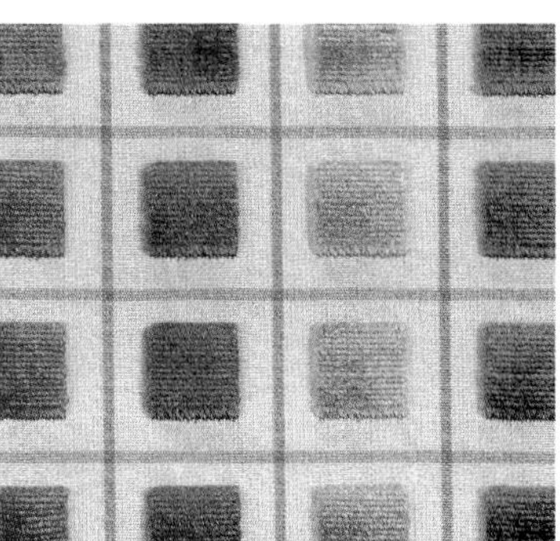

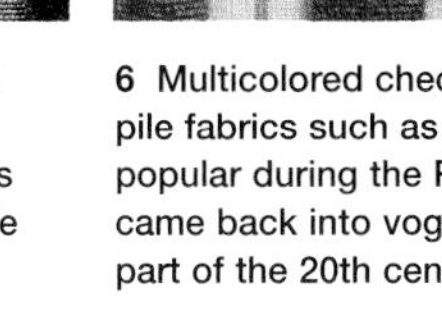

6 Multicolored checkerboard-pattern pile fabrics such as this one were popular during the Renaissance, and came back into vogue during the latter part of the 20th century.

1 **Scalamandré/Bacchus** Color **maize on green** Alternative colors **available** Composition **52% rayon, 48% cotton** Width **51in/130cm** Repeat **30in/76cm** Price ★★★★★ T

2 **Hill & Knowles/Canbury** Color **banana** Alternative colors **available** Composition **100% cotton** Width **51in/130cm** Repeat **14in/36cm** Price ★★

3 **Hodsoll McKenzie/Empire Chenille** Color **141** Alternative colors **available** Composition **100% cotton** Width **50in/127cm** Repeat **2¼in/5.5cm** Price ★★★ W

4 **RBI International/Brazil** Color **5522** Alternative colors **available** Composition **60% cotton, 40% viscose** Width **54½in/138cm** Repeat **14in/36cm** Price ★★★ LC

5 **Percheron/Robespierre** Color **green/blue** Alternative colors **available** Composition **69% viscose, 31% cotton** Width **51in/130cm** Repeat – Price ★★ W

6 **Old World Weavers/San Marco Square** Color **multi** Alternative colors **available** Composition **69% cotton, 31% silk** Width **51in/130cm** Repeat – Price ★★★★★

Patterned Pile: **Pre-20th century**

Prior to the 20th century, pile fabrics were produced in numerous colors and patterns. Silk Genoa velvet (made since the Renaissance) has always been the most expensive. It features a multicolored pile (cut or uncut) on a satin ground and is patterned during weaving. Less costly Utrecht and *gaufrage* velvets have stamped patterns. The alternatives include moquette (produced since the 16th century), which has a wool warp pile (usually cut) on a linen ground, and woven or stamped patterns; chenille (first seen in the 19th century), a fabric woven from cut and twisted cloth, with a fuzzy pile; plush (from the late 17th century), which is a double-warp fabric, of wool and hair (or silk) with woven or stamped patterns and a longer but less dense pile than velvet; and, since the 18th century, Manchester velvet (*see* page 67) and velour–the latter having a dense, short, lustrous, cotton-warp pile.

1

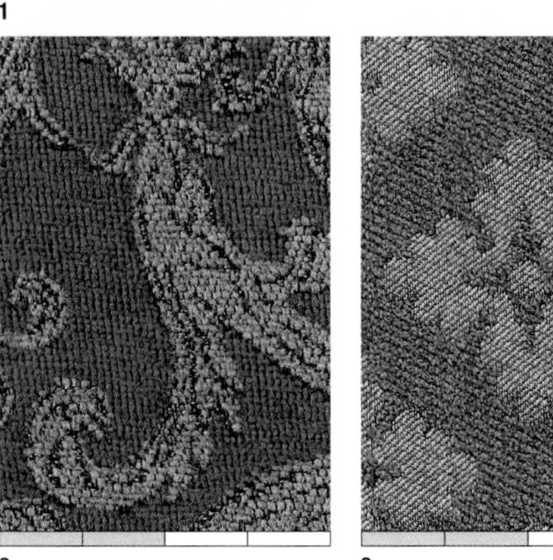

2

3

5

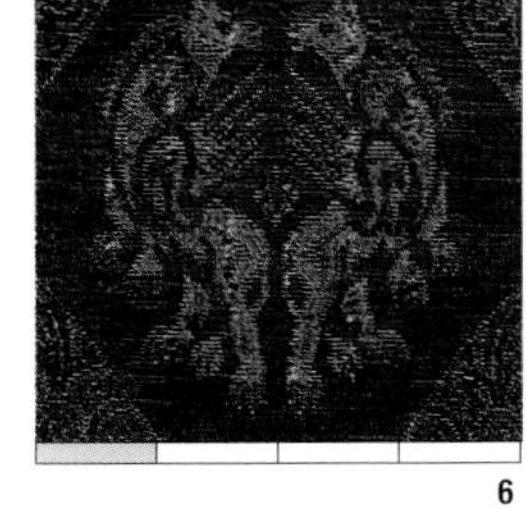

6

5 The Silk Gallery/Cantabile Color **maroon silk, gold chenille** Alternative colors **available** Composition **83% cotton, 17% silk** Width **50in/127cm** Repeat **15in/38cm** Price ★★★

6 Old World Weavers/Aracelis Color **wine** Alternative colors **available** Composition **54% viscose, 43% acrylic, 3% polypropylene** Width **54in/137cm** Repeat **9½in/24cm** Price ★★★

7 Ian Sanderson/Pendragon Color **coral** Alternative colors **available** Composition **58% cotton, 24% polyacrylic, 18% viscose** Width **55in/140cm** Repeat **24¾in/63cm** Price ★★

8 Old World Weavers/Corda Matisse Color **gold** Alternative colors **not available** Composition **67% viscose, 33% cotton** Width **51in/130cm** Repeat **26in/66cm** Price ★★★★

1 Old World Weavers/Sahara SX 02342149 Color **beige and green** Alternative colors **available** Composition **47% rayon, 32% acrylic, 21% cotton** Width **55in/140cm** Repeat **18½in/47cm** Price ★★★

2 Beaumont & Fletcher/Augustus 10050 Color **red/gray** Alternative colors **available** Composition **90% cotton, 10% wool** Width **55in/140cm** Repeat **11¼in/28.5cm** Price ★★★

3 Hodsoll McKenzie/Turkish Flower 303/103 Color **blue** Alternative colors **available** Composition **100% cotton** Width **50in/127cm** Repeat **3in/8cm** Price ★★★

4 Lelièvre/Florence 93104 Color **soleil** Alternative colors **available** Composition **60% wool, 40% acrylic** Width **59in/150cm** Repeat **25in/64cm** Price ★★★

4

7

8

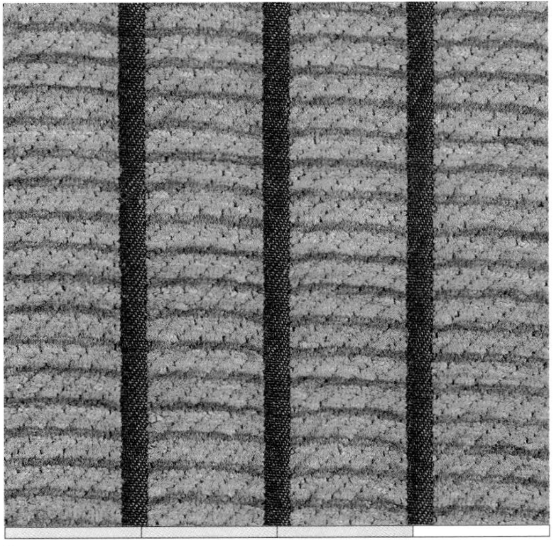

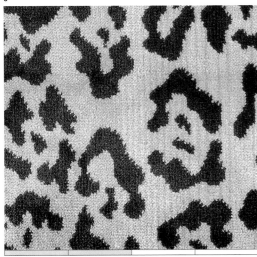

9

9 **The Silk Gallery/Chenille II** Color **henna and gold** Alternative colors **available** Composition **83% cotton, 17% silk** Width **50in/127cm** Repeat **–** Price ★★★

10 **Old World Weavers/Leopard Velvet Y00 6900001** Color **gold and brown** Alternative colors **not available** Composition **57% silk, 30% cotton, 13% viscose** Width **51¾in/132cm** Repeat **29in/73.5cm** Price ★★★★★

11 **Hodsoll McKenzie/Star Chenille 301** Color **106** Alternative colors **available** Composition **100% cotton** Width **50in/127cm** Repeat **4in/10.5cm** Price ★★★

12 **Watts of Westminster/Pine** Color **brick and leaf green** Alternative colors **available** Composition **100% cotton/chenille** Width **48¾in/ 124cm** Repeat **31in/ 79cm** Price ★★★★

13 **Mulberry/Aubusson Chenille FD001/508** Color **5103** Alternative colors **available** Composition **75% cotton, 25% wool** Width **59in/150cm** Repeat **51½in/131cm** Price ★★★

14 **Old World Weavers/Velours Marmara FV6 7028007** Color **green** Alternative colors **available** Composition **75% rayon, 25% cotton** Width **53in/135cm** Repeat **–** Price ★★★

11

12

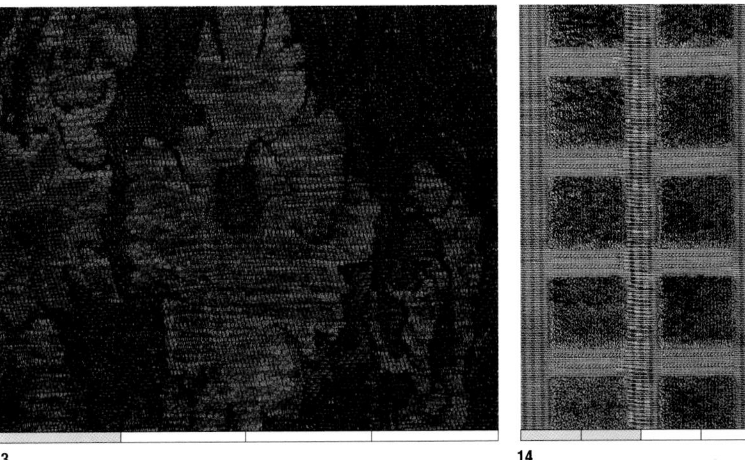

13

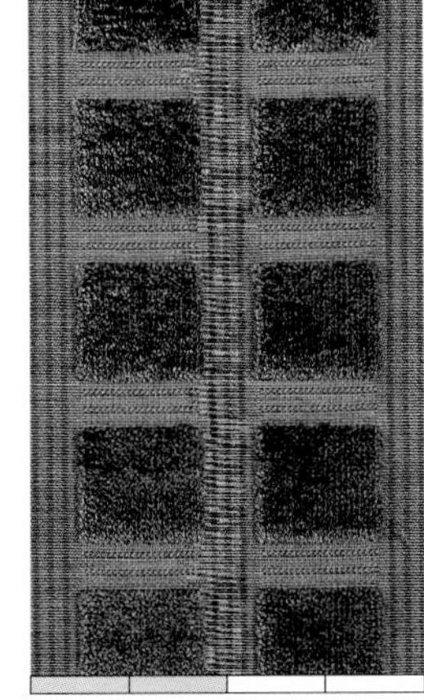

14

10

15 **Zoffany/VCB11** Color **green** Alternative colors **available** Composition **74% cotton, 26% linen** Width **51in/130cm** Repeat **–** Price ★★★

16 **Zimmer & Rohde/Bilkis 5014** Color **217** Alternative colors **available** Composition **100% cotton** Width **51in/130cm** Repeat **¾in/2cm** Price ★★★

17 **Sahco Hesslein/Eroica 04630** Color **green and yellow** Alternative colors **available** Composition **57% cotton, 43% viscose** Width **51in/130cm** Repeat **–** Price ★★★★

18 **RBI International/Brazil GFB78** Color **5444** Alternative colors **available** Composition **60% cotton, 30% viscose, 10% polyester** Width **54in/137cm** Repeat **9in/23cm** Price ★★★

15

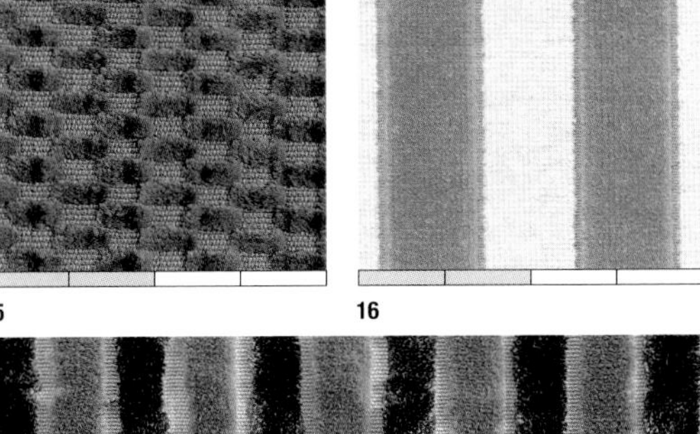

16

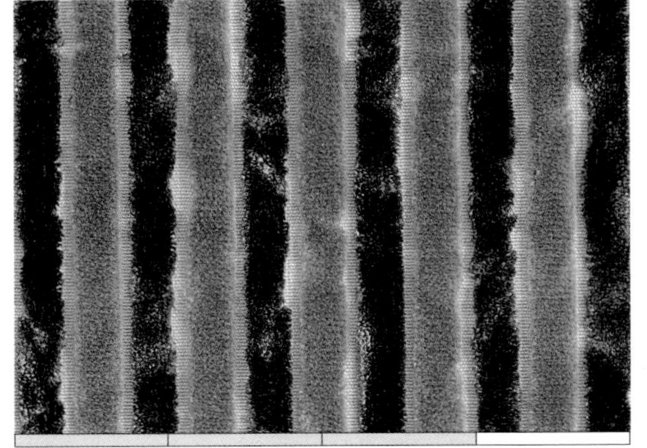

17

18

Patterned Pile: **20th century**

Toward the end of the 19th century, patterned pile fabrics suffered a drop in popularity. Because of their densely woven pile, they were viewed by many arbiters of household taste as dust traps, particularly when heavily draped around beds, over doors, or in front of windows; as the latter, they were also deemed to hinder the entrance of "health-giving" sunlight. In reality, such views were less a concern for health and more an aesthetic reaction to overfurnished and often gloomy "High Victorian" interiors. At the beginning of the 20th century, patterned pile fabrics enjoyed a resurgence of popularity, and except in minimal Modernist interiors, their use has continued to this day.

Manufacturers produced a wide range of patterned pile fabrics, notably Genoa and *gaufrage* velvets, as well as chenille and velour. Most are intended for curtains and as top covers for upholstery. Generally, patterns remained traditional, with floral, leaf, or fruit motifs, and stripes and checks in highest demand. As in previous centuries, silk, mohair, wool, and cotton yarns were still used in the production of pile fabrics, although since 1945, synthetic yarns, such as Dralon, were also employed.

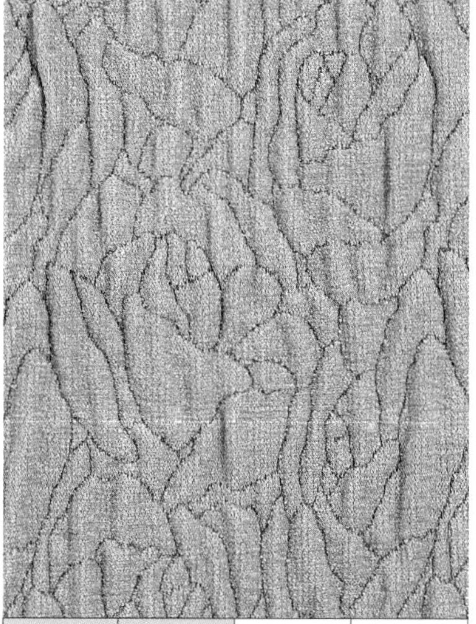

Donghia/Rugose 0556/6480-10 Color **cavolo-cream** Alternative colors **available** Composition **80% viscose, 12% polyester, 8% polyacrylic** Width **52in/133cm** Repeat **3½in/9cm** Price ★★★★

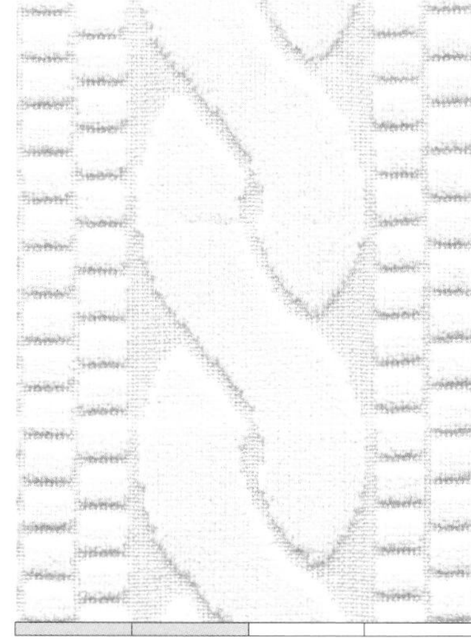

Ian Sanderson/Spiral Color **cream** Alternative colors **available** Composition **100% cotton** Width **55in/140cm** Repeat **4in/10.5cm** Price ★★

Zimmer & Rohde/Danko 1259 Color **989** Alternative colors **available** Composition **100% cotton** Width **55in/140cm** Repeat **9in/23cm** Price ★★★

Sahco Hesslein/Akka 04614 Color **cream** Alternative colors **not available** Composition **100% cotton** Width **55in/140cm** Repeat – Price ★★★

Zimmer & Rohde/Dina 1260 989 Color **black and cream** Alternative colors **available** Composition **100% cotton** Width **55in/140cm** Repeat **¾in/2cm** Price ★★★

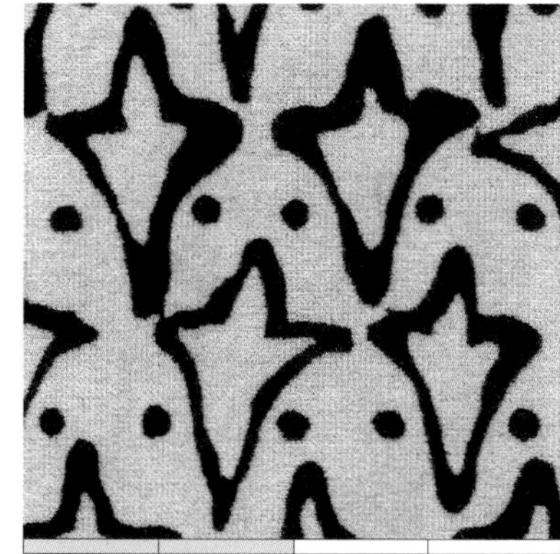

Bentley & Spens/Lilies Color **black/gray** Alternative colors **not available** Composition **100% cotton** Width **51in/130cm** Repeat **19¼in/49cm** Price ★★ LC W

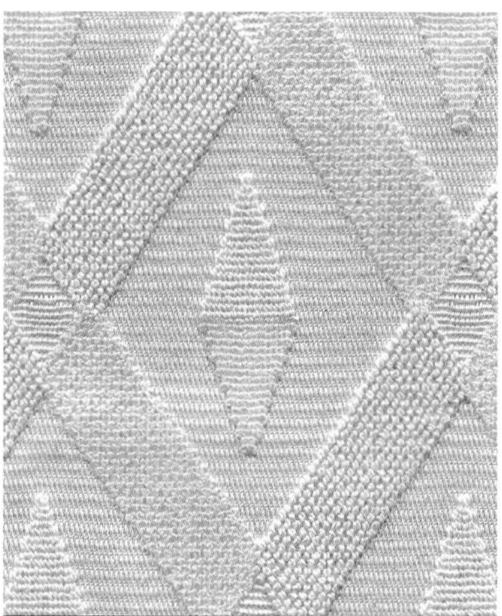

Sahco Hesslein/Akkord 04625 Color **cream** Alternative colors **not available** Composition **68% cotton, 32% viscose** Width **55in/140cm** Repeat **5in/13cm** Price ★★★

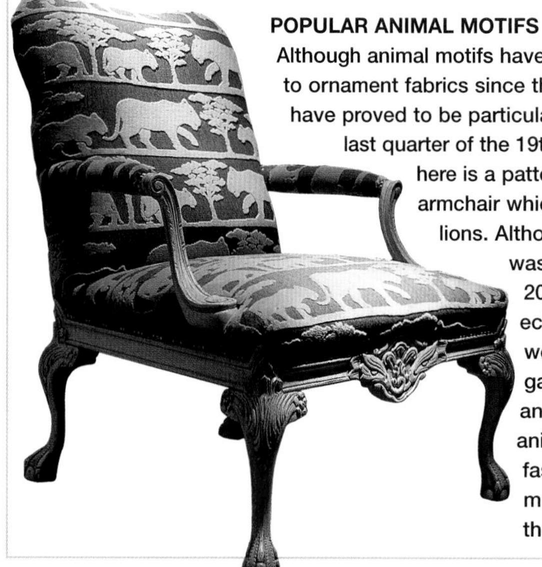

POPULAR ANIMAL MOTIFS

Although animal motifs have been used regularly to ornament fabrics since the Middle Ages, they have proved to be particularly popular since the last quarter of the 19th century. Shown here is a patterned-pile upholstered armchair which displays a pride of lions. Although the textile design was created in the late 20th century, it strongly echoes the fabrics that were embellished with gazelles, antelopes, lions, and other exotic African animals and were in fashion throughout much of Europe during the 1920s and 1930s.

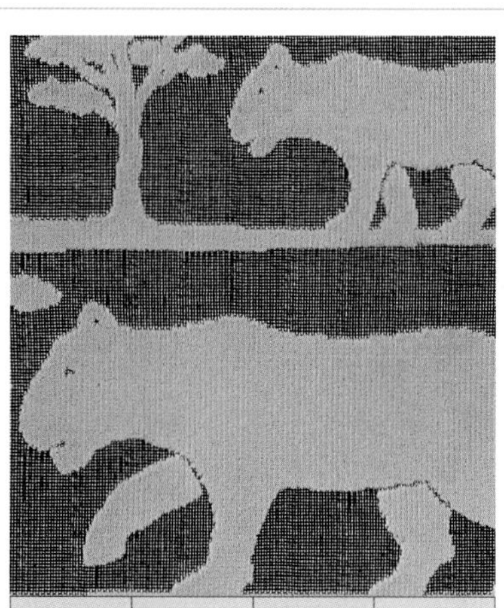

Andrew Martin/Pride Color **taupe** Alternative colors **available** Composition **face: 100% cotton; back: 72% polyester, 28% rayon** Width **55in/140cm** Repeat **11¾in/30cm** Price ★★

Pierre Frey/Brigitte Bardot/Rivoli 2150 Color **anthracite** Alternative colors **available** Composition **77% viscose, 23% cotton** Width **51in/130cm** Repeat **¾in/2cm** Price ★★★

Glant/Labyrinth 9020 Color **aqua** Alternative colors **available** Composition **100% cotton** Width **51in/130cm** Repeat – Price ★★★★

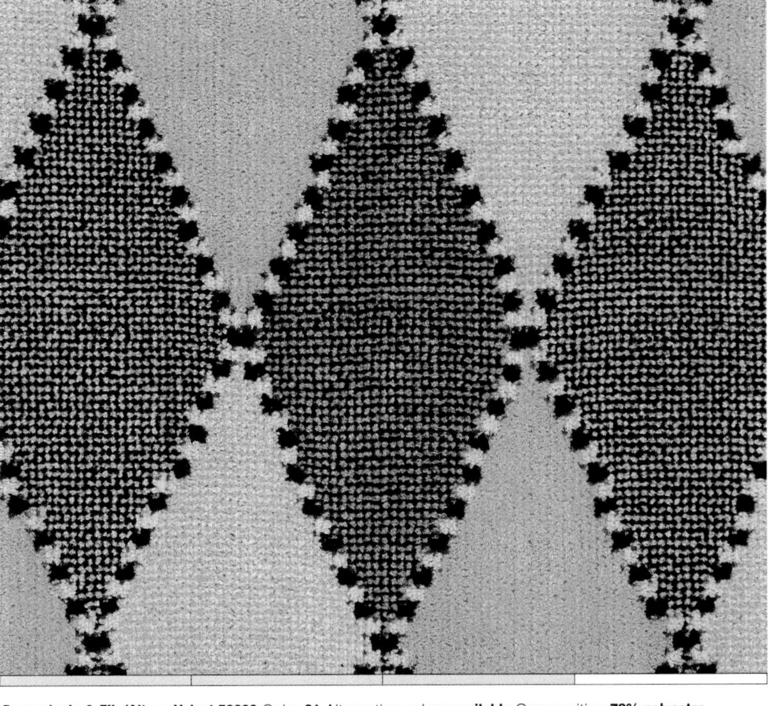

Brunschwig & Fils/Altena Velvet 53293 Color **01** Alternative colors **available** Composition **78% polyester, 22% cotton** Width **55in/140cm** Repeat **9in/23cm** Price ★★★★

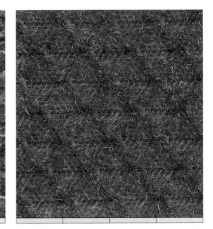

Brunschwig & Fils/Bichon Chenille Plaid 46091 Color **02** Alternative colors **available** Composition **60% rayon, 40% cotton** Width **55¾in/142cm** Repeat **6in/15cm** Price ★★★★

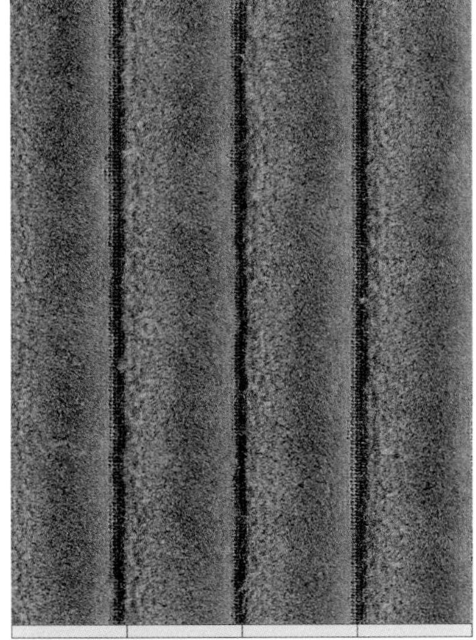

Osborne & Little/Patara F1141 Color **green** Alternative colors **available** Composition **100% cotton** Width **50½in/127cm** Repeat – Price ★★★

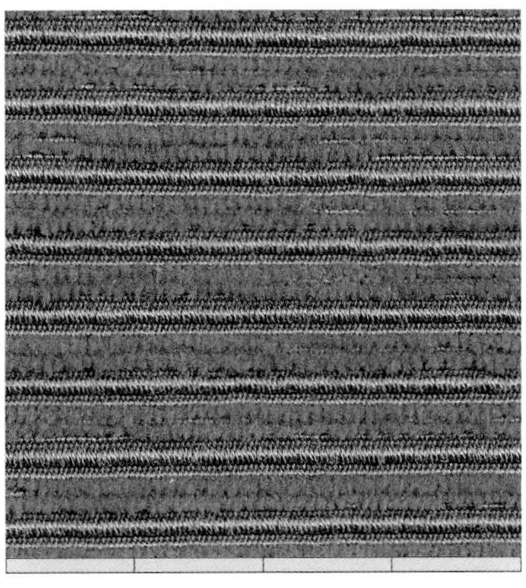

Jab/Tampa 1-2011-581 Color **green and blue** Alternative colors **available** Composition **100% cotton** Width **55in/140cm** Repeat – Price ★★★

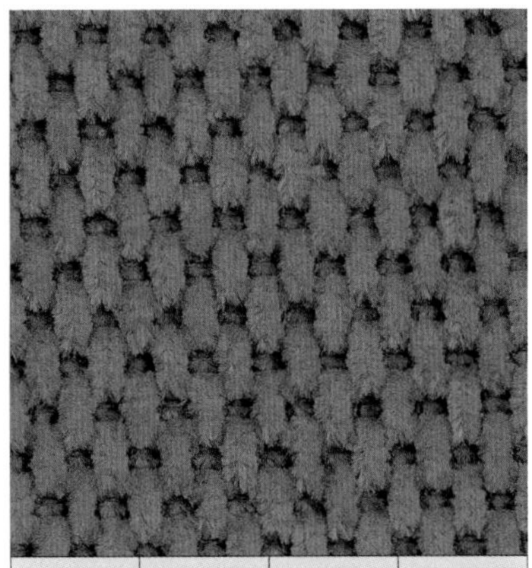

Glant/Chaine 3050 Color **forget-me-not** Alternative colors **available** Composition **100% cotton** Width **51in/130cm** Repeat – Price ★★★★

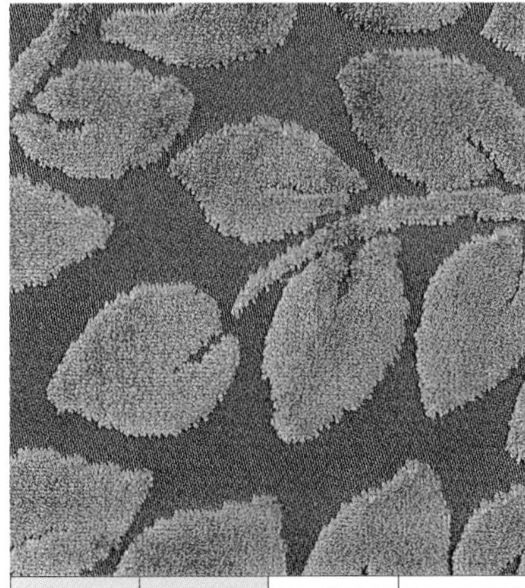

Jack Lenor Larsen/Solace 8590/93 Color **coral** Alternative colors **available** Composition **52% viscose, 48% polyester** Width **51in/130cm** Repeat **13in/33cm** Price ★★★★★

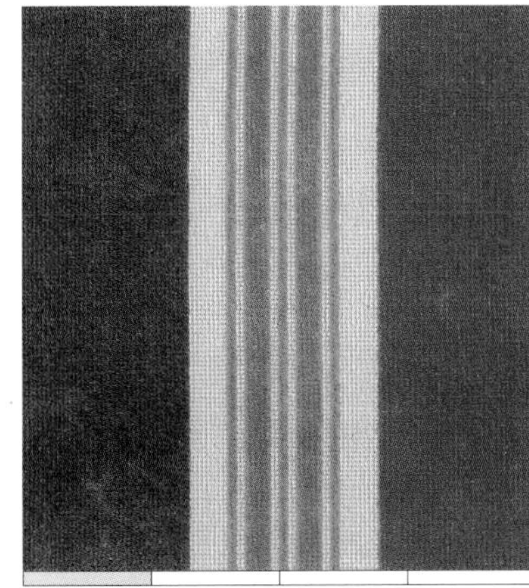

Osborne & Little/Hussar F1421 Color **05** Alternative colors **available** Composition **95% cotton, 5% polyester** Width **50½in/128cm** Repeat – Price ★★★

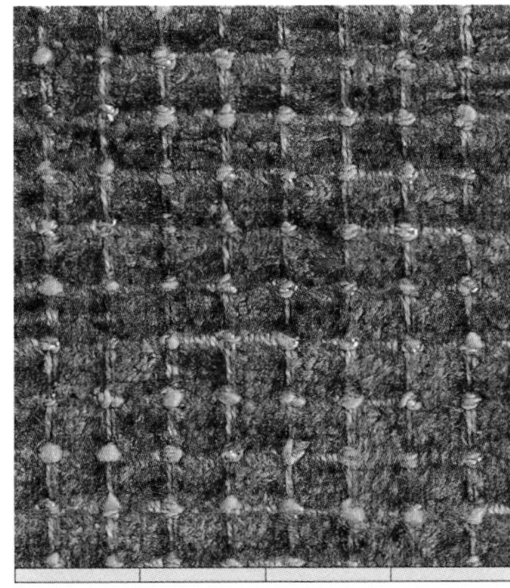

Old World Weavers/Cubic PW 00930005 Color **rust/putty** Alternative colors **available** Composition **60% cotton, 40% rayon** Width **55in/140cm** Repeat – Price ★★★

Brunschwig & Fils/Brigham Mohair Figured Velvet 32 38 01 Color **5** Alternative colors **available** Composition **50% cotton, 50% mohair** Width **51in/130cm** Repeat – Price ★★★★

Damask & Brocade

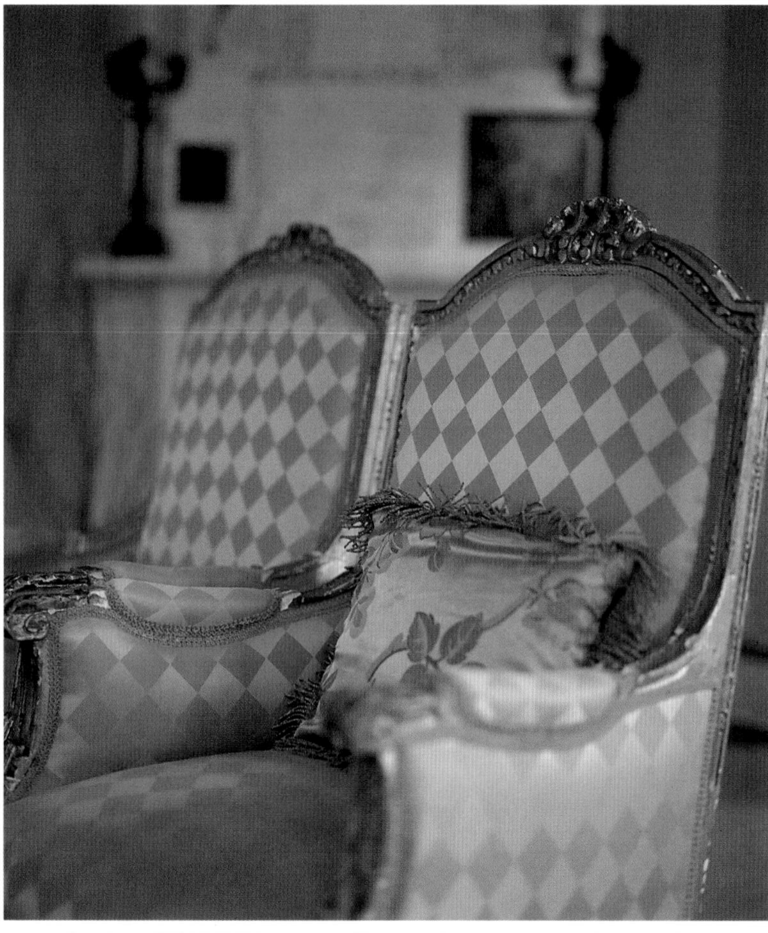

ABOVE Residing in the drawing room of a house in Charleston, South Carolina, this pair of 18th-century, French gilt armchairs have been recovered in a 20th-century, checker-pattern silk damask. The geometric design was inspired by upholstery fabrics fashionable in France since the 17th century.

FLORAL DAMASK
The late 18th-century French armchair shown here has been sympathetically reupholstered in a rose-pattern silk damask. Floral patterns have proved to be among the most enduringly popular of damask designs since they were first produced in Europe during the early Renaissance. Many of the examples created since then have featured stylized and often exotic flowers and vegetation. However, during the late 18th century, the floral patterns, as here, tended to be more naturalistic depictions of cultivated and wild flowers native to the European countryside.

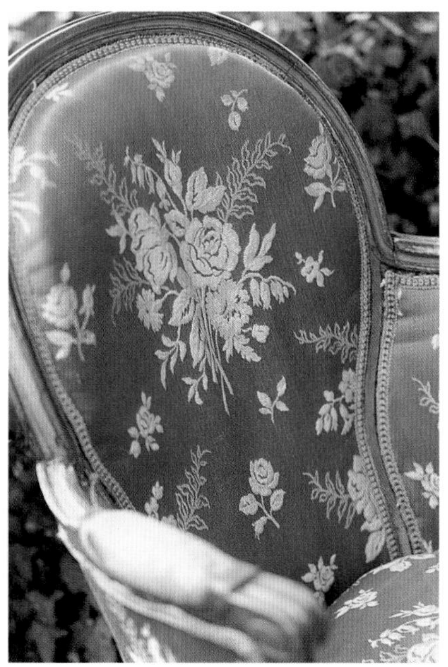

Damasks were first produced in the Syrian capital, Damascus, during the 4th century A.D. The first European damasks were made in Italy during the 15th century, and thereafter were mainly produced in the Netherlands, France, Ireland, Switzerland, and Britain. True damask is a monochrome reversible fabric displaying fluid but formal patterns created by the contrast between a shiny, satin-weave ground and matte, sateen-weave figuring. However, damasks that incorporate two or more colors have also been produced. Originally, damasks were made of silk, but linen, wool, cotton, and synthetic fibers have also been used. Traditional motifs include stylized flowers and leaves, and exotic fruits such as the pomegranate. Brocatelle is a variant of damask and incorporates a satin or twill figuring that is contrasted with a plain- or satin-weave ground. Brocade is also damask based, but distinguished by figured patterns raised against the ground by the embroidery-like technique of spooling additional colored threads through the weave.

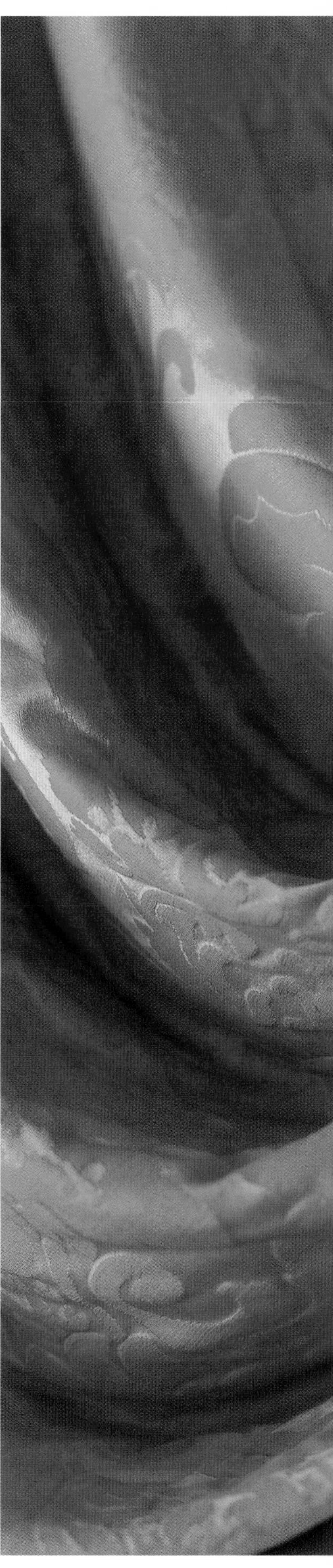

RIGHT A detail of one of a pair of heavy, yellow silk damask curtains, with silk rope-and-tassel tiebacks, in Rosalie, a mid-19th-century house in Natchez, Mississippi. The floral-pattern damask is late 20th century, but it was copied from the fabric originally used in the house when it was first furnished and decorated.

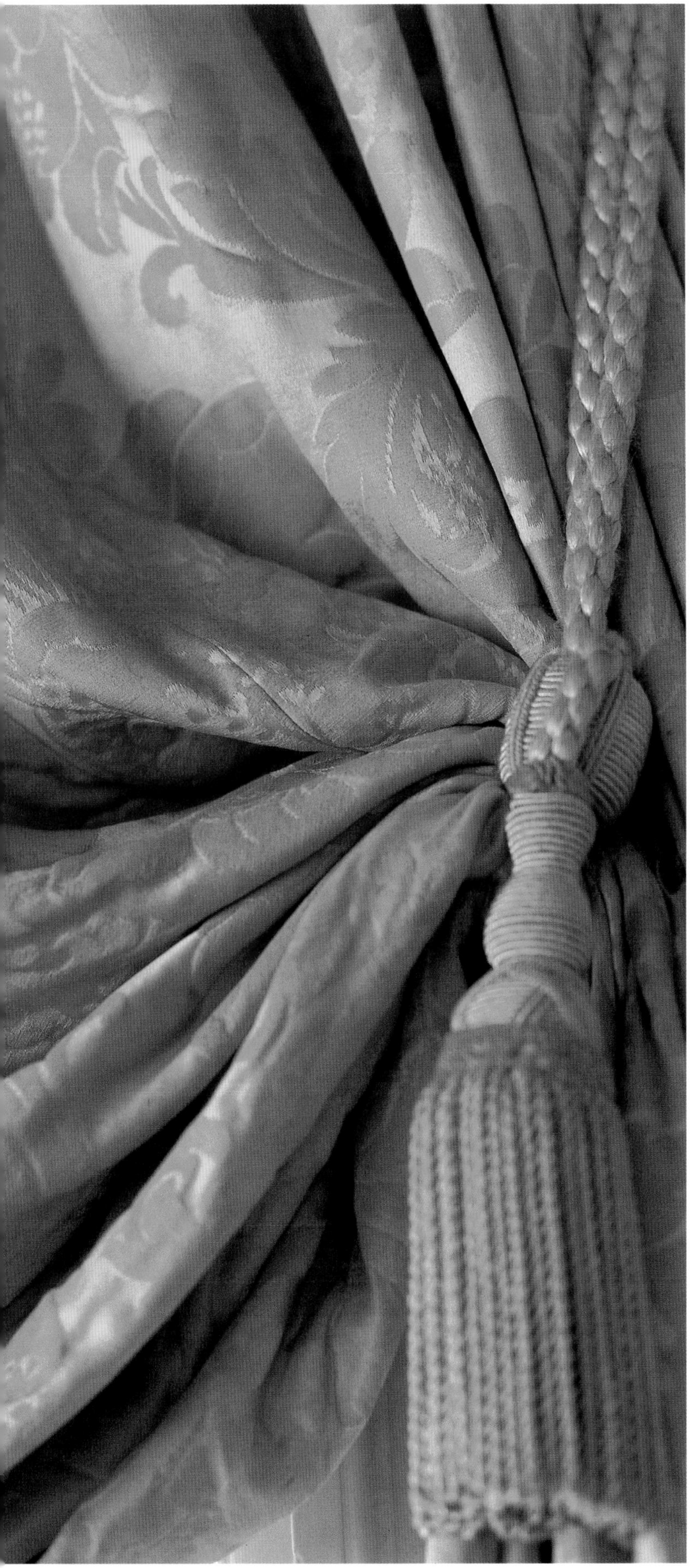

KEY DESIGNS

1 Stylized interlaced foliage patterns (arabesques) were derived from Near Eastern ornament and favored on European (and later American) damasks from the mid-16th to early 17th centuries.

2 Vegetal patterns incorporating ripening fruits and seedpods–notably thistles and pomegranates–are among the most traditional damask designs. They were first used during the early Renaissance.

3 Floral patterns on damasks are often flat and highly stylized. However, more naturalistic "three-dimensional" elements are sometimes used, such as the shading in this 19th-century damask.

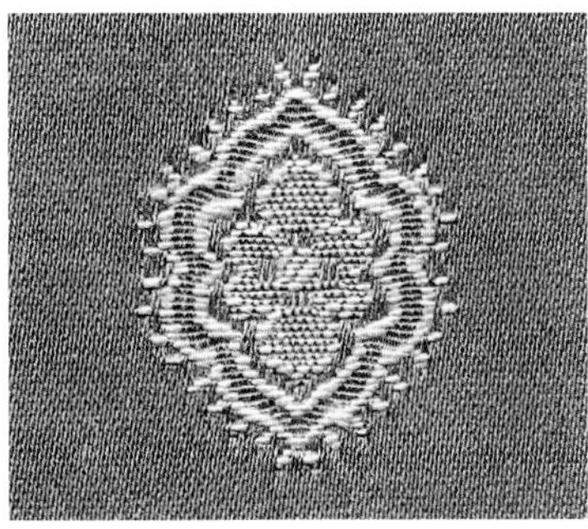

4 Damasks and brocades embellished with small, repeated motifs became increasingly popular from the early 19th century, particularly on fabrics intended for use on upholstered seating.

5 Diaper-patterned damasks, such as this small trellis design with stylized flowers, have been produced since the Renaissance, but were a notable feature of 19th-century Victorian interiors.

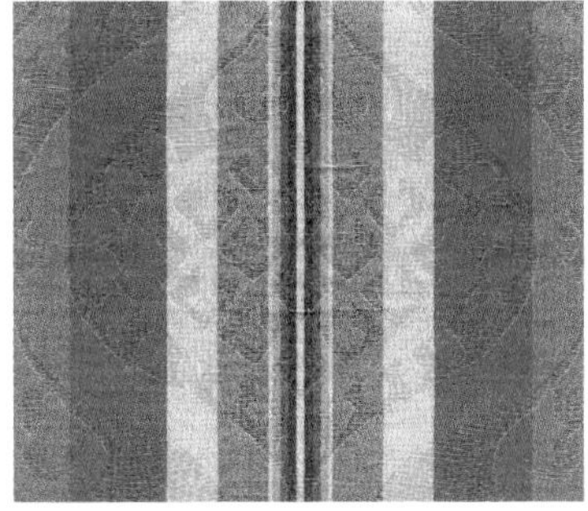

6 While true damasks are monochromatic, multicolored damasks are also produced. Striped versions were fashionable during the Renaissance and the late 18th and early 19th centuries.

---

1 **Lelièvre/Carnavalet** Color **Bordeaux** Alternative colors **available** Composition **57% linen, 43% viscose** Width **51in/130cm** Repeat **22¾in/58cm** Price ★★★

2 **Scalamandré/Newport Damask** Color **tile blue** Alternative colors **available** Composition **100% silk** Width **55in/140cm** Repeat **18½in/47cm** Price ★★★ W T

3 **Liberty/Sutrana** Color **sky** Alternative colors **available** Composition **56% viscose, 33% cotton, 11% nylon** Width **53in/135cm** Repeat **20½in/52cm** Price ★★

4 **John Wilman/Laurel** Color **celadon** Alternative colors **available** Composition **63% cotton, 37% polyester** Width **54in/137cm** Repeat **2¾in/7cm** Price ★

5 **Gainsborough Silk Weaving/F841** Color **gold** Alternative colors **available** Composition **100% cotton** Width **50in/127cm** Repeat **3¾in/9.5cm** Price ★★★ LC

6 **Zimmer & Rohde/Bela** Color **cream** Alternative colors **available** Composition **54% linen, 46% cotton** Width **51in/130cm** Repeat **7in/18cm** Price ★★★

Damask & Brocade: **Pre-18th century**

During the Renaissance, Italy led the way in the production of silk damasks and heavier silk brocatelles and brocades, the latter often augmented with gold and silver thread. Favored designs–stylized flowers, fruits, and leaves–had large pattern repeats particularly suitable for wall-, bed-, window-, and door-hangings in grander interiors. After the Netherlands began large-scale production in the late 15th century, less expensive linen weaves became fashionable. During the 16th century, Flemish weavers also introduced new designs–such as hunting scenes–and made traditional patterns with smaller repeats, better suited for upholstery. By the early 17th century, production had spread to France, notably the Huguenot city of Lyons, and, following the emigration of the Huguenots to England, Ireland, and Switzerland in the late 17th century, these countries also began to produce large quantities of silk, linen, and even cheaper woolen and worsted weaves for use as both hangings and upholstery.

1

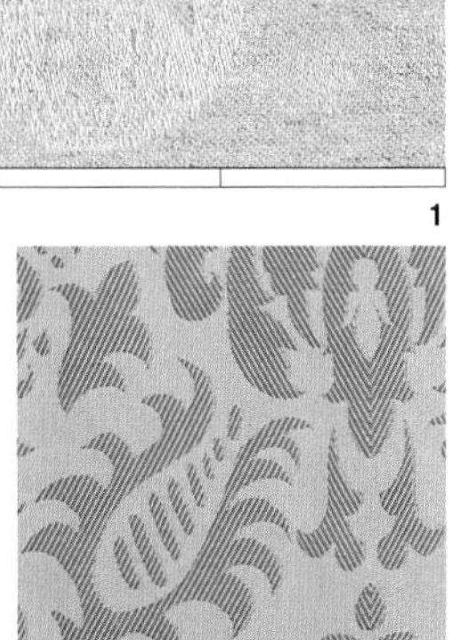
2

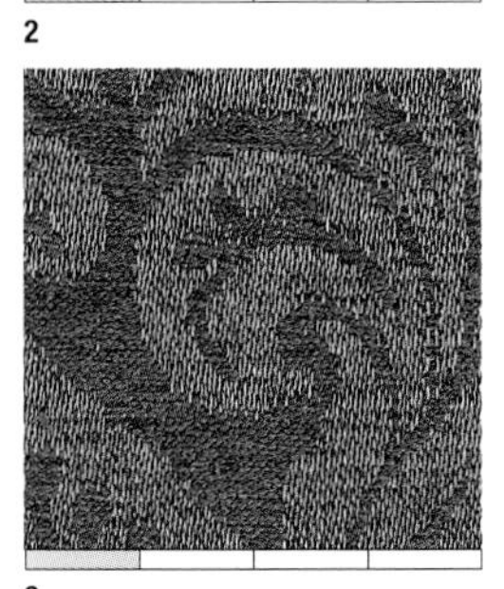
3

1 **Claremont Fabrics/Orkney J00** Color **natural beige** Alternative colors **available** Composition **85% cotton, 15% linen** Width **55¾in/142cm** Repeat **26¾in/68cm** Price ★

2 **The Silk Gallery/Ceres Damask** Color **ivory/antique green** Alternative colors **available** Composition **82% silk, 18% cotton** Width **50in/127cm** Repeat **15in/38cm** Price ★★★★

3 **Antico Setificio Fiorentino/Doria D1** Color **green on green** Alternative colors **available** Composition **100% silk** Width **47in/120cm** Repeat **21½in/55cm** Price ★★★★ W

4

5

6

7

8

4 **Gainsborough Silk Weaving/F832** Color **8** Alternative colors **available** Composition **85% cotton, 15% viscose** Width **50in/127cm** Repeat **26in/66cm** Price ★★

5 **Watts of Westminster/Crevelli** Color **gold and pearl** Alternative colors **available** Composition **51% cotton, 29% lumiyarn, 20% silk** Width **48¾in/124cm** Repeat **34½in/88cm** Price ★★★★

6 **Ian Sanderson/Florin** Color **red clay** Alternative colors **available** Composition **70% cotton, 30% rayon** Width **50in/127cm** Repeat **15¼in/39cm** Price ★★

7 **Stuart Interiors/Fiori** Color **burgundy and gold** Alternative colors **available** Composition **60% wool, 40% linen** Width **68¾in/175cm** Repeat **23¾in/60cm** Price ★★★★ LC W

8 **Stuart Interiors/Medici** Color **gold-gold/red** Alternative colors **available** Composition **100% wool** Width **57in/145cm** Repeat **18½in/47cm** Price ★★★ LC W

BIRDS

Usually displayed in flight or sitting in foliage, birds are among the most traditional of damask and brocade motifs. "Uccellini," shown right, which dates from the 16th century, is typical of Florentine Renaissance design, and was inspired by the drapery in paintings by Benozzo Gozzoli and Ghirlandaio. "Love Bird," shown far right, dates from the 17th century, and is representative of the symbolism of birds in fabric patterns. For example, two birds in a tree were emblematic of the Holy Ghost and the Virgin Mary.

Antico Setificio Fiorentino/Uccellini UC1 Color **silver/green** Alternative colors **not available** Composition **100% silk** Width **51in/130cm** Repeat **4¼in/11cm** Price ★★★ W

Scalamandré/Love Bird 1098004 Color**old ivory** Alternative colors **available** Composition **100% silk** Width **50in/127cm** Repeat **18in/46cm** Price ★★★★★ T

9

9 Crowson/Palazzo 03097 P02 Color **red and gold** Alternative colors **available** Composition **56% viscose, 44% polyester** Width **54in/137cm** Repeat **26¾in/68cm** Price ★★

10 Stuart Interiors/Genoa Color **blue and rust** Alternative colors **available** Composition **100% wool** Width **48¾in/124cm** Repeat **34½in/88cm** Price ★★★ LC W

11 Zoffany/Flower 334405 Color **blue** Alternative colors **available** Composition **61% wool, 29% cotton, 10% nylon** Width **57in/145cm** Repeat **4in/10.5cm** Price ★★

12 Zimmer & Rohde/Otello 3000-351 Color **gold** Alternative colors **available** Composition **54% linen, 46% cotton** Width **51in/130cm** Repeat **22in/56cm** Price ★★★★

13 Scalamandré/Georgian 1225M-044 Color **rose and burgundy** Alternative colors **available** Composition **100% silk** Width **55in/140cm** Repeat **24in/61cm** Price ★★★★★ T

13

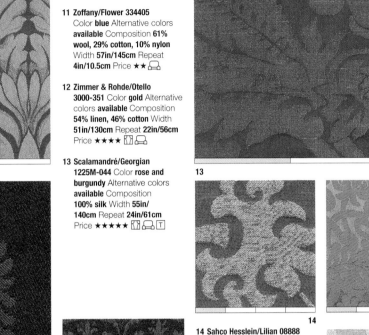

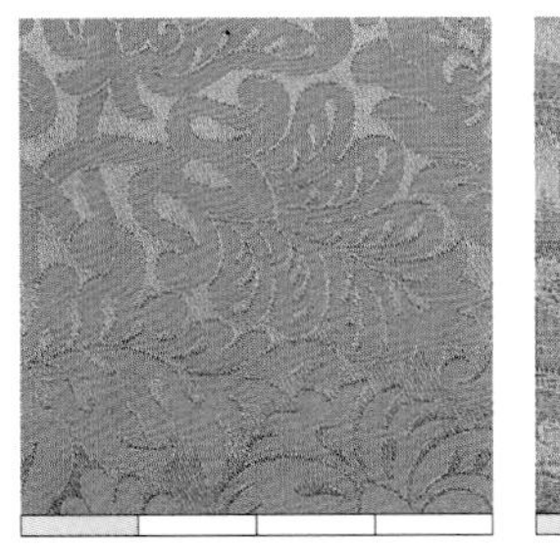
14

15

16

10

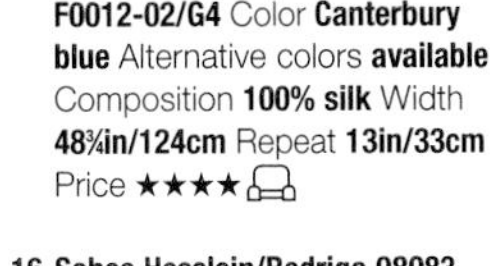
11

14 Sahco Hesslein/Lilian 08888 Color **red and gold** Alternative colors **available** Composition **57% linen, 43% cotton** Width **55in/140cm** Repeat **26¾in/68cm** Price ★★★

15 Watts of Westminster/Holbein F0012-02/G4 Color **Canterbury blue** Alternative colors **available** Composition **100% silk** Width **48¾in/124cm** Repeat **13in/33cm** Price ★★★★

16 Sahco Hesslein/Rodrigo 08083 Color **gold** Alternative colors **available** Composition **60% cotton, 40% viscose** Width **51in/130cm** Repeat **21in/53cm** Price ★★★★

17 Zimmer & Rohde/Berytos 5004 175 Color **yellow** Alternative colors **available** Composition **54% linen, 46% cotton** Width **51in/130cm** Repeat **7in/18cm** Price ★★★

18 Lelièvre/Carnavalet 4043 07 Color **persan** Alternative colors **available** Composition **57% linen, 43% viscose** Width **51in/130cm** Repeat **22¾in/58cm** Price ★★★

17

12

18

STUART

Damask & Brocade: **18th century**

The increased production of damasks during the second half of the 17th century was sustained throughout the 18th century. Silk and linen damask upholstery was a feature of Palladian, Rococo-style, and Neoclassical interiors in England and Europe, and was often coordinated with wall-hangings and curtains. Damask upholstery and hangings, mostly of a woolen or worsted variety imported from England, were also fashionable in North American Adam-style interiors of the late 18th century.

Favored colors of the period included magenta and crimson, deep green, dark blue, and pastel pinks and blues. Flower, leaf, and fruit patterns remained fashionable, although pastoral designs, in which traditional motifs were combined with musical instruments and birds, also came into vogue. In grander interiors, silk brocade hangings were much in evidence. Many were multicolored, with exotic designs such as coral motifs and Indo-Chinoiserie patterns featuring elephants and buddhas.

Donghia/Sogno 0387/9315 Color **09** Alternative colors **available** Composition **38% silk, 35% linen, 27% cotton** Width **54in/137cm** Repeat **31in/79cm** Price ★★★★★

Andrew Martin/Avignon Color **black** Alternative colors **available** Composition **100% cotton** Width **53½in/136cm** Repeat **26½in/67cm** Price ★★

Scalamandré/Classical Lampas 26035-005 Color **multi cream on lacquer** Alternative colors **available** Composition **45% spun rayon, 34% linen, 21% silk** Width **53½in/136cm** Repeat **29in/74cm** Price ★★★★★

Beaumont & Fletcher/Marlowe 1012b Color **gold/red** Alternative colors **available** Composition **92% wool, 8% nylon** Width **55in/140cm** Repeat **17¾in/45cm** Price ★★

CHINOISERIE

During the 18th century, *chinoiserie*-patterned damasks became highly fashionable throughout Europe, notably in French Rococo- and English Gothick-style interiors. Inspired by the decorations on imported Chinese artifacts, particularly lacquerwares and ceramics, designers produced Europeanized interpretations of some traditional Oriental motifs. Typical subjects included exotic birds, dragons, and monkeys (*singeries*).

Percheron/Damas-Les Chinois 10237 Color **40** Alternative colors **available** Composition **71% cotton, 29% silk** Width **51in/130cm** Repeat **27in/69cm** Price ★★★★

John Wilman/Laurel 170177 Color **salmon** Alternative colors **available** Composition **63% cotton, 37% polyester** Width **54in/137cm** Repeat **2¾in/7cm** Price ★★

Dovedale/Harvard HARV005 Color **05** Alternative colors **available** Composition **100% cotton** Width **57in/145cm** Repeat **15¾in/40cm** Price ★

Marvic Textiles/Damask Rosario 5201-4 Color **rose** Alternative colors **available** Composition **71% cotton, 29% silk** Width **51in/130cm** Repeat **18½in/47cm** Price ★★★

Hodsoll McKenzie/Turkish Tulip 357/101-109 Color **natural** Alternative colors **available** Composition **100% silk** Width **50in/127cm** Repeat **25½in/65cm** Price ★★★★ W

Ian Sanderson/Dijon Damask Color **shrimp** Alternative colors **available** Composition **63% rayon, 37% cotton** Width **58in/147cm** Repeat **26¾in/68cm** Price ★★

Hodsoll McKenzie/Venetian Damask 352/101 Color **dusty pink** Alternative colors **available** Composition **61% flax, 26% cotton, 13% silk** Width **50in/127cm** Repeat **26in/66cm** Price ★★★★

Warner Fabrics/Hilliard T 114004 Color **cedar** Alternative colors **available** Composition **100% silk** Width **55in/140cm** Repeat **15in/38cm** Price ★★★

The Silk Gallery/Campana Color **henna/cedar ground** Alternative colors **available** Composition **82% silk, 18% cotton** Width **50in/127cm** Repeat **23¾in/60cm** Price ★★★★

Damask & Brocade: **Early 19th century**

The most significant development in the production of woven fabrics during the first half of the 19th century was technological. The invention, in 1805, of the automated Jacquard loom resulted in a speeding up of the weaving process, and by removing the number of operators needed, also achieved a cut in labor costs. Damasks, brocatelles, and, to a lesser extent, partly hand-worked brocades, therefore became more affordable, and damask-covered upholstery gradually found its way into middle-class homes, particularly on sofas and chairs. The "dobby" loom, invented in 1824 and designed to supplement the Jacquard loom, also made it easier to produce patterns with smaller repeats–the type most suited to upholstering furniture.

While linen, woolen, and worsted damasks, brocatelles, and brocades became cheaper and more accessible, the more expensive silk versions continued to be produced not only for upholstery but also for wall- and bed-hangings, curtains, and lambrequins (valances). During this period, the new looms of Genoa in Italy, Lyons in France, and Spitalfields in England turned out increasingly complex and elaborate patterns well suited to the grander French Empire, English Regency, and American Federal interiors.

2

3

1

4

5

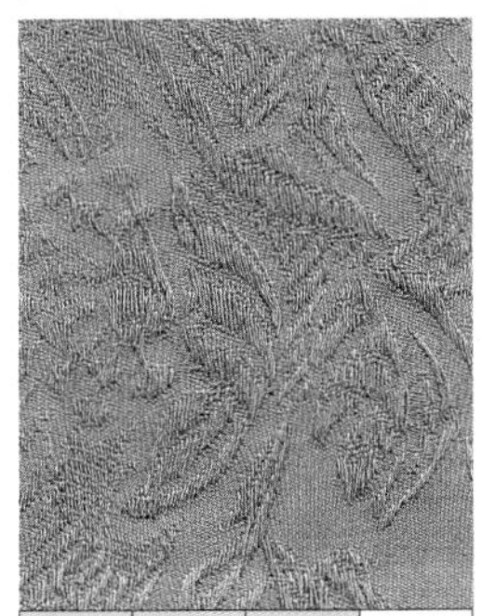

6

1 **Watts of Westminster/Gaheris F0048-01/N6** Color **rose/linen** Composition **64% cotton/36% linen** Width **55in/140cm** Repeat **7in/18cm** Price ★★★

2 **Guy Evans/Palmerston Damask** Color **red/gold** Alternative colors **available** Composition **50% wool, 50% silk** Width **42in/107cm** Repeat **19½in/49.5cm** Price ★★★★

3 **Mary Fox Linton/Tancredi** Color **03** Alternative colors **available** Composition **67% cotton, 33% viscose** Width **55in/140cm** Repeat **14½in/37cm** Price ★★★★

4 **Warner Fabrics/Eugene Damask T 851001F** Color **azure/jade** Alternative colors **available** Composition **54% cotton, 46% modacrylic** Width **51in/130cm** Repeat **17¼in/44cm** Price ★★

5 **Mary Fox Linton/Laveno** Color **04** Alternative colors **available** Composition **100% silk** Width **55in/140cm** Repeat **15¼in/39cm** Price ★★★★

6 **Osborne & Little/Eglantine F870** Color **14** Alternative colors **available** Composition **70% cotton, 30% viscose** Width **55in/140cm** Repeat **7in/18cm** Price ★★

7

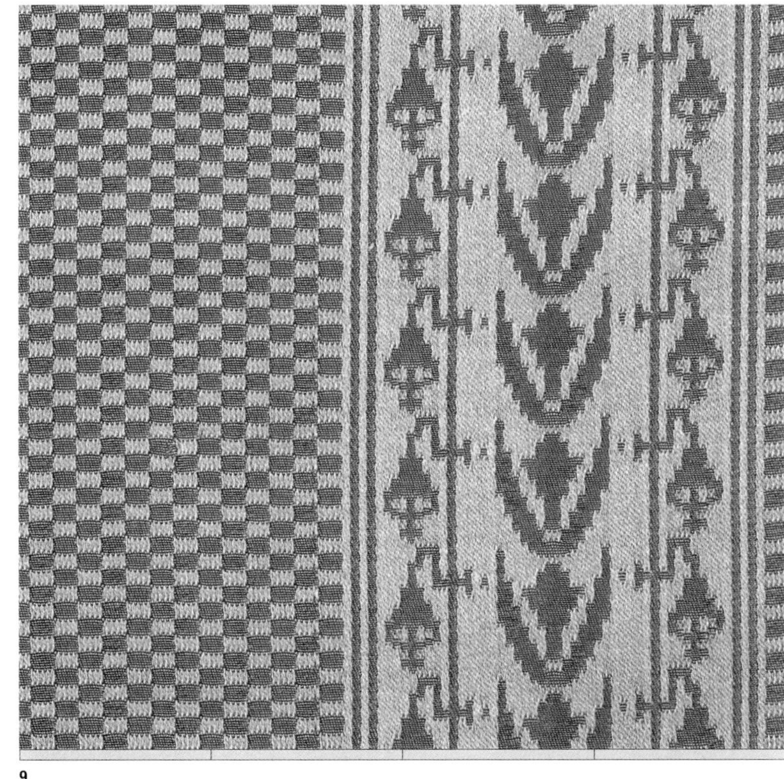

9

7 Today Interiors/Court Weaves FRW 1332 Color **gold** Alternative colors **available** Composition **52% modacrylic, 36% cotton,12% nylon** Width **55in/140cm** Repeat **2½in/6.5cm** Price ★★

8 Mary Fox Linton/Belgarbo Color **02** Alternative colors **available** Composition **79% cotton, 21% silk** Width **55in/140cm** Repeat **2in/5cm** Price ★★★★

9 Percheron/Damas Clochettes 10414 Color **5** Alternative colors **available** Composition **100% silk** Width **51in/130cm** Repeat **4¼in/11cm** Price ★★★★★

10

11

12

10 Watts of Westminster/Giovanna Damask F0052-01/B4 Color **white/butter** Alternative colors **available** Composition **100% silk** Width **48¾in/124cm** Repeat **8in/20cm** Price ★★★★

11 Northwood Designs/Scala 001 Color **natural** Alternative colors **available** Composition **55% polyester, 45% cotton** Width **118in/300cm** Repeat **7½in/19cm** Price ★

12 Garin/Alhambra 07082722 Color **oro/uno** Alternative colors **available** Composition **60% linen, 40% cotton** Width **55in/140cm** Repeat **20½in/52cm** Price ★★★

13 Crowson/Ricco 030 97 R44 Color **gold** Alternative colors **available** Composition **56% viscose, 44% polyester** Width **54in/137cm** Repeat **4¾in/12cm** Price ★★

13

8

Damask & Brocade: **Late 19th–20th century**

From the mid-19th century to the present day, damasks, brocatelles, and brocades have remained in widespread use, with colored damasks particularly favored for upholstery, and brocades primarily produced as curtain fabrics. Traditional white linen damask tablecloths and napkins, the preserve of the aristocracy during the 16th and 17th centuries, can also now be found in numerous households. However, damask wall-, bed-, and door-hangings tend to be confined to grander period-style interiors.

Over the last 150 years, silk, linen, and wool have continued to be used for the manufacture of these fabrics, although cotton damask has become increasingly popular (particularly for upholstery). Traditional designs have also remained fashionable: stylized flowers and leaves, pomegranates and acorns, and, recently, Napoleonic motifs (such as swans, bees, and Ns encircled by laurel wreaths) are all much in demand. However, there have been design innovations of note, including late 19th-century Gothic-style polychrome brocatelles incorporating traditional motifs set within geometric grids; 1920s gold brocades featuring stylized floral motifs overprinted with Jazz Age motifs in black; and post-1940s damasks with abstract figuring and designs inspired by 16th- and 17th-century needlework patterns.

Abbott & Boyd/Damasco Estambul 47942-2 Color **beige/cream** Alternative colors **available** Composition **100% cotton** Width **53in/135cm** Repeat **19in/48cm** Price ★★★

The Design Archives/Marivaux 51018CU/004 Color **cream on gold** Alternative colors **available** Composition **77% cotton, 23% silk** Width **55in/140cm** Repeat **24in/61cm** Price ★

Scalamandré/Vanderbilt 97429-002 Color **coral and ivory** Alternative colors **available** Composition **66% cotton, 34% silk** Width **50½in/ 128cm** Repeat **11¼in/29cm** Price **to quote** T

Watts of Westminster/Hilliard F0011-07/J4 Color **old gold and medici** Alternative colors **available** Composition **100% silk** Width **48¾in/124cm** Repeat **8½in/22cm** Price ★★★★

Dovedale/Yale Color **02** Alternative colors **available** Composition **100% cotton** Width **56in/143cm** Repeat **24¾in/63cm** Price ★
LC

Scalamandré/Breaker's–Dining Room 20183-002 Color **white** Alternative colors **available** Composition **53% linen, 47% silk** Width **50in/127cm** Repeat **70in/178cm** Price ★★★★★ T

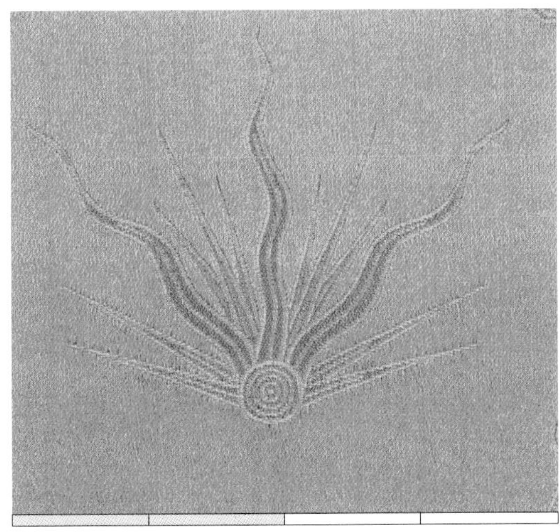

Watts of Westminster/Flame F0007-02/J17 Color **gold** Alternative colors **available** Composition **51% cotton, 29% lumiyarn, 20% rayon** Width **48¾in/124cm** Repeat **8¼in/21cm** Price ★★★★

Warner Fabrics/Melodie T 217005F Color **beige** Alternative colors **available** Composition **59% cotton, 41% modacrylic** Width **51in/130cm** Repeat **12½in/32cm** Price ★★ LC

Gainsborough Silk Weaving/S590 Color **19** Alternative colors **available** Composition **61% silk, 39% cotton** Width **50in/127cm** Repeat **27in/69cm** Price ★★★★

G. P. & J. Baker/Arabica K0240 Color **118** Alternative colors **available** Composition **57% cotton, 43% modacrylic** Width **57in/145cm** Repeat **¾in/2cm** Price ★★

MATELASSÉ

Derived from the French verb *matelasser*, which means to quilt or wad, *matelassé* is a term used to describe double-woven damasks and other fabrics that incorporate raised figures or motifs on their surface. The decorative puckered effect, which has the appearance of machine quilting, is achieved by weaving in an interlocking "wadding weft" in order to accentuate relief. The "Hibiscus" design shown here is typical of the floral patterns that were fashionable during the 19th and 20th centuries.

Northwood Designs/Hibiscus Color **miel** Alternative colors **available** Composition **100% cotton** Width **110¼in/280cm** Repeat **13¼in/34cm** Price ★★ LC W

Bentley & Spens/Day By Night BS09 Color **natural** Alternative colors **available** Composition **50% linen, 50% cotton** Width **53in/135cm** Repeat **27½in/70cm** Price ★★

Lelièvre/Lotus 929 01 Color **12** Alternative colors **available** Composition **95% cotton, 5% polyamide** Width **57½in/146cm** Repeat **10½in/27cm** Price ★★★

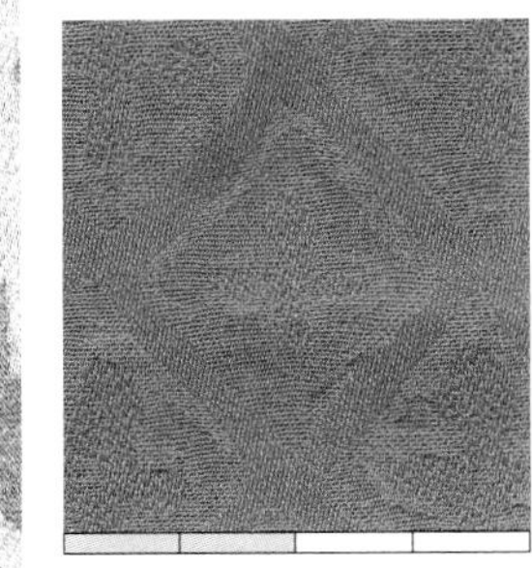

Designers Guild/Marquetry F542 Color **14** Alternative colors **available** Composition **44% cotton, 41% modacrylic, 15% polyacrylic** Width **54in/137cm** Repeat **5½in/14cm** Price ★★

Tapestry

A heavy, durable material, similar in appearance to embroidery, tapestry has been used since the Middle Ages for wall-hangings, bed-hangings, portieres, screens, and cushion covers; since the 17th century this fabric has also been utilized as a top cover for upholstered furniture. Tapestry consists of different-colored warp and weft threads that are woven to form motifs, or, more commonly, narrative accounts of important religious or historical events, or scenes from everyday life. The designs were often based on drawings or paintings that were followed as a guide. Before the late 19th century, all tapestry was handwoven with bobbins and worked on a loom, but since then many tapestries have been machine-made (jacquard woven). Traditional yarns used include wool, linen, and cotton. The grandest tapestries incorporate silk or gilt thread, while in recent years synthetic fibers, such as viscose, have also been used. The number of colors in any one tapestry can range from as few as eight to as many as three hundred.

LEFT A pictorial tapestry portiere hangs in an arch-top doorway at Parham House in Sussex, England. Since the Middle Ages, heavier-weight fabrics, including tapestry, velvet, and brocatelle, have been favored for portieres because of their draft- and sound-proofing qualities. However, lighter fabrics, such as chintz and silk taffeta, have also been used, particularly in the better-insulated houses of the 20th century.

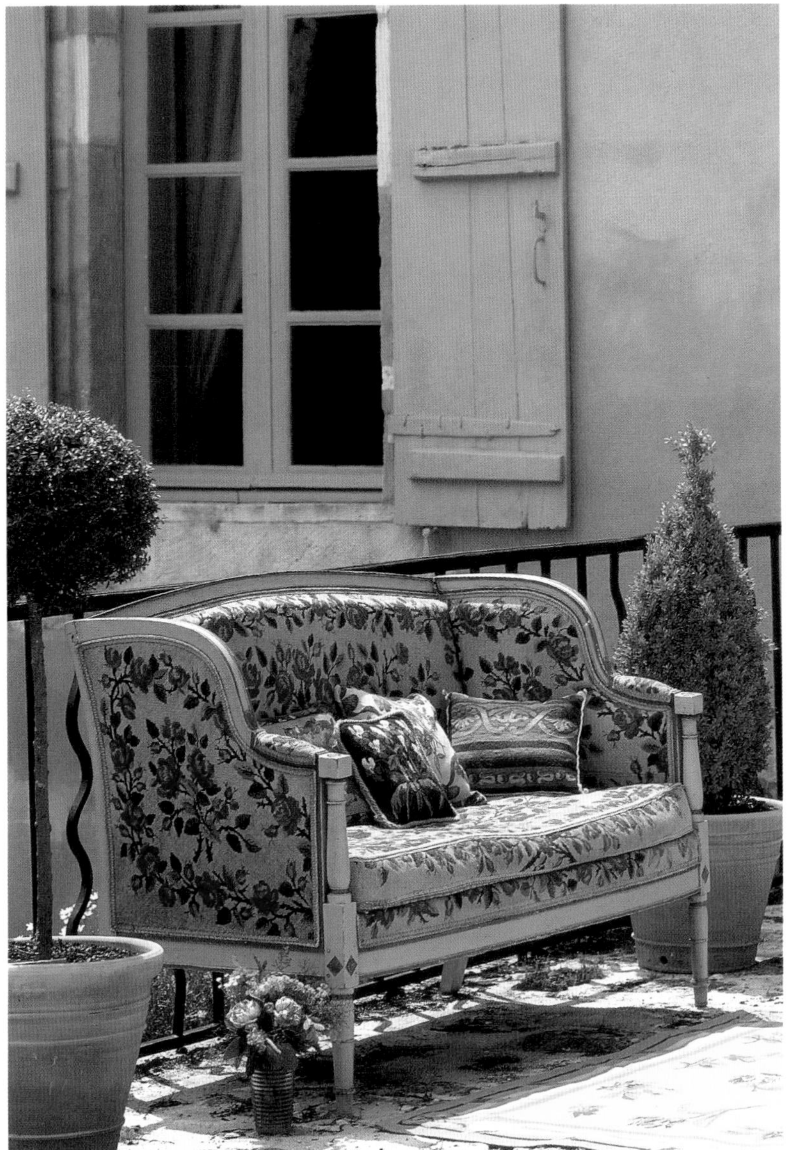

ABOVE The tapestry upholstery on this 19th-century, painted French settee temporarily displayed on the terrace of a medieval *manoir* in Monflanquin, France, is original and particularly well preserved. The floral rose pattern is typical of the period.

KEY DESIGNS

1 Over the centuries many tapestry wall-hangings have featured patterns simulating architectural fixtures and fittings such as pilasters, cornices, dados, and, as here, bookcases.

2 Scenes of Indian origin, such as these elephants, first appeared on early 17th-century tapestries. They became notably fashionable again during the second half of both the 18th and the 19th centuries.

3 Elaborate floral-patterned tapestries designed for hangings and upholstery were especially popular during the 17th, the first half of the 18th, and the second half of the 19th centuries.

4 Tapestries feature an array of heraldic motifs. The lion, featured on Medieval, Renaissance, early 18th-century, and 20th-century Classical Revival tapestries, symbolizes majesty, courage, and pride.

1 **Nobilis-Fontan/Bibliothèque** Color **red, black, green, yellow** Alternative colors **available** Composition **88% cotton, 12% polyester** Width **51in/130cm** Repeat **26¼in/67cm** Price ★★★★

2 **Nobilis-Fontan/Les Animaux** Color **amber on green** Alternative colors **available** Composition **89% cotton, 11% polyester** Width **51in/130cm** Repeat **30¾in/78cm** Price ★★★★

3 **Jab/Monti** Color **195** Alternative colors **available** Composition **68% viscose, 28% polyacrylic, 3% polyester, 1% nylon** Width **55in/140cm** Repeat **21½in/55cm** Price ★★★

4 **Belinda Coote Tapestries/Parisian Lions** Color **rust** Alternative colors **available** Composition **58% viscose, 21% polyester, 21% cotton** Width **55in/140cm** Repeat **23in/59cm** Price ★★

TAPESTRY UPHOLSTERY

When chairs with upholstered seats and backs, such as English "farthingales," first appeared in the 1620s, many were covered with handwoven tapestry. Providing comfort and durability, tapestry remained a popular top cover on chairs and settees until the Classical and Neoclassical Revivals of the late 18th century and early 19th century. Tapestry-upholstered seating came back into fashion in Jacobean Revival, Gothic Revival, and Arts and Crafts interiors from the 1860s to the 1920s, and has remained popular ever since.

ABOVE Classical mythology and pastoralism are combined in the 19th-century scallop-edged tapestry that extends the canopy to the headboard of this fruitwood four-poster. The bed resides in an 18th-century French hunting lodge.

Tapestry: **Pre-19th century**

Prior to the 17th century, the vast majority of tapestries were narrative pictorials produced for wall-, bed-, and door-hangings. However, non-narrative tapestries were also woven, with the fashionable patterns including animals, scrolled ribbons, and *millefleurs*. During the 17th and 18th centuries, tapestry also became a popular top cover on upholstered furniture. Production increased throughout the world–most notably in Flanders, at Aubusson, Gobelins, and Beauvais in France, and at Mortlake and Worcester in England. "Picturesque" designs ranged from military conflicts, cities, and castles to scenes from nature and Aesop's fables. Elaborate floral arrangements also remained fashionable, while in the 18th century *chinoiserie* and *verdure* tapestries came into vogue.

Changing tastes and the preference for wallpaper over wall-hangings resulted in a decline in tapestry production toward the end of the 18th century that was to last until the second half of the 19th century.

Monkwell/Calcot 05178 Color **2** Alternative colors **available** Composition **62% cotton, 38% modacrylic** Width **54in/137cm** Repeat **5in/13cm** Price ★★

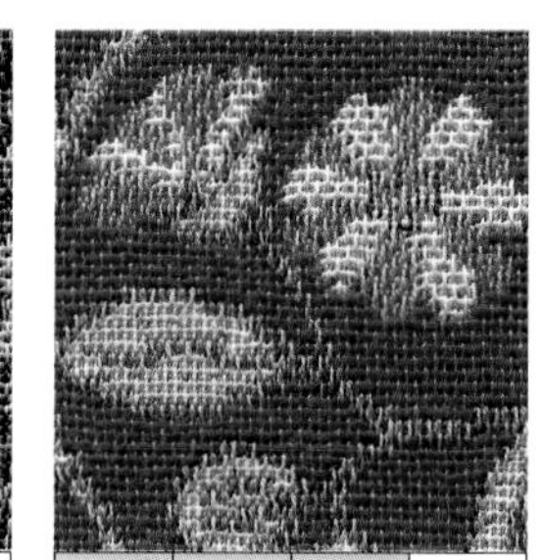

Fired Earth/Carolean Caroleanta Color **red** Alternative colors **not available** Composition **100% cotton** Width **59in/150cm** Repeat **18in/46cm** Price ★★

Stuart Interiors/Rose & Pansy Color **gold background** Alternative colors **available** Composition **100% wool** Width **57in/145cm** Repeat **11½in/29cm** Price ★★★★ LC W

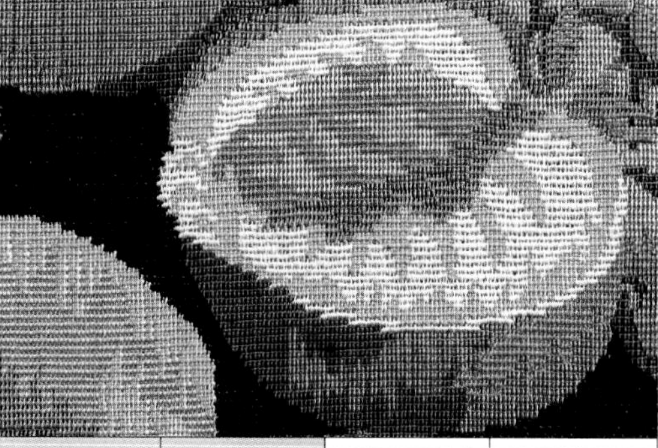

Jab/Tilburg 1-2054-144 Color **brown and sage** Alternative colors **not available** Composition **100% cotton** Width **55in/140cm** Repeat **–** Price ★★★

Percheron/Perceval 14862 Color **blue** Alternative colors **available** Composition **73% cotton, 25% acrylic, 2% rayon** Width **51in/130cm** Repeat **15in/38cm** Price ★★★★

Belinda Coote Tapestries/Jacobean Brocade Color **beige and terracotta** Alternative colors **available** Composition **66% viscose, 34% cotton** Width **53½in/136cm** Repeat **24in/61cm** Price ★★★★ LC

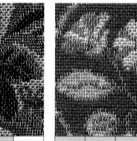

AUTHENTIC EARLY COLORS

The design of "Windsor," the tapestry-woven fabric shown here, is based on an early 17th-century embroidered bed-hanging. The pattern is produced in a limited color range on a plain ground and contains rudimentary areas of shading. In these respects it bears a much closer resemblance to the flat and highly stylized tapestries of the Middle Ages than to the multicolored, subtly shaded, "three-dimensional" realism of the tapestries that began to be produced during the Renaissance. The thistles and the birds-of-prey that are depicted in the pattern of this fabric are motifs that recur frequently in both English and French medieval tapestries.

Watts of Westminster/Windsor F0033-01/23 Color **Windsor** Alternative colors **available** Composition **100% cotton** Width **48¾in/124cm** Repeat **22½in/57cm** Price ★★★

Old World Weavers/Spoccia EB-3943 Color **0056** Alternative colors **available** Composition **50% rayon, 49% cotton, 1% nylon** Width **55in/140cm** Repeat **7in/18cm** Price ★★★

Jab/Aleppo 1-2066 Color **155** Alternative colors **available** Composition **100% cotton** Width **55in/140cm** Repeat **3in/8cm** Price ★★★

Fired Earth/Blue Jug Color **blue** Alternative colors **available** Composition **100% cotton** Width **57in/145cm** Repeat **25½in/65cm** Price ★★

G. P. & J. Baker/Dean Fr 1 V1229-44 Color **reds on sand** Alternative colors **available** Composition **66% cotton, 34% modacrylic** Width **55in/140cm** Repeat **16½in/42cm** Price ★★

Jab/Gent 1-2052-189 Color **multi** Alternative colors **not available** Composition **100% cotton** Width **55in/140cm** Repeat **–** Price ★★★

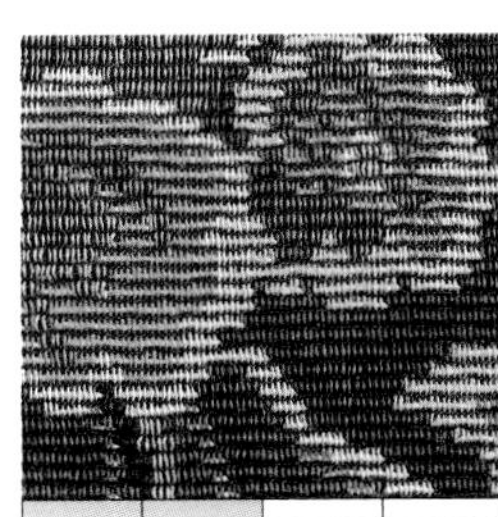

Old World Weavers/Beethoven BD648/0001 Color **brown** Alternative colors **not available** Composition **86% cotton, 14% rayon** Width **55in/140cm** Repeat **34in/86.5cm** Price ★★★

Old World Weavers/Clermont ND495 40088 Color **gold/green/beige** Alternative colors **available** Composition **100% cotton** Width **50in/127cm** Repeat **28¼in/72cm** Price ★★★★

Tapestry: **19th–20th century**

Following a fifty-year decline, tapestry production enjoyed a resurgence during the late 19th century. Medieval-style designs were predominant, although hanging baskets of flowers set within scrolling wreaths and cartouches also proved highly popular.

Most 20th-century tapestries were machine-made, and many were designed specifically for upholstery. Although heavy and durable, they were softer than their handwoven counterparts and were suitable for curtains. Many of the *verdure* tapestries favored in the early 20th-century Baronial-style and Jacobean-Revival interiors featured foliage in soft greens, tans, and browns set against a dark blue background. Similarly, numerous late-20th-century tapestries displayed stylized floral-and-trellis, or geometric, patterns. Machine-made and handwoven pictorial tapestries were still produced, primarily as wall-hangings. However, in terms of artistic approach, handwoven designs changed, with a gradual move away from narrative pictorial realism, instigated in the early 20th century at Aubusson, by Frenchman Jean Lurçat. Many late- 20th-century designs relied on the interaction between the weave's texture and the colors employed, mirroring the innovation and developments of modern art.

5

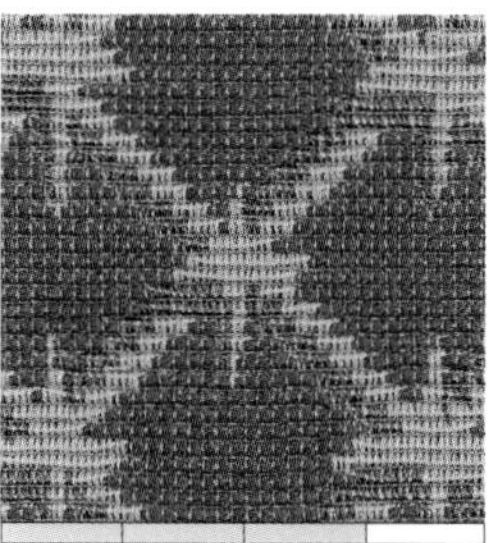

1

2

3

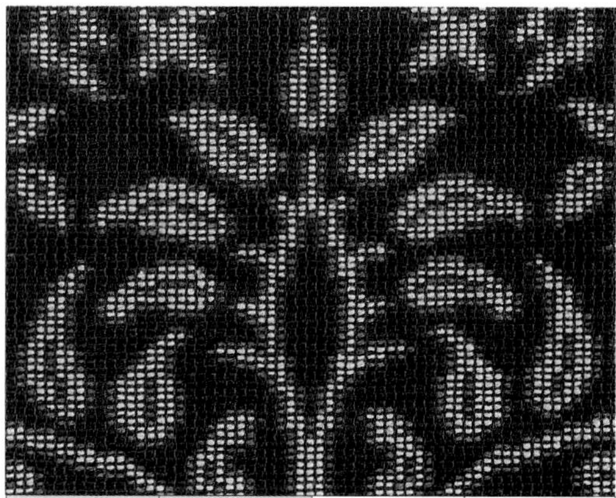

4

6

7

1 **Marvic Textiles/Criss Cross 3903-5** Color **russet** Alternative colors **available** Composition **100% cotton** Width **55in/140cm** Repeat **2¾in/7cm** Price ★★

2 **Marvic Textiles/Maple Leaf 3902-5** Color **russet** Alternative colors **available** Composition **100% cotton** Width **55in/140cm** Repeat **3¼in/8.5cm** Price ★★

3 **Belinda Coote Tapestries/ Parisian Lions** Color **rgreen** Alternative colors **available** Composition **68% viscose, 21% polyester, 21% cotton** Width **55in/140cm** Repeat **23in/59cm** Price ★★

4 **Stroheim & Romann/Pugin 4847N-0550** Color **blue and cream** Alternative colors **available** Composition **100% cotton** Width **54in/137cm** Repeat **15¾in/40cm** Price ★★★

5 **Old World Weavers/Boboli TV 25240001** Color **cinnabar** Alternative colors **available** Composition **50% rayon, 47% acrylic, 3% cotton** Width **55in/140cm** Repeat **46¾in/119cm** Price ★★★★

6 **Watts of Westminster/Rose & Fleur de Lys** Color **navy** Alternative colors **available** Composition **60% cotton, 40% velicren** Width **55in/ 140cm** Repeat **17in/43cm** Price ★★★

7 **Watts of Westminster/Benson** Color **Westminster** Alternative colors **available** Composition **62% cotton, 38% silk** Width **48¾in/124cm** Repeat **24¾in/ 63cm** Price ★★★★★

8

8 **G. P. & J. Baker/Caliph Chenille J0235-74** Color **green, red, and blue** Alternative colors **available** Composition **100% cotton** Width **57in/145cm** Repeat **22½in/57cm** Price ★ LC

9 **Ian Sanderson/Pompom** Color **bottle** Alternative colors **available** Composition **100% cotton** Width **58in/147cm** Repeat **29¼in/74.5cm** Price ★★

10

11

9

10 **Brunschwig & Fils/Guirlande Tapestry 40231.01** Color **red** Alternative colors **not available** Composition **100% cotton** Width **54in/137cm** Repeat **22in/56cm** Price ★★★

11 **Garin/Vinanoz 66754891** Color **beige** Alternative colors **available** Composition **70% cotton, 30% viscose** Width **55in/140cm** Repeat **20½in/52cm** Price ★★

12 **Garin/Denia 66754881** Color **buttermilk** Alternative colors **available** Composition **80% cotton, 20% viscose** Width **55in/140cm** Repeat **15¼in/39cm** Price ★★

13 **Brunschwig & Fils/Jacinthe Tapestry 53122.01** Color **ultramarine** Alternative colors **available** Composition **100% cotton** Width **54in/137cm** Repeat **4½in/11.5cm** Price ★★★

14 **Marvic Textiles/Grapes 3901-3** Color **yellow** Alternative colors **available** Composition **100% cotton** Width **55in/140cm** Repeat **9in/23cm** Price ★★★ LC

12

ART NOUVEAU

The revival in tapestry production that took place in the Arts and Crafts Movement was also evident in the output of designers working in the Art Nouveau style from the late 19th century to the early years of the 20th century. Liberty of London commissioned a number of designs, one of which was the late 19th-century tapestry-weave, "Ianthe," shown here. Highly typical of Art Nouveau and its fascination with the forms of nature, the pattern depicts stylized stems, roots, elongated blooms, and foliage within highly sinuous, interlaced lines.

Liberty/Ianthe 1485004 Color **B** Alternative colors **available** Composition **61% cotton, 37% modacrylic, 2% polypropylene** Width **54in/137cm** Repeat **14in/36cm** Price ★★★ LC

13

14

Motif Fabrics

Woven and printed cloths displaying patterns made up of systematically repeated images are traditionally referred to as "motif fabrics." Their enduring appeal through the centuries can be explained by their decorative qualities such as strong visual repetition, and by the ease with which they allow hangings, upholstery, and floor coverings to be coordinated not only with each other, but also with architectural fixtures and fittings and pieces of furniture embellished with the same motifs. The attractiveness of such fabrics also resides in the huge variety of motifs that can be represented–a catalog of architectural, mythological, animal, and plant-form imagery, both stylized and naturalistic, that has been accumulated from around the globe from the Middle Ages onward, with much of it disseminated via pattern books in circulation from the late Renaissance until the early 20th century. The inherent symbolism of most motifs is particularly appealing to fabric designers, because it allows them to convey "hidden meanings" via the pattern. For example, a wreath motif is not merely a "still life" of bound laurel, oak, or olive leaves, it is also a symbol of sovereignty, honor, glory, poetic achievement, or of victory over death.

ABOVE The silk top cover of this early 19th-century saber-legged mahogany tub chair from France features a repeat wreath motif. Consisting of a garland or crown of leaves (laurel, oak, or olive), the wreath was a popular motif during the early Renaissance, and was revived under the Neoclassical Empire style of the late 18th and early 19th centuries. The Emperor Napoleon chose a golden wreath of laurel for his coronation to recall the sovereignty, honor, glory, and victories of the Ancient Roman emperors.

LEFT "Palmiers," the yellow, linen-cotton top cover on this late 18th-century French settee and footstool, displays a repeat palm tree motif. Comoglio derived and adapted the pattern from an 18th-century Marseilles pattern book. Naturalistic and stylized palm trees, a species native to North Africa, became fashionable fabric motifs during the late 18th and early 19th centuries following Napoleon's military campaigns in Egypt.

CYPHERS

Traditionally, cyphers–initials interwoven to form a flat linear design– are used on fabrics to denote ownership or patronage. Prior to the 18th century, they were the almost exclusive preserve of monarchies, a notable example being the interlaced L's of Louis XI of France. However, following the publication in 1726 of Samuel Sympson's *A New Book of Cyphers*, which contained "every possible combination of two intertwining scrolling letters embellished with flourishes of foliage," they were increasingly commissioned by other sections of society on both sides of the Atlantic, and proved especially popular in 19th-century Gothic Revival interiors.

KEY DESIGNS

1 The bee was a symbol of industry and order, rebirth and immortality in the ornaments of Ancient Greece and China. Adopted by Napoleon, it became a prevalent motif on Empire-style textiles.

2 Originally from France, the fleur-de-lis (a stylized three- or five-petal lily) has been one of the most popular of all motifs, and was prominent in Medieval, Renaissance, and Gothic Revival interiors.

3 A crown or garland of leaves, the wreath symbolized sovereignty, honor, glory, and victory in Ancient Greece and Rome. In fashion during the Renaissance, it was revived under Empire style.

4 The swan was associated with Apollo (music) and Venus (love) in classical mythology, and was widely used as a motif on Medieval, Regency, Empire, Biedermeier, and Art Nouveau fabrics.

5 This pear motif is late 20th century, but pear and other fruit motifs–from apples and raspberries to figs and pineapples–have been favored on textiles since the Middle Ages.

6 The oak leaf symbolizes civic virtue and steadfastness and has appeared on numerous fabrics, notably in Ancient Roman, Renaissance, Gothic, Neo-classical, and Arts and Crafts interiors.

---

1 **Scalamandré/Bee U.SA. (S)** Color **multi on cream ground** Alternative colors **available** Composition **100% silk** Width **50in/127cm** Repeat **2¼in/5.5cm** Price ★★★★★ T

2 **Percheron/Fleur de Lys** Color **red** Alternative colors **available** Composition **69% viscose, 31% cotton** Width **55in/140cm** Repeat **–** Price ★★★★

3 **Scalamandré/Rosecliff** Color **cranberry** Alternative colors **available** Composition **100% silk** Width **55in/140cm** Repeat **6½in/16.5cm** Price ★★★★★ W T

4 **Stuart Interiors/Medieval Swan** Color **blue and gold** Alternative colors **available** Composition **100% wool** Width **57in/145cm** Repeat **6¼in/16cm** Price ★★★★ W

5 **Liberty/Pears** Color **blue/tan** Alternative colors **available** Composition **100% cotton** Width **54in/137cm** Repeat **21in/53cm** Price ★★

6 **Lee Jofa/Oak Leaf Weave** Color **green** Alternative colors **available** Composition **85% rayon, 15% cotton** Width **52in/132cm** Repeat **3in/8cm** Price ★★★

Motifs: **Pre-18th century**

In addition to Islamic ornament, such as arabesques, favored European motifs of the Middle Ages included stylized heraldic decorations and naturalistic depictions of animals and plant forms, particularly *millefleurs* (roses, anemones, violas, pinks, and columbines), ivy, grapevines, wild strawberries, chestnuts, and acorns. Heraldic motifs remained fashionable during the Renaissance, as did military and emblematic symbols. However, Renaissance fabrics were largely characterized by sculptural-like classical forms, such as swags, festoons, dolphins, and scallop shells, and realistically depicted acanthus leaves, scrolling foliage, pomegranates, thistles, and other plant forms. During the later Renaissance, rambling foliage, luxuriant blooms, and exotic fruits and birds also embellished imported Indian chintzes. The classical ornamentation of the Renaissance was further consolidated in the Baroque interiors of the 17th century, with fabric motifs including angels, cupids, human figures, scrolls, urns, flaming torches, swags, and leafy scrolls. Vying with these motifs, however, were *chinoiserie* pagodas, bells, mandarins, dragons, and birds; these were very popular in the late 1600s following the publication in several languages of J. Nieuhof's illustrated travel book, *Atlas Chinois* (1665).

1

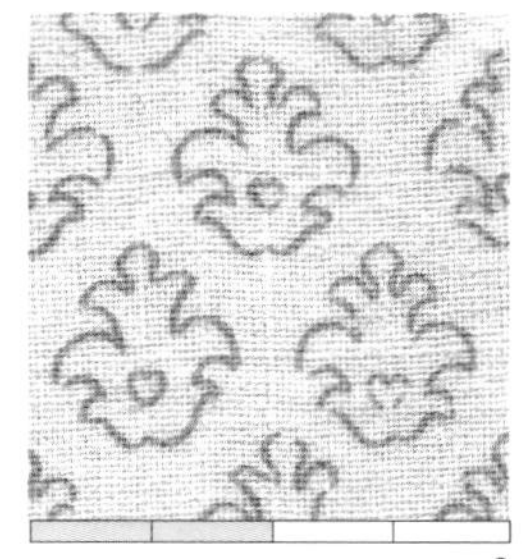

2

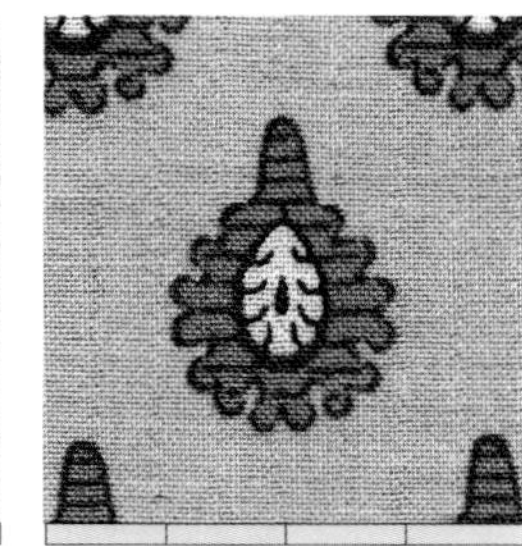

3

5

1 **The Silk Gallery/Fleur Weave** Color **antique gold and green** Alternative colors **available** Composition **68% silk, 32% polyester** Width **50in/127cm** Repeat **2½in/6cm** Price ★★★

2 **Elizabeth Eaton/Saighton** Color **green on white** Alternative colors **available** Composition **100% linen** Width **48in/122cm** Repeat **2in/5cm** Price ★★

3 **Les Olivades/Indianaire TRT 0064** Color **yellow/blue** Alternative colors **available** Composition **100% cotton** Width **59in/150cm** Repeat **1¼in/3cm** Price ★★

4 **Stuart Interiors/Heraldic Beasts** Color **rust/beige** Alternative colors **available** Composition **70% wool, 30% linen** Width **67¾in/172cm** Repeat **35in/89cm** Price ★★★★

4

5 **Stuart Interiors/Fleur de Lys** Color **blue** Alternative colors **available** Composition **75% wool, 25% silk** Width **48¾in/124cm** Repeat **11½in/ 29cm** Price ★★★★

6 **Jason D'Souza/Siena SIE01** Color **coral** Alternative colors **available** Composition **51% modacrylic, 37% cotton, 12% nylon** Width **53in/135cm** Repeat **1½in/4cm** Price ★★

7 **Baer & Ingram/Troubadour TRO 04** Color **yellow gold** Alternative colors **available** Composition **100% cotton** Width **55in/140cm** Repeat **10¾in/27.5cm** Price ★★

8 **Baer & Ingram/Blazon BLF** Color **09** Alternative colors **available** Composition **100% cotton** Width **55in/140cm** Repeat **17¾in/45cm** Price ★★

6

7

8

9

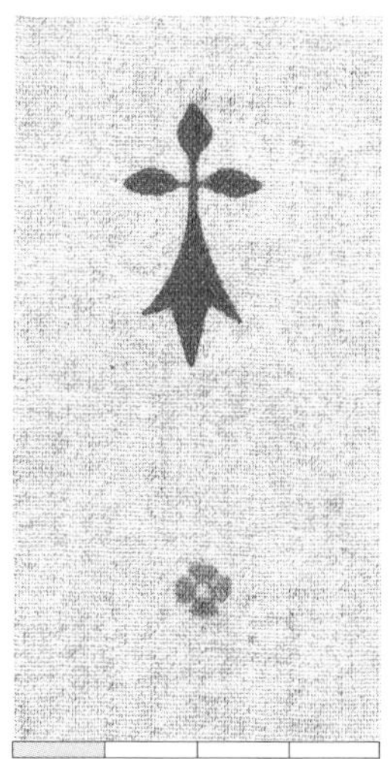

10

11

12

9 Tissunique/Jardin de Traconnade 35/2341/F Color **jaune rouge** Alternative colors **available** Composition **50% cotton, 50% viscose** Width **55in/140cm** Repeat **4¼in/11cm** Price ★★★★

10 Zoffany/Gothic Flower 37BT Color **04** Alternative colors **available** Composition **100% cotton** Width **54in/137cm** Repeat **15¼in/38.5cm** Price ★★

11 The Silk Gallery/Dis print Color **stone 235** Alternative colors **available** Composition **100% silk** Width **50in/127cm** Repeat **5½in/14cm** Price ★★★

12 Bernard Thorp & Co/Daisy Time Color **blue** Alternative colors **available** Composition **100% jute** Width **47in/120cm** Repeat **21in/53cm** Price ★★

13 George Spencer Decorations/ Orlando 004C Color **moss** Alternative colors **available** Composition **100% cotton** Width **47in/120cm** Repeat **12in/31cm** Price ★★★

14 Monkwell/Alhambra MP9367 Color **red** Alternative colors **available** Composition **62% cotton, 38% jute** Width **54in/137cm** Repeat **25in/64cm** Price ★★

13

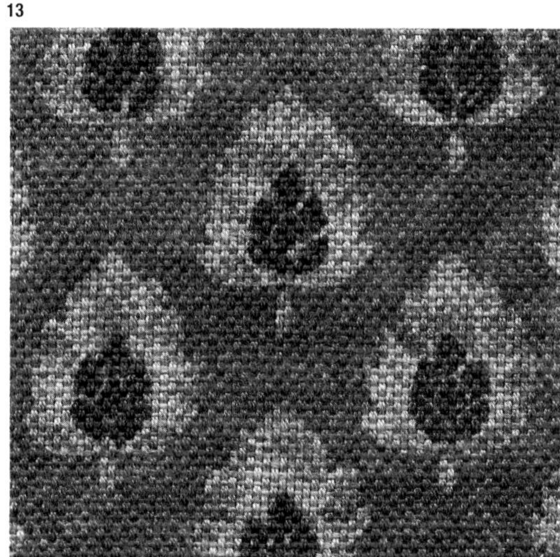

14

HERALDIC MOTIFS

First used in the 12th century to denote position and status in a feudal society, heraldic emblems rapidly became a form of decoration that also conveyed pride of ownership and pedigree. Typical motifs, often within achievements-of-arms, include helmets and shields, cyphers, and draperies. Stylized beasts, for example stags, dogs, lions or porcupines, griffins or harpies, unicorns, and enfields or ypotrylls, were also popular.

Andrew Martin/Magna Carta Color **red** Alternative colors **available** Composition **100% cotton** Width **52½in/133cm** Repeat **44in/112cm** Price ★★

"Magna Carta" is a printed cotton from Andrew Martin's "Conqueror Collection," a range of fabrics inspired by heraldic motifs and English chivalry. The central shield bears a Latin inscription that translates to: "One does not value things easily obtained."

Motifs: **18th century**

Access to the numerous pattern books in international circulation during the 18th century allowed fabric designers to draw on a rich and varied catalog of historical ornamentation. Early in the century, fabrics adorning Palladian interiors featured herms, eagles, dolphins, and masks that were inspired by Classical Roman and Renaissance ornament, while fabrics in Picturesque schemes displayed pastoral and rustic scenes and *fêtes galantes*–the latter also appearing on the Rococo-style fabrics in vogue until the middle of the century. Other motifs that were typical of the Rococo Period included *singeries*, *rocaille*, scrollwork, and *chinoiserie* birds and lanterns. In the Neoclassical Adam- and Federal-style schemes of the late 18th century, Roman motifs–lion masks, rosettes, urns, vases, griffins, and delicate scrolling foliage–were prevalent, while the Gothick Revival at the end of the century saw Gothick ornament, such as flora, fauna, the seasons, and portraits of masons and clerics, portrayed in a historically accurate manner.

1

2

3

4

5

6

7

1 Hodsoll McKenzie/Toile d'Avignon 221/101-10 Color **red/blue** Alternative colors **available** Composition **50% spun rayon, 50% cotton** Width **50in/127cm** Repeat **16in/40.5cm** Price ★★★

2 Brunschwig & Fils/Canton Cotton Print 79512.04 Color **blue fish on white** Alternative colors **available** Composition **100% cotton** Width **52¾in/134cm** Repeat **25in/64cm** Price ★★

3 The Design Archives/Cachet 51028 Color **2** Alternative colors **available** Composition **56% cotton, 44% modacrylic** Width **57in/145cm** Repeat **7½in/19cm** Price ★★

4 Donghia/Islamica 0365/9310-07 Color **bordeaux** Alternative colors **available** Composition **52% viscose, 48% cotton** Width **54in/137cm** Repeat **47in/120cm** Price ★★★★★

5 Colefax and Fowler/Osterley 2063/03 Color **coral and green** Alternative colors **available** Composition **52% linen, 36% cotton, 12% nylon** Width **52¾in/134cm** Repeat **16in/40.5cm** Price ★★

6 Busby & Busby/Heavenly Bodies 4212 Color **black on gold** Alternative colors **available** Composition **100% silk** Width **48in/122cm** Repeat **7½in/19cm** Price ★★

7 Busby & Busby/Amaretti 4913 Color **gold, crimson, and stone** Alternative colors **available** Composition **100% cotton** Width **55in/140cm** Repeat **25in/64cm** Price ★★

8

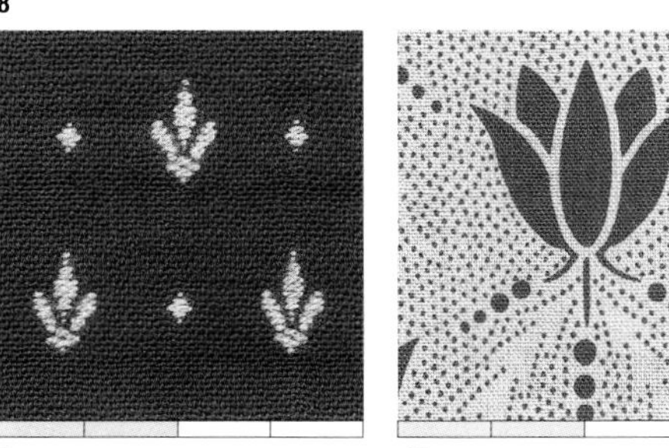

9

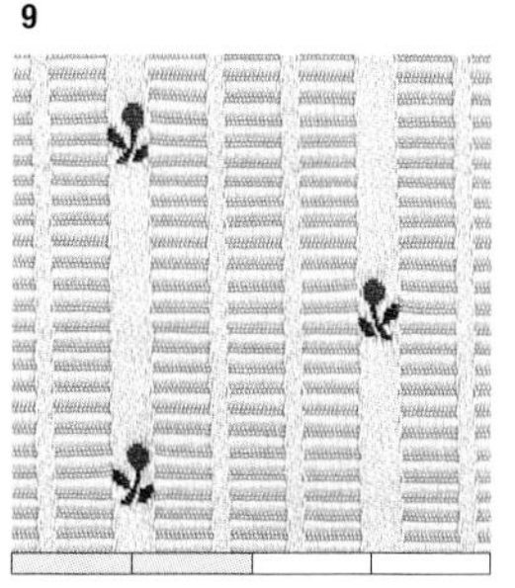

10

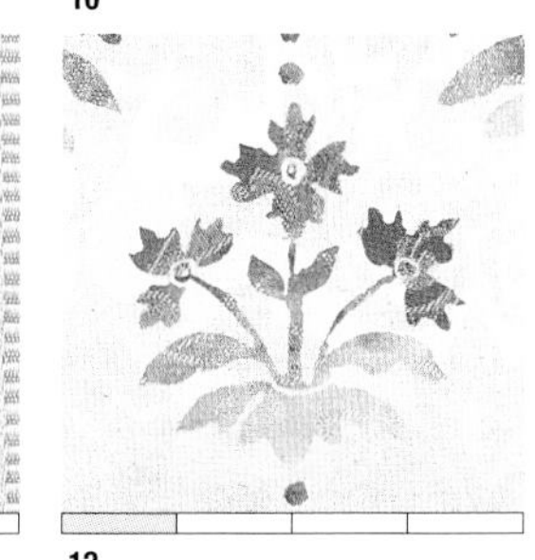

11

12

8 Apenn/Hampton linen LN 476-8/9 Color **red-blue** Alternative colors **available** Composition **100% linen** Width **49in/125cm** Repeat **8in/20cm** Price ★★

9 The Isle Mill/Red Fintry Color **red** Alternative colors **available** Composition **100% wool** Width **54in/137cm** Repeat **2¼in/6cm** Price ★★

10 Tissunique/Candide 35/10948/1 Colors **red and yellow** Alternative colors **not available** Composition **55% cotton, 45% linen** Width **51in/130cm** Repeat **3in/8cm** Price ★★★

11 Tissunique/Paola 35/3000/P Color **ecru** Alternative colors **available** Composition **50% cotton, 50% viscose** Width **55in/140cm** Repeat **2in/5cm** Price ★★★★

12 Claremont Fabrics/Domino JOLD18 Color **claret** Alternative colors **available** Composition **60% cotton, 40% polyester** Width **55in/140cm** Repeat **6¾in/17cm** Price ★

13

14

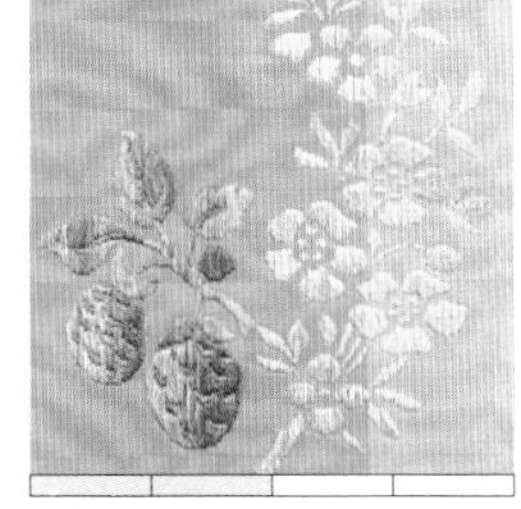

15

16

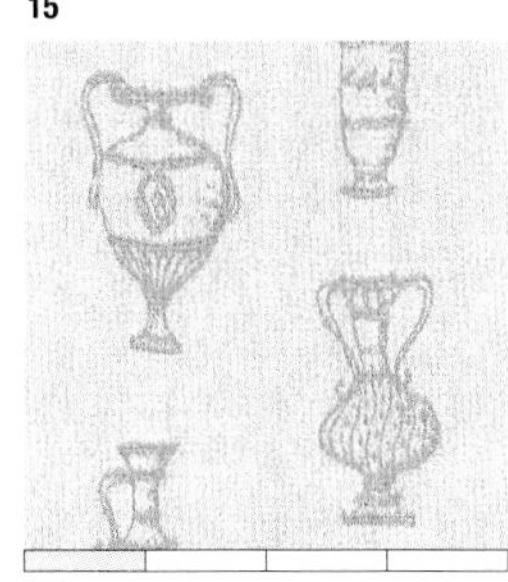

17

13 Bennison Fabrics/China Birds Color **1** Alternative colors **not available** Composition **70% linen, 30% cotton** Width **46½in/118cm** Repeat **17in/43cm** Price ★★

14 Marvic Textiles/Pineapple Plaid 414-10 Color **holly** Alternative colors **available** Composition **62% linen, 23% cotton, 15% viscose** Width **51in/130cm** Repeat **2½in/6.5cm** Price ★★

15 Scalamandré/Strawberry Design 205-003 Color **multi on blue and ivory** Alternative colors **available** Composition **100% silk** Width **50in/127cm** Repeat **2½in/6.5cm** Price ★★★★★

16 Percheron/Lampas–Les Lyres 10087 Color **1** Alternative colors **available** Composition **100% silk** Width **51in/130cm** Repeat **8¾in/22cm** Price ★★★★★

17 Timney Fowler/Amphorae TF0192/07 Color **silver alloy** Alternative colors **available** Composition **100% wool** Width **58in/147cm** Repeat **10¾in/27cm** Price ★★★

18 Timney Fowler/Roman Heads TF0027.04 Color **red and ecru** Alternative colors **available** Composition **100% cotton** Width **47in/120cm** Repeat **42½in/108cm** Price ★★

18th century

NEOCLASSICISM

The Louis XVI-style lampas shown here was designed in 1779 and used to upholster chairs in Marie Antoinette's private apartments at the Château de Versailles, outside Paris, France. In 1859 the pattern was reproduced for Empress Eugénie's apartments in the Palais des Tuileries. The pattern is typical of late 18th-century Neoclassicism. Although predominantly floral, the center contains an oval medallion encompassing a fluted torch encircled with flowers and entwined crumpled ribbons.

Percheron/Lampas–Marie Antoinette 10481 Color **2** Alternative colors **available** Composition **100% silk** Width **51in/130cm** Repeat **¾in/2cm** Price ★★★★★

18

Motifs: **Early 19th century**

Underpinning the Empire, Regency, and Federal styles of decoration prevalent during the early 19th century was a revival of Classicism in its original purity. Initiated in France by architects Percier and Fontaine (under the patronage of Napoleon), Empire style was encapsulated in their influential book *Recueil des Décorations Intérieures* (1801), spread rapidly to Federal America, and was strongly reflected in the Regency interiors of England. Early 19th-century Classicism was made up of two major historical strands: "le Style Etrusque" and Roman. Favored Etruscan motifs for fabrics included palmettes, palm leaves, and anthemia, as well as vases, medallions, winged lions, and eagles. Roman motifs and emblems proved even more popular, especially in France, largely due to Napoleon's desire to identify the country with the greatness of the Roman Empire. Therefore, laurel and oak wreaths, lances, arrows and fasces, griffins, winged torches, and figures of victory and fame were much in evidence. An additional historical influence was fueled by archaeological excavations in Egypt and by Napoleon's Nile campaign, with ancient Egyptian motifs, such as scarabs, sphinxes, lotus flowers, and hieroglyphics, appearing soon after being copied from drawings in Baron Denon's *Voyages dans la Basse et la Haute Egypte* (1802-3).

7

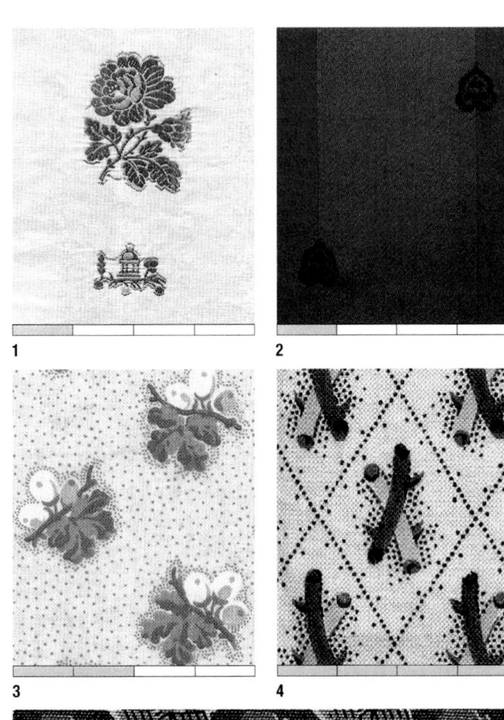

1 2 3 4

6 8

1 Brunschwig & Fils/Lindsey's Garden Lisère 53451 Color **01** Alternative colors **available** Composition **55% cotton, 45% rayon** Width **54in/137cm** Repeat **6¾in/17cm** Price ★★★

2 Mary Fox Linton/Orlando Color **03** Alternative colors **available** Composition **83% cotton, 17% viscose** Width **55in/140cm** Repeat **8in/20cm** Price ★★★★

3 Warner Fabrics/Little Acorns CS 336080 Color **petrol/buff** Alternative colors **available** Composition **100% cotton** Width **54in/137cm** Repeat **4in/10cm** Price ★

4 Guy Evans/Rose Cuttings Color **1** Alternative colors **not available** Composition **100% cotton** Width **51in/130cm** Repeat **1¼in/3cm** Price ★★

5 Liberty/Eugene LF 4003 Color **03** Alternative colors **available** Composition **100% cotton** Width **58¼in/148cm** Repeat **7½in/19cm** Price ★★

6 Zoffany/Blois Trellis 335505 Color **blue/honey** Alternative colors **available** Composition **45% modacrylic, 41% cotton, 14% nylon** Width **54in/137cm** Repeat **3in/8cm** Price ★★

7 The Silk Gallery/Astra Stripe Color **henna/Italian gold** Alternative colors **available** Composition **68% silk, 32% polyester** Width **50in/127cm** Repeat **5½in/14cm** Price ★★★

8 Mary Fox Linton/Gonzaga Color **05** Alternative colors **available** Composition **100% cotton** Width **55in/140cm** Repeat **3½in/9cm** Price ★★★

9 Lelièvre/Prudhon 4147 07 Color **marine** Alternative colors **available** Composition **55% cotton, 45% silk** Width **51in/130cm** Repeat **8½in/22cm** Price ★★★

5

9

10

11

12

10 Scalamandré/Lampas–Rosecliff Laurel 20221-007 Color **cranberry** Alternative colors **available** Composition **100% silk** Width **55in/140cm** Repeat **6¾in/17cm** Price ★★★★★

11 Monkwell/Hugo Stripe 51015CU/012 Color **gold on red** Alternative colors **available** Composition **56% viscose, 44% polyester** Width **55in/140cm** Repeat **13in/33cm** Price ★

12 Lelièvre/Vernet 414606 Color **bleu** Alternative colors **available** Composition **55% cotton, 45% silk** Width **51in/130cm** Repeat **6¼in/16cm** Price ★★★★

13 Percheron/Lampas–Bernadotte 10474 Color **3** Alternative colors **available** Composition **63% cotton, 37% viscose** Width **51in/130cm** Repeat **4½in/11.5cm** Price ★★★★★

14 Monkwell/Zola 51014CU/004 Color **gold** Alternative colors **available** Composition **56% viscose, 44% polyester** Width **55in/140cm** Repeat **9in/23cm** Price ★

13

14

NAPOLEONIC MOTIFS

There are three recurring Napoleonic motifs: the bee, the swan, and the palm tree. Napoleon adopted the bee as his emblem primarily because it was an Ancient Greek symbol of order and industry, but also because metal bees found in the tomb of Chilperic I (a 6th-century Frankish king) provided a link with the early French rulers. The black swan was the Empress Josephine's emblem, chosen because swans pulled the chariot of Venus. The palm tree was an emblem of fame and victory, and, being indigenous to Africa, it was viewed as symbolic of Napoleon's Egyptian campaigns.

1

2

3

1 Percheron/Lampas–Les Abeilles 10085 Color **1** Alternative colors **available** Composition **63% cotton, 37% viscose** Width **51in/130cm** Repeat **5½in/14cm** Price ★★★★

2 Percheron/Les Cygnes 18429 Color **green and red** Alternative colors **available** Composition **60% viscose, 40% cotton** Width **51in/130cm** Repeat **12½/32cm** Price ★★★★★

3 Pierre Frey/Palmiers 2525 Color **original** Alternative colors **available** Composition **64% linen, 36% cotton** Width **53½in/136cm** Repeat **10in/25.5cm** Price ★★★

Motifs: **Mid-19th century**

The majority of fabric motifs favored during the middle of the 19th century fell into one of two stylistic categories–Classical Revival and Gothic Revival, and in that respect mirrored the "battle of the styles" that was taking place in contemporary architecture. Typical Gothic-Revival motifs, employed by noted designers such as the English architect A. W. N. Pugin, included stylized scrolling leaves and heraldic motifs (such as fleur-de-lis), usually set within a flat pattern of basic ogival structure. Mythical beasts, gargoyles, and patrons of the arts, presented within medallions, were also recurring motifs of the style.

Classical ornamentation of the period was wide-ranging. In Renaissance-Revival interiors, naturalistic, Roman-influenced acanthus leaves, scrolling foliage, swags, and festoons vied with grotesques and *grisaille* panels incorporating the Elements and the Muses, while in the Baroque-Revival (Second Empire) designs that followed, leafy scrolls, swags, urns, flaming torches, angels, cupids, and putti were all much in evidence. Further enriching the ornamentation of fabrics during this period were Moorish motifs, such as arabesques, and Indian designs, such as the paisley patterns derived from Kashmiri shawls and consisting of formalized representations of pinecones, palms, and almonds.

Borderline/Forget Me Not Color **A** Alternative colors **available** Composition **100% cotton** Width **54in/137cm** Repeat **14¾in/37.5cm** Price ★★

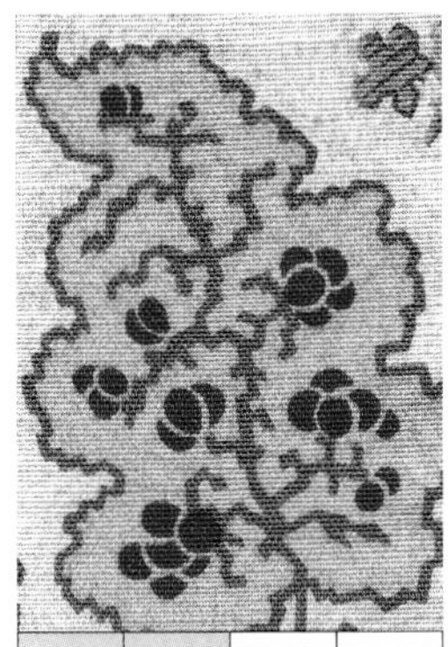

George Spencer Decorations/ Elisabeth Color **apricot** Alternative colors **available** Composition **66% cotton, 34% linen** Width **54in/137cm** Repeat **8in/20cm** Price ★★★

The Design Archives/Cachet 51032 Color **3** Alternative colors **available** Composition **60% cotton, 40% modacrylic** Width **54in/137cm** Repeat **16in/40.5cm** Price ★★ LC

Bennison Fabrics/Jubilee Stripe Color **red** Alternative colors **available** Composition **70% linen, 30% cotton** Width **54¾in/139cm** Repeat **17in/43cm** Price ★★★

Galliards/Francesco Color **beige and brown** Alternative colors **available** Composition **100% cotton** Width **54in/137cm** Repeat **6¼in/16cm** Price ★★

Hodsoll McKenzie/Chinese Fans Color **yellow** Alternative colors **available** Composition **52% linen, 36% cotton, 12% nylon** Width **54in/137cm** Repeat **19¾in/50cm** Price ★★★ LC W

Watts of Westminster/Wexford Welby 21WWB/3 Color **Geneva** Alternative colors **available** Composition **100% cotton** Width **48¾in/124cm** Repeat **8¼in/21cm** Price ★★★

Watts of Westminster/Tudor Badge F0026-01/U1 Color **lichen/old gold** Alternative colors **available** Composition **100% cotton** Width **48¾in/124cm** Repeat **5½in/14cm** Price ★★★

Mary Fox Linton/Fedra Color **01** Alternative colors **available** Composition **50% cotton, 50% viscose** Width **55in/140cm** Repeat **6¼in/16cm** Price ★★★

Watts of Westminster/Trellis Z1TR/M30FR Color **bottle green** Alternative colors **available** Composition **64% cotton, 46% Velicren** Width **55in/140cm** Repeat **7in/18cm** Price ★★★

Garin/Mauricio 67083003 Color **oro/grana** Alternative colors **available** Composition **60% viscose, 40% cotton** Width **55in/140cm** Repeat **7½in/19cm** Price ★★

Mary Fox Linton/Corona Color **6806** Alternative colors **available** Composition **100% silk** Width **55in/140cm** Repeat **8¾in/22.5cm** Price ★★★★

Zoffany/Gothic Flower 3 FL04 Color **5** Alternative colors **available** Composition **100% cotton** Width **54in/137cm** Repeat **15in/38cm** Price ★★

Northwood Designs/Chambord Rubis Color **05** Alternative colors **available** Composition **55% cotton, 45% viscose** Width **54in/137cm** Repeat **27½in/70cm** Price ★★

Zuber/Alcove Chambre de la Reine T9222 Color **1** Alternative colors **not available** Composition **100% cotton** Width **51in/130cm** Repeat **29in/74cm** Price ★★★★

Motifs: **Late 19th century**

The diversity of fabric motifs in evidence during the late 19th century was as wide-ranging as the contemporary styles of architecture and decoration. On both sides of the Atlantic an eclectic mix of revivalist styles, such as Gothic, Louis XIV, Rococo, and Pompeiian, were often employed in different rooms in the same house. However, a reaction to this jumbled ornamentation set in, and more uniform decorative schemes, derived from the Aesthetic, Arts and Crafts, and Art Nouveau Movements, soon emerged.

Fabric motifs favored by the Aesthetic Movement included flowers (particularly sunflowers), which were mostly depicted in a conventionalized, flat, circular form, but sometimes with almost botanical accuracy; Japanese-style sparrows, kingfishers, and peacocks; Renaissance-style putti, dolphins, and grotesques; and scrollwork inspired by Turkish, Persian, and Cretan embroideries. Arts and Crafts fabrics–the most popular of the period–featured birds and flowers rhythmically presented within a medieval-style pattern structure. Stylized birds and floral and vegetative motifs, notably scrolling acanthus leaves, were also favored by Art Nouveau designers. However, these motifs were more sinuously illustrated than their Arts and Crafts counterparts.

2

1

1 Bennison Fabrics/India Stripe Color **red** Alternative colors **available** Composition **70% linen, 30% cotton** Width **48in/122cm** Repeat **19¼in/49cm** Price ★★★

2 Watts of Westminster/Malvern WF0016-03/T5 Color **brick/rust/old gold** Alternative colors **available** Composition **63% cotton, 37% flax** Width **51in/130cm** Repeat **48¾in/124cm** Price ★★★★

3 Scalamandré/Coronet 16266 Color **005** Alternative colors **available** Composition **100% cotton** Width **54in/137cm** Repeat **28in/71cm** Price ★★★★ T

3

4 Stroheim & Romann/Roycroft 4843N-0130 Color **flesh** Alternative colors **available** Composition **100% cotton** Width **55in/140cm** Repeat **8½in/22cm** Price ★★★

5 Hodsoll McKenzie/Small Ottoman 263/101-106 Color **blue** Alternative colors **available** Composition **100% cotton** Width **50in/127cm** Repeat **8¼in/21cm** Price ★★★

6 Stroheim & Romann/Eastlake 4845N-0130 Color **gold and red** Alternative colors **available** Composition **100% cotton** Width **54in/137cm** Repeat **4¾in/12cm** Price ★★★

7 Scalamandré/Coeur de Lion 26315-002 Color **crimson** Alternative colors **available** Composition **52% acrylic, 48% cotton** Width **55¾in/142cm** Repeat **7in/18cm** Price ★★★

8 Watts of Westminster/Memlinc F0017-07/A5 Color **taupe/oatmeal** Alternative colors **available** Composition **100% cotton** Width **48¾in/124cm** Repeat **38½in/98cm** Price ★★★

9 Warner Fabrics/Etiennes Folly CS 8060 Color **stone/cream** Alternative colors **available** Composition **68% linen, 32% cotton** Width **54in/137cm** Repeat **24¼in/62cm** Price ★★

4

5

6

7

8

9

Motifs: **Early 20th century**

For the first five years of the 20th century, Art Nouveau motifs, such as stems, roots, elongated blooms, and dreamlike figures of women, retained their popularity, while Arts and Crafts fabrics, featuring daisies, wild roses, and medieval motifs such as the fleur-de-lis, remained fashionable well into the 1930s. Also in vogue were Tudor- and Jacobean-Revival fabrics, which were ornamented with birds of paradise, the "Tree of Life," Tudor roses, and furled, bannerlike ribbons.

Less revivalist and more innovative were the Art Deco fabrics. The earliest examples of these fabrics were embellished with rounded and romantic motifs, such as garlands and baskets of flowers, stylized rosebuds, fawns, doves, and ropes of pearls. Such images were gradually superseded by Egyptian motifs, including the scarab, and Aztec symbols, such as stepped shapes and sun motifs. However, all of these motifs were in turn supplanted by streamlined geometric and abstract images that provoked French designer Paul Iribe to observe in exasperation, "They [have] sacrificed the flower on the altar of Cubism and the machine."

1

2

1 Abbott & Boyd/Orphée Color **red and gold** Alternative colors **available** Composition **51% acrylic, 49% viscose** Width **55in/140cm** Repeat **11¼in/28.5cm** Price ★★★★

2 Watts of Westminster/French Stripe F0042-01/K7 Color **black and taupe** Alternative colors **not available** Composition **70% cotton, 30% Velicren** Width **55in/140cm** Repeat **9½in/24cm** Price ★★★

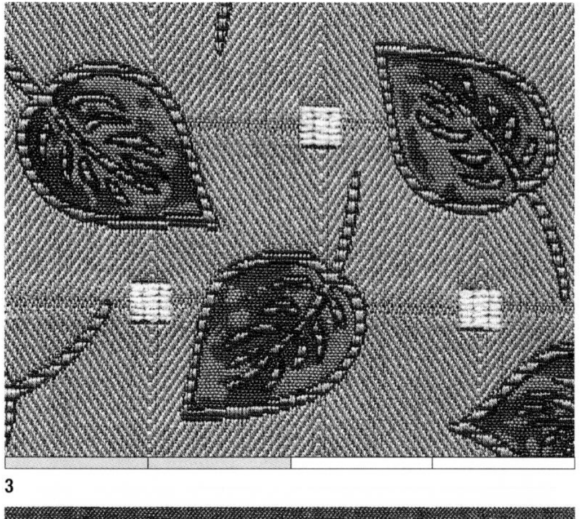

3

4

3 Jab/Aviano 1-2020-178 Color **178** Alternative colors **available** Composition **58% cotton, 31% viscose, 11% polyester** Width **55in/140cm** Repeat **7in/18cm** Price ★★★

4 Zimmer & Rohde/Scirell 4820295 Color **rust** Alternative colors **available** Composition **100% silk** Width **55in/140cm** Repeat **4¾in/12cm** Price ★★★

5 John Wilman/Rio 500 Color **papaya** Alternative colors **available** Composition **100% cotton** Width **54in/137cm** Repeat **2¾in/7cm** Price ★

6 Marvic Textiles/Medaillon Empire SCF 954-1 Color **blue and beige** Alternative colors **available** Composition **100% cotton** Width **55in/140cm** Repeat **17¾in/45cm** Price ★★

7 Hill & Knowles/Fleumont Hestia CK9103F Color **gray** Alternative colors **available** Composition **100% cotton** Width **56½in/144cm** Repeat **35½in/90cm** Price ★★

5

6

7

8

9

10

8 Donghia/Fleur d'Hiver 0475/3310 Color **01** Alternative colors **available** Composition **88% cotton, 12% viscose** Width **54in/137cm** Repeat **26¾in/68cm** Price ★★★★

9 Jab/Verbania 1-7054 Color **115** Alternative colors **available** Composition **46% cotton, 34% polyester, 20% cotton** Width **118in/300cm** Repeat **2¾in/7cm** Price ★★

10 Brunschwig & Fils/Sycamore Floral Plaid 53373.01 Color **mandarin plaid** Alternative colors **available** Composition **100% cotton** Width **51in/130cm** Repeat **6¼in/16cm** Price ★★

11 Zimmer & Rohde/Plumito 7008 910 Color **1** Alternative colors **not available** Composition **57% viscose, 23% cotton, 20% linen** Width **55in/140cm** Repeat **24¼in/62cm** Price ★★★★

12 Celia Birtwell/Orphée 1013 Color **beige** Alternative colors **available** Composition **100% silk** Width **55in/140cm** Repeat **35¾in/91cm** Price ★★★

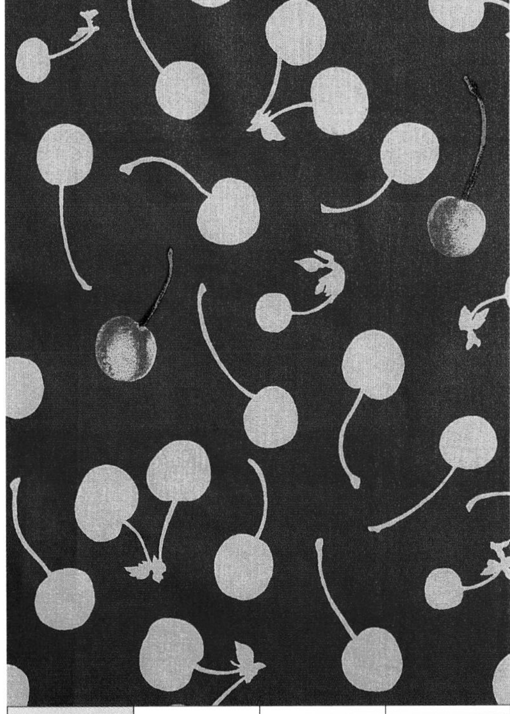

13

11 12

14

THE OAK LEAF

The fabric shown here is adapted from a hand-blocked tapestry woven in the Arthur H. Lee factory in Birkenhead, England, until the early 1970s, when the factory closed. The pattern dates from the early 20th century. However, the oak-leaf motif was first used much earlier, for example, in ancient Rome as a symbol of civic virtue and in naturalistic decorations of the Middle Ages and the Renaissance. Similarly, the acorn–a symbol of life, fecundity, and immortality–notably recurs in ancient Roman, Celtic, and Scandinavian designs, and has been consistently favored since the Middle Ages.

Lee Jofa/Oak Leaf Weave 854252 Color **carmine** Alternative colors **available** Composition **85% rayon, 15% cotton** Width **52in/132cm** Repeat **32½in/82.5cm** Price ★★★★

15

13 Liberty/Cherries 1125005 Color **E** Alternative colors **available** Composition **100% cotton** Width **54in/137cm** Repeat **21in/53.5cm** Price ★★

14 Apenn/Knot Garden AV478-5 Color **sand and rose** Alternative colors **available** Composition **100% cotton** Width **54in/137cm** Repeat **13¾in/35cm** Price ★★

15 Brunschwig & Fils/Ormseby Glazed Chintz 62315.01 Color **jade and terracotta** Alternative colors **available** Composition **100% cotton** Width **55in/140cm** Repeat **4¾in/12cm** Price ★★★

Motifs: **Late 20th century**

Fashionable fabric motifs of the 1950s included abstract, geometric, and Cubist-inspired images, as well as crystalline shapes derived from scientific observations under the microscope and produced by designers working in a style known as Organic Modernism. Small repeat motifs of fruits such as apples and pears were also popular. Depicted in both stylized and naturalistic form, and often set on a plain background, they remained in demand for much of the rest of the century.

The 1960s gave rise to a profusion of decorative styles and accompanying motifs: Art Nouveau fabrics (harboring sinuous plant stems and roots and elongated blooms) enjoyed a great revival; foliage, flowers, animals, birds, and insects appeared in repeating patterns taken from Persian paintings and ceramics; Renaissance-style classical figures, vases, and urns–sometimes set within geometric patterns and sometimes in mosaic form–came into vogue; and Pop Art crossed over from canvas and concrete to textiles. As the 1960s drew to a close, a new ruralism emerged, the significant consequences of which were the enduring "English country house" look and the accompanying revival in the manufacture of chintzes incorporating traditional foliage, flower, fruit, and bird motifs.

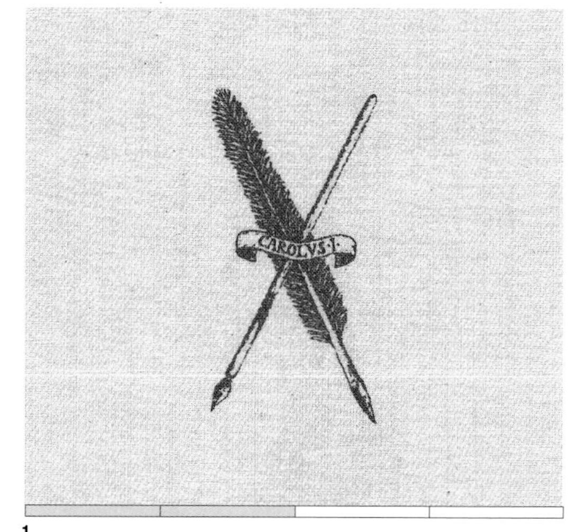

1

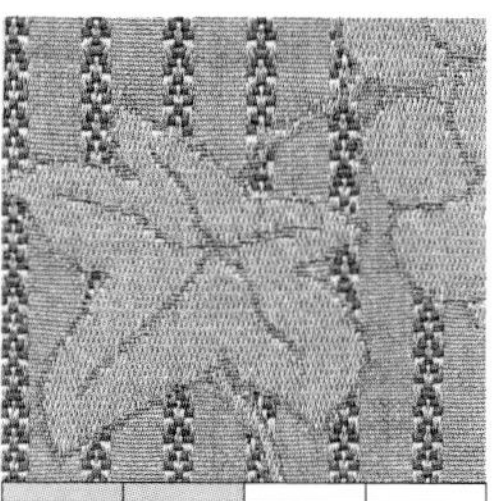
2

3

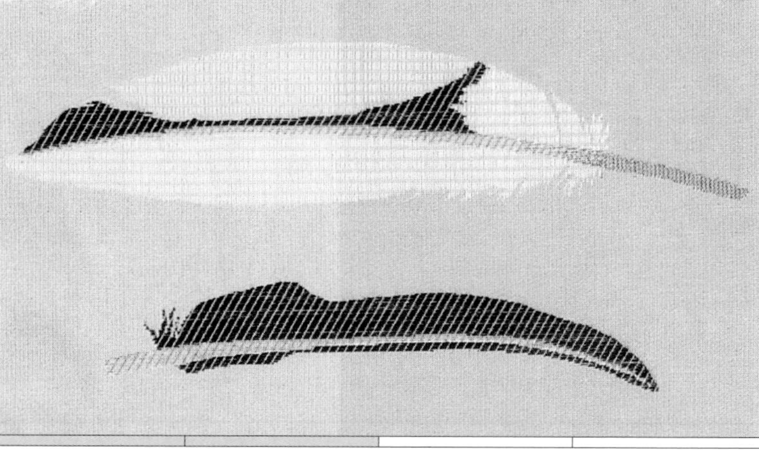
4

5

6

1 **Andrew Martin/Guinevere** Color **taupe** Alternative colors **available** Composition **100% cotton** Width **52¼in/133cm** Repeat **10½in/26.5cm** Price ★★

2 **Tissunique/Savigny 35/2415** Color **green and beige** Alternative colors **available** Composition **50% cotton, 50% viscose** Width **55in/140cm** Repeat **10½in/27cm** Price ★★★

3 **Jab/Osman 2735** Color **173** Alternative colors **available** Composition **59% polyester, 30% cotton, 11% metal** Width **55in/140cm** Repeat **9¾in/25cm** Price ★★★

4 **Sahco Hesslein/Indiana 12906** Color **cream** Alternative colors **available** Composition **55% cotton, 45% polyacrylic** Width **55in/140cm** Repeat **19¾in/50cm** Price ★★★

5 **Knowles & Christou/Amphora** Color **stone** Alternative colors **available** Composition **100% cotton** Width **52in/132cm** Repeat **11¾in/30cm** Price ★★

6 **Sahco Hesslein/Apollo 12180** Color **black and gold** Alternative colors **available** Composition **70% cotton, 30% cupro** Width **55in/140cm** Repeat **12½in/32cm** Price ★★★

7

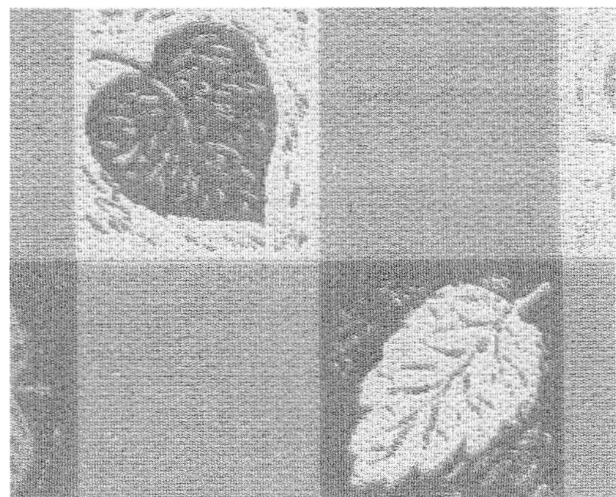

10

11

7 Donghia/Crown Jewels 2000 Color **18** Alternative colors **available** Composition **81% rayon, 19% polyester** Width **54in/137cm** Repeat **12½in/32cm** Price ★★★★★

8 Liberty/Pears 1125003 Color **blue** Alternative colors **available** Composition **100% cotton** Width **54in/137cm** Repeat **24¾in/63cm** Price ★★

9 Sahco Hesslein/Taranto 09681 Color **multi** Alternative colors **available** Composition **47% cotton, 26% wool, 22% polyacrylic, 5% viscose** Width **55in/140cm** Repeat **13in/33cm** Price ★★★★

10 Abbott & Boyd/Abeto 50054-2 Color **beige and cream** Alternative colors **available** Composition **100% cotton** Width **54in/137cm** Repeat **13¼in/34cm** Price ★★★

12

11 Osborne & Little/Rondo F1413 Color **02** Alternative colors **available** Composition **57% cotton, 43% viscose** Width **55in/140cm** Repeat **14in/36cm** Price ★★

12 Busby & Busby/Aspen 5009 Color **desert** Alternative colors **available** Composition **100% cotton** Width **55in/140cm** Repeat **25in/64cm** Price ★★

13 Andrew Martin/Tempo Color **buff** Alternative colors **available** Composition **80% cotton, 20% linen** Width **63in/160cm** Repeat **61¾in/157cm** Price ★★

8

9

13

20th century

Motifs: **Late 20th century**

Many of the fabric motifs favored during the last three decades of the 20th century reflected a widespread nostalgia for previous eras and the accompanying boom in "period-style" interiors. Apart from chintz-style flowers, foliage, and birds, revivals included late 19th-century William Morris- and other Arts and Crafts-style flowers, animal motifs derived from 16th- and 17th-century needlework patterns, and, in America, "Native Orders," first popular in the late 18th and early 19th centuries. Significant among the latter were corncobs, tobacco, and cotton balls, stars, turkeys, and bald eagles, as well as Native American motifs such as feathered arrow shafts, bison, and bison horns. Some of the most striking motifs were classical architectural elements rendered in black and white. At the same time, more short-term nostalgia resulted in "space age" motifs inspired by the Apollo program and the moon landings.

On an international basis, the late 20th century also witnessed a further consolidation of the links between contemporary fine art and fabric design, with some of the most fashionable motifs including artistic images of fruits and berries, a diverse range of domestic artifacts ranging from crockery to buttons, and photographic images and photocopied prints.

Pierre Frey/Minton Color **rose ancien 5** Alternative colors **available** Composition **100% cotton** Width **54in/137cm** Repeat **30¼in/77cm** Price ★★★★

John Wilman/Giovanni 888140 Color **Aegean** Alternative colors **available** Composition **100% cotton** Width **54in/137cm** Repeat **8½in/22cm** Price ★

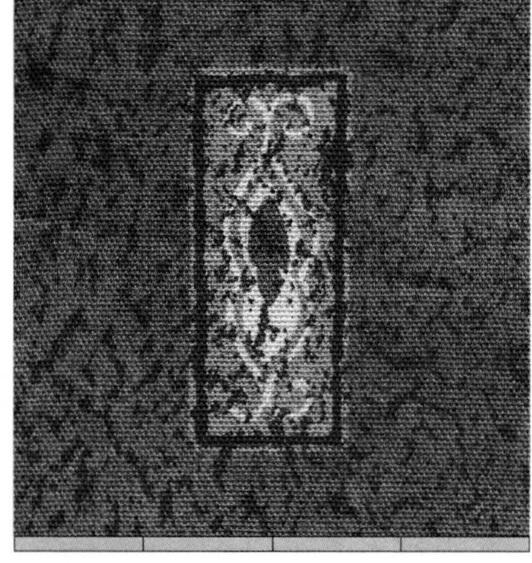

Harlequin/Orissa Color **191** Alternative colors **available** Composition **100% cotton** Width **54in/137cm** Repeat **25in/64cm** Price ★

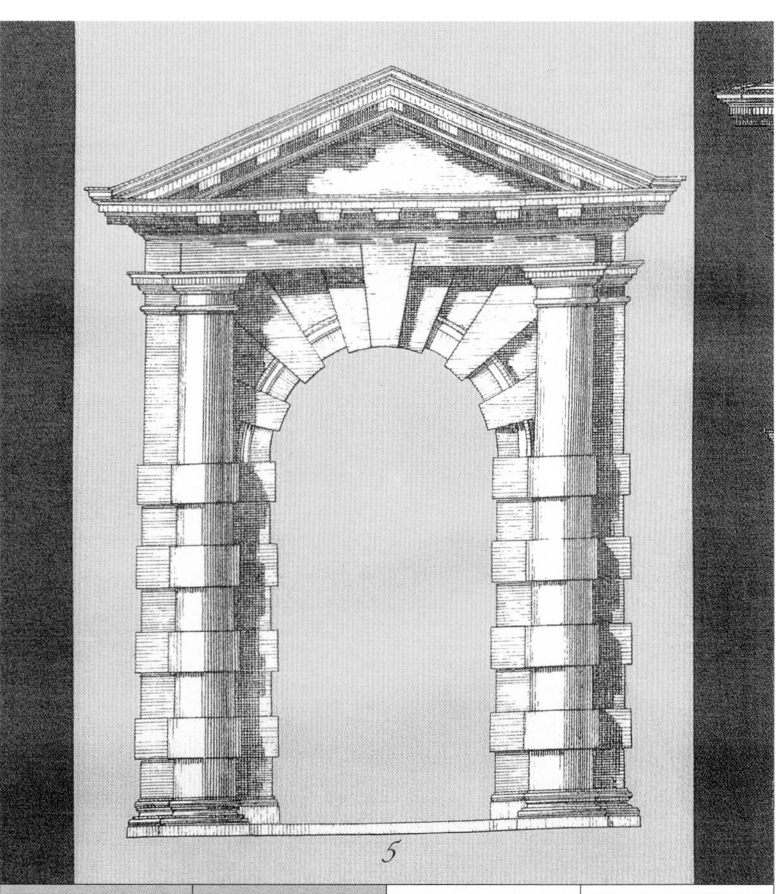

Timney Fowler/Porticos TF0203/03 Color **03** Alternative colors **available** Composition **100% cotton** Width **54in/137cm** Repeat **38in/96.5cm** Price ★★

Anna French/Tintagel Color **green** Alternative colors **available** Composition **100% cotton** Width **54in/137cm** Repeat **25in/64cm** Price ★★ LC

Osborne & Little/Merlin F583 Color **gold and yellow** Alternative colors **available** Composition **100% cotton** Width **55in/140cm** Repeat **5in/13cm** Price ★★

Designers Guild/Latika F538/05 Color **red** Alternative colors **available** Composition **100% cotton** Width **54in/137cm** Repeat **25in/64cm** Price ★★

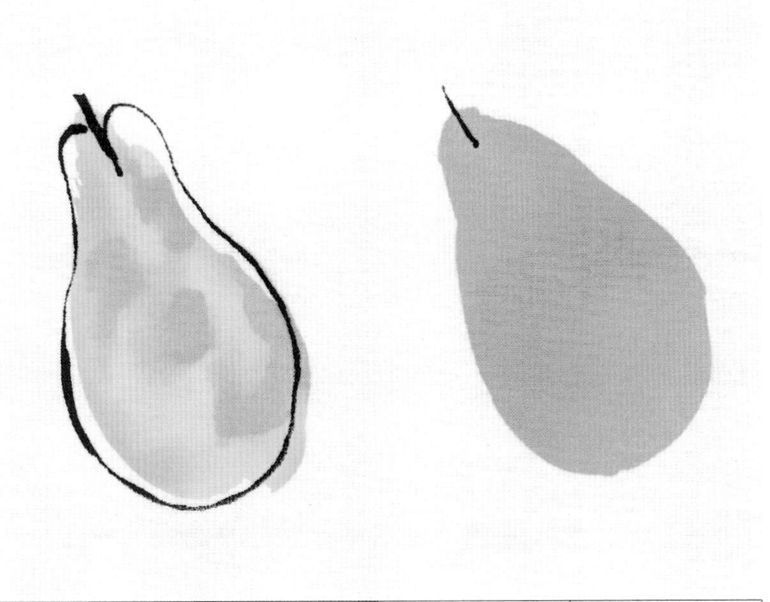

Garin/Nashi 8319 Color **yellow** Alternative colors **available** Composition **100% cotton** Width **55in/140cm** Repeat **35¾in/91cm** Price ★★

Manuel Canovas/Tilda 4423/21 Color **rose/jaune** Alternative colors **available** Composition **73% viscose, 27% cotton** Width **55in/140cm** Repeat **3¼in/8.5cm** Price ★★★

Manuel Canovas/Mazurka 4425 Color **paille 28** Alternative colors **available** Composition **100% cotton** Width **58¼in/148cm** Repeat **1½in/4cm** Price ★★★

Monkwell/Imaria 09332CU/003 Color **orange** Alternative colors **available** Composition **100% cotton** Width **54in/137cm** Repeat **12½in/32cm** Price ★

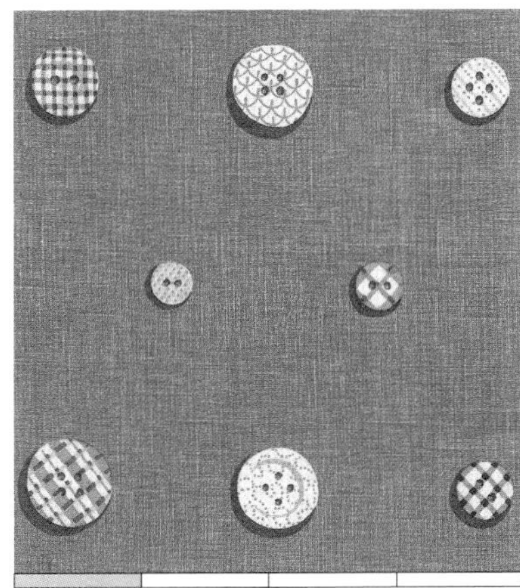

Osborne & Little/Button Up F1174 Color **02** Alternative colors **available** Composition **100% cotton** Width **55in/140cm** Repeat **12½in/32cm** Price ★

Jab/Magao 1-2071-148 Color **yellow, rust** Alternative colors **available** Composition **100% cotton** Width **55in/140cm** Repeat **15¾in/40cm** Price ★★

Anna French/Chalice Color **28** Alternative colors **available** Composition **100% cotton** Width **54in/137cm** Repeat **25in/64cm** Price ★★

Floral Fabrics

Throughout history textile designers have made extensive use of plant motifs, especially floral subjects. In Europe, prior to the end of the 16th century, floral patterns were featured on a wide variety of fabrics, including tapestry, embroidery, and woven damasks and velvets. However, the diversity of plants and the accuracy of their depiction was restricted by the limitations of early weaving techniques and a lack of botanical reference material. Then two events occurred that resulted in a proliferation of floral-patterned fabrics that has endured to this day. The first was the publication in 1586 of *La Clef des Champs*, by French artist and traveler Jacques le Moyne de Morgues. Depicting flowers, fruits, and animals in a simple but accurate style, this early pattern book provided textile designers with a wealth of inspiration, and also set the precedent for more extensive publications in the future. The second was the importation of the first colorfast, hand-blocked calicoes (*indiennes*) from India, which confirmed that floral decoration could be most dramatically exploited on printed fabrics.

LEFT Printed cotton curtains grace the window of a medieval house in a *bastide* (a fortified town) in the Lot-et-Garonne region in France. The floral design, which is augmented with a pattern of foliage and birds, is elegantly rendered in white, red, and shades of pink.

BELOW LEFT *Chinoiserie* patterns on 17th- and 18th-century delftware provided the inspiration for the bed-hangings and upholstered seating in this bedroom at the Château de Morsan in France.

BELOW The walls of this room, designed by Roger Banks Pye, are decorated with a machine-woven, crewelwork fabric, its stylized floral pattern inspired by 17th-century Eastern designs. Various blue-and-white and black-and-white checks cover the cushions and screen.

ROSE MOTIFS

Rich in symbolism, the rose has been one of the most enduringly popular floral motifs. In Christian iconography it is an attribute of the Virgin Mary and paradise, while in classical mythology it is a token of Venus (and love), and of secrecy (*sub rosa*). Other notable associations of the rose include martyrdom (red rose) and piety (white rose). Over the centuries, wild and cultivated roses have provided inspiration for fabric designs. Wild roses are closely associated with Medieval, Jacobean, and Arts and Crafts fabrics, while cultivated roses appear on both Victorian and Edwardian designs.

KEY DESIGNS

1 Naturalistic floral patterns were especially popular in the 18th and 19th centuries, but they first began to appear in the 17th century as designers gained access to illustrated botanical studies.

2 Flowering-vine patterns were prevalent in Egyptian, Ancient Roman, and early eastern Mediterranean decorations, and were favored on Renaissance and 17th-, 18th-, and mid-19th-century fabrics.

3 Stylized floral patterns have been seen since the Middle Ages. They were particularly popular during the late 19th century, and were a feature of Arts and Crafts and Art Nouveau fabrics.

4 Flowers are a feature of *chinoiserie* and *japonaiserie* fabrics, many of which were derived from traditional porcelain designs. Popular imagery included blossom sprigs, peonies, and chrysanthemums.

5 Patterns of densely packed blooms and foliage were highly fashionable in Victorian interiors, especially on chintzes, and were to come back into fashion in the Art Deco schemes of the 20th century.

6 Since the Middle Ages, typical embellishments to naturalistic and stylized floral patterns have included trelliswork, hanging baskets, and, as in this rose pattern, decorative ribbons.

1 **Bennett Silks/Basket and Ribbon** Color **multi** Alternative colors **available** Composition **100% silk** Width **51in/130cm** Repeat **24in/61cm** Price ★★

2 **Schumacher/Imperial Vine** Color **document cream and multi** Alternative colors **available** Composition **100% cotton** Width **54in/137cm** Repeat **25¼in/64.5cm** Price ★★★

3 **Liberty/Clementina** Color **S** Alternative colors **available** Composition **100% cotton** Width **53in/135cm** Repeat **10½in/27cm** Price ★

4 **Old World Weavers/Lasalle** Color **multi/brown** Alternative colors **available** Composition **100% rayon** Width **55in/140cm** Repeat **25in/64cm** Price ★★★

5 **Jason D'Souza/Blenheim** Color **plum/rust** Alternative colors **available** Composition **64% linen, 36% cotton** Width **53in/135cm** Repeat **36¼in/92cm** Price ★★★

6 **Lelièvre/Watteau** Color **ivoire** Alternative colors **available** Composition **68% viscose, 32% silk** Width **51in/130cm** Repeat **3in/8cm** Price ★★★ LC

Florals: **Pre-18th century**

With the notable exception of the often highly naturalistic *millefleurs* in medieval tapestries, the majority of floral-patterned fabrics produced before the 17th century featured stylized flowers. Most Renaissance damasks and velvets employed symmetrical floral designs, while the brightly colored calicoes (*indiennes*) imported from India at the end of the 16th century used stylized flowers, as did the European copies that followed. However, during the 17th century, naturalistic renderings of an ever-greater number of flowers became increasingly common as knowledge of plant forms grew and pattern books on the subject proliferated. Influential publications included Pierre Vallet's *Le Jardin du Roi* (1608), which introduced many flower species, such as the tulip, and P. A. Ducerceau's *Bouquets Propres pour les Etoffes de Tours* (ca.1660-70), which was specifically intended for silk designers and illustrated flower species as diverse as narcissi, snake head and crown fritillaries, lilies, orchids, roses, pinks, clematis, and campanula.

1

2

3

1 **Hodsoll McKenzie/English Crewelwork 220/103** Color **olive** Alternative colors **available** Composition **60% spun rayon, 40% cotton** Width **50in/127cm** Repeat **24½in/62cm** Price ★★★

2 **Chelsea Textiles/Queen Anne F101A** Color **rust** Alternative colors **available** Composition **60% linen, 40% cotton with cotton crewelwork** Width **45in/114cm** Repeat **42in/107cm** Price ★★★★

3 **Stroheim & Romann/Haskell 4704N-0020** Color **multi on cream** Alternative colors **available** Composition **100% cotton** Width **54in/137cm** Repeat **11¾in/30cm** Price ★★

4

5

4 **Watts of Westminster/Langton F0064-01/ZIF** Color **natural** Alternative colors **available** Composition **100% linen** Width **49in/125cm** Repeat **31½in/80cm** Price ★★★

5 **RBI International/Benares GFB 75** Color **11621** Alternative colors **available** Composition **65% cotton, 35% viscose** Width **54in/137cm** Repeat **27½in/70cm** Price ★★★

6 **Chelsea Textiles/Grapes Fine Crewelwork F032** Color **multi** Alternative colors **available** Composition **100% cotton with wool crewelwork** Width **59in/150cm** Repeat **37¾in/96cm** Price ★★★★

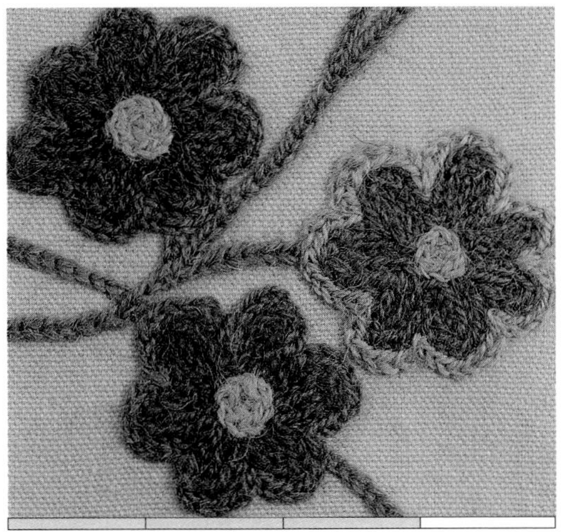

6

SYMBOLISM

The inspiration for "Darnley," which is shown here, came from a 16th-century needlework panel that has been attributed to Mary, Queen of Scots. Now part of the historic Hardwick Hall collection in Derbyshire, England, it features interlaced thistles, lilies, and roses, which are symbolic of Mary's double crown of France and Scotland and of her claim to the throne of England. The fabric is woven in muted shades of the original (but now faded) ivory, gold, rose, and green.

Stuart Interiors/Darnley Color **ivory** Alternative colors **available** Composition **60% wool, 40% cotton** Width **49in/125cm** Repeat **11¾in/30cm** Price ★★★★

7

8

9

CREWELWORK

A form of outline embroidery, crewelwork was fashionable during the 17th and 18th centuries; it has since enjoyed revivals in the late 19th and 20th centuries. Stitched with crewel, which is a loose-spun worsted yarn, on a linen or cotton ground, crewelwork is traditionally used for bed furnishings and covers for cushions. Popular stitches include stem, double-back, and chain, while satin, rope coral, buttonhole, and French knot are used for the fillings. The motifs are often Eastern in origin, and usually include naïvely depicted flowers, leaves, animals, and birds.

Nice Irma's/Rosemary CWF 39 Color **pastels on cream** Alternative colors **available** Composition **100% cotton with wool crewelwork** Width **51¾in/132cm** Repeat **37in/95cm** Price ★

10

11

7 **Jason D'Souza/Medici MED03** Color **burgundy/blue** Alternative colors **available** Composition **70% linen, 30% cotton** Width **53½in/136cm** Repeat **19½in/49.5cm** Price ★★★

8 **Bernard Thorp & Co/Jane** Color **blue and red** Alternative colors **available** Composition **100% jute** Width **47in/120cm** Repeat **33in/84cm** Price ★★

9 **Zimmer & Rohde/Meriana 7049 821** Color **red and green** Alternative colors **available** Composition **100% linen** Width **55in/140cm** Repeat **25in/64cm** Price ★★★

10 **Beaumont & Fletcher/Tyger 2337a** Color **madder/indigo** Alternative colors **available** Composition **52% linen, 36% cotton, 12% nylon** Width **52½in/133.5cm** Repeat **31½in/80cm** Price ★★★

11 **Liberty/Moray LF4010** Color **02** Alternative colors **available** Composition **100% cotton** Width **55in/140cm** Repeat **15¼in/39cm** Price ★★

12 **Abbott & Boyd/Floralia Barroca 45314-5** Color **deep multi on gray** Alternative colors **not available** Composition **100% linen** Width **55in/140cm** Repeat **43¼in/110cm** Price ★★★

13 **Lee Jofa/Rose Stripe Weave 845014** Color **blue/cream/multi** Alternative colors **available** Composition **100% cotton** Width **55¾in/142cm** Repeat **3in/8cm** Price ★★★

12

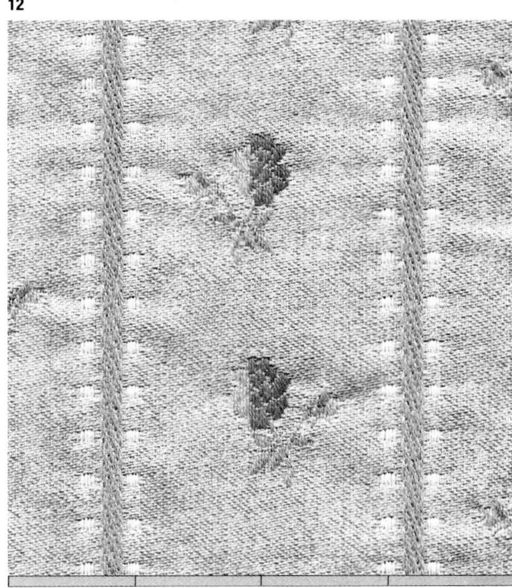

13

Florals: **Early 18th century**

The first half of the 18th century saw developments in the design of floral-patterned fabrics. A new influence came from the East in the form of Chinese lacquerwares and ceramics showing exotic floral ornamentation. These provided the inspiration to copy unfamiliar flowers, such as the chrysanthemum, and to produce *chinoiserie* designs that imitated Oriental compositions, notably the *famille rose* and *Kakiemon* patterns. During the Rococo Period the pursuit of the exotic even extended to devising imaginary species, such as the "umbrella" flower.

Running parallel to the adoption of Chinese forms of decoration was a growth in the production of French and English floral chintzes, developed from the imported Indian calicoes (*indiennes*) of the previous century. By 1721 these printed cotton fabrics were sufficiently popular to threaten the future of woven fabrics, and in England an Act of Parliament forbade their manufacture for the home market. However, due to popular demand the English cotton industry was allowed to renew production in the 1730s (restrictions were removed totally in the 1770s), using a linen-cotton cloth known as fustian. Similar legislation was introduced in France in the 1680s and rescinded in 1759.

5

1

2

3

4

1 **Beaumont & Fletcher/Aubusson Rose 2209** Color **coral** Alternative colors **available** Composition **52% linen, 36% cotton, 12% nylon** Width **52½in/133.5cm** Repeat **33in/84cm** Price ★★★

2 **Jab/Siljan 1-8105-114** Color **burgundy/cream** Alternative colors **available** Composition **100% cotton** Width **55in/140cm** Repeat **25in/64cm** Price ★

3 **Hodsoll McKenzie/Indian Iris 105/503** Color **red/ocher** Alternative colors **available** Composition **52% linen, 36% cotton, 12% nylon** Width **54in/137cm** Repeat **8in/20cm** Price ★★

4 **Marvic Textiles/Baronscourt 474** Color **4** Alternative colors **available** Composition **54% viscose, 28% cotton, 18% linen** Width **53½in/136cm** Repeat **25in/64cm** Price ★★

5 **Scalamandré/Louis XV 2770M-005** Color **Chinese red** Alternative colors **available** Composition **100% silk** Width **55in/140cm** Repeat **21in/53cm** Price ★★★★★

6 **Warner Fabrics/Indian** Color **multi on ecru** Alternative colors **available** Composition **63% flax, 28% cotton, 9% nylon** Width **48in/122cm** Repeat **22in/56cm** Price ★★

6

7 Jason D'Souza/Verona Color **pink and blue** Alternative colors **available** Composition **70% linen, 30% cotton** Width **53½in/136cm** Repeat **29in/74cm** Price ★★★

8 Garin/Janini 96455041 Color **rojo** Alternative colors **available** Composition **69% cotton, 21% viscose, 10% linen** Width **59in/150cm** Repeat **22in/56cm** Price ★★

9 Lee Jofa/Hollyhock Minor 849016 Color **multi** Alternative colors **available** Composition **100% cotton** Width **54in/137cm** Repeat **25in/64cm** Price ★★

10 Abbott & Boyd/Vienna Color **05** Alternative colors **available** Composition **100% cotton** Width **63in/160cm** Repeat **22in/56cm** Price ★★

11 Jason D'Souza/Colonne Fleurie CF1 Color **tonal pink** Alternative colors **available** Composition **70% linen, 30% cotton** Width **47½in/121cm** Repeat **18½in/47cm** Price ★★★

7

8

9

10

11

12

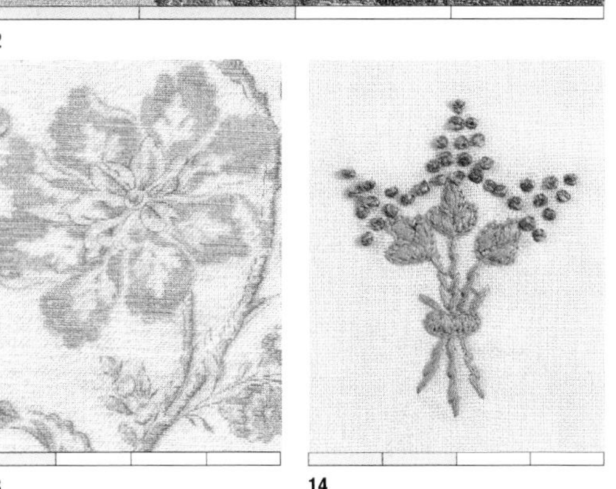

13

14

12 Zimmer & Rohde/Adrastos 2556 Color **184** Alternative colors **available** Composition **70% cotton, 30% viscose** Width **54in/138cm** Repeat **14in/36cm** Price ★★★

13 Colefax and Fowler/Lincoln 2061/03 Color **cream and aqua** Alternative colors **available** Composition **60% linen, 20% cotton, 20% modacrylic** Width **54in/137cm** Repeat **18¼in/46.5cm** Price ★★

14 Chelsea Textiles/Wisteria Pink F057P Color **pink** Alternative colors **available** Composition **60% linen, 40% cotton with cotton crewelwork** Width **45in/114cm** Repeat **8in/20cm** Price ★★★ LC W

15 Old World Weavers/Lisere Romano II AO 27513222 Color **rose/green** Alternative colors **available** Composition **100% silk** Width **19¾in/50cm** Repeat **13¾in/35cm** Price ★★★★★

16 Hodsoll McKenzie/English Ribbon 223/101-108 Color **blue** Alternative colors **available** Composition **61% spun rayon, 39% cotton** Width **50in/127cm** Repeat **8in/20.5cm** Price ★★★ W

15

16

Florals: **Late 18th century**

The proliferation of floral-patterned fabrics in Europe was further fueled during the second half of the 18th century by the English government's removal, in the 1770s, of previously imposed restrictions on the manufacture of cotton chintzes. Moreover, the development of copperplate printing during the mid-1700s revolutionized the fabric industry by increasing output, reducing costs, and improving the sophistication and quality of designs. By the end of the 18th century, Americans began to produce their own chintzes following the emigration of a number of English printers to Philadelphia.

Aesthetically, floral patterns of the second half of the century were characterized by a move away from the exotic and toward naturalistic renditions of less complicated (often wild) flowers. Examples included larkspurs, roses, carnations, poppies, and cornflowers, as well as the daisies, stocks, violets, and anemones embellishing many of the fabrics used in 1768 to decorate Marie Antoinette's bedroom at the Petit Trianon in Versailles, France.

1

2

3

4

5

6

7

1 Tissunique/Jehan Rose Color **red, cream, and green** Alternative colors **available** Composition **100% cotton** Width **51in/130cm** Repeat **8in/20cm** Price ★★★

2 Lennox Money/Miramar 2433C Color **green and yellow** Alternative colors **available** Composition **100% cotton** Width **53¾in/136.5cm** Repeat **46⅞in/119cm** Price ★★

3 Bennison Fabrics/Corne Fleurie Color **blue and yellow** Alternative colors **available** Composition **70% linen, 30% cotton** Width **50¾in/129cm** Repeat **16½in/42cm** Price ★★★

4 Watts of Westminster/Edenwood F0063-02/N15 Color **Dorchester** Alternative colors **available** Composition **100% linen** Width **50in/127cm** Repeat **30in/76cm** Price ★★★★

5 Percheron/Lampas Diane 10491 Color **3** Alternative colors **available** Composition **100% silk** Width **51in/130cm** Repeat **11¼in/28.5cm** Price ★★★★★

6 Jab/Appiano 2719-136 Color **136** Alternative colors **available** Composition **100% viscose** Width **55in/140cm** Repeat **6¾in/17cm** Price ★★★

7 Brunschwig & Fils/Ukiyo Glazed Chintz 65043.01 Color **01** Alternative colors **available** Composition **100% cotton** Width **54in/137cm** Repeat **14¾in/37.5cm** Price ★★★

8 **Montgomery/Damask Rose Color No. 4** Color **green on beige** Alternative colors **available** Composition **100% cotton satin** Width **54in/137cm** Repeat **24¾in/63.5cm** Price ★

9 **Hodsoll McKenzie/Florentine 126/403** Color **green** Alternative colors **available** Composition **100% cotton** Width **54in/137cm** Repeat **11in/28cm** Price ★★

10 **Anne & Robert Swaffer/Amy** Color **32** Alternative colors **available** Composition **100% cotton** Width **55in/140cm** Repeat **8½in/22cm** Price ★

11 **Schumacher/Imperial Vine 168360** Color **white** Alternative colors **available** Composition **100% cotton** Width **54in/137cm** Repeat **25in/64cm** Price ★★★

12 **Bennison Fabrics/Wheatflower** Color **1** Alternative colors **not available** Composition **70% linen, 30% cotton** Width **49½in/126cm** Repeat **22¾in/57.5cm** Price ★★★

13 **Brunschwig & Fils/Empress of China Stripe 51305** Color **01** Alternative colors **available** Composition **100% cotton** Width **55in/140cm** Repeat **42in/107cm** Price ★★★

14 **Lennox Money/Chekian Lotus** Color **1** Alternative colors **not available** Composition **100% cotton** Width **53in/135cm** Repeat **25in/64cm** Price ★★★

8

9

10

11

12

13

14

DOCUMENTARY DESIGNS

A "document" is a historic fabric that serves as the source for a reproduction–a documentary fabric. In its purest form a documentary fabric is an exact copy of the fibers, width, repeat, colors, and every detail of the original design. However, as is often the case, if one or more of the original elements is altered, then the reproduction is referred to as an "adaptation." Typical examples include a change from silk to synthetic fibers, adjustments of scale to accommodate modern power looms, and variations in color caused by different dyes or printing techniques.

The fabrics below are based on the original documents shown above, with some modifications: alteration to the size of the pattern, and, in the case of "Tulip Stripe," replacement of the roses by a broken stripe.

Apenn/Surrey Rose Garland AV464-1/2/3 Color **1** Alternative colors **available** Composition **100% cotton** Width **48in/122cm** Repeat **19in/48cm** Price ★★

Apenn/Tulip Stripe AV466-1/2/3 Color **red and blue** Alternative colors **available** Composition **100% cotton** Width **48¾in/124cm** Repeat **9in/23cm** Price ★★

18th century

Bennison Fabrics
16 Holbein Place, London, SW1W 8NL • 76 Greene Street, New York, N.Y.10012

Florals: **Early 19th century**

During the early 19th century, the naturalistically rendered flowers that had been a feature of 18th-century Neoclassical ornamentation remained fashionable, although in Empire-style interiors they were eventually abandoned in favor of militaristic motifs and mythical beasts. At the beginning of the century, many French, British, and American chintzes with a glazed finish did show flowers in stylized form, but they too became even more naturalistic as the century progressed.

As before, the realistic depiction of flowers was aided by the publication of botanical reference books, with the English nurseryman Robert Furber's late 18th-century seed catalog, *The Flower Garden Display'd,* published throughout Europe, continuing to be a source of inspiration. Technical advances–the discovery of mineral colors, such as manganese (bronze), antimony (orange), and a "solid" green (instead of indigo penciled over yellow)–also made more realistic floral representations possible. On a more esoteric level, floral patterns were further popularized by the publication, from the 1820s onward, of numerous books on "floral emblems" and "flower language." However, the symbolic meaning attributed to particular flowers was often tenuous with, for example, the poppy, known to induce sleep, representing consolation.

Guy Evans/Adelaide Urn Color **multi** Alternative colors **available** Composition **100% cotton** Width **50½in/128cm** Repeat **15¾in/40cm** Price ★★★

Schumacher/Williamsburg Parrots & Blossoms 168212 Color **red** Alternative colors **available** Composition **100% cotton** Width **54in/137cm** Repeat **12½in/32cm** Price ★★★

Scalamandré/Amazonia 16232 Color **001** Alternative colors **available** Composition **100% cotton** Width **55in/140cm** Repeat **36in/91.5cm** Price ★★★★ T

George Spencer Decorations/Clare's Leaf 00CL/02 Color **blue and rust** Alternative colors **available** Composition **100% cotton** Width **51in/130cm** Repeat **9in/23cm** Price ★★

Garin/Alameda 66823853 Color **Isabelino** Alternative colors **available** Composition **42% rayon, 37% cotton, 21% silk** Width **51in/130cm** Repeat **28¼in/72cm** Price ★★★★

Brunschwig & Fils/Candace Glazed Chintz 79442 Color **04** Alternative colors **available** Composition **100% cotton** Width **54in/137cm** Repeat **36in/91.5cm** Price ★★

G. P. & J. Baker/Directoire Stripe B0851 03 Color **mustard on white** Alternative colors **available** Composition **100% cotton** Width **54in/137cm** Repeat **24¾in/63cm** Price ★★ LC

Hamilton Weston/ Swakely 6137175 Color **pink** Alternative colors **available** Composition **100% cotton** Width **54in/ 137cm** Repeat **14in/36cm** Price ★★ LC

DIFFERENT PRINTING TECHNIQUES

Today, many more fabric manufacturers have begun to produce less expensive screen-printed versions of their hand-blocked documentary fabrics. Shown far right is "Althea" (taken from the Latin for hollyhock), Lee Jofa's screen-printed alternative to their classic hand-blocked "Hollyhock," shown right, which was adapted for printing in the 1920s from an early 19th-century document.

Lee Jofa/Hollyhock Handblock Print 7129 Color **multi** Alternative colors **available** Composition **100% linen** Width **47in/120cm** Repeat **15¾in/40cm** Price ★★★★

Lee Jofa/Althea 879001 Color **multi** Alternative colors **available** Composition **100% cotton** Width **51¾in/132cm** Repeat **31½in/80cm** Price ★★★

Hodsoll McKenzie/Exotic Column 009/413 Color **gray** Alternative colors **available** Composition **100% cotton** Width **54in/137cm** Repeat **14½in/37cm** Price ★★ LC W

Warner Fabrics/Chintz Garden CS 4620 Color **multi/stone** Alternative colors **available** Composition **100% cotton** Width **54in/137cm** Repeat **32¼in/82cm** Price ★★ LC

Bennison Fabrics/Dragon Flower Color **spice** Alternative colors **available** Composition **70% linen, 30% cotton** Width **55in/140cm** Repeat **30¾in/78cm** Price ★★★

Borderline/Kirmani 2340 Color **blue** Alternative colors **available** Composition **61% linen, 39% cotton** Width **54in/137cm** Repeat **18in/46cm** Price ★ LC

Northwood Designs/Folia Color **natural** Alternative colors **available** Composition **55% polyester, 45% cotton** Width **118in/300cm** Repeat **8¼in/21cm** Price ★ W

Nina Campbell/Viola NCF3132 Color **03** Alternative colors **available** Composition **100% cotton** Width **55in/140cm** Repeat **15¾in/40cm** Price ★★

Florals: **Mid-19th century**

Two technological developments served to expand the production and popularity of floral-patterned fabrics during the middle of the 19th century. The first was the introduction of the power loom, which came into widespread use during the mid-1820s, and served to increase the speed as well as reduce the costs of production. The second development was the discovery of coal tar and aniline dyes in the mid-1850s, which enabled manufacturers to produce deeper and more vivid colors. The result was an outburst of naturalistic, often overblown, floral ornament. For example, many Rococo-style ("Louis Quatorze") fabrics displayed floral patterns augmented with scrolls and cartouches shaded for "three-dimensional effect." Similarly, a typical mid-19th-century chintz incorporated "three-dimensional" scrolling acanthus leaves and flowers in various shades of green, blue, white, violet, and yellow. The rationale for this heightened naturalism was expressed by the Jury of the Great Exhibition, held in London, England in 1851: "The task is to cover the surface almost entirely with large, coarse flowers: dahlias, hollyhocks, roses, hydrangeas, or others which [give] scope for strong or vivid colouring, and which are often magnified by the designer much beyond the scale of nature."

1

2

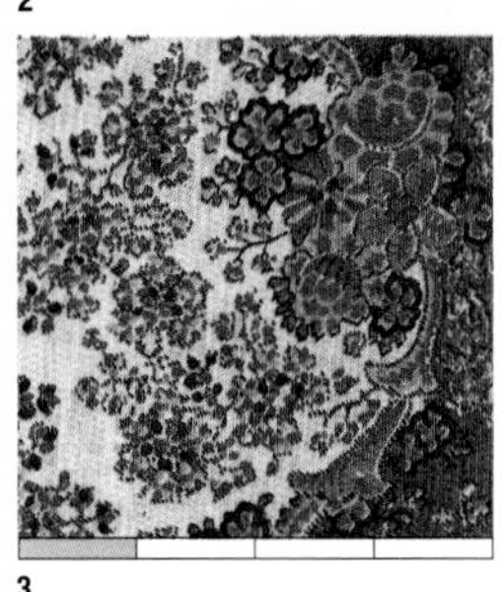

3

4

5

6

7

1 **Tissunique/Le Pavilion 35/9324/1** Color **green and gray** Alternative colors **available** Composition **100% cotton** Width **51in/130cm** Repeat **3in/8cm** Price ★★★

2 **Beaumont & Fletcher/Baroque Floral 2239** Color **beige and pink** Alternative colors **available** Composition **52% linen, 36% cotton, 12% nylon** Width **52½in/133.5cm** Repeat **20½in/52cm** Price ★★★

3 **Borderline/Indica 2463** Color **blue and yellow** Alternative colors **available** Composition **100% wool** Width **54in/137cm** Repeat **9½in/24.5cm** Price ★

4 **George Spencer Decorations/Thistle 108L** Color **red** Alternative colors **available** Composition **100% linen** Width **47in/120cm** Repeat **18½in/47cm** Price ★★

5 **Lee Jofa/Floral Bouquet 88903** Color **03** Alternative colors **available** Composition **100% cotton** Width **50¾in/129cm** Repeat **33in/84cm** Price ★★★

6 **Ramm, Son & Crocker/Ludlow E7536** Color **ivory/green** Alternative colors **available** Composition **100% cotton** Width **50in/127cm** Repeat **25in/64cm** Price ★★

7 **Colefax and Fowler/Coniston F1314** Color **stone** Alternative colors **available** Composition **52% linen, 36% cotton, 12% nylon** Width **53in/135cm** Repeat **17in/43cm** Price ★★

8 **Warner Fabrics/Montpelier Chintz CS 4190/93** Color **blue ribbon** Alternative colors **available** Composition **100% cotton** Width **54in/137cm** Repeat **17in/43cm** Price ★★★

9 **Jane Churchill/Pansies JY20F 03** Color **blue/yellow** Alternative colors **available** Composition **100% cotton** Width **54½in/138cm** Repeat **40in/101.5cm** Price ★★

10 **Ramm, Son & Crocker/Bagatelle E8048** Color **blue/peach** Alternative colors **available** Composition **100% cotton** Width **55in/140cm** Repeat **9in/23cm** Price ★★

11 **Jim Thompson/Montague 1055** Color **04** Alternative colors **available** Composition **100% silk** Width **48in/122cm** Repeat **18in/46cm** Price ★★★

8

9

10

11

FADED CHINTZ

One of chintz's most aesthetically pleasing characteristics is that its original bright colors gradually mellow and fade, a process that is caused by exposure to sunlight, laundering, and general usage. This explains why 18th- and 19th-century chintzes are sought after today, and why, since the 1970s, designers and manufacturers have been producing "artificially aged" chintzes to meet the demand. Soaking the fabric in a weak solution of tea is a simple method of achieving subtle discoloration, and sandwashing produces fading. However, most fabric manufacturers make adjustments in their dyes and use chemical solutions to achieve the desired effect.

Bennison Fabrics/Rosevine Color **faded pink, green** Alternative colors **available** Composition **70% linen, 30% cotton** Width **52in/132cm** Repeat **19¼in/49cm** Price ★★★

Bennison Fabrics/Damask Rose Color **green/pink** Alternative colors **available** Composition **70% linen, 30% cotton** Width **46¾in/119cm** Repeat **24¾in/ 63cm** Price ★★★

Hodsoll McKenzie/Faded Bouquet 110/403 Color **blue** Alternative colors **available** Composition **100% cotton** Width **54in/137cm** Repeat **23¼in/59.5cm** Price ★★★ W

Florals: **Late 19th century**

The last two decades of the 19th century witnessed a reaction to the highly naturalistic floral patterns favored earlier. For example, the Aesthetic Movement espoused the use of simple flowers, such as the lotus (a Japanese influence), pinks, and sunflowers, the latter appearing as a recurring motif in the designs (some highly stylized, some botanically accurate) of Walter Crane. Similarly, William Morris and the Arts and Crafts Movement promoted a return to simple, uncomplicated flowers–as illustrated in medieval herbals–and the use of traditional vegetable, rather than chemical, dyes.

Morris's designs included columbines, poppies, honeysuckle, pinks, anemones, marigolds, daisies, and jasmine, and had a rhythmical, sensuous quality absent from the flat, static patterns produced by many followers of the Aesthetic Movement. This sensuality was later reflected in the work of some Art Nouveau designers. Many of them had rejected floral forms altogether and turned to "vegetal" motifs (roots, buds, and seedpods) to fit the dynamic lines of Art Nouveau. However, others such as E. A. Séguy in his book *Les Fleurs et Leurs Applications Décoratives* (1899), employed a wide selection of sinuous plant forms, such as passionflowers, poppies, wisteria, and water lilies.

5

1

2

6

7

3

4

1 **Sanderson/Fruit RR8048** Color **1** Alternative colors **available** Composition **100% cotton** Width **54in/137cm** Repeat **25in/64cm** Price ★

2 **G. P. & J. Baker/Avalon R1285 02** Color **greens** Alternative colors **available** Composition **60% linen, 22% cotton, 18% viscose** Width **54in/137cm** Repeat **24¼in/62cm** Price ★★ LC

3 **Old World Weavers/Vera Linen B1886L01** Color **07 multi** Alternative colors **available** Composition **58% linen, 42% cotton** Width **55in/140cm** Repeat **37¾in/96cm** Price ★★★★

4 **Lee Jofa/Kingsworthy Print 929070** Color **multi** Alternative colors **available** Composition **100% linen** Width **52in/132cm** Repeat **19¾in/50cm** Price ★★★ LC

5 **Brunschwig & Fils/Ogden House Cotton Print 79308** Color **176 pomegranate** Alternative colors **available** Composition **100% cotton** Width **54¼in/138cm** Repeat **15in/38cm** Price ★★★

6 **Borderline/Pomegranate 2170B** Color **jade/pink** Alternative colors **available** Composition **60% linen, 40% cotton** Width **5¾in/14.5cm** Repeat **12in/30cm** Price ★

7 **Beaumont & Fletcher/Wisteria & Rose 2196a** Color **rust** Alternative colors **available** Composition **52% linen, 36% cotton, 12% nylon** Width **52¾in/134cm** Repeat **28in/71cm** Price ★★★

8

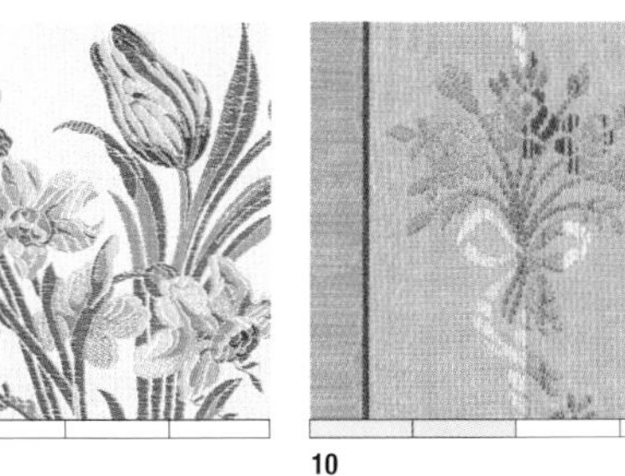

9

10

8 Lelièvre/Bouquet Champêtre 4317 Color **ivory 01** Alternative colors **available** Composition **100% silk** Width **51in/130cm** Repeat **40½in/103cm** Price ★★★★★

9 Lelièvre/Les Tulipes 4138 Color **ivoire 01** Alternative colors **not available** Composition **100% silk** Width **51in/130cm** Repeat **21in/53cm** Price ★★★★★

10 Scalamandré/Newport–Moiréd Lisère 96495 Color **multi on beige and salmon stripe** Alternative colors **available** Composition **100% silk** Width **50in/127cm** Repeat **3in/8cm** Price ★★★★★

11 Lee Jofa/Southdown Rose 909403 Color **03** Alternative colors **available** Composition **100% cotton** Width **52in/132cm** Repeat **17¾in/45cm** Price ★★

12 Jim Thompson/Botanica PDB 3014 Color **A** Alternative colors **available** Composition **100% silk** Width **48in/122cm** Repeat **36in/91.5cm** Price ★★★★

13 Marvic Textiles/Baudouin 8247 Color **blue 6** Alternative colors **available** Composition **52% linen, 48% viscose** Width **55in/140cm** Repeat **24in/61cm** Price ★★

11

12

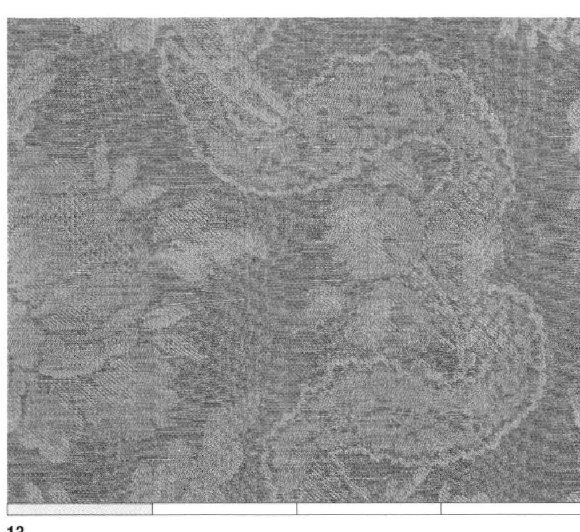

13

ARTS & CRAFTS STYLE

"Anyone wanting to produce dyed textiles with any artistic quality in them must forego the modern and commercial methods in favour of those that are at least as old as Pliny, who speaks of them as being old in his time," pronounced William Morris. For Morris (and the other Arts and Crafts designers) this meant using block- rather than roller-printing, and vegetable rather than chemical dyes. The rhythmical and elaborate patterns that they created, which incorporated simple but sinuous flowers and other plant forms, remains fashionable until today.

Liberty/Burnham 1061036 Color **J** Alternative colors **available** Composition **100% cotton** Width **54in/137cm** Repeat **12½in/32cm** Price ★

Liberty/Snakeshead 1095020 Color **blue/green** Alternative colors **available** Composition **53% linen, 35% cotton, 12% polyacrylic** Width **54in/137cm** Repeat **17¼in/44cm** Price ★★

Florals: **Early 20th century**

Despite the earlier protestations of the Aesthetic Movement, largely on the grounds of "poor taste," naturalistically depicted floral chintzes remained highly popular among the general public around the end of the 19th century. However, the majority of the Art Deco fabrics that were fashionable during the early 20th century incorporated stylized flowers, although they were usually confined (in the "classical style") to baskets, festoons, or garlands, or were densely packed. An example of this is E. A. Séguy's influential *Bouquets de Fronaisons*, first published in Paris, France in 1927, which contained illustrations of tightly packed rosebuds and composites such as marguerites, daisies, and zinnias.

William Morris's floral designs (*see* page 118) remained fashionable in the later Arts and Crafts interiors of the first three decades of the century, as did the cheaper, machine-printed copies of his designs that were produced. However, the designers of fabrics in the Modernist style largely rejected floral ornamentation altogether.

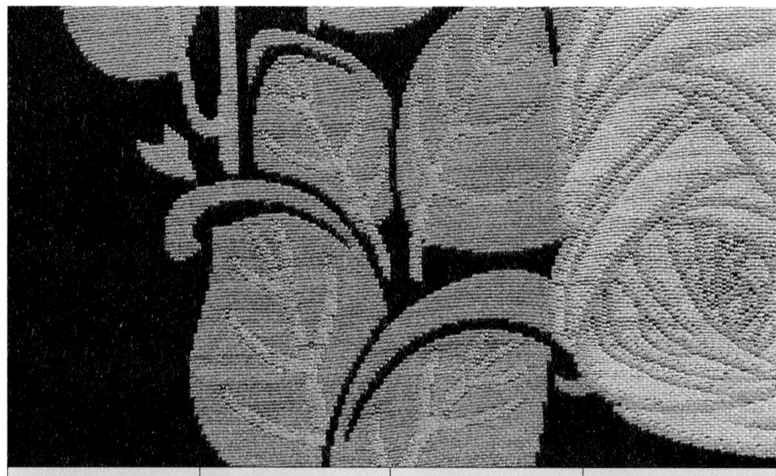

Percheron/Lampas les Roses 10522 Color **2** Alternative colors **available** Composition **100% silk** Width **51in/130cm** Repeat **8½in/22cm** Price ★★★★★

Jab/Bardelli 1-2038 Color **170/cream** Alternative colors **available** Composition **55% cotton, 36% viscose, 9% polyester** Width **55in/140cm** Repeat **–** Price ★★★

Galliards/Lucca 01-05 Color **yellow** Alternative colors **available** Composition **60% linen, 30% cotton, 10% nylon** Width **54in/137cm** Repeat **12½in/32cm** Price ★★

Liberty/Cottage Garden 1067026 Color **browns** Alternative colors **available** Composition **100% cotton** Width **53in/135cm** Repeat **21¼in/54cm** Price ★

Garin/Villajoyosa 66364921 Color **fuchsia** Alternative colors **available** Composition **70% cotton, 30% viscose** Width **55in/140cm** Repeat **16½in/42cm** Price ★★★

Osborne & Little/Marigold F1007 Color **01** Alternative colors **available** Composition **100% cotton** Width **55in/140cm** Repeat **19¾in/50cm** Price ★

Tissunique/Graslin 35/10946/1 Color **red/cream/green** Alternative colors **not available** Composition **100% cotton** Width **51in/130cm** Repeat **9½in/24cm** Price ★★★

Crowson/Sweet Briar 025 03 596 Color **green** Alternative colors **available** Composition **100% cotton** Width **54in/137cm** Repeat **12½in/32cm** Price ★

Manuel Canovas/Serendip 11300 Color **Ecru/95** Alternative colors **available** Composition **100% cotton** Width **53in/135cm** Repeat **61in/155cm** Price ★★★★★

Brunschwig & Fils/Sconset Quilted Floral 32833.01 Color **gold and red** Alternative colors **available** Composition **100% cotton** Width **55in/140cm** Repeat **19in/48cm** Price ★★★

Lee Jofa/Harrogate Handblock 697115 Color **multi** Alternative colors **not available** Composition **100% linen** Width **48in/122cm** Repeat **30in/76cm** Price ★★★★★

Warner Fabrics/Edwardian Roses CS 336910. Color **pink/blue/cream** Alternative colors **available** Composition **100% cotton** Width **54in/137cm** Repeat **25in/64cm** Price ★★

Osborne & Little/Mughal F1005 Color **02** Alternative colors **available** Composition **100% cotton** Width **55in/140cm** Repeat **5½in/14cm** Price ★★

Florals: **Late 20th century**

Floral chintzes became less popular after the Second World War, at the same time that abstract and geometric patterns started to come into vogue. Chintzes remained largely out of favor for some 40 years, but during the late 1980s interest in them was revived, particularly for use in bedrooms. As a consequence, many companies produced reproductions of 19th-century chintzes, with the original patterns and colors virtually unchanged, and many contemporary designers returned to nature for inspiration and created floral chintzes in "new" pastel colors. Demand for woven floral damasks increased during the last decades, especially for use in upholstery. William Morris designs began to be fashionable once again, as were some of the designs originated by Sybil Colefax and John Fowler earlier in the century. Notable among these was an "English" adaptation of the Indian "Tree of Life," in which lilies, roses, and briars were portrayed in small sprigs and garlands.

1

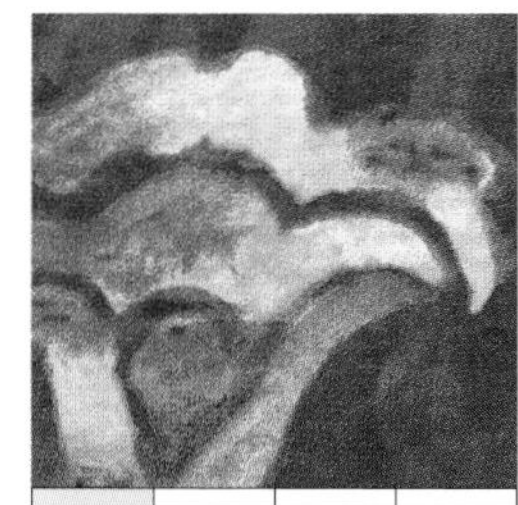

2

3

4

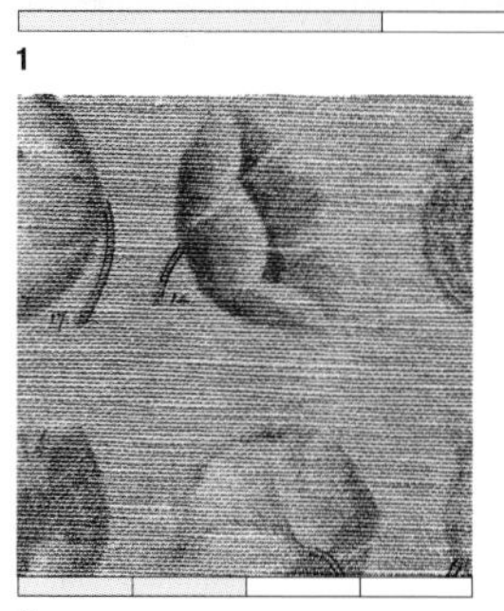

5

6

7

1 **Michael Szell/Flower Show** Color **1** Alternative colors **available** Composition **100% cotton** Width **47in/120cm** Repeat **41¼in/105cm** Price ★★

2 **Anna French/Jester** Color **26** Alternative colors **available** Composition **100% cotton** Width **54in/137cm** Repeat **25in/64cm** Price ★★ LC

3 **Anna French/Marguerite** Color **blue** Alternative colors **available** Composition **100% cotton** Width **54in/137cm** Repeat **25in/64cm** Price ★★ LC

4 **George Spencer Decorations/Andrea Celadon 105L/04** Color **green** Alternative colors **available** Composition **100% linen** Width **50in/127cm** Repeat **11in/28cm** Price ★★

5 **Interdesign/Opium 30921** Color **beige/red** Alternative colors **available** Composition **100% cotton** Width **55in/140cm** Repeat **9in/23cm** Price ★★★

6 **Garin/Kaminari 8160** Color **11** Alternative colors **available** Composition **100% cotton** Width **55in/140cm** Repeat **35¾in/91cm** Price ★★

7 **Lelièvre/Nougatine 5983** Color **ivoire** Alternative colors **available** Composition **90% viscose, 10% linen** Width **54in/137cm** Repeat **26¾in/68cm** Price ★★★ LC

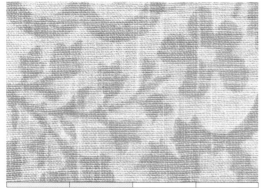

8

9

10

8 **Manuel Canovas/Pali 11146** Color **bleu 59** Alternative colors **available** Composition **100% cotton** Width **51in/130cm** Repeat **40½in/103cm** Price ★★★★★ LC W

9 **Brunschwig & Fils/Amandine Glazed Chintz 77730-04** Color **multi on white** Alternative colors **not available** Composition **100% cotton** Width **52in/132cm** Repeat **33½in/85.5cm** Price ★★★

10 **Garin/Oas 8231** Color **red** Alternative colors **available** Composition **60% cotton, 40% linen** Width **59in/150cm** Repeat **25in/64cm** Price ★★

11 **Montgomery/Jardinière No. 2** Color **yellow and blue** Alternative colors **available** Composition **100% cotton** Width **55in/140cm** Repeat **25in/64cm** Price ★ LC

12 **Pippa & Hale/Minerva MIF015** Color **yellow** Alternative colors **available** Composition **100% cotton** Width **54in/137cm** Repeat **14in/36cm** Price ★

11

12

13

15

16

14

13 **Harlequin/Pattari 186** Color **blue** Alternative colors **available** Composition **100% cotton** Width **54in/137cm** Repeat **25in/64cm** Price ★

14 **Claremont Fabrics/Octavia P99013** Color **sapphire** Alternative colors **available** Composition **100% cotton** Width **54in/137cm** Repeat **26¾in/68cm** Price ★

15 **G. P. & J. Baker/Pine Cone R128701** Color **burgundy on stone** Alternative colors **available** Composition **60% linen, 22% cotton, 18% viscose** Width **54in/137cm** Repeat **17in/43cm** Price ★★ LC

16 **Osborne & Little/Turfan F1162** Color **04** Alternative colors **available** Composition **100% cotton** Width **55in/140cm** Repeat **17in/43cm** Price ★★

20th century

Pictorial Fabrics

Pictorial fabrics have appeared in various guises since the Middle Ages. The best known of these are the woven tapestries and printed *toiles de Jouy*. Others pictorial fabrics of note include Chinese and Middle Eastern pictorial silks, Indonesian *batiks*, Indian calicoes (called *indiennes*), European chintzes, ethnic African weaves and prints, and European and American hand-blocked and screen-printed synthetics.

Long regarded as a mirror of civilization, narrative pictorial fabrics depict a wide range of human activities (both real and mythical), from biblical scenes, military conquests, and political events, to harvesting, hunting, and theatergoing. However, this reflection of life is also evident in non-narrative pictorials, such as "still life" fruits and flowers, views of animals in movement, birds in flight, and "drawings" of architectural components. In each of these, the subject matter, and the manner in which it is portrayed, reflects both the preoccupations of, and the styles of ornament that were available to, different cultures at different times.

LEFT **Shown here is a detail of a late 18th-century oval-back, gilt open armchair that resides in a manor house in Norfolk, England. The top cover, which is original, is exquisitely worked in petit point, and depicts cherubs at play. This was a popular subject for the pictorial fabrics that were used in classical interiors on both sides of the Atlantic during the latter part of the 18th century.**

INDUSTRIAL ESPIONAGE

Toile de Jouy fabrics originated in 1770, in a factory established by the German Oberkampf brothers in the French village of Jouy-en-Josas. Intent on expansion, the brothers traveled to England in 1810 in an attempt to discover secret advances that had been made in copper-plate printing techniques. The brothers managed to smuggle out the information by writing it on cotton percale fabric using an alum solution tinted with red dye, then dipping the fabric in vinegar to render the writing invisible. Once they were back in France, they immersed the fabric in red dye to retrieve the concealed information.

ABOVE This late 20th-century settee is upholstered with a hand-printed, modern pictorial fabric designed by Janet Milner. The hairdressing imagery, particularly the exaggerated "beehive" hairdo, is wryly amusing, but the design is potentially classic, largely due to the sophisticated combination of black, cream, and caramel coloring.

KEY DESIGNS

1 Historically significant naval and land battles were popular subject matter for pictorial fabrics, particularly Medieval and Renaissance tapestries, and, as here, 18th- and 19th-century printed *toiles*.

2 Oriental scenes, incorporating human figures, buildings, and exotic animals, birds, and plant forms, appeared on numerous European textiles from the mid-17th century to the late 19th century.

3 Printed cottons and linens featuring pictorial patterns copied from or inspired by Chinese export porcelain and delftware were highly fashionable in Europe during the 18th century.

4 Fabrics patterned with a series of scenes, framed within decorative plaques or cartouches, have been popular since the Renaissance. This Empire-style print displays classical imagery.

5 Ethnic weaves and prints have long been a source of inspiration for 20th-century European and North American pictorial textiles.

6 The playing card pattern is 20th century, but its portrayal of royalty, clerics, and theatrical figures is within a genre that extends back to the Middle Ages.

1 **Manuel Canovas/Hispaniola** Color **groseille/ecru 05** Alternative colors **available** Composition **100% cotton** Width **70in/178cm** Repeat **37¾in/96cm** Price ★★★ W

2 **Apenn/Chelworth Linen** Color **heather/ navy blue** Alternative colors **available** Composition **60% linen, 30% cotton, 10% nylon** Width **48in/122cm** Repeat **32¾in/83cm** Price ★★★ LC

3 **Bennison Fabrics/Chinese Toile** Color **blue and white** Alternative colors **available** Composition **70% linen, 30% cotton** Width **48in/122cm** Repeat **17½in/44.5cm** Price ★★★ LC

4 **Marvic Textiles/Empire** Color **red on sand** Alternative colors **available** Composition **100% cotton** Width **55in/140cm** Repeat **30¾in/78cm** Price ★ LC W

5 **John Wilman/Salvador** Color **amazon** Alternative colors **available** Composition **100% cotton** Width **54in/137cm** Repeat **27½in/70cm** Price ★

6 **Osborne & Little/Snap** Color **multi** Alternative colors **available** Composition **100% cotton** Width **55in/140cm** Repeat **24¾in/63cm** Price ★★

Pictorials: **Pre-18th century**

Medieval pictorial fabrics–mainly tapestry wall-hangings–depicted subject matter and were executed in a style that bore close resemblance to illustrated manuscripts of the period. Typical subjects ranged from ecclesiastical scenes and narratives of significant matters of state to everyday life at court. Pageantry was also depicted, including military sieges, parades, and tournaments, often augmented with motifs such as coats of arms. Hunting scenes, featuring stylized heraldic beasts such as stags, dogs, lions, griffins, unicorns, and enfields, were also widely used.

Much of the subject matter of medieval pictorial fabrics, particularly hunting and battle scenes, also appeared during the Renaissance. However, biblical stories, classical mythology, and pastoral images became increasingly fashionable, and all images were rendered with a much greater use and understanding of perspective. By the 17th century, pictorial wall-hangings had become even more spectacular and sophisticated in terms of both color and realism, especially in the grandest French and English Baroque interiors, where classical, mythological, historical, religious, and pastoral images remained popular, and were often coordinated with upholstered furniture.

3

3 **Donghia/Theodora 0390/9320-10** Color **ecru** Alternative colors **available** Composition **52% silk, 48% linen** Width **54in/137cm** Repeat **8¼in/21cm** Price ★★★★★

4 **Brunschwig & Fils/Palio Cotton and Linen Print 79821.04** Color **rosso** Alternative colors **available** Composition **54% linen, 46% cotton** Width **54in/137cm** Repeat **18in/46cm** Price ★★★★

5 **Brunschwig & Fils/C'era Una Volta 50984.01** Color **sage** Alternative colors **available** Composition **100% cotton** Width **55¾in/142cm** Repeat **35in/89cm** Price ★★★

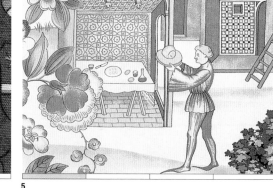

1

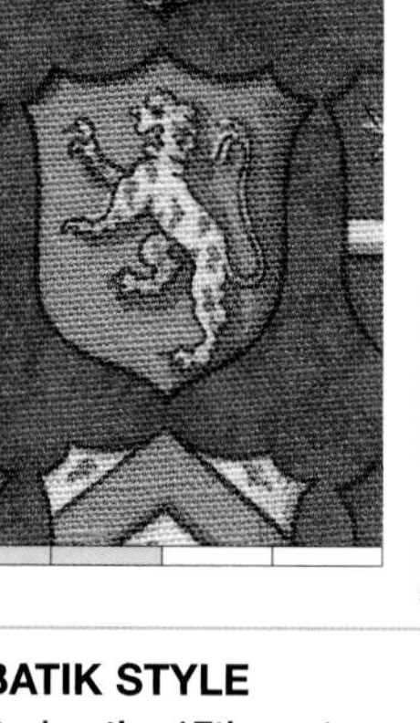

4

5

1 **Claremont Fabrics/Merrydown C74 M53** Color **chintz** Alternative colors **available** Composition **100% cotton** Width **54in/137cm** Repeat **26¾in/68cm** Price ★

2 **Liberty/Leone 1063064** Color **blue and gold** Alternative colors **available** Composition **100% cotton** Width **54in/137cm** Repeat **12½in/32cm** Price ★★

2

BATIK STYLE

During the 17th century, imported Indonesian cottons that displayed pictorial patterns of stylized buildings, human figures, animals, and birds became very fashionable in Europe. They were produced by "batik," which is a form of printing that involves applying hot wax to the fabric around the pattern before applying dyes or inks. The wax resists the dyes or inks, which adhere to the unwaxed areas and the pattern is revealed once the wax is removed with hot water.

Monkwell/Batumi 09358 Color **5** Alternative colors **available** Composition **100% cotton** Width **54in/137cm** Repeat **24¼in/62cm** Price ★★

6

6 Abbott & Boyd/Codice 49094 Color **1** Alternative colors **not available** Composition **100% cotton** Width **59in/150cm** Repeat **21in/53cm** Price ★★

7 Mulberry/Tudor Animals FD101/521 Color **natural** Alternative colors **available** Composition **60% linen, 22% cotton, 18% viscose** Width **54in/137cm** Repeat **32¼in/82cm** Price ★★

8 Celia Birtwell/Beasties Color **green** Alternative colors **available** Composition **100% cotton** Width **55in/140cm** Repeat **25in/64cm** Price ★★

9 Abbott & Boyd/Escritura 47658 Color **4** Alternative colors **available** Composition **100% cotton** Width **63in/160cm** Repeat **25in/64cm** Price ★★

10 Monkwell/Salamanca 09371CU/004 Color **gold on blue/green** Alternative colors **available** Composition **100% cotton** Width **54in/137cm** Repeat **32¼in/82cm** Price ★★

7

8

9

10

11 Monkwell/Tamburlaine 09370 Color **red and green** Alternative colors **available** Composition **100% cotton** Width **54in/137cm** Repeat **25in/64cm** Price ★

12 Abbott & Boyd/Caciera Medieval 49009 Color **yellow/beige ground** Alternative colors **not available** Composition **100% cotton** Width **63in/160cm** Repeat **26¾in/68cm** Price ★★

13 Abbott & Boyd/Cenera Medieval 49131 Color **yellow/beige ground** Alternative colors **not available** Composition **100% cotton** Width **63in/160cm** Repeat **37¾in/96cm** Price ★★

14 Abbott & Boyd/Officios Catalanes 49136 Color **5** Alternative colors **available** Composition **100% cotton** Width **63in/160cm** Repeat **15¼in/39cm** Price ★★

15 Lee Jofa/Stuart Tree Print 858271 Color **multi** Alternative colors **available** Composition **100% linen** Width **54in/137cm** Repeat **28¼in/72cm** Price ★★★

11

12

13

14

15

Pictorials: **Early 18th century**

Stylistically, some of the pictorial fabrics produced during the early 18th century were rather heavy and somber in appearance and echoed the Baroque ornamentation of the previous century. The vast majority, however, increasingly reflected the lighter-hearted, less formal, more colorful, and often frivolous approach of the Rococo style that became fashionable across most of Europe as the century progressed.

Much of this change of style can be attributed to an expansion of trade with the Orient and the importation of Chinese silks, ceramics, and wallpapers, and hand-painted and hand-printed Indian calicoes (*indiennes*), all of which provided inspiration for European pictorial silk, cotton, and tapestry hangings. Typical subject matter included interpretations of Chinese, Indian, Arabian, Moorish, and Persian landscapes filled with indigenous flora and fauna. Also common were native figures engaged in a diverse range of activities, including hunting, fishing, harvesting, tax collecting, tea drinking, playing musical instruments, and bartering with colonial traders. Other subjects in evidence were trading ships in the South China seas, and, as the first half of the century drew to a close, images of life in the English countryside.

1

2

1 **Brunschwig & Fils/Clipper Ships 79680.04** Color **cream** Alternative colors **available** Composition **55% linen, 45% cotton** Width **53in/135cm** Repeat **44¾in/113.5cm** Price ★★★

2 **Brunschwig & Fils/Meissen Cotton Print 50552.01** Color **blue** Alternative colors **available** Composition **100% cotton** Width **54in/137cm** Repeat **33¾in/86cm** Price ★★★★

18th century

3

4

5

EASTERN INFLUENCE

Inspired by imported Chinese goods, some 18th-century designers, including Antoine Watteau, Jean Pillement, and Thomas Chippendale, devised *chinoiserie* patterns and motifs that were suitable for textiles, wallpaper, furniture, and paneling. Such was the popularity of the designs that Lady Mary Wortley Montagu ironically remarked, "Sick of Grecian eloquence and symmetry or Gothic grandeur, we must all seek the barbarous gaudy gout of the Chinese."

Tissunique/Xiang 35/1945 Color **coral vert** Alternative colors **available** Composition **100% cotton** Width **59in/150cm** Repeat **23¾in/60cm** Price ★★★

3 **The Design Archives/Rosendal Griffin 54143** Color **gold on blue** Alternative colors **available** Composition **100% cotton** Width **54in/137cm** Repeat **34¼in/87cm** Price ★★

4 **Timney Fowler/Ionic Capital TF 0190/01** Color **black and white** Alternative colors **available** Composition **100% wool** Width **58in/147cm** Repeat **39¼in/100cm** Price ★★★

5 **Brunschwig & Fils/Fishing Lady 79654.04** Color **stone green** Alternative colors **available** Composition **65% linen, 35% cotton** Width **54in/137cm** Repeat **31¾in/81cm** Price ★★

6 **George Spencer Decorations/Philippe 111L/01** Color **red/blue** Alternative colors **available** Composition **100% linen** Width **55in/140cm** Repeat **11¾in/30cm** Price ★★★

6

7

8

7 Old World Weavers/Voyage en Chine FBA 02A 0002 Color **black** Alternative colors **available** Composition **59% linen, 41% cotton** Width **54in/137cm** Repeat **45in/114cm** Price ★★★

8 Brunschwig & Fils/Chinoiserie Glazed Chintz 75460.04 Color **lacquer red** Alternative colors **available** Composition **100% cotton** Width **48in/122cm** Repeat **36in/91.5cm** Price ★★

9 Percheron/Planter Café 7135 Color **tabac/blue** Alternative colors **available** Composition **100% cotton** Width **53in/135cm** Repeat **37¾in/96cm** Price ★★★

10 Manuel Canovas/La Source 11349/89 Color **ficelle** Alternative colors **available** Composition **100% cotton** Width **53½in/136cm** Repeat **29in/74cm** Price ★★★

11

12

11 Percheron/Tea Introduction 7134 Color **famille rose** Alternative colors **available** Composition **100% cotton** Width **53in/135cm** Repeat **4¾in/12cm** Price ★★★

12 Brunschwig & Fils/West Indies Toile Cotton 79522.04 Color **blue on white** Alternative colors **available** Composition **100% cotton** Width **52¾in/134cm** Repeat **34¼in/87cm** Price ★★

13 Busby & Busby/Serenata 4956 Color **red/gold** Alternative colors **available** Composition **100% cotton** Width **55in/140cm** Repeat **35¾in/91cm** Price ★★

14 Brunschwig & Fils/Bromley Hall Toile 50151.01 Color **red** Alternative colors **available** Composition **100% cotton** Width **41¾in/106.5cm** Repeat **36in/91.5cm** Price ★★★

9

10

13

14

Pictorials: **Late 18th century**

As pictorial tapestry production declined during the second half of the 18th century, the manufacture of pictorial silks and printed calicoes, particularly from Jouy in France, increased. Much of the subject matter favored in earlier Rococo interiors remained fashionable, except in North America where the style never really took hold. The *chinoiserie* and Indian scenes that were produced were more authentically depicted than in the past, the reason being that fabric designers now had access to the illustrated recollections of Europeans who had traveled to the Orient.

In addition, pastoral and rustic images, such as the *fêtes galantes*, were very much in evidence. This was also the case with theatrical scenes and accounts of important contemporary events, such as the American Revolution, the French Revolution, and the first ascents by hot air balloon. Mythological and Ancient Greek and Roman subjects returned to favor in the Neoclassical interiors that came into vogue during the latter part of the century.

Guy Evans/Volunteer Chintz Color **1** Alternative colors **not available** Composition **100% cotton** Width **63in/160cm** Repeat **31½in/80cm** Price ★★★

George Spencer Decorations/Goose & Fox 110C/02/01 Color **blue** Alternative colors **available** Composition **100% cotton** Width **50in/127cm** Repeat **11¼in/29½cm** Price ★★★

Abbott & Boyd/Elefantes 47654 Color **2** Alternative colors **available** Composition **100% cotton** Width **57in/145cm** Repeat **22in/56cm** Price ★★

The Design Archives/Stove Tiles 54139 Color **blue on cream** Alternative colors **available** Composition **100% cotton** Width **54in/137cm** Repeat **31½in/80cm** Price ★★ LC

Schumacher/Journal de la Mode 168181 Color **aqua and multi** Alternative colors **available** Composition **100% cotton** Width **54in/137cm** Repeat **25in/64cm** Price ★★★

Monkwell/Chatsworth 09320CU/002 Color **red and yellow** Alternative colors **available** Composition **100% cotton** Width **54in/137cm** Repeat **24¼in/62cm** Price ★

The Design Archives/Gustavian Cameo Color **black and gray on yellow** Alternative colors **available** Composition **100% cotton** Width **54in/137cm** Repeat **19¼in/49cm** Price ★★ LC

Brunschwig & Fils/Dancing Ladies Toile 51142.01 Color **blue** Alternative colors **available** Composition **100% cotton** Width **54in/137cm** Repeat **41in/104cm** Price ★★

John Wilman/La Bohème 888249 Color **Aegean** Alternative colors **available** Composition **100% cotton** Width **54in/137cm** Repeat **8½in/22cm** Price ★

Nina Campbell/Canto Cargo NCF6741 Color **02** Alternative colors **available** Composition **100% cotton** Width **55in/140cm** Repeat **35¾in/91cm** Price ★★

The Design Archives/Pavilions 54138 Color **red and green** Alternative colors **available** Composition **100% cotton** Width **54in/137cm** Repeat **24¼in/62cm** Price ★★

Zoffany/Emperor's Musicians APO 603 Color **03** Alternative colors **available** Composition **100% cotton** Width **58½in/149cm** Repeat **52½in/133.5cm** Price ★★

TOILE DE JOUY

The majority of printed cottons, or *toiles*, which were made at the famous Jouy factory in France prior to 1775, were either one of two design types, striped or floral. After this time, however, an enormous variety of narrative patterns were produced. Apart from *chinoiserie*, the most popular subject matter included idealized or romanticized depictions of rural life and well-known scenes from the theater. Such patterns were to remain popular in both Europe and America well into the 19th century.

Guy Evans/Chatsworth Color **red and white** Alternative colors **available** Composition **100% cotton** Width **51in/130cm** Repeat **2¾in/7cm** Price ★★

Monkwell/Milton 09321 Color **blue on beige** Alternative colors **available** Composition **100% cotton** Width **54in/137cm** Repeat **11¾in/30cm** Price ★

Timney Fowler/Passage of Time TF0200/02 Color **neutral** Alternative colors **available** Composition **100% cotton** Width **54in/137cm** Repeat **33in/84cm** Price ★★

The Design Archives/Liaisons 54044 Color **brown on cream** Alternative colors **available** Composition **100% cotton** Width **54in/137cm** Repeat **18in/46cm** Price ★★

Marvic Textiles/Les Enfants 5440-005 Color **black on sand** Alternative colors **available** Composition **100% cotton** Width **55in/140cm** Repeat **34½in/88cm** Price ★★

Pictorials: **Early 19th century**

The first three decades of the 19th century witnessed a further expansion of the printed cotton industry to meet the ever-increasing demand for pictorial *toiles* and floral chintzes. Moreover, advances in the techniques of copperplate printing, when combined with traditional pigments, such as madder (pinks and reds) and indigo and woad (blues), and newly discovered mineral dyes, such as manganese (bronze) and antimony (orange), enabled manufacturers to produce increasingly ambitious and sophisticated images.

Chinoiserie, Indian, and similarly exotic scenes retained their popularity from the previous century, while narratives depicting Napoleon's campaigns in Egypt became widespread. However, in keeping with the Neoclassical styles of decoration fashionable on both sides of the Atlantic, mythological and classical subjects proved the most popular. Typically elaborate *toiles* consisted of medallions or cartouches incorporating classical figures or ancient buildings, framed by allegorical figures, animals, scrolls, and trophies of arms, and linked by scrolling flowers or sheaves of wheat. Such imagery drew heavily on the decorative motifs and styles of ornamentation that had been unearthed during archaeological excavations at Pompeii and Herculaneum in the late 18th century.

4

1

2

3

5

6

1 **Schumacher/Athena Toile 166845** Color **cadet** Alternative colors **available** Composition **100% cotton** Width **54in/137cm** Repeat **20½in/52cm** Price ★★★

2 **Tissunique/Les Angelots 35/1973** Color **vert** Alternative colors **available** Composition **100% cotton** Width **59in/150cm** Repeat **14in/36cm** Price ★★★

3 **Guy Evans/Lord Byron's Chintz** Color **1** Alternative colors **not available** Composition **100% cotton** Width **51in/130cm** Repeat **16¼in/41cm** Price ★★★

4 **Marvic Textiles/Les Amours 5330-007** Color **blues on off-white** Alternative colors **available** Composition **100% cotton** Width **55in/140cm** Repeat **21in/53cm** Price ★★

5 **Marvic Textiles/Les Vues de Paris 6203-6** Color **charcoal** Alternative colors **available** Composition **100% cotton** Width **55in/140cm** Repeat **18½in/47cm** Price ★★

6 **Brunschwig & Fils/Mount Vernon 79668-04** Color **wheat** Alternative colors **available** Composition **100% cotton** Width **54in/137cm** Repeat **36in/91.5cm** Price ★★

7

8

9

7 Turnell & Gigon/DX 1647 Color **green** Alternative colors **available** Composition **39% viscose, 38% cotton, 23% linen** Width **55in/140cm** Repeat **22½in/57cm** Price ★★★

8 Brunschwig & Fils/Hunting Toile 70932.04 Color **blue** Alternative colors **available** Composition **50% cotton, 50% linen** Width **48in/122cm** Repeat **11in/28.5cm** Price ★★★

9 Brunschwig & Fils/Bunny Business Glazed Chintz 79781 Color **04** Alternative colors **available** Composition **100% cotton** Width **54in/137cm** Repeat **28in/71cm** Price ★★★

10 Ian Sanderson/Farmer Color **plum** Alternative colors **available** Composition **100% cotton** Width **53½in/136cm** Repeat **25in/64cm** Price ★

11 Guy Evans/Northanger Abbey Color **1** Alternative colors **available** Composition **100% cotton** Width **51in/130cm** Repeat **14½in/37cm** Price ★★★

10

11

12

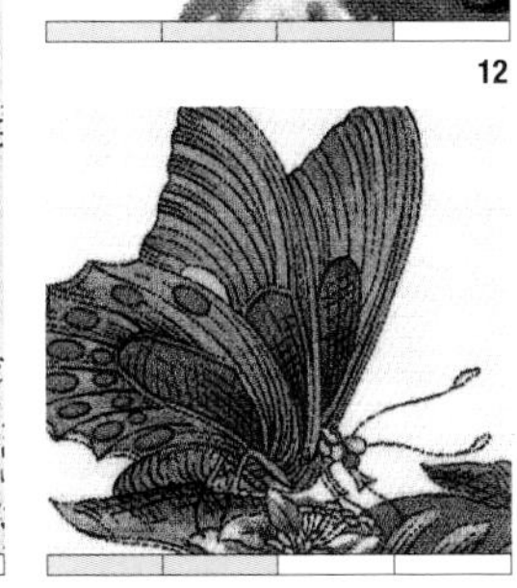

13

12 G. P. & J. Baker/Directoire Parrot B0849 Color **01** Alternative colors **available** Composition **100% cotton** Width **54in/137cm** Repeat **25in/64cm** Price ★★

13 Zoffany/Butterflies AP0702 Color **02** Alternative colors **available** Composition **100% cotton** Width **52¾in/134cm** Repeat **19in/48cm** Price ★★

14 Timney Fowler/Lady in Waiting Color **multi** Alternative colors **available** Composition **100% cotton** Width **52½in/133cm** Repeat **46in/117cm** Price ★★

BRIGHTON

The printed cotton fabric shown here was inspired by fabric wall-panels that were commissioned in 1801 by the Prince of Wales (subsequently Prince Regent, and then George IV of England) for the famous Brighton Pavilion. Like many French and English printed cottons of the late 18th and early 19th centuries, the pattern includes birds of paradise, exotic insects such as dragonflies and butterflies, colorful flowers, and luxuriant foliage. These are depicted in a style that owes a great deal to contemporary imported Indian textiles and even more to the ornamentation found on imported Chinese artifacts.

Scalamandré/Brighton 16121-002 Color **multi on framboise** Alternative colors **available** Composition **100% cotton** Width **54in/137cm** Repeat **39¾in/101cm** Price ★★★★★ T

14

19th century

Pictorials: **Mid-19th century**

To meet the requirements of the increasingly numerous middle classes on both sides of the Atlantic, large quantities of printed pictorial cottons continued to be produced in the mid-19th century. But one consequence of the Gothic Revival was a renewed demand for woven pictorial fabrics (notably tapestries) depicting medieval images. Gothic-arched windows with elaborate tracery provided typical subject matter, and were often augmented with heraldic motifs such as banners, emblems, and achievements-of-arms.

As far as printed pictorials were concerned, *chinoiserie*, Indian, and African scenes remained popular, and featured exotic and indigenous figures, animals, birds, and plant forms. In the grander European and American Renaissance-Revival interiors, classical ornamentation was considered the height of fashion. Some of the most interesting pictorial hangings were inspired by the 15th century artist Della Robbia, whose earthenware plaques were decorated with festoons of fruit and flowers and white figures on pale blue grounds. The pictorial designs of children and animals that found favor in more ordinary households were garish in comparison, and were despised for their sentimentality by the emerging Aesthetic and Arts and Crafts Movements.

2

1

3

4 5

6

1 **Scalamandré/Daktari 26270** Color **002** Alternative colors **available** Composition **65% cotton, 30% rayon, 5% polyester** Width **54in/137cm** Repeat **16¼in/41cm** Price ★★★

2 **Abbott & Boyd/Westminster 46673-0** Color **green, blue, and gold** Alternative colors **available** Composition **100% cotton** Width **59in/150cm** Repeat **26¼in/67cm** Price ★★

3 **Schumacher/Fruitier 168253** Color **biscuit and red** Alternative colors **available** Composition **100% cotton** Width **54in/137cm** Repeat **17¾in/46cm** Price ★★

4 **Nina Campbell/Sir Oliphant NCF 3124** Color **04** Alternative colors **available** Composition **60% linen, 20% cotton, 20% viscose** Width **55in/140cm** Repeat **19¾in/50cm** Price ★★

5 **Nina Campbell/Lord Lyon NCF 31201** Color **06** Alternative colors **available** Composition **100% cotton** Width **55in/140cm** Repeat **25in/64cm** Price ★★

6 **Marvic Textiles/Vivarais 7542-001** Color **blue on red** Alternative colors **available** Composition **100% cotton** Width **59in/150cm** Repeat **11¼in/28.5cm** Price ★★★

7

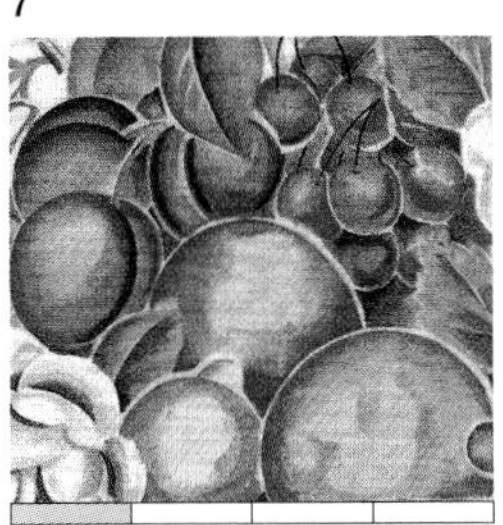

8

9

10

11

12

13

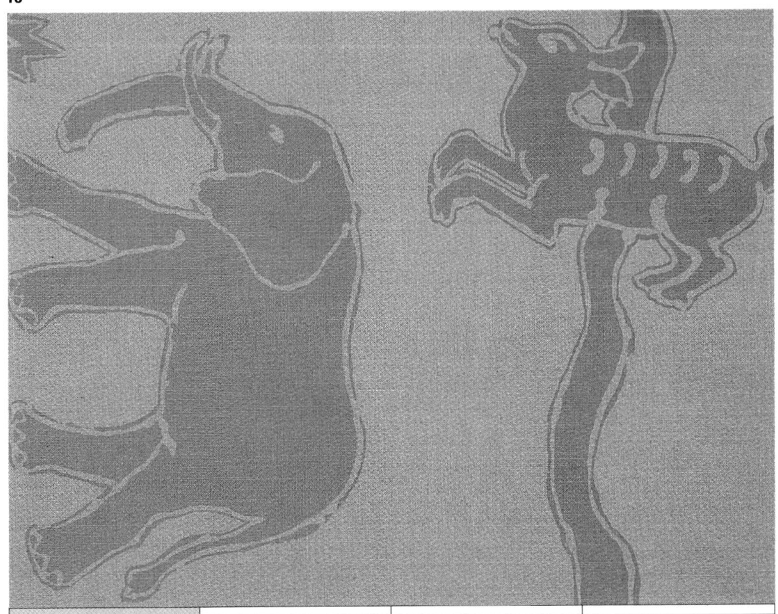

14

7 **Busby & Busby/Fête 4936** Color **charcoal** Alternative colors **available** Composition **100% cotton** Width **55in/140cm** Repeat **35¾in/91cm** Price ★★

8 **Jane Churchill/Ophelia JY50F-04** Color **cream/green** Alternative colors **available** Composition **100% cotton** Width **54in/137cm** Repeat **18in/45.5cm** Price ★★

9 **Percheron/Black Pepper 7137** Color **jaune/rose** Alternative colors **available** Composition **100% cotton** Width **53in/135cm** Repeat **44in/112cm** Price ★★★

10 **Abbott & Boyd/Flora Antilana 48076** Color **9** Alternative colors **available** Composition **100% cotton** Width **59in/150cm** Repeat **37¾in/96cm** Price ★★

11 **Zoffany/Cherubs AP0404** Color **blue/cream** Alternative colors **available** Composition **52% linen, 36% cotton, 12% nylon** Width **54in/137cm** Repeat **46½in/118cm** Price ★★

12 **Today Interiors/L'Orient China Garden FR 2243** Color **blue** Alternative colors **available** Composition **63% linen, 28% cotton, 9% nylon** Width **54in/137cm** Repeat **6¾in/17.5cm** Price ★★

13 **Liberty/Hammada 1062042** Color **black and cream** Alternative colors **available** Composition **100% cotton** Width **54in/137cm** Repeat **18in/46cm** Price ★★

14 **Bentley & Spens/Animal Magic B201** Color **3** Alternative colors **available** Composition **70% linen, 30% cotton** Width **53in/135cm** Repeat **41¾in/106cm** Price ★★ LC W

TIMNEY-FOWLER-LONDON
Europa
Africa
Asia
TIMNEY · FOWLER
Fabrics and Wallpapers
Timney Fowler
388 Kings Road London SW3 5UZ
Telephone 00 44 171 352 2263
Fax 00 44 171 352 0351

GALA

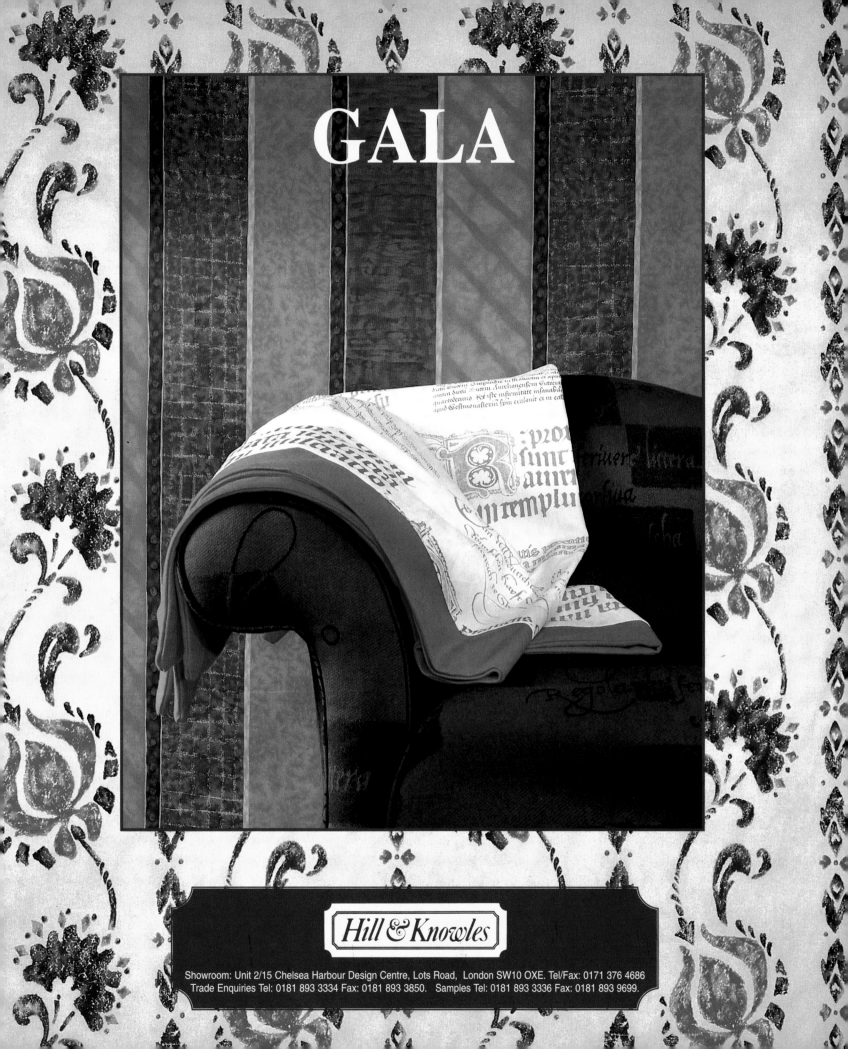

Pictorials: **Late 19th century**

Although the leading exponents of the Aesthetic and Arts and Crafts Movements were dismissive of many of the mass-produced, aniline-dyed pictorial fabrics fashionable since the mid-19th century, such designs still found favor outside the confines of these aesthetic elites. Woven and printed pictorials of cats, dogs, horses, children, and railway trains were still much in evidence in ordinary homes until the end of the century. Conversely, Aesthetic Movement *japonaiserie* fabrics, displaying images of dragons, birds (sparrows, kingfishers, peacocks), and flowers (chrysanthemums, prunus blossoms) derived from *Kakiemon*-pattern porcelain, were rarely admired except by the artistically minded.

More universally popular, however, were the Gothic-Revival pictorials that used medieval ornamentation as their source. Notable among these were the vegetable-dyed Arts and Crafts designs, many of which depicted human figures set against a floral ground. Similarly, *chinoiserie*, Indian, and African pictorials remained in vogue, as did classically inspired architectural prints rendered in black and white. Yet, the most innovative pictorials were produced by Art Nouveau designers: dreamlike figures of women, set among sinuous, entwining plant forms (*"femme fleurs"*) were a recurring theme of their work.

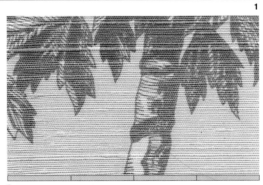

1

4

5

2

3

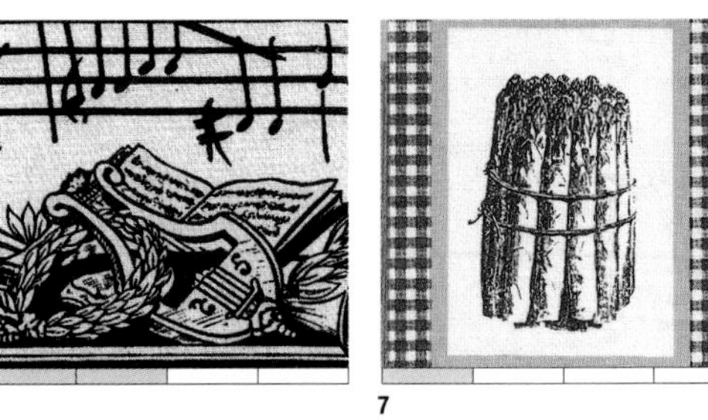

6

7

8

1 **Brunschwig & Fils/Balmoral Glazed Chintz 50112** Color **01** Alternative colors **available** Composition **100% cotton** Width **54in/137cm** Repeat **26in/66cm** Price ★★★

2 **Jim Thompson/Chinoiserie PMS 2991** Color **B** Alternative colors **available** Composition **100% silk** Width **48in/122cm** Repeat **36in/91.5cm** Price ★★★

3 **Jim Thompson/Dedar** Color **green/yellow** Alternative colors **available** Composition **100% cotton** Width **55in/140cm** Repeat **52in/132cm** Price ★★★

4 **Brunschwig & Fils/Komodie 39866.01** Color **coral/beige** Alternative colors **available** Composition **60% acrylic, 40% linen** Width **54¾in/139cm** Repeat **11in/28cm** Price ★★★

5 **Colefax and Fowler/Ditchley F1508/06** Color **yellow** Alternative colors **available** Composition **52% linen, 36% cotton, 12% nylon** Width **53½in/136cm** Repeat **28in/71.5cm** Price ★★

6 **Abbott & Boyd/Pentagramma 45832** Color **8** Alternative colors **available** Composition **100% cotton** Width **59in/150cm** Repeat **37¾in/96cm** Price ★★

7 **Abbott & Boyd/Granja** Color **04** Alternative colors **available** Composition **100% cotton** Width **63in/160cm** Repeat **14in/35.5cm** Price ★★

8 **Abbott & Boyd/Silos II 49008-9** Color **1** Alternative colors **available** Composition **100% cotton** Width **61in/155cm** Repeat **31½in/80cm** Price ★★

9

9 Borderline/Palmyra 2303 Color **A** Alternative colors **available** Composition **52% linen, 48% cotton** Width **54in/137cm** Repeat **22in/56cm** Price ★★

10 Warner Fabrics/Damask Fantasie CS7840 Color **sapphire and buff** Alternative colors **available** Composition **100% cotton** Width **54in/137cm** Repeat **25in/64cm** Price ★★

11 Timney Fowler/Tunnel Plan TF0055 Color **black and white** Alternative colors **available** Composition **100% cotton** Width **47in/120cm** Repeat **21in/53cm** Price ★★

12 Borderline/Samarkand 2341A Color **burgundy** Alternative colors **available** Composition **52% linen, 36% cotton, 12% nylon** Width **54in/137cm** Repeat **20½in/52cm** Price ★★

13 Borderline/Water Garden Color **blue** Alternative colors **available** Composition **100% cotton** Width **49in/125cm** Repeat **16¾in/42.5cm** Price ★

12

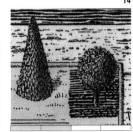

13

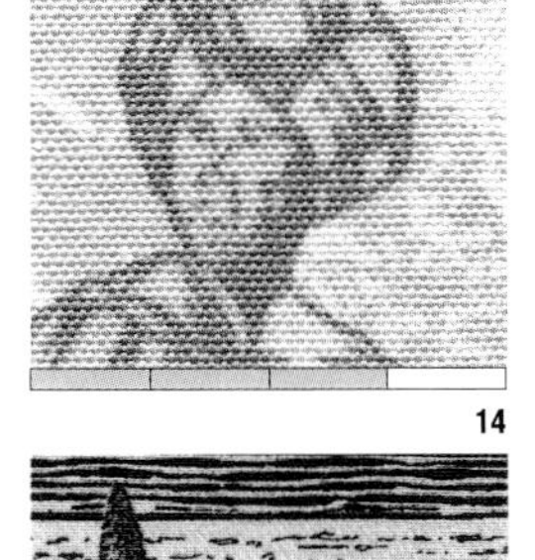

14

15

14 Jim Thompson/Parade 1040 Color **02** Alternative colors **available** Composition **100% cotton** Width **50in/127cm** Repeat **25in/64cm** Price ★★

15 Monkwell/Eden 09318 CU Color **002** Alternative colors **available** Composition **100% cotton** Width **54in/137cm** Repeat **28¼in/73cm** Price ★★★

16 Borderline/Otaka 2424 Color **blue/pink** Alternative colors **available** Composition **100% cotton** Width **54in/137cm** Repeat **19in/48cm** Price ★★

17 Mulberry/Naval Ensigns FD116/569 V113 Color **red/navy** Alternative colors **available** Composition **100% cotton** Width **53in/135cm** Repeat **26in/66cm** Price ★★

16

10

11

17

19th century

Pictorials: **Early 20th century**

Although rarely employed in Art Deco and Modernist interiors, pictorial furnishing fabrics continued to be produced in considerable quantities and in a diverse range of styles during the first half of the 20th century. Prominent examples included chintzes that were either reproductions of or inspired by the "Tree of Life" and birds of paradise designs favored during the 17th and 18th centuries. Primarily used in Jacobean Revival interiors, they tended to be made in more somber and muted colors than the flamboyant originals. Pictorial tapestries also appeared in some Jacobean- and Arts and Crafts-style schemes, although most of the tapestries produced during this period departed from the pictorial tradition and displayed geometric and abstract designs. In addition to birds of paradise, scenes depicting animals and fish also proved fashionable. Especially popular were printed examples primarily intended for use in kitchens and bathrooms, many of which appeared in stylized form and were often humorously augmented with pertinent objects such as kitchenware and vegetables, or perfume bottles, bars of soap, and shaving equipment. Exotic animals, such as African elephants and Indian tigers, were also in vogue, as were groups of "humanized" animals derived from nursery stories, the latter designed for children's rooms.

4

3

1

2

5

6

1 **Liberty/Dante 1095015** Color **A** Alternative colors **available** Composition **53% linen, 35% cotton, 12% polyacrylic** Width **54in/137cm** Repeat **10½in/27cm** Price ★★

2 **Scalamandré/Under the Ice 16263-003** Color **multi on sky blue** Alternative colors **available** Composition **51% linen, 37% cotton, 12% nylon** Width **54¼in/138cm** Repeat **34½in/88cm** Price ★★★ T

3 **Warner Fabrics/Souvenir d'Afrique CS6140** Color **straw yellow** Alternative colors **available** Composition **100% cotton** Width **54in/137cm** Repeat **25in/64cm** Price ★★★ LC

4 **Scalamandré/Kilkenny Cats 16259-004** Color **pink** Alternative colors **available** Composition **100% cotton** Width **54in/137cm** Repeat **34½in/88cm** Price ★★ T

5 **Hodsoll McKenzie/Circus 120/401** Color **blue** Alternative colors **available** Composition **100% cotton** Width **54in/137cm** Repeat **47¼in/120.5cm** Price ★★ W

6 **Guy Evans/Petrushka** Color **green and black** Alternative colors **available** Composition **100% cotton** Width **54in/137cm** Repeat **31¾in/80.5cm** Price ★★ LC

20th century

7

10

11

7 Hill & Knowles/Spats Day Out 43103F Color **blue and peach** Alternative colors **available** Composition **100% cotton** Width **54in/137cm** Repeat **32in/81.5cm** Price ★

8 Scalamandré/Akabar's Stables 16236-004 Color **tan and black** Alternative colors **available** Composition **100% cotton** Width **55in/140cm** Repeat **27in/68.5cm** Price ★★★ T

9 Celia Birtwell/History Color **gold** Alternative colors **available** Composition **100% silk** Width **48in/122cm** Repeat **37½in/95cm** Price ★★

10 Jane Churchill/Dancing Vegetables JY29F Color **multi on cream** Alternative colors **available** Composition **100% cotton** Width **54in/137cm** Repeat **24¾in/63cm** Price ★★

11 Marvic Textiles/Parterre de Roses SCF 951-1 Color **yellow and pink** Alternative colors **available** Composition **100% cotton** Width **55in/140cm** Repeat **19¼in/49cm** Price ★★ LC

8

9

TREE OF LIFE

This hand-blocked linen fabric incorporates an early 20th-century version of the "Tree of Life" design. The original pattern, which has at its center a tree symbolizing the "life force," was first seen in ancient Persian and Indian fabrics. However, the manner in which it is depicted here–with branches and shoots, and exotic flowers and fruits interwoven with birds of paradise–is in the style of the English "Tree of Life" designs developed during the 17th century and most commonly found on contemporary Jacobean crewelwork and on 19th-century Jacobean-Revival chintzes.

Lee Jofa/Tree of Life 667069 Color **multi** Alternative colors **not available** Composition **100% linen** Width **98¾in/251cm** Repeat **50in/127cm** Price ★★★★★ W

Pictorials: **Late 20th century**

Much of the subject matter that was depicted in the pictorial fabrics favored during the first half of the 20th century has remained popular to this day, in particular stylized and naturalistic, and Indian-influenced, animal scenes and Persian-style hunting scenes. Printed classical and Neoclassical images inspired by or adapted from designs that were first produced during the Renaissance and the 17th and 18th centuries also came into vogue. Typical examples of such designs included biblical events, as well as Ancient Greek and Roman figures in architectural settings, many of which were produced in black and white or shades of gray. At the same time, a large number of fabric manufacturers also mass-produced machine-printed pictorials in the style of 18th- and 19th-century hand-printed *toiles* (*see* pages 130-3), while innovations included highly stylized medieval scenes (such as knights on horseback), and diverse landscapes and still lifes that were executed in styles mirroring the developments in 20th-century fine art.

1

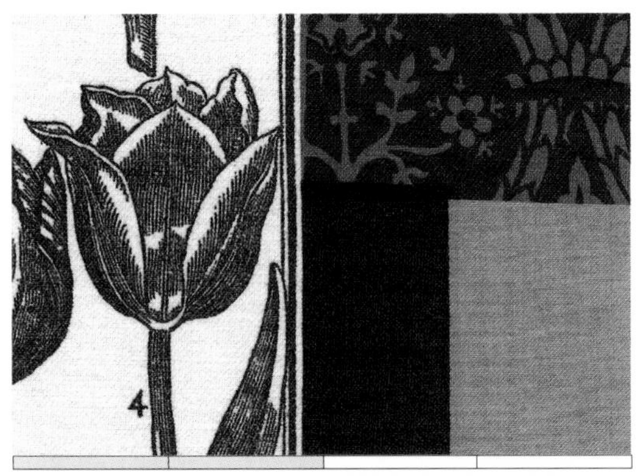

2

3

4

5

6

1 **Bentley & Spens/Fruit with Bowls** Color **red** Alternative colors **available** Composition **55% linen, 34% cotton, 11% nylon** Width **54in/137cm** Repeat **65in/165cm** Price ★★★

2 **Timney Fowler/Draughtsman's Collage TF0172/20** Color **multi** Alternative colors **available** Composition **100% cotton** Width **52¼in/133cm** Repeat **43¼in/110cm** Price ★★

3 **Percheron/Newmarket 10005** Color **1** Alternative colors **available** Composition **100% cotton** Width **52¼in/133cm** Repeat **24in/61cm** Price ★★

4 **Ivo Prints/Cox** Color **black, white, and green** Alternative colors **available** Composition **100% cotton** Width **47in/120cm** Repeat **15¾in/40cm** Price ★★

5 **Timney Fowler/Madonna TF0196** Color **black and white** Alternative colors **available** Composition **100% cotton** Width **52¼in/133cm** Repeat **25½in/65cm** Price ★★

6 **Osborne & Little/Toad Hall F11781** Color **2** Alternative colors **available** Composition **100% cotton** Width **55in/140cm** Repeat **35¾in/91cm** Price ★★

7 Claremont Fabrics/Maryland Color **apricot** Alternative colors **available** Composition **100% cotton** Width **54in/137cm** Repeat **26¾in/68cm** Price ★

8 Jane Churchill/Jousting JY32F-03 Color **dark red** Alternative colors **available** Composition **100% cotton** Width **55½in/141cm** Repeat **16in/40.5cm** Price ★★

9 John Wilman/Salvador 500417 Color **mango** Alternative colors **available** Composition **100% cotton** Width **54in/137cm** Repeat **23½in/60cm** Price ★★★

7

10

8

9

11

12

13

14

10 Bruno Triplet/Modula Color **cream** Alternative colors **available** Composition **100% cotton** Width **59in/150cm** Repeat **25in/64cm** Price ★★★

11 Jab/Bardera 1-8057 Color **174** Alternative colors **available** Composition **100% cotton** Width **55in/140cm** Repeat **12½in/32cm** Price ★

12 Donghia/Housepets 0450/5850-18 Color **nana** Alternative colors **available** Composition **100% cotton** Width **54in/137cm** Repeat **13¼in/34cm** Price ★★★★

13 Andrew Martin/Mungo Park Color **blue and red** Alternative colors **available** Composition **60% cotton, 40% jute** Width **51in/130cm** Repeat **36¼in/92cm** Price ★★

14 G. P. & J. Baker/Tiger Tiger J0248 Color **green** Alternative colors **available** Composition **100% silk** Width **55in/140cm** Repeat **24¾in/63cm** Price ★★★★

20th century

Overall Pattern

ABOVE A flame-stitch pattern fabric has been glued to the walls in this contemporary recreation of a turn-of-the-18th-century English interior. Handwoven flame-stitch fabrics were fashionable, especially in America, during the late 18th and early 19th centuries. The example shown here is machine-woven.

BLOCK PRINTING
One of the oldest methods of printing designs on textiles is still used today and involves hand-pressing wooden blocks against the surface of the fabric, the pattern having been carved in relief onto the underside of the blocks, and the dyes or inks being carried on the raised sections of the carving. The number of blocks required depends upon the complexity of the design, and can range from one for a simple repeat monochrome to up to a thousand or more for incredibly complex, multicolored pictorial patterns. Many scrolling, vegetal patterns have been produced in this way.

Of all the imagery that has provided inspiration for fabric patterns from the Middle Ages to the present day, organic forms (especially plants) have proved the most universal. Fabrics with floral patterns have been produced in such diverse styles that they merit discussion and illustration elsewhere (*see* pages 106-123). However, running a close second are the patterns based on fruits, buds, stems, leaves, shoots, roots, and organic forms such as animal skins and bird feathers.

Most plant ornament–both naturalistic and stylized–can be traced to specific cultures or periods. For example, the pomegranate is Middle Eastern in origin, the palm Asian and African, and the anthemion Ancient Greek and Oriental. Since the Renaissance, however, the expansion of the export trade in fabrics has "internationalized" these forms, a development that has also been fueled by archaeological discoveries of ancient civilizations, travel overseas, and the publication of numerous botanical studies and pattern books.

RIGHT The windows and seating in this 19th-century interior are furnished with woven and printed fabrics from Baumann's "Casa Blanca" range. The window sheers, the jacquard-woven top covers on the daybed and oval-back, painted armchair, and the jacquard-woven curtains, all feature traditional trailing foliage patterns. The fabrics covering the screen and foreground cushion display fruit-and-foliage patterns printed in complementary colors.

KEY DESIGNS

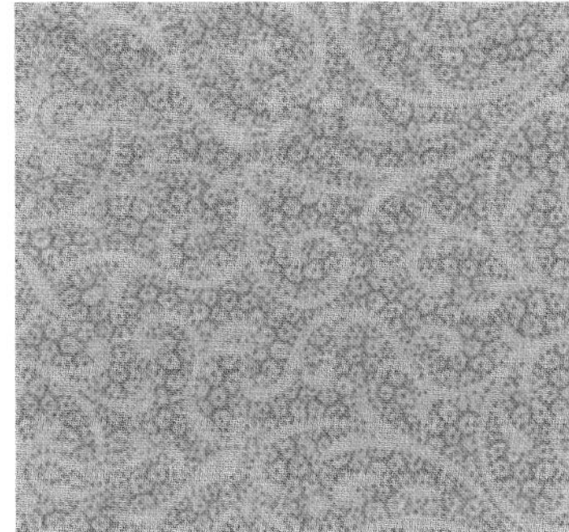

1 Stylized interlaced foliage, scrolling or trailing, has been one of the most popular fabric patterns since the late Middle Ages. This example is set on a *millefleurs* (thousand flower) ground.

2 Paisley patterns–stylized pinecones surrounded by vegetation–are derived from Oriental decoration. Paisley fabrics have been fashionable on both sides of the Atlantic since the mid-19th century.

3 Historically, most interlaced foliage patterns have been highly stylized. Naturalistic renderings have also been produced, however, particularly during the early 19th and 20th centuries.

4 Symbolizing immortality, foresight, and beauty, peacock feathers are often found on Oriental textiles. Other notable applications include Renaissance silks and Aesthetic Movement fabrics.

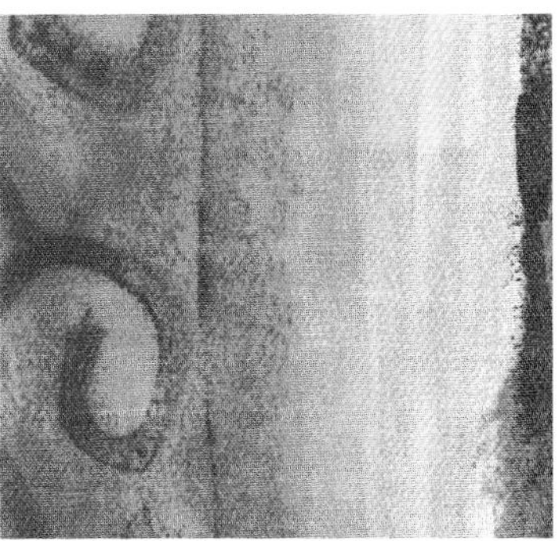

5 Fabric designers have often drawn inspiration from decorative plaster and wooden moldings. Typical examples since the Renaissance include fluting, *guilloche,* and wave patterns.

6 Woven and printed fabric patterns simulating exotic animal skins, such as zebra, tiger, and leopard, became fashionable from the middle of the 19th century onward, particularly in Europe.

1 **Nina Campbell/Hertford Scroll** Color **red** Alternative colors **available** Composition **100% cotton** Width **55in/140cm** Repeat **10½in/27cm** Price ★★

2 **G. S. Fabrics/Paisley Weave** Color **maize** Alternative colors **available** Composition **100% cotton** Width **54in/137cm** Repeat **15in/38cm** Price ★★

3 **Bennison Fabrics/Oakleaf** Color **green** Alternative colors **available** Composition **100% cotton** Width **46¼in/117.5cm** Repeat **11in/28cm** Price ★★★

4 **Liberty/Hera** Color **green** Alternative colors **available** Composition **36% modacrylic, 33% cotton, 31% polyester** Width **54in/137cm** Repeat **21¼in/54cm** Price ★

5 **Harlequin/Morelli** Color **multi** Alternative colors **available** Composition **100% cotton** Width **54in/137cm** Repeat **27in/68.5cm** Price ★

6 **Garin/Teseus** Color **black/cream** Alternative colors **available** Composition **50% wool, 25% cotton, 25% polyester** Width **55in/140cm** Repeat **22in/56cm** Price ★★★★

Overall Pattern: **Pre-18th century**

Prior to the 18th century, the vast majority of overall-patterned fabrics were decorated with stylized or naturalistic plant forms. During the Middle Ages, the ability of European fabric designers to depict such images accurately was restricted by the limitations of early weaving techniques and also by a scarcity of botanical reference material such as medieval herbals. Nevertheless, patterns based on grapevines, ivy, parsley, waterleafs, oak leaves, and acorns were very much in evidence, as were patterns with palms, which had been adopted as a heraldic emblem following the Crusades.

During the Renaissance, European fabric designers began to gain access to a much wider catalog of plant ornament, notably those forms used in Classical Greco-Roman and Middle Eastern decoration. These included the stylized pomegranate and pine forms set within repeat leaf patterns, favored for damasks and velvets, and scrolling foliage patterns based on the acanthus leaf. In the 17th century, the proliferation of botanical pattern books, such as Guillaume Toulouze's *Livre de Fleurs, Feuilles et Oyzéaus* (1656), further fueled the fashion for overall plant-form patterns, and made possible highly naturalistic renderings of fruit and extravagant scrolling foliage.

4

1

2

3

5

1 **Warwick/Marseille 105461506620** Color **burgundy** Alternative colors **available** Composition **100% cotton** Width **54in/137cm** Repeat **25in/64cm** Price ★★

2 **Bernard Thorp & Co/Faisan** Color **multi** Alternative colors **available** Composition **88% flax, 12% silk** Width **47in/120cm** Repeat **38in/97cm** Price ★★★

3 **Jason D'Souza/Riccio RIC04** Color **peach** Alternative colors **available** Composition **50% linen, 50% cotton** Width **53½in/136cm** Repeat **6¾in/17cm** Price ★★ LC

4 **Beaumont & Fletcher/Ottoman 1000a** Color **red** Alternative colors **available** Composition **100% cotton** Width **55in/140cm** Repeat **25½in/65cm** Price ★★★

5 **Bernard Thorp/Lucien** Color **multi** Alternative colors **available** Composition **58% flax, 42% cotton** Width **47in/120cm** Repeat **14½in/37cm** Price ★★

6 Percheron/Lampas les Ananas 2181 Color **1** Alternative colors **available** Composition **100% silk** Width **21¼in/54cm** Repeat **58in/147cm** Price ★★★★

7 Tissunique/Toile D'Artagnan 35/10943 Color **blue and beige** Alternative colors **available** Composition **54% linen, 46% cotton** Width **51in/130cm** Repeat **37in/94cm** Price ★★★

8 Monkwell/Segovia 09369CU/001 Color **green and beige** Alternative colors **available** Composition **62% cotton, 38% jute** Width **54in/137cm** Repeat **25in/64cm** Price ★

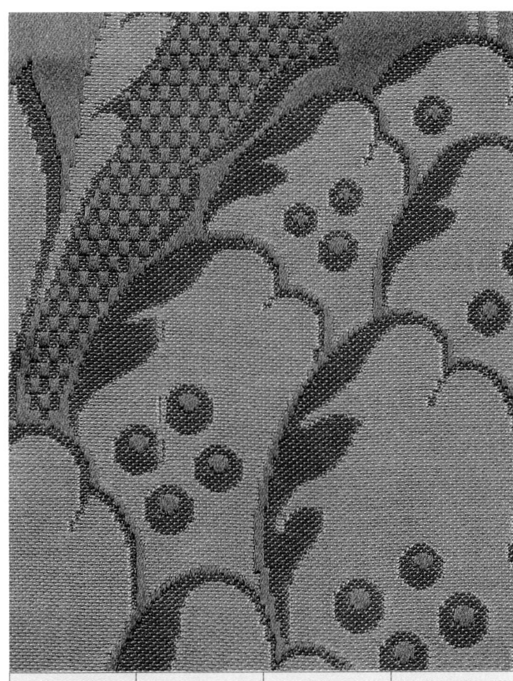

6

8

7

MORESQUE

The fabric shown here was derived from a panel of English ivory and white silk damask over-worked in embroidery, and dated ca. 1554. The pattern is "moresque," a term that is used to describe the stylized foliage patterns that were fashionable in Europe from the mid-16th to the early 17th centuries. Also known as "arabesques," the patterns originated in the damascened and engraved metalwork of Mesopotamia, Persia, and Syria, and were introduced into Europe by Muslim craftsmen who settled in Venice during the 15th century.

Stuart Interiors/Walsingham MC/LA Color **ecru, bottle, and cherry** Alternative colors **available** Composition **60% cotton, 40% wool** Width **57in/145cm** Repeat **23¾in/60cm** Price ★★★

Overall Pattern: **18th century**

The library of plant forms utilized by fabric designers was substantially augmented during the 18th century. The factors fueling this development included a greater understanding of plant ornament used in Classical Greece and Rome, following significant archaeological discoveries; the importation of Chinese silks and ceramics and Indian chintzes decorated with Oriental plant forms; and the increasing fashionableness of horticulture and gardening, and the attendant publication of botanical pattern books such as J. G. Huquier's *Nouveau Livre de Trophées de Fleurs Etrangers* (ca. 1750) and Philip Miller's *Figures of the Most Beautiful and Uncommon Plants* (1752). Many plant-form patterns on fabrics in Palladian interiors were based on acanthus and waterleafs, while in Rococo schemes numerous designs were based on light, scrolling foliage, palms, *chinoiserie* and Indian lotus leaves, artichokes, and cauliflower florets. In the Neoclassical interiors of the second half of the century, anthemia, laurels, lotus leaves, oak leaves, palmettes, and seaweed were fashionable, the latter often combined with coral on silk damasks. Ivy patterns also became popular in Gothick schemes, as the plant's association with ruined buildings was in tune with the Gothick taste for rustic decay. *Guilloche* patterns (*see* page 162) were also very popular.

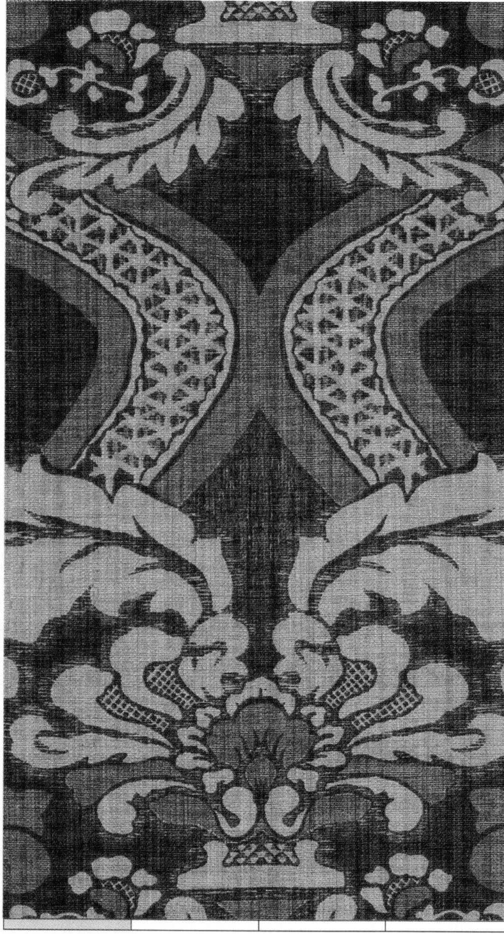

3

1

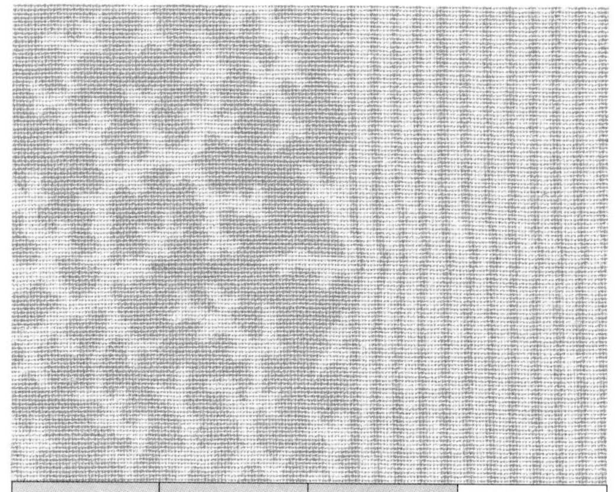

2

18th century

1 **The Silk Gallery/Persephone** Color **new gold 278** Alternative colors **available** Composition **100% silk** Width **50in/127cm** Repeat **35½in/90cm** Price ★★★

2 **George Spencer Decorations/ Woody 001W/01/06** Color **stone and green** Alternative colors **available** Composition **100% cotton** Width **52¾in/ 134cm** Repeat **12in/31cm** Price ★★

3 **Nina Campbell/Meredith NCF 3060** Color **09** Alternative colors **available** Composition **100% cotton** Width **55in/ 140cm** Repeat **17¼in/44cm** Price ★★

4 **Timney Fowler/Agra Ironwork TF004/3** Color **green and ecru** Alternative colors **available** Composition **100% cotton** Width **53in/135cm** Repeat **11in/28cm** Price ★★

5 **Watts of Westminster/Alwyne Zial/CSC4C4** Color **beige and oatmeal** Alternative colors **available** Composition **100% cotton** Width **48¾in/ 124cm** Repeat **38in/97cm** Price ★★★

4

5

6 Apenn/Hayward AV469-1 Color **green** Alternative colors **available** Composition **100% cotton** Width **47½in/121cm** Repeat **3in/8cm** Price ★★

7 Brunschwig & Fils/Benoa Contrefond Cotton Print 51251 Color **01** Alternative colors **available** Composition **100% cotton** Width **53in/134.5cm** Repeat **7in/17.75cm** Price ★★

8 Apenn/Marietta AV440-12 Color **terracotta** Alternative colors **available** Composition **100% cotton** Width **52in/132cm** Repeat **6in/15cm** Price ★

9 Zoffany Ltd/Vine 347706 Color **wedish blu** Alternative colors **available** Composition **45% modacrylic, 41% cotton, 14% nylon** Width **54in/137cm** Repeat **4in/10.3cm** Price ★★

10 Brunschwig & Fils/Rampur Stripe Cotton Print 79637 Color **04** Alternative colors **available** Composition **100% cotton** Width **54in/137cm** Repeat **18in/45.75cm** Price ★★

11 Bennison/Cinnabar Color **beige** Alternative colors **available** Composition **70% linen, 30% cotton** Width **54in/137cm** Repeat **19¼in/49cm** Price ★★★

12 Templeton Field 63270 Color **grass** Alternative colors **available** Composition **100% cotton** Width **54in/137cm** Repeat **¾in/2cm** Price ★

13 Percheron/Feuilles de Chenes 81117 Color **green** Alternative colors **not available** Composition **100% cotton** Width **51in/130cm** Repeat **10in/25cm** Price ★★★★

7

8

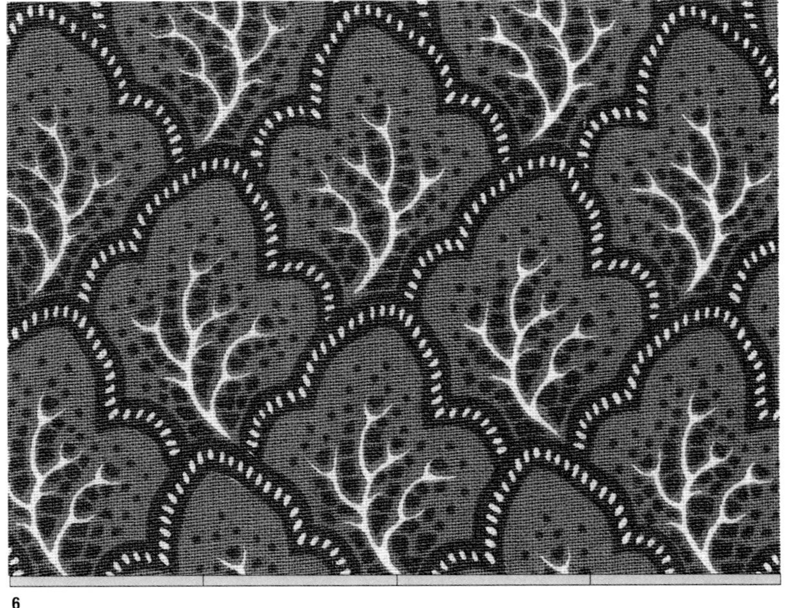

6

9

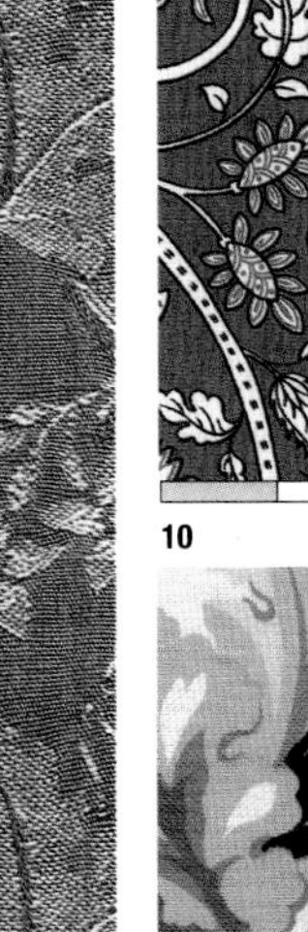

10

11

12

13

18th century

Overall Pattern: **Early 19th century**

In early 19th-century Neoclassical interiors, fashionable plant-form-patterned fabrics were based on stylized anthemia (especially popular in France and America), laurels, Egyptian-style lotus and palm leaves, seaweed, and the waterleaf. However, as the century wore on, increasingly naturalistic renderings of plant patterns were produced. Sometimes "sculptured" with shading, favored patterns included acanthus leaf, grapevine, oak leaf, thistle, and various fruits.

Around the middle of the century, there was a reaction against naturalistic patterns, with influential designers such as A. W. N. Pugin and Owen Jones producing heavily stylized designs. For example, many of the fabrics that were designed by Pugin in the 1840s were "flat-patterned" with a basic ogival structure featuring scrolling leaves and fleurs-de-lis, while Jones's designs incorporated stylized classical and Moorish ornament. Abstract patterns derived from motifs were also very popular at this time, as were "ironwork" designs.

1

2

3

4

5

1 Ramm, Son & Cocker/Oakley 65251 Color **red** Alternative colors **available** Composition **52% linen, 36% cotton, 12% nylon** Width **55in/140cm** Repeat **10in/25cm** Price ★

2 Hill & Knowles/Trefoil–Cornelia 83624F Color **green** Alternative colors **available** Composition **57% linen, 43% cotton** Width **54in/137cm** Repeat **8¼in/21cm** Price ★★

3 Lennox Money/Araz 2149A Color **beige on green** Alternative colors **available** Composition **100% cotton sateen** Width **55in/140cm** Repeat **47in/120cm** Price ★★
LC

4 Brunschwig & Fils/Coraux Glazed Chintz 62702.01 Color **blueberry** Alternative colors **available** Composition **100% cotton** Width **55in/140cm** Repeat **5½in/14cm** Price ★★

5 Hodsoll McKenzie/Arabesque 222/105 Color **green** Alternative colors **available** Composition **56% cotton, 44% spun rayon** Width **50in/127cm** Repeat **14¼in/36.5cm** Price ★★★
W

6

7

8

9

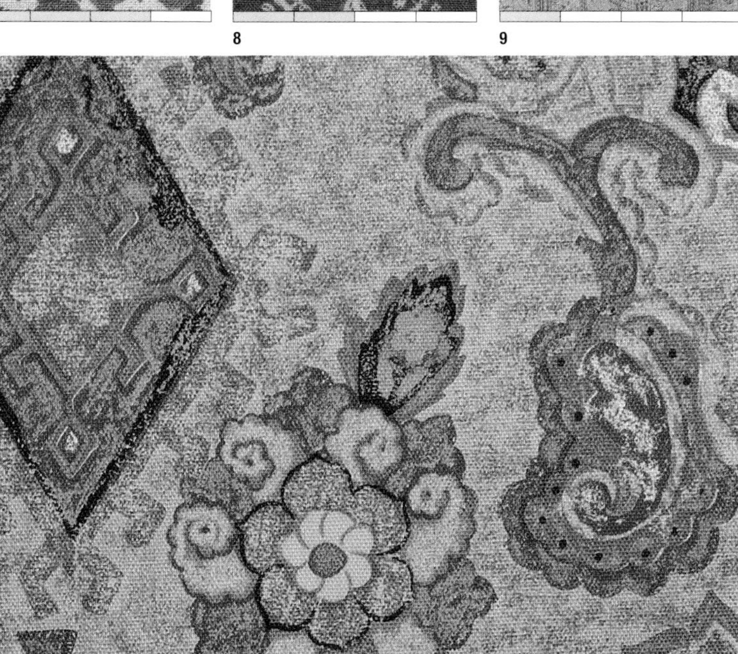

10

6 Belinda Coote Tapestries/ Provence 1 Color **sage green** Alternative colors **available** Composition **66% cotton, 22% viscose, 12% polyester** Width **55in/ 140cm** Repeat **4in/11cm** Price ★★

7 Busby & Busby/Jujube 494 Color **3** Alternative colors **available** Composition **100% cotton** Width **55in/140cm** Repeat **3½in/9cm** Price ★★

8 Anne and Robert Swaffer/ Pavane Color **103** Alternative colors **available** Composition **100% cotton** Width **55in/140cm** Repeat **6¼in/16cm** Price ★

9 Brunschwig & Fils/45989 Color **02** Alternative colors **available** Composition **100% cotton** Width **54in/137cm** Repeat **6¾in/17cm** Price ★★

10 Hill & Knowles/Afshar Zanda BT6703F Color **rust and turquoise** Alternative colors **available** Composition **100% cotton** Width **54in/137cm** Repeat **25in/64cm** Price ★★

11

12

13

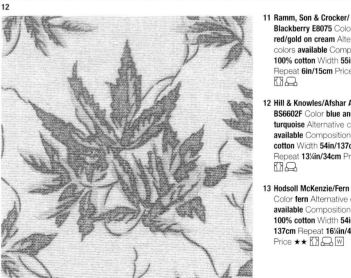

11 Ramm, Son & Crocker/ Blackberry E8075 Color **red/gold on cream** Alternative colors **available** Composition **100% cotton** Width **55in/140cm** Repeat **6in/15cm** Price ★

12 Hill & Knowles/Afshar Azar BS6602F Color **blue and turquoise** Alternative colors **available** Composition **100% cotton** Width **54in/137cm** Repeat **13¼in/34cm** Price ★★

13 Hodsoll McKenzie/Fern 222/402 Color **fern** Alternative colors **available** Composition **100% cotton** Width **54in/ 137cm** Repeat **16¼in/41.5cm** Price ★★

Overall Pattern: **Late 19th century**

Although naturalistically rendered plant-form patterns continued to appear on fabrics during the second half of the 19th century, stylized versions proved more fashionable. For example, designers from the Aesthetic Movement drew inspiration from Classical, Medieval, Renaissance, Middle Eastern, and Japanese flat-patterns and plant motifs. These include E. W. Godwin's rigid geometric designs, which incorporated highly conventionalized flowers and leaves reduced to flat, circular forms, and Christopher Dresser's formalized lotus patterns. Many Arts and Crafts fabrics also featured stylized, rhythmical plant forms, such as the willow, worked within Medieval-style pattern structures, while Art Nouveau fabrics displayed sinuous vegetal patterns based on pomegranates, thistles, buds, and seedpods, and leaflike peacock feathers.

Of special note during the second half of the century were the paisley-pattern fabrics widely employed in English and American Victorian interiors, and also popular in France. Inspired by imported Kashmiri shawls, they featured formalized representations of pinecones filled in with small, incidental motifs commonly found in Indian textile designs, and surrounded by stylized vegetation based on palms, cypress, and other plant forms.

4

1

2

3

1 **Lennox Money/Mangosteen 2152c** Color **dark green on beige** Alternative colors **available** Composition **100% cotton sateen** Width **54in/137cm** Repeat **44½in/113cm** Price ★★

2 **Tissunique/Les Symbolistes 35/10944/1** Color **1** Alternative colors **not available** Composition **100% cotton** Width **51in/130cm** Repeat **6¼in/16cm** Price ★★★

3 **Zuber/Volutes 3000S** Color **celadon** Alternative colors **available** Composition **100% cotton** Width **51in/130cm** Repeat **17in/43.5cm** Price ★★★

4 **Watts of Westminster/Bodley F0041** Color **English beige** Alternative colors **available** Composition **54% cotton, 46% Velicren** Width **55in/140cm** Repeat **14in/36cm** Price ★★★

5 **Watts of Westminster/Villiers F0028-01/MI5** Color **01** Alternative colors **available** Composition **100% linen** Width **49in/125cm** Repeat **35in/89cm** Price ★★★

5

6 Borderline/Juniper 2528a Color **red** Alternative colors **available** Composition **100% wool** Width **54in/137cm** Repeat **17¼in/44cm** Price ★★ LC

7 Bennison/Pacific Willow Color **beige** Alternative colors **available** Composition **70% linen, 30% cotton** Width **52½in/132.5cm** Repeat **5in/13cm** Price ★★★

8 Warner Fabrics/Cranford Coral C8 7930 Color **scarlet** Alternative colors **available** Composition **100% cotton** Width **54in/137cm** Repeat **5in/13cm** Price ★ LC

6

9

10

9 Tissunique/Sanchi 35/9840/1 Color **rouge** Alternative colors **available** Composition **100% cotton** Width **62½in/159cm** Repeat **5in/13cm** Price ★★★★ W

10 Watts of Westminster/Wyvern F0034-01 Color **green and blue** Alternative colors **available** Composition **100% linen** Width **53in/135cm** Repeat **21in/53cm** Price ★★★

11 Liberty/Hera 1067032 Color **G** Alternative colors **available** Composition **100% cotton** Width **54in/137cm** Repeat **14in/36cm** Price ★

12 Brunschwig & Fils/Chiang Mai 51224.01 Color **malachite** Alternative colors **available** Composition **65% cotton, 35% viscose** Width **54in/137cm** Repeat **13in/33cm** Price ★★★

11

7

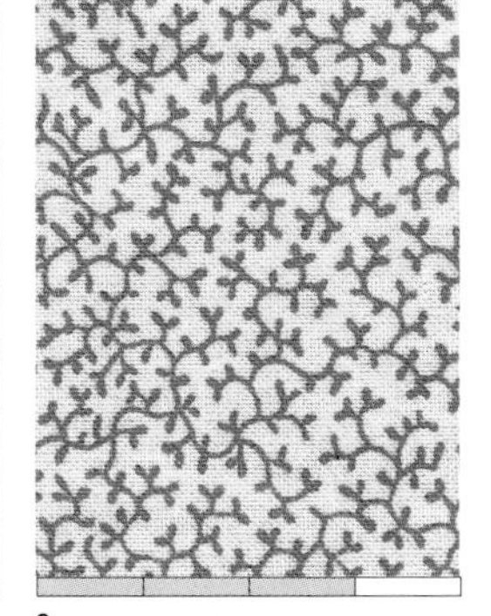

8

FLAME STITCH

The flame stitch pattern enjoyed a resurgence in popularity during the late 19th century, and, as a consequence, machine-made versions were produced to meet the demand. A form of embroidery that was primarily used as a cover for chairs, couches, and fire screens, flame stitch consists of "flames" of color. The technique, which allows large areas of backing canvas to be covered rapidly and to dramatic effect, was a fashionable pastime in England and America during the 18th century.

Brunschwig & Fils/Verona Flame Stitch 40064 Color **01** Alternative colors **not available** Composition **100% cotton** Width **51in/130cm** Repeat **9in/23cm** Price ★★★★★

12

19th century

Overall Pattern: **Early 20th century**

Woven and printed fabric patterns consisting of stylized plant forms remained fashionable during the first half of the 20th century. For example, sinuously depicted foliage was an important element in late Art Nouveau designs, and thistle, poppy, wisteria, and water lily patterns were especially favored. Similarly, Arts and Crafts designers continued to explore new areas of plant ornament. L. F. Day, whose influential *Nature and Ornament* was published in the United States and Europe (1908-9), noted: "The rose has been variously treated but comparatively little use has been made [to date] of the fruit, or of the thorns, or of the broad stipules at the base of the leaves."

More traditional plant-form patterns were also much in evidence during the first half of the century. Significant examples included the Renaissance-style pomegranate- and acorn-patterned damasks that were found in Tudor- and Jacobean-Revival interiors. Also prevalent were the Classical Greco-Roman palms and palmettes that appeared on some of the Art Deco fabrics. However, the increasing influence of fine art on textile design also resulted in the appearance of radically new organic forms, such as abstract depictions of aquariums and pond life.

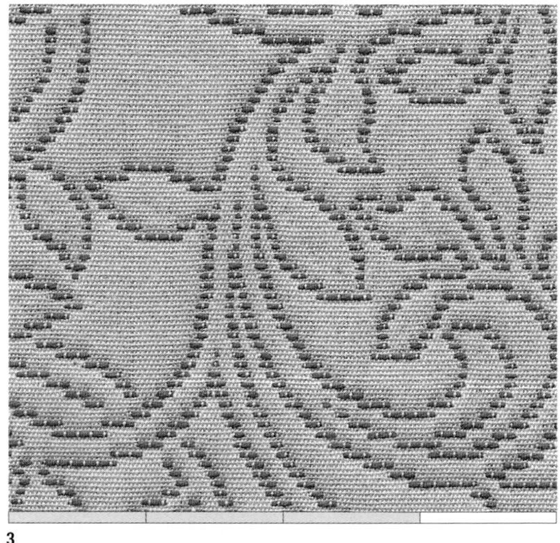

3

1

2

1 **Jab/Monza 1-2019** Color **170** Alternative colors **available** Composition **60% cotton, 30% viscose, 10% polyester** Width **55in/140cm** Repeat **11½in/29cm** Price ★★★

2 **Zuber/Chambord Brodé 10174** Color **white/gold** Alternative colors **available** Composition **100% cotton** Width **55in/140cm** Repeat **26¼in/67cm** Price ★★★★

3 **Northwood Designs/Winter-Sheherazade** Color **coquille** Alternative colors **available** Composition **100% cotton** Width **110¼in/280cm** Repeat **2in/5cm** Price ★★

4 **Brunschwig & Fils/Angelina Figured Texture 53591.01** Color **shell** Alternative colors **available** Composition **60% cotton, 20% silk, 20% polyester** Width **52in/132cm** Repeat **4¼in/11cm** Price ★★★★

4

5

5 **Brunschwig & Fils/Rampur Multi-Stripe 53412** Color **01** Alternative colors **available** Composition **100% cotton** Width **53in/135cm** Repeat **4¼in/11cm** Price ★★★★

6 **Donghia/Magic 0392/5725-03** Color **harvest** Alternative colors **available** Composition **100% silk** Width **55in/140cm** Repeat **5in/13cm** Price ★★★★★

6

7

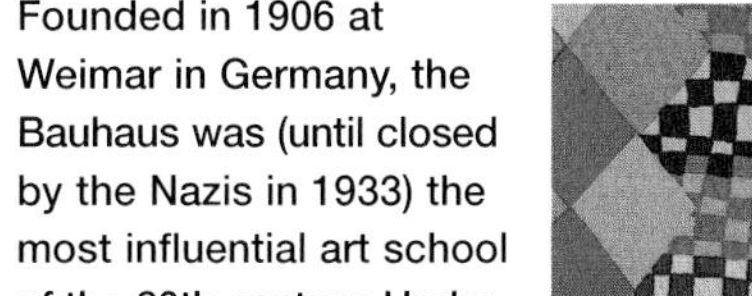

8

9

7 Lee Jofa/Pardah Print 91930 Color **0** Alternative colors **available** Composition **52% linen, 36% cotton, 12% nylon** Width **54in/137cm** Repeat **28¼in/72cm** Price ★★

8 Monkwell/Folium 09331 Color **blue** Alternative colors **available** Composition **100% cotton** Width **54in/137cm** Repeat **25in/64cm** Price ★

9 Warner Fabrics/Aquarium CS 7900 Color **orange** Alternative colors **available** Composition **100% cotton** Width **54in/137cm** Repeat **28¼in/72cm** Price ★★

10 Brunschwig & Fils/Villandry Cotton Print 72151 Color **04** Alternative colors **not available** Composition **100% cotton** Width **48in/122cm** Repeat **6in/15cm** Price ★★

11 Zimmer & Rohde/Lyra 6997 Color **717** Alternative colors **available** Composition **100% silk** Width **55in/140cm** Repeat **3½in/9cm** Price ★★★★

12 Monkwell Firifiss/Luna–Atlas FF74028 Color **2** Alternative colors **available** Composition **100% cotton** Width **59¾in/152cm** Repeat **49in/125cm** Price ★★

13 Brunschwig & Fils/Involve Silk Texture 53462.01 Color **imperial blue** Alternative colors **available** Composition **76% silk, 24% cotton** Width **55in/140cm** Repeat **12in/30.5cm** Price ★★★

10

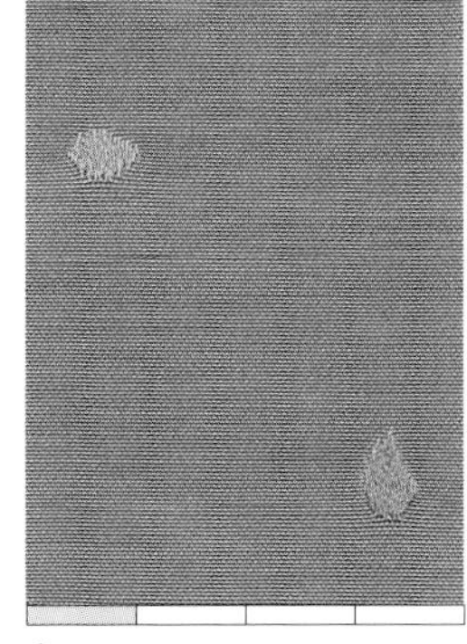

11

12

13

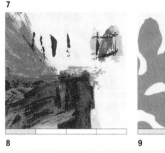

THE BAUHAUS MOVEMENT

Founded in 1906 at Weimar in Germany, the Bauhaus was (until closed by the Nazis in 1933) the most influential art school of the 20th century. Under the banner of International Modernism, the school promoted a close link between the artist and industry, as well as experimenting with new materials like rayon. Its tutors (such as Gunta Stölzl and Paul Klee) and pupils produced numerous innovative textile designs of stark cubic simplicity.

Liberty/Bauhaus 1069663 Color **B** Alternative colors **available** Composition **100% cotton** Width **54in/137cm** Repeat **25in/64cm** Price ★

14

14 Brunschwig & Fils/Jazzywoven Damask 46033.02 Color **camel** Alternative colors **available** Composition **100% cotton** Width **54in/137cm** Repeat **21in/53cm** Price ★★★★

15 Firifiss/Merino FF71006 Color **8** Alternative colors **available** Composition **100% wool** Width **54in/137cm** Repeat **21in/53cm** Price ★★

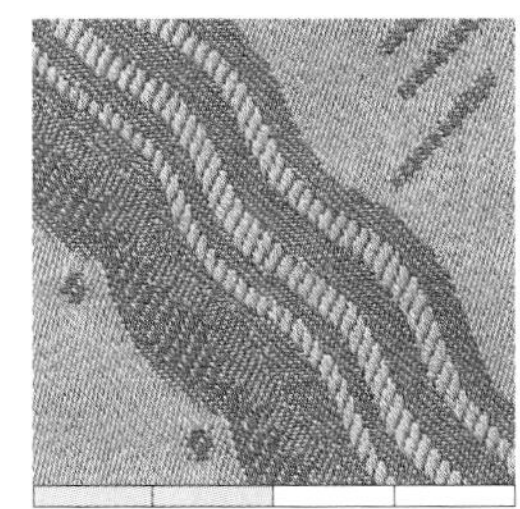

15

Overall Pattern: **Late 20th century**

Woven and printed fabrics with traditional-style leaf patterns were much in demand during the second half of the 20th century. Highly stylized–sometimes shaded, sometimes flat–they were often presented on a contrasting plain ground to give them a contemporary feel. Sinuous Art Nouveau and rhythmical Arts and Crafts plant-form patterns (*see* pages 150-3) came back into fashion in the 1960s and the 1980s respectively. Pointillist-style patterns comprising small, repeated fruit motifs, such as strawberries and raspberries, also found favor, while stylized and naturalistic animal prints proved popular, especially as top covers for upholstered seating.

Among some of the most recent and important additions to the catalog of organic ornamentation were colorful woven fabrics showing stylized "three-dimensional" basket weave patterns, and literally three-dimensional fabrics that were comprised of plain- or neutral-colored grounds "embroidered" with highly textured threadwork.

1

2

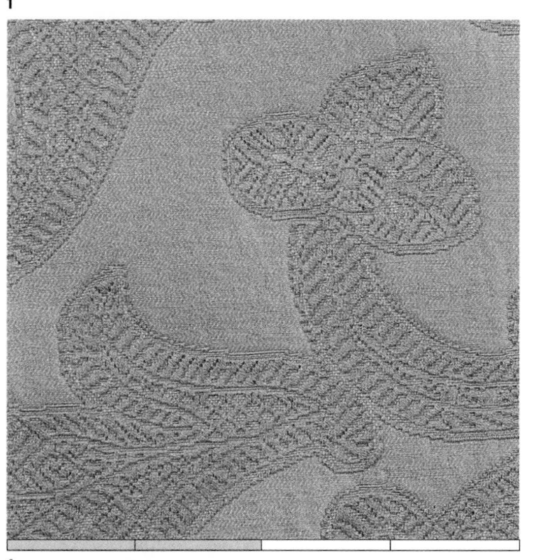

4

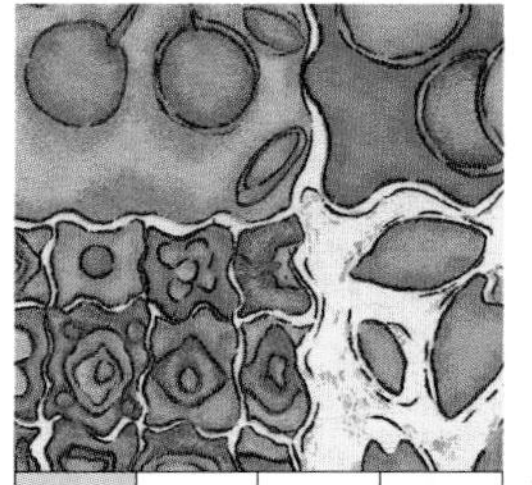

5

6

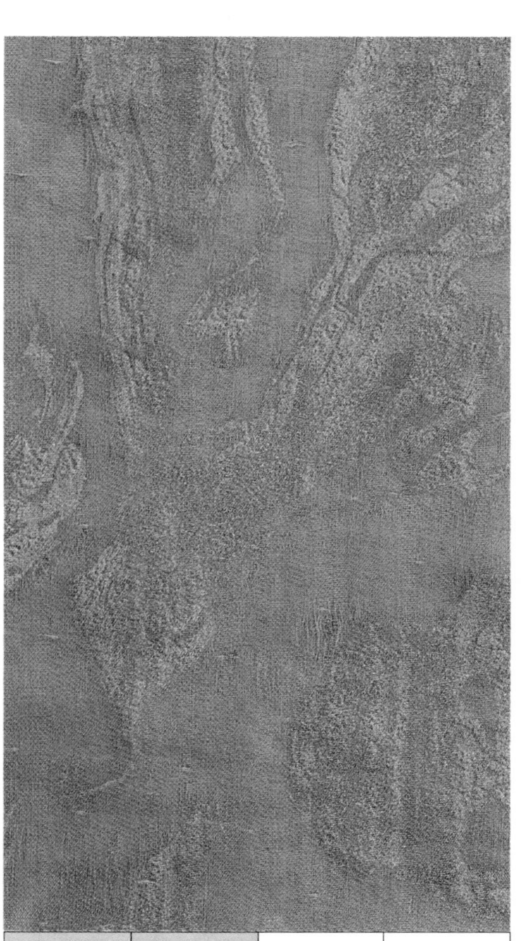

3

7

1 **Harlequin/Sangiori 5601** Color **multi** Alternative colors **available** Composition **100% cotton** Width **54in/137cm** Repeat **27in/68.5cm** Price ★

2 **Guy Evans/Stromboli** Color **multi** Alternative colors **available** Composition **100% cotton** Width **54in/137cm** Repeat **27½in/70cm** Price ★★★★★

3 **Sahco Hesslein/Teatro 50384** Color **gold and blue** Alternative colors **available** Composition **62% viscose, 38% silk** Width **55in/140cm** Repeat **35½in/90cm** Price ★★★★

4 **Sahco Hesslein/Elektra 08814** Color **cream and gold** Alternative colors **available** Composition **55% viscose, 24% cotton, 21% linen** Width **55in/140cm** Repeat **23¾in/60cm** Price ★★★

5 **Fine Decor/Toscano TY1184** Color **pink** Alternative colors **available** Composition **100% cotton satin** Width **54in/137cm** Repeat **25in/64cm** Price ★

6 **Knowles & Christou/Cabouchon KG403a** Color **opal and lilac** Alternative colors **available** Composition **100% cotton** Width **52in/132cm** Repeat **4in/10cm** Price ★★★ W

7 **Manuel Canovas/Africa 11336 82** Color **taupe** Alternative colors **available** Composition **59% linen, 41% cotton** Width **67in/170cm** Repeat **55in/140cm** Price ★★ W

20th century

8 **Bruno Triplet/Stella Color** Color **cream** Alternative colors **available** Composition **44% linen, 33% cotton, 23% polyester** Width **47in/120cm** Repeat **3in/8cm** Price ★★★

9 **Bruno Triplet/BAO** Color **brown** Alternative colors **available** Composition **55% linen, 45% polyester and raffia** Width **59in/150cm** Repeat **9½in/24cm** Price ★★★★

10 **Jim Thompson/Image 1023** Color **07** Alternative colors **available** Composition **100% cotton** Width **54in/137cm** Repeat **–** Price ★★★

11 **Knowles & Christou/Wicker** Color **blue** Alternative colors **available** Composition **100% linen** Width **52in/132cm** Repeat **1¼in/3cm** Price ★★★

12 **Montgomery/Bahia Color No.1** Color **blues** Alternative colors **available** Composition **100% cotton satin** Width **54in/137cm** Repeat **24¾in/63.5cm** Price ★

8

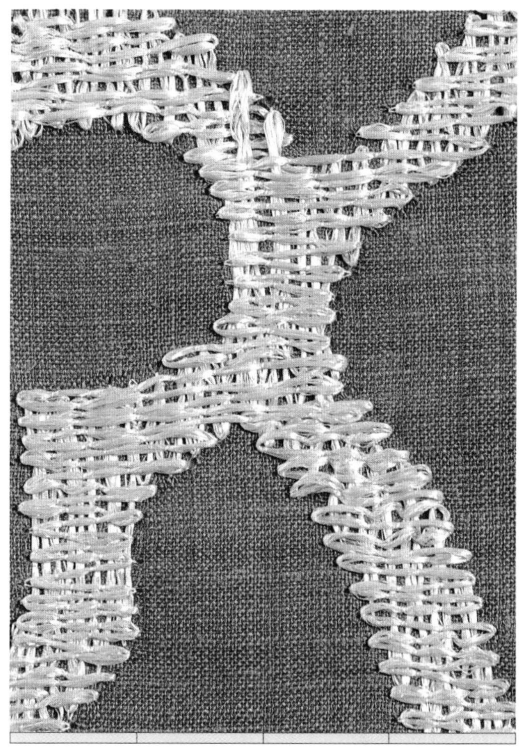

9

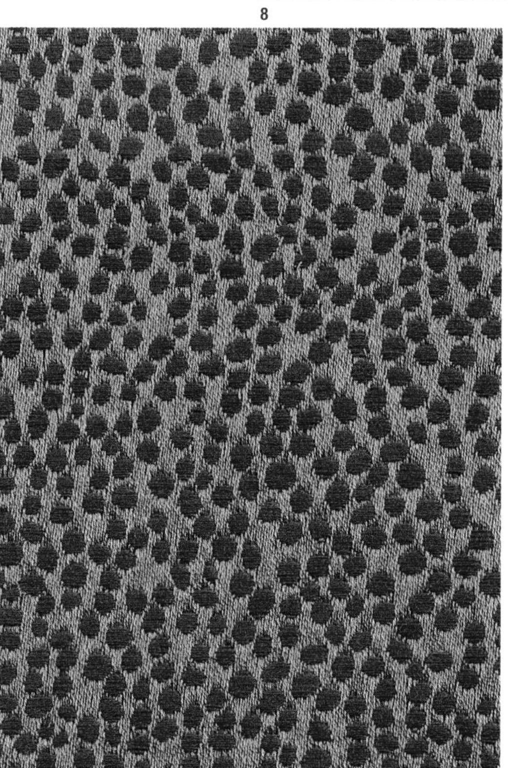

10

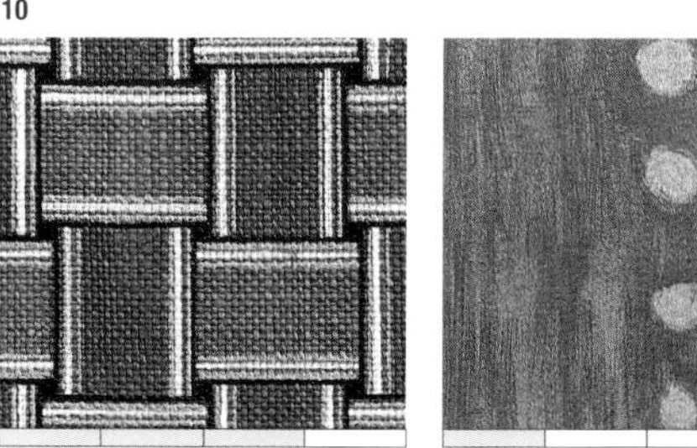

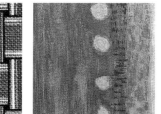

11

12

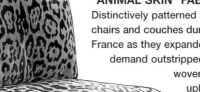

"ANIMAL SKIN" FABRIC

Distinctively patterned animal skins provided fashionable covers for chairs and couches during the 19th century, particularly in Britain and France as they expanded their empires into Africa. However, even then demand outstripped supply and thus faux skins made of both woven and printed fabrics were also produced for upholstery. With animals such as the leopard, tiger, panther, and some species of zebra hunted close to extinction, it was the fabric substitutes that enjoyed a resurgence in popularity during the second half of the 20th century.

G. P. & J Baker/Panther J0257-220 Color **black and cream** Alternative colors **available** Composition **86% cotton, 14% polyacrylic** Width **54in/137cm** Repeat **15in/38cm** Price ★★

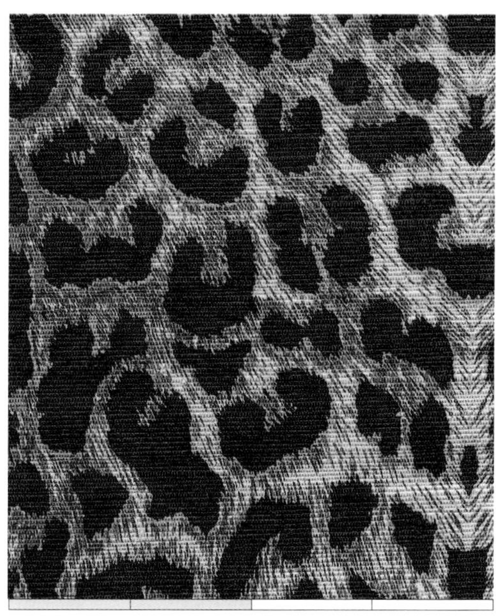

Jim Thompson/Leopard PDB 2798A Color **A** Alternative colors **not available** Composition **100% silk** Width **48in/122cm** Repeat **18in/46cm** Price ★★★★

20th century

Geometric Fabrics

A wide range of geometric-patterned fabrics, woven and printed, has been produced from the Middle Ages to the present day. Much of the geometric ornament employed originated in Classical and Oriental civilizations or in medieval Europe. Stylistically, geometric-patterned fabrics can be divided into two basic categories. In the first, the pattern consists of geometric or linear forms. In the second, a basic geometric pattern, sometimes comprised of nongeometric repeat motifs, frames or provides the ground for nongeometric imagery. "Pure" geometric patterns include woven or printed stripes; checks, such as woven plaids and printed madras; and combinations of irregular geometric forms inspired by Cubist art. Geometric-based patterns include trelliswork or latticework grounds that are formed from stylized leaves and covered with scrolling foliage, and *guilloche,* which is an overall repeating pattern (*see* pages 142-155) of interlacing curved bands that is often encircled with floral motifs.

LEFT The squab seat of the lyre-back chair in the background is upholstered with a red, horsehair-weave, cut-pile velvet, while the armchair in the foreground is covered with a trellis-pattern, red-and-gold silk lampas by Scalamandré. Both chairs date from the early to mid-19th century, and are located in the parlor of the 19th-century Andrew Low House in Savannah, Georgia.

ABOVE Linear stripe patterns are particularly suitable for pull-up, pull-down window shades, and were very fashionable in late 18th- and early 19th-century interiors. These Roman shades are located in a late Georgian house in Brighton, England.

TICKING

This 19th-century French wirework child's bed has been converted into a small bench seat, with a bolster added for comfort. The squab and bolster are both covered with a modern, blue-and-white striped bed ticking, a fabric that has been produced in various patterns over the centuries, although striped examples are certainly the most common. Blue-and-white striped ticking such as this example, which is woven in either cotton or linen, has changed little in appearance since the late 18th century, and has remained very fashionable on both sides of the Atlantic.

KEY DESIGNS

1 Popular since the 19th century, checked ginghams have vertical and horizontal stripes of equal width. They are woven from only two colors, but display a third color where these overlap.

2 Thick-textured, multicolored fabrics patterned with woven stripes of various widths were used during the Renaissance, and are not restricted to 20th-century interiors.

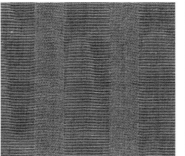

3 Striped fabrics incorporating alternating weaves and colors have been popular since the Middle Ages, but were especially fashionable during the late 18th and early 19th centuries.

4 Plaids have been widely used as furnishing fabrics since the 19th century. They are produced in various patterns and colors ("sets"), each associated with a particular Scottish clan.

5 Diaper patterns have consistently appeared on fabrics since the Middle Ages. Favored designs include trellis or lattice frameworks containing repeated geometric or nongeometric motifs.

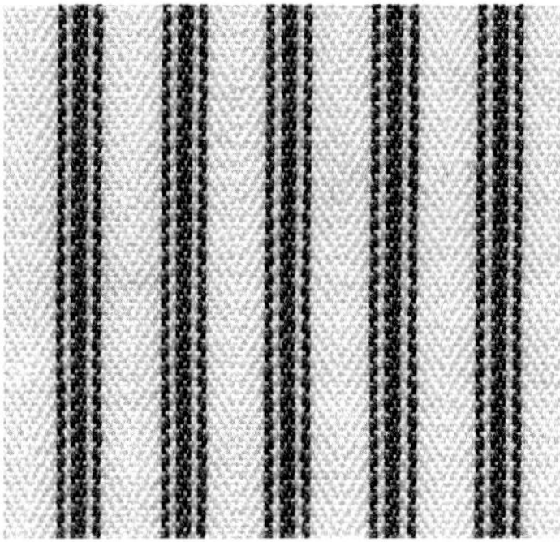

6 Originally a mattress covering, striped herringbone-weave ticking is now widely employed for hangings and upholstery. Classic colors are black, green, blue, or red on white or beige.

1 **Hill & Knowles/Square Dance** Color **black/beige** Alternative colors **available** Composition **100% cotton** Width **54in/137cm** Repeat **2in/5cm** Price ★

2 **Henderson Woven Designs/Kaleidoscope** Color **blue, green, vert, red, orange, yellow** Alternative colors **available** Composition **80% cotton, 20% mohair** Width **49¼in/125cm** Repeat **1¼in/3cm** Price ★★★★ LC

3 **Nobilis-Fontan/Rodolphe** Color **red** Alternative colors **available** Composition **100% silk** Width **51in/130cm** Repeat **–** Price ★★★

4 **The Isle Mill/Tullochcan** Color **multi** Alternative colors **not available** Composition **100% wool** Width **55in/140cm** Repeat **10in/25cm** Price ★★★ LC

5 **G. P. & J. Baker/Roi Soleil** Color **green** Alternative colors **available** Composition **57% cotton, 43% modacrylic** Width **57in/145cm** Repeat **2½in/6cm** Price ★★ LC LC

6 **Ian Mankin/Ticking I** Color **spruce** Alternative colors **available** Composition **100% cotton** Width **47in/120cm** Repeat **–** Price ★ LC

Geometrics: **Pre-18th century**

During the Middle Ages, diaper patterns were often employed on woven fabrics, and usually took the form of trellis grounds filled with motifs such as diamonds, squares, scales, or formalized flowers and leaves. Checked patterns (regularly spaced squares of alternating colors) were also popular, as were chevrons (V-shapes, used either singly in vertical series, or strung to form zigzags), nailheads (small pyramid forms), and powdered ornament (evenly spaced scatterings of small flowers or stars).

Diaper, checked, and nailhead patterns continued to appear on Renaissance fabrics. Strapwork patterns (twisted and intertwined bands similar to ribbons or strips of leather) were also fashionable, and Islamic influence was notable in *guilloche* (repeated interlacing curved bands, sometimes forming circles and usually enriched with floral motifs). However, aside from plaids (*see* opposite), which were primarily used as clothing and blankets during this period, the most notable late 16th- and 17th-century addition to this rich catalog of geometric ornament was jeweled strapwork–an elaboration of its plainer forerunner in which increasingly intricate banding was embellished with studs or diamonds shaded in imitation of faceted, prismatic jewels.

5

1

2

3

4

6

1 **Jason D'Souza/Stripe 561** Color **green** Alternative colors **available** Composition **50% linen, 50% cotton** Width **54in/137cm** Repeat **3in/8cm** Price ★★

2 **Warwick/Matour** Color **burgundy 1** Alternative colors **available** Composition **100% cotton** Width **54in/137cm** Repeat **25in/64cm** Price ★★ LC

3 **Jason D'Souza/San Marco SAN 01** Color **walnut and coral** Alternative colors **available** Composition **50% linen, 50% cotton** Width **52¼in/133cm** Repeat **2in/5.5cm** Price ★★

4 **Thomas Dare/Cavalli CAV 199125** Color **green and blue** Alternative colors **available** Composition **100% silk** Width **47in/120cm** Repeat **¾in/2cm** Price ★★ LC

5 **Zimmer & Rohde/Orlando** Color **rust** Alternative colors **available** Composition **54% linen, 46% cotton** Width **51in/130cm** Repeat **2½in/6cm** Price ★★★★

6 **Hill & Knowles/Troubadour** Color **green and red** Alternative colors **available** Composition **100% cotton** Width **54in/137cm** Repeat **12½in/32cm** Price ★★

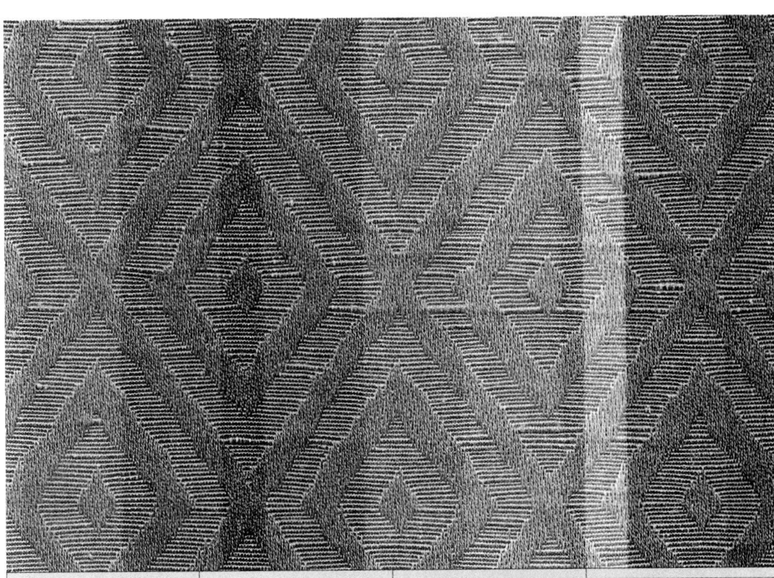

7

10 **Warwick/Loire 105442506620** Color **burgundy 1** Alternative colors **available** Composition **100% cotton** Width **54in/137cm** Repeat **25in/64cm** Price ★★

11 **Anta/Ballone 955** Color **blue/green** Alternative colors **not available** Composition **100% wool** Width **55in/140cm** Repeat **19¾in/50cm** Price ★★★

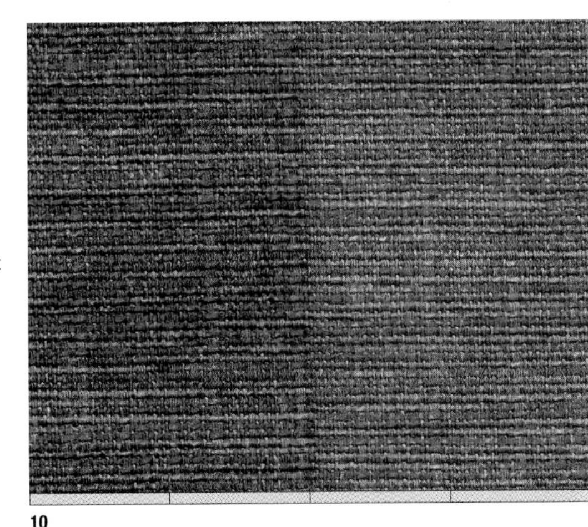

10

7 **Zimmer & Rohde/Orazio 3002 600** Color **multi** Alternative colors **available** Composition **54% linen, 46% cotton** Width **51in/130cm** Repeat **2½in/6cm** Price ★★★★

8 **Zimmer & Rohde/Lucca 3042** Color **590** Alternative colors **available** Composition **42% viscose, 40% cotton, 18% linen** Width **51in/130cm** Repeat **1½in/4cm** Price ★★★

9 **John Wilman/Bolivia 500394** Color **tabasco** Alternative colors **available** Composition **100% cotton** Width **54in/137cm** Repeat **25in/64cm** Price ★

8

11

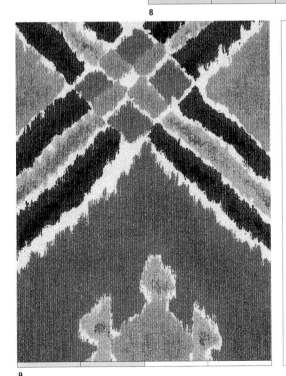

9

PLAIDS

In the 19th century, when plaids became fashionable furnishing fabrics, many manufacturers outside of Scotland produced them in sets (patterns and colors) that sometimes bore very little resemblance to the authentic designs of the Scottish clans. This arose because of three factors: financial opportunism; the use of synthetic aniline rather than vegetable dyes; and a lack of knowledge, a result of the fact that many pre-18th-century sets were never recorded, but instead were passed down by generations of Scottish dyers and weavers.

Seamoor Fabrics/Hay Tartan 96720/22 Color **red and black** Alternative colors **not available** Composition **100% cotton** Width **55in/140cm** Repeat **4¼in/11cm** Price ★

Seamoor Fabrics/Macalpine Tartan 96720/27 Color **green and cream** Alternative colors **not available** Composition **100% cotton** Width **55in/140cm** Repeat **4¼in/11cm** Price ★

Geometrics: **Early 18th century**

Diaper ornament continued to appear on furnishing fabrics produced during the first half of the 18th century. Indeed, early Rococo-style fabrics were characterized by trellis and latticework patterns (often constructed from leaf motifs), while bandwork (the 18th-century term for strapwork) was also much in evidence, and usually provided the ground for light, scrolling foliage. Other Medieval and Renaissance geometric patterns that either remained popular or were revived included V-shape chevrons (particularly popular in mid-18th-century Gothick interiors), dogteeth (symmetrically arranged, starlike decorations developed from pyramid-shaped nailheads–*see* page 158), and, to a lesser extent, plaids.

Also increasingly popular during the early 18th century were vertical-stripe patterns. Varying in width, alternating in two or more colors, and sometimes incorporating additional small motifs, the stripes either made up the main body of the fabric pattern, or they were superimposed over other patterns (often floral) in the weave.

George Spencer Decorations/Ottoman Stripe 006V/01 Color **green-gold** Alternative colors **available** Composition **82% viscose, 18% linen** Width **50in/127cm** Repeat **–** Price ★★★

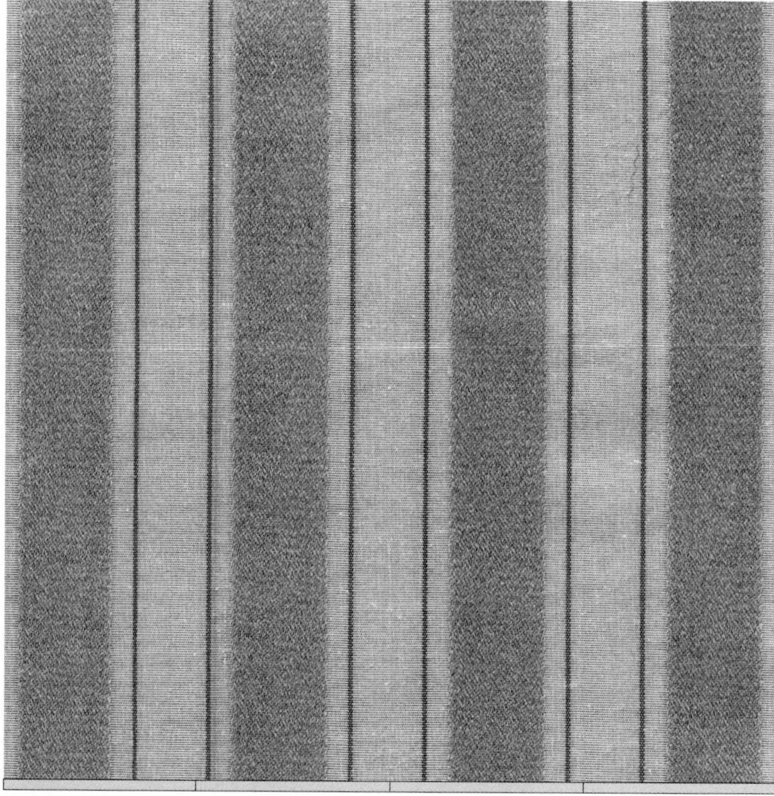

Scalamandré/Province 154-007 Color **yellow and pale blue** Alternative colors **available** Composition **100% silk** Width **50in/127cm** Repeat **1in/2.5cm** Price ★★★★★

George Spencer Decorations/Check 001C/11 Color **green/plum** Alternative colors **available** Composition **100% cotton** Width **50in/127cm** Repeat **¾in/2cm** Price ★★★

Zimmer & Rohde/Oreste 3003 Color **600** Alternative colors **available** Composition **54% linen, 46% cotton** Width **51in/130cm** Repeat **21½in/55cm** Price ★★★★

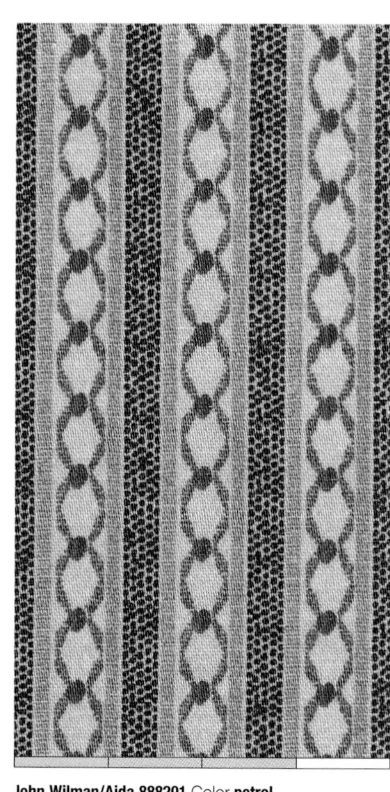

John Wilman/Aida 888201 Color **petrol** Alternative colors **available** Composition **100% cotton satin** Width **54in/137cm** Repeat **¾in/2cm** Price ★

The Isle Mill/Black Watch 801 Color **black and green** Alternative colors **not available** Composition **100% wool** Width **55in/140cm** Repeat **10in/25cm** Price ★★

The Isle Mill/Campbell, Ancient Muted 1203 Color **green and blue** Alternative colors **not available** Composition **100% wool** Width **55in/140cm** Repeat **11¾in/30cm** Price ★★

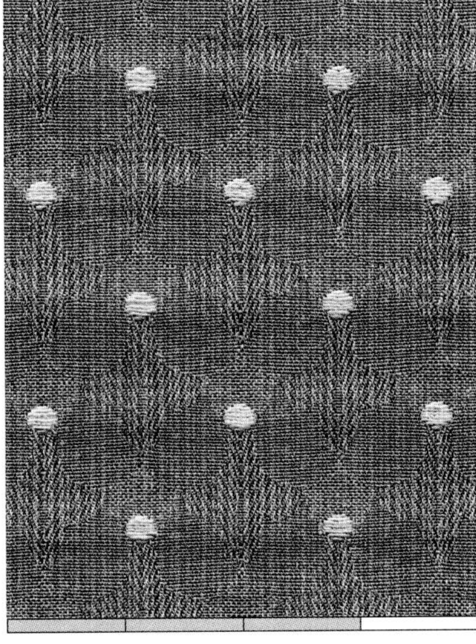

Zimmer & Rohde/Arena 6996 684 Color **green and yellow** Alternative colors **available** Composition **54% cotton, 46% viscose** Width **55in/140cm** Repeat **1in/ 2.5cm** Price ★★★

Ian Sanderson/Ducane Color **brick** Alternative colors **available** Composition **100% cotton** Width **54in/137cm** Repeat **1¼in/3cm** Price ★★

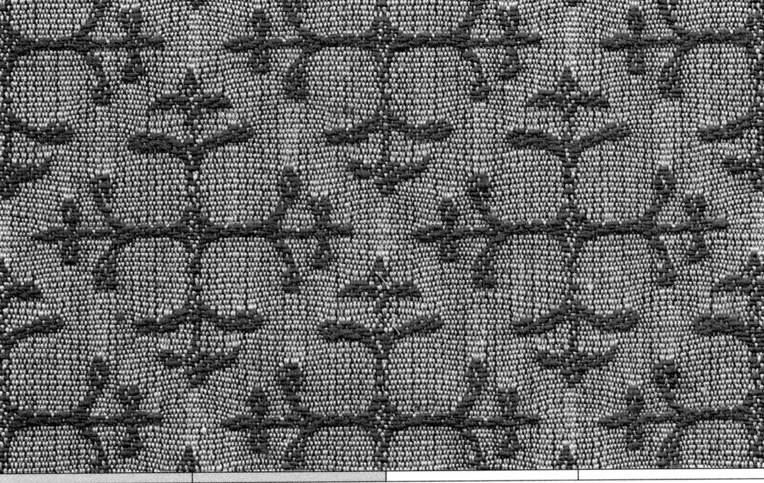

Zoffany/Domino 336602 Color **rust** Alternative colors **available** Composition **53% modacrylic, 35% cotton, 12% nylon** Width **57in/145cm** Repeat **2in/5cm** Price ★★

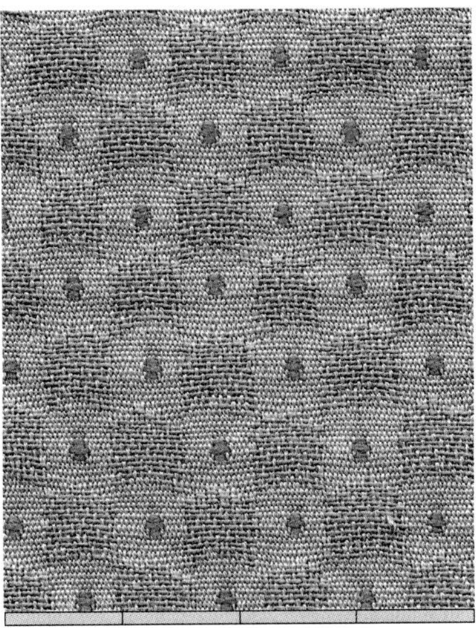

Zoffany/Dice 348804 Color **green and red** Alternative colors **available** Composition **38.6% cotton, 34.8% modacrylic, 13.8% wool, 12.8% nylon** Width **55¾in/142cm** Repeat **½in/1.5cm** Price ★★

SWEDISH STYLE

The trellis pattern was a much-favored fabric design in both Rococo and Neoclassical interiors of the 18th century, especially for upholstery. The example shown here is made up of small leaves and is typical of the fabrics found on Swedish furniture during this period. Such fabrics were characterized by their elegant, symmetrical shapes, restrained ornamentation, and cool, pale colors. As well as this muted ("Swedish") blue, pearl gray and straw yellow remained fashionable throughout the century.

Zoffany/Trellis 349907 Color **Swedish blue** Alternative colors **available** Composition **45% modacrylic, 41% cotton 14% nylon** Width **54in/137cm** Repeat **2½in/6.5cm** Price ★★

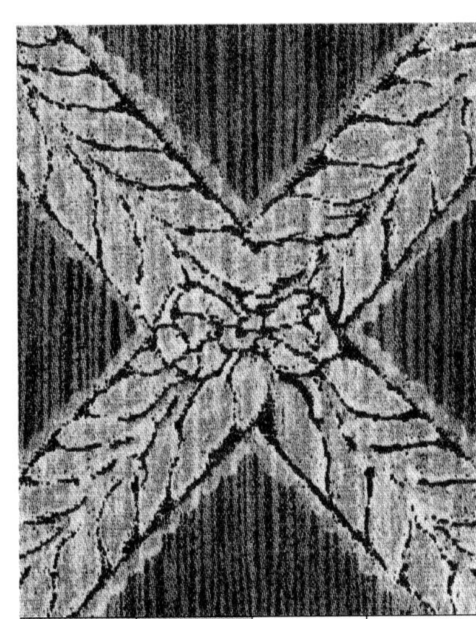

John Wilman/Figaro 888065 Color **granite** Alternative colors **available** Composition **100% cotton** Width **54in/137cm** Repeat **–** Price ★

Geometrics: **Late 18th century**

Striped fabrics were to be found in many Neoclassical interiors during the second half of the 18th century. The alternation of the widths and colors of woven stripes also became increasingly sophisticated following technical improvements made to the looms. Typical designs included thin bands of vertically stacked single chevrons alternating with contrasting-colored wider bands of horizontally linked pairs of chevrons; Etruscan-style vertical stripes composed of leaves, tripods, urns, chimeras, half-figures, and other classical motifs; and *guilloche* patterns (*see* pages 146-7).

In Greek-Revival interiors, the Greek key pattern was often used as a border on fabrics–the interlocking right-angled and vertical lines often doubled up to create a perspective effect–and was sometimes intermittently embellished with either *paterae* or rosettes. Latticework patterns were also fashionable, often as grounds for *chinoiserie* and Indian motifs, as were multicolored woven checks, their squares sometimes decorated with small classical or floral motifs. Toward the end of the century, ticking also came into vogue. Initially employed as a cover for feather mattresses–its herringbone-weave stripes designed to keep feathers in and ticks out–its used subsequently spread to furnishings.

4

1

1 **Timney Fowler/Architect's Stripe TF0194/24** Color **taupe** Alternative colors **available** Composition **100% wool** Width **58in/147cm** Repeat **4in/10cm** Price ★★★

2 **Sahco Hesslein/Bellevue 14790** Color **brown** Alternative colors **available** Composition **71% cotton, 29% silk** Width **51in/130cm** Repeat **–** Price ★★★★

3 **Ian Sanderson/Pym Stripe** Color **brick** Alternative colors **available** Composition **100% cotton** Width **55in/140cm** Repeat **–** Price ★★

2

3

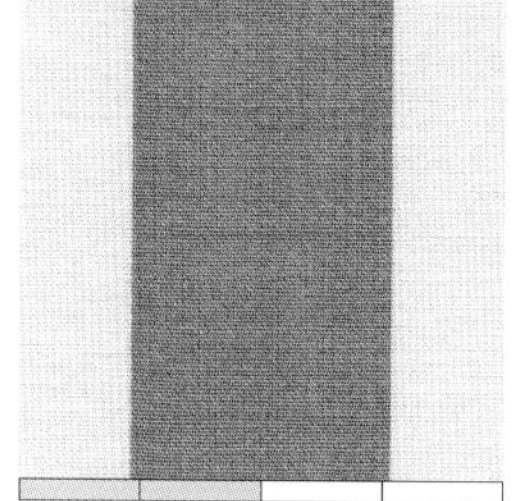

5

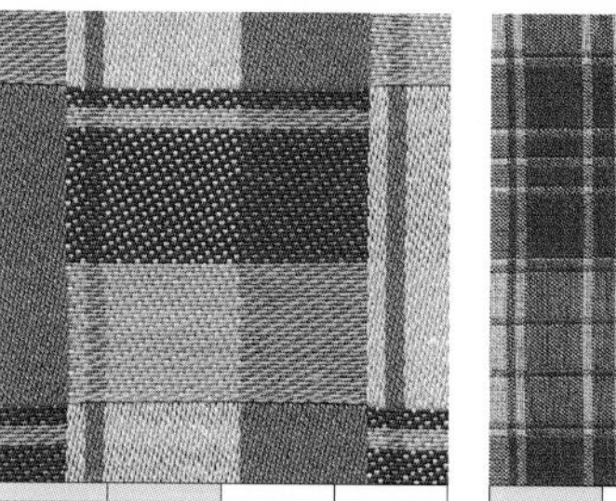

6

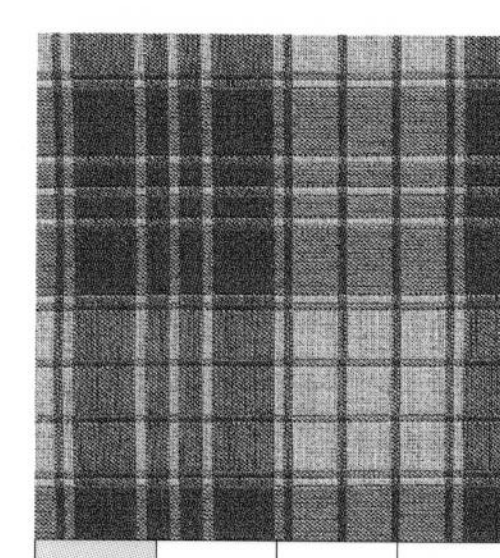

7

4 **Zimmer & Rohde/Stradino 4818** Color **245** Alternative colors **available** Composition **100% silk** Width **55in/140cm** Repeat **¾in/2cm** Price ★★★

5 **Jab/Regis 1-8107-169** Color **pink/cream** Alternative colors **available** Composition **100% cotton** Width **55in/140cm** Repeat **2¾in/7cm** Price ★

6 **The Design Archives/Cachet 51031** Color **12** Alternative colors **available** Composition **60% cotton, 40% velicren** Width **54in/137cm** Repeat **3½in/9cm** Price ★★

7 **Tissunique/Carreaux** Color **red/gold** Alternative colors **available** Composition **100% cotton** Width **55in/140cm** Repeat **4¾in/12cm** Price ★★★

8 **Sahco Hesslein/Majestic 15144** Color **brown** Alternative colors **available** Composition **45% cotton, 45% silk, 10% linen** Width **155in/40cm** Repeat **–** Price ★★★★

8

9 **Sahco Hesslein/Bizet 08896** Color **gold** Alternative colors **available** Composition **79% cotton, 21% silk** Width **55in/140cm** Repeat **2½in/6cm** Price ★★★

10 **Zimmer & Rohde/Sciro 4819 707** Color **13** Alternative colors **available** Composition **100% silk** Width **55in/140cm** Repeat **6½in/16.5cm** Price ★★★

11 **Colefax and Fowler/Maplehurst Check F1305/03** Color **green** Alternative colors **available** Composition **48% cotton, 44% Velicren, 8% linen** Width **55in/140cm** Repeat **2½in/6cm** Price ★★

9

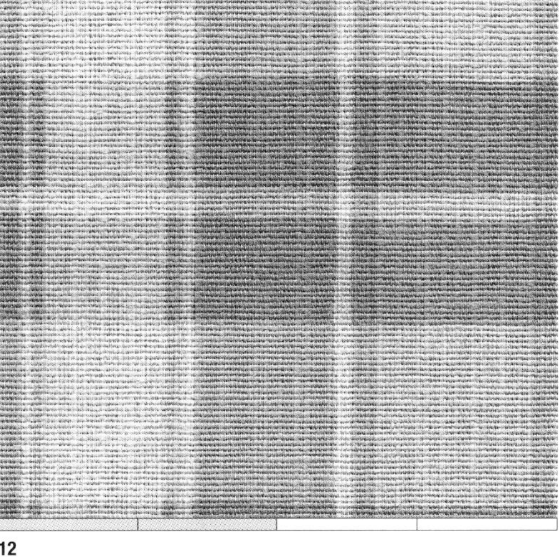

12

12 **Warwick/Washcott Fairford 118192414580** Color **dusk 20** Alternative colors **available** Composition **100% cotton** Width **54in/137cm** Repeat **6in/15.5cm** Price ★★

13 **Ian Sanderson/Glen Plaid** Color **orchid** Alternative colors **not available** Composition **100% wool** Width **55in/140cm** Repeat **8½in/22cm** Price ★★

14 **Scalamandré/Roma 1205-001** Color **multi on ivory** Alternative colors **available** Composition **100% silk** Width **50in/127cm** Repeat **4¾in/12cm** Price ★★★★★

15 **Old World Weavers/Ombre Thien JN00030001** Color **multi/gold** Alternative colors **available** Composition **100% silk** Width **48in/122cm** Repeat – Price ★★★★

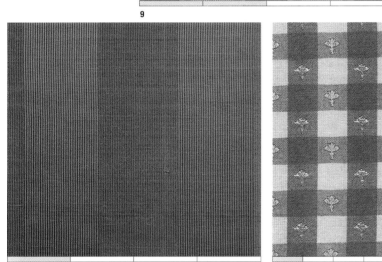

10

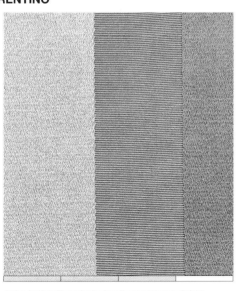

11

13

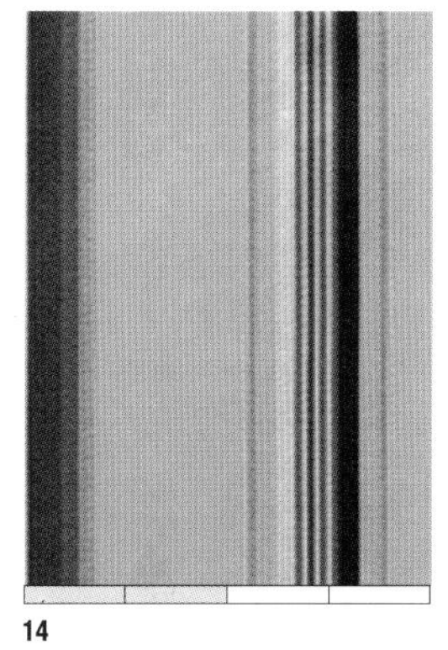

14

18th century

ANTICO SETIFICIO FIORENTINO

The Italian cloth factory Antico Setificio Fiorentino has made woven fabrics since the Renaissance, and produces most of its document fabrics on the original looms, some of which were donated in 1780 by the Grand Duke of Tuscany. The factory also retains an ancient thread-winding machine that is based on a design by Leonardo da Vinci. In view of their illustrious history, it has been said that when you order a brocade or a damask from this company it is similar to ordering a custom-made Ferrari.

Antico Setificio Fiorentino/Le Roy Color **gold/orange/bright beige** Alternative colors **available** Composition **100% silk** Width **47in/120cm** Repeat **11½in/29cm** Price ★★★

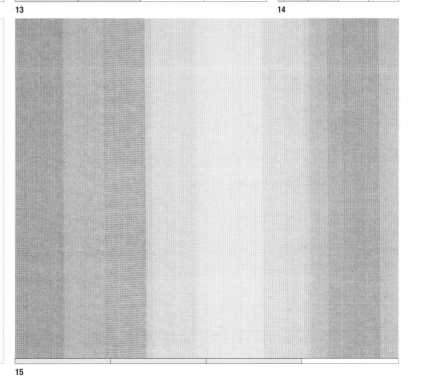

15

Geometrics: **Early 19th century**

Stripes remained fashionable up until the 1830s, particularly for upholstered seating (*see* "Striped Fabrics," opposite), while during the 1840s jeweled strapwork patterns and powdered ornament (*see* page 158) reappeared in Gothic-Revival interiors. However, a tremendous range of check-patterned fabrics was also produced throughout the first half of the 19th century. For example, rectangular shapes surrounding small Neoclassical and Napoleonic motifs were popular in Empire-style interiors, and twill-weave plaidbegan to be more widely employed in furnishing fabrics in both Britain and America.

Typical of the printed checks that became increasingly fashionable were the imported Indian ginghams. These were lightweight cottons, brightly colored with vegetable dyes. Unfortunately, they were not colorfast, a problem that also affected silk. Indeed, red-and-black check Indian cotton madras became known as "bleeding madras" because of the instability of its colors.

1

2

1 **The Isle Mill/Macnaughton Muted 1229** Color **red and green** Alternative colors **not available** Composition **100% wool** Width **55in/140cm** Repeat **10in/25cm** Price ★★

2 **The Isle Mill/Lindsay S912** Color **black and red** Alternative colors **not available** Composition **100% silk** Width **39¼in/100cm** Repeat **4in/10cm** Price ★★

3

4

3 **Warner Fabrics/Versailles Marble CS 336220** Color **celadon and apricot** Alternative colors **available** Composition **100% cotton** Width **54in/137cm** Repeat **25in/64cm** Price ★★

4 **Marvic Textiles/Fabiola 8249-5** Color **olive** Alternative colors **available** Composition **52% linen, 48% viscose** Width **55in/140cm** Repeat **3in/8cm** Price ★★

5 **Baer & Ingram/Daisy DSF 05** Color **dark pink** Alternative colors **available** Composition **100% cotton** Width **55in/140cm** Repeat **4¼in/11cm** Price ★★

6 **Nina Campbell/Violet Plaid NCF3131** Color **01** Alternative colors **available** Composition **100% cotton** Width **55in/140cm** Repeat **3½in/9cm** Price ★★

7 **Ian Mankin/Empire 1** Color **Air Force** Alternative colors **available** Composition **100% cotton** Width **54in/137cm** Repeat – Price ★

5

6

7

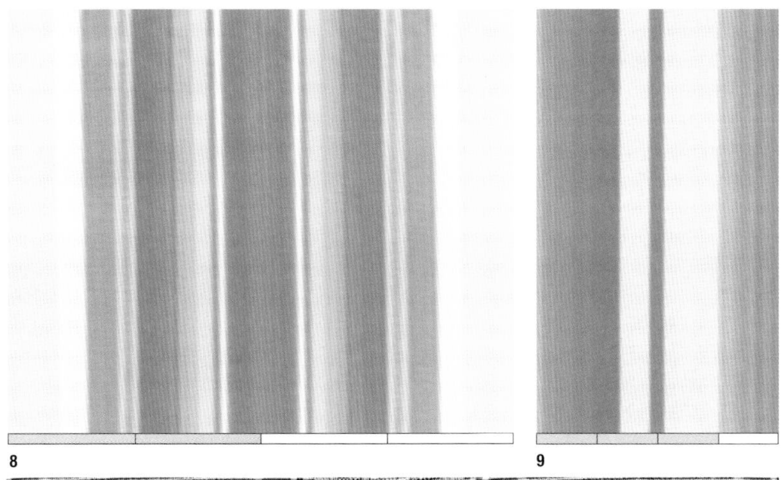

8

9

8 Scalamandré/Simbolo 90010-001 Color **multi on peach** Alternative colors **available** Composition **100% silk** Width **50in/127cm** Repeat **17in/43cm** Price ★★★★ T

9 Mary Fox Linton/Marquis 8351 Color **blue and yellow** Alternative colors **available** Composition **100% silk** Width **55in/140cm** Repeat **4¾in/12cm** Price ★★★★

10 Brunschwig & Fils/Valmy Lisère Stripe 32482.01 Color **blue stripe** Alternative colors **available** Composition **100% cotton** Width **51in/130cm** Repeat **2¾in/7cm** Price ★★★

11 The Silk Gallery/Pergamon Color **henna and Italian gold** Alternative colors **available** Composition **68% silk, 32% polyester** Width **50in/127cm** Repeat – Price ★★★ W

12 Hodsoll McKenzie/Campaign Stripe 353/103 Color **red/green** Alternative colors **available** Composition **76% cotton, 24% silk** Width **50in/127cm** Repeat – Price ★★★ W

11

10

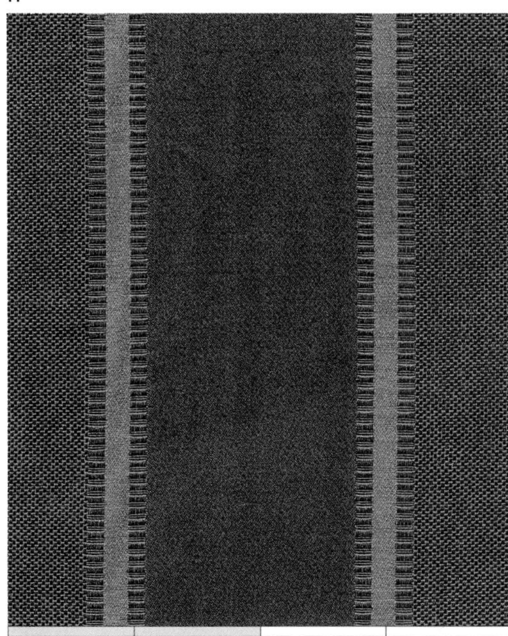

12

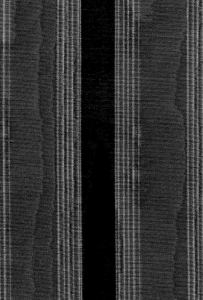

STRIPED FABRICS

Silk, linen, and horsehair fabrics in striped designs became fashionable in France at the beginning of the 19th century, and were initially inspired by the striped bunting hung from the exteriors of buildings to celebrate the Emperor Napoleon's victories on the battlefield against other European powers. Striped hangings and upholstery proved equally popular in America and elsewhere in Europe, particularly in Britain, up until the 1830s. In England, the diverse range of colorful woven and printed striped fabrics produced during this period (under the Regency and then reign of George IV) came to be known collectively as "Regency stripes."

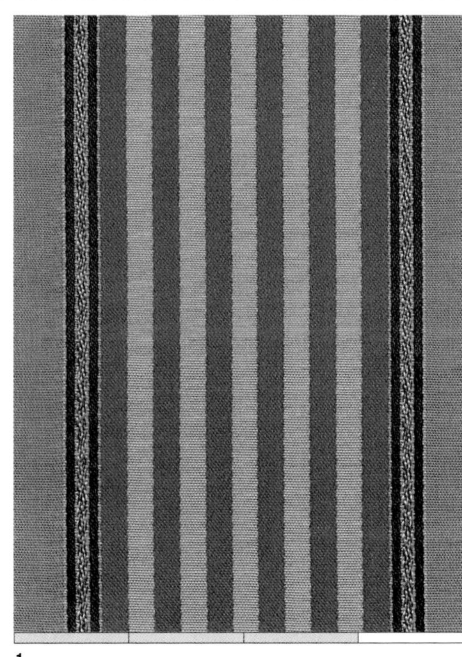

1

2

1 Jim Thompson/Flotilla II 1002 Color **02** Alternative colors **available** Composition **100% silk** Width **48in/122cm** Repeat **4in/10cm** Price ★★★

2 Marvic Textiles/Emilio FR 1302-7 Color **red and black** Alternative colors **available** Composition **63% viscose, 37% modacrylic** Width **55in/140cm** Repeat **2¾in/7cm** Price ★★ LC

Geometrics: **Late 19th century**

Proposition Eight of Owen Jones's *Grammar of Ornament* (published in 1856 and reprinted until 1910) stipulated that "all ornament should be based on geometric construction." Jones's view, much inspired by his studies of Chinese, Japanese, Indian, Indonesian, African, South American, Celtic, and Medieval patterns, proved highly influential during the second half of the 19th century, especially among designers in the Aesthetic and Arts and Crafts Movements. Indeed, many of the theories of Jones and his contemporaries also found favor with the general public once they had been translated onto fabrics.

Typical examples included trelliswork, latticework, and other diaper patterns, used as frames or grounds for Medieval, Jacobean, or Oriental motifs, such as fleur-de-lis, thistles, and pomegranates. Jeweled strapwork, chevrons, stripes, and powdered ornament (*see* page 158) were fashionable, as were Celtic triquetra and triskele. Imported Indonesian *ikats*, featuring kaleidoscopic blocks, circles, and stripes, and Indian checked gingham and madras were also much in evidence. Particularly fashionable, however, were the striped and checked plaids now widely employed for hangings and covers–a trend fueled by Queen Victoria's establishment of a royal residence in Balmoral, Scotland.

4

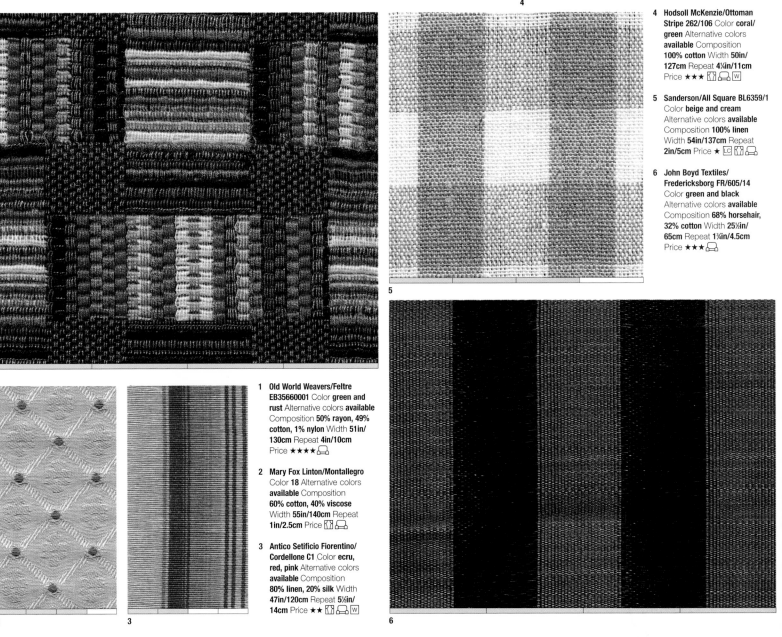

1

2

3

5

6

1 **Old World Weavers/Feltre EB35660001** Color **green and rust** Alternative colors **available** Composition **50% rayon, 49% cotton, 1% nylon** Width **51in/130cm** Repeat **4in/10cm** Price ★★★★

2 **Mary Fox Linton/Montallegro** Color **18** Alternative colors **available** Composition **60% cotton, 40% viscose** Width **55in/140cm** Repeat **1in/2.5cm** Price

3 **Antico Setificio Fiorentino/Cordellone C1** Color **ecru, red, pink** Alternative colors **available** Composition **80% linen, 20% silk** Width **47in/120cm** Repeat **5½in/14cm** Price ★★

4 **Hodsoll McKenzie/Ottoman Stripe 262/106** Color **coral/green** Alternative colors **available** Composition **100% cotton** Width **50in/127cm** Repeat **4¼in/11cm** Price ★★★

5 **Sanderson/All Square BL6359/1** Color **beige and cream** Alternative colors **available** Composition **100% linen** Width **54in/137cm** Repeat **2in/5cm** Price ★

6 **John Boyd Textiles/Fredericksborg FR/605/14** Color **green and black** Alternative colors **available** Composition **68% horsehair, 32% cotton** Width **25½in/65cm** Repeat **1¾in/4.5cm** Price ★★★

7 **The Isle Mill/Duke of Fife 509** Color **red, green, and black** Alternative colors **available** Composition **100% wool** Width **55in/140cm** Repeat **6¼in/16cm** Price ★★

8 **Sahco Hesslein/Dundee 12073** Color **445** Alternative colors **available** Composition **60% viscose, 25% cotton 15% polyacrylic** Width **55in/140cm** Repeat **6in/15cm** Price ★★★

7

8

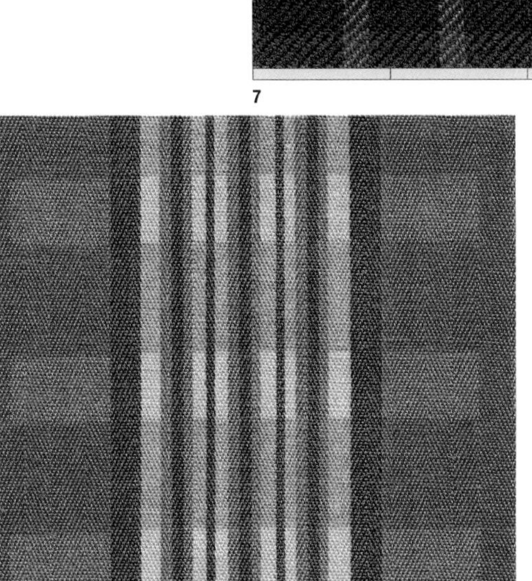

9

10

9 **Zoffany/Check Stripe 37 CS01** Color **05** Alternative colors **available** Composition **100% cotton** Width **54in/137cm** Repeat **1¼in/3cm** Price ★★

10 **Dedar/Manon** Color **cream and black** Alternative colors **available** Composition **58% cotton, 23% viscose, 19% polyester** Width **55in/140cm** Repeat **–** Price ★★★

11 **Pippa & Hale/Delphi MIF 100** Color **red** Alternative colors **available** Composition **100% cotton** Width **54in/137cm** Repeat **–** Price ★

12 **Old World Weavers/Shantung Albatross SB14862201** Color **multi** Alternative colors **not available** Composition **100% silk** Width **55in/140cm** Repeat **13¼in/34cm** Price ★★★★★

13 **Antico Setificio Fiorentino/Spinato SP1** Color **orange, green, yellow, blue** Alternative colors **available** Composition **70% silk, 30% linen** Width **47in/120cm** Repeat **6¼in/16cm** Price ★★

14 **John Boyd Textiles/Neapolitan NE/637/2** Color **green and beige** Alternative colors **available** Composition **100% horsehair** Width **25½in/65cm** Repeat **2in/5cm** Price ★★★

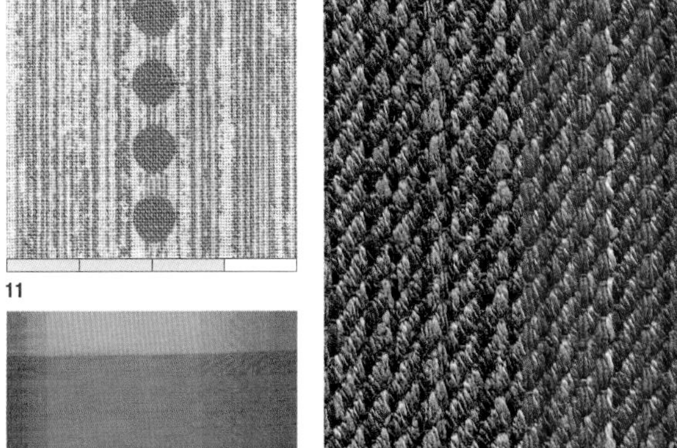

11

12

13

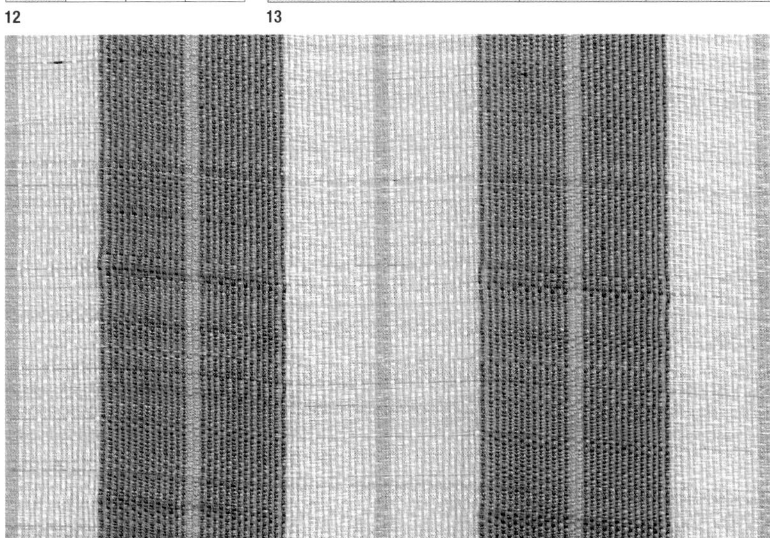

14

Geometrics: **Early 20th century**

Geometrically patterned fabrics were very fashionable from the end of the 19th century until the outbreak of the Second World War. Many of these patterns had been popular in previous centuries: striped and checked plaids in Baronial-style interiors; strapwork and jeweled strapwork patterns in Elizabethan- and Jacobean-Revival schemes; and chevrons, Aztec-stepped shapes, and prismatic triangles in Art Deco rooms. Also, herringbone-weave ticking began to be increasingly used for curtains, upholstery, and shades.

However, the most innovative fabric patterns of the period were designed by artists bridging the gap between fine and applied art. Examples included the woodblock-printed, Cubist-inspired, irregular shapes from Raoul Dufy in the first two decades of the 20th century; the strong geometric forms and bold stripes, often combined with abstract floral forms, produced by Paul Poiret in 1911; and the colorful shapes and lines of Sonia Delaunay in the 1920s and 1930s (*see* "Kasak," opposite).

1

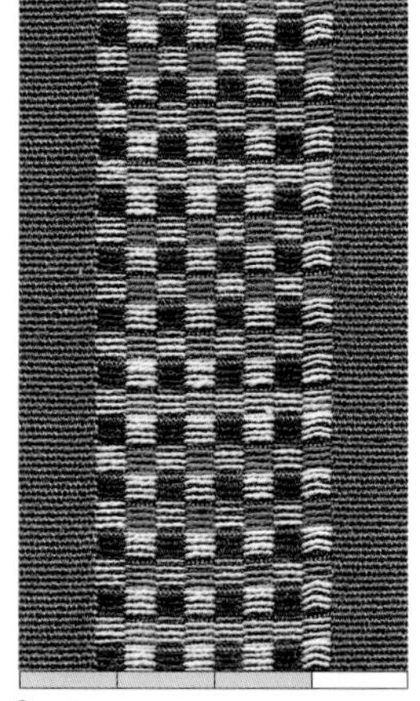

2

1 **Bennison Fabrics/Tooth Check** Color **greens** Alternative colors **available** Composition **70% linen, 30% cotton** Width **54in/137cm** Repeat **6¼in/16cm** Price ★★★

2 **Abbott & Boyd/Ajedrez Listada 49881-2** Color **blue, multi checker/stripe** Alternative colors **available** Composition **100% cotton** Width **55in/ 140cm** Repeat **3¼in/8.5cm** Price ★★★

3

4

3 **G. P. & J. Baker/Gallery J0242** Color **755** Alternative colors **available** Composition **100% silk** Width **55in/140cm** Repeat **7in/18cm** Price ★★★

4 **Donghia/Righe 9305** Color **05** Alternative colors **available** Composition **100% silk** Width **55in/140cm** Repeat **2in/5cm** Price ★★★★★

5 **Ian Mankin/Ticking 1** Color **sage** Alternative colors **available** Composition **100% cotton** Width **47in/120cm** Repeat **–** Price ★

6 **Northwood Designs/Maya** Color **brick** Alternative colors **available** Composition **100% cotton** Width **114¼in/290cm** Repeat **2in/5cm** Price ★★ LC W

7 **Manuel Canovas/Vita 4424** Color **pêche, veronse** Alternative colors **available** Composition **58% viscose, 42% cotton** Width **51in/130cm** Repeat **1½in/4cm** Price ★★★

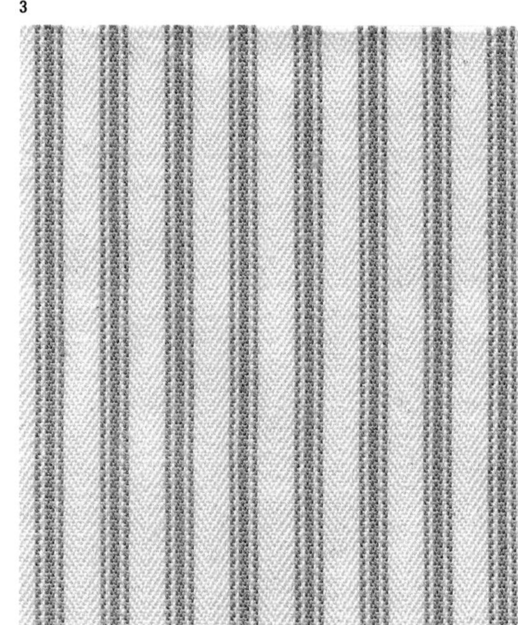

5

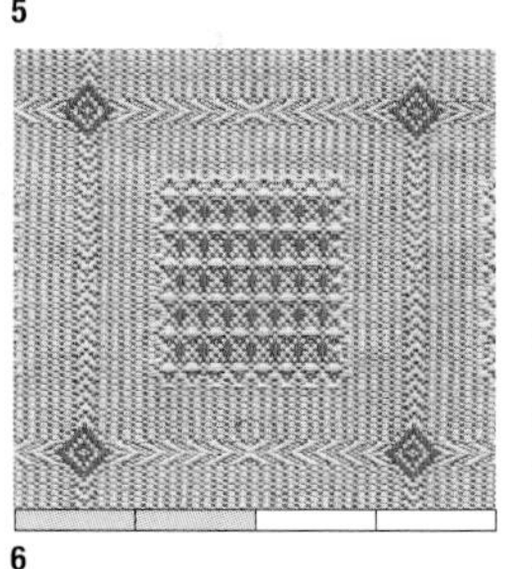

6

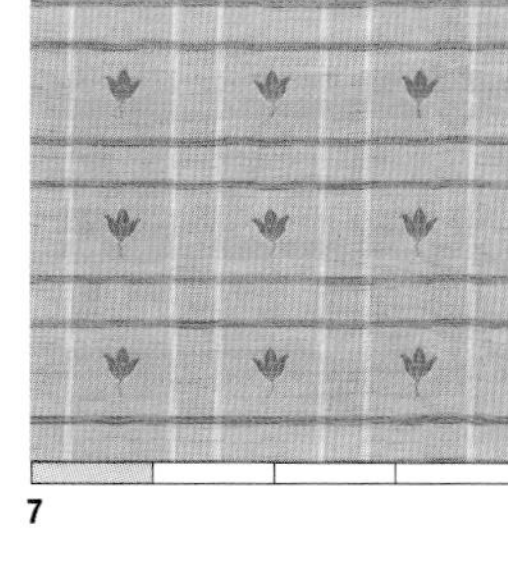

7

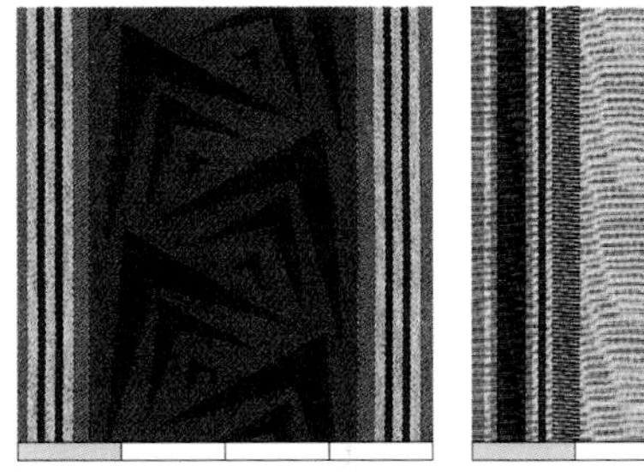

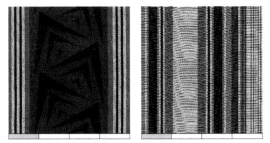

8

9

8 Firifiss/Lalaine FF71012 Color **cheviot 6** Alternative colors **available** Composition **100% wool** Width **54in/137cm** Repeat **2¾in/7cm** Price ★★

9 Nina Campbell/Wide Stripe NCF 3140 Color **01** Alternative colors **available** Composition **60% cotton, 40% modacrylic** Width **55in/140cm** Repeat **–** Price ★★

10 Sahco Hesslein/Ambassador 15013 Color **green** Alternative colors **available** Composition **70% wool, 25% silk, 5% polyester** Width **51in/130cm** Repeat **8½in/22cm** Price ★★★★

11 The Isle Mill/Dress Gordon 5863 Color **multi** Alternative colors **not available** Composition **100% silk** Width **39¼in/100cm** Repeat **4in/10cm** Price ★★

12 Garin/Bolero 66754441 Color **cream, black** Alternative colors **available** Composition **100% cotton** Width **55in/140cm** Repeat **½in/1cm** Price ★★

13 The Isle Mill/Glen Morar GT112 Color **blue, red, and cream** Alternative colors **available** Composition **100% wool** Width **55in/140cm** Repeat **2½in/6cm** Price★★

14 Firifiss/Lalaine FF71008 Color **Soay** Alternative colors **available** Composition **100% wool** Width **54in/137cm** Repeat **½in/1cm** Price ★★

11

10

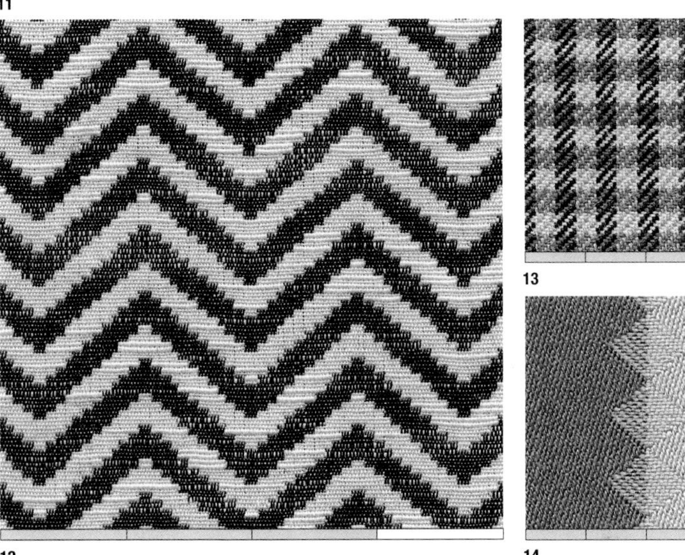

12

13

14

15

15 Lee Jofa/Parquet Matelassé 934007 Color **apricot/sage** Alternative colors **available** Composition **54% cotton, 46% rayon** Width **53in/135cm** Repeat **1½in/4cm** Price ★★★

16 Donghia/Double Diamond 0259/8200-08 Color **natural oyster** Alternative colors **not available** Composition **60% linen, 40% cotton** Width **54in/137cm** Repeat **19¾in/50cm** Price ★★★★

16

KASAK

"Kasak," shown here, was designed by Susan Collier when she worked in the Liberty Studio during the 1970s. It was inspired by the work of Sonia Delaunay, a painter and decorative artist who was based in Paris during the first 30 years of the 20th century. Delaunay, who was born in the Ukraine, favored geometric patterns in which vibrant color was used to suggest a feeling of space and movement. Thus in this respect Delaunay's designs reveal the influence of traditional Russian patchwork quilts.

Liberty/Kasak 1069624 Color **C** Alternative colors **available** Composition **100% cotton** Width **54in/137cm** Repeat **16¼in/41cm** Price ★★

Geometrics: **Late 20th century**

Many of the geometrically patterned fabrics that proved fashionable for curtains and upholstery during the second half of the 20th century originated from European and American designers. In the 1950s and 1960s, for example, numerous late Modernist-style fabrics were embellished with schematized geometric or abstract patterns; these consisted of modified versions of the irregular geometric forms found in Cubist paintings from earlier in the century. Crystalline structures (such as insulin viewed under a microscope) presented within diaper ground patterns also provided the inspiration for many designs of the period, and symmetrically spaced triangles, squares, and dots were much in evidence.

Among the imported fabrics that became increasingly fashionable were ginghams, *ikats,* and madras. Indonesian *ikats*, which are woven in silk or in fine cotton yarn, were particularly appreciated for the way in which their geometric blocks, circles, and stripes were softened by a vegetable-dyeing process, a procedure that feathered the edges of the colors into one another. Similarly, silk, cotton, and rayon check madras, which at one time was only dyed black and red, became even more popular when manufacturers began to produce many other vibrant colors.

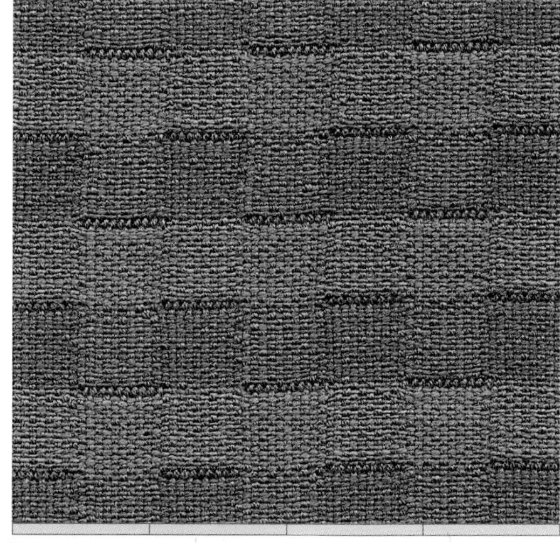
5

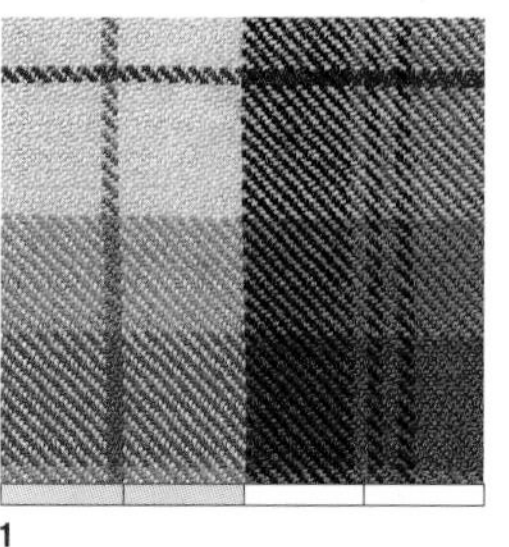
1

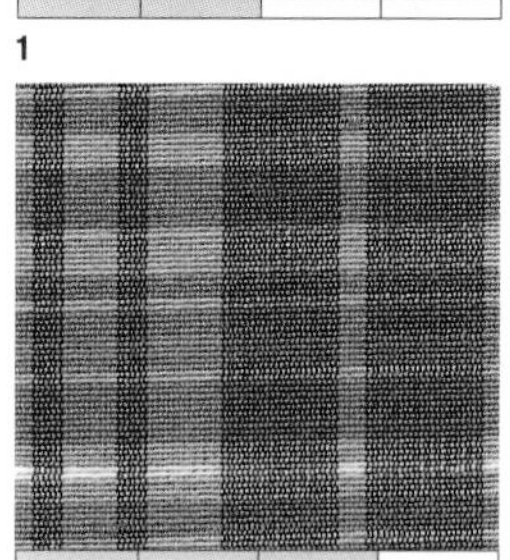
2

3

6

4

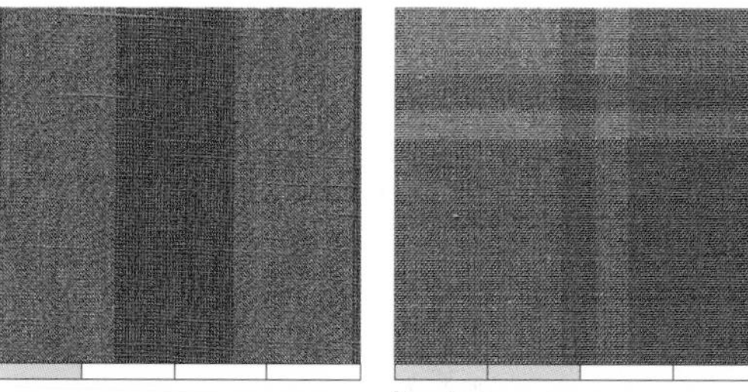
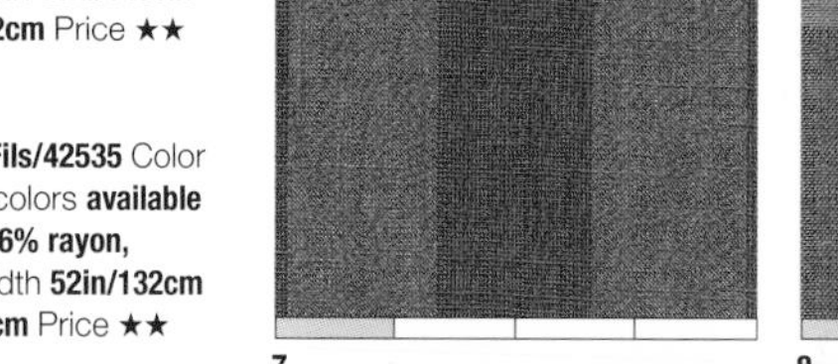

7 8

9

1 **Ian Sanderson/Glen Plaid** Color **orchid** Alternative colors **available** Composition **100% wool** Width **55in/140cm** Repeat **8½in/22cm** Price ★★

2 **Brunschwig & Fils/42535** Color **02** Alternative colors **available** Composition **86% rayon, 14% dacron** Width **52in/132cm** Repeat **1½in/4cm** Price ★★

3 **Hill & Knowles/Checkers 20952F** Color **green, beige, white** Alternative colors **available** Composition **100% cotton** Width **54in/137cm** Repeat **2¼in/5.5cm** Price ★

4 **Donghia/Quadri 0375/9300** Color **05** Alternative colors **available** Composition **100% silk** Width **55in/140cm** Repeat **1¼in/3cm** Price ★★★★★

5 **Jab/Disentis 1-2040** Color **184** Alternative colors **available** Composition **100% cotton** Width **53in/135cm** Repeat **–** Price ★★★

6 **Percheron/Tartar 7316** Color **grigio 8** Alternative colors **available** Composition **100% cotton** Width **55in/140cm** Repeat **1¾in/4.5cm** Price ★★★ LC

7 **Crowson/Zaria 03097Z91** Color **red/orange** Alternative colors **available** Composition **76% cotton, 24% viscose** Width **54in/137cm** Repeat **3in/8cm** Price ★

8 **Tissunique/St Malo 35/20341/5** Color **celadon green** Alternative colors **available** Composition **100% cotton** Width **51in/130cm** Repeat **9½in/24cm** Price ★★ W

9 **Monkwell/Mistri 05413 CU/012** Color **red and gold** Alternative colors **available** Composition **88% cotton, 12% polyacrylic** Width **54in/137cm** Repeat **3½in/9cm** Price ★★

10 Baumann Fabrics/Bristol Color **186** Alternative colors **available** Composition **90% cotton, 10% polyester** Width **59in/150cm** Repeat **1½in/3.5cm** Price ★★★

11 Jab/Samos 1-2047 Color **171** Alternative colors **available** Composition **100% cotton** Width **55in/140cm** Repeat – Price ★★★

12 Marvic Textiles/Valencia Stripe 5013 Color **browns** Alternative colors **not available** Composition **54% viscose, 46% linen** Width **55in/140cm** Repeat – Price ★★

13 Percheron/Ascot Taffeta HAP 10001 Color **cream ground** Alternative colors **available** Composition **57% viscose, 43% cotton** Width **51in/130cm** Repeat – Price ★★★

14 The Isle Mill/Kildonan STR016 Color **multi** Alternative colors **not available** Composition **100% wool** Width **55in/140cm** Repeat **5½in/14cm** Price ★★

10

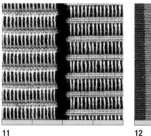

11 12 13

14

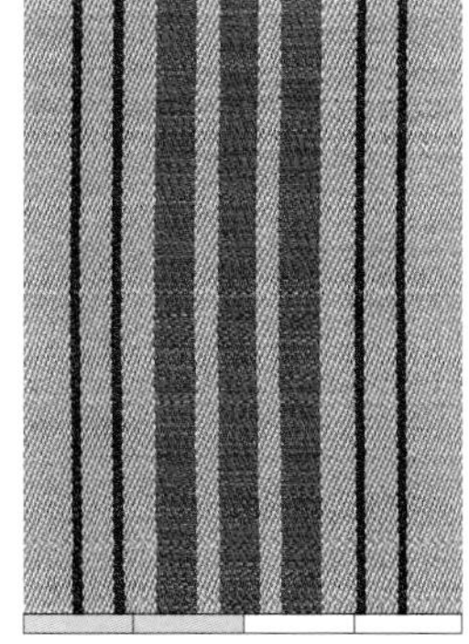

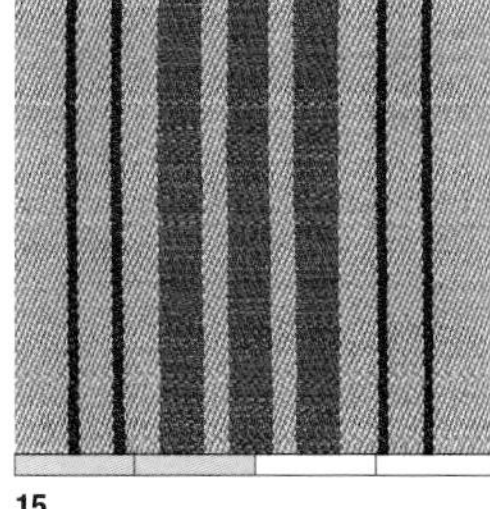

15

16

17

15 John Boyd Textiles/Ardennais AR/SK 100/74 Color **beige, black, and red** Alternative colors **available** Composition **68% horsehair, 32% cotton** Width **22in/56cm** Repeat **3in/8cm** Price ★★★★

16 Percheron/Corfu 7246-2 Color **junior navy 2** Alternative colors **available** Composition **43% viscose, 39% cotton, 18% linen** Width **55in/140cm** Repeat **4¾in/12cm** Price ★★★

17 Zimmer & Rohde/Askuni 2557 Color **347** Alternative colors **available** Composition **52% viscose, 29% cotton, 19% linen** Width **54¾in/139cm** Repeat **13¾in/35cm** Price ★★★

18 Ottilie Stevenson/Monty Check VF0052 Color **mustard** Alternative colors **available** Composition **100% cotton** Width **54in/137cm** Repeat – Price ★

18

20th century

Geometrics: **Late 20th century**

During the last three decades of the 20th century, geometric-patterned Indonesian *ikats* and Indian ginghams and madras (*see* page 170) retained their popularity as furnishing fabrics, particularly for hangings and slipcovers. Also fashionable were various ethnic weaves and prints from Africa, including the woven "kente" silks and cottons, particularly from Ghana and Nigeria, which displayed brightly colored, eclectic combinations of stripes, checks, chevrons, and other geometric forms. South American weaves, with geometric, abstract, and iconographic patterns derived from ancient Aztec and Inca cultures, were in demand, and provided inspiration for European and North American designers.

During the late 20th century, there was also a vogue for striped and checked plaids, and printed fabrics embellished with repeat classical motifs; these were either framed by traditional diaper grounds, or set within vertical stripes that resembled strips of movie film.

1

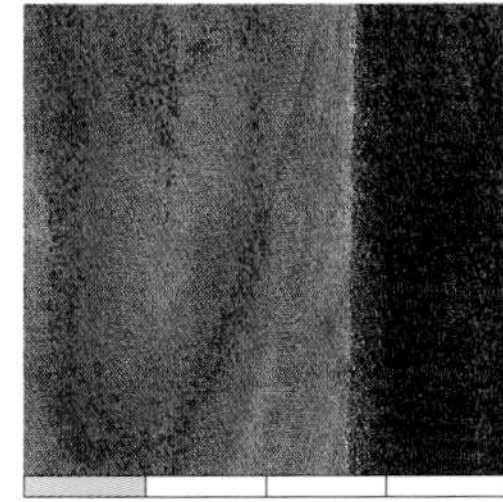

2

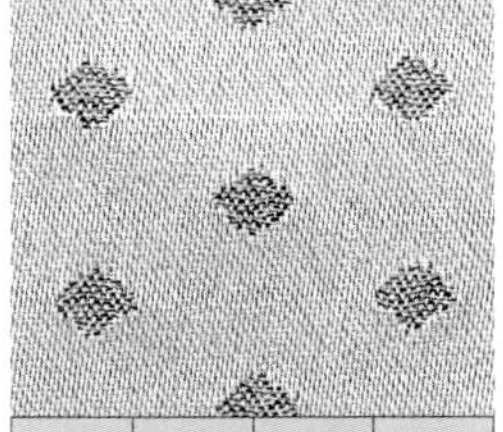

3

4

1 **Bentley & Spens/New Geometrics** Color **beige** Alternative colors **available** Composition **52% velicron modacrylic, 37% cotton, 11% nylon** Width **56½in/144cm** Repeat **19¼in/49cm** Price ★★ W

2 **Harlequin/Treviso 5606** Color **blue** Alternative colors **available** Composition **100% cotton** Width **54in/137cm** Repeat **24¾in/63.5cm** Price ★

3 **Jab/Sindbad 1-7055-146** Color **gold/cream** Alternative colors **available** Composition **88% polyester, 12% nylon** Width **59in/150cm** Repeat **–** Price ★★

4 **Anna French/Spangle** Color **78** Alternative colors **available** Composition **100% cotton** Width **54in/137cm** Repeat **18in/46cm/** Price ★★ LC

5

5 **Jim Thompson/Mirage Check P4011** Color **taupe** Alternative colors **available** Composition **100% silk** Width **48in/122cm** Repeat **1½in/4cm** Price ★★★★

6 **Ian Sanderson/Ripley Check** Color **lettuce** Alternative colors **available** Composition **100% cotton** Width **55in/140cm** Repeat **4¾in/12cm** Price ★★ LC

7 **Ian Sanderson/Box Check** Color **cornflower** Alternative colors **available** Composition **100% cotton** Width **55in/140cm** Repeat **1in/2.5cm** Price ★★

8 **Jim Thompson/Pavilion Cloth 1018** Color **01** Alternative colors **available** Composition **60% silk, 40% cotton** Width **48in/122cm** Repeat **½in/1cm** Price ★★★

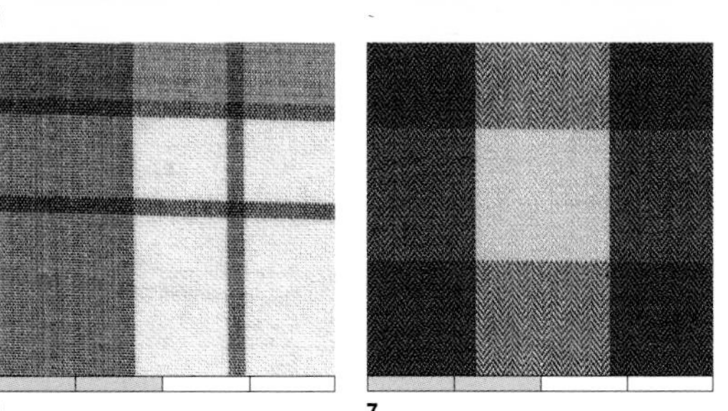

6 7

8

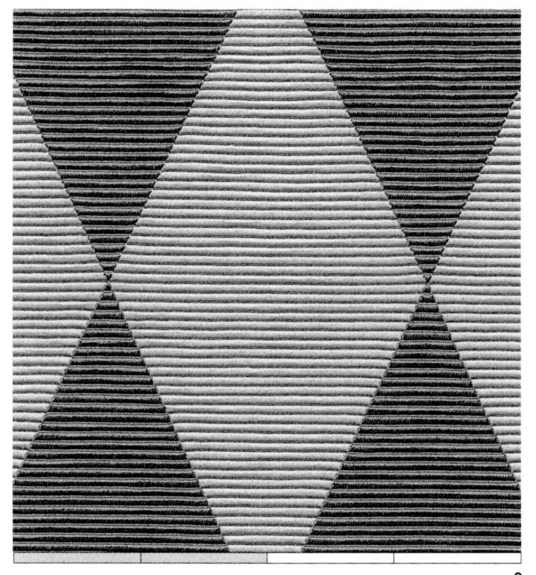

9

COLOR AND WEAVE

The plotting of "color and weave" on graph paper is a technique that is used by many textile designers to explore the effects of different combinations of patterns, yarns, and colors. It is an excellent means of experimenting with a design before committing it to the finished fabric. As designers have found, even very small adjustments in the weave or type of yarn used can produce startlingly wide variations in pattern.

Henderson Woven Designs/Sunburst Color **blue/green/orange** Alternative colors **not available** Composition **50% cotton, 25% nylon, 25% mohair** Width **6¼in/16cm** Repeat **–** Price ★★★

9 Zimmer & Rohde/Nomen 1264-707 Color **green/yellow** Alternative colors **available** Composition **80% cotton, 20% viscose** Width **55in/140cm** Repeat **3½in/9cm** Price ★★★

10 Knowles & Christou/Tambour KG208 Color **topaz** Alternative colors **available** Composition **100% cotton** Width **52in/132cm** Repeat **6in/15cm** Price ★★★

11 Knowles & Christou/Taffeta Silk Stripe Color **date** Alternative colors **available** Composition **100% silk** Width **47in/120cm** Repeat **6¼in/16cm** Price ★★★

12 Sahco Hesslein/Zeus 12109 Color **black and cream** Alternative colors **available** Composition **70% cotton, 30% Cupro** Width **53½in/136cm** Repeat **–** Price ★★★

13 Harlequin/Summer Check Color **blue/green** Alternative colors **available** Composition **100% cotton** Width **54in/137cm** Repeat **12½in/32cm** Price ★

14 Designers Guild/Isika F537/03 Color **turquoise** Alternative colors **available** Composition **100% cotton** Width **54in/137cm** Repeat **25in/64cm** Price ★★

15 Michael Szell/Safari Color **multi** Alternative colors **available** Composition **100% cotton** Width **47in/120cm** Repeat **19¾in/50cm** Price ★★

10

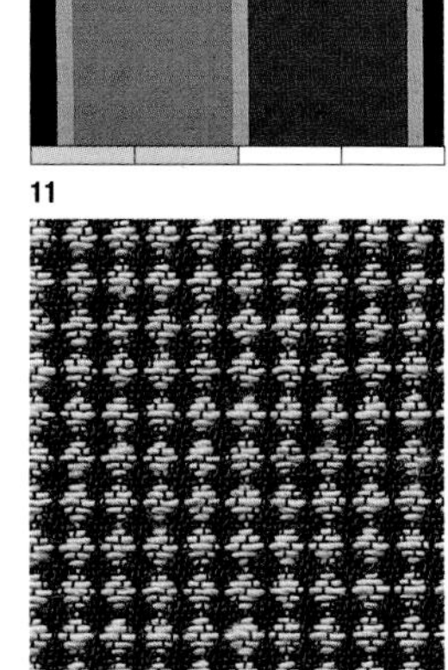

11

12

16

13

14

15

17

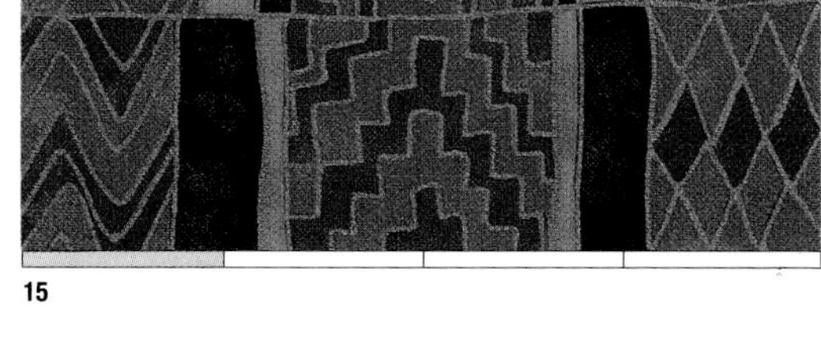

16 Designers Guild/Kashipur F517/03 Color **fuschia** Alternative colors **available** Composition **100% cotton** Width **54in/137cm** Repeat **16¼in/41cm** Price ★★

17 Elizabeth Eaton/Lanka Check Color **pink** Alternative colors **not available** Composition **100% cotton** Width **50in/127cm** Repeat **1in/2.5cm** Price ★★

Lace & Sheers

Lace is an ornamental openwork fabric that is traditionally made from flaxen thread or silk, wool, or cotton yarns. Before the late 18th century it was exclusively handmade, either by buttonhole stitching with a needle and thread (needle lace), or by twisting bobbins carrying the threads around pins outlining the pattern and stuck into a pillow (bobbin lace). A less expensive alternative is machine-woven Nottingham (or Swiss) lace, which was first produced in quantity during the early 19th century. Lace has been used as decorative bed and table covers, but it has also been employed as bed-hangings and under-curtains (sheers) designed to diffuse sunlight, provide a degree of privacy, and keep out insects. Other materials used include muslin, which is a soft, open-mesh fabric that is woven from finely spun cotton or silk; organza, a stiffer version of muslin; voile, a crisp and finely woven fabric made from cotton, silk, or synthetics; and leno, a cross-woven gauze made from natural or synthetic fibers.

RIGHT The use of lace and sheers as both under-curtains (insertions) and the main drapes in a window treatment has flourished during the 20th century, especially in bedrooms. Here, laces are simply pleated for the insertions, tassel fringed, and tied back for the main drapes, and elaborately swagged and tailed for the heading. They are coordinated with the bed-hangings, cushion covers, and bedspread, a fashion that dates back to the late 17th century.

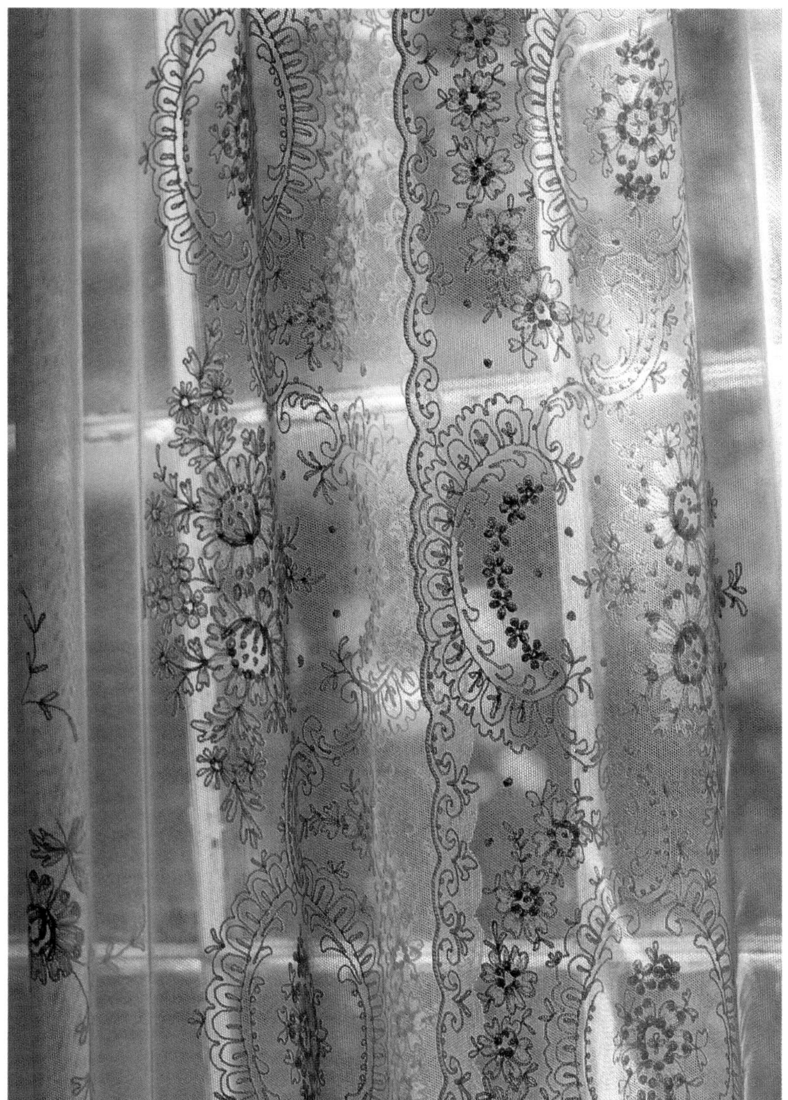

ABOVE These lace under-curtains are in a 19th-century American house. Their sage green, stylized flower-and-leaf pattern was particularly fashionable toward the end of the 19th century. Like much of the lace used in American interiors during this period, these examples are machine-made and imported from Brussels, Belgium.

ANTIQUING LACE

Pre-20th-century handmade lace is highly sought after today, and can be bought from specialist antique dealers and at textile auctions. However, it is now becoming increasingly expensive. Consequently, when asked to create a period look on a tight budget, many interior designers mimic the appearance and feel of handmade antique lace simply by soaking inexpensive, white, machine-made lace in a weak solution of cold tea (or coffee). The lace emerges with a subtle, straw-colored tint and a softer, less crisp texture than it had before the treatment.

KEY DESIGNS

1 In the 16th and 17th centuries, woven stylized floral patterns were popular on lace and sheers; more naturalistic floral weaves became fashionable during the early 19th century.

2 Stylized birds, particularly exotic Oriental species, as well as architectural components, such as pillars and arches, have been frequent embellishments to lace and sheers since the 19th century.

3 Silk bobbin net (tulle) was first produced in France at the end of the 18th century, and has been used primarily for insertions and bed-hangings, notably in hot climates as insect barriers.

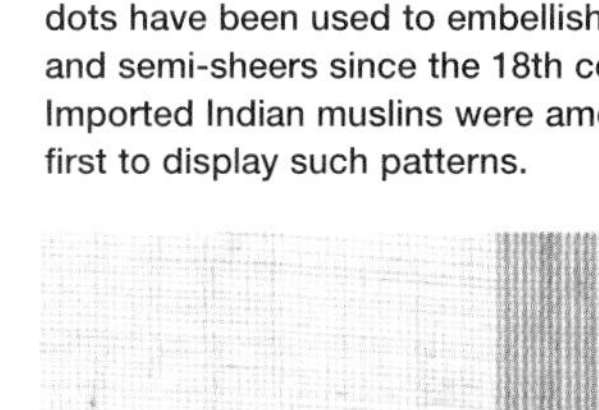

4 Repeats of small, woven or printed dots have been used to embellish sheers and semi-sheers since the 18th century. Imported Indian muslins were among the first to display such patterns.

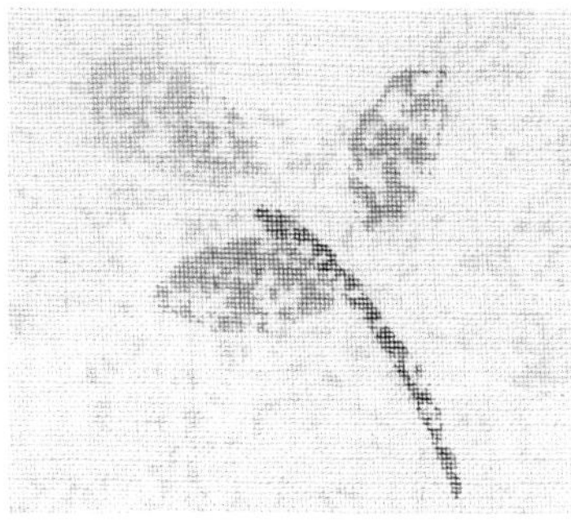

5 During the course of the 20th century, increasingly colorful patterns, mostly printed, such as this floral-and-leaf-patterned voile, have been employed on sheers and semi-sheers.

6 Before the 20th century, finely woven voiles were made from cotton or silk; thereafter, synthetic yarns have also been used. Voiles in colored stripes were fashionable during the early 19th century.

1 **Jab/Sonate** Color **white** Alternative colors **available** Composition **50% acrylic, 25% viscose, 25% polyester** Width **71in/180cm** Repeat **7½in/19cm** Price ★★★

2 **Parkertex Fabrics/My Lady's Garden** Color **white** Alternative colors **available** Composition **93% cotton, 7% polyester** Width **59in/150cm** Repeat **25in/64cm** Price ★

3 **Bennett Silks/Annelle** Color **91** Alternative colors **available** Composition **100% silk** Width **72in/180cm** Repeat – Price ★

4 **Abbott & Boyd/Visillo Plumeti** Color **white** Alternative colors **available** Composition **100% polyester** Width **118in/300cm** Repeat **¾in/2cm** Price ★★

5 **Anna French/Moss Rose Voile** Color **32** Alternative colors **available** Composition **100% cotton** Width **54in/137cm** Repeat **32¼in/82cm** Price ★★

6 **Nice Irma's/Blue Stripe Voile** Color **blue and white** Alternative colors **available** Composition **100% cotton** Width **39¼in/100cm** Repeat – Price ★

Lace & Sheers: **Pre-19th century**

During the 16th century, leading centers of lace production were established in Italy (in Venice, Genoa, and Milan), the Netherlands (in Brussels, Mechlin, and Antwerp), and Spain and Portugal; during the 17th century they were established in France (in Alençon, Argenton, Paris, and Chantilly) and England (in Honiton). Lace production in the United States took hold during the 18th century, notably in Ipswich, Massachusetts. Fashionable needle lace included *Punto in Aria*, *Gros Point*, *Point Plat*, *Point de Neige* ("Venetian"), *Point de France,* and *Hollie Point*. From the early 17th century, bobbin lace was produced in greater quantity and was equally sought after. Popular patterns included stylized flowers linked by scrolling stems, and Moorish geometric designs such as the wheel and the sun.

Throughout this period, handmade lace was used for bed and table covers and bed-hangings, but rarely for under-curtains. However, many shutterless 17th- and 18th-century windows were covered with "sashes" (thin silks or linens stretched over frames and soaked with oil to make them transparent). Sheers draped at 18th-century windows included "quinze-seize" (thin taffeta), leno (a gauze often painted with Indian motifs), and Indian muslin (white or cream and sometimes woven with a ribbed stripe or small motif).

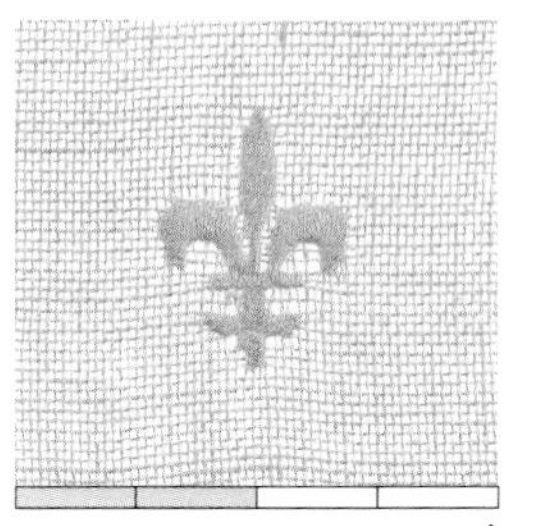

1

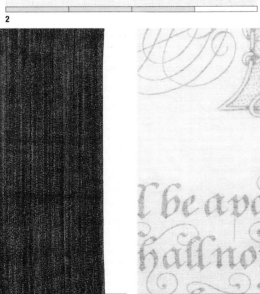

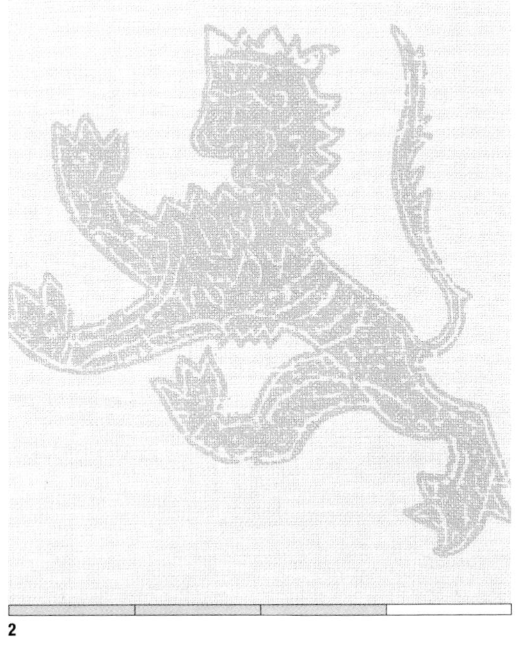

2

3

4

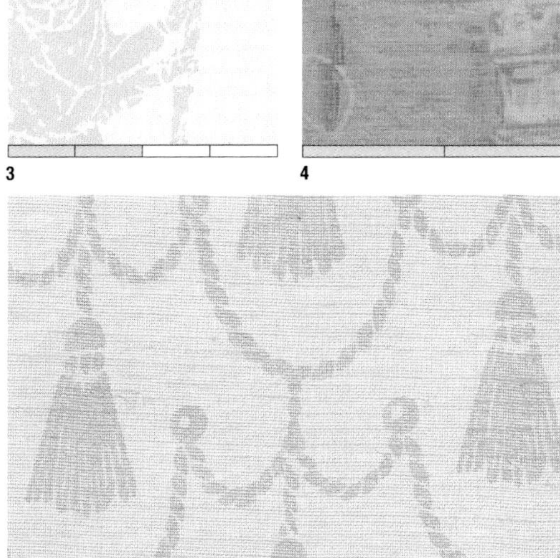

5

6

7

1 **Interdesign/Rio Fleur de Lys 2301/3** Color **white** Alternative colors **available** Composition **100% linen** Width **82½in/210cm** Repeat – Price ★★★★

2 **Knowles & Christou/Cardoban Lion KSC03** Color **white** Alternative colors **available** Composition **60% polyester, 40% cotton** Width **47in/120cm** Repeat **9½in/24cm** Price ★★

3 **Knowles & Christou/Angels KSC05** Color **white** Alternative colors **available** Composition **60% polyester, 40% cotton** Width **47in/120cm** Repeat **9½in/24cm** Price ★★

4 **Claremont Fabrics/Campanile JOL COA** Color **green** Alternative colors **available** Composition **100% polyester** Width **55in/140cm** Repeat **27in/69cm** Price ★

5 **Ian Sanderson/Curtain Call Gala** Color **ecru** Alternative colors **available** Composition **90% polyester, 10% linen** Width **57in/145cm** Repeat **2¾in/7cm** Price ★

6 **Thomas Dare/Vivaldi Tapestry VIV 266 530** Color **blue/red/yellow** Alternative colors **available** Composition **100% silk** Width **47in/120cm** Repeat **7½in/19cm** Price ★★

7 **Crowson/Script 02579S97** Color **02** Alternative colors **available** Composition **67% polyester, 33% cotton** Width **54in/137cm** Repeat **25in/64cm** Price ★

8 Nice Irma's/Yellow Stripe Voile Color **yellow and white striped** Alternative colors **available** Composition **100% cotton** Width **40¼in/102cm** Repeat **16in/40.5cm** Price ★

9 Claremont Fabrics/Domino V05 D18 Color **claret** Alternative colors **available** Composition **100% polyester** Width **55in/140cm** Repeat **6¾in/17cm** Price ★

10 Firifiss/Luna 74030 Color **Alpes 3** Alternative colors **available** Composition **100% cotton** Width **59¾in/152cm** Repeat **48in/122cm** Price ★★

11 Hill & Knowles/Fantasy Voiles–Cherubim VF91F Color **white on white** Alternative colors **available** Composition **67% polyester, 33% cotton** Width **59in/150cm** Repeat **25in/64cm** Price ★

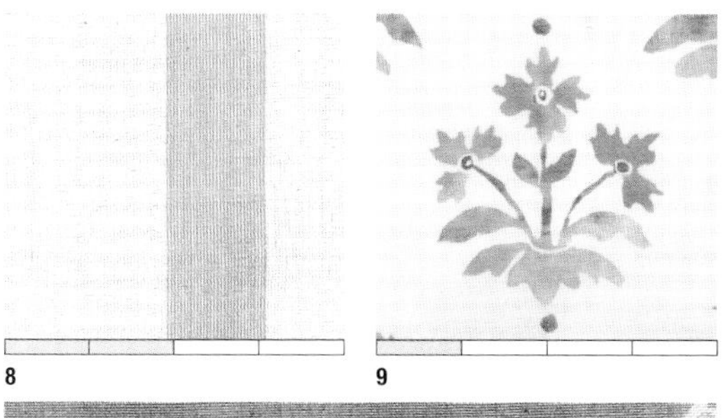

8

9

10

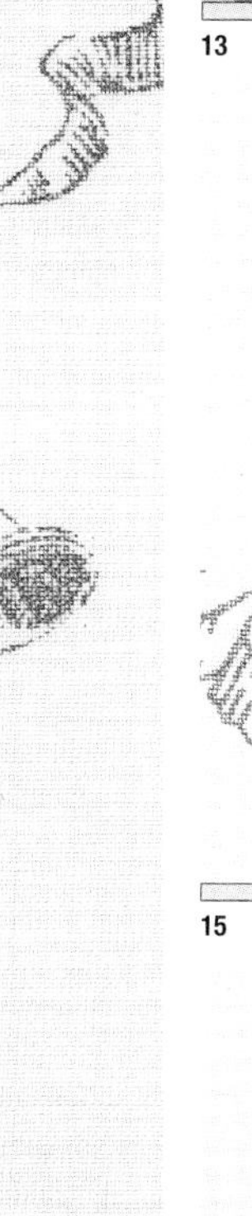

11

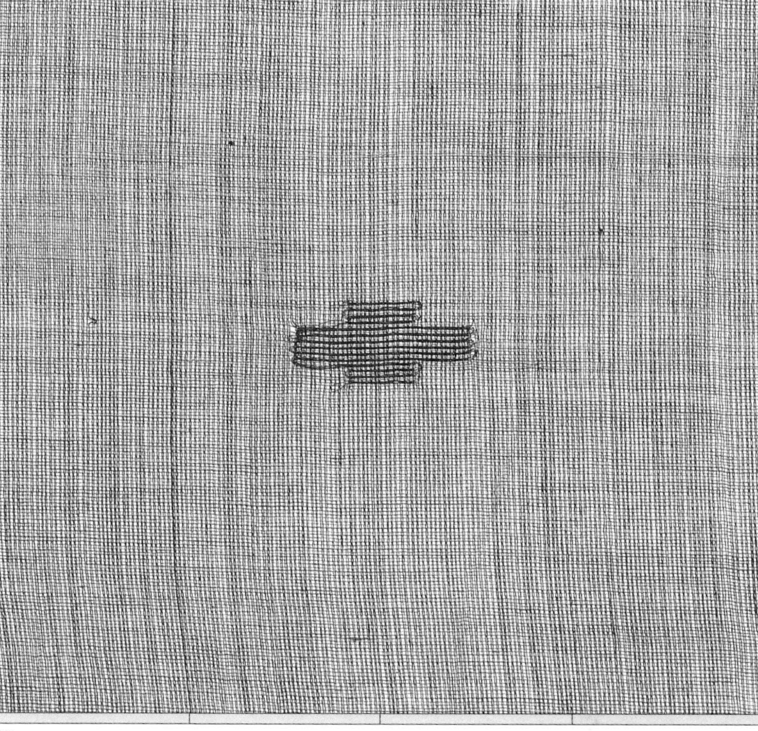

12

12 Nice Irma's/Voile Color **burnt orange on gold** Alternative colors **available** Composition **100% cotton** Width **39¾in/101cm** Repeat **–** Price ★

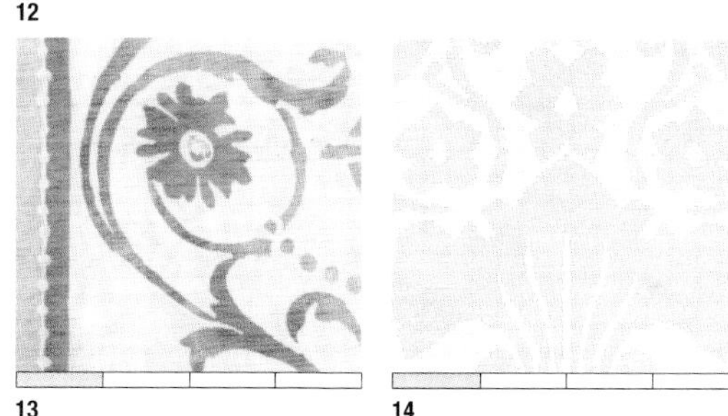

13

14

13 Claremont Fabrics/Terazzo JOL T08 Color **ocher** Alternative colors **available** Composition **100% polyester** Width **55in/140cm** Repeat **25in/64cm** Price ★

14 Bernard Thorp & Co/French Damask Color **white** Alternative colors **not available** Composition **91% polyester, 9% flax/linen** Width **47in/120cm** Repeat **34¼in/87cm** Price ★★

15 Hill & Knowles/Jubilee Voiles VJ25F Color **gold on cream** Alternative colors **available** Composition **67% polyester, 33% cotton** Width **59in/150cm** Repeat **29½in/75cm** Price ★

16 Hill & Knowles/Fantasy Voiles–Calligraphy VK31F Color **gold on cream** Alternative colors **available** Composition **67% polyester, 33% cotton** Width **59in/150cm** Repeat **25in/64cm** Price ★

17 Bennett Silks/Como 5111DCO Color **54170L** Alternative colors **available** Composition **100% silk** Width **41¼in/105cm** Repeat **35in/89cm** Price ★★★

15

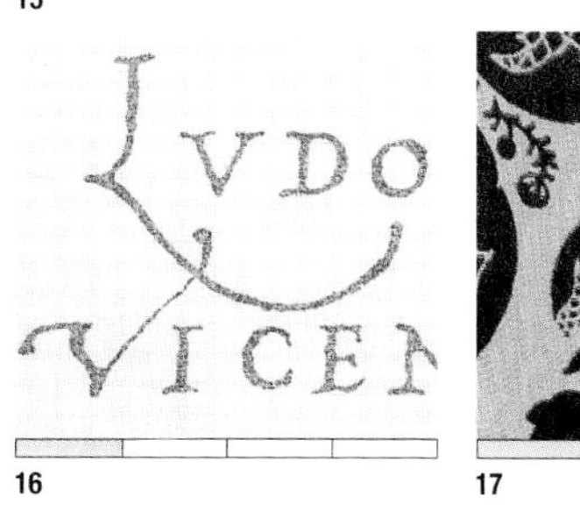

16

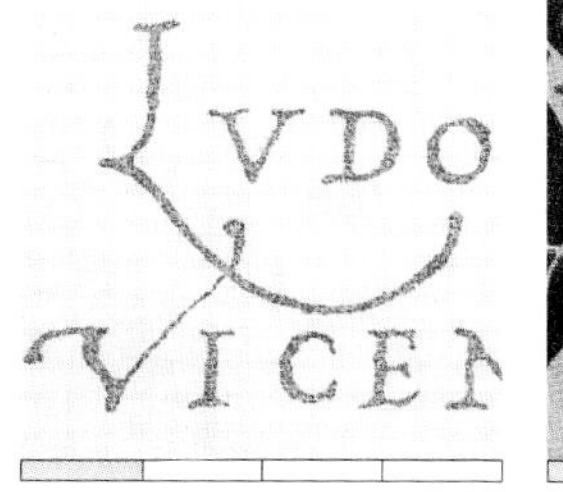

17

Lace & Sheers: **19th century**

By the early 19th century, under-curtains had become a fairly standard window treatment in fashionable European (particularly English Regency and French Empire) and American Federal interiors. Thin silks or muslin (the latter by this time made in Europe and America, as well as in India) were the preferred choice, and in many cases they were augmented with delicate fringing or border designs in contrasting colors–green or yellow on white being a popular combination.

The production of lace had undergone a revolution throughout Europe and America at the end of the 18th century. Expensive handmade lace was still being manufactured in traditional centers of production (*see* page 176), but the invention of cheaper, machine-woven lace dramatically expanded the market to include less affluent homeowners. Made in large quantities in Nottingham, England, machine-woven lace was largely intended for use as more decorative under-curtains and bed-hangings, and featured exuberant patterns of hothouse flowers and other designs derived from 16th- and 17th-century handmade lace.

1

2

3

4

5

6

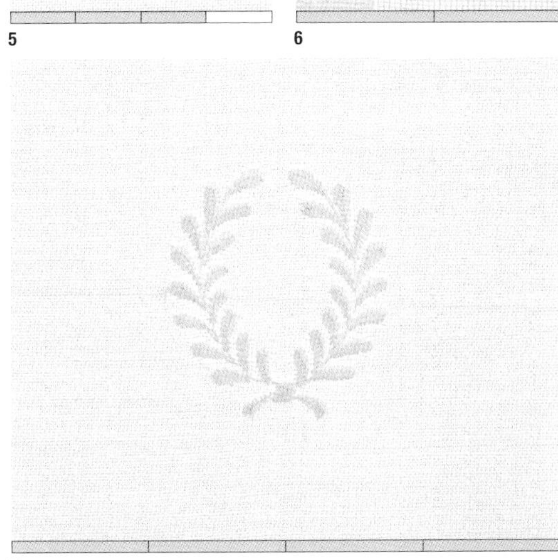
7

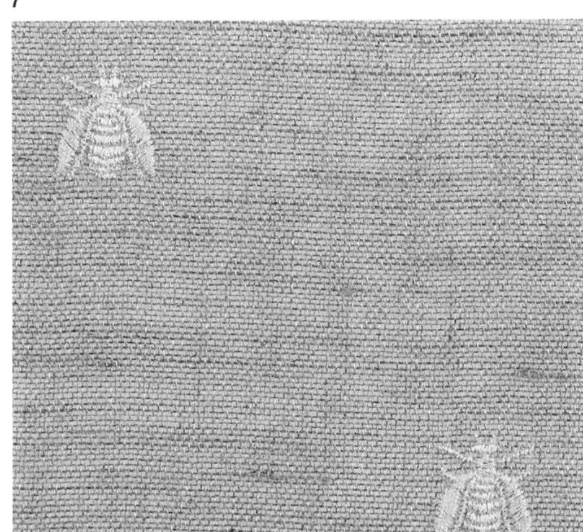
8

1 **Old World Weavers/Vera Sheer B/1886S0108** Color **multi** Alternative colors **available** Composition **100% cotton** Width **54¾in/139cm** Repeat **38in/97cm** Price ★★★★

2 **Sahco Hesslein/Mizar 16012** Color **white** Alternative colors **not available** Composition **70% cotton, 30% polyester** Width **118in/300cm** Repeat **24¾in/63cm** Price ★★★

3 **Anna French/Fondant Lace** Color **68** Alternative colors **available** Composition **100% cotton** Width **59in/150cm** Repeat **28¼in/72cm** Price ★★

4 **Elizabeth Eaton/Muslin 59908** Color **white** Alternative colors **not available** Composition **100% cotton** Width **59in/150cm** Repeat **4in/10cm** Price ★★

5 **Hill & Knowles/Pineapples VP61F** Color **white** Alternative colors **available** Composition **67% polyester, 33% cotton** Width **59in/150cm** Repeat **5in/13cm** Price ★

6 **Sanderson/Rococo BL6420/1** Color **off white** Alternative colors **available** Composition **100% cotton** Width **48in/122cm** Repeat **23¾in/60cm** Price ★★

7 **Elizabeth Eaton/Muslin 9550/3837** Color **ivoire** Alternative colors **available** Composition **100% cotton** Width **59in/150cm** Repeat **4¼in/11cm** Price ★★

8 **Interdesign/Ric Api 230/09** Color **tan** Alternative colors **available** Composition **100% linen** Width **63in/160cm** Repeat **4¾in/12cm** Price ★★★★

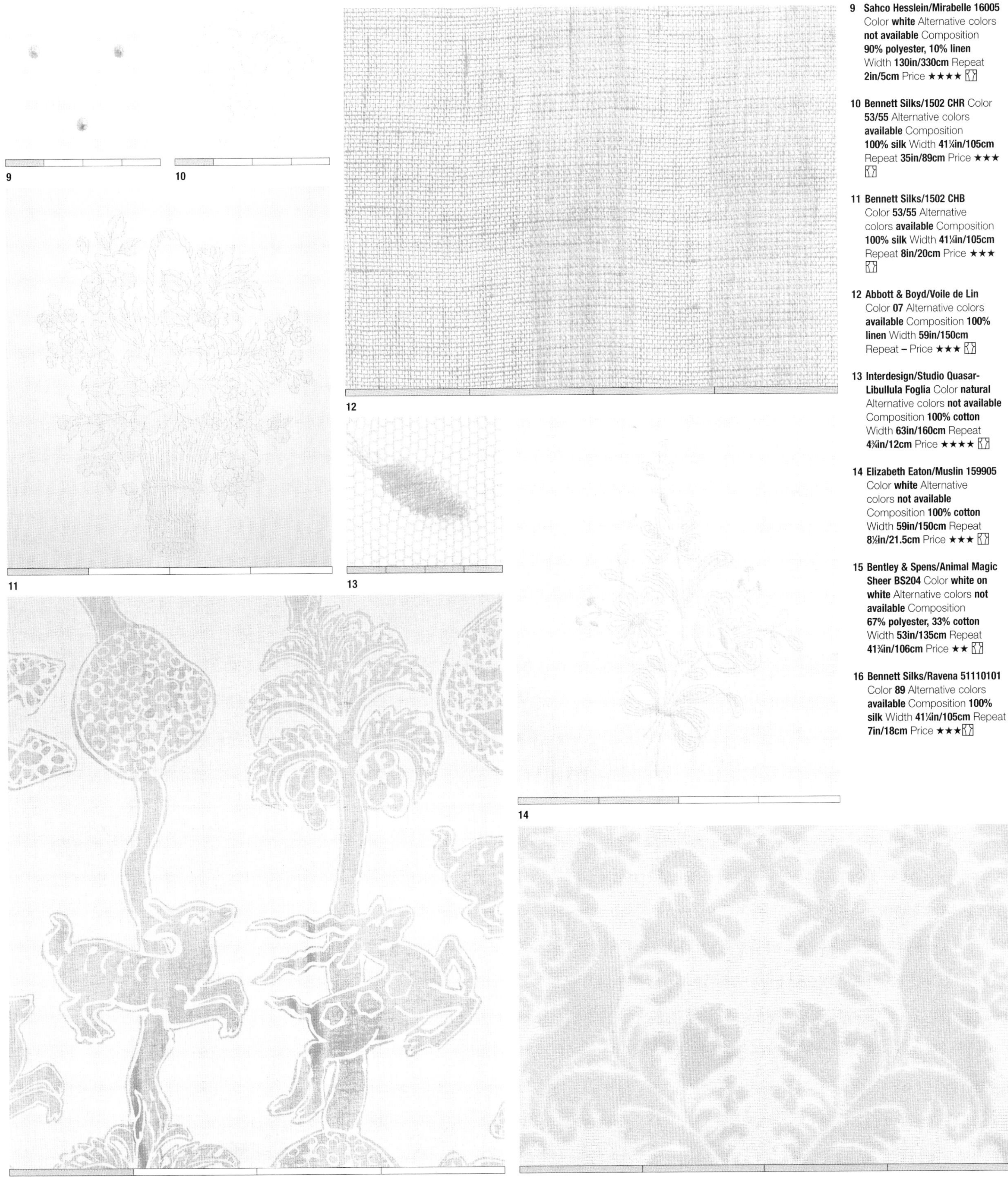

9

10

11

12

13

14

15

16

9 Sahco Hesslein/Mirabelle 16005 Color **white** Alternative colors **not available** Composition **90% polyester, 10% linen** Width **130in/330cm** Repeat **2in/5cm** Price ★★★★

10 Bennett Silks/1502 CHR Color **53/55** Alternative colors **available** Composition **100% silk** Width **41¼in/105cm** Repeat **35in/89cm** Price ★★★

11 Bennett Silks/1502 CHB Color **53/55** Alternative colors **available** Composition **100% silk** Width **41¼in/105cm** Repeat **8in/20cm** Price ★★★

12 Abbott & Boyd/Voile de Lin Color **07** Alternative colors **available** Composition **100% linen** Width **59in/150cm** Repeat **–** Price ★★★

13 Interdesign/Studio Quasar-Libullula Foglia Color **natural** Alternative colors **not available** Composition **100% cotton** Width **63in/160cm** Repeat **4¾in/12cm** Price ★★★★

14 Elizabeth Eaton/Muslin 159905 Color **white** Alternative colors **not available** Composition **100% cotton** Width **59in/150cm** Repeat **8½in/21.5cm** Price ★★★

15 Bentley & Spens/Animal Magic Sheer BS204 Color **white on white** Alternative colors **not available** Composition **67% polyester, 33% cotton** Width **53in/135cm** Repeat **41¾in/106cm** Price ★★

16 Bennett Silks/Ravena 51110101 Color **89** Alternative colors **available** Composition **100% silk** Width **41¼in/105cm** Repeat **7in/18cm** Price ★★★

Lace & Sheers: **Early 20th century**

Around the beginning of the 20th century, a reaction set in to the extensive use of lace and sheers in 19th-century interiors. In some quarters this was an aesthetic judgement–the American writer Edith Wharton dismissed them, particularly at windows, on the grounds that "lingerie effects do not commune well with architecture." Other commentators were more concerned with the welfare of the homeowner. For example, the English architect and writer Charles Eastlake believed it was healthier to sleep without being surrounded by layers of (dust trap) draperies, and thus recommended metal or wooden bedsteads without hangings, although he did make an exception for warm, humid climates, such as the southern states of America and Australia, where muslin or organza could be draped over a four-poster or half-tester, or from a corona, to protect sleepers from mosquitoes and other insects.

However, with the exception of Eastlake, whose views proved to be highly influential in America, most householders during the first half of the 20th century chose to ignore such advice and continued to employ sheers such as muslin, organza, and voile at windows. Favored patterns included woven stripes and woven or printed spots and figurative patterns.

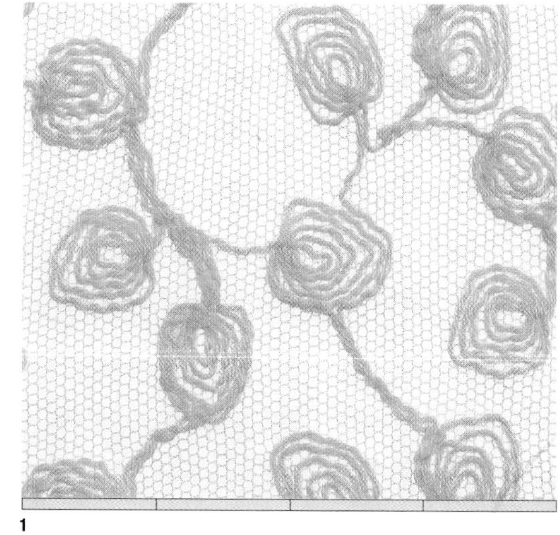

1

2

4

3

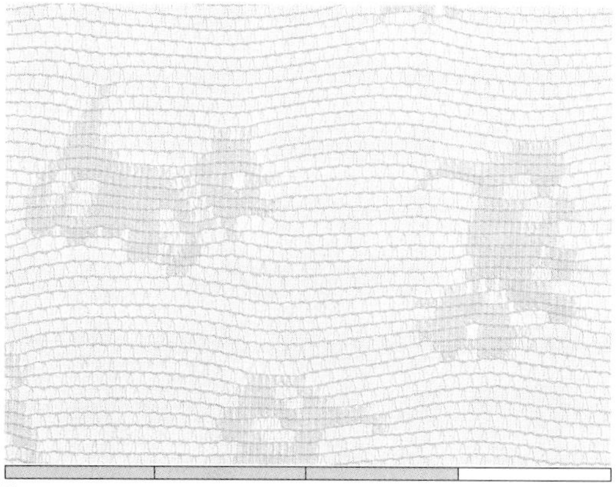

5

6

1 **Interdesign/Studio Quasar–Fiore** Color **natural** Alternative colors **not available** Composition **100% cotton** Width **63in/160cm** Repeat **4¾in/12cm** Price ★★★★

2 **Hill & Knowles/Jubilee Voiles Ghost Stripe VC95F** Color **gold on cream** Alternative colors **available** Composition **67% polyester, 33% cotton** Width **59in/150cm** Repeat **–** Price ★

3 **Anna French/Collioure Madras** Color **white** Alternative colors **available** Composition **100% cotton** Width **68¾in/175cm** Repeat **21in/53cm** Price ★★★

4 **Anna French/Savernak Lace** Color **white** Alternative colors **available** Composition **100% cotton** Width **59in/150cm** Repeat **22in/56cm** Price ★★

5 **Scalamandré/Angus 26366-001** Color **white** Alternative colors **not available** Composition **95% cotton, 5% polyester** Width **59½in/151cm** Repeat **–** Price ★★★

6 **Jab/Eleganza 7324** Color **197** Alternative colors **available** Composition **55% polyester, 45% silk** Width **47in/120cm** Repeat **11in/28cm** Price ★★★★★

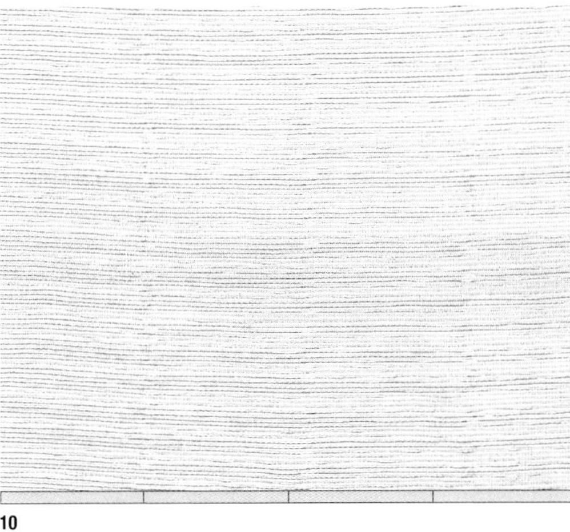

10

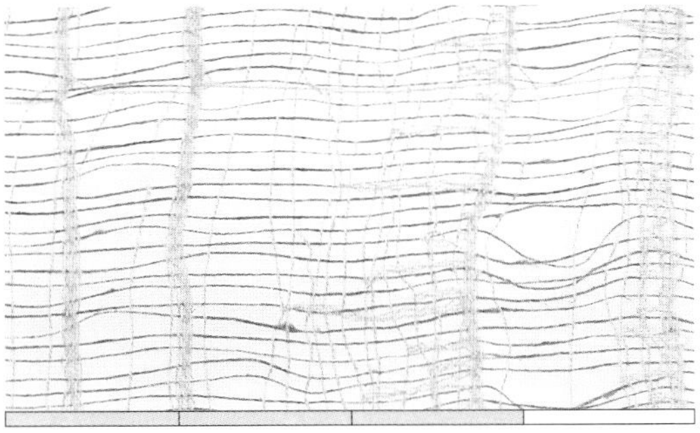

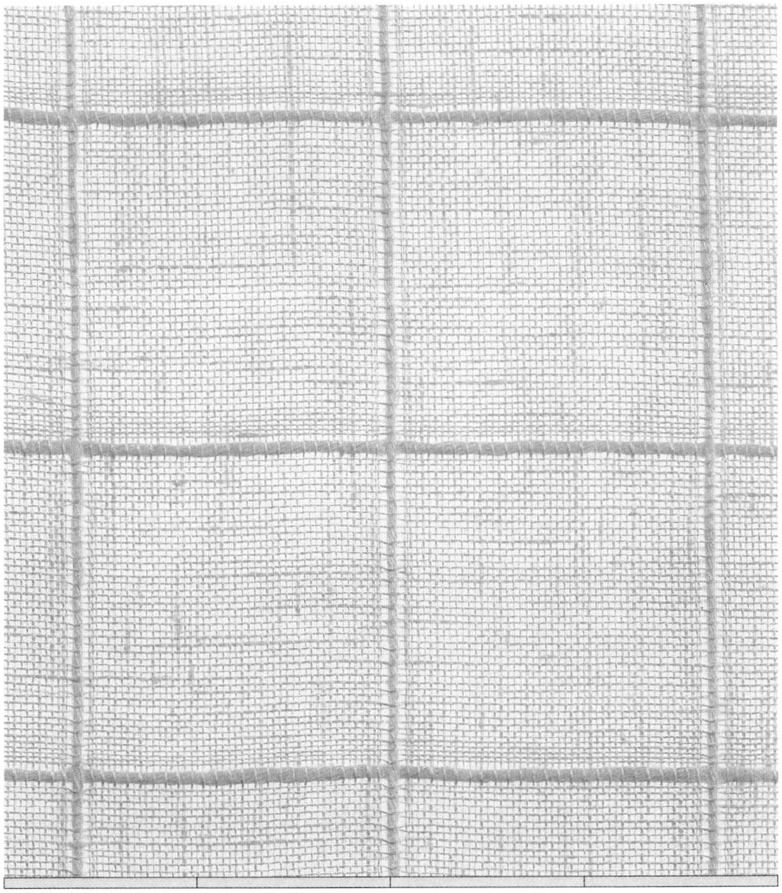

COLORED SHEERS

Historically, most sheers–particularly muslins and organzas–have been produced either in white or "off-white" colors. However, colored versions have proved very fashionable, notably during the 20th century. While very pale pastel-colored sheers are widely available, it is worth bearing in mind that when they are exposed to strong sunlight their coloring can be rendered overly subtle. To compensate for this, slightly stronger tones, such as the blue and green shown below, can be employed.

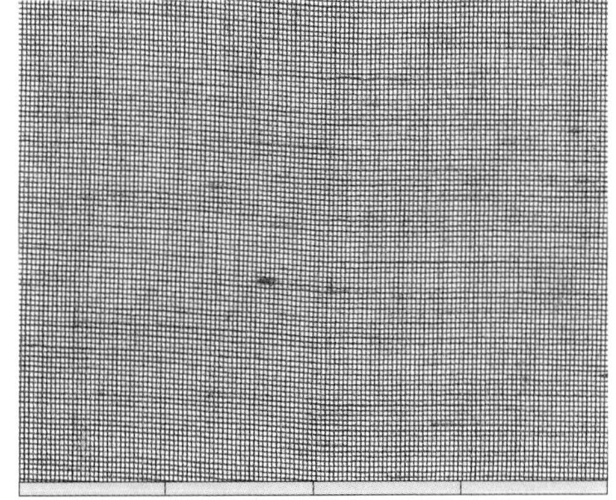

Crowson/Cashel 03097 CC9 Color **11** Alternative colors **available** Composition **67% polyester, 33% cotton** Width **54in/137cm** Repeat **25in/64cm** Price ★

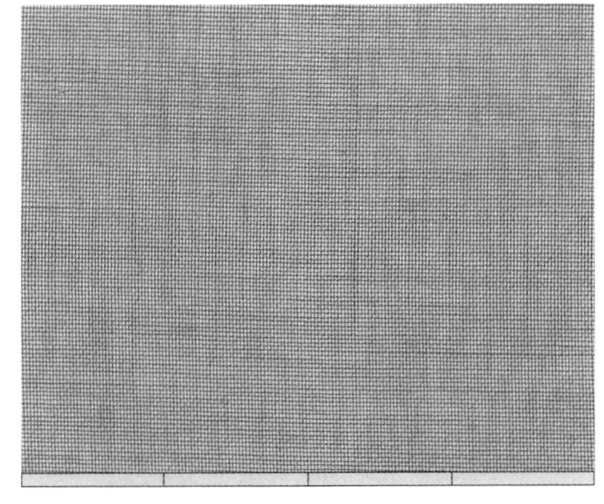

Baumann Fabrics/Sinfonia Color **730** Alternative colors **available** Composition **100% polyester** Width **118in/300cm** Repeat – Price ★

7 **Garin/Pling 1532** Color **white** Alternative colors **available** Composition **64% cotton, 36% linen** Width **59in/150cm** Repeat – Price ★★

8 **Donghia/Rete 0378/9335-10** Color **ecru** Alternative colors **available** Composition **100% linen** Width **51in/130cm** Repeat – Price ★★★★

9 **Celia Birtwell/Classical Stripe French Voile** Color **yellow and white** Alternative colors **available** Composition **67% polyester, 33% cotton** Width **55in/140cm** Repeat **25in/64cm** Price ★★

10 **Sahco Hesslein/Gold 50401** Color **gold** Alternative colors **not available** Composition **64% metal, 26% cotton, 10% polyester** Width **62¼in/158cm** Repeat – Price ★★★

11 **Sanderson/Foursome BL6437/1** Color **cream** Alternative colors **available** Composition **100% cotton** Width **59in/150cm** Repeat **1½in/4cm** Price ★★

20th century

Lace & Sheers: **Late 20th century**

During the second half of the 20th century there was renewed demand for traditional handmade lace, particularly for use as decorative bedcovers. Machine-woven lace, notably incorporating floral, animal, and bird patterns, was a popular choice for under-curtains in period houses, while plain or patterned muslin, organza, and voile sheers–the latter more often made from synthetic fibers–was widely employed as bed-hangings.

Although these fabrics were used to some extent in the first half of the 20th century, manufacturers increasingly produced colored versions such as pastel lemons, plaster pinks, pale blues, blue-grays, and warm hues. Other trends included stretching sheers over wooden frames to make screens or room dividers that were similar to traditional Japanese *shojis*; these were especially well suited to large warehouse conversions and to loft apartments. The 19th-century practice of bordering sheers such as muslin with contrasting fabrics was further developed by some designers in the 20th century, who alternated and joined strips of semitransparent muslin with strips of closely woven fabrics, such as damask or leather, to produce weblike effects.

1

2

3

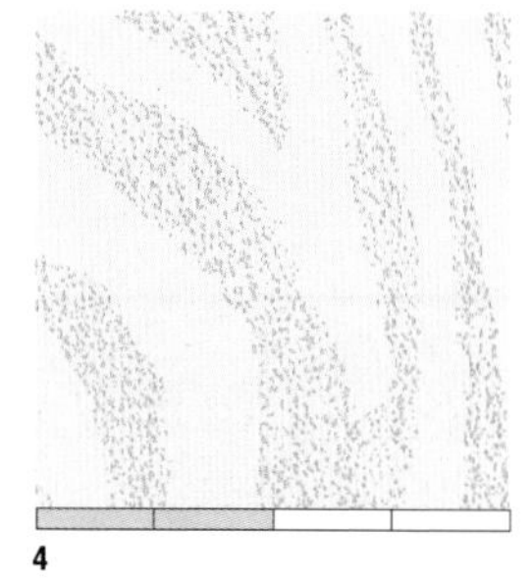

4

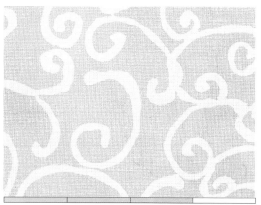

1 **Sahco Hesslein/Obelisk 50386** Color **cream** Alternative colors **available** Composition **100% polyester** Width **53in/135cm** Repeat **31½in/80cm** Price ★★★

2 **Elizabeth Eaton/Muslin** Color **white** Alternative colors **not available** Composition **100% cotton** Width **59in/150cm** Repeat **4¾in/12cm** Price ★★

3 **Bentley & Spens/Cornelli Sheers B50712** Color **white on white** Alternative colors **not available** Composition **67% polyester, 33% cotton** Width **51in/130cm** Repeat **23¾in/60cm** Price ★★

4 **Hill & Knowles/Zebra VW14F** Color **gold on cream** Alternative colors **available** Composition **67% polyester, 33% cotton** Width **59in/150cm** Repeat **25in/64cm** Price ★

5 **Hill & Knowles/Columbine Star VG97F** Color **gold/cream** Alternative colors **available** Composition **67% polyester, 33% cotton** Width **59in/150cm** Repeat **12½in/32cm** Price ★

SEMI-SHEERS

The main difference between sheers and semi-sheers is their degree of translucency. Sheers such as muslin, organza, and voile are highly translucent, and therefore they allow considerable quantities of diffused light to enter a room. At the same time, however, sheers can provide some degree of privacy without completely obliterating the view. The semi-sheers, which are more opaque, are generally made from half-silks, open-weave linens, taffetas, cottons, and synthetic fabrics.

1

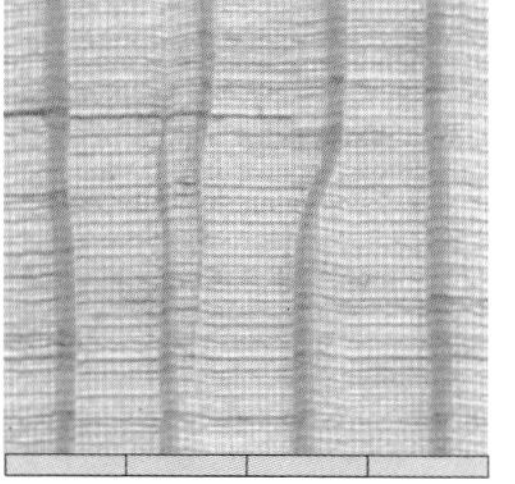

2

1 **Jack Lenor Larsen/Luminescence** Color **topaz** Alternative colors **available** Composition **66% metal, 22% cotton, 12% polyester** Width **55in/140cm** Repeat – Price ★★★

2 **Sahco Hesslein/Caprice 50262** Color **gold** Alternative colors **available** Composition **50% viscose, 21% silk, 15% acrylic, 14% linen** Width **55in/140cm** Repeat – Price ★★★

5

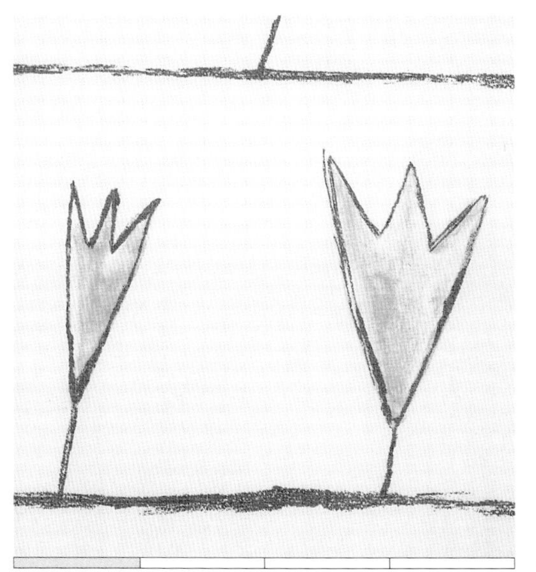

6

7

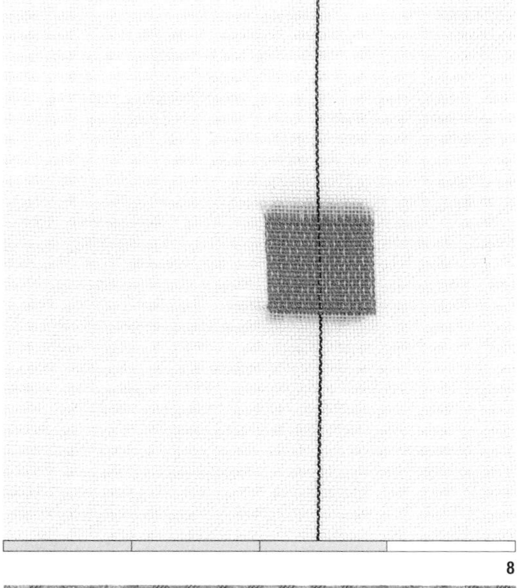

8

6 Garin/Mayo 3159 Color **peach** Alternative colors **available** Composition **100% cotton** Width **59in/150cm** Repeat **35¾in/91cm** Price ★★★

7 Hill & Knowles/Pigs Promenade VW47F Color **gold on cream** Alternative colors **available** Composition **67% polyester, 33% cotton** Width **59in/150cm** Repeat **12½in/32cm** Price ★

8 Garin/Rut 5327 Color **blues on white** Alternative colors **available** Composition **100% polyester** Width **59in/150cm** Repeat **3½in/9cm** Price ★★

9 Interdesign/Ricamati Color **natural** Alternative colors **available** Composition **100% cotton** Width **106¼in/270cm** Repeat **4¾in/12cm** Price ★★★★

10 Hill & Knowles/Feather Dance VF86F Alternative colors **gold on cream** Alternative colors **available** Composition **67% polyester, 33% cotton** Width **59in/150cm** Repeat **25in/64cm** Price ★

11 Bentley & Spens/Shells B5044 Voile Color **bronze, silver, white** Alternative colors **not available** Composition **67% polyester, 33% cotton** Width **52¾in/134cm** Repeat **26¼in/67cm** Price ★★

9

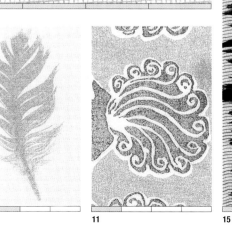

10

11

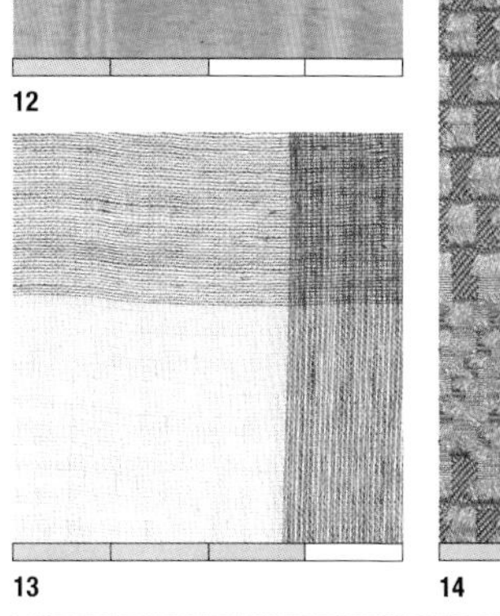

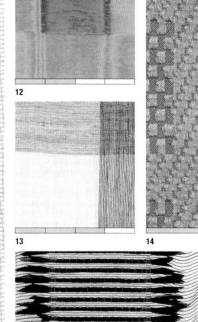

12

13

14

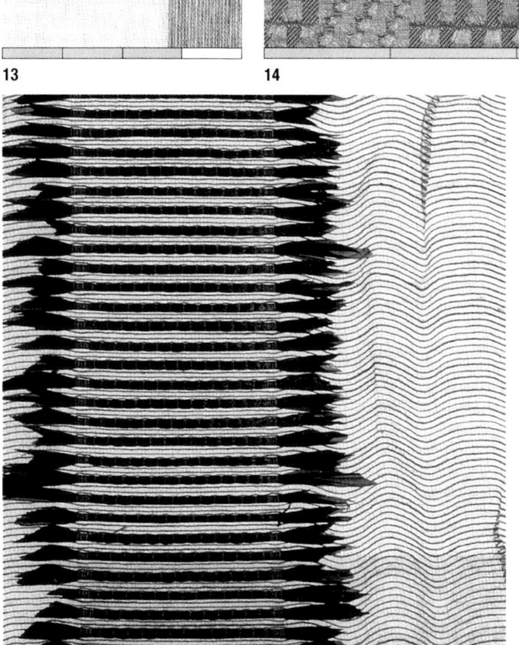

15

12 Sahco Hesslein/Carnival 50179 Color **pink** Alternative colors **available** Composition **72% acrylic, 22% silk, 6% linen** Width **59in/150cm** Repeat **8¼in/21cm** Price ★★★

13 Designers Guild/Oola F495/08 Color **fuchsia** Alternative colors **available** Composition **100% cotton** Width **45¼in/115cm** Repeat **4in/10cm** Price ★

14 Jack Lenor Larsen/Fielding 7478-01 Color **hazelnut** Alternative colors **available** Composition **100% polyester** Width **44in/112cm** Repeat **2¼in/6cm** Price ★★★

15 Sahco Hesslein/Uris 50271 Color **gray** Alternative colors **available** Composition **55% viscose, 24% cotton, 21% linen** Width **61in/155cm** Repeat **–** Price ★★★

Braids & Trimmings

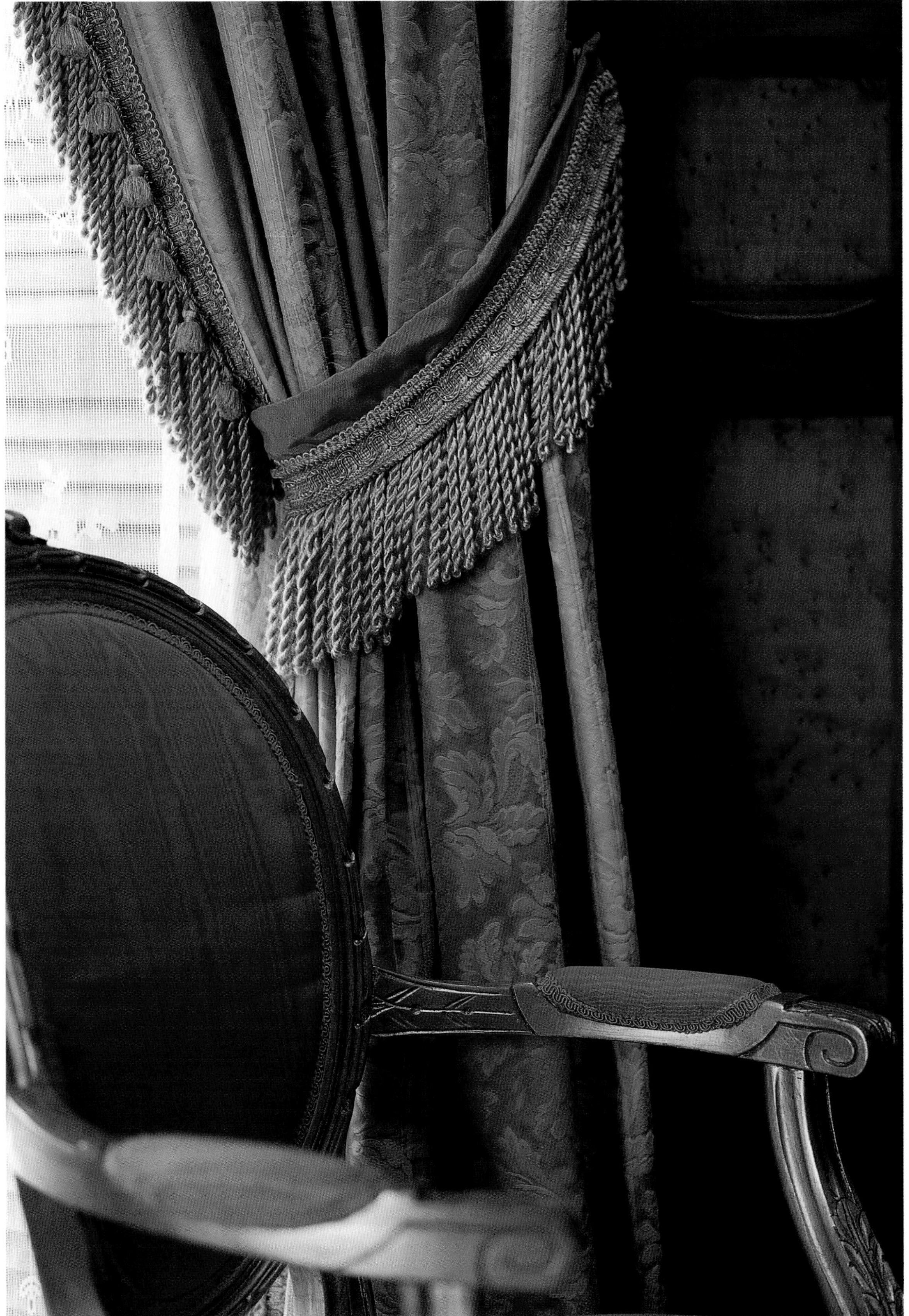

Decorative hand-sewn trimmings (*passements*), such as tassels, fringing, braids, and galloons (tapes and ribbons), were originally designed to disguise the seams and edges of wall-, bed-, and window-hangings. In the 15th and 16th centuries *passements* were popular in Italy, but they were rarely used elsewhere. However, in the 17th century, following the emigration of skilled Milanese textile workers to the court of Louis XIV of France, *passements* became fashionable among the French nobility. And, as drapery and upholstered furniture became more common in the houses of other sections of society, demand for decorative trimmings grew. Much of this was met by the French Huguenot communities who, in order to escape religious persecution, emigrated at the end of the century from France to England, Ireland, Switzerland, Germany, and the Netherlands at the end of the century, taking their *passementerie* skills with them. The result was a proliferation of these intricate trimmings throughout Europe and, later, America, during the 18th and 19th centuries. Demand for *passements* has continued to this day.

LEFT This oval-back gilt armchair at the Calhoun Mansion in Charleston, South Carolina, features edging braid around the pink moiré silk upholstery. It is coordinated with the wire-braid tiebacks and the deep bullion fringing on the silk damask curtains.

ABOVE These silk damask curtains at the 19th-century Calhoun Mansion (*see* opposite) were designed to imitate mid-19th-century originals. They are edged with multicolored, rope-twist bullion fringing made from silk.

CAMPAIGN FRINGE

Numerous styles of decorative trimmings for curtains and upholstery have been produced since the 15th century, including fringes made up of braid (or sometimes rope), from which hang a row or rows of tassels. Often highly elaborate, most tassels were worked around wooden forms carved in a variety of shapes, such as arrows, domes, and balls. However, the most enduringly popular type of edging has proved to be the "campaign fringe." First devised in Italy in the 17th century, it is so called because the tassels have a bell-like shape, the Italian for bell being *campana*.

KEY DESIGNS

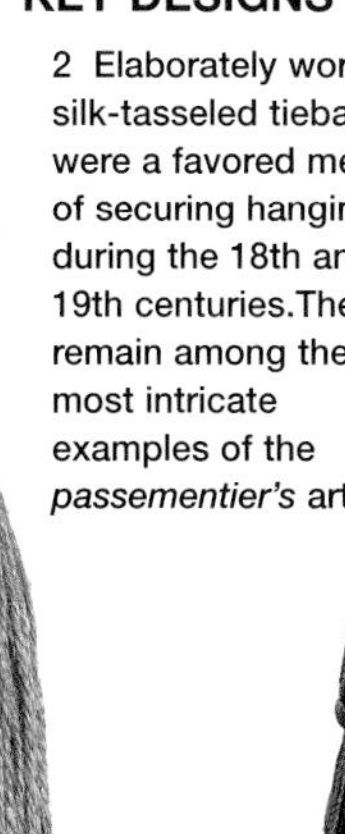

1 While the tops of many of the tassels produced since the Renaissance have been worked around plain wooden forms, some have been enclosed within decorative forms made from carved wood, cut glass, or engraved or plain metal. This tassel is made of jute and bound with a simple tin band.

2 Elaborately worked silk-tasseled tiebacks were a favored means of securing hangings during the 18th and 19th centuries.They remain among the most intricate examples of the *passementier's* art.

3 Bullion fringe, which was originally made from gold or silver thread, has been in widespread use as a decorative edging for curtains, pelmets, and upholstery since the mid-19th century.

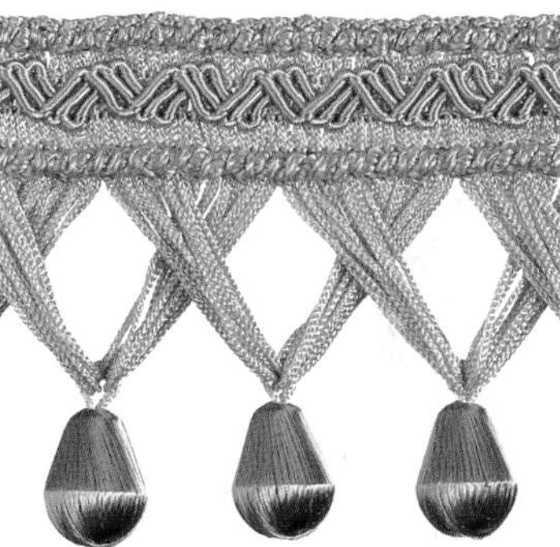

4 Decorative braid edgings, such as this silk campaign fringe featured prominently on curtains, pelmets, upholstery, cushions, and lamp shades in Victorian interiors.

5 Ribbons and galloons (tapes and ribbons) have been produced in numerous patterns and colors from the Renaissance onward. This example is designed to be used as a disguise for upholstery seams.

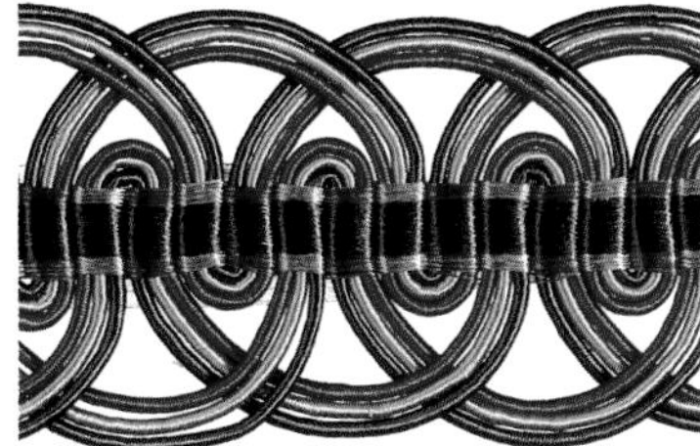

6 Multicolored, interlaced braids were especially popular during the last quarter of the 19th century. This particular design, however, can be traced back to 17th-century France when such braids were in fashion among the nobility.

1 **V. V. Rouleaux/Tin Tassel** Color **jute** Alternative colors **available** Composition **100% jute, tin** Depth **6in/15cm** Width **–** Price ★

2 **Scalamandré/T2906-010** Color **multi** Alternative colors **available** Composition **100% silk, wood** Depth **23¾in/60cm** Width **–** Price ★★★

3 **Henry Newbery & Co/Selkirk Fringe** Color **multi** Alternative colors **available** Composition **100% Dralon** Depth **6¾in/17cm** Width **–** Price ★★

4 **Henry Newbery & Co/Carlos Fringe** Color **gold** Alternative colors **available** Composition **100% Dralon** Depth **2½in/6cm** Width **–** Price ★

5 **Abbott & Boyd/Braid** Color **bottle green, golden maize, and silver gray** Alternative colors **available** Composition **100% cotton** Depth **–** Width **1½in/4cm** Price ★

6 **Percheron/Richelieu Brele** Color **752** Alternative colors **available** Composition **100% rayon** Depth **–** Width **1½in/4cm** Price ★★★

Tassels & Tiebacks

Decorative tassels and tiebacks have been used to embellish drapery since the Renaissance. At their simplest, tassels are ornamental tufts of thread incorporated into fringing and edgings (*see* pages 190-5) and applied to bed-hangings, window curtains, lambrequins, pelmets, portieres, and upholstery. Many of the more elaborate tassels, notably those used as, or as part of, tiebacks for bed- and window-hangings and portieres, are among the most intricate examples of the *passementier's* art. Working around flat-, dome-, arrow-, ball-, or screw-shaped wooden forms covered with fabrics such as silk or velvet, the *passementier* could apply a range of embellishments, such as braid or cord edgings, appliquéd motifs, and long or short skirts, many of which were made of gold or silver thread fringing. During the 18th century, relatively small arrow- and rectangular-shaped heads were popular, as were proportionately short skirts trimmed with appliquéd bows or smaller, fabric-covered wooden forms. Such ornamentation, however, was discrete when compared to the elaborate tassels produced during the 19th century.

1 **V. V. Rouleaux/Acorns** Color **emerald, gold, and blue** Alternative colors **available** Composition **100% polyester** Depth **1½in/3.5cm** Width – **Price** ★

2 **V. V. Rouleaux/MOK-05-L** Color **black and silver** Alternative colors **available** Composition **70% rayon, 30% polyester** Depth **1½/ 3.5cm** Width – Price ★

3 **V. V. Rouleaux/Waxed Turk Hen Knot Tassel** Color **navy** Alternative colors **available** Composition **100% acrylic** Depth **1½in/3.5cm** Width – Price ★★

4 **Nice Irma's/Wood Tieback CTB-10N** Color **navy** Alternative colors **available** Composition **100% cotton, wood** Depth **8½in/21.5cm** Width – Price ★

5 **Nice Irma's/CTB-17** Color **cream** Alternative colors **available** Composition **100% cotton** Depth **10¼in/26cm** Width – Price ★

6 **Nice Irma's/Wood Tieback CTB10** Color **natural** Alternative colors **available** Composition **100% cotton, wood** Depth **8½in/21.5cm** Width – Price ★

7 **Nice Irma's/CTB-02** Color **cream** Alternative colors **available** Composition **100% cotton** Depth **11¾in/30cm** Width – Price ★

8 **Henry Newbery & Co/ Cambridge** Color **wine (1)** Alternative colors **available** Composition **100% Dralon** Depth **8in/20cm** Width – Price ★★

RENAISSANCE INFLUENCE

From the Renaissance to today, the manufacture of decorative trimmings (*passements*) for furnishings has remained a specialist activity. However, as far as the design of these often exquisite trimmings is concerned, there has always been considerable cross-fertilization of ideas existing between different areas of textile production. These elaborate tassels were inspired by dressmakers' embellishments and key fobs that were considered the height of fashion during the Italian Renaissance.

1 **Wendy Cushing Trimmings/ Traditional Key Tassel 39112** Color **silver** Alternative colors **available** Composition **100% cotton** Depth **4in/10cm** Width – Price ★★

2 **V. V. Rouleaux/Terracotta Tassel** Color **burgundy and gold** Alternative colors **available** Composition **50% terracotta, 50% rayon** Depth **9½in/24cm** Width - Price ★★★★★

9 10

11 12 13

14

9 **Abbott & Boyd/Single Tassel Tieback 613** Color **jute/red** Alternative colors **available** Composition **50% jute, 50% cotton** Depth **11¾in/30cm** Width – Price ★★

10 **Henry Newbery & Co/Fitzherbert** Color **wine and aquamarine** Alternative colors **available** Composition **100% viscose** Depth **6½in/16.5cm** Width – Price ★★★

11 **Wendy Cushing Trimmings/Gothic Tiebacks 39033** Color **black and white** Alternative colors **available** Composition **100% cotton** Depth **7in/17.75cm** Width – Price ★★★★★

12 **Altfield/Fruit Tieback FT2** Color **gold** Alternative colors **not available** Composition **100% silk, wood** Depth **32¾in/83cm** Width – Price ★★★

13 **V. V. Rouleaux/OP-8612** Color **63–light blue** Alternative colors **available** Composition **100% polyester** Depth **5½in/14cm** Width – Price ★

14 **Abbott & Boyd/Double Tassel Tieback 614** Color **jute** Alternative colors **available** Composition **50% jute, 50% cotton** Depth **11¾in/30cm** Width – Price ★★★

ROSETTES

Strictly defined as a circular, formalized flower ornament, but generally accepted as any type of circular ornament with decorative elements radiating from its center, the rosette has been frequently employed as a trimming for fabrics and upholstery since the Renaissance. As shown here, the basic circular shape is often augmented with tassels. Since the early Renaissance it has recurred on Classical and Neoclassical furnishings. However, it is an almost universal motif that can be traced back to both Ancient Greece and Mesopotamia, ca. 2500 B.C., where it was frequently applied to furnishings and and also to other decorative and religious artifacts.

1 2 3

1 **Zoë Barlow Passementerie/Button and Tassel EP/P20/Sg/Sp** Color **pink and green** Alternative colors **available** Composition **100% cotton, wood** Depth **21½in/55cm** Width – Price ★★★★

2 **Zoë Barlow Passementerie/Button Med/D10/Sp** Color **pastel** Alternative colors **available** Composition **100% cotton, wood** Depth **11¾in/30cm** Width – Price ★★★

3 **V. V. Rouleaux/Cherry Ball** Color **neutral** Alternative colors **not available** Composition **100% jute** Depth **5in/13cm** Width – Price ★

Pre-17th century
17th century
18th century
19th century
20th century

Tassels & Tiebacks

During the 19th century, tassels generally became more ornate and played an even more prominent role in the furnishing of interiors. As in previous centuries they were incorporated into fringes and edgings on drapes, pelmets, lambrequins, and upholstery. However, the most elaborate examples tended to be reserved for tiebacks and–a new use–bellpulls. In this context their increased complexity mirrored that of related items, such as the bronze and gilt rosettes, disks, and cloak pins that were used to secure the tiebacks. Notable examples from the 19th century included multitiered tassels worked around a maximum of six carved or turned wooden forms. Arrow- and dome-shaped heads, appliquéd with golden leaves or shells, proved very popular, as were long, onion-shaped skirts.

During the Art Deco and the Modernist Periods of the 20th century, tassels became both smaller and simpler, although there were some innovations; these included, for example, the use of heads made from uncovered cut glass. However, to meet renewed demand, manufacturers and designers have once again begun to produce highly intricate and elaborate tassels, which are based on, or inspired by, authentic period designs.

1

2 3 4 5 6

1 **Henry Newbery & Co/Tivoli** Color **pink, green, and cream** Alternative colors **available** Composition **100% viscose** Depth **9½in/24cm** Width – Price ★★ [symbol]

2 **Scalamandré/Tassel Tie T2906-10** Color **black and sand** Alternative colors **available** Composition **100% silk** Depth **6in/15cm** Width – Price ★★★★★ [symbol] [T]

3 **Henry Newbery & Co/Melrose–Single Tassel** Color **pink** Alternative colors **available** Composition **100% viscose** Depth **7in/17.5cm** Width – Price ★★ [symbol]

4 **Wendy Cushing Trimmings/Celtic Tieback 39063** Color **blue** Alternative colors **available** Composition **50% cotton, 50% artificial silk** Depth **9in/23cm** Width – Price ★★★★★ [symbol]

5 **Scalamandré/T2790-12** Color **green and gold** Alternative colors **available** Composition **100% silk** Depth **7in/18cm** Width – Price ★★★★★ [symbol] [T]

6 **Henry Newbery & Co/Blenheim** Color **green and sand** Alternative colors **available** Composition **100% viscose** Depth **9½in/24cm** Width – Price ★★★ [symbol]

7 **Claremont/Embrasse Neker Guirlande** Color **blue and gold** Alternative colors **available** Composition **100% fibranne** Depth **11in/29cm** Width – Price ★★★★★ [symbol] [T]

7

8

9

10

11

12

13

14

8 **Zoë Barlow Passementerie/ Tassel Electric Blue** Color **blue** Alternative colors **available** Composition **100% cotton, wood** Depth **11in/28cm** Width – Price ★★★★

9 **Henry Newbery & Co/Beta** Color **bright gold** Alternative colors **available** Composition **47% cotton, 43% metallic thread, 10% wood** Depth **10½in/27cm** Width – Price ★★★★

10 **V. V. Rouleaux/Mosaic Tassel** Color **multi** Alternative colors **available** Composition **100% acrylic, colored glass, iron** Depth **made to order** Width – Price ★★★★★

11 **Zoë Barlow Passementerie/ Double Tieback Tassel MEX/P2/M** Color **blue, green, yellow, and rust** Alternative colors **available** Composition **100% cotton, wood** Depth **4½in/11.5cm** Width – Price ★★★★★

12 **Claremont/Embrasse Raisins** Color **green** Alternative colors **available** Composition **100% fibranne** Depth **7in/18cm** Width – Price ★★★★★ T

13 **Zoë Barlow Passementerie/ Tassel Siamese Fighting Fish (A)** Color **rusty orange/bottle green** Alternative colors **available** Composition **100% cotton, wood** Depth **8¾in/22.5cm** Width – Price ★★★★

14 **V. V. Rouleaux/Sev–Special** Color **red and gold** Alternative colors **available** Composition **100% acrylic** Depth **15¾in/40cm** Width – Price ★★★★★

TIEBACKS

Historically, the majority of tiebacks used to restrain window drapes, bed-hangings, and portieres have been embellished with intricately worked *passements*. However, relatively simple arrangements have also found favor. For example, during the 17th century most tiebacks simply consisted of braided rope cords made from fibers as diverse as silk, cotton, and hemp. Ribbons or galloons were popular during the 18th century, and plain cords reemerged during the 19th century, although some were as thick as an elephant's trunk.

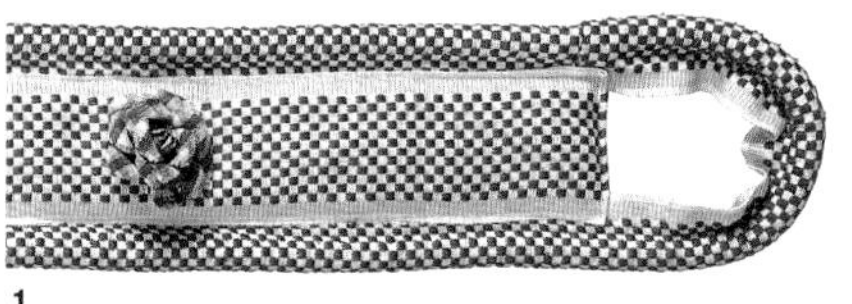
1

2

3

1 **Nobilis-Fontan/ Embrasses Damier 1202.89** Color **navy and white** Alternative colors **available** Composition **65% viscose, 15% wood, 10% polyester, 10% cotton** Length **35½in/90cm** Width **2¾in/7cm** Price ★★★★

2 **Claremont/S & S Cable Tieback** Color **green, pink, and white** Alternative colors **available** Composition **100% cotton** Length **29½in/75cm** Width – Price ★★★ T

3 **Nobilis-Fontan/Embrasses Club 1201.87** Color **gold and blue** Alternative colors **available** Composition **70% viscose, 15% silk, 15% cotton** Length **35½in/90cm** Width **1¼in/3cm** Price ★

4 **Abbott & Boyd/211** Color **58** Alternative colors **available** Composition **95% cotton, 5% viscose** Length **28½in/73cm** Width **1¼in/3cm** Price ★

4

Fringes

As the influential 19th-century English architect, designer, and ornamentalist A. W. N. Pugin noted, fringe was at one time "nothing more than the threads of a silk or woolen stuff knotted together at a ragged edge, to prevent it unravelling further." In terms of its original purpose, this was undeniably true. However, since the 17th century fringe has been produced in a wide variety of styles, some of which have been simple and functional, others highly elaborate and decorative (*see* pages 192-3).

During the 19th century, extremely elaborate upholstery fringing was the height of fashion. Prior to that, fringes were often relatively plain, with typical examples consisting of braid (or sometimes lace) tops hung with simple tufts or tassels. The depth of such fringes essentially depended on their purpose. Shorter versions (which did not droop) were designed for the vertical edges of hangings and upholstered seating, while longer fringes were intended for the bottom edges. Some simple fringes were also made during this period specifically for the leading edges of mantelshelves (*tours de cheminées*) and bookcases, the purpose of the latter being to dust a book each time it was removed from and returned to its shelf.

4

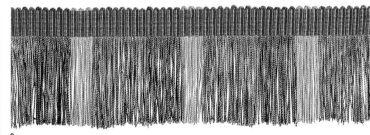

1

5

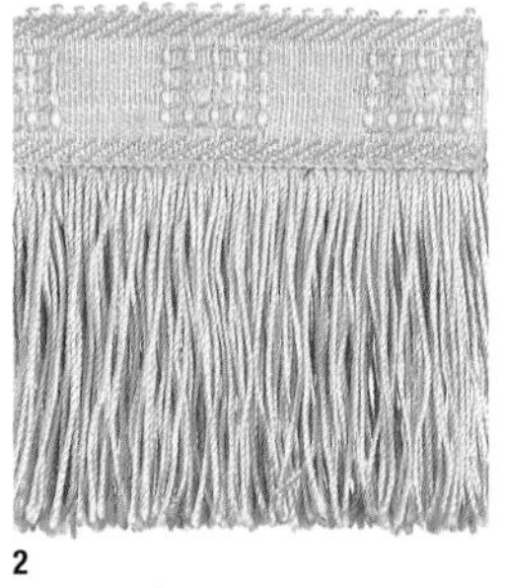

2

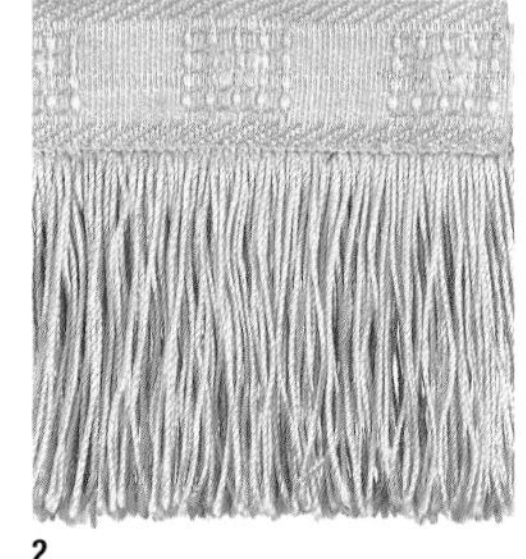

6

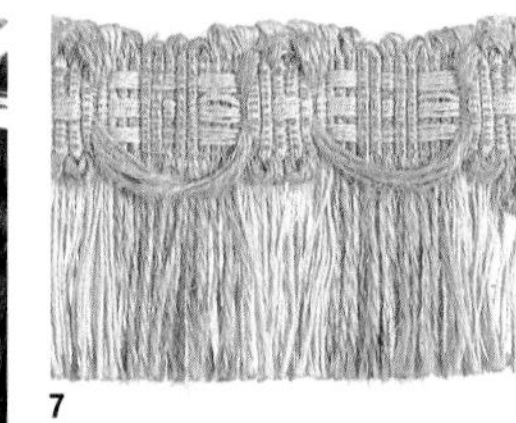

7

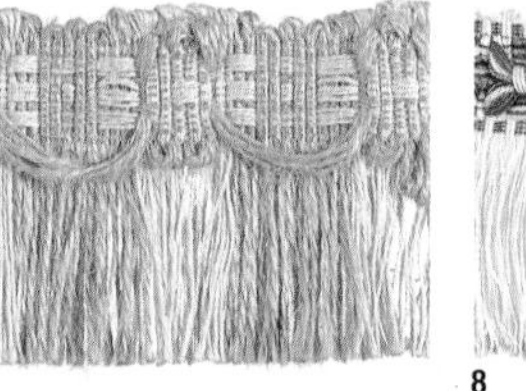

8

3

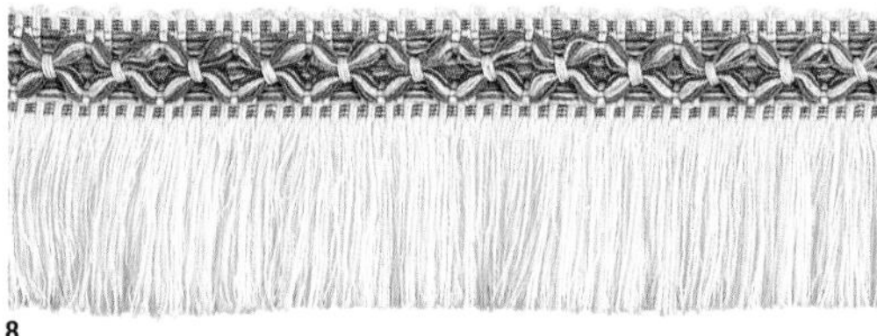

9

1 **Wemyss Houlès/Toinette 33127** Color **royal blue (light blue) with white** Alternative colors **available** Composition **100% viscose** Depth **2¾in/7cm** Width – Price ★

2 **Scalamandré/Cut Fringe FC1195** Color **red and parchment** Alternative colors **available** Composition **90% silk, 10% rayon** Depth **3¾in/9.5cm** Width – Price ★★★

3 **Wendy Cushing Trimmings/ Roll Top Bullion Fringe** Color **black and white** Alternative colors **available** Composition **100% rayon** Depth **4¾in/12cm** Width – Price ★★

4 **Wendy Cushing Trimmings/ Silk Bullion with Gimp Heading and Silk Acorns 39120** Color **silver** Alternative colors **available** Composition **100% silk** Depth **4in/10cm** Width – Price ★★★★★

5 **Nice Irma's/Cotton Fringing** Color **unbleached cotton** Alternative colors **available** Composition **100% cotton** Depth **10in/25cm** Width – Price ★

6 **Claremont/Block Fringe Long** Color **mauve, mustard, and green** Alternative colors **available** Composition **100% fibranne** Depth **2½in/ 6.5cm** Width – Price ★★

7 **Percheron/Effilé Naturel 906** Color **two-tone natural (3)** Alternative colors **available** Composition **93% linen, 7% viscose** Depth **2½in/6cm** Width – Price ★★

8 **Henry Newbery & Co/Madison** Color **5** Alternative colors **available** Composition **100% viscose** Depth **2in/5cm** Width – Price ★

9 **Henry Newbery & Co/Callas Ruche** Color **2** Alternative colors **available** Composition **80% viscose, 20% wool** Depth **1¾in/4.5cm** Width – Price ★

10

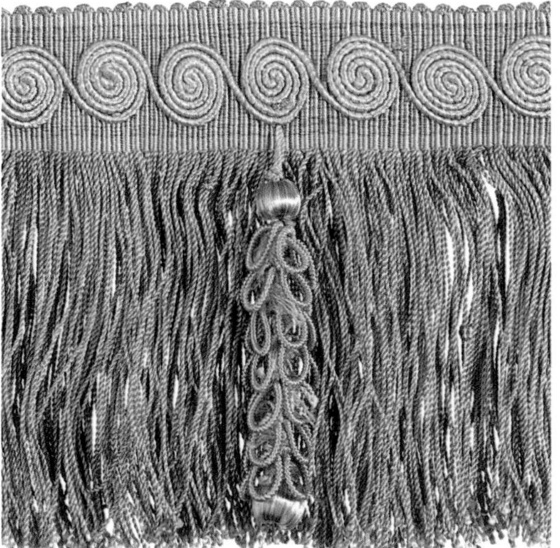

11

12

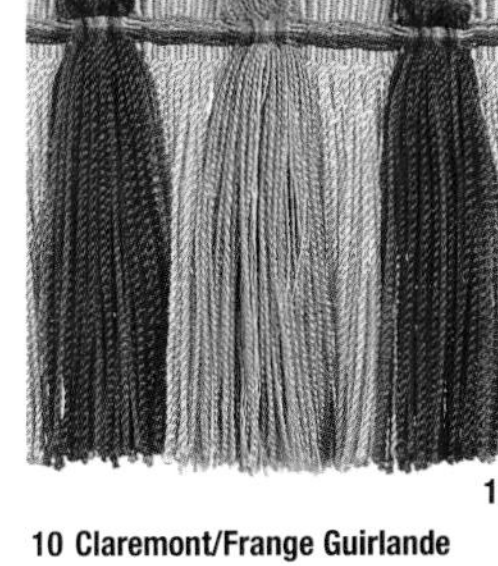

13

10 Claremont/Frange Guirlande Color **blue and gold** Alternative colors **available** Composition **100% fibranne** Depth **6¾in/17cm** Width – Price ★★★★★ T

11 Wendy Cushing Trimmings/Spiral Silk Fringe with Hangers 39121 Color **gray** Alternative colors **available** Composition **100% silk** Depth **4in/10cm** Width – Price ★★★★★

12 Percheron/Cut Fringe Richelieu 110421 Color **navy and gold** Alternative colors **available** Composition **100% viscose** Depth **4¾in/12cm** Width – Price ★★★★

13 Wemyss Houlès/Cordelia Trim 33063 Color **9582** Alternative colors **available** Composition **100% viscose** Depth **2½in/6.5cm** Width – Price ★★

14 V. V. Rouleaux/Feather Trim Color **brown and black** Alternative colors **available** Composition **100% feathers** Depth **6¼in/16cm** Width – Price ★★★

BULLION FRINGE

So called because its twisted lengths of hanging rope were often made from gold, silver, or metallic fibers, bullion fringe was particularly fashionable during the mid-19th century. Its primary use was as a skirt for the base of upholstered armchairs and couches. Single and multi- colored linen and cotton versions also proved popular in mid-20th-century "country house"-style interiors.

1

2

1 Henry Newbery & Co/Melrose Black Color **black** Alternative colors **available** Composition **100% viscose** Depth **4in/10cm** Width – Price ★★

2 Percheron/Vérone Frange Torse 119612 Color **green/gold, red, and brown (859)** Alternative colors **available** Composition **100% viscose** Depth **4¾in/12cm** Width – Price ★★ LC

14

Fringes

During the late 18th and early 19th centuries, fringe was generally regarded as unfashionable. Napoleon I, for example, described it as a "useless" ornament and banned it from his apartments at the Tuileries in Paris, France. There was also a reaction against it among the followers of the Aesthetic Movement during the second half of the 19th century. However, for most of the Victorian era and for much of the 20th century an enormous variety of intricate and highly elaborate fringing was used on drapes and upholstery. For example, from the 1830s to the 1850s, long spiral and bullion fringes (*see* page 191), embellished with appliquéd flowers and topped with picot or gimp braids, were very fashionable. In the second half of the 19th century, Persian fringe incorporating a wide braid border supporting fabric-covered balls ("teardrops") was popular. During the 20th century, many Art Deco and Modernist furnishings featured long, skirtlike fringes with deep, crochet-work headings. These are but a few of the many fashionable types of fringing. Other significant types include inch, caul, block, campaign, vellum, trellis, butterfly, snailing, tufted, twisted, knotted, netted, fagoted, and swagged, all of which are still produced by the *passementiers* of today.

1

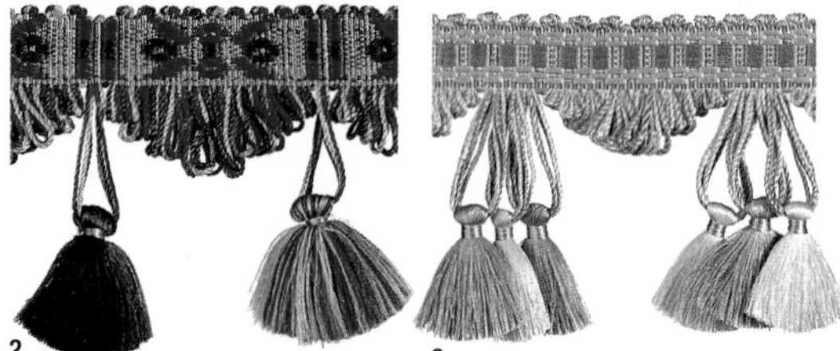
2
3

4

5

6

1 **Henry Newbery & Co/Blenheim** Color **green and beige** Alternative colors **available** Composition **50% cotton, 50% viscose** Depth **2¾in/7cm** Width – Price ★

2 **Scalamandré/Tassel Fringe** Color **multi** Alternative colors **available** Composition **100% silk** Depth **2½in/6cm** Width – Price ★★

3 **Scalamandré/Tassel Fringe FT44** Color **1** Alternative colors **available** Composition **100% silk** Depth **2½in/6cm** Width – Price ★★★★

4 **Wemyss Houlès/Cap-Ferret** Color **yellow-maize, green** Alternative colors **available** Composition **82% viscose, 18% wool** Depth **3in/7.5cm** Width – Price ★★

5 **Abbott & Boyd/Antigua Tassel Fringe** Color **pink, black, and white** Alternative colors **available** Composition **50% cotton, 50% viscose** Depth **2½in/6cm** Width – Price ★

6 **Brunschwig & Fils/Applause Tasseled Fringe** Color **multi** Alternative colors **available** Composition **100% viscose** Depth **3in/8cm** Width – Price ★★★

7

7 **Percheron/Richelieu–Fringe & Mèches 110422** Color **752** Alternative colors **available** Composition **100% viscose** Depth **4¼in/11cm** Width – Price ★★★★

8 **Wemyss Houlès/Cordelia 33376** Color **9573** Alternative colors **available** Composition **85% wool, 15% viscose** Depth **3½in/9cm** Width – Price ★★★

9 **Wemyss Houlès/Sultane 33379** Color **9574** Alternative colors **available** Composition **90% viscose, 5% cotton, 5% metal** Depth **2½in/6.5cm** Width – Price ★★★★

8
9

10 **Henry Newbery & Co/Imperial Fringe** Color **blue, red, and green** Alternative colors **available** Composition **100% viscose** Depth **4¾in/12cm** Width – Price ★★

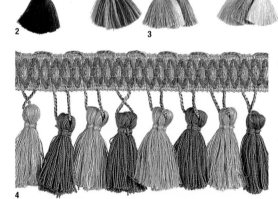

11 **Henry Newbery & Co/Tivoli Fringe** Color **pink, fern, and cream** Alternative colors **available** Composition **100% viscose** Depth **3½in/9cm** Width – Price ★★

10

11

12 Wendy Cushing Trimmings/ Gilded Bell Hanger Fringe 39045 Color **gold** Alternative colors **available** Composition **50% cotton, 50% wool** Depth **4in/10cm** Width – Price ★★★★★

13 V. V. Rouleaux/3-Drop Bauble Fringe Color **terracotta** Alternative colors **available** Composition **75% cotton, 25% jute** Depth **4in/10cm** Width – Price ★★

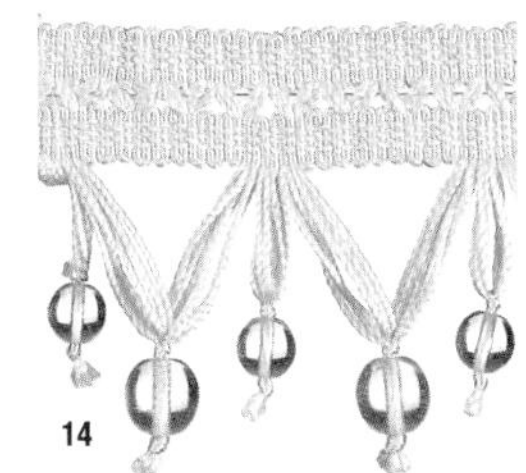

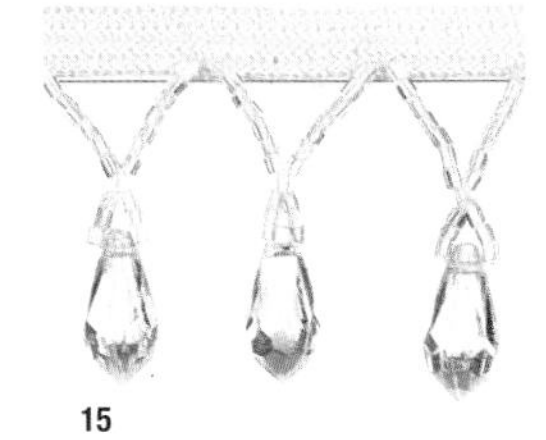

14 Brunschwig & Fils/Paulina Beaded Fringe 905861.05 Color **creme** Alternative colors **available** Composition **50% silk, 50% glass** Depth **2¼in/5.5cm** Width – Price ★★★★★

15 Scalamandré/Clear Crystal Fringe ST5401 Color **white** Alternative colors **available** Composition **50% rayon, 50% lucite** Depth **1½in/4cm** Width – Price ★★

16 Henry Newbery & Co/Carlos Fringe Color **14** Alternative colors **available** Composition **100% Dralon** Depth **4in/10cm** Width – Price ★

17 Brunschwig & Fils/Tourner Wood Mould Fringe 90580.05/2 Color **natural** Alternative colors **available** Composition **75% wood, 25% cotton** Depth **3½in/9cm** Width – Price ★★★★

18 Henry Newbery & Co/Opera Color **4** Alternative colors **available** Composition **100% viscose** Depth **2in/ 5cm**Width – Price ★★

19 V. V. Rouleaux/3 Bauble Drop R5 Color **oyster** Alternative colors **available** Composition **100% polyester** Depth **6in/ 15cm** Width – Price ★★★

20 Wendy Cushing Trimmings/ Classical Hanger for Fringes 39052 Color **green, red, and gold** Alternative colors **available** Composition **100% silk, wood** Depth **4in/10cm** Width – Price ★★

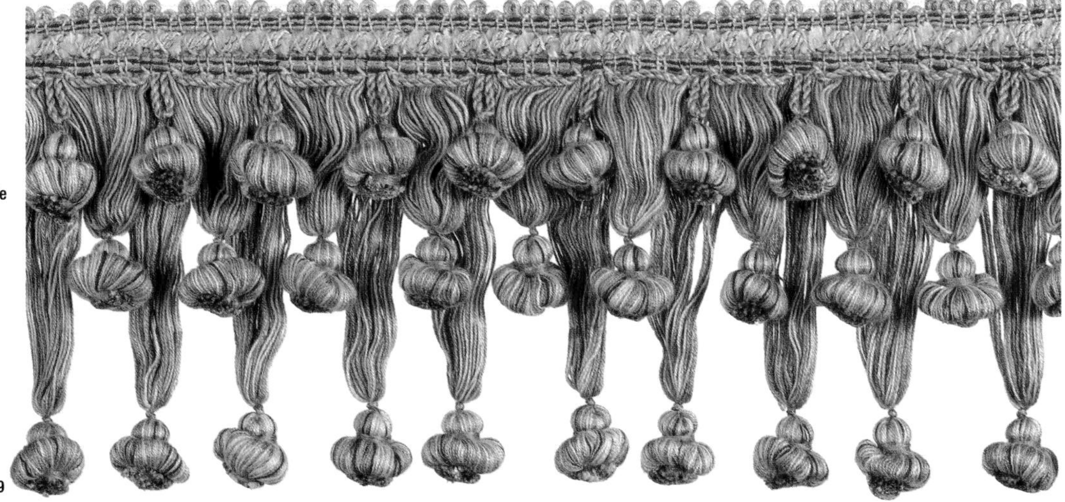

Braids & Ribbons

Primarily used to disguise seams and raw edges, braids–flat, narrow woven textiles–also serve to add decorative embellishments to drapes and upholstery, often in conjunction with tassels and fringing. In the 17th century braids of plaited silk and gold thread were fashionable, as were velour braids that featured stylized flowers and lozenges. Starting in the 18th century many tiebacks were edged with substantial braids embellished with flowers, bows, rosettes, and butterfly shapes, and picot or gimp braids served as headings for fringing. Early 19th-century braids tended to be delicate, mid-century examples were generally larger, while end-of-century braids were often multicolored, curved, and interlaced. In the 20th century, neater, straighter braids with geometric motifs were favored.

Decorative ribbons (galloons) have also been widely used for embellishments. In Paris, France, there were over 700 *rubaniers* producing bows and artificial flowers from ribbons during the mid-18th century. These embellishments were used as trim on drapes, pelmets, valances, tiebacks, and table coverings. Many examples, such as *à la cocque*, *au mirlton*, *à la quadrille*, and *à l'allure*, took their names from current events, personalities, popular songs, and dances, and are still available today.

7

8

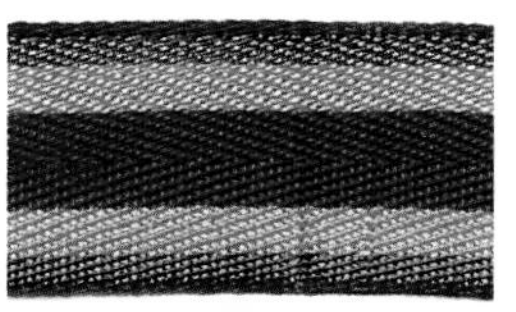
9

10

1

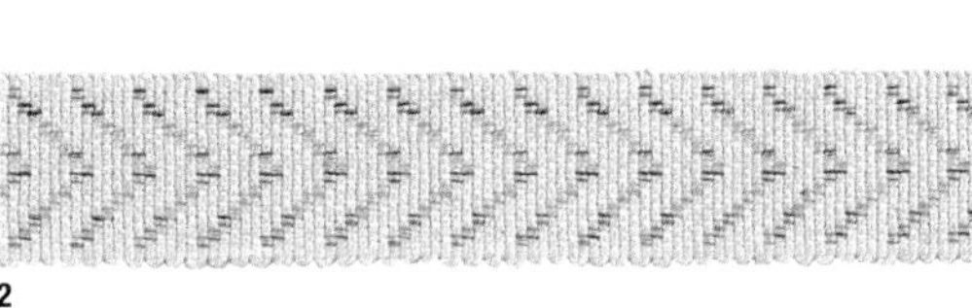
2

3

4

5

6

11

12

13

14

1 **Claremont/Galon Chenille** Color **pink, green, cream, and black** Alternative colors **available** Composition **100% cotton** Depth – Width **2in/5cm** Price ★★

2 **Brunschwig & Fils/B128-5** Color **cream background with colors** Alternative colors **available** Composition **100% cotton** Depth – Width **¾in/2cm** Price ★

3 **Wendy Cushing Trimmings/Tabby Braid 39038** Color **black, cream** Alternative colors **available** Composition **100% cotton** Depth – Width **½in/1.5cm** Price ★★

4 **Scalamandré/Braid V772-4** Color **paprika** Alternative colors **available** Composition **100% rayon** Depth – Width **1in/2.5cm** Price ★

5 **Abbott & Boyd/Antigua Braid 121** Color **black, red, and cream** Alternative colors **available** Composition **95% cotton, 5% viscose** Depth – Width **1½in/4cm** Price ★

6 **Wemyss Houlès/Cap-Ferret 32179** Color **9171** Alternative colors **available** Composition **100% viscose** Depth – Width **1½in/4cm** Price ★★

7 **Nobilis-Fontan/Galon et Boutons de Roses** Color **blue, white** Alternative colors **available** Composition **100% viscose** Depth – Width **1¾in/4.5cm** Price ★★

8 **George Spencer Decorations/Braid 506C** Color **manila and terracotta** Alternative colors **available** Composition **100% cotton** Depth – Width **2½in/6.5cm** Price ★

9 **Scalamandré/Military Ribbon V161-48** Color **jade green, maize, and old glory red** Alternative colors **available** Composition **100% rayon** Depth – Width **¾in/2cm** Price ★★

10 **Abbott & Boyd/Braid 621** Color **jute, white** Alternative colors **available** Composition **70% jute, 30% cotton** Depth – Width **1½in/3.5cm** Price ★

11 **Claremont/Galon** Color **burgundy, green, and cream** Alternative colors **available** Composition **100% fibranne** Depth – Width **5in/13cm** Price ★★★

12 **V. V. Rouleaux/Indian Figure of Eight** Color **jute** Alternative colors **not available** Composition **100% jute** Depth – Width **2½in/6cm**Price ★

13 **V. V. Rouleaux/Petersham** Color **6** Alternative colors **available** Composition **64% viscose, 36% cotton** Depth – Width **⅜in/1cm** Price ★

14 **Claremont/Greek Key Border** Color **gold, white, and black** Alternative colors **available** Composition **100% fibranne** Depth – Width **2¼in/5.5cm** Price ★★

15 Scalamandré/Braid V635-4 Color **seaspray, teal blue, and cream** Alternative colors **available** Composition **100% silk** Depth – Width **2in/5cm** Price ★★

16 Brunschwig & Fils/30434-M21 Color **wine, red, turquoise, cream, gold mix** Alternative colors **available** Composition **100% viscose** Depth – Width **2in/5cm** Price ★

17 Scalamandré/Braid V713-4 Color **taupe and pink** Alternative colors **available** Composition **90% silk, 5% rayon, 5% Bemberg** Depth – Width **2in/5cm** Price ★★★

18 Scalamandré/Braid V417-12 Color **salmon pink, tarragon, and parchment** Alternative colors **available** Composition **100% silk** Depth – Width **1½in/4cm** Price ★★★

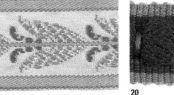

15

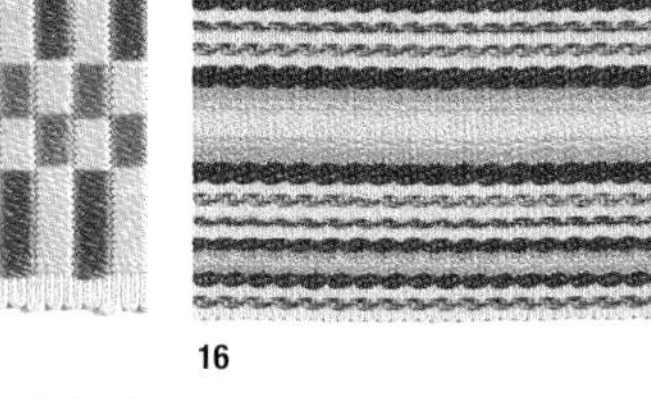

16

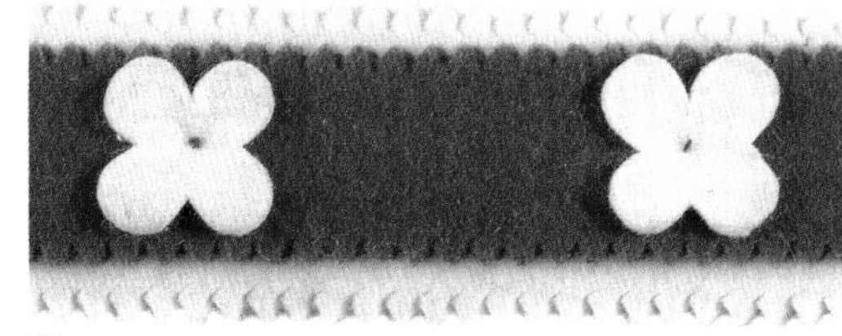

19

17

18

20

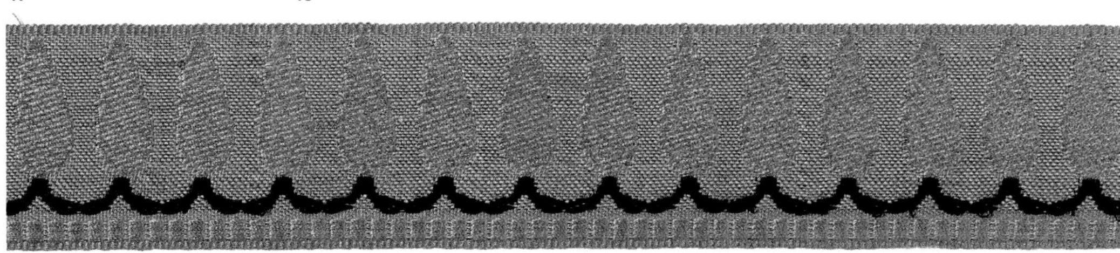

21

22

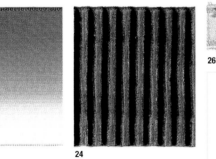

23

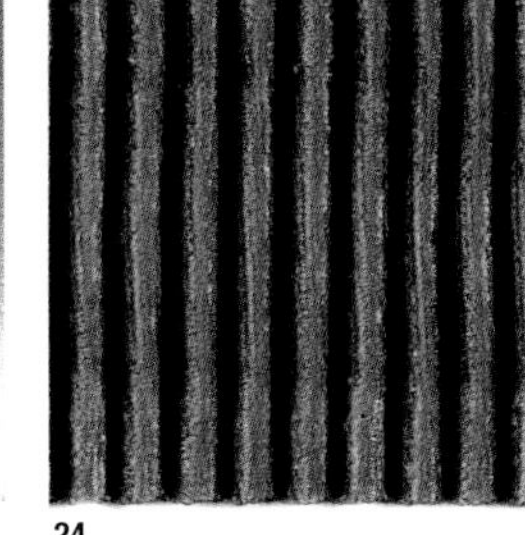

24

26

25

19 V. V. Rouleaux/VL-0204/12 Color **red, fern, and brown** Alternative colors **available** Composition **100% felt** Depth – Width **1½in/4cm** Price ★★★

20 Claremont/Galon d'Olives Color **red museum** Alternative colors **available** Composition **100% wool** Depth – Width **1¼in/3cm** Price ★★

21 Claremont/Palmette Color **tan, green, and black** Alternative colors **available** Composition **100% viscose** Depth – Width **1½in/4cm** Price ★★

22 V. V. Rouleaux/Mokuba–Flower Tape 9313 Color **yellow, blue, and red** Alternative colors **available** Composition **100% polyester** Depth – Width **¼in/7mm** Price ★★

23 V. V. Rouleaux/1359 No. 12 Color **7** Alternative colors **available** Composition **100% silk** Depth – Width **2in/5cm** Price ★

24 V. V. Rouleaux/Mokuba–Flower Ribbon/MOK 0500 Color **moss green 16** Alternative colors **available** Composition **50% polyester, 50% rayon** Depth – Width **2in/5cm** Price ★

25 Nice Irma's/Brocade Sari Ribbon Color **multi** Alternative colors **available** Composition **100% silk** Depth – Width **5½in/14cm** Price ★

26 V. V. Rouleaux/Ribbon Picot Edge Color **cayenne, green, and cream** Alternative colors **available** Composition **100% polyester** Depth – Width **1in/2.5cm** Price ★

UPHOLSTERY BRAIDS

Braid was first used extensively as a means of decoratively masking the seams and raw edges of drapes and pelmets during the reign of Louis XIV in France. However, the profusion of braid designs that emerged from the late 17th to the end of the 19th century largely resulted from the development of numerous styles of upholstered seating. In that instance, braid provided a complementary (or contrasting) edging material, and served to define the diverse shapes of seating as varied as wing and bergère chairs, occasional and corner chairs, and settees and chaise longues.

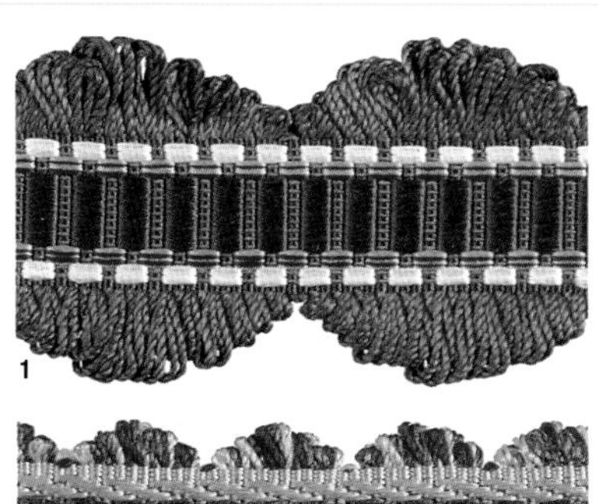

1

2

3

1 Scalamandré/Double Scallop Braid V640-43 Color **emerald green, paprika, flax, and white** Alternative colors **available** Composition **100% silk** Depth – Width **1¾in/4.5cm** Price ★★

2 Scalamandré/Scalloped Braid V704-4 Color **old gold, fern, and wine** Alternative colors **available** Composition **100% silk** Depth – Width **1in/2.5cm** Price ★★

3 Scalamandré/Braid V780-7 Color **royal blue, wine, and gold** Alternative colors **available** Composition **90% cotton, 10% rayon** Depth – Width **1in/2.5cm** Price ★★★

Wallpapers

Plain Wallpapers

Although most wallpapers that have been made since the 15th century have been embellished with patterns and motifs, a very considerable number have been produced in plain or mottled colors. The plainest of these wallpapers present a solid expanse of a single color. The types of dyes and inks–animal, vegetable, mineral, aniline, and chemical–that have been used to print them, together with the method of printing, have varied, and have also determined the purity, strength, and vivacity of color available (*see* page 200). However, the primary purpose of these plain wallpapers has always been to introduce color into a room, and also to provide both an uncluttered and complementary background for architectural fixtures and fittings, furniture, and soft furnishings. Also within the plains category are those wallpapers that exhibit subtle gradations or mottling of color. Many of the 20th-century Modernist wallpapers are purely abstract, but others are intended as simulations of stone, wood, and textiles, such as burlap and tweed, and a few also exhibit embossing or applied texturing across their surface.

RIGHT In the Victorian era, pictures were often displayed against plain wallpapers. Crimson and magenta papers were deemed the most appropriate as they accentuated the warm glow of gilded and polished wooden picture frames, while providing a contrast for ebony and black-lacquered frames.

PAINT-EFFECT PAPERS

Wallpapers that reproduce the appearance of decorative paint effects have been particularly popular since the 1980s. Most are imitations of colorwashing, ragging, rag-rolling, sponging, and stippling. Known as "broken color" techniques, all of these effects display, to varying degrees, subtle gradations and patterning of color. Some–such as sponging or rag-rolling–are often used in recreations of period interiors. They simulate the mottling that occurred in many pre-20th century paint finishes as a result of a chemical breakdown in their pigments following exposure to light.

ABOVE Since the late 19th century, dark blue papered walls have often been used as complementary backgrounds for displays of silverware and gray marble and granite artifacts.

KEY DESIGNS

1 Many plain wallpapers have been produced in imitation of plain-woven fabrics. This late 20th-century example imitates the warp and weft of the weave in its two-color surface printing.

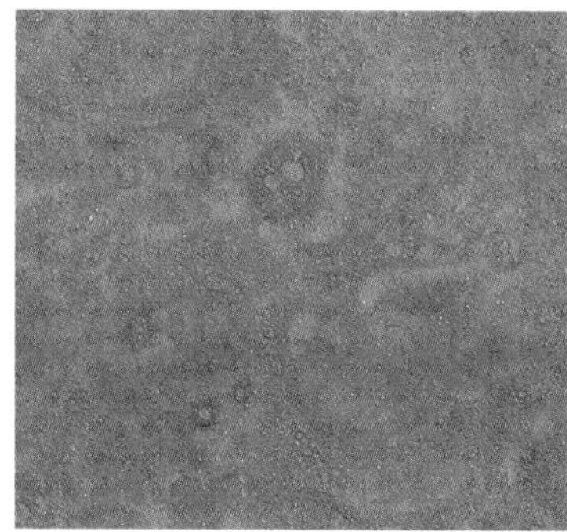

2 Finely figured hardwoods are often simulated in wallpapers. This modern design displays the configurations and mottled coloring associated with stained and polished walnut.

3 During the 19th and 20th centuries a number of papers were produced in imitation of leather wall-hangings. Some, like this "suede" paper, actually do have the texture of leather.

4 This paper, inspired by iridescent Roman glassware, exhibits subtle gradations and luminosities of color which are very typical of late 20th-century wallpaper design.

5 Some plain wallpapers give the appearance of stonework or patinated metal surfaces. They can also display subtle and random variations in tonality that can be appreciated in their own right.

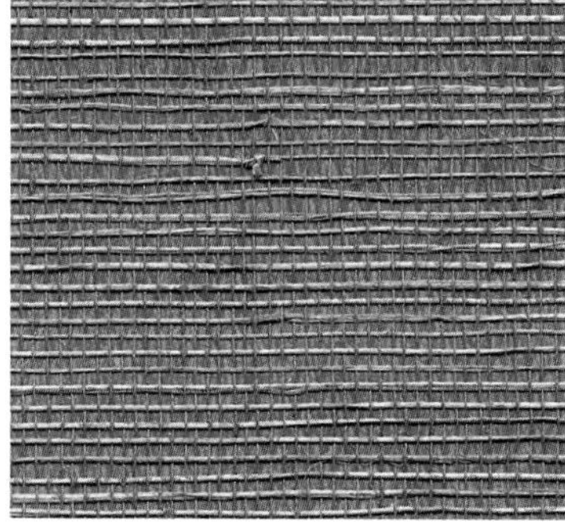

6 Grass cloths have been used as wall coverings for centuries, particularly in Japan and Korea. They were very fashionable in Europe and America from the 1960s until the 1980s.

---

1 **Jane Churchill/Texture JY15W-03** Color **manilla** Alternative colors **available** Width **20½in/52cm** Length **11yd/10m** Repeat – Price ★

2 **Maya Romanoff/Patina MR-T35-176-G** Color **golden taupe** Alternative colors **available** Width **30in/76cm** Length **to order** Repeat – Price ★★★★★ [T]

3 **Northwood Designs/Suedel** Color **48 Chine** Alternative colors **available** Width **39¼in/100cm** Length **to order** Repeat – Price ★★

4 **Harlequin/57020** Color **orange/yellow** Alternative colors **available** Width **20½in/ 52cm** Length **11yd/10m** Repeat – Price ★

5 **Osborne & Little/Glissando W1443/01** Color **silver** Alternative colors **available** Width **20½in/52cm** Length **11yd/10m** Repeat – Price ★

6 **Donghia/Hemps Wallcovering G970/01** Color **red** Alternative colors **available** Width **35¾in/91cm** Length **3¾yd/3.5m** Repeat – Price ★★★★★

Plains

Wallpapers printed with a single block of color (usually blues, reds, and greens) appeared in the 15th century as grounds for paper cutouts of religious and heraldic imagery. During the 18th century, plain blue, crimson, and yellow wallpapers were employed in "print rooms" (*see* page 239). In 19th-century interiors, single-colored wallpapers (especially shades of red) were favored for displaying ebony- and gilt-framed pictures, while in the 20th century, plain-colored papers have proved particularly popular in Modernist and post-Modernist interiors.

Prior to the 1850s, papers that had been hand-blocked with animal, vegetable, or mineral dyes exhibited a notable delicacy and purity of color. In comparison, the hand-blocked or roller-printed aniline dyes of the mid- and late 19th century were more vibrant, but sometimes rather garish. The synthetic chemical dyes of the 20th century have increased the color range but, partly due to the slight loss of crispness associated with photogravure and screen-printing, they have often failed to match the even coverage given by vegetable dyes, a fact that explains the revival of hand-blocking with traditional vegetable and mineral dyes during the late 20th century.

Nina Campbell/Lawn NCW2025/06 Color **yellow** Alternative colors **available** Width **20½in/52cm** Length **11yd/10m** Repeat **–** Price ★

G. P. & J. Baker/Carrara W0110-01 Color **01** Alternative colors **available** Width **20½in/52cm** Length **11yd/10m** Repeat **–** Price ★★

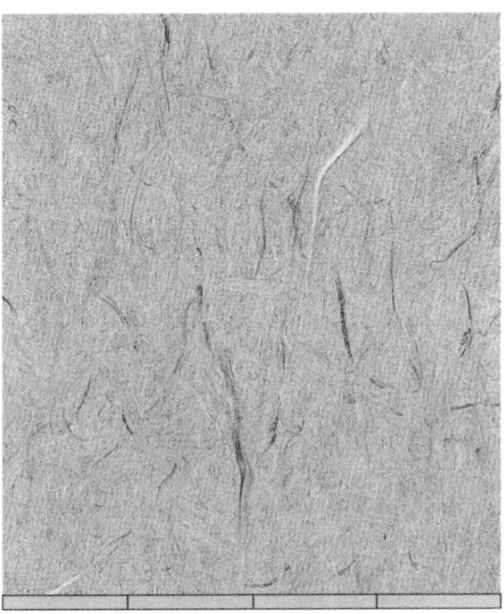

Maya Romanoff/Washi Tsuchikabe Color **green** Alternative colors **available** Width **36½in/93cm** Length **to order** Repeat **–** Price ★★★★ T

Zoffany/Stucco PC81905 Color **05** Alternative colors **available** Width **20½in/52cm** Length **11yd/10m** Repeat **–** Price ★

Ornamenta/Lysander Cirrus GIR306 Color **gray** Alternative colors **available** Width **20½in/52cm** Length **11yd/10m** Repeat **–** Price ★

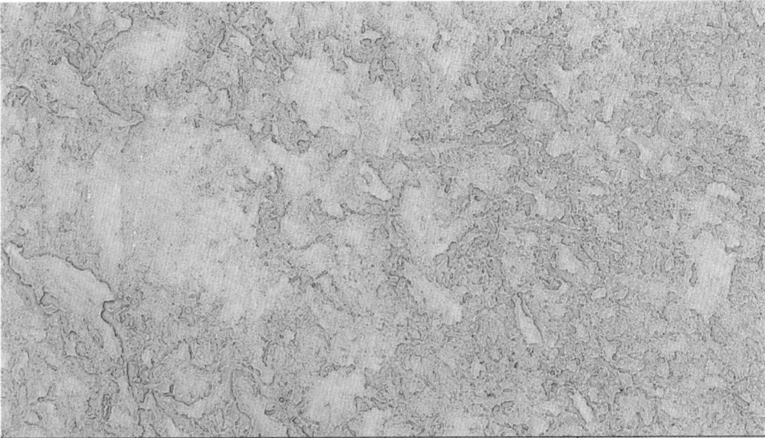

Maya Romanoff/Stucco MR-RV-2071 Color **adobe** Alternative colors **available** Width **37½in/95cm** Length **to order** Repeat **–** Price ★★★★ T

Harlequin/95002 Color **pastel** Alternative colors **available** Width **20½in/52cm** Length **11yd/10m** Repeat **–** Price ★

Maya Romanoff/Patina MR-T35-163 Color **mustard** Alternative colors **available** Width **30¼in/77cm** Length **to order** Repeat **–** Price ★★★★ T

Ornamenta/Woodgrain WGR808 Color **beige, pink, and rose** Alternative colors **available** Width **21in/53cm** Length **11yd/10m** Repeat – Price ★★

Anya Larkin/Moondust Teapaper Color **236 pueblo** Alternative colors **available** Width **40¼in/102cm** Length **3½yd/3m** Repeat – Price ★★★★★

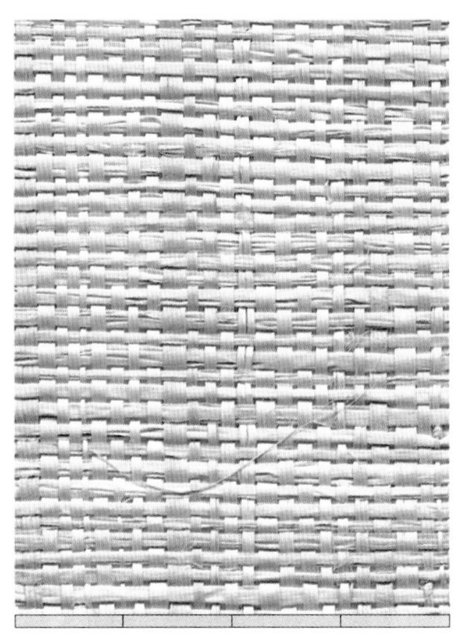

Andrew Martin/Raffia Medium Color **natural** Alternative colors **not available** Width **30in/76cm** Length **6½yd/6m** Repeat – Price ★★★

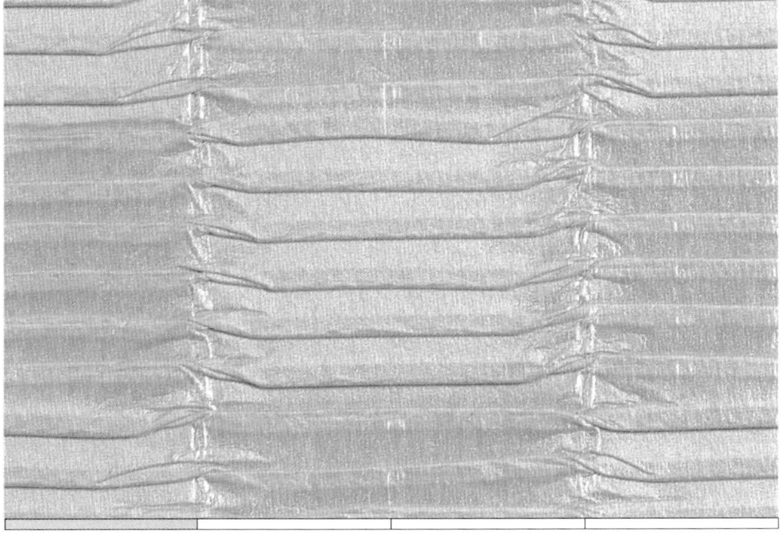

Anya Larkin/Concertina Color **430 ivory** Alternative colors **available** Width **29in/74cm** Length **3½yd/3m** Repeat – Price ★★★★★

Maya Romanoff/Jewel Collection Color **moonstone** Alternative colors **available** Width **36½in/93cm** Length **to order** Repeat – Price ★★★ T

David Bonk/Light Fawn Color **709** Alternative colors **available** Width **36½in/93cm** Length **2¾yd/2.5m** Repeat – Price ★★★★★

Anya Larkin/Flat Teapaper Color **104 gold** Alternative colors **available** Width **40¼in/102cm** Length **3½yd/3m** Repeat – Price ★★★★★

GRASS CLOTHS

Textured wallpapers with a "natural" look have been popular since the mid-1960s, especially in northern Europe and Scandinavia. Examples include loose-weave burlap (laminated to a paper backing), suedes, and grass cloths (as shown here). The latter, which consists of parallel strips of dried grass or seaweed glued or woven to a coarse paper ground, had been used as wall coverings in Korea and Japan for centuries. Many of the grass cloths employed in Western interiors are imported from the Far East, but some are produced in Europe (notably France), and these often have a flame-retardant coating.

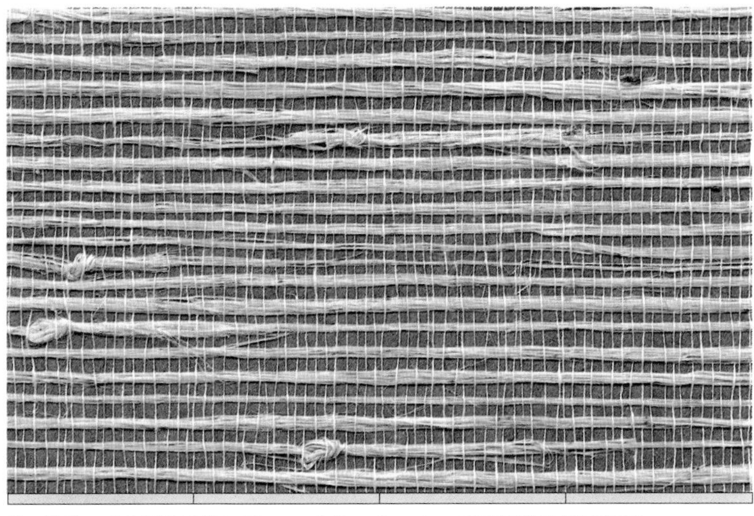

Donghia/Grasscloth G946-04 Color **04 seaweed** Alternative colors **available** Width **35¾in/91cm** Length **3¾yd/3.5m** Repeat – Price ★★★★

Plains

Wallpapers displaying subtle mottling and gradations of color printed in imitation of stonework, such as marble, limestone, granite, and porphyry, were produced in Italy and France as early as the 16th century. As a cheaper substitute for the often unavailable raw material, they have remained in widespread use ever since. Papers simulating the colors, figuring, and grain of hardwoods, such as mahogany, oak, maple, and birch, have also proved fashionable since the 17th century and have been primarily employed as an alternative to increasingly expensive dado, half-height, or full-height wall-paneling. Throughout the 20th century, other special-effect papers appeared featuring abstract patterns not dissimilar to faux stone and wood. Among the most notable and influential are the Modernist papers of the 1930s, which displayed blurred, streaky patches of graduated color, and were sometimes enlivened with gilt powders.

4

1

2

3

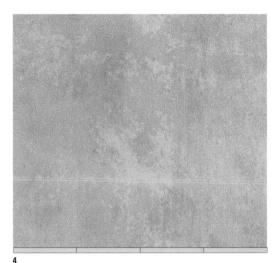

1 **K and K Designs/16214** Color **gold** Alternative colors **available** Width **21in/53cm** Length **11yd/10m** Repeat – Price ★

2 **De Gournay/"E" Red Silk** Color **red** Alternative colors **available** Width **36½in/93cm** Length **3¼yd/3m** Repeat – Price ★★★ ♣

3 **Fine Decor/Milano 14122** Color **lemon** Alternative colors **available** Width **20½in/52cm** Length **11yd/10m** Repeat **21in/53cm** Price ★

5

6

4 **Coloroll/Lindsey 528401** Color **rust** Alternative colors **available** Width **20½in/52cm** Length **11yd/10m** Repeat – Price ★

5 **Ornamenta/Pelham Moiré MOI 106** Color **terracotta** Alternative colors **available** Width **20½in/52cm** Length **11yd/10m** Repeat – Price ★

6 **Nobilis-Fontan/Louisiane LOS313** Color **sunset** Alternative colors **available** Width **27½in/70cm** Length **11yd/10m** Repeat – Price ★

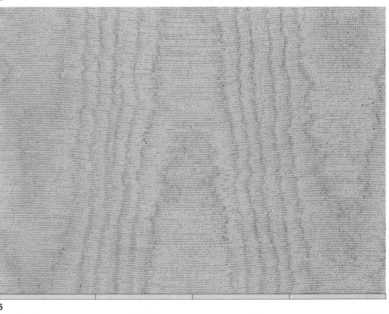

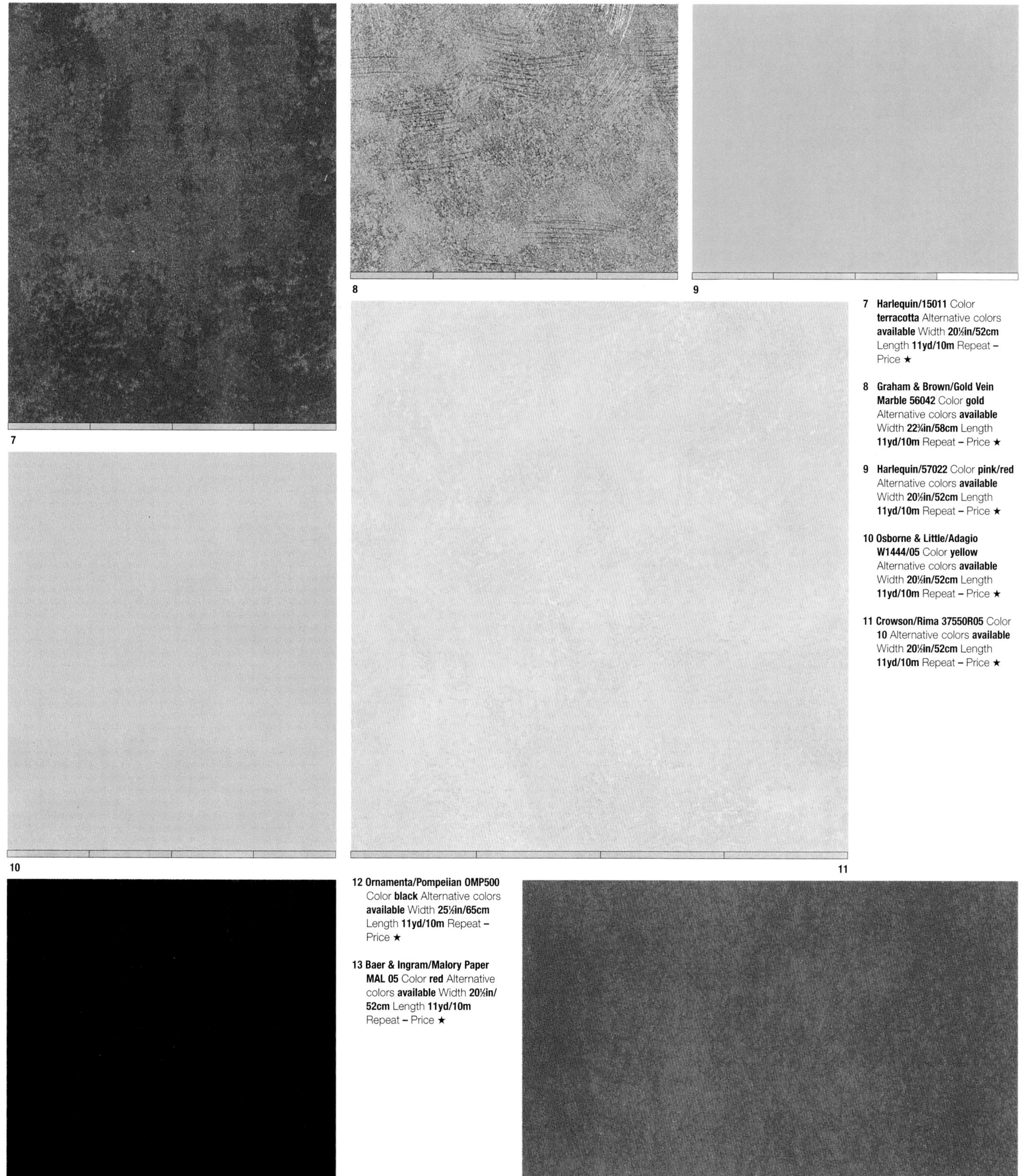

7 **Harlequin/15011** Color **terracotta** Alternative colors **available** Width **20½in/52cm** Length **11yd/10m** Repeat **–** Price ★

8 **Graham & Brown/Gold Vein Marble 56042** Color **gold** Alternative colors **available** Width **22¾in/58cm** Length **11yd/10m** Repeat **–** Price ★

9 **Harlequin/57022** Color **pink/red** Alternative colors **available** Width **20½in/52cm** Length **11yd/10m** Repeat **–** Price ★

10 **Osborne & Little/Adagio W1444/05** Color **yellow** Alternative colors **available** Width **20½in/52cm** Length **11yd/10m** Repeat **–** Price ★

11 **Crowson/Rima 37550R05** Color **10** Alternative colors **available** Width **20½in/52cm** Length **11yd/10m** Repeat **–** Price ★

12 **Ornamenta/Pompeiian OMP500** Color **black** Alternative colors **available** Width **25½in/65cm** Length **11yd/10m** Repeat **–** Price ★

13 **Baer & Ingram/Malory Paper MAL 05** Color **red** Alternative colors **available** Width **20½in/52cm** Length **11yd/10m** Repeat **–** Price ★

Plains

Over the centuries, but particularly since the mid-19th century, wallpapers produced in imitation of plain textiles have proved just as popular as those simulating the appearance of wood and stone (*see* page 202).

Favored "fabrics" during this period have included canvas, cambric, calico, burlap, tweed, moiré silks, seersuckers, and Lurex. In many cases the simulation is achieved by flat-printing the weave and subtle gradations of color that characterize the fabrics. Screen-printing and photogravure have proved particularly suitable for simulating texture, the latter achieving this *trompe l'oeil* effect by building up the finish with a series of small colored dots of varying degrees of opacity (*see* page 275.)

However, some of the faux fabrics produced, notably pile fabrics such as velvet and corduroy, have actually been textured, either by embossing the paper or by flocking it, while other fabric papers, such as Korean and European grass cloths (*see* page 201) are textured in their own right.

1

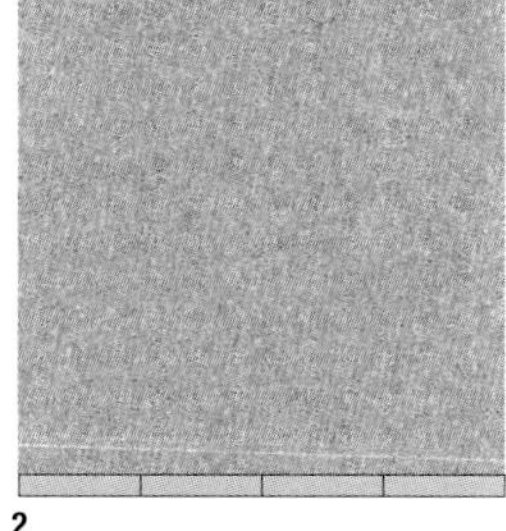

2

3

1 **Fardis/Pompeii 2510-28** Color **28** Alternative colors **available** Width **27½in/70cm** Length **11yd/10m** Repeat **21in/53cm** Price ★

2 **Northwood Designs/Senza 22023** Color **blue** Alternative colors **available** Width **35½in/90cm** Length **to order** Repeat – Price ★★

3 **Coloroll/Moiré 401810** Color **green** Alternative colors **available** Width **20½in/52cm** Length **11yd/10m** Repeat – Price ★

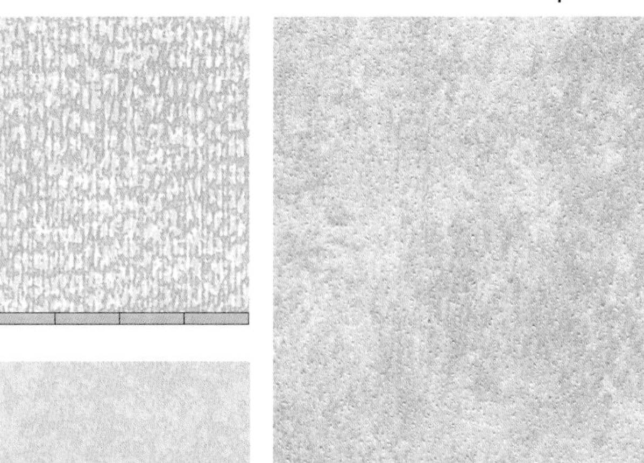

4

7

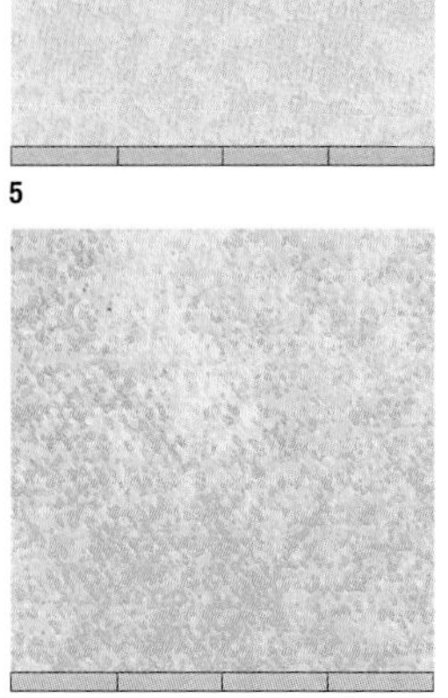

5

6

8

4 **Jane Churchill/Eliot JY60W-04** Color **blue** Alternative colors **available** Width **20½in/52cm** Length **11yd/10m** Repeat – Price ★

5 **Ornamenta/Pompeiian OMP508** Color **blue** Alternative colors **available** Width **25½in/65cm** Length **11yd/10m** Repeat – Price ★

6 **Anna French/Atelier** Color **ATEWP014** Alternative colors **available** Width **20½in/52cm** Length **11yd/10m** Repeat – Price ★

7 **Warwick/Hampton** Color **sapphire 5** Alternative colors **available** Width **20½in/52cm** Length **11½yd/10.5m** Repeat – Price ★

8 **Fardis/Oregon 5506-17** Color **17** Alternative colors **available** Width **27½in/70cm** Length **11yd/10m** Repeat – Price ★

9 **Fine Decor/Siena 18083** Color **green** Alternative colors **available** Width **20½in/52cm** Length **11yd/10m** Repeat **10½in/27cm** Price ★

10 **Cole & Son/Jaspé 57/2512/PR** Color **blue** Alternative colors **available** Width **20½in/52cm** Length **11yd/10m** Repeat **11¾in/30cm** Price ★

9

10

11 **J. W. Bollom/Brushed Suede** Color **purple** Alternative colors **available** Width **54¼in/138cm** Length **11yd/10m** Repeat **–** Price ★★

12 **Ornamenta/Pompeiian OMP509** Color **green** Alternative colors **available** Width **25½in/65cm** Length **11yd/10m** Repeat **–** Price ★

13 **Fine Decor/Milano 14118** Color **blue** Alternative colors **available** Width **20½in/52cm** Length **11yd/10m** Repeat **21in/53cm** Price ★

14 **Malabar/Shaha Malachite** Color **WCSH/13** Alternative colors **available** Width **20½in/52cm** Length **11yd/10m** Repeat **–** Price ★

15 **G. P. & J. Baker/Palissandrie 1500-04** Color **04** Alternative colors **available** Width **20½in/52cm** Length **11yd/10m** Repeat **–** Price ★

16 **Mauny/Faux Marbres FM14** Color **pink** Alternative colors **available** Width **22in/56cm** Length **11yd/10m** Repeat **–** Price ★★★ ♣

17 **Sheila Coombes/Ray W612-5** Color **5** Alternative colors **available** Width **21in/53cm** Length **11yd/10m** Repeat **–** Price ★★

18 **Crowson/Sancerre 37550S04** Color **71** Alternative colors **available** Width **20½in/52cm** Length **11yd/10m** Repeat **–** Price ★

Motif Wallpapers

LEFT This grand, 19th-century American dining room displays the papered tripartite division of walls–frieze, field, and dado–that was the height of fashion in reception rooms during this period. The ceiling is also compartmentalized with complementary papers in imitation of polychromatic plaster moldings. The motifs, which include stars and shells, are of classical origin.

The vast catalog of motifs that wallpaper designers have been able to draw on has accumulated since the late Middle Ages as Oriental, Asian, and African styles of ornament have gradually been added to those of European origin. In addition, the types of motifs favored at different periods have invariably reflected the cultural, aesthetic, and political preoccupations of the time.

For example, heraldic imagery remained very much in evidence during the early Renaissance and resurfaced during the Gothic Revival of the 19th century. Classical motifs began to appear during the Renaissance and were added to and refined up until the mid-19th century as knowledge of Ancient Greek and Roman civilizations increased. Chinese motifs were adopted from the late 17th century onward as European fascination with the Orient developed through trade. In the early 19th century, Egyptian motifs were assimilated during Napoleon's military campaigns. And during the 20th century, the imagery of Cubist, Pop Art, and Constructivist paintings found its way onto wallpapers.

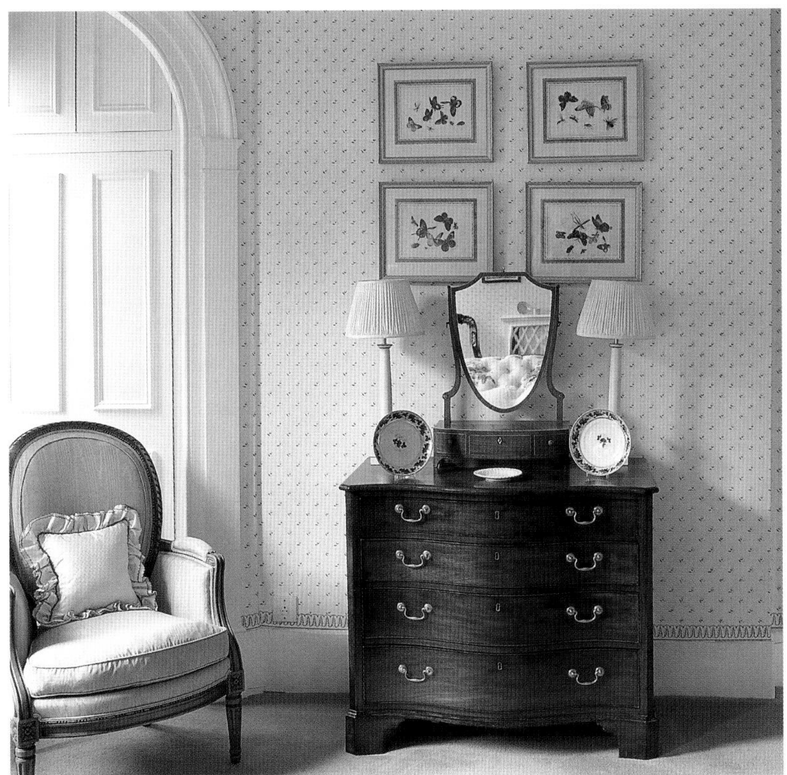

ABOVE While wallpapers embellished with classical imagery were much in evidence during the late 18th and early 19th centuries, patterns made up of small, regularly spaced leaf motifs, similar in appearance to medieval powdered ornament, were also fashionable.

WATTS OF WESTMINSTER

British architects G. F. Bodley, Thomas Garner, and Gilbert Scott the Younger founded Watts & Company in 1874 in order to produce wallpapers, textiles, needlework, and furniture in the Gothic Revival and early English Renaissance style, which they were unable to obtain elsewhere. Many of their hand-blocked wallpapers were inspired by A. W. N. Pugin's Gothic Revival designs, of which this diaper-patterned paper with floral motifs is a typical example. It is representative of what was to become the accepted decorative style of the Church of England and the British Establishment.

KEY DESIGNS

1 Highly conventionalized leaves and flowers, combined with repeat geometric motifs in imitation of Islamic tiles, were featured on many late Victorian papers, notably those by Christopher Dresser.

2 The stylized, three-petal lily flower–or fleur-de-lis–is a heraldic motif that has been in widespread use since the Middle Ages. It appeared on many 19th-century Gothic Revival wallpapers.

3 A heraldic symbol, also much used in Islamic ornament, the star has often appeared on wallpapers, notably in Regency England, and in America in the first years after independence.

4 Animal motifs, such as those derived from heraldic ornament, were frequently employed on wallpapers in 18th-century, Neoclassical, and Victorian interiors. The lion is a symbol of strength and pride.

5 Medieval and early Renaissance motifs, such as the rose and the coronet, appeared on many Gothic Revival papers of the 19th century. This example was designed by A. W. N. Pugin.

6 The lyre motif, here embellished with leaves, dates back to classical antiquity. There were revivals in the Neoclassical Empire and Regency interiors of the late 18th and early 19th centuries.

1 **Bradbury & Bradbury/Algernon AGW** Color **210** Alternative colors **available** Width **27in/68.5cm** Length **5yd/4.5m** Repeat **13½in/34.5cm** Price ★★★ ♣

2 **Baer & Ingram/CHEB 05** Color **red and gold** Alternative colors **available** Width **20½in/52cm** Length **11yd/10m** Repeat **–** Price ★

3 **Watts of Westminster/Cleopatra Star W0012** Color **Llewellyn** Alternative colors **available** Width **21¼in/54cm** Length **11yd/10m** Repeat **3in/8cm** Price ★★

4 **Zuber/Lions 40028** Color **gris et vert** Alternative colors **available** Width **18½in/47cm** Length **11yd/10m** Repeat **9in/23cm** Price ★★★ ♣

5 **Watts of Westminster/Tudor Badge W0058-04/B11** Color **I14** Alternative colors **available** Width **20½in/52cm** Length **11yd/10m** Repeat **5in/13cm** Price ★

6 **The Design Archives/Rosemonde 58035** Color **2** Alternative colors **available** Width **20½in/52cm** Length **11yd/10m** Repeat **6in/15cm** Price ★

Motifs: **Pre-19th century**

The most commonly used motifs on late 15th- and 16th-century papers were heraldic and floral, and were mainly woodcut-printed or stenciled. Typical heraldic imagery were coats of arms, emblems, cyphers, and fleur-de-lis, while notable flowers and plant forms included Tudor roses, anemones, columbines, thistles, chestnuts and acorns, and stylized pomegranates and pinecones derived from European damasks. On many papers these motifs were applied to plain grounds, but on others they were printed on faux marble or framed by simple diaper patterns. Heraldic motifs and stylized plant forms remained fashionable during the 17th century. Naturalistic flowers, fruits, caterpillars, and butterflies, as found on "Spanish stitch" textiles, were also in evidence, as were classical motifs such as cupids, putti, vases, and urns. Classical imagery remained popular throughout the 18th century, when it also included eagles, dolphins, masks, rosettes, griffins, and architectural components inspired by archaeological discoveries at Herculaneum and Pompeii. Also favoredr in the late 17th and 18th centuries were motifs that were taken from Oriental pictorials, including pagodas, dragons, and exotic birds and flowers (*see* pages 128-9).

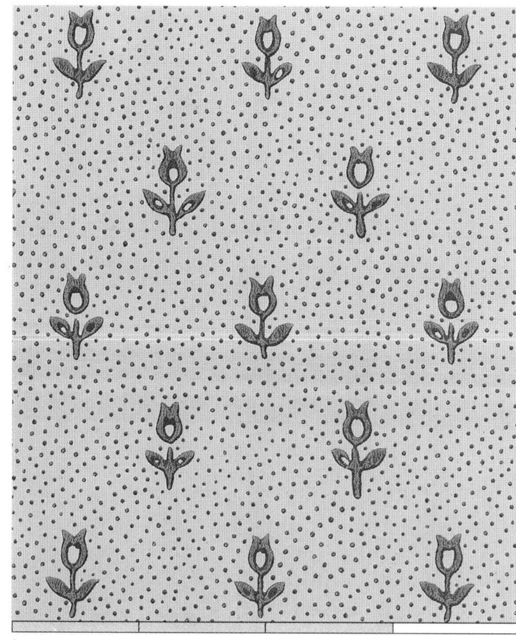
1

1 Cole & Son/Sprig & Spot 12/094/PR Color **blue on buff** Alternative colors **available** Width **21in/53cm** Length **11yd/10m** Repeat **2in/5cm** Price ★

2 Hamilton Weston/Archway House Color **white, green, and black on gray** Alternative colors **available** Width **20½in/52cm** Length **11yd/10m** Repeat **3½in/9cm** Price ★★

3 Elizabeth Eaton/Saighton Color **No. 4** Alternative colors **available** Width **22½in/57cm** Length **11yd/10m** Repeat **2in/5cm** Price ★

4 Cole & Son/Temple Newsam Color **special** Alternative colors **available** Width **20½in/52cm** Length **11yd/10m** Repeat **21¼in/54cm** Price ★★

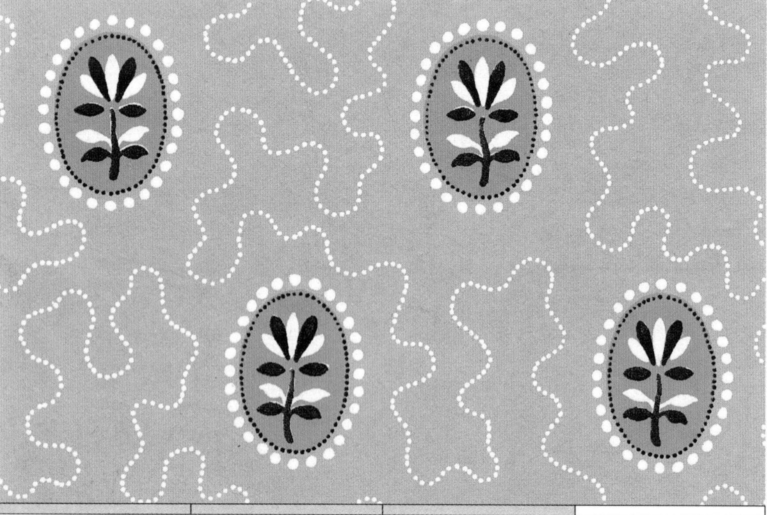
2

3

4

5

7

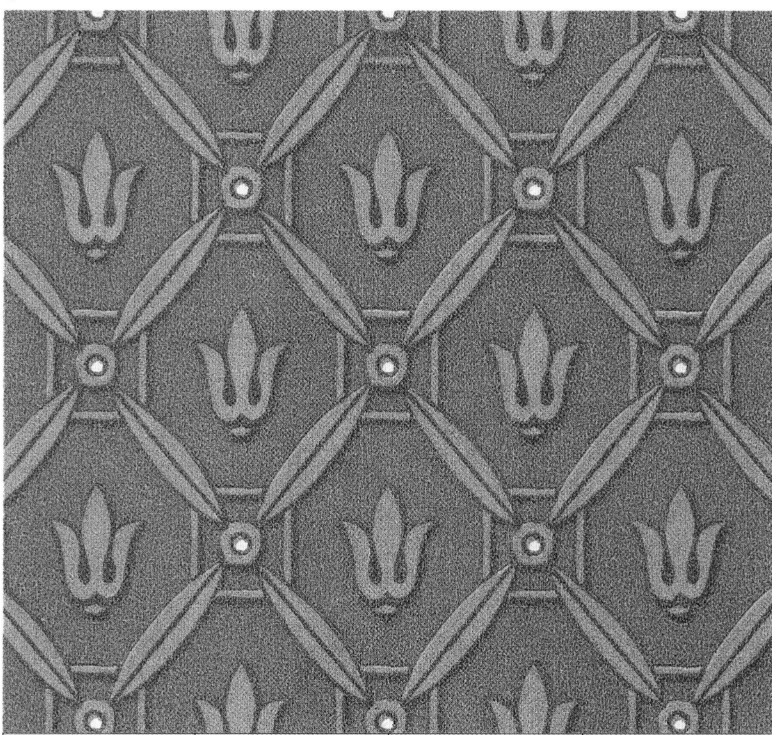

6

5 Hamilton Weston/Guilloche BD43 Color **ocher** Alternative colors **available** Width **1½in/ 4cm** Length **11yd/10m** Repeat **–** Price ★ ♛

6 The Design Archives/Delphi 58020 Color **3** Alternative colors **available** Width **20½in/52cm** Length **11yd/ 10m** Repeat **1¾in/4.5cm** Price ★

7 Hamilton Weston/Embroidery BD21 Color **gray** Alternative colors **available** Width **1½in/ 4cm** Length **11yd/10m** Repeat **–** Price ★ ♛

8 Cole & Son/Georgian Button 12-101/PR Color **red on cream** Alternative colors **available** Width **21in/53cm** Length **11yd/10m** Repeat **1¾in/4.5cm** Price ★

8

9

10

9 Ornamenta/Gothick Shadow GTK 408 Color **beige** Alternative colors **available** Width **20½in/52cm** Length **11yd/10m** Repeat **11¾in/ 30cm** Price ★★ ♛

10 Baer & Ingram/Blazon BLAB 09 Color **blue on red** Alternative colors **available** Width **5in/ 12.5cm** Length **11yd/10m** Repeat **21in/53cm** Price ★

11 Zoffany/Brittany 36BY03 Color **03** Alternative colors **available** Width **20½in/52cm** Length **11yd/10m** Repeat **3in/8cm** Price ★

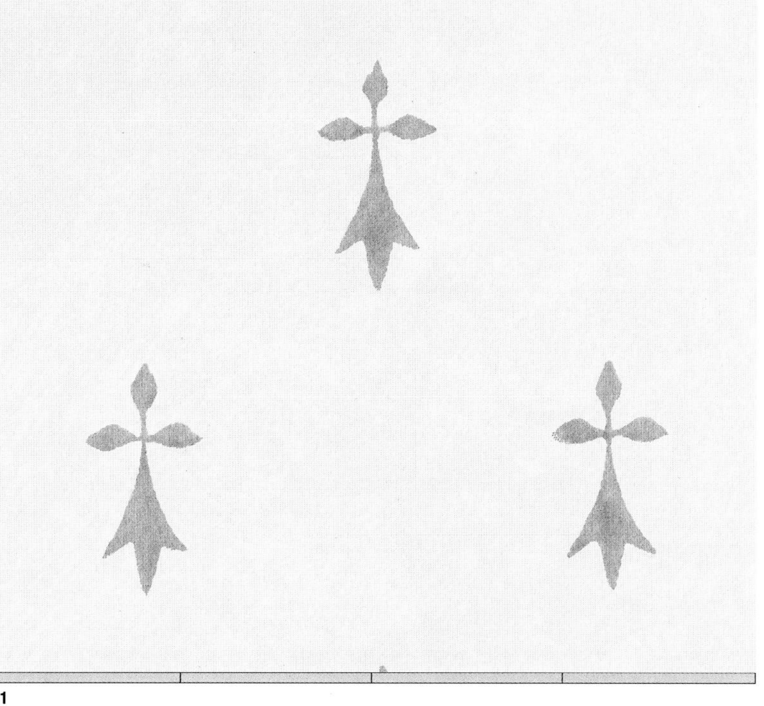

11

Motifs: **Early 19th century**

Many of the early 19th-century papers patterned with repeat motifs were printed in England where, unlike in France, a stringent government tax based on the weight of the wallpaper inhibited the production of large pictorial designs. The majority of motif patterns produced for the French Empire, English Regency, and American Federal interiors in the first 30 years of the century were derived from the classical vocabulary of ornament, particularly Roman and Etruscan. Egyptian motifs, including scarabs, sphinxes, and lotus flowers, were also much in evidence following the Peninsular War fought between France and England.

Typical Roman motifs, popular in America and Europe, and especially in France under the empire of Napoleon Bonaparte, included laurel, oak, and olive wreaths, rosettes, arrows and lances, winged torches, lions, eagles, and griffins. Favored Etruscan motifs–which were in fact Ancient Greek in origin–included palm leaves, anthemia, festoons, vases, medallions, and chimeras, while Egyptian influence was evident in lotus flowers, scarabs, and sphinxes. Also popular during this period were *trompe l'oeil* border papers made in imitation of acanthus leaf, Greek key, rope, dentil, and egg-and-dart plaster or stucco moldings.

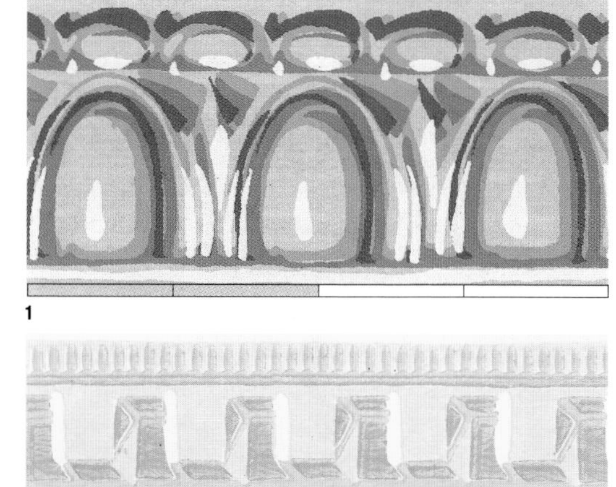

1

2

1 **Alexander Beauchamp/Egg and Dart Border** Color **gray** Alternative colors **available** Width **2½in/6.5cm** Length **25m/27½yd** Repeat **2in/5cm** Price ★★★★ ♛

2 **G. P. & J. Baker/Keystone Border W0122-02** Color **02** Alternative colors **available** Width **2⅜in/6cm** Length **11yd/10m** Repeat **3in/8cm** Price ★

3 **Zuber/Petits Lauriers 40084** Color **JSD** Alternative colors **available** Width **18½in/47cm** Length **11yd/10m** Repeat **21½in/55cm** Price ★★★

4 **The Design Archives/Zola 58032** Color **4** Alternative colors **available** Width **20½in/52cm** Length **11yd/10m** Repeat **9in/23cm** Price ★

3

4

5

5 **Osborne & Little/Couronne W590-05** Color **pale green** Alternative colors **available** Width **20½in/52cm** Length **11yd/10m** Repeat **10½in/27cm** Price ★

6 **G. P. & J. Baker/Corinth Border W0119-01** Color **01** Alternative colors **available** Width **4¾in/12cm** Length **11yd/10m** Repeat **4¾in/12cm** Price ★

7 **Hamilton Weston/Anthemion** Color **BC13 blue** Alternative colors **available** Width **1½in/4cm** Length **11yd/10m** Repeat – Price ★ ♛

6

7

8

9

10

11

8 Osborne & Little/Zoroaster B1072/01 Color **blue** Alternative colors **available** Width **6¾in/ 17.5cm** Length **11yd/10m** Repeat **–** Price ★

9 Hamilton Weston/Green Park Color **210** Alternative colors **available** Width **20½in/52cm** Length **11yd/10m** Repeat **1½in/4cm** Price ★

10 Jane Churchill/Colbrooke Sprig JY58W-07 Color **yellow** Alternative colors **available** Width **20½in/52cm** Length **11yd/10m** Repeat **1¾in/ 4.5cm** Price ★

11 G. P. & J. Baker/Heraldic Damask W0113-02 Color **02** Alternative colors **available** Width **20½in/52cm** Length **11yd/10m** Repeat **21in/ 53cm** Price ★

12

13

12 Hamilton Weston/Regency Rosette Color **mint green on pale green** Alternative colors **available** Width **20½in/52cm** Length **11yd/ 10m** Repeat **2in/5cm** Price ★★

13 Cole & Son/Victorian Star 55/3017/PR Color **gold on red** Alternative colors **available** Width **20½in/52cm** Length **11yd/10m** Repeat **1¾in/4.5cm** Price ★

14 Zoffany/Blois V32201 Color **01** Alternative colors **available** Width **20½in/52cm** Length **11yd/10m** Repeat **3½in/9cm** Price ★

15 Colefax and Fowler/Rosace Border 7068/04 Color **coral** Alternative colors **available** Width **3½in/9cm** Length **11yd/10m** Repeat **–** Price ★

14

15

Motifs: **Mid-19th century**

The majority of classical motifs that had appeared on wallpapers during the early 19th century also found favor in the Renaissance and Baroque Revival interiors fashionable on both sides of the Atlantic around the middle of the century. In contrast to these predominantly naturalistic and often "three-dimensionalized" classical motifs were the stylized, flat motifs employed on Gothic Revival wallpapers throughout Europe, notably those devised by influential English designers such as A. W. N. Pugin (*see* opposite) and Owen Jones.

Conventionalized plant forms, often presented within a geometrical pattern structure, lay at the heart of many of Pugin's and Jones's designs. However, while Pugin drew heavily and precisely from the Gothic and heraldic vocabulary of ornament prevalent during the Middle Ages and the early Renaissance, Jones's sources were more wide-ranging. These were primarily Oriental–Chinese, Far Eastern, Persian, Indian, Arabic, and Moorish–but they also embraced medieval imagery and primitive art.

Watts of Westminster/Quatre Foil W0042-06/B11 Color **I16** Alternative colors **available** Width **20½in/52cm** Repeat **11yd/10m** Repeat **3½in/9cm** Price ★

Hodsoll McKenzie/Fleur de Lys 504/631 Color **yellow** Alternative colors **available** Width **20½in/52cm** Length **11yd/10m** Repeat **3in/7.5cm** Price ★

Watts of Westminster/Pineapple W0039-03/I12 Color **Seton** Alternative colors **available** Width **21¼in/54cm** Length **11yd/10m** Repeat **10½in/27cm** Price ★★

Zuber/Alcove Chambre de la Reine 9222 Color **gold, terracotta, and gray** Alternative colors **not available** Width **20in/51cm** Length **10yd/9m** Repeat **34½in/88cm** Price ★★★★

Cole & Son/The Strawberry 10-HP117 Color **stock** Alternative colors **available** Width **20½in/52cm** Length **11yd/10m** Repeat **14½in/37cm** Price ★★★

Zoffany/Owen Jones Narrow Border BLK412 Color **412** Alternative colors **available** Width **4¾in/12cm** Length **11yd/10m** Repeat **–** Price ★

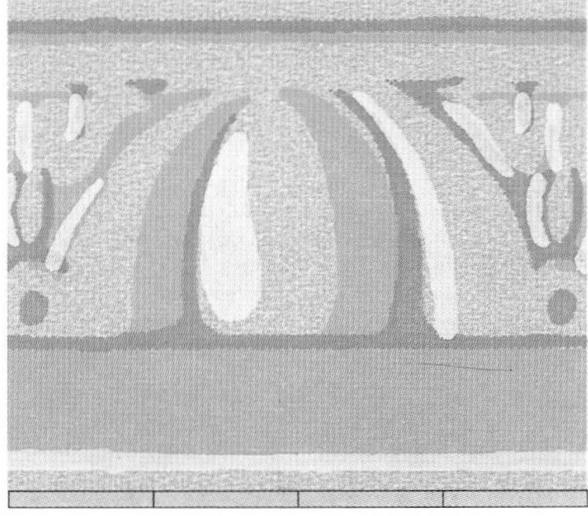

Zoffany/Egg and Dart Border BLM207 Color **07** Alternative colors **available** Width **1½in/4cm** Length **11yd/10m** Repeat **–** Price ★

Cole & Son/Block 015 Color **yellow on green** Alternative colors **available** Width **20½in/52cm** Length **11yd/10m** Repeat **–** Price ★★★ ♣

Watts of Westminster/Rose & Coronet Color **Stuart** Alternative colors **available** Width **21¼in/54cm** Length **11yd/10m** Repeat **17¾in/45cm** Price ★★

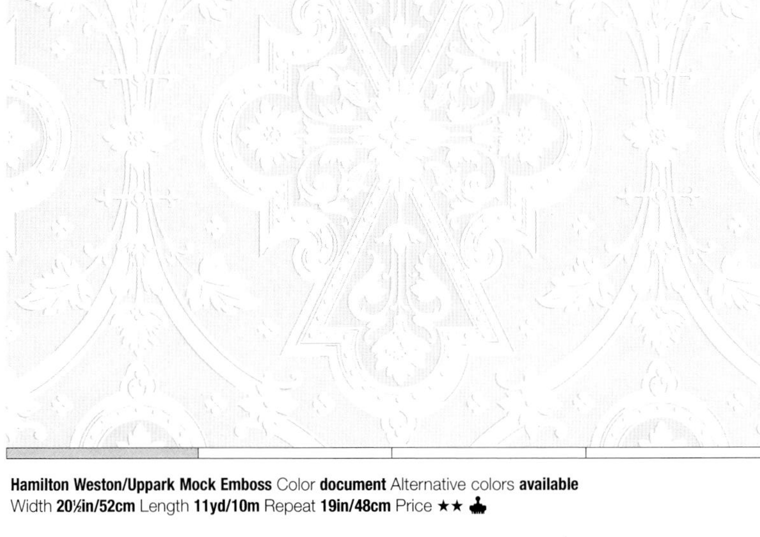

Hamilton Weston/Uppark Mock Emboss Color **document** Alternative colors **available** Width **20½in/52cm** Length **11yd/10m** Repeat **19in/48cm** Price ★★ ♣

Watts of Westminster/Shrewsbury W0050 Color **Walton** Alternative colors **available** Width **21¼in/54cm** Length **11yd/10m** Repeat **18½in/47cm** Price ★★

Zoffany/Owen Jones Broad Border BLJ507 Color **07** Alternative colors **available** Width **4¾in/12cm** Length **11yd/10m** Repeat **–** Price ★

Zoffany/Gothic Flower 36GF04 Color **04** Alternative colors **available** Width **20½in/52cm** Length **11yd/10m** Repeat **12½in/32cm** Price ★

PUGIN'S PAPERS

The English designer and architect A. W. N. Pugin (1812-52) designed hundreds of wallpapers in the mid-19th century, notably for the New Palace of Westminster, in London, England. Dismissive of eclecticism, and scornful of *trompe l'oeil* papers for creating "dishonest" illusions of depth on "two-dimensional" surfaces, his flat and conventionalized treatments of imagery were derived from Gothic art. Typical patterns included heraldic emblems and stylized fruit and foliage forms found on medieval manuscripts and textiles, and geometric patterns based on medieval tiles and stenciling.

Watts of Westminster/Trellis W0056-06/I12 Color **Padgett** Alternative colors **available** Width **21¼in/54cm** Length **11yd/10m** Repeat **7in/18cm** Price ★★

Watts of Westminster/Triad W5057-15/A13 Color **Amsterdam** Alternative colors **available** Width **21¼in/54cm** Length **11yd/10m** Repeat **31½in/80cm** Price ★★

Motifs: **Late 19th century**

The tremendous variety of motifs employed on wallpapers during the last three decades of the 19th century reflected the eclectic mixture of decorative styles favored at this time in both Europe and the United States. Classical and Pompeiian motifs of the 18th century (*see* pages 208-9) reemerged, and A. W. N. Pugin's Gothic Revival imagery endured, especially in Britain, while the Oriental- and Moresque-based patterns of Owen Jones remained internationally influential.

However, the most distinctive, and in many respects the most innovative, wallpapers of the late 19th century were produced by designers working under the aegis of the Arts and Crafts, Aesthetic, and Art Nouveau Movements. Many Arts and Crafts-patterned wallpapers, particularly those devised by William Morris, were characterized by stylized, rhythmical plant forms, usually English, floral, and medieval in origin. Conventionalized as well as naturalistic plant forms, together with exotic bird and insect motifs, were also an important feature of both Aesthetic and Art Nouveau papers, and were inspired not only by medieval imagery, but also by Renaissance, Rococo, Chinese, and, especially, Japanese styles of ornament.

1

2

3

4

1 **Zuber/Fleur de Lys 4805 BRD** Color **blue** Alternative colors **available** Width **18½in/47cm** Length **11yd/10m** Repeat **13in/33cm** Price ★★★

2 **Hamilton Weston/Victorian Leaf Quatrefoil** Color **cream, gray, and gray/blue** Alternative colors **available** Width **20½in/52cm** Length **11yd/10m** Repeat **6¼in/15cm** Price ★★ ♣

3 **Zoffany/Maple V43805** Color **05** Alternative colors **available** Width **20½in/52cm** Length **11yd/10m** Repeat – Price ★

4 **Zoffany/Lennel BLY02** Color **02** Alternative colors **available** Width **20½in/52cm** Length **11yd/10m** Repeat **12½in/32cm** Price ★

5 **G. P. & J. Baker/Fleur de Lys W0097-09** Color **red** Alternative colors **available** Width **20½in/52cm** Length **11yd/10m** Repeat **2in/5cm** Price ★

5

6

7

8

6 Bradbury & Bradbury/Roland RLW-130 Color **130** Alternative colors **available** Width **26¾in/68cm** Length **5yd/ 4.5m** Repeat **10½in/27cm** Price ★★ ♣

7 Malabar/Cherimoya WCTA/10 Color **10** Alternative colors **available** Width **20½in/52cm** Length **11yd/10m** Repeat **–** Price ★

8 Watts of Westminster/Gaheris WW0017-02/E12 Color **Garbot** Alternative colors **available** Width **18½in/47cm** Length **11yd/10m** Repeat **7½in/19cm** Price ★★

9 Cole & Son/Butterflies 54/4717/PR Color **red on green** Alternative colors **available** Width **20½in/52cm** Length **11yd/10m** Repeat **12in/30.5cm** Price ★

9

10

10 Manuel Canovas/Daphnis 8089 Color **27 jaune** Alternative colors **available** Width **27in/69cm** Length **11yd/10m** Repeat **12½in/ 32cm** Price ★★★★ ♣

11 Zoffany/Florentine Lily ZV0503 Color **03** Alternative colors **available** Width **20½in/52cm** Length **11yd/10m** Repeat **3in/8cm** Price ★

11

Motifs: **Early 20th century**

Although plant-form motifs were generally excluded from Modernist designs, they were widely employed in the other fashionable decorative styles of the early 20th century. For example, Art Nouveau wallpapers featured roots, stems, and elongated blooms, while small leaves, fruits, and cup-shaped blossoms appeared on Deutscher Werkbund papers. Arts and Crafts papers were characterized by conventionalized flowers and leaves, while early Art Deco designs incorporated stylized floral motifs (*see* pages 120-1). Many wallpapers were also produced in imitation of 18th- and 19th-century floral chintzes. Even the highly mathematical Cubist-patterned papers of the 1920s and 1930s were sometimes softened with small flower or leaf motifs.

Apart from Egyptian motifs (*see* opposite), heraldic imagery on Tudor Revival papers, and bows, swags, shells, insects, and architectural scrollwork inspired by 18th-century, French Rococo, and Neoclassical decoration, the majority of other fashionable motifs were either geometric or abstract in form. These included medieval and Oriental diaper patterns, the stepped shapes and overlapping squares and oblongs of Art Deco, and the shaded circles, triangles, and rectangles inspired by Constructivist principles of painting.

2

1

FINISHING LINCRUSTA

Machine-embossed Lincrusta papers–a composite of linseed oil, gum, resins, and wood pulp on canvas (*see* page 233)–provided a substantially cheaper alternative to traditional wood, plaster, leather, and tile paneling and moldings. Lincrusta was particularly suited to avant-garde use. The example shown here was designed for dado paneling and features a stylized flower and foliage pattern typical of early 20th-century Art Nouveau. Its faux tile finish was created by lightly distressing a blue-green oil-based glaze, applied over a bronze-gold base coat.

Akzo Nobel/Edwardian Dado RD1950 Color **white** Alternative colors **not available** Width **24in/61cm** Length **40¼in/102cm** Repeat **–** Price ★★★★

1 **Graham & Brown/Motif 56460** Color **green** Alternative colors **available** Width **20½in/52cm** Length **11yd/10m** Repeat **4in/10.5cm** Price ★

2 **Bradbury & Bradbury/Neo-Grecian Dado NGD-210** Color **210** Alternative colors **available** Width **27in/69cm** Length **sold by yard** Repeat **13¾in/35cm** Price ★★★

3 **Coloroll/Cabriolet 401605** Color **pink** Alternative colors **available** Width **20½in/52cm** Length **11yd/10m** Repeat **5½in/14cm** Price ★

4 **Watts of Westminster/French Stripe WW0016-11/I11** Color **M22** Alternative colors **available** Width **20½in/52cm** Length **11yd/10m** Repeat **10½in/27cm** Price ★

5 **Coloroll/Fleur de Lys** Color **M22** Alternative colors **available** Width **20½in/52cm** Length **11yd/10m** Repeat **10½in/27cm** Price ★

6 **Alexander Beauchamp/Florence** Color **red, gold, and black** Alternative colors **available** Width **21in/53cm** Length **11yd/10m** Repeat **30in/76cm** Price ★★★

3

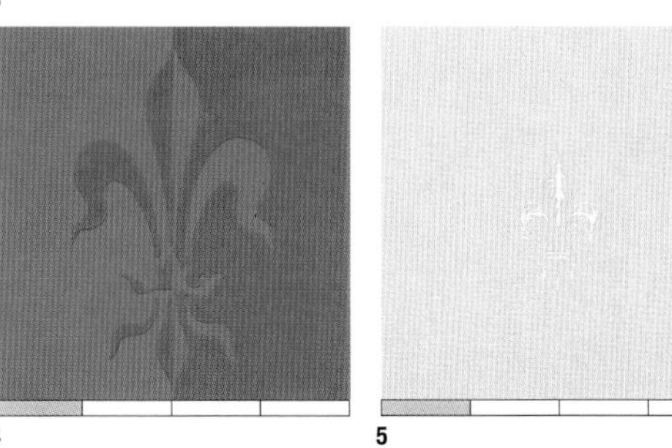

4 5

6

EGYPTIAN MOTIFS

Wallpapers that were patterned with Egyptian motifs first became fashionable in early 19th-century Neoclassical interiors, particularly in France and England, following Napoleon Bonaparte's military campaigns in Egypt. They also appeared on English wallpapers during the last quarter of the 19th century as the British Empire consolidated its rule over Egypt. However, during the first half of the 20th century Egyptian motifs such as scarabs, sphinxes, lotus leaves, and, as shown here, palm trees and camels enjoyed a revival. Egyptian elements and features appeared frequently in Art Deco schemes of the period.

Andrew Martin/Khartoum Color **red** Alternative colors **available** Width **20½in/52cm** Length **11yd/10m** Repeat **10¼in/26cm** Price ★

9

10

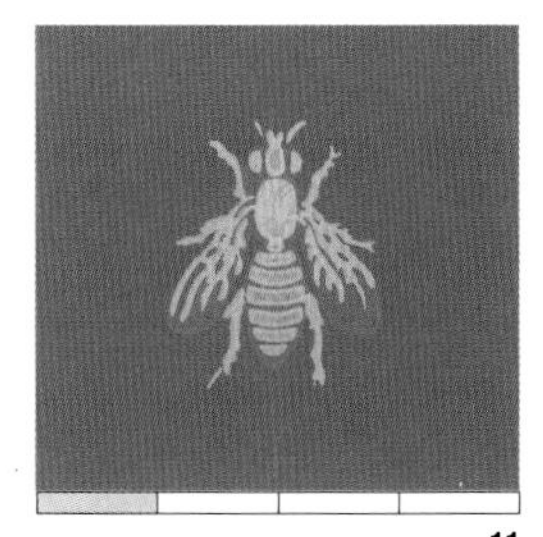

11

7

8

12

13

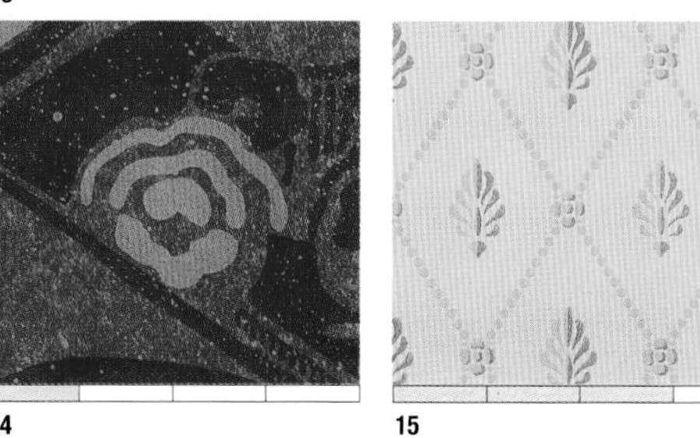

14

15

7 **Osborne & Little/Beachcomber W841/04** Color **blue** Alternative colors **available** Width **20½in/52cm** Length **11yd/10m** Repeat **5½in/14cm** Price ★

8 **Ramm, Son & Crocker/Millbrook Border W1246** Color **sea foam** Alternative colors **available** Width **3½in/9cm** Length **11yd/10m** Repeat **3in/7.5cm** Price ★

9 **Graham & Brown/Fleur de Lys 16537** Color **cream** Alternative colors **available** Width **20½in/52cm** Length **11yd/10m** Repeat **3in/8cm** Price ★

10 **Osborne & Little/Chantilly VW1223/04** Color **terracotta** Alternative colors **available** Width **20½in/52cm** Length **11yd/10m** Repeat **4¼in/11cm** Price ★

11 **Zuber/Grandes Abeilles 30118V0** Color **green** Alternative colors **available** Width **18½in/47cm** Length **11yd/10m** Repeat **9½in/24cm** Price ★★★

12 **Harlequin/1553** Color **terracotta** Alternative colors **available** Width **3¼in/8.5cm** Length **5½yd/5m** Repeat – Price ★

13 **Graham & Brown/Shantou 96273** Color **green** Alternative colors **available** Width **4in/10cm** Length **5½yd/5m** Repeat – Price ★

14 **Alexander Beauchamp/Art Deco Fans** Color **special** Alternative colors **available** Width **21in/53cm** Length **11yd/10m** Repeat **21½in/55in** Price ★★★ ♣

15 **Cole & Son/Alma Trellis 55/3062/PR** Color **yellow and gold** Alternative colors **available** Width **20½in/52cm** Length **11yd/10m** Repeat **5¼in/13.5cm** Price ★

Motifs: **Late 20th century**

During the 1950s and 1960s, wallpapers embellished with geometric and abstract motifs retained their popularity from earlier in the century. Apart from Cubist-inspired squares and oblongs, motif designs from the 1950s included diamonds, suns, stars, checks, "worm-casts," prisms, sound waves, and sketchy squiggles and organic shapes based on amoeba and crystalline structures. In the 1960s, sunbursts, giant circles, and even flying saucer shapes appeared.

Plant-form motifs also remained prevalent during this period, especially in the United States and Scandinavia, where many designers were preoccupied with bringing nature indoors. Papers of this genre designed to appeal to traditionalists displayed patterns such as large-scale tropical flowers or leaves, single roses in cartouches, and Victorian sprigs or stylized flowers on diaper grounds derived from Persian art and ceramics, as well as sinuous Art Nouveau–style roots, stems, and elongated blooms. More modern designs included wild strawberries, marine fauna, and cow parsley, while papers intended for kitchens featured not only fruits and vegetables, but also kitchenware, recipes, and bottles of "foreign" wine (*see* page 138), the latter reflecting the substantial increase in international leisure travel at this time.

1

2

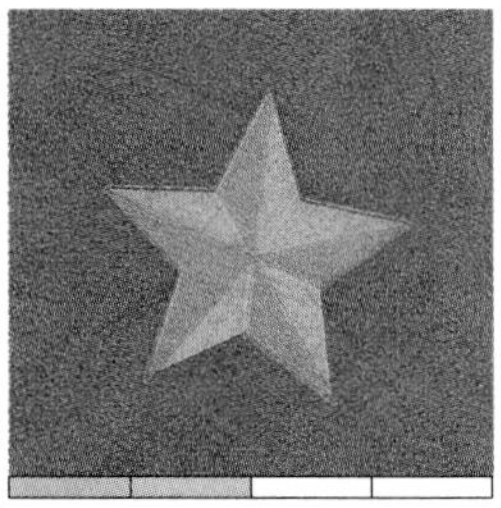

3

4

6

5

7

1 **Coloroll/Tournament 703372** Color **red** Alternative colors **available** Width **20½in/52cm** Length **11yd/10m** Repeat **6¾in/17.5cm** Price ★

2 **Coloroll/Holdenby Border 400325** Color **red** Alternative colors **available** Width **6¾in/17cm** Length **5½yd/5m** Repeat **10½in/26.5cm** Price ★

3 **Coloroll/Castille 703433** Color **green** Alternative colors **available** Width **20½in/52cm** Length **11yd/10m** Repeat **10½in/26.5cm** Price ★

4 **Zoffany/Palm NC9802** Color **peach** Alternative colors **available** Width **20½in/52cm** Length **11yd/10m** Repeat **–** Price ★

5 **Zoffany/Star 36ST05** Color **05** Alternative colors **available** Width **20½in/52cm** Length **11yd/10m** Repeat **12½in/32cm** Price ★

6 **Ciel Decor/Bonis PPA 0078.047** Color **blanc marine** Alternative colors **available** Width **59in/150cm** Length **11yd/10m** Repeat **1in/2.5cm** Price ★

7 **Osborne & Little/Consul B592/10** Color **blue** Alternative colors **available** Width **4in/10.5cm** Length **11yd/10m** Repeat **–** Price ★

8

9

8 Warwick/Monarc Border 6 Color **jade 6** Alternative colors **available** Width **5¼in/13.5cm** Length **11yd/10m** Repeat **6¾in/17cm** Price ★

9 Osborne & Little/Sundance W844/05 Color **blue** Alternative colors **available** Width **20½in/52cm** Length **11yd/10m** Repeat **10½in/27cm** Price ★

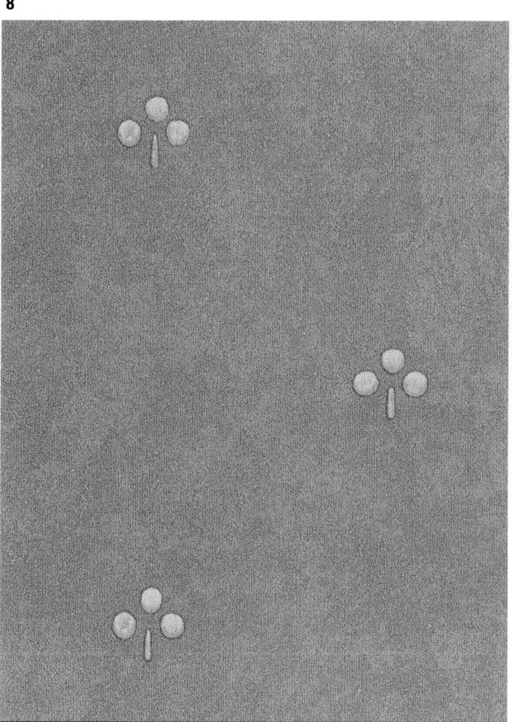

10

10 Zoffany/Blois Plain V43005 Color **05** Alternative colors **available** Width **20½in/52cm** Length **11yd/10m** Repeat **3¼in/8.5cm** Price ★

11 Coloroll/Garcia 400523 Color **pink** Alternative colors **available** Width **20½in/52cm** Length **11yd/10m** Repeat **10½in/26.5cm** Price ★

12 Coloroll/Castille Border 703785 Color **red** Alternative colors **available** Width **4in/10cm** Length **5½yd/5m** Repeat **10½in/26.5cm** Price ★

13 Nina Campbell/Wallace Sprig NCW513/04 Color **pink** Alternative colors **available** Width **20½in/52cm** Length **11yd/10m** Repeat **2¾in/7cm** Price ★

12

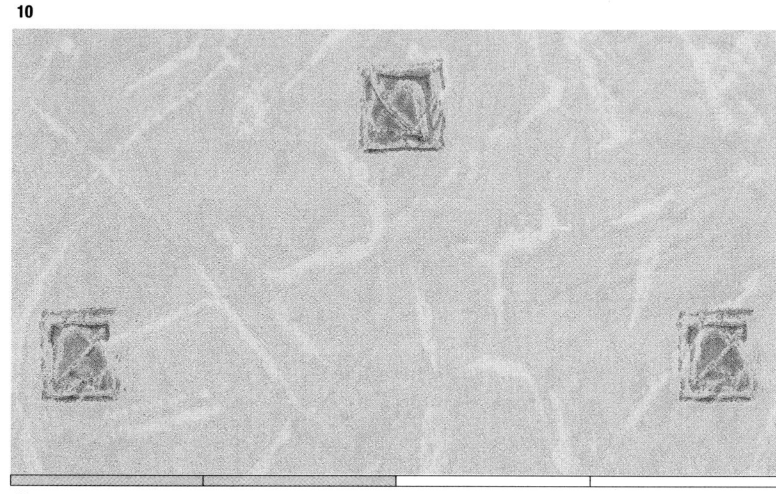

11

13

20th century

Motifs: **Late 20th century**

The last three decades of the 20th century witnessed a significant revival of interest in the wallpaper patterns of the previous centuries. As a consequence of this, the favored motifs were drawn from an extremely rich and varied catalog of international ornament that had gradually been accumulating since the Middle Ages (*see* pages 206-219), with much of that imagery consisting of plant forms (especially floral motifs), geometric or abstract shapes, and various emblems and imitations of architectural moldings.

In many cases, wallpaper companies reproduced the original designs using traditional dyes and the original method of printing. In other cases, however, designers adapted and updated the motifs by stylizing and recoloring them to suit a more modern aesthetic. Generally, this reworking took the form of a reduction in the numbers of colors that were used in any one design or pattern. There was also a distinct favoring of colors that, although saturated, had a noticeably soft and chalky appearance.

1

1 Pippa & Hale/Opal Color **MIB 073** Alternative colors **available** Width **2¼in/5.5cm** Length **11yd/10m** Repeat – Price ★

2 Osborne & Little/Catalpa W1010/07 Color **green** Alternative colors **available** Width **20½in/52cm** Length **11yd/10m** Repeat **8¼in/21cm** Price ★

3 Harlequin/88040 Color **yellow** Alternative colors **available** Width **20½in/52cm** Length **11yd/10m** Repeat **5in/13cm** Price ★

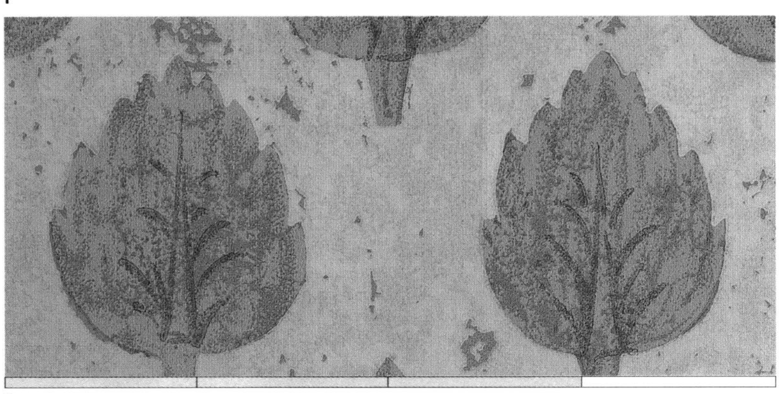

2

3

4

4 Anna French/Chalice Color **CHAWP02** Alternative colors **available** Width **20½in/52cm** Length **11yd/10m** Repeat **18in/46cm** Price ★

5 Harlequin/57035 Color **biscuit** Alternative colors **available** Width **20½in/52cm** Length **11yd/10m** Repeat **24in/61cm** Price ★

6 Osborne & Little/Sundance Border B854/04 Color **blue** Alternative colors **available** Width **4¼in/11cm** Length **11yd/10m** Repeat – Price ★

7 Designers Guild/Pushpa P243/03 Color **ultramarine** Alternative colors **available** Width **21in/53cm** Length **11yd/10m** Repeat **21in/53cm** Price ★

8 K and K Designs/16232 Color **azure blue with green** Alternative colors **available** Width **21in/53cm** Length **11yd/10m** Repeat **10½in/26.5cm** Price ★

5

6

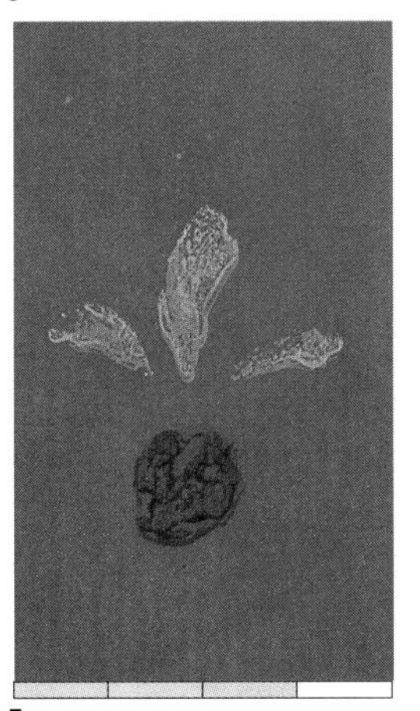

7

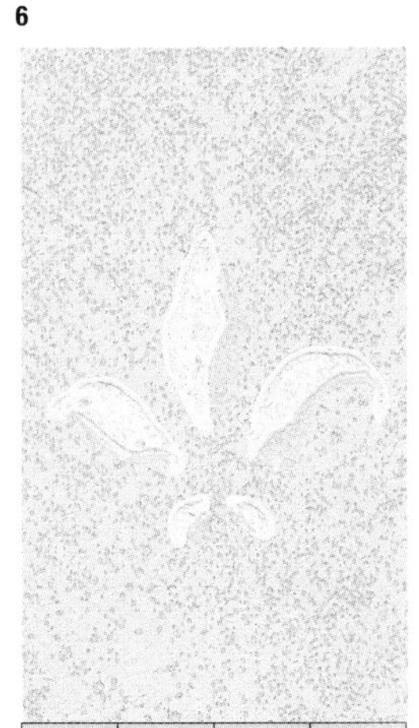

8

9

10

11

12

STENCIL EFFECT

Border papers that are intended for use as friezes or dados were in great demand during the last quarter of the 20th century. Among the most popular patterns were repeat stenciled motifs of stylized flowers and foliage. Although updated, the original inspiration for many of these designs came from the painted stenciled borders that had been favored in Medieval and Renaissance houses. It is also derived from late 19th-century wallpaper friezes, and, as here, from marble and stone terrazzo work of both Western and Eastern origin.

Warwick/Terrazzo Border 3 Color **coral** Alternative colors **available** Width **5in/13cm** Length **11yd/10m** Repeat **8in/20cm** Price ★

13

14

15

16

17

9 Anna French/Savernake Color **SAVWP011** Alternative colors **available** Width **20½in/52cm** Length **11yd/10m** Repeat **24in/61cm** Price ★

10 Osborne & Little/Coronata W1065/04 Color **green** Alternative colors **available** Width **20½in/52cm** Length **11yd/10m** Repeat **10½in/27cm** Price ★

11 Monkwell/Lavris 7530/472 Color **472** Alternative colors **available** Width **27½in/70cm** Length **11yd/10m** Repeat **6¼in/16cm** Price ★

12 Coloroll/Penshurst 400356 Color **blue** Alternative colors **available** Width **20½in/52cm** Length **11yd/10m** Repeat **21in/53cm** Price ★

13 Fine Decor/Barleta Border B2423 Color **multi** Alternative colors **available** Width **6¾in/17.5cm** Length **5½yd/5m** Repeat **6¾in/17cm** Price ★

14 Crowson/Tiarella 37550T81 Color **20** Alternative colors **available** Width **20½in/52cm** Length **11yd/10m** Repeat **6¾in/17.5cm** Price ★

15 Crowson/Stars 37550S79 Color **15** Alternative colors **available** Width **4in/10.5cm** Length **11yd/10m** Repeat **–** Price ★

16 Coloroll/Garcia Border 400707 Color **green** Alternative colors **available** Width **5in/13cm** Length **5½yd/5m** Repeat **10½in/26.5cm** Price ★

17 Fine Decor/Toscano Border B2410 Color **pink** Alternative colors **available** Width **5in/13cm** Length **5½yd/5m** Repeat **5in/13cm** Price ★

Floral Wallpapers

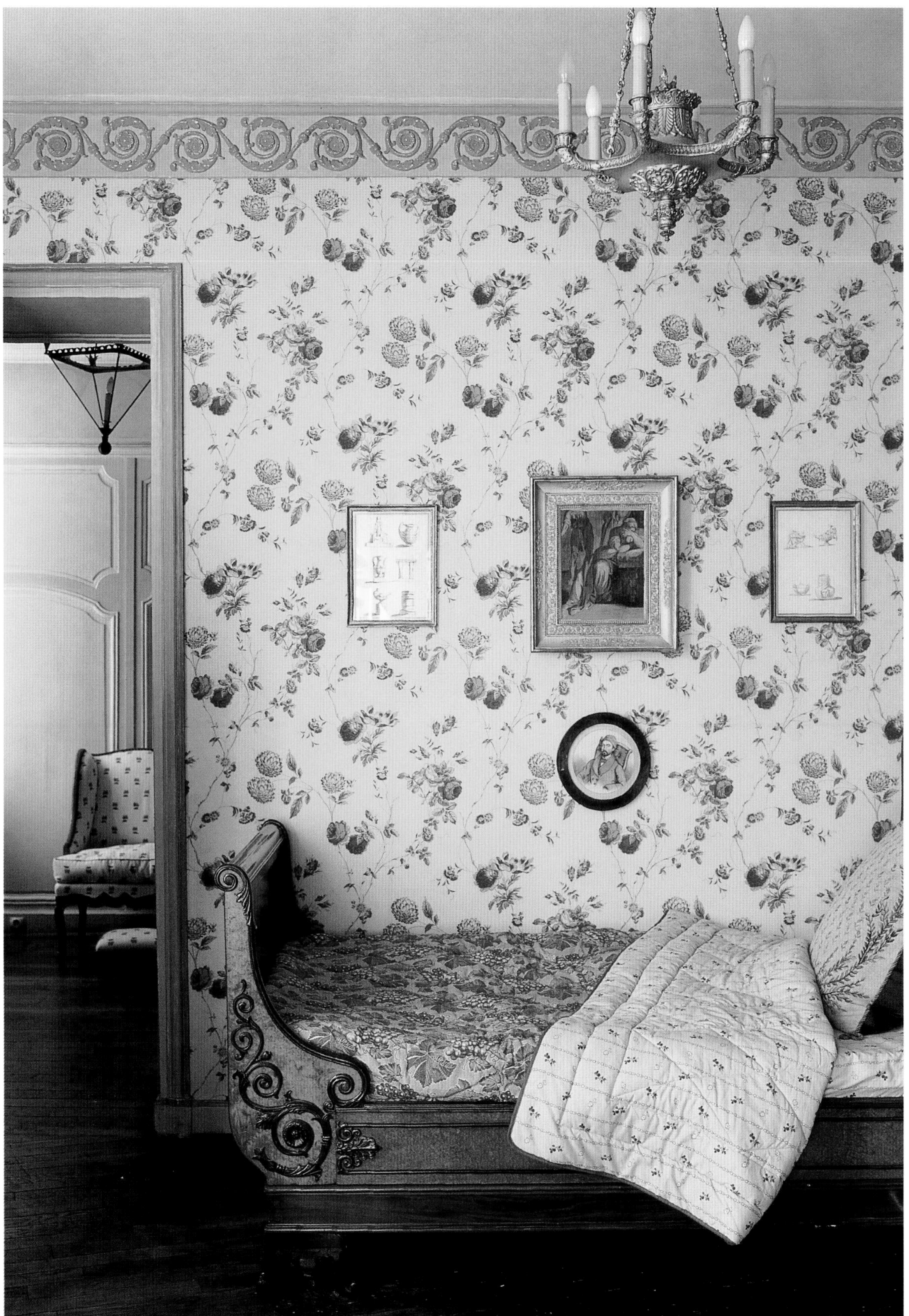

From the early Renaissance up until the present day, both naturalistic and conventionalized flowers have proved the most enduringly fashionable and universal form of imagery that has been employed on wall-papers. Only in the Modernist interiors of the first half of the 20th century were floral designs considered unpopular.

Sources of inspiration for floral wallpaper patterns have been many and varied. For example, before the 19th century, numerous wallpapers replicated the floral designs found on textiles, particularly damasks and chintzes. During the 20th century, the manner in which flowers were depicted in fine art was avidly adopted by the wallpaper industry. Some wallpaper designers also produced floral patterns and motifs that were drawn from their own observations of nature. However, since the initial use of this imagery, the primary reference material for floral designs has been the pattern books and the illustrated botanical studies that have been published–first in Europe, and, later, also in the United States–since the 17th century.

LEFT This provincial-style bedroom is in a late 18th-century Parisian town house. The wallpaper displays a naturalistic floral pattern printed in shades of red on a pale yellow background. It echoes the other plant-form motifs on the bedding, and is typical of the horticultural and rustic imagery that was fashionable in many parts of Europe during the second half of the 18th century.

EMPIRE-STYLE FLORALS

This floral-patterned wallpaper is in a drawing room of the Jumel Mansion in New York. The mansion was decorated and furnished in French Empire style during the 1820s after the Jumels returned from a trip to Paris with a collection of hand-blocked wallpapers and other furnishings that were considered the height of fashion and quality on both sides of the Atlantic. Naturalistic bouquets set against contrasting colored backgrounds were among the most popular of Empire-style patterns.

KEY DESIGNS

1 Small repeats of native European flowers, such as roses, daisies, poppies, violets, larkspurs, and anemones, were generally favored over exotic Oriental blooms in the late 18th century.

2 Uncomplicated floral patterns of delicately trailing flowers printed on pale backgrounds were fashionable in France during the 1770s and 1780s, and remained popular until the 1840s.

3 Botanically accurate, large-scale floral patterns, characterized by realistic colors and subtle use of highlighting and shading, appeared in many Victorian interiors in the mid-19th century.

4 From the late 18th century onward, wallpaper manufacturers in both France and England produced numerous floral-patterned wallpapers that imitated *toile de Jouy* fabrics.

5 Since the early 18th century, many floral wallpapers were designed to imitate floral-patterned, silk damask wall-hangings. This late 18th-century French paper has a lotus flower pattern.

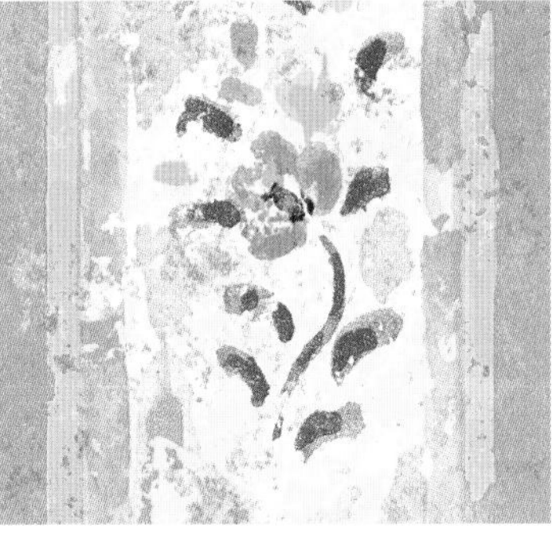

6 Small repeat floral motifs are often used to embellish striped wallpapers. This example is late 20th century, but floral-decorated stripes were also popular in the late 18th and early 19th centuries.

---

1 Colefax and Fowler/Petits Fleurs 7202/01 Color **terracotta/green** Alternative colors **available** Width **20½in/52cm** Length **11yd/10m** Repeat **10¼in/26cm** Price ★

2 Brunschwig & Fils/Georgette 16171-06 Color **scarlet on white** Alternative colors **available** Width **27in/68.5cm** Length **5yd/4.5m** Repeat **25in/64cm** Price ★★★★

3 Colefax and Fowler/Ormesson 7038/03 Color **ivory** Alternative colors **available** Width **20½in/52cm** Length **11yd/10m** Repeat **20in/51cm** Price ★

4 Ornamenta/English Musick EMK702 Color **blue** Alternative colors **available** Width **20½in/52cm** Length **11yd/10m** Repeat **35¾in/91.5cm** Price ★★

5 Schumacher/Lotus Damask 510334 Color **malachite** Alternative colors **available** Width **27in/68.5cm** Length **4½yd/4m** Repeat **25in/64cm** Price ★★

6 Anna French/Daisy Rose Stripe Color **DAIWP077** Alternative colors **available** Width **20½in/52cm** Length **11yd/10m** Repeat **25in/64cm** Price ★

Florals: **Medieval to mid-18th century**

Many of the black-and-white woodcut-printed papers of the late 16th and early 17th centuries featured floral patterns based on "black stitch" embroidery (black silk embroidery executed on a white ground). Sophisticated, stylized floral patterns derived from velvets and brocades were also highly fashionable during the 17th century, with many examples featuring additional hand-painted elements, as were naturalistically depicted flowers and fruit in imitation of "Spanish stitch" textiles.

Other 17th-century, floral-patterned papers of note displayed elaborate arrangements of flowers, such as tulips, narcissi, orchids, and roses, set in classical vases and surrounded by stylized foliation and strapwork. Such designs were to remain popular for much of the 18th century, and became increasingly realistic as knowledge of plant forms grew via illustrated pattern books and methods of printing improved. Also fashionable in the first half of the 18th century were English flock papers styled in imitation of floral-patterned damasks, and Chinese and *chinoiserie* papers that featured flowering shrubs, roses, chrysanthemums, poppies, peonies, and bamboo, often augmented with exotic birds and insects.

1

2

1 **Ramm, Son & Crocker/ Lampas W1615** Color **green** Alternative colors **available** Width **20½in/52cm** Length **11yd/10m** Repeat **12in/ 30.5cm** Price ★

2 **Alexander Beauchamp/Ghintez** Color **green** Alternative colors **available** Width **18½in/47cm** Length **11yd/10m** Repeat **18½in/47cm** Price ★★★ ♣

3 **Elizabeth Eaton/Wheat Damask 154504** Color **04** Alternative colors **available** Width **24in/61cm** Length **6yd/5.5m** Repeat **24¾in/63cm** Price ★★

4 **Alexander Beauchamp/Jacobean** Color **special** Alternative colors **available** Width **15¼in/39cm** Length **11yd/10m** Repeat **20in/51cm** Price ★★★ ♣

5 **G. P. & J. Baker/Solomon's Seal W0087-63** Color **63** Alternative colors **available** Width **20½in/ 52cm** Length **11yd/10m** Repeat **21in/53cm** Price ★

3

4

5

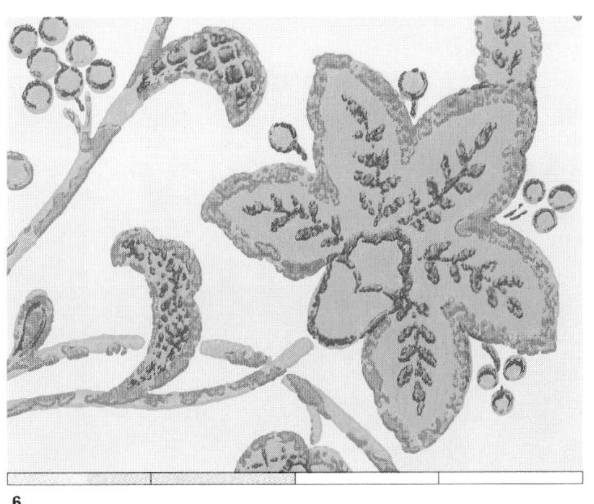

6

6 Sheila Coombes/Heversham 614-2 Color **2** Alternative colors **available** Width **21in/53cm** Length **11yd/10m** Repeat **21in/53cm** Price ★

7 Hamilton Weston/Twickenham Color **gray, black, and white on green** Alternative colors **available** Width **20½in/52cm** Length **11yd/10m** Repeat **8¼in/21cm** Price ★★ ♣

8 G. P. & J. Baker/Nocturne W0095-44 Color **44** Alternative colors **available** Width **20½in/52cm** Length **11yd/10m** Repeat **18in/46cm** Price ★

9

7

10

9 Alexander Beauchamp/Melton Color **green and white** Alternative colors **available** Width **17¼in/44cm** Length **11yd/10m** Repeat **28½in/72.5cm** Price ★★★ ♣

10 Cole & Son/St Cloud 54/4666/PR Color **green** Alternative colors **available** Width **20½in/52cm** Length **11yd/10m** Repeat **15in/38cm** Price ★

11 Ciel Decor/Maianenco PPA0010-391 Color **jaune florence** Alternative colors **available** Width **59in/150cm** Length **11yd/10m** Repeat **1in/2.5cm** Price ★

12 Brunschwig & Fils/Rêve du Papillon 12473.06 Color **yellow** Alternative colors **available** Width **27¼in/69.5cm** Length **5yd/4.5m** Repeat **38½in/98cm** Price ★★★★ ♣

8

11

12

Florals: **Late 18th century**

Floral-patterned wallpapers, like floral-patterned textiles, were very popular during the second half of the 18th century. Chinese and European *chinoiserie* floral papers were especially in vogue, and many other papers displayed imagery that was half-Chinese and half-classical in origin, with a typical example combining Oriental peacocks and parrots with classical vases of flowers.

Fashionable French papers included *papiers marbres* stenciled with floral patterns; floral flocks made from silk shearings in imitation of silk wall-hangings; floral arabesques; and papers with patterns composed of flowers bound with ribbons. Fashionable English papers featured flowers with large petals, flowering bushes, and diapered bouquets. Leading designers of the period were the Frenchman Jean-Baptiste Réveillon and the Englishman John Baptist Jackson. Many papers by these designers, along with others from France and England, were exported in large numbers to the increasingly prosperous American Colonies.

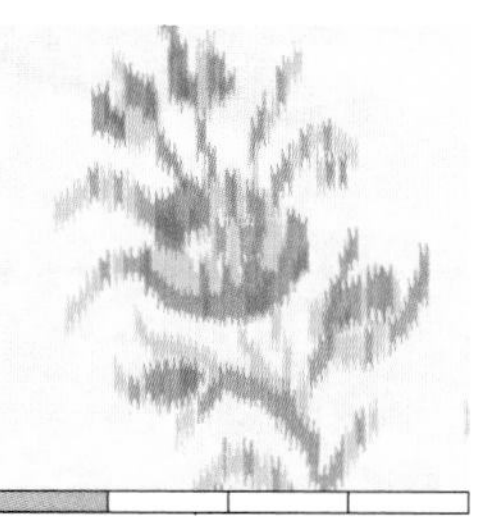

1

2

3

4

5

6

7

FABRIC IMITATIONS

Many of the floral wallpapers that were produced during the 18th century derived their patterns from contemporary textiles, particularly Chinese silks, French and English printed floral chintzes, and, especially, woven damasks and brocades. This is not surprising, given that during this period wallpapers were beginning to be employed as a less expensive alternative to textile wall-hangings in all but the grandest of houses. The late 18th-century French paper shown here is an imitation of a typical stylized, floral-patterned damask.

Scalamandré/Tekko TE1B-932 Color **maize and vermeil** Alternative colors **available** Width **31½in/80cm** Length **5yd/4.5m** Repeat **28in/71cm** Price ★★★★★ [T]

8

1 **Hamilton Weston/Mayfair 404** Color **green** Alternative colors **available** Width **20½in/52cm** Length **11yd/10m** Repeat **21in/53cm** Price ★

2 **Elizabeth Eaton/East India** Color **158269** Alternative colors **available** Width **20½in/52cm** Length **7yd/6.5m** Repeat **22in/56cm** Price ★★

3 **Hamilton Weston/Kew Green Border** Color **pink, dark turquoise on cream** Alternative colors **available** Width **2½in/6.5cm** Length **11yd/10m** Repeat **13¼in/34cm** Price ★★★

4 **Hamilton Weston/Kew Green** Color **pink, dark turquoise on cream** Alternative colors **available** Width **19¾in/50cm** Length **11yd/10m** Repeat **13¼in/34cm** Price ★★★

5 **Brunschwig & Fils/Suffield Arabesque 15690.06** Color **white** Alternative colors **available** Width **22½in/57cm** Length **5yd/4.5m** Repeat **21½in/55cm** Price ★★★★★

6 **Nobilis-Fontan/Sarah** Color **BGL 132** Alternative colors **available** Width **26¾in/68cm** Length **9yd/8.2m** Repeat **13¾in/35cm** Price ★

7 **Brunschwig & Fils/Marianthi 13900.06** Color **white** Alternative colors **available** Width **27in/68.5cm** Length **5yd/4.5m** Repeat **27in/68.5cm** Price ★★★★★

8 **Brunschwig & Fils/Lallarookh 15636.06** Color **coral and forest** Alternative colors **available** Width **27in/68.5cm** Length **5yd/4.5m** Repeat **18in/46cm** Price ★★★

9 Schumacher/Imperial Vine Color **turquoise and rose** Alternative colors **available** Width **27in/ 68.5cm** Length **4½yd/4m** Repeat **25in/64cm** Price ★★★

10 Elizabeth Eaton/Cape Cod Floral 209489 Color **green** Alternative colors **available** Width **21in/ 53cm** Length **7yd/6.5m** Repeat **12½in/32cm** Price ★★

11 Colefax and Fowler/Torsade Color **pink and green** Alternative colors **available** Width **20½in/52cm** Length **11yd/10m** Repeat **20½in/ 52cm** Price ★

12 Schumacher/Waistcoat Florets Color **cream** Alternative colors **available** Width **27in/68.5cm** Length **4½yd/4m** Repeat **12½in/32cm** Price ★★

13 Schumacher/Solomon's Seal Color **aqua** Alternative colors **available** Width **27in/68.5cm** Length **4½yd/4m** Repeat **36½in/93cm** Price ★★★

9

14

10

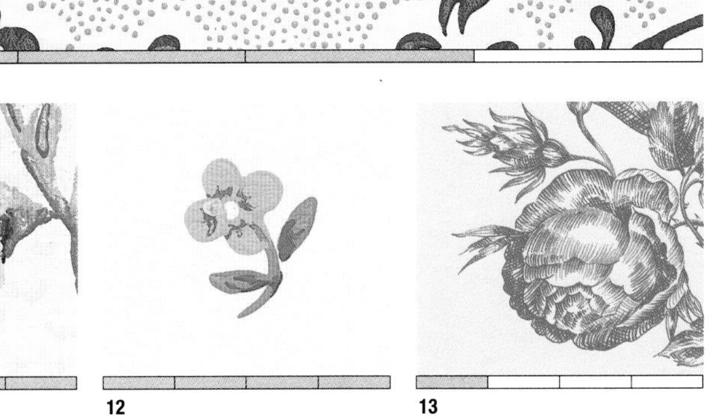
11 12 13

14 Alexander Beauchamp/Genoa Color **yellow** Alternative colors **available** Width **21in/53cm** Length **11yd/10m** Repeat **28¼in/72cm** Price ★★★★

15 Cole & Son/Chippendale 58/1020/PR Color **gold on coral** Alternative colors **available** Width **20½in/52cm** Length **11yd/10m** Repeat **39¼in/100cm** Price ★★

16 Colefax and Fowler/Liseron 7201/04 Color **blue and green** Alternative colors **available** Width **20½in/52cm** Length **11yd/10m** Repeat **15in/38cm** Price ★

15

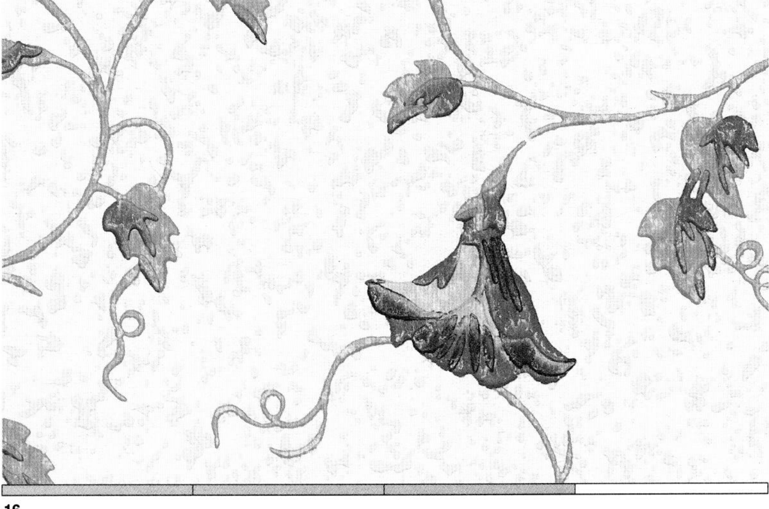
16

Florals: **Early 19th century**

At the beginning of the 19th century, some British, French, and American manufacturers produced stylized floral-patterned papers in imitation of fashionable glazed floral chintzes. More popular, however, were the naturalistically depicted floral patterns that had first come into vogue in the classical interiors of the late 18th century. Many of these were also inspired by contemporary textiles, such as elaborate floral-patterned silks.

The tendency to represent flowers in a naturalistic way, as opposed to conventionalizing them, became more marked as the century progressed. Apart from aesthetic considerations, the main factors that fueled this greater realism were the publication of numerous illustrated botanical studies, which provided designers with increasingly accurate reference material, and the development of new mineral dyes, including various oranges and greens, that closely resembled the vivid colors displayed in many natural plant forms. Also playing a part was the increasingly sophisticated use of hand-blocked printing (*see* opposite) to create subtle shading and "three-dimensionality" within patterns, a quality further, and literally, enhanced on the flocked papers that proved popular during this period.

4

4 Hamilton Weston/Kingston Market Color **8132** Alternative colors **available** Width **21in/53cm** Length **11yd/10m** Repeat **10½in/26.5cm** Price ★★

5 Zoffany/Trianon 7701003 Color **03** Alternative colors **available** Width **20½in/52cm** Length **11yd/10m** Repeat **25in/64cm** Price ★

6 Colefax and Fowler/Sudbury Park 7046/01 Color **red/red** Alternative colors **available** Width **20½in/52cm** Length **11yd/10m** Repeat **3in/7.5cm** Price ★

7 Zoffany/Hopetoun Bud 215203 Color **03** Alternative colors **available** Width **20½in/52cm** Length **11yd/10m** Repeat **–** Price ★

1

1 Schumacher/Fruitier Vine 5190402 Color **periwinkle & royal** Alternative colors **available** Width **27in/68.5cm** Length **4½yd/4m** Repeat **20in/51cm** Price ★★★

2 Osborne & Little/Strawberry House W1373-03 Color **dark pink** Alternative colors **available** Width **20½in/52cm** Length **11yd/10m** Repeat **3½in/9cm** Price ★

3 Colefax and Fowler/Dentelle 7032/01 Color **pink** Alternative colors **available** Width **20½in/52cm** Repeat **6in/15.5cm** Price ★

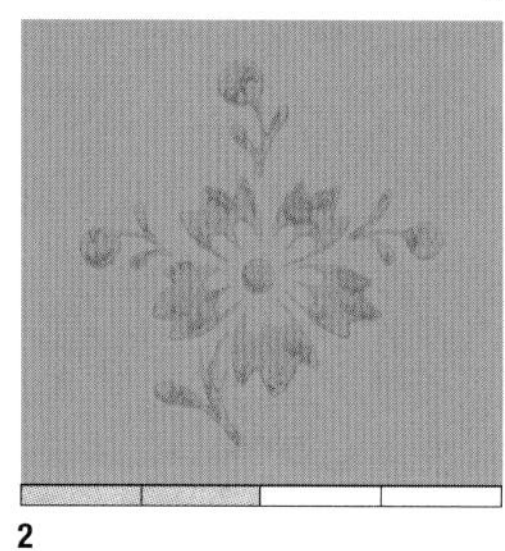

2

5

3

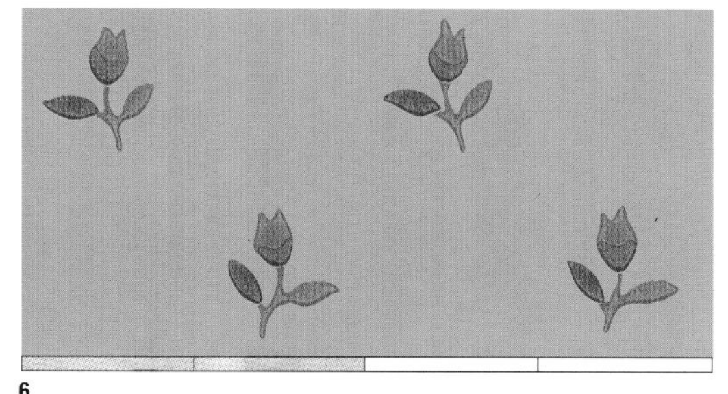

6

7

19th century

8

8 **Cole & Son/Sweet Pea 54/4682/PR** Color **yellow** Alternative colors **available** Width **20½in/52cm** Length **11yd/10m** Repeat **15in/38cm** Price ★

9 **Schumacher/Waistcoat Florets Border 519140** Color **yellow** Alternative colors **available** Width **4in/15cm** Length **11yd/10m** Repeat **15in/38cm** Price ★★★

10 **Hamilton Weston/Hortensia Border** Color **document** Alternative colors **available** Width **4in/10.5cm** Length **5½yd/5m** Repeat **–** Price ★★

9

11

11 **Schumacher/Williamsburg Parrots 519002** Color **document** Alternative colors **available** Width **6in/15.5cm** Length **to order** Repeat **–** Price ★★★ W

12 **Hamilton Weston/Fuchsia St James** Color **8155** Alternative colors **available** Width **21in/53cm** Length **11yd/10m** Repeat **10¾in/27.5cm** Price ★★

13 **Elizabeth Eaton/Classic Damask** Color **207624** Alternative colors **available** Width **20½in/52cm** Length **7yd/6.5m** Repeat **22in/56cm** Price ★★

14 **Zoffany/Hopetoun Flower 7704004** Color **04** Alternative colors **available** Width **20½in/52cm** Length **11yd/10m** Repeat **10½in/26.5cm** Price ★

10

12

HAND-BLOCKED PRINTING

Despite the introduction of hand-operated cylinder printing in 1764, and machine-driven roller printing in the 1830s, the best quality wallpapers were those that had been hand-blocked. The subtle shading, the purity of color, and the crispness of detail that is evident in this early 19th-century naturalistic floral border wallpaper is a perfect example of traditional hand-blocking. The hand-blocking process involves each color of the pattern being allotted an individual wooden block that bears part of the pattern in relief. These individual blocks are then skillfully pressured into position one at a time.

Scalamandré/Prestwould Saloon Border WB81504/001 Color **01** Alternative colors **not available** Width **21¾in/55.5cm** Length **7yd/6.5m** Repeat **43¼in/110cm** Price ★★

13

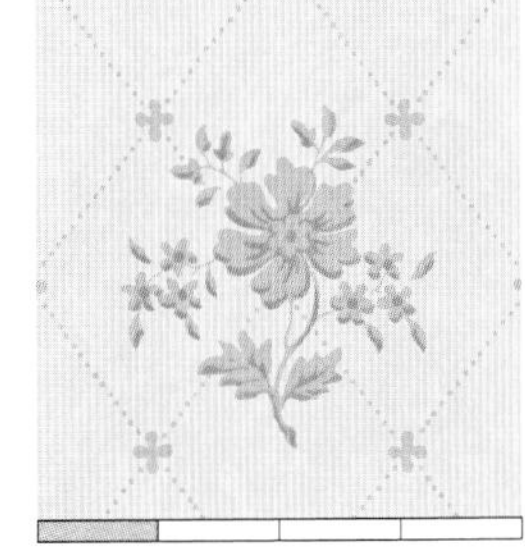

14

Florals: **Mid-19th century**

Although conventionalized flowers figured in the flat wallpaper patterns of internationally influential designers such as A. W. N. Pugin and Owen Jones around the middle of the 19th century, most of the floral-patterned papers produced during this period were naturalistically depicted, and subsequently given far greater depth either by shading and highlighting, or by flocking. Indeed, many floral designs were rendered realistic almost to the point of caricature. This effect was largely a result of designers favoring large, coarse flowers, such as dahlias, hollyhocks, and hydrangeas, and of manufacturers printing them with new synthetic aniline dyes that produced sharp yellows, vivid blues, and acid greens of a chemical intensity not always matched by the natural coloring of the real blooms and foliage. More authentically realistic were many of the popular "satin" papers produced in imitation of floral silk hangings, their silklike appearance having been created by polishing the surface with French chalk.

1

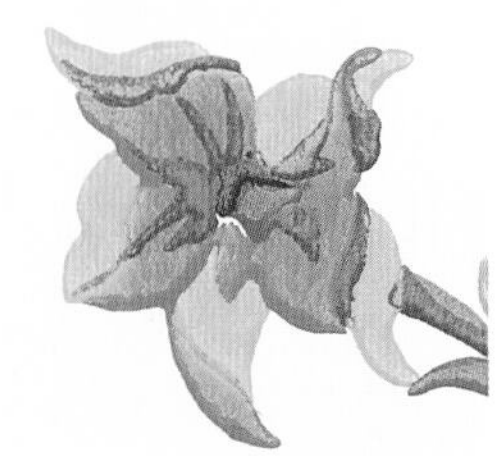

2

3

1 **Hodsoll McKenzie/Dorset Rose 502/607** Color **red** Alternative colors **available** Width **20½in/52cm** Length **11yd/10m** Repeat **18in/46cm** Price ★

2 **Ramm, Son & Crocker/Wendover 14715.06** Color **pink** Alternative colors **available** Width **20½in/52cm** Length **11yd/10m** Repeat **16¼in/41cm** Price ★

3 **Cole & Son/Madras Violet 54/4625/PR** Color **cream ground** Alternative colors **available** Width **20½in/52cm** Length **11yd/10m** Repeat **21in/53cm** Price ★

4

5

4 **Ramm, Son & Crocker/Ludlow Border W1000** Color **blue** Alternative colors **available** Width **7in/18cm** Length **11yd/10m** Repeat **20½in/52cm** Price ★

5 **Warwick/Document Border 3** Color **ice** Alternative colors **available** Width **5in/13cm** Length **11½yd/10.5m** Repeat **6¾in/17cm** Price ★

6 **Nobilis-Fontan/Volubilis BOR3101** Color **pink, yellow, and green on cream** Alternative colors **available** Width **9in/23cm** Length **10yd/9m** Repeat **18½in/47cm** Price ★★★

7 **Sanderson/Josephine WR7599/1** Color **1** Alternative colors **available** Width **21in/53cm** Length **11½yd/10.5m** Repeat **21in/53cm** Price ★

8 **Colefax and Fowler/Geranium Moiré 7402/01** Color **coral/aqua** Alternative colors **available** Width **20½in/52cm** Length **11yd/10m** Repeat **18in/45.5cm** Price ★

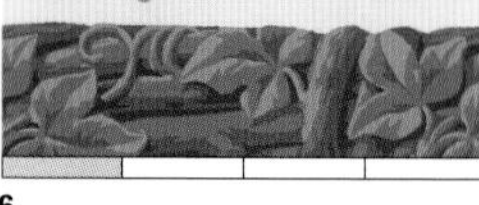

6

7

8

19th century

9 Watts of Westminster/Gawdelyn Border W0018-01/A12 Color **Oslo** Alternative colors **available** Width **9in/23cm** Length **2½yd/2m** Repeat **18½in/47cm** Price ★★★

10 Sanderson/Sheraton WR7943/2 Color **2** Alternative colors **available** Width **21in/53cm** Length **11½yd/10.5m** Repeat **5in/13cm** Price ★

11 Sanderson/Ornamental Garden WR7835/1 Color **1** Alternative colors **available** Width **21in/53cm** Length **11½yd/10.5m** Repeat **9in/23cm** Price ★

12 Hodsoll McKenzie/Faded Bouquet 610/604 Color **cream/yellow** Alternative colors **available** Width **20½in/52cm** Length **11yd/10m** Repeat **24in/61cm** Price ★

13 Elizabeth Eaton/New England Floral Color **203J07** Alternative colors **available** Width **20½in/52cm** Length **7yd/6.5m** Repeat **22in/56cm** Price ★★

14 Sanderson/Antoinette WR7946/2 Color **2** Alternative colors **available** Width **21in/53cm** Length **11½yd/10.5m** Repeat **10½in/27cm** Price ★

9

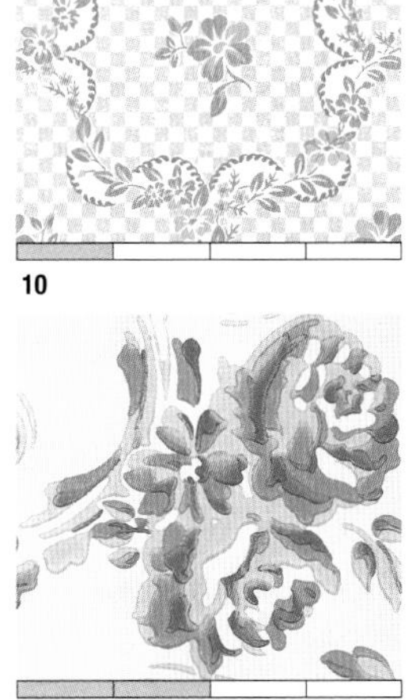

10

11

12

15

13

16

17

14

18

15 Hamilton Weston/Yellow Bedroom Color **document** Alternative colors **available** Width **20½in/52cm** Length **11yd/10m** Repeat **21½in/54.5cm** Price ★★★ ♣

16 Watts of Westminster/Nimue W0031 Color **Grant** Alternative colors **available** Width **18½in/47cm** Length **11yd/10m** Repeat **17¼in/44cm** Price ★★

17 Colefax and Fowler/Camilla 7017/03 Color **yellow/blue** Alternative colors **available** Width **20½in/52cm** Length **11yd/10m** Repeat **9in/23cm** Price ★

18 Ramm, Son & Crocker/Rosedale W1030 Color **chintz** Alternative colors **available** Width **20½in/52cm** Length **11yd/10m** Repeat **20½in/52cm** Price ★

Florals: **Late 19th century**

Naturalistically depicted flowers continued to appear on wallpapers produced during the last 30 years of the 19th century. However, as a reaction to the overblown naturalism of many mid-19th-century papers, conventionalized floral patterns were more in evidence, especially in Arts and Crafts, Aesthetic, and Art Nouveau interiors, where they were often employed as the field ("filling") in a tripartite (frieze-field-dado) division of the walls. Undoubtedly the most popular were the Arts and Crafts papers of William Morris and his followers. These featured relatively simple flowers, such as poppies, daisies, marigolds, and jasmine, hand-blocked with traditional vegetable dyes and depicted within formal pattern structures.

Aesthetic papers, notably those by the influential English designer E. W. Godwin (publicized in Britain and America by Charles Eastlake), were also characterized by uncomplicated blooms such as sunflowers, pinks, and the Japanese lotus. Although many were botanically correct, they were generally highly stylized and rather static. These were in marked contrast to the sinuous poppy, wisteria, and water lily patterns of Art Nouveau designers, which, although conventionalized, had a marked rhythmical and sensuous quality.

4

5

4 Brunschwig & Fils/Kyoto 15908-06 Color **pongee** Alternative colors **available** Width **27in/68.5cm** Length **5yd/4.5m** Repeat **36in/91.5cm** Price ★★★★★ ♣

5 Cole & Son/Plumbago 54/4648/PR Color **black** Alternative colors **available** Width **20½in/52cm** Length **11yd/10m** Repeat **21in/53cm** Price ★

6 Colefax and Fowler/Bowood 7401/04 Color **yellow/blue** Alternative colors **available** Width **20½in/52cm** Length **11yd/10m** Repeat **11¾in/30cm** Price ★

7 Cole & Son/Block 0265 Color **special** Alternative colors **available** Width **21in/53cm** Length **11yd/10m** Repeat **–** Price ★★★ ♣

8 Graham & Brown/Anshan Floral Color **red and green** Alternative colors **available** Width **20½in/52cm** Length **11yd/10m** Repeat **21in/53cm** Price ★

9 Colefax and Fowler/Durham 7605/07 Color **yellow** Alternative colors **available** Width **20½in/52cm** Length **11yd/10m** Repeat **12in/31cm** Price ★

10 Cole & Son/Sunflower 12/062/PR Color **yellow and blue** Alternative colors **not available** Width **21in/53cm** Length **11yd/10m** Repeat **7in/18cm** Price ★

11 Graham & Brown/Emporio 96284 Color **rose and gold** Alternative colors **available** Width **4¾in/12cm** Length **5½yd/5m** Repeat **–** Price ★

1

1 Cole & Son/Ormond Color **pink on cream** Alternative colors **available** Width **20½in/52cm** Length **11yd/10m** Repeat **5in/13cm** Price ★

2 Watts of Westminster/Sunflower W0055-01/P12 Color **xanthe** Alternative colors **available** Width **21¼in/54cm** Length **11yd/10m** Repeat **20½in/52cm** Price ★★

3 Colefax and Fowler/Rose Damask 7407/03 Color **yellow** Alternative colors **available** Width **20½in/52cm** Length **11yd/10m** Repeat **24in/61cm** Price ★

2

6 7

8

9

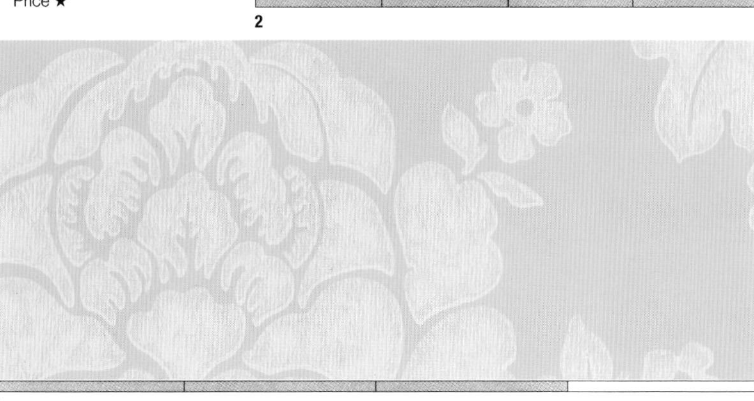

3

10

11

19th century

12 Alexander Beauchamp/Oleander Trellis 161/20 Color **multi** Alternative colors **available** Width **18½in/47cm** Length **11yd/10m** Repeat **18in/46cm** Price ★★★★★ ♣

13 Elizabeth Eaton/Wellington House Color **198635** Alternative colors **not available** Width **27in/69cm** Length **15¼yd/14m** Repeat **19in/48cm** Price ★

12

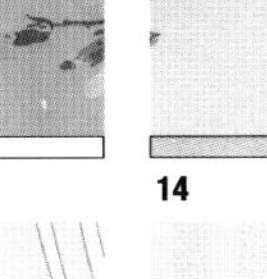

14

15

14 Manuel Canovas/Eglantine 8081 Color **92 ecru** Alternative colors **available** Width **26¾in/68cm** Length **11yd/10m** Repeat **16¼in/41cm** Price ★★★★★ ♣

15 Coloroll/Shayla Border 401964 Color **brown** Alternative colors **available** Width **7¾in/19.5cm** Length **5½yd/5m** Repeat **21in/53cm** Price ★

16 Ramm, Son & Crocker/Romney W1050 Color **rose** Alternative colors **available** Width **20½in/52cm** Length **11yd/10m** Repeat **24in/61cm** Price ★

17 Elizabeth Eaton/Chinese Poppy Color **blue and cream** Alternative colors **available** Width **22½in/57cm** Length **11yd/10m** Repeat **18½in/47cm** Price ★★★ ♣

18 Bradbury & Bradbury/Antique Rose Panels ARP-550 Color **550** Alternative colors **available** Width **27in/69cm** Length **15¼yd/14m** Repeat **19in/48cm** Price ★★★★ ♣

13

16

LINCRUSTA & ANAGLYPTA

Lincrusta was developed in 1877 by Frederick Walton. Made of linseed oil, gum, resins, and wood pulp spread over canvas, its surface was embossed with patterns (such as this stylized floral) by engraved metal rollers. Waterproof and durable, Lincrusta could be painted, stained, or gilded to simulate traditional relief moldings of wood, plaster, leather, or tiles. A cheaper and lighter alternative–Anaglypta–was invented in 1886 by Thomas Palmer. Made from cotton fiber pulp, its relief patterns were created by hollow molding. Both Lincrusta and Anaglypta remained in demand well into the 20th century, and are still in production today.

Akzo Nobel/Italian Renaissance RD1952 Color **white** Alternative colors **not available** Width **20½in/52cm** Length **40in/101.5cm** Repeat **40¼in/102cm** Price ★★★

17

18

19th century

Florals: **Early 20th century**

Numerous floral-patterned wallpapers were manufactured during the first half of the 20th century. Designs included the stylized, long-stemmed lilies and poppies that featured on Art Nouveau papers, and the cup-shaped blossoms favored by the Deutscher Werkbund. Bizarre, dusty-colored "magic flowers," with elongated, lancet-shaped leaves and slender blossoms, were characteristic of later Wiener Werkstätte papers, while Arts and Crafts floral patterns (*see* pages 232-3) retained their popularity from the previous century. Roses, daisies, and dahlias were also among the floral motifs preferred in Art Deco interiors, their round heads "two-dimensionally" stylized, strongly outlined, densely packed, and often presented in baskets, festoons, or garlands.

Floral-patterned papers featured in early 20th-century interiors inspired by 18th-century French decoration, and took the form of "fillings" in imitation of floral damasks, topped by friezes of swagged roses and ribbons, or of combined friezes and "fillings" in which roses or wisteria cascaded down the wall. The "English country house" look (fashionable in both Britain and America) also gave rise to many designs based on 18th- and 19th-century floral chintz patterns.

1

1 Graham & Brown/Traditional Rose Color **gold** Alternative colors **available** Width **24¼in/62cm** Length **11yd/10m** Repeat **25in/64cm** Price ★

2 Colefax & Fowler/Jessica Color **yellow/blue** Alternative colors **available** Width **20½in/52cm** Length **11yd/10m** Repeat **10in/25.5cm** Price ★

3 Mauny/Bouquets Color **document** Alternative colors **available** Width **21½in/55cm** Length **11yd/10m** Repeat **7½in/19cm** Price ★★★★ ♣

4 Ramm, Son & Crocker/Chesham Color **pink/tan** Alternative colors **available** Width **20½in/52cm** Length **11yd/10m** Repeat **10¼in/26cm** Price ★

2

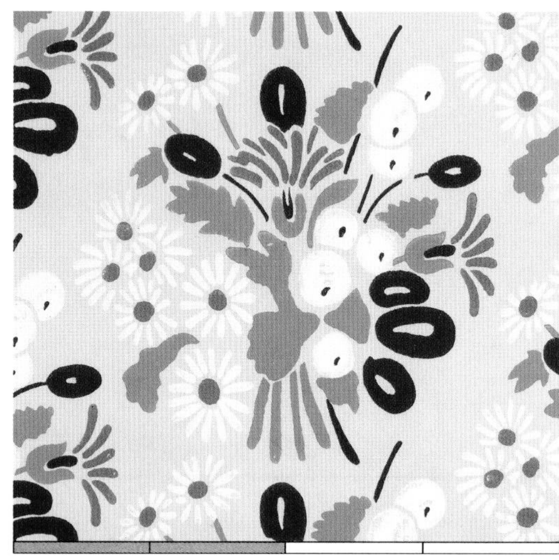
3

4

5 Bradbury & Bradbury/Honeysuckle Color **HSW-900** Alternative colors **available** Width **27in/68.5cm** Length **5yd/4.5m** Repeat **15¾in/40cm** Price ★★ ♣

6 Colefax and Fowler/Lydia 7611/02 Color **yellow/sage** Alternative colors **available** Width **20½in/52cm** Length **11yd/10m** Repeat **1¾in/4.5cm** Price ★

7 Jane Churchill/Tulip Sprig JY67W-02 Color **blue on white** Alternative colors **available** Width **20½in/52cm** Length **11yd/10m** Repeat **5in/13cm** Price ★

8 Bradbury & Bradbury/Thistle Wall Color **THW-970** Alternative colors **available** Width **23in/58.5cm** Length **sold by yard** Repeat **21in/53cm** Price ★★ ♣

5

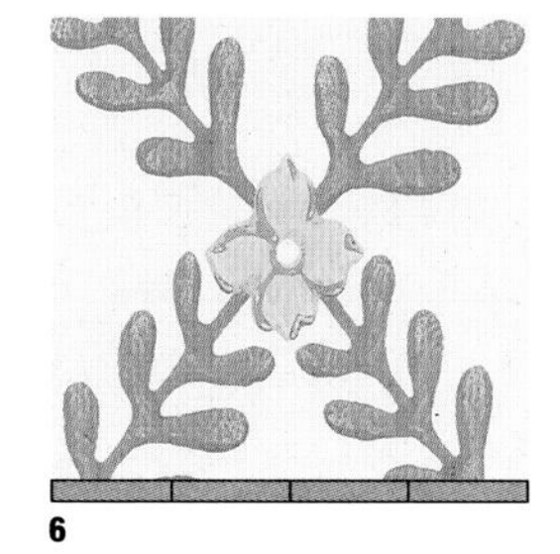
6

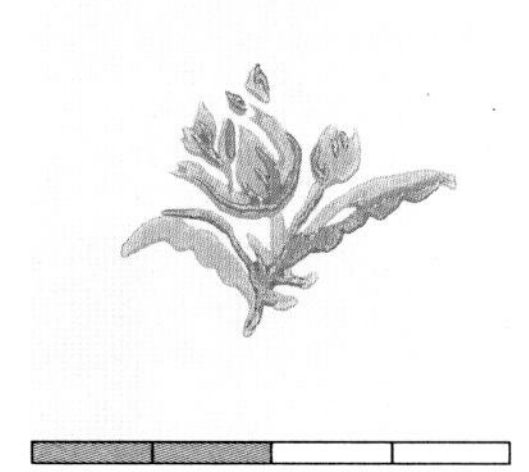
7

8

9

9 Mauny/Tarterres 5044 Color **document** Alternative colors **available** Width **18½in/47cm** Length **11yd/10m** Repeat **26¾in/68cm** Price ★★★★

10 Bradbury & Bradbury/Glasgow Panel Color **GWP-970** Alternative colors **available** Width **27in/ 68.5cm** Length **2¼yd/2m** Repeat – Price ★★★

11 G. P. & J. Baker/Rose & Hummingbird W0092-11 Color **11** Alternative colors **available** Width **20½in/52cm** Length **11yd/10m** Repeat **21in/53cm** Price ★

12 Cath Kidston/Rose Bouquet Color **blue** Alternative colors **available** Width **20½in/52cm** Length **11yd/10m** Repeat **18in/46cm** Price ★

13 Coloroll/Japonica 527770 Color **rust** Alternative colors **available** Width **20½in/52cm** Length **11yd/10m** Repeat **21in/53cm** Price ★

14

15

18

14 Coloroll/Chesterton Border 528180 Color **pink** Alternative colors **available** Width **6¾in/17cm** Length **5½yd/5m** Repeat **21in/53cm** Price ★

15 Cole & Son/Wild Rose Trellis Color **green, pink on white** Alternative colors **available** Width **21in/53cm** Length **11yd/10m** Repeat – Price ★★★★

16 Graham & Brown/Regency 96111 Color **beige and blue** Alternative colors **available** Width **5in/12.5cm** Length **5½yd/5m** Repeat – Price ★

17 Sanderson/Rose & Peony WR7670 Color **1** Alternative colors **available** Width **21in/53cm** Length **11½yd/ 10.5m** Repeat **21in/53cm** Price ★

18 Coloroll/Foxley 528296 Color **white** Alternative colors **available** Width **20½in/52cm** Length **11yd/10m** Repeat **21in/53cm** Price ★

10

16

11

12

13

17

Florals: **Late 20th century**

The post-war years were characterized by innovative designs as much as they were by period ones. Frequently seen during the 1950s were large, flamboyantly colored tropical flowers, and, for feature walls, photoengraved prints of single fantasy flowers, or screen-printed, freelyspaced flowers embellished with metallic highlights and displayed on dark grounds. Floral damask and *chinoiserie* patterns were also fashionable, but often recolored, rescaled, and applied over textured grounds–brown, gray,or pink flowers on white grass cloth being a typical example.

In the 1960s, Victorian sprigs and floral trails and sinuous Art Nouveau designs vied with sketchily realistic blooms and simplified flowers in bold, bright colors–the latter superseded during the romanticism of the mid-1970s by chalkily rendered, tiny floral repeats. Starting in the early 1980s there was a significant growth of interest in documentary floral papers dating from the late Renaissance to the early 20th century. Floral chintz patterns from the 18th and 19th centuries were especially popular, having fallen out of favor from 1945 until the late 1970s. Bright, impressionistic floral designs–inspired by painters such as Monet and Matisse–also became fashionable.

Crowson/Malura Color **36** Alternative colors **available** Width **6¾in/17.5cm** Length **11yd/10m** Repeat – Price ★

Jean Louis Seigner/Jardin d'Hiver 50 Color **white** Alternative colors **available** Width **21in/53cm** Length **11yd/10m** Repeat **17¾in/45cm** Price ★

Designers Guild/Quite Contrary Color **orange** Alternative colors **available** Width **20½in/52cm** Length **11yd/10m** Repeat **20½in/52cm** Price ★

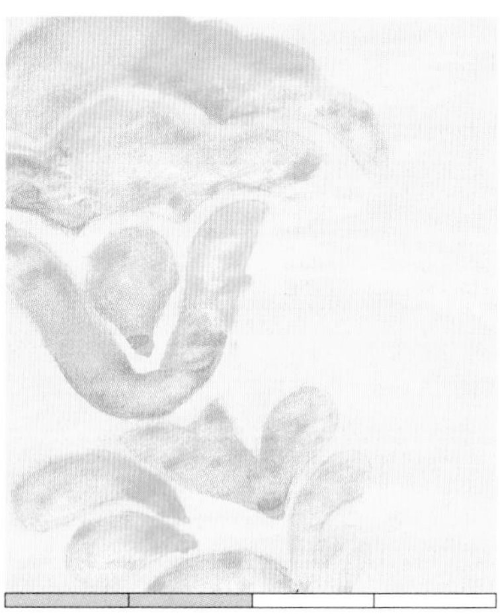

Anna French/Jester Color **JESWP036** Alternative colors **available** Width **20½in/52cm** Length **11yd/10m** Repeat **24in/61cm** Price ★

Brunschwig & Fils/Johanna 16140.06 Color **ivory** Alternative colors **available** Width **27in/68.5cm** Length **5yd/4.5m** Repeat **50¾in/129cm** Price ★★★★★

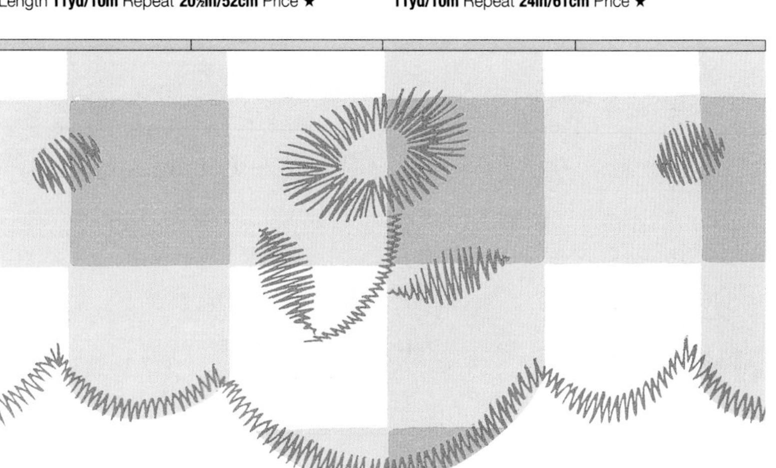

Baer & Ingram/Daisy Border DSB16 Color **blue** Alternative colors **available** Width **4in/10cm** Length **11yd/10m** Repeat **3½in/9cm** Price ★

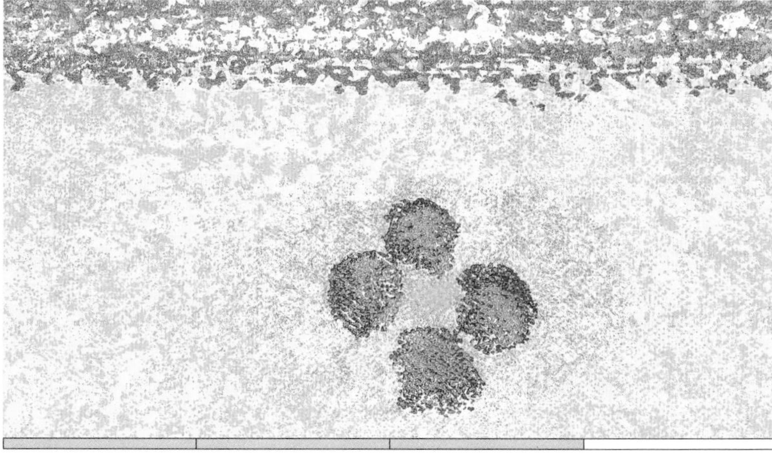

Anna French/Manila Color **MANWP025** Alternative colors **available** Width **20½in/52cm** Length **11yd/10m** Repeat **20½in/52cm** Price ★

Harlequin/8710 Color **multi** Alternative colors **available** Width **9½in/24cm** Length **5½yd/5m** Repeat **–** Price ★

Graham & Brown/Flower Basket 16540 Color **pink** Alternative colors **available** Width **42in/107cm** Length **11yd/10m** Repeat **25in/64cm** Price ★

Ciel Decor/Maianenco Border PFR0123.001 Color **blanc** Alternative colors **available** Width **3in/8cm** Length **11yd/10m** Repeat **–** Price ★

Anna French/Isolde Color **ISOWP063** Alternative colors **available** Width **20½in/52cm** Length **11yd/10m** Repeat **24in/61cm** Price ★

VINYL WALL COVERINGS

The first vinyl wall coverings, introduced in 1947, consisted of a coating of polyvinyl chloride (PVC) bonded to a patterned or plain paper backing. Their attraction was durability, washability–grease, lipstick, and ink could be scrubbed off with soap and water, and a resistance to yellowing with age. During the 1980s, however, more sophisticated relief vinyls were developed. This floral-patterned example is textured and "three-dimensionalized" in two ways: first, an additional "in-register" vinyl coating has been engraved exactly over the top of the pattern; second, some of the pattern is "blown"–printed with vinyl inks containing a catalyst that expands when heated.

Fine Decor/Palencia 20100 Color **dark blue** Alternative colors **available** Width **20½in/52cm** Length **11yd/10m** Repeat **21in/53cm** Price ★

Jean Louis Seigner/Les Fraises 1976 Color **multi** Alternative colors **not available** Width **21in/53cm** Length **11yd/10m** Repeat **19in/48cm** Price ★

Coloroll/Sella Rose Border 528371 Color **blue** Alternative colors **available** Width **6¾in/17.5cm** Length **5½yd/5m** Repeat **21in/53cm** Price ★

Fine Decor/Teleno 20086 Color **blue** Alternative colors **available** Width **20½in/52cm** Length **11yd/10m** Repeat **21in/53cm** Price ★

Pictorial Wallpapers

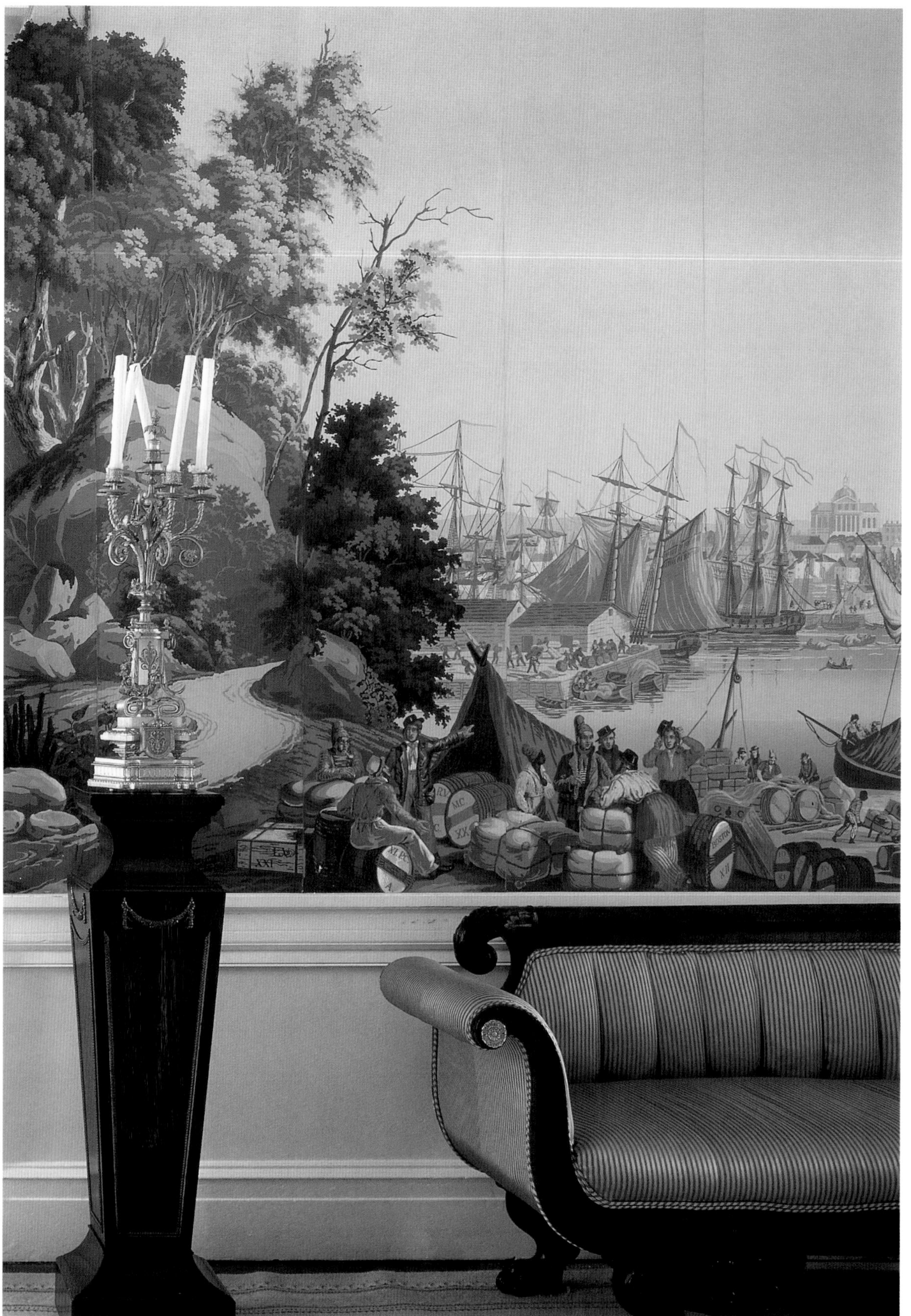

Pictorial wallpapers were first documented in 1481, when Louis XI of France paid Jean Bourdichon to paint 50 rolls of paper blue, and to add a Latin inscription held by three painted angels. Colored papers with pictures of religious and allegorical subjects were also used in Europe during the 16th and 17th centuries. However, it was not until the 18th century that pictorial wallpapers were produced in quantity, many of them inspired by Chinese wall-hangings. In England, John Baptist Jackson was the first to use papers imitating architectural features. But the finest pictorial papers were hand-printed in France during the late 18th and early 19th centuries, notably by paper-stainers such as Boulgard, Réveillon, Zuber, and Dufour. Many of these wallpapers were exported to Britain and America where, due to their high cost, they remained the preserve of the wealthy. However, the introduction of the cylinder-printing process in the 1850s meant that mass-produced pictorials could be made at more affordable prices and available to the middle class.

LEFT A mid-19th-century Zuber pictorial wallpaper, hung in the Monmouth Mansion in Natchez, Mississippi. Never having visited North America, the French designer painted this scene from his imagination, with Mississippi steamboats at Niagara Falls, Spanish moss at the Boston Tea Party, and Native Americans in African dress.

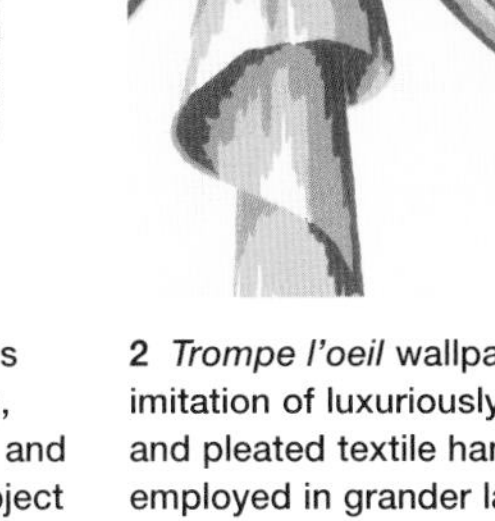

KEY DESIGNS

1 Human figures engaged in activities as diverse as military battles, hunting, shooting, harvesting, trading, sailing, and tea drinking have proved popular subject matter for pictorial papers.

2 *Trompe l'oeil* wallpapers produced in imitation of luxuriously swagged, tailed, and pleated textile hangings were often employed in grander late 18th- and early 19th-century Neoclassical interiors.

3 *Chinoiserie*-patterned wallpapers were fashionable throughout the 18th and early 19th centuries. Much of the imagery was heavily Europeanized by designers who had only scant knowledge of the Orient.

4 Imported Chinese papers and artifacts provided much of the inspiration for bird motifs during the 17th and 18th centuries. Audubon's *Birds of America* (1827) was also influential in the 19th century.

5 Pictorial papers patterned with naturalistic still-life images of flowers, fruit, and foliage were popular in the late 18th and mid-19th centuries, and enjoyed a revival in the late 20th century.

6 Nursery motifs were first introduced during the late 19th century. Subjects have included characters from children's tales and nursery rhymes, and, in the 20th century, from movies and cartoons.

1 **Joanna Wood/Vauxhall Gardens LW09** Color **azure** Alternative colors **available** Width **20½in/52cm** Length **11yd/10m** Repeat **21in/53cm** Price ★

2 **Hamilton Weston/Swag Border** Color **yellow/umber** Alternative colors **available** Width **9½in/24cm** Length **26¼in/66.5cm** Repeat **12½in/32cm** Price ★★★★ ♣

3 **Scalamandré/Ch'in Ling WP81212-10** Color **old gold and bark on lacquer red** Alternative colors **available** Width **24in/61cm** Length **6yd/5.5m** Repeat **38in/96.5cm** Price ★★★ ♣ [T]

4 **Cole & Son/Humming Bird** Color **special** Alternative colors **available** Width **21in/53cm** Length **11yd/10m** Repeat **20½in/52cm** Price ★★★★★ ♣

5 **Anna French/Sweet Plum** Color **WP041BI** Alternative colors **available** Width **20½in/52cm** Length **11yd/10m** Repeat **20½in/52cm** Price ★

6 **Jane Churchill/Check Bears JY21W/02** Color **yellow/blue** Alternative colors **available** Width **20½in/52cm** Length **11yd/10m** Repeat **20½in/52cm** Price ★

PRINT ROOMS

The fashion for decorating rooms with prints pasted over painted walls originated in the mid-18th century. Many print rooms featured black-and-white prints and borders simply pasted in rows; others, such as those designed by Thomas Chippendale, were more flamboyant and incorporated *trompe l'oeil* paper cutouts of swags, garlands, bows, and chains "supporting" and embellishing the prints. This decorative convention continued well into the 19th century. In the late 20th century, there was a revival of this fashion, with books of prints and borders designed for this purpose.

Pictorials: **Pre-19th century**

Many pictorial papers of the 16th and early 17th centuries depicted subject matter similar to that of pictorial tapestries, including figures emblematic of the four seasons surrounded by coats of arms, hunting scenes, and characters and events from Christian and classical mythology. Imported Chinese pictorial papers also became fashionable during the late 17th century. Typical patterns included landscapes of naturalistic flowering plants and trees, rivers and pools, exotic birds and insects, architectural images, and Oriental figures engaged in diverse activities–both urban and rural, secular and religious.

These Chinese-export papers provided the inspiration for the European *chinoiserie* pictorials that proved popular throughout the 18th century, especially in Rococo interiors. Equally fashionable, however, were *chiaroscuro*-printed imitations of fine art (notably the paintings of Titian and Tintoretto) and of Greco-Roman statuary and architecture. Also popular in the latter part of the century were French arabesques inspired by Roman wall paintings, Gothic ruins, and exceptionally large panoramas or "panoramic papers" of subject matter as varied as the Grand Tour, the exploration of the South Pacific, *fêtes galantes,* and scenes from the French Revolution.

6

1

2

3

4

5

1 **Schumacher/Children's Pastimes 519035** Color **green on white** Alternative colors **available** Width **27in/68.5cm** Length **11yd/10m** Repeat **23¾in/60cm** Price ★★★

2 **Zoffany/Réveillon Landscape 81004** Color **04** Alternative colors **available** Width **21in/53cm** Length **11yd/10m** Repeat **38½in/98cm** Price ★★

3 **The Design Archives/Persephone 58021** Color **32** Alternative colors **available** Width **20½in/52cm** Length **11yd/10m** Repeat **20½in/52cm** Price ★

4 **Schumacher/Journal de la Mode** Color **32** Alternative colors **available** Width **27in/68.5cm** Length **4½yd/4m** Repeat **25in/64cm** Price ★★★

5 **Timney Fowler/Sphinx Border** Color **black** Alternative colors **not available** Width **4¼in/11cm** Length **11yd/10m** Repeat **24in/61cm** Price ★

6 **Scalamandré/Pillement Toile** Color **4** Alternative colors **available** Width **27in/69cm** Length **5yd/4.5m** Repeat **27in/69cm** Price ★★★ T

7 **Manuel Canovas/Grand Khan** Color **jaune rouge** Alternative colors **available** Width **28¼in/72cm** Length **10yd/9m** Repeat **17½in/44.5cm** Price ★★★★★ ♣

8 **Nobilis-Fontan/L'Arbre Nantais** Color **red on cream** Alternative colors **available** Width **21½in/55cm** Length **11yd/10m** Repeat **23¾in/60cm** Price ★

7

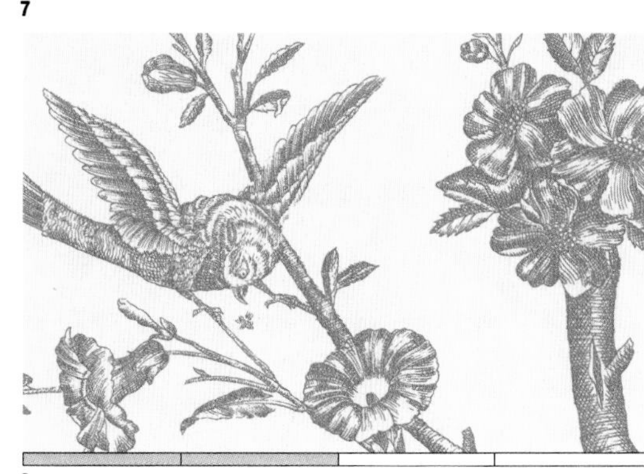
8

9 Sanderson/Canton WR7938/1 Color **1** Alternative colors **available** Width **21in/53cm** Length **11yd/10m** Repeat **11¾in/30cm** Price ★

10 Manuel Canovas/Merlin 8083 Color **30 ocher** Alternative colors **available** Width **26¾in/68cm** Length **11yd/10m** Repeat **11⅝in/29.5cm** Price ★★★★★ ♣

11 Schumacher/Jungle Kingdom 519011 Color **document** Alternative colors **available** Width **27in/68.5cm** Length **4½yd/4m** Repeat **36⅝in/93cm** Price ★★★

9

10

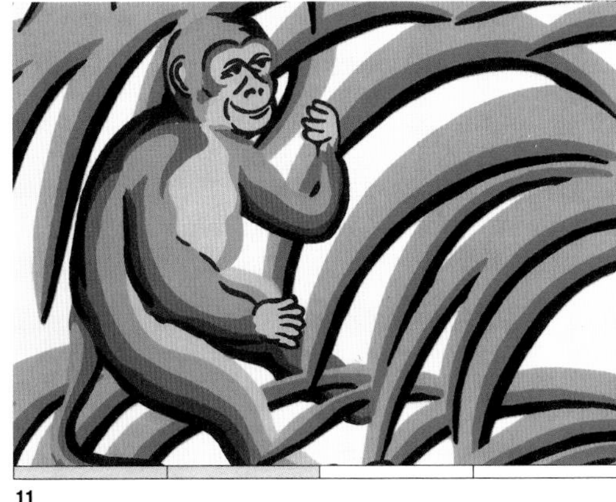

11

12

13

14

15

16

12 Alexander Beauchamp/Hunting Scene Color **multi** Alternative colors **available** Width **19¾in/50cm** Length **11yd/10m** Repeat **15½in/39.5cm** Price ★★★★ ♣

13 Zoffany/Réveillon Mini 8515004 Color **04** Alternative colors **available** Width **20½in/52cm** Length **11½yd/10.5m** Repeat **18in/46cm** Price ★

14 Sanderson/Garden Toile WR7929/2 Color **2** Alternative colors **available** Width **21in/53cm** Length **11yd/10m** Repeat **11¾in/30cm** Price ★

15 Hamilton Weston/Lambeth Saracen Color **8116** Alternative colors **available** Width **20¼in/51.5cm** Length **11yd/10m** Repeat **8in/20cm** Price ★★ ♣

16 De Gournay/Askew J-018 Color **verdigris** Alternative colors **available** Width **35¾in/91cm** Length **2¾yd/2.5m** Repeat – Price ★★★★★ ♣

ARABESQUES

The term "arabesque" refers to the stylized, interlaced foliage patterns that were derived from Islamic art. It was introduced to Europe via the engraved metalwork of Muslim craftsmen who emigrated to Venice during the 15th century. These foliage patterns appeared on wallpapers from the 17th to the 20th centuries. However, in the 18th century, arabesques acquired an additional meaning: French designers used the term to describe grotesque patterns, based on Roman wall paintings, which incorporated figures, vases, bandwork, flowers, and scrolling foliage.

Zuber/Arabesques 2402N Color **black** Alternative colors **available** Width **18½in/47cm** Length **10m/11yd** Repeat **18in/46cm** Price ★★★

Pictorials: **Early 19th century**

The French panoramics produced during the late 18th century (*see* page 240) became even more popular during the early 19th century, although few were exported until the end of the Napoleonic Wars in 1815. Apart from *chinoiserie* designs (*see* opposite), fashionable subject matter included classical deities (in *chiaroscuro*), views of English, European, and American cities, monuments and landscapes, hunting and horse-racing scenes, wars and battles, and episodes from literature.

Also widespread in the early 19th century were religious pictures portrayed in *grisaille* and paper friezes produced in imitation of stuccowork and sculpture depicting Ancient Greek or Roman figures, legends, and architectural elements. Of special note were the hand-blocked *trompe l'oeil* papers (*see* right), of mostly French manufacture, that simulated silk and velvet hangings realistically swagged and tailed, pleated, or button-backed, and often embellished with decorative *passements* such as cords, braids, and tassels.

1

2

1 **Zoffany/Empire Damask 36ED05** Color **05** Alternative colors **available** Width **20½in/52cm** Length **11yd/10m** Repeat **18in/46cm** Price ★

2 **Brunschwig & Fils/Vaison 15760.06** Color **sand** Alternative colors **available** Width **27in/68.5cm** Length **5yd/4.5m** Repeat **18¼in/46.5cm** Price ★★★★

3 **Brunschwig & Fils/Bunny Business 15892-06** Color **bluebell** Alternative colors **available** Width **27in/68.5cm** Length **5yd/4.5m** Repeat **27in/68.5cm** Price ★★

3

TROMPE L'OEIL

A characteristic of many of the pictorial wallpapers that were produced for Neoclassical interiors of the early 19th century was an enhanced use of perspective. The "three-dimensional" effect displayed by these *trompe l'oeil* papers, such as the pleated textile (right) and the Greek frieze (below), was primarily achieved by strengthening both the shadows and the highlights in the pattern.

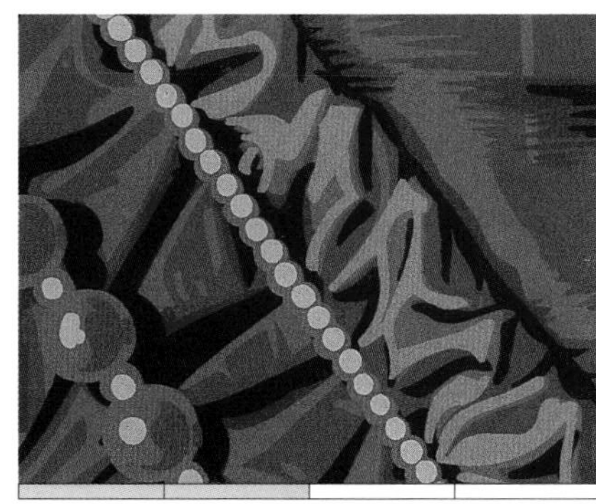

Zuber/Eugénie 9013 Color **rouge** Alternative colors **available** Width **18½in/47cm** Length **10yd/9m** Repeat **26¼in/66.5cm** Price ★★★

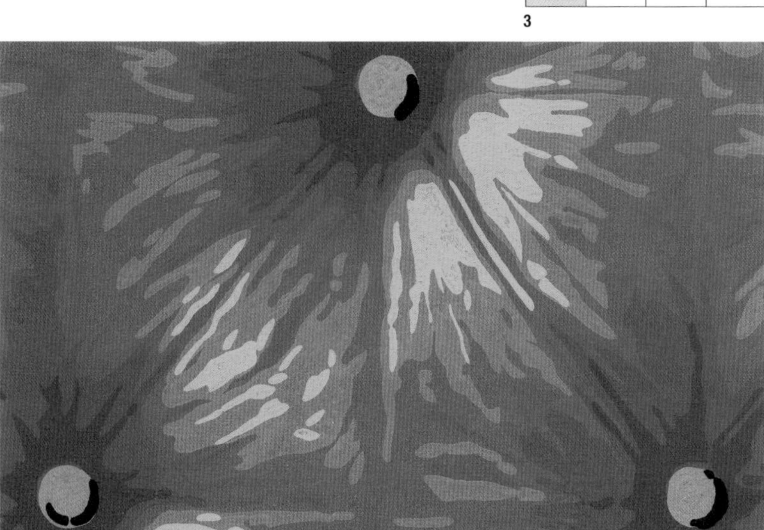

4

4 **Zuber/Capiton 30023** Color **rouge** Alternative colors **available** Width **18½in/47cm** Length **11yd/10m** Repeat **8in/20cm** Price ★★★

5 **Zuber/Bordure Draperie Empire 20047** Color **vert** Alternative colors **available** Width **13¼in/34cm** Length **11yd/10m** Repeat **18½in/47cm** Price ★★

5

Scalamandré/Prestwould Saloon Dado WB81504 Color **document** Alternative colors **available** Width **21in/53cm** Length **7yd/6.5m** Repeat – Price ★★ ♣ T

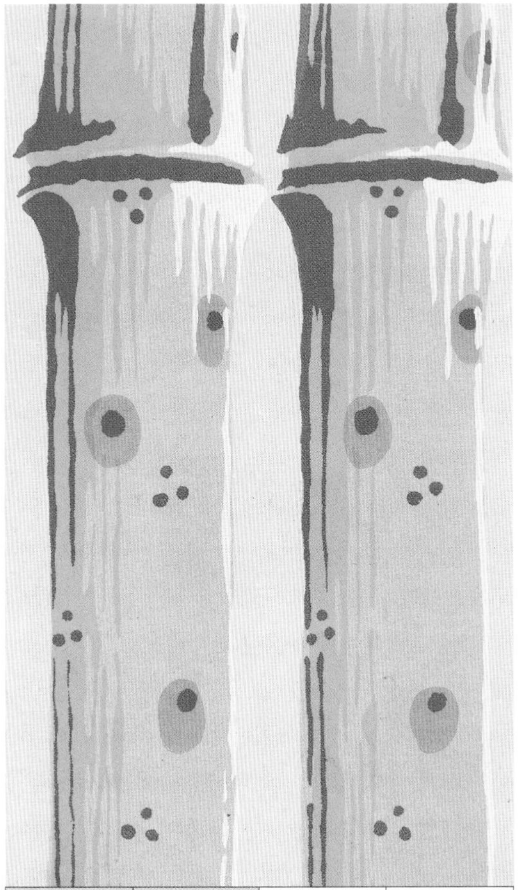

6

7

8

6 Alexander Beauchamp/Regency Bamboo Border Color **multi** Alternative colors **available** Width **6½in/16.5cm** Length **11yd/10m** Repeat **27in/68.5cm** Price ★★★★★

7 Schumacher/Athena Toile Color **capet** Alternative colors **available** Width **27in/68.5cm** Length **4½yd/4m** Repeat **25in/64cm** Price ★★★

8 Nina Campbell/Leapfrog NCB2032/07 Color **07** Alternative colors **available** Width **4in/10.5cm** Length **11yd/10m** Repeat – Price ★

9 Today Interiors/China Grove LOW2295 Color **red** Alternative colors **available** Width **21in/53cm** Length **11yd/10m** Repeat **6¾in/17cm** Price ★

9

PANORAMIC DESIGNS

During the first half of the 19th century, panoramic wallpapers were very fashionable on both sides of the Atlantic. Some papers were particularly large (up to 52½ft/16m long by 10ft/3m high), and designed to be placed in sequence around the four walls of a room. Some panoramics were so complicated that they required up to 1,500 separate printing blocks to produce. Especially popular were *chinoiserie* designs, such as scenes of everyday life in China, and landscapes that were populated with flowering trees, exotic birds, butterflies, and insects.

De Gournay/Coutts Color **antique finish** Alternative colors **available** Width **36in/91.5cm** Length **3¾yd/3.5m** Repeat – Price ★★★★★

De Gournay/Coutts Color **Painted Paper** Alternative colors **available** Width **36in/91.5cm** Length **3¾yd/3.5m** Repeat – Price ★★★★★

De Gournay/Earlham J040 Color **dark blue** Alternative colors **available** Width **36in/91.5cm** Length **3¾yd/3.5m** Repeat – Price ★★★★★

Pictorials: **Late 19th century**

During the second half of the 19th century, the development of roller-printing and the introduction of new synthetic dyes made it much easier for wallpaper manufacturers on both sides of the Atlantic to produce sophisticated but reasonably inexpensive pictorial patterns. Favored subject matter of the period was diverse. Notable examples included "three-dimensional" depictions of animals, flowers, fruits, and other plant forms–many indigenous to Europe and the United States, but others derived from more exotic *chinoiserie*, *japonaiserie*, and Indian and African imagery. Rural landscapes, scenes from industry, and commemorative pictorials of significant military and political events also proved popular. Particularly fashionable in the various Classical Revival interiors of grander European and American homes were *trompe l'oeil* simulations of architectural elements, such as statuary, pillars, plaster moldings, and wood carvings. On the other hand, favored pictorial papers in Gothic Revival houses were generally flatter-patterned and incorporated medieval imagery ranging from Gothic-arched windows with elaborate tracery to beasts-of-the-field, all invariably augmented with stylized or naturalistic plant forms, or with heraldic motifs such as emblems and coats of arms.

1

3

1 **Warner Fabrics/Temples of Antiquity** Color **cream** Alternative colors **available** Width **20½in/52cm** Length **11yd/10m** Repeat **16¼in/41cm** Price ★

2 **Sanderson/Fruit** Color **1** Alternative colors **available** Width **21in/53cm** Length **11yd/10m** Repeat **–** Price ★

3 **Watts of Westminster/Bird** Color **blue** Alternative colors **available** Width **25in/64cm** Length **11yd/10m** Repeat **23in/59cm** Price ★★

4 **Bradbury & Bradbury/Pomegranate Panel** Color **410** Alternative colors **available** Width **27in/68.5cm** Length **to order** Repeat **27in/68.5cm** Price ★★★

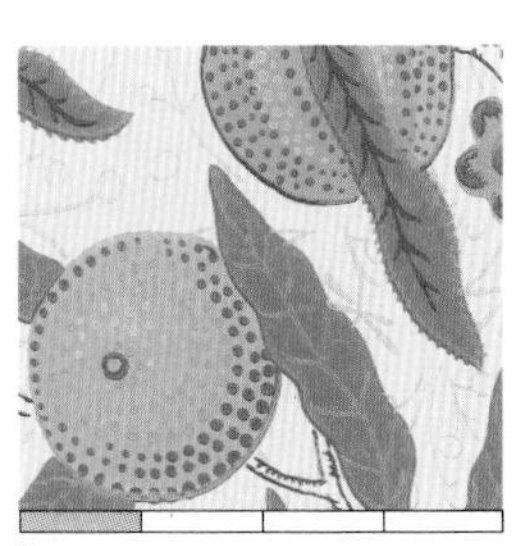

2

4

5

6

5 **Brunschwig & Fils/Bartlett 16043-06** Color **gold** Alternative colors **available** Width **27in/68.5cm** Length **5yd/4.5m** Repeat **25in/64cm** Price ★★★★★

6 **Sanderson/Trellis Morris** Color **document** Alternative colors **not available** Width **21in/53cm** Length **11yd/10m** Repeat – Price ★★★★

7 **Bradbury & Bradbury/Lion & Dove Frieze LDF** Color **001** Alternative colors **not available** Width **26¼in/67cm** Length **to order** Repeat **46in/117cm** Price ★★★★

7

8

9

11

8 Brunschwig & Fils/Shimo 15414.06 Color **green** Alternative colors **available** Width **24¾in/63.5cm** Length **5yd/4.5m** Repeat **25in/64cm** Price ★★★

9 Schumacher/Painted Scroll Border 519174 Color **red** Alternative colors **available** Width **15¾in/40cm** Length **to order** Repeat **38in/96.5cm** Price ★★★

10 Alexander Beauchamp/ Etiene Frieze Color **multi** Alternative colors **available** Width **21in/53.5cm** Length **11yd/10m** Repeat **10in/ 25.5cm** Price ★★★★

11 Schumacher/Fruitier Border 519152 Color **periwinkle and royal** Alternative colors **available** Width **9¼in/23.5cm** Length **to order** Repeat **20in/51cm** Price ★★★

12 Watts of Westminster/ Ettalde W0015-01/Z12 Color **Stockholm** Alternative colors **available** Width **2¾in/7cm** Length **2⅛yd/2m** Repeat **21in/53cm** Price ★★★

13 Alexander Beauchamp/ Moorish Dado Color **multi** Alternative colors **available** Width **18½in/47cm** Length **11yd/10m** Repeat **22¼in/ 56.5cm** Price ★★★★★

10

12

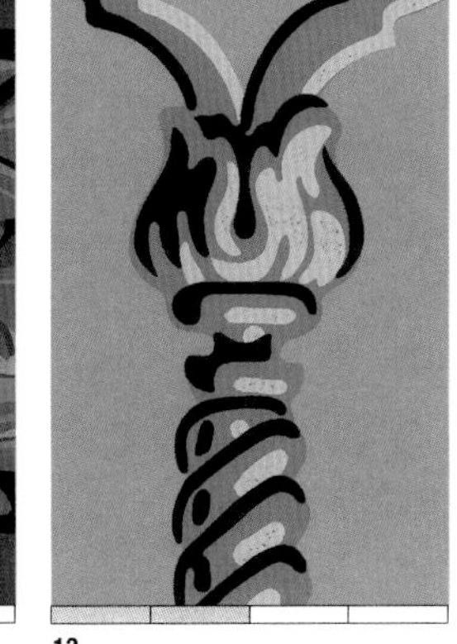

13

CEILING PAPERS

A tremendous variety of wallpapers designed specifically for use on ceilings and adjacent cornices were made during the 19th century, and were fashionable in Classical Revival interiors. As a result of new printing techniques, many examples, especially those of French origin, were sophisticated in terms of color and shading–elements employed to produce *trompe l'oeil* simulations of both floral and faunal imagery, as well as plasterwork molding such as fan- and star-shaped roses and geometrical strapwork.

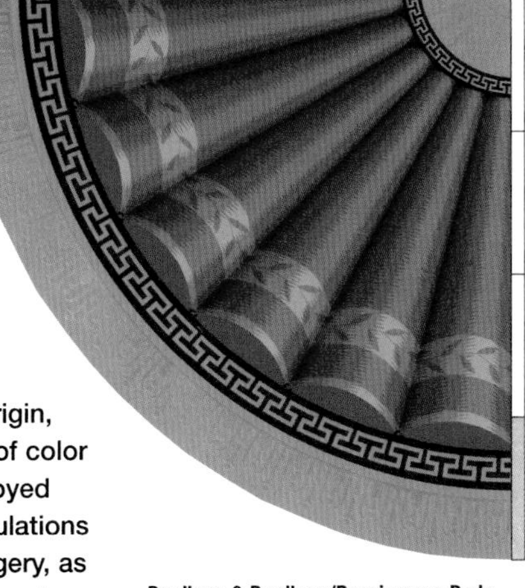

Bradbury & Bradbury/Renaissance Dado RED Color **550** Alternative colors **available** Width **27in/68.5cm** Length **5yd/4.5m** Repeat **27in/68.5cm** Price ★★★

Bradbury & Bradbury/Gossamer Ceiling GSC Color **610** Alternative colors **available** Width **27in/68.5cm** Length **5yd/4.5m** Repeat **27in/ 68.5cm** Price ★★

Detail of an American Italianate or Second Empire ceiling. Individual papers include a scrolling foliage Renaissance frieze, Italianate borders, and Roman corner fans.

Pictorials: **Early 20th century**

Scenic wallpapers similar to those produced in early 19th-century France enjoyed a revival during the early 20th century, especially in the United States. The subject matter was diverse and ranged from horse-racing to views of important cities and monuments, with woodland and hunting scenes favored in dining rooms and seascapes appearing in bathrooms. Imitations of both Medieval and Renaissance narrative tapestries also proved very popular in Arts and Crafts and Tudor and Jacobean Revival interiors.

Apart from nursery papers (*see* opposite), other pictorial-patterned wallpapers of note included designs inspired by 18th-century *chinoiserie* papers, Egyptian desert imagery, and exotic wild animals from the jungles and plains of central and southern Africa. In the 1940s, fine art also exerted a strong influence, with manufacturers offering screen-printed murals by great artists such as Matisse, Miró, and Raphael, including the latter's decorations for the loggia of the Vatican in Rome.

Osborne & Little/Jester Border B1210/05 Color **yellow/red/blue** Alternative colors **available** Width **5in/13cm** Length **11yd/10m** Repeat **–** Price ★

Scalamandré/Akabar's Stable WP81542-1 Color **1** Alternative colors **available** Width **27½in/70cm** Length **5yd/4.5m** Repeat **27½in/70cm** Price ★★★★ T

Osborne & Little/Toad Hall W1199-03 Color **green** Alternative colors **available** Width **20½in/52cm** Length **11yd/10m** Repeat **28¼in/72cm** Price ★

Colefax and Fowler/Check Bears JY22B-02 Color **yellow/blue** Alternative colors **available** Width **10¼in/26cm** Length **11yd/10m** Repeat **–** Price ★

Mauny/Les Singes 5042 Color **multi** Alternative colors **available** Width **18½in/47cm** Length **11yd/10m** Repeat **20½in/52cm** Price ★★★★ ♣

Cole & Son/Pekin Color **blue/gold/black** Alternative colors **available** Width **20½in/52cm** Length **11yd/10m** Repeat **21in/53cm** Price ★★ ♣

Nobilis-Fontan/Fanny BOR2101 Color **terracotta on cream** Alternative colors **available** Width **10¼in/26cm** Length **11yd/10m** Repeat **19in/48cm** Price ★★★ ♣

Cath Kidston/Bathtime Color **multi** Alternative colors **available** Width **20½in/52cm** Length **11yd/10m** Repeat **18in/46cm** Price ★

Jane Churchill/Picture Book JY16B-01 Color **green** Alternative colors **available** Width **10¼in/26cm** Length **11yd/10m** Repeat – Price ★

Mauny/Martin Pêcheur 5035 Color **multi** Alternative colors **available** Width **18½in/47cm** Length **11yd/10m** Repeat **24¼in/62cm** Price ★★★ ♣

Jane Churchill/St Paul JY01W-04 Color **yellow** Alternative colors **available** Width **20½in/52cm** Length **11yd/10m** Repeat **20½in/52cm** Price ★

Marthe Armitage/Willow Pattern Color **multi** Alternative colors **available** Width **21in/53cm** Length **11yd/10m** Repeat **16½in/42cm** Price ★

Mauny/Chinoiseries 5059 Color **multi** Alternative colors **available** Width **18½in/47cm** Length **11yd/10m** Repeat **18½in/47cm** Price ★★★★ ♣

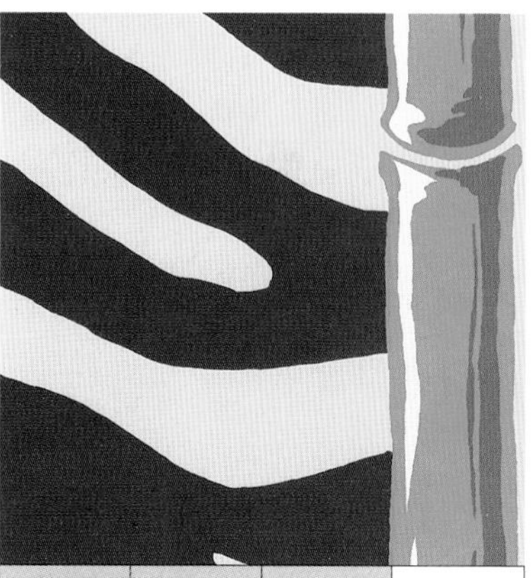

Nobilis-Fontan/Zèbra et Léopard Color **BOR2901 black/white** Alternative colors **available** Width **6¼in/16cm** Length **11yd/10m** Repeat – Price ★★★★★ ♣

NURSERY PAPERS

Pictorial wallpapers that were designed specifically for children's rooms first appeared in the late 19th century, when leading illustrators of the time, including Walter Crane, Kate Greenaway, and Mabel Attwell, devised patterns based on children's stories and nursery rhymes. While the nursery paper genre was established in the 19th century, it proliferated in the 20th. Some early 20th-century designs, notably those that were based on *The Tales of Beatrix Potter* and cartoon characters such as Disney's Mickey Mouse™, are still very popular today and compete with subject matter as diverse as soldiers, airplanes, farm animals, vintage cars, humorous vegetables, and famous film and television characters.

Osborne & Little/Lords & Ladies B1211/02 Color **blue** Alternative colors **available** Width **5in/13cm** Length **11yd/10m** Repeat – Price ★

Jane Churchill/Dancing Vegetables JY17W-04 Color **green/yellow** Alternative colors **available** Width **20½in/52cm** Length **11yd/10m** Repeat **20½in/52cm** Price ★

Pictorials: **Late 20th century**

The revival of mural wallpapers that took place in the early 19th century has been largely sustained to the present day. However, there have been some significant changes of style and content that reflect developments in both urban and rural life, and in printing techniques. For example, in the United States during the 1950s and 1960s, fashionable photomurals showed subjects such as the New York skyline, groups of commuting office workers, and Route 66 cutting the age of the automobile through its desert landscape. Similarly, the Pop Art and Op Art of the 1960s was readily translated onto still life pictorial papers.

Nursery papers were also produced in increasing quantities in the latter part of the 20th century. Many were photogravure murals designed to cover modern flush doors ("photodoors") in a child's bedroom. And, while some of the subject matter, such as Disney's Mickey Mouse, *The Tales of Beatrix Potter*, life on the farm, and Thomas the Tank Engine™, is as popular today as it was earlier in the century, the genre has constantly accommodated new characters–familiar comic book and cartoon figures such as BarbieTM™, Batman™, The Simpsons™, and the Power Rangers™ being among the most popular.

4

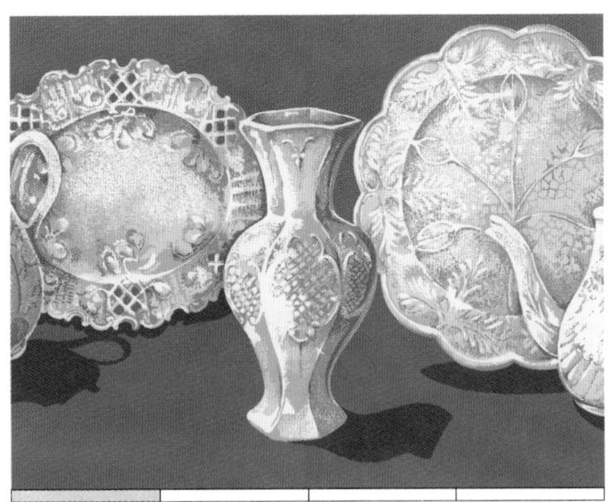

1

2

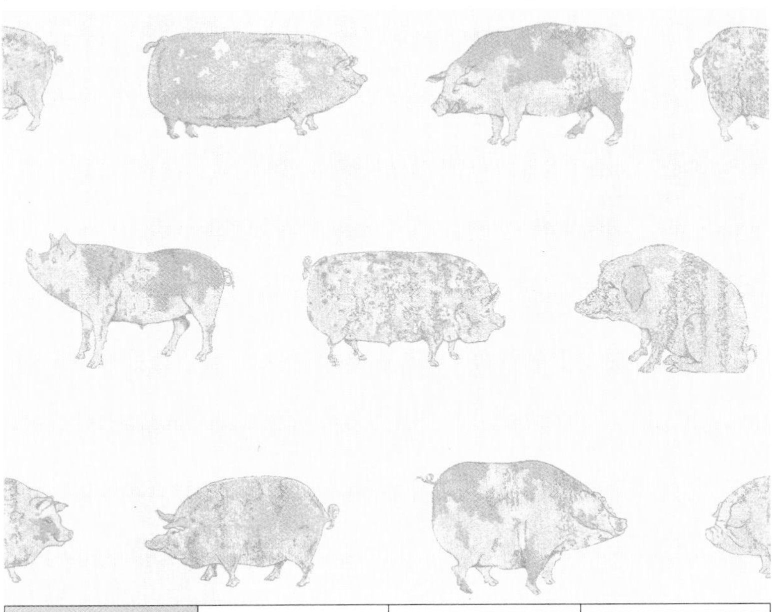

3

1 **Schumacher/Wetherburn Stoneware Border 519163** Color **blue** Alternative colors **available** Width **10½in/27cm** Length **to order** Repeat **31⅞in/81cm** Price ★★★

2 **Jean Louis Seigner/Egyptian Popylus** Color **black and white** Alternative colors **available** Width **27½in/70cm** Length **11yd/10m** Repeat **3½in/9cm** Price ★★

3 **Osborne & Little/Piggy W1195-04** Color **green** Alternative colors **available** Width **20½in/52cm** Length **11yd/10m** Repeat **21in/53cm** Price ★

4 **Marthe Armitage/Italian Garden** Color **black and white** Alternative colors **available** Width **23in/59cm** Length **11yd/10m** Repeat **16½in/42cm** Price ★

5 **Osborne & Little/Aviary W1196-06** Color **red** Alternative colors **available** Width **20½in/52cm** Length **11yd/10m** Repeat **21in/53cm** Price ★

6 **Osborne & Little/Safari W1192-04** Color **green** Alternative colors **available** Width **20½in/52cm** Length **11yd/10m** Repeat **21in/53cm** Price ★

5

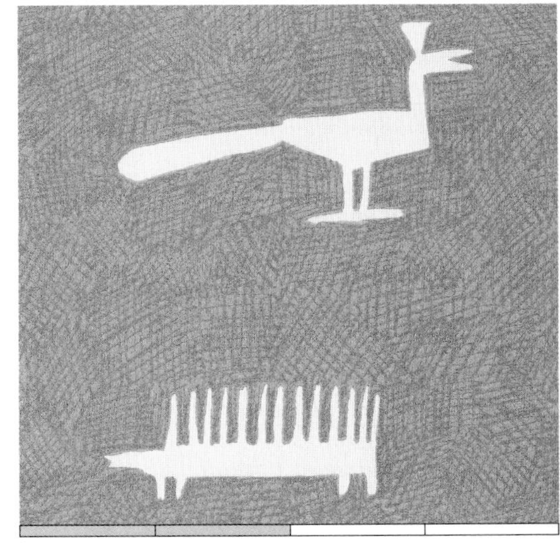

6

7

8

9

10

7 Jane Churchill/Farmyard Antics JY20B-04 Color **red/green** Alternative colors **available** Width **5in/13cm** Length **11yd/10m** Repeat **–** Price ★

8 Jane Churchill/Jousting J Y13W-07 Color **red/parchment** Alternative colors **available** Width **20½in/52cm** Length **11yd/10m** Repeat **20½in/ 52cm** Price ★

9 Jean Louis Seigner/Jardin du Luxembourg Color **21** Alternative colors **available** Width **27½in/70cm** Length **11yd/10m** Repeat **19¼in/ 49cm** Price ★

10 Vymura/Thomas the Tank Engine Color **multi** Alternative colors **not available** Width **20½in/ 52cm** Length **11yd/10m** Repeat **21in/53cm** Price ★

11 Coloroll/Chevalier Border 703907 Color **red** Alternative colors **available** Width **5in/ 13cm** Length **5½yd/5m** Repeat **21in/53cm** Price ★

12 Crowson/Cannes 37650CB9 Color **40** Alternative colors **available** Width **5in/13cm** Length **11yd/10m** Repeat **–** Price ★

13 Crowson/Alphabet 37650A14 Color **10** Alternative colors **available** Width **5in/13cm** Length **11yd/10m** Repeat **–** Price ★

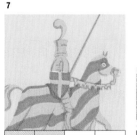

11

12

13

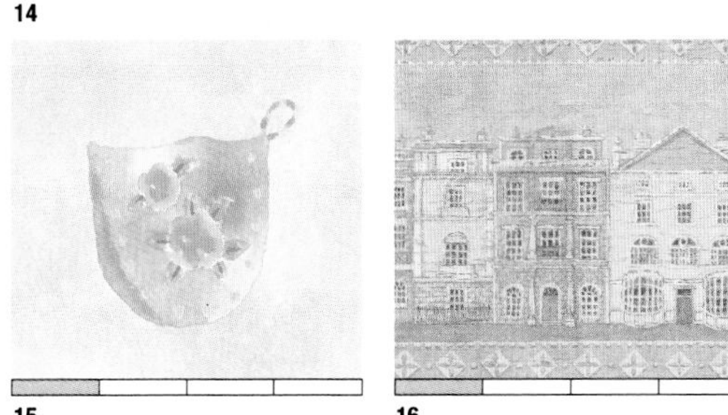

14

15

16

14 Vymura/Barbie™ Color **multi** Alternative colors **not available** Width **20½in/52cm** Length **11yd/10m** Repeat **21in/53cm** Price ★

15 Anna French/Purses PRWP072 Color **072** Alternative colors **available** Width **20½in/52cm** Length **11yd/10m** Repeat **20½in/52cm** Price ★

16 G. P. & J. Baker/Castle Street Border W0117-01 Color **01** Alternative colors **available** Width **7in/18cm** Length **11yd/10m** Repeat **7in/18cm** Price ★

Overall Pattern Wallpapers

Of the numerous patterns that have appeared on wallpapers from the late 15th century to the present day, a substantial number have been based on plant forms. Vying for popularity with floral designs have been patterns depicting fruits, nuts, vegetables, and foliage. Since the Renaissance, the gradual assimilation of Oriental, Middle Eastern, Asian, and African styles of decoration into the vocabulary of European, and, later, American ornament, has resulted in a steady increase in the types of plant forms available to wallpaper designers. The vagaries of fashion have also resulted in these organic forms being either conventionalized or depicted naturalistically during different periods. For example, naturalistic renderings were common for much of the 17th century, as well as in the late 18th and mid-19th centuries, while stylized representations were a feature of the late 19th and early 20th centuries. Other popular overall patterns used since the 17th century have included imitations of decorative plaster and wooden moldings; simulations of the figuring and grain of various hardwoods; replicas of the random crazing found on craquelure-varnished paneling; and abstract designs inspired by microphotography and 20th-century fine art.

PLANT-FORM REPEATS
Chinese wallpapers that displayed many different kinds of exotic Oriental imagery were highly sought after in Britain and Europe during the early 18th century. However, they were generally confined to reception rooms. In bedrooms of this period it was much more usual to find wallpapers embellished with indigenous plant-form patterns. The example shown here in the Prince's Room at Temple Newsam near Leeds in England has a repeating pattern of fruit, vegetables, and leaves. The wallpaper is a reproduction of the original that was hung in the room in 1827.

ABOVE & LEFT A large number of foliage-patterned wallpapers, designed for use on both ceilings and walls, were produced throughout the 19th century and proved popular on both sides of the Atlantic. Early in the century, laurel leaf and fern patterns were fashionable. By the middle of the century, acanthus leaves, oak leaves, grapevines, and ivy were popular, while in the later Aesthetic and Arts and Crafts interiors, formalized oak, acanthus, and lotus leaves were much in evidence. Colors–mostly shades of green and brown–remained realistic throughout the 19th century.

FAR LEFT Wallpapers produced to imitate blocks of stone have been much in demand since the beginning of the 20th century, particularly in Medieval Revival interiors. Some examples are flat-patterned, and therefore little more than a pastiche of stonework, but others employ subtle highlights and shading in the areas of the mortar joints to achieve quite realistic *trompe l'oeil* effects.

KEY DESIGNS

1 Small-scale scrolling patterns (leaf or ironwork) have been used on wallpapers since the 17th century. The contemporary example shown here was inspired by a 19th-century printed fabric document.

2 This large-scale leaf pattern dates from the late 19th century. Like many two-tone leaf-patterned wallpapers that have appeared since the late 17th century, it is produced in imitation of a silk damask.

3 Willow-pattern wall- and ceiling-papers were especially fashionable during the second half of the 19th and early 20th centuries, notably in Aesthetic and Arts and Crafts interiors.

4 Stylized patterns were popular during the late 19th century. The sinuous, rhythmical qualities inherent in this late Victorian example heralded the Art Nouveau designs of the early 20th century.

5 Naturalistic, small-scale, overall leaf patterns were a feature of late 17th-century interiors. This mid-20th-century example was an adaptation of a French document paper from around 1800.

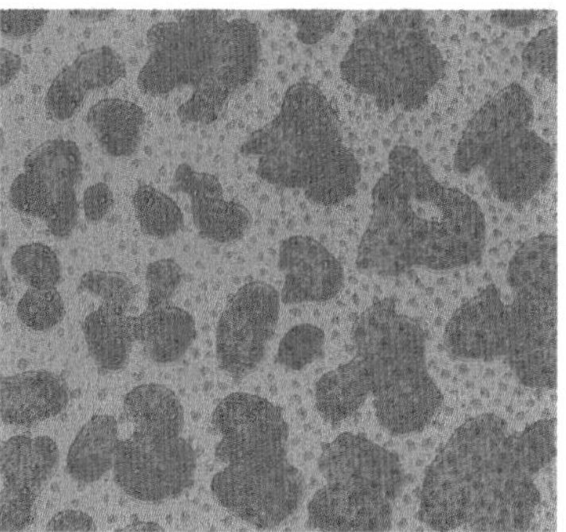

6 Wallpapers featuring animal-print patterns can present an effective overall pattern, especially when viewed from a distance. Similar abstract designs have imitated this type of patterning.

1 **Colefax and Fowler/New Paris 7603/10** Color **stone** Alternative colors **available** Width **20½in/52cm** Length **11yd/10m** Repeat **21in/53cm** Price ★

2 **Osborne & Little/Pompadour W1372/03** Color **neutral** Alternative colors **available** Width **20½in/52cm** Length **11yd/10m** Repeat **12in/31cm** Price ★

3 **Sanderson/Willow** Color **Morris 66** Alternative colors **available** Width **21in/53cm** Length **11½yd/10.5m** Repeat **18in/46cm** Price ★ ♣

4 **Hodsoll McKenzie/Neoclassic 503/620** Color **green** Alternative colors **available** Width **20½in/52cm** Length **11yd/10m** Repeat **9in/23cm** Price ★

5 **Colefax and Fowler/Langley 7607/02** Color **leaf green** Alternative colors **available** Width **20½in/52cm** Length **11yd/10m** Repeat **10¼in/26cm** Price ★

6 **Nina Campbell/Bagatelle Spot NCW511/01** Color **green** Alternative colors **available** Width **20½in/52cm** Length **11yd/10m** Repeat **8in/20cm** Price ★

Overall Pattern: **Pre-19th century**

From the mid-16th to the late 18th century, the majority of overall-patterned papers depicted conventionalized or naturalistic fruit or foliage, with many of the designs produced in imitation of fashionable textiles such as damasks. Favored plant forms during the Renaissance and the 17th century included grapevines, ivy, parsley, waterleafs, oak leaves, and palms, as well as pomegranates and pines (usually set within scrolling acanthus leaves). These were also used during the 18th century, when they vied with plants of Oriental origin, such as lotus leaves, artichokes, Neoclassical anthemia, laurels, and seaweed.

Apart from fruit and foliage, overall-patterned papers of the 18th century often imitated decorative architectural features traditionally made of plaster or wood. Typical examples, mostly *chiaroscuro*-printed to achieve the required "three-dimensional" effect, included elements such as *grisaille* paneling and scrollwork, while in Sweden wood-effect designs were particularly popular.

1

2

3

1 **Hamilton Weston/Royal Crescent** Color **gray, brown, and white on blue** Alternative colors **available** Width **20½in/52cm** Length **11yd/10m** Repeat **21in/53cm** Price ★★ ♣

2 **Schumacher/Antebellum Blocks 512930** Color **document** Alternative colors **available** Width **27in/68.5cm** Length **4½yd/4m** Repeat **25in/64cm** Price ★★★

3 **Alexander Beauchamp/Seaton** Color **multi** Alternative colors **available** Width **18in/46cm** Length **11yd/10m** Repeat **24in/61cm** Price ★★★★ ♣

4 **Alexander Beauchamp/Gainsborough** Color **blue/white** Alternative colors **available** Width **17in/43cm** Length **11yd/10m** Repeat **18¼in/46.5cm** Price ★★★ ♣

5 **Ciel Decor/Campano PPA 0029.399** Color **bleu Santorin** Alternative colors **available** Width **4in/10.5cm** Length **22yd/20m** Repeat **3in/7.5cm** Price ★

6 **Watts of Westminster/Napoleon W5030** Color **green, black, and gold** Alternative colors **available** Width **18in/46cm** Length **11yd/10m** Repeat **21in/53cm** Price ★★★

5

4

6

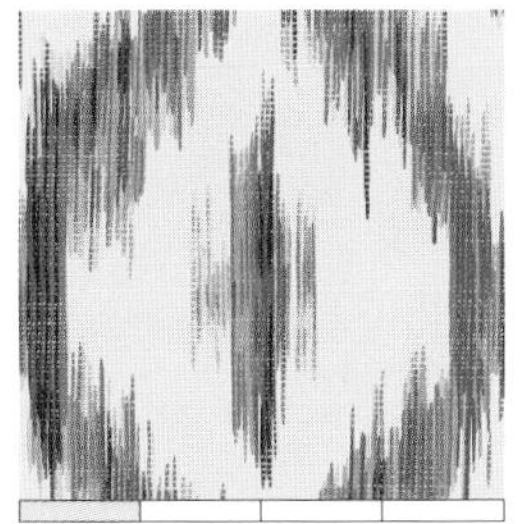

7

8

9

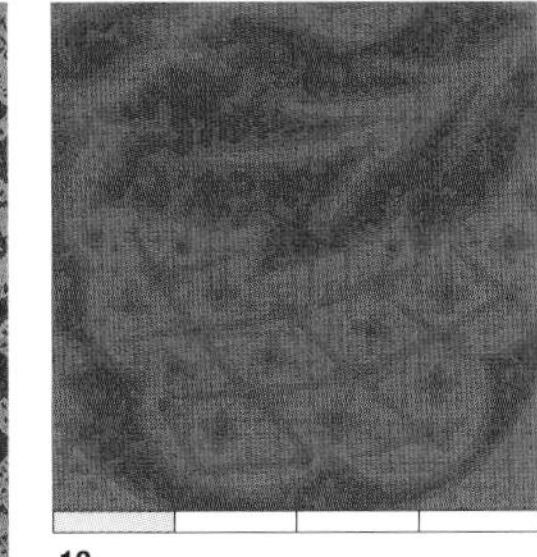

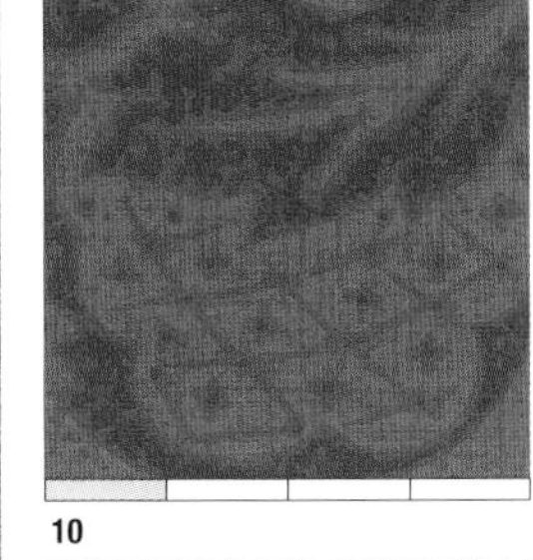

10

11

12

7 **Schumacher/Diamond Ikat** Color **gray** Alternative colors **available** Width **27in/68.5cm** Length **5yd/4.5m** Repeat **21in/53cm** Price ★★★

8 **Zuber/Damas/Or 40068** Color **red and gold** Alternative colors **available** Width **21in/53cm** Length **11yd/10m** Repeat – Price ★★★

9 **Alexander Beauchamp/Holcombe** Color **red and gold** Alternative colors **available** Width **19¾in/50cm** Length **11yd/10m** Repeat **15½in/39.5cm** Price ★★★

10 **G. P. & J. Baker/Venetian Damask W0112-05** Color **05** Alternative colors **available** Width **20½in/52cm** Length **11yd/10m** Repeat **21in/53cm** Price ★

11 **Alexander Beauchamp/Urn & Acanthus** Color **red** Alternative colors **available** Width **21in/53cm** Length **11yd/10m** Repeat **18½in/47cm** Price ★★★

12 **Alexander Beauchamp/Italian Damask** Color **green** Alternative colors **available** Width **21in/ 53cm** Length **11yd/10m** Repeat **23¾in/60.5cm** Price ★★★★

SMALL-SCALE DESIGNS

The wallpaper shown here, called "Satin Grass," was one of eleven fine-quality papers purchased in 1799 from the English paper-stainer James Duppa by Lady Jean Skipworth for her new house, Prestwould Plantation, in Clarksville, Virginia. The paper features a striking, interlaced foliage pattern on a highly polished satin ground. It is typical of the simple, small-scale repeating designs (which also included stripes and floral patterns) that became fashionable in grander London town houses and substantial American mansions during the 1790s and the first decade of the 19th century.

Scalamandré/Satin Grass WP81527-7 Color **07** Alternative colors **available** Width **21in/53cm** Length **5yd/4.5m** Repeat **21in/53cm** Price ★★★ T

Overall Pattern: **Early 19th century**

In the 1830s and 1840s, cylinder-printed papers with patterns produced in imitation of arabesque-shaped plasterwork and set on *irisé* (blended color) grounds proved very popular. Also fashionable were abstract-patterned papers in imitation of moiré silks. Nevertheless, as in previous centuries, the vast majority of overall-patterned papers produced during the first half of the 19th century were of the hand-blocked variety, with the imagery depicted on them derived from plant forms, particularly foliage.

In French, British, and American Neoclassical interiors at the beginning of the century, the favored forms included laurels, waterleafs, anthemia, and seaweed. Most of these forms were conventionalized, but, as the century progressed, more naturalistic imagery, incorporating a greater use of shading (and sometimes flock) came into vogue. Popular patterns included acanthus and oak leaves, parsley, thistles, grapevines, ivy, and various fruits. However, by the 1840s a reaction to highly naturalistic and "three-dimensional" imagery was beginning to set in, as evidenced by the appearance during this period of many flat foliage patterns of stylized palmettes and anthemia that had been derived from both classical and Indian ornament.

5

1

2

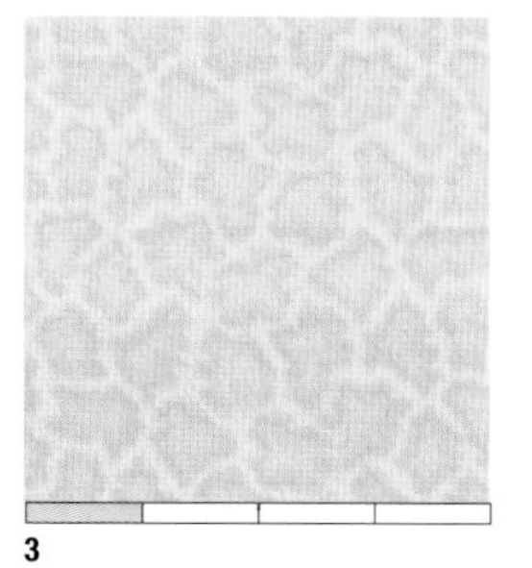

3

4

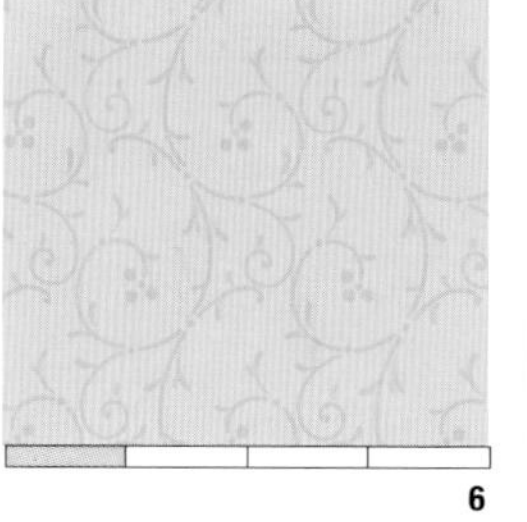

6

7

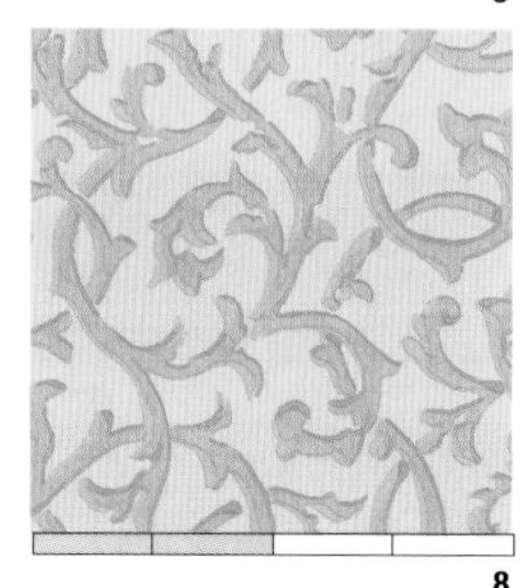

8

9

10

11

1 Hamilton Weston/Jasmine Color **red and gold on olive green** Alternative colors **available** Width **20½in/52cm** Length **11yd/10m** Repeat **12in/30.5cm** Price ★★ ♣

2 Hamilton Weston/Covent Garden Floral Color **red on peach** Alternative colors **available** Width **21in/53cm** Length **11yd/10m** Repeat **11¼in/28.5cm** Price ★ ♣

3 Colefax and Fowler/Livingstone 7304/03 Color **beige** Alternative colors **available** Width **20½in/52cm** Length **11yd/10m** Repeat **3¾in/9.5cm** Price ★

4 Cole & Son/Emma 25/PK303 Color **white and green** Alternative colors **available** Width **21in/53cm** Length **11yd/10m** Repeat **7in/18cm** Price ★

5 Ramm, Son & Crocker/Oakley 14661.06 Color **red** Alternative colors **available** Width **20½in/52cm** Length **11yd/10m** Repeat **10¼in/26cm** Price ★

6 Cole & Son/Scroll 12/085/PR Color **coral on peach** Alternative colors **available** Width **21in/53cm** Length **11yd/10m** Repeat **3in/8cm** Price ★

7 K and K Designs/Impressions 16203 Color **burnt orange** Alternative colors **available** Width **21in/53cm** Length **11yd/10m** Repeat **10½in/26.5cm** Price ★

8 Ramm, Son & Crocker/Turville 14783.06 Color **gold on wheat** Alternative colors **available** Width **20½in/52cm** Length **11yd/10m** Repeat **6in/15cm** Price ★

9 Ramm, Son & Crocker/Latimer 14684.06 Color **green** Alternative colors **available** Width **20½in/52cm** Length **11yd/10m** Repeat **11¾in/30cm** Price ★

10 Warner Fabrics/Madame Eugenia EY 2070 Color **cream** Alternative colors **available** Width **20½in/52cm** Length **11yd/10m** Repeat **10¼in/26cm** Price ★

11 Nina Campbell/Hertford Scroll NCW512/04 Color **neutral** Alternative colors **available** Width **20½in/52cm** Length **11yd/10m** Repeat **5in/13cm** Price ★

12

13

14

15

12 Cole & Son/Clandon 52/7000 Color **yellow and gold** Alternative colors **available** Width **21in/53cm** Length **11yd/10m** Repeat **5½in/14cm** Price ★

13 Jane Churchill/Colbrooke Trellis JW62W-04 Color **red** Alternative colors **available** Width **20½in/52cm** Length **11yd/10m** Repeat **6¾in/17.5cm** Price ★

14 Zuber/Volutes 30005 Color **20** Alternative colors **available** Width **18½in/47cm** Length **11yd/10m** Repeat **18½in/47cm** Price ★★★

15 Hamilton Weston/Cyfarthfa Damask Color **cream on white** Alternative colors **available** Width **20½in/52cm** Length **11yd/10m** Repeat **5in/13cm** Price ★★ ♣

16 Watts of Westminster/Kinnersley WW5025-01/B Color **blue** Alternative colors **available** Width **21¼in/54cm** Length **11yd/10m** Repeat **35in/89cm** Price ★★

16

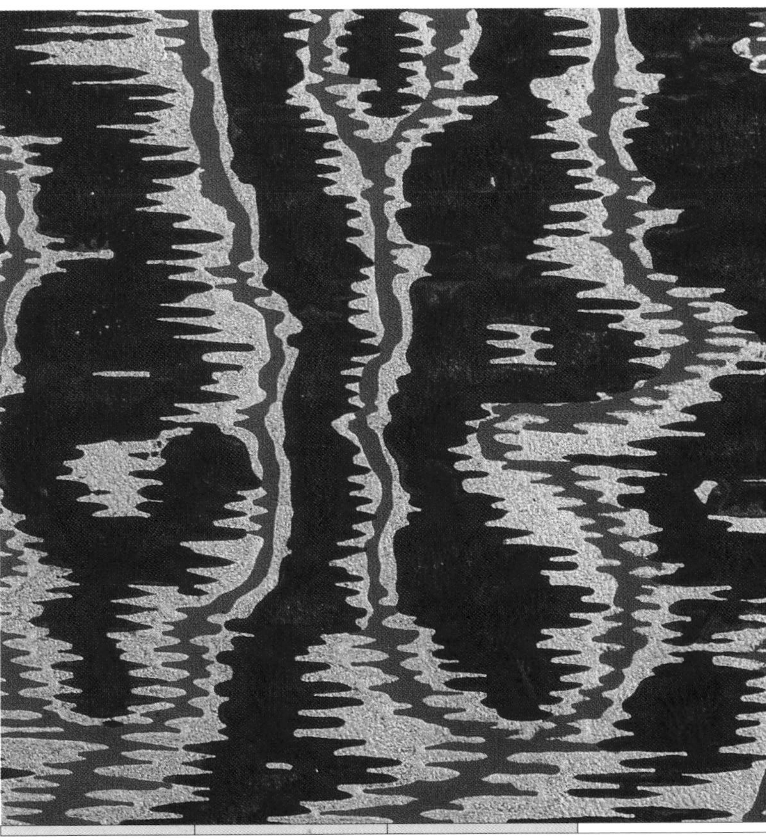

17

17 Zuber/Moiré 1265 Color **rouge** Alternative colors **available** Width **18½in/47cm** Length **11yd/10m** Repeat **26in/66cm** Price ★★★

18 Coloroll/Millgreen 528197 Color **green** Alternative colors **available** Width **20½in/52cm** Length **11yd/10m** Repeat **3½in/9cm** Price ★

19 Hamilton Weston/Chester Square Color **green** Alternative colors **available** Width **20½in/52cm** Length **11yd/10m** Repeat **5½in/14cm** Price ★

20 Colefax and Fowler/Couronne 7207/04 Color **olive** Alternative colors **available** Width **20½in/52cm** Length **11yd/10m** Repeat **1¾in/4.5cm** Price ★

21 Nina Campbell/Pushkin NCW645/04 Color **green** Alternative colors **available** Width **20½in/52cm** Length **11yd/10m** Repeat **8¼in/21cm** Price ★

22 Nina Campbell/Benedict Strie NCW684/03 Color **blue** Alternative colors **available** Width **20½in/52cm** Length **11yd/10m** Repeat **5¼in/13.5cm** Price ★

18

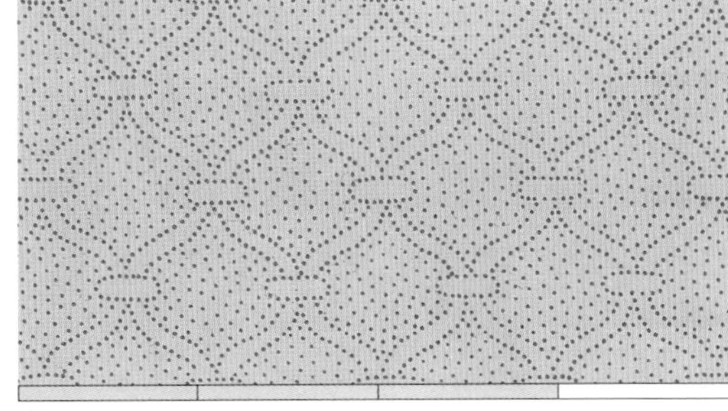

19

20

21

22

19th century

Overall Pattern: **Late 19th century**

Victorian designers Owen Jones and William Morris believed that, because wallpaper was intended to cover flat surfaces, the only appropriate form of pattern for it had to be "two-dimensional" in appearance; any *trompe l'oeil* and other "three-dimensional" effects were simply "dishonest." Their opinion was to prove particularly influential during the second half of the 19th century when naturalistic foliage patterns continued to appear, but were generally supplanted by conventionalized Arts and Crafts, Aesthetic, and Art Nouveau designs in which any shading was usually limited to dots, lines, and hatching. Arts and Crafts designs, including those by Elbert Hubbard, were frequently based on willow and acanthus leaves. Aesthetic patterns, such as those by E. W. Godwin and Christopher Dresser, included formalized bamboo and lotus leaves, while many of C. F. A. Voysey's and the Silver Studio's Art Nouveau papers featured sinuously depicted pomegranates, thistles, various roots, and leaflike peacock feathers.

1

1 **Joanna Wood/Bourne Street L/W3354** Color **Chinese yellow** Alternative colors **available** Width **20½in/52cm** Length **11yd/10m** Repeat **10½in/27cm** Price ★

2 **Cole & Son/Aspen 12/052/PR** Color **052** Alternative colors **available** Width **21in/53cm** Length **11yd/10m** Repeat **22in/56cm** Price ★

3 **Ramm, Son & Crocker/Rosedale Leaf W1042** Color **mauve** Alternative colors **available** Width **20½in/52cm** Length **11yd/10m** Repeat **20½in/52cm** Price ★

2

3

4

5

4 **Alexander Beauchamp/Langley** Color **blue** Alternative colors **available** Width **18¼in/46.5cm** Length **11yd/10m** Repeat **19in/48cm** Price ★★★★♣

5 **Osborne & Little/Sherringham W1371/03** Color **red and green** Alternative colors **available** Width **20½in/52cm** Length **11yd/10m** Repeat **5in/13cm** Price ★

6 **Cole & Son/Owen Jones 52/7040** Color **red** Alternative colors **available** Width **21in/53cm** Length **11yd/10m** Repeat **2¾in/7cm** Price ★

7 **Zuber/40068** Color **130** Alternative colors **available** Width **21½in/55cm** Length **11yd/10m** Repeat **26¼in/66.5cm** Price ★★★

6

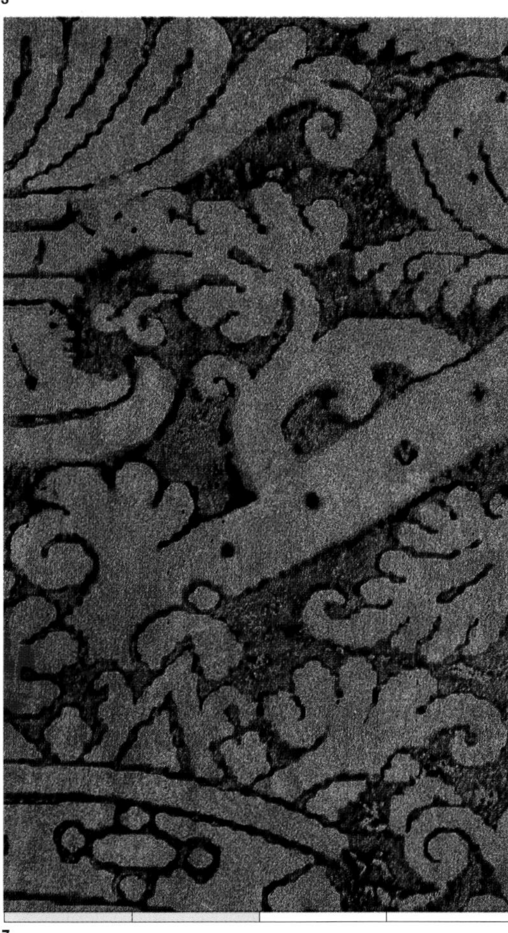

7

8 Graham & Brown/Leaf Trail 56455 Color **green/gold** Alternative colors **available** Width **20½in/52cm** Length **11yd/10m** Repeat **21in/ 53cm** Price ★

9 Hodsoll McKenzie/Fern 616/ 605 Color **blue** Alternative colors **available** Width **20½in/52cm** Length **11yd/ 10m** Repeat **21¼in/53.5cm** Price ★

10 Cole & Son/Dielytra 25/PK352/PR Color **blue and white** Alternative colors **available** Width **21in/ 53cm** Length **11yd/10m** Repeat **15in/38cm** Price ★

11 Watts of Westminster/Clarence W0011 Color **rose** Alternative colors **available** Width **21¼in/ 54cm** Length **11yd/10m** Repeat **10¼in/26cm** Price ★★

12 Watts of Westminster/Melias W5028-02/A12 Color **cream** Alternative colors **available** Width **18½in/47cm** Length **11yd/10m** Repeat **13¾in/ 35cm** Price ★★

13 Bradbury & Bradbury/Eastlake Dado ELD Color **550** Alternative colors **available** Width **27in/ 69cm** Length **to order** Repeat **3in/8cm** Price ★★★

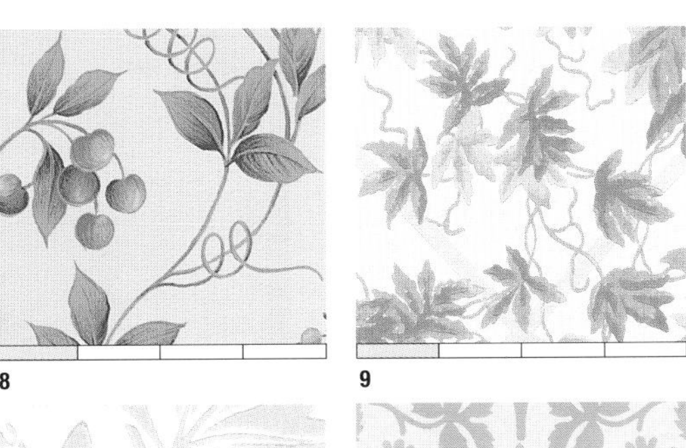

8

9

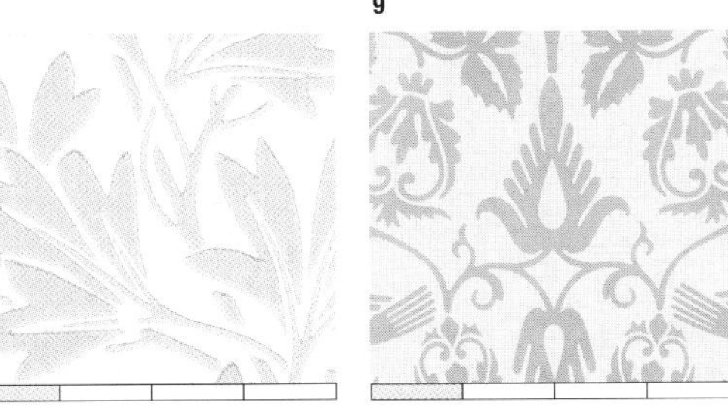

10

11

14

15

14 Cole & Son/Lee Priory 12/082 Color **082** Alternative colors **available** Width **21in/53cm** Length **11yd/10m** Repeat **2in/5cm** Price ★

15 Cole & Son/Owen Jones Shell Pattern Color **pink and turquoise** Alternative colors **available** Width **21in/53cm** Length **11yd/10m** Repeat **4¼in/11cm** Price ★★

16 Cole & Son/Sussana 25/ PK307/ PR Color **yellow** Alternative colors **available** Width **21in/53cm** Length **11yd/10m** Repeat **7in/ 18cm** Price ★

12

16

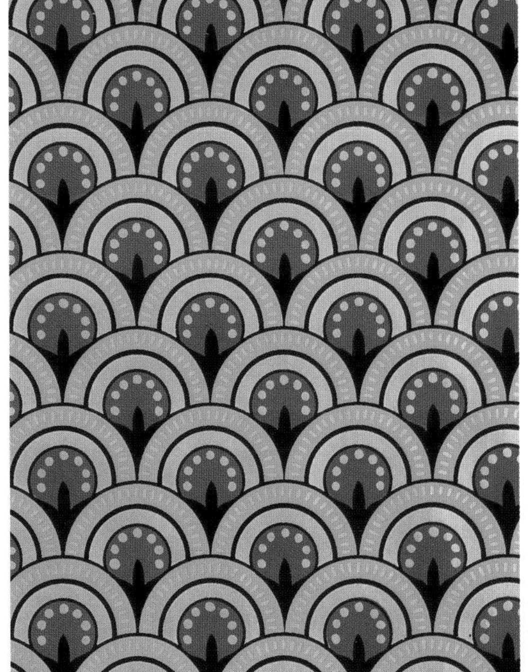

13

SANITARY PAPERS

In 1871, the English firm of Heywood, Higginbottom & Smith pioneered the first washable wallpapers. They were known as "sanitaries" because they were easy to clean, and were printed with engraved metal rollers that built up the pattern from a series of small dots of thin, oil-based inks or varnish colors. The technique produced a very smooth surface that was water-repellent, and also allowed for considerable subtlety in the shading and blending of colors.

Watts of Westminster/Cogges Manor Farm W5061-01/B13 Color **Oxford** Alternative colors **available** Width **21½in/54cm** Length **11yd/10m** Repeat **21in/53cm** Price ★★★

19th century

Overall Pattern: **Early 20th Century**

Botanic and organic forms continued to provide much of the inspiration for overall-patterned wallpapers during the first half of the 20th century. Scrolling acanthus, stylized thistles, sweeping and curving wisteria, and reed and water lily patterns featured large in Art Nouveau designs, while small leaves with undulating stems articulated the surface of many Deutscher Werkbund papers. Stenciled leaf patterns were characteristic of the later Arts and Crafts papers of the 1920s and 1930s, and numerous early Art Deco designs consisted of fantastically stylized abstractions of plant forms. Also fashionable in the 1930s were realistic sketches of branches, leaves, and blossoms, and stylized large-scale leaf patterns rendered in "tea stain" colors and sometimes highlighted with silver or gold. In the 1940s ivy leaf trellis papers proved especially popular.

Also much in evidence during the first half of the 20th century were papers displaying spattered patterns similar to those found on contemporary ceramics. In addition, papers were produced in imitation of 17th-century tooled-leather wall-hangings, classical moldings, faux marble paint finishes, and paneling made of decoratively figured hardwoods such as maple and birch.

Crowson/Malory Color **50** Alternative colors **available** Width **20½in/52cm** Length **11yd/10m** Repeat **6¾in/17.5cm** Price ★

Jane Churchill/Sparkle JY19W-04 Color **multi** Alternative colors **available** Width **20½in/52cm** Length **11yd/10m** Repeat **10¼in/26cm** Price ★

Zuber/Damas Or 10174 Color **111** Alternative colors **available** Width **18½in/47cm** Length **11yd/10m** Repeat **24¼in/62cm** Price ★★★

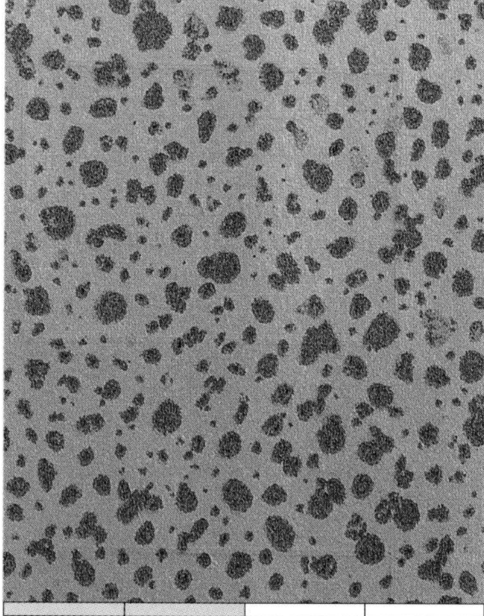

Osborne & Little/Nocturne W1442-04 Color **04** Alternative colors **available** Width **20½in/52cm** Length **11yd/10m** Repeat **–** Price ★

John Wilman/Figaro 170426 Color **red** Alternative colors **available** Width **20½in/52cm** Length **11yd/10m** Repeat **3in/7.5cm** Price ★

Osborne & Little/Madrigal W1441/10 Color **green** Alternative colors **available** Width **20½in/52cm** Length **11yd/10m** Repeat **–** Price ★

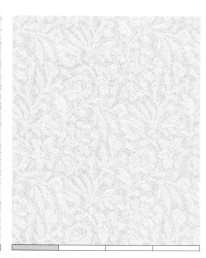

Zoffany/Viola Plain V21704 Color **04** Alternative colors **available** Width **20½in/52cm** Length **11yd/10m** Repeat **5in/13cm** Price ★

Cole & Son/Fantail 12-096 Color **peach and black** Alternative colors **not available** Width **21in/53cm** Length **11yd/10m** Repeat **3in/8cm** Price ★

RAISED RELIEF DESIGNS

White or neutral-colored wallpapers with raised relief patterns, intended for painting, were popular throughout the 20th century. Made of paper (or paper and vinyl), they proved cheaper to produce than Lincrusta and Anaglypta (*see* page 223), and thus supplanted these earlier relief coverings in the mass-market. Prior to the 1980s all raised relief papers were produced by mechanical embossing, but thereafter "blown" vinyl techniques were also employed. Favored designs ranged from traditional geometrics to abstracts, such as bubble patterns, impasto-like doodlings, and "cracked ice."

Akzo Nobel/Arundel RD100 Color **white** Alternative colors **not available** Width **20½in/52cm** Length **11yd/10m** Repeat **–** Price ★

Akzo Nobel/Westminster RD101 Color **white** Alternative colors **not available** Width **20½in/52cm** Length **11yd/10m** Repeat **21in/53cm** Price ★

Akzo Nobel/Berkeley RD125 Color **white** Alternative colors **not available** Width **20½in/52cm** Length **11yd/10m** Repeat **5in/13cm** Price ★

Watts of Westminster/Northmore W0032-01/E11 Color **B08** Alternative colors **available** Width **20½in/52cm** Length **11yd/10m** Repeat **6in/15cm** Price ★

Fardis/Reliure UP654 Color **54** Alternative colors **available** Width **27½in/70cm** Length **11yd/10m** Repeat **21in/53cm** Price ★

Jane Churchill/Delphi JY45W-04 Color **green** Alternative colors **available** Width **20½in/52cm** Length **11yd/10m** Repeat **20½in/52cm** Price ★

Harlequin/95026 Color **peach** Alternative colors **available** Width **20½in/52cm** Length **11yd/10m** Repeat **20½in/52cm** Price ★

Graham & Brown/Mosaic 16518 Color **rust** Alternative colors **available** Width **40¼in/102cm** Length **11yd/10m** Repeat **8½in/21.5cm** Price ★

Marthe Armitage/Solomon's Seal Color **orange** Alternative colors **available** Width **21in/53cm** Length **11yd/10m** Repeat **17in/43cm** Price ★

Sheila Coombes/Belle Isle 607-10 Color **10** Alternative colors **available** Width **21in/53cm** Length **11yd/10m** Repeat **10½in/27cm** Price ★

Overall Pattern: **Late 20th century**

Conventionalized and naturalistic plant-form patterns seen in the previous century reappeared on numerous "filling" and border papers produced during the 1950s and 1960s. For example, the late 19th-century rhythmical Arts and Crafts designs of William Morris and J. H. Dearle were hand-printed again with the original wooden blocks, and sinuous Art Nouveau vegetal patterns came back into fashion. American designers also created leaf patterns, either overlaid with lines, dots, diamonds, and checks or combined with simulations of tweed textiles, while many Scandinavian and other American papers featured intricate patterns depicting marine flora and fauna.

Microphotographic views of the molecular structure of materials such as myoglobin and insulin provided additional inspiration for wallpaper designers during the 1950s and 1960s, and a general preoccupation with naturally occurring forms and phenomena was further evident in those patterns based on "worm-casts," spiderwebs, amoebas, and rainfall. Also fashionable as earlier in the century were printed replicas of the figuring and grain of various species of wood, as well as realistic and fantastic simulations of decorative stone finishes such as those seen on marble and porphyry.

1

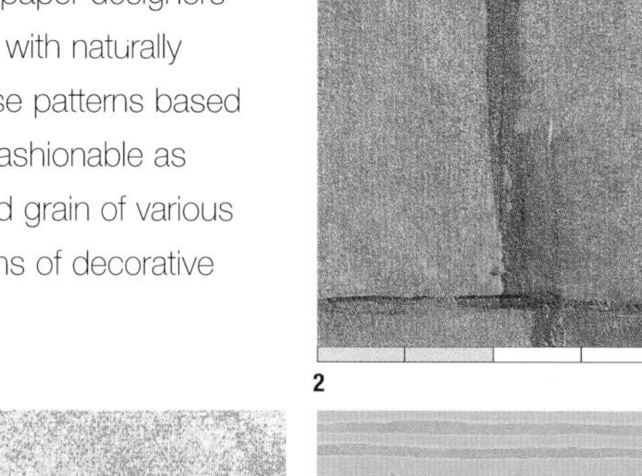
2

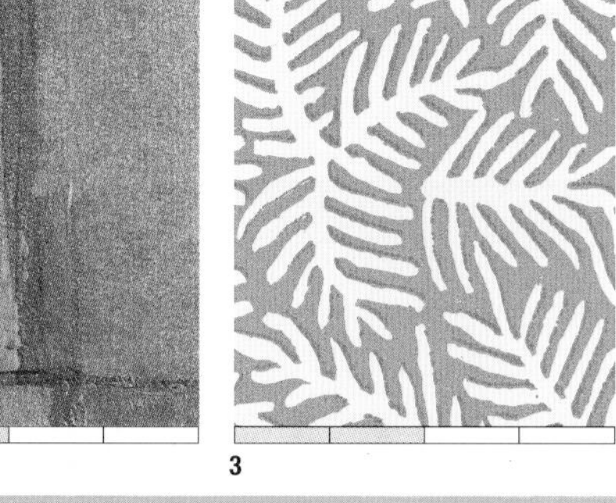
3

1 **Maya Romanoff/Mica MR-SK-1402** Color **Ishtar** Alternative colors **available** Width **36½in/93cm** Length **to order** Repeat – Price ★★★★ T

2 **Donghia/Fluxus 2001** Color **silver** Alternative colors **available** Width **40¼in/102cm** Length **3⅓yd/3m** Repeat **6in/15cm** Price ★★★★

3 **Cath Kidston/Fernleaf** Color **red** Alternative colors **available** Width **20½in/52cm** Length **11yd/10m** Repeat **3½in/9cm** Price ★

4

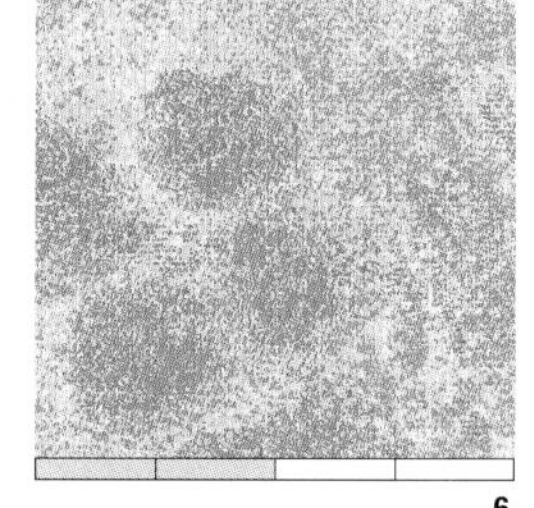
6

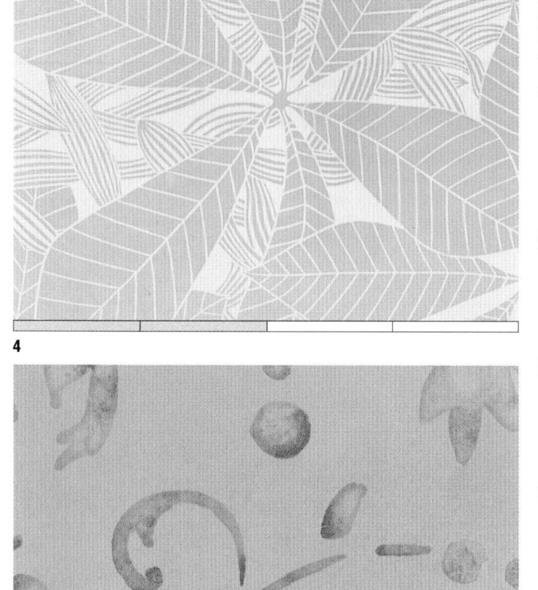
5

4 **Marthe Armitage/Chestnut** Color **green** Alternative colors **available** Width **23in/59cm** Length **11yd/10m** Repeat **31¾in/81cm** Price ★

5 **Anna French/Fondant** Color **WP075BI** Alternative colors **available** Width **20½in/52cm** Length **11yd/10m** Repeat **20½in/52cm** Price ★

6 **Anna French/Fougère** Color **FOUWP011** Alternative colors **available** Width **20½in/52cm** Length **11yd/10m** Repeat **23¾in/60cm** Price ★

7 **Harlequin/8713 border** Color **orange and terracotta** Alternative colors **available** Width **3in/7.5cm** Length **11yd/10m** Repeat – Price ★

8 **Jean Louis Seigner/Apollo** Color **1A** Alternative colors **available** Width **26¼in/67cm** Length **11yd/10m** Repeat **38½in/98cm** Price ★

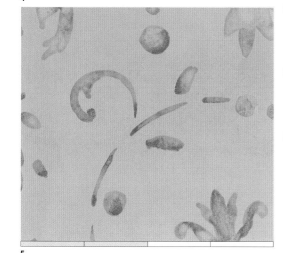

7

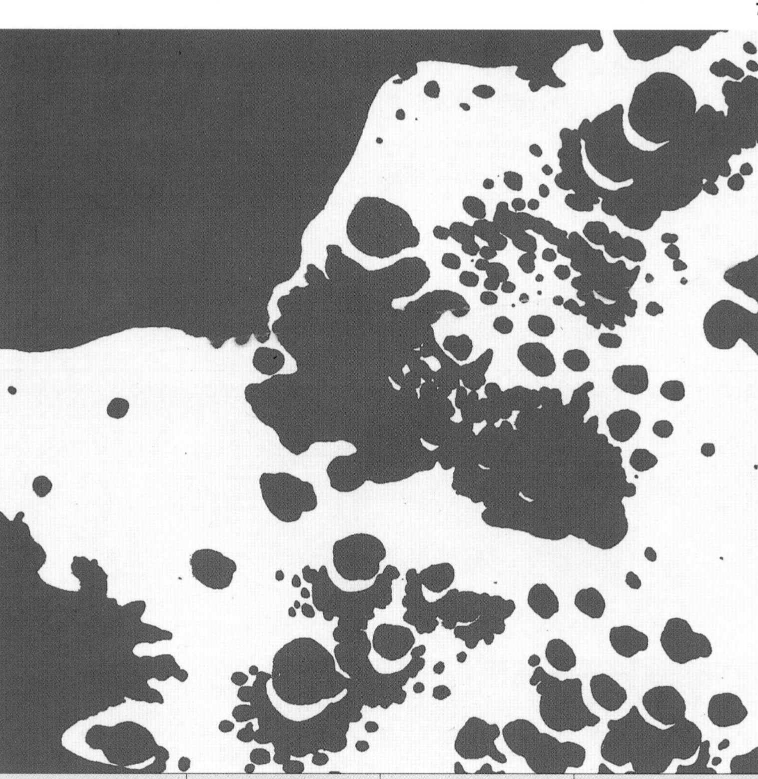
8

20th century

9 Coloroll/Hoghton Border 400271 Color **yellow** Alternative colors **available** Width **4in/10.5cm** Length **5½yd/5m** Repeat **21in/53cm** Price ★

10 Coloroll/Lindsey Border 400776 Color **brown** Alternative colors **available** Width **3in/7.5cm** Length **5½yd/5m** Repeat **10¼in/26cm** Price ★

11 Osborne & Little/Oratorio W1440/06 Color **06** Alternative colors **available** Width **20½in/52cm** Length **11yd/10m** Repeat **21in/53cm** Price ★

9

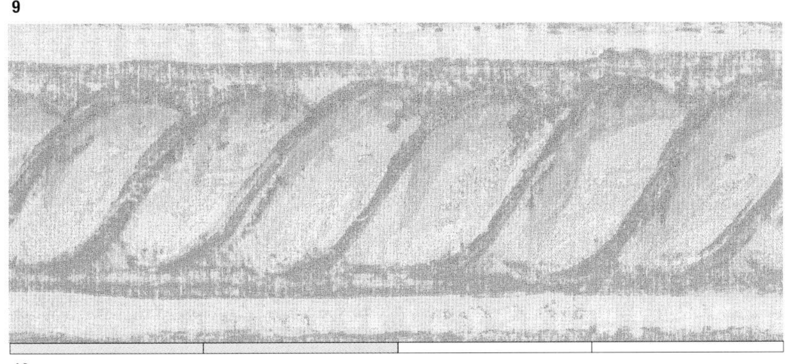

10

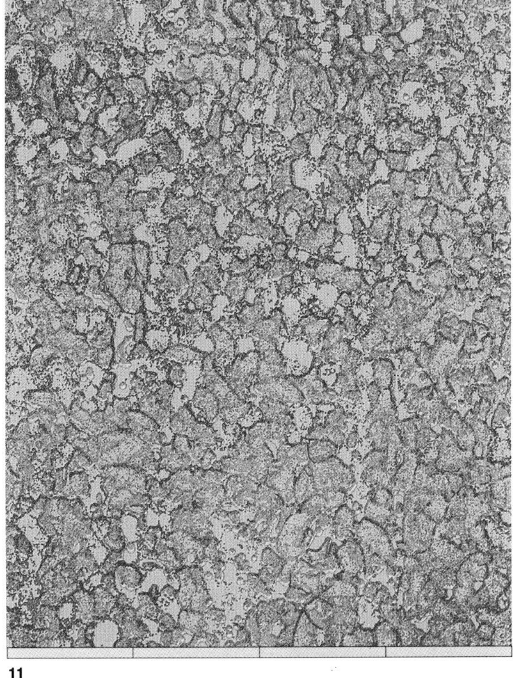

11

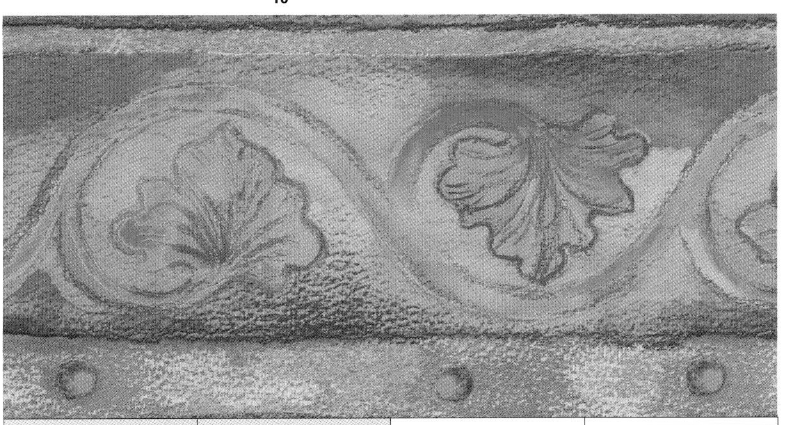

12

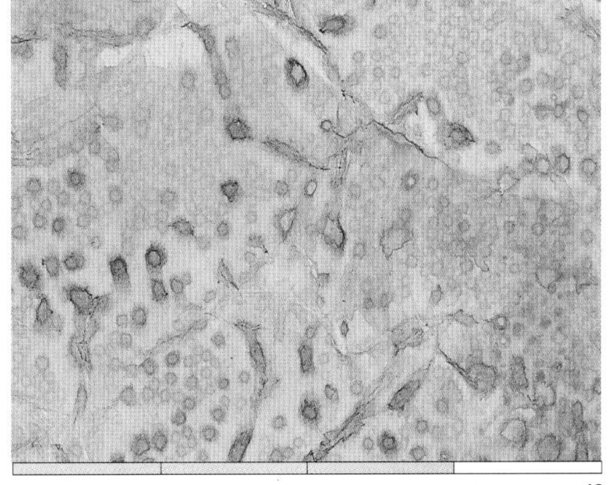

13

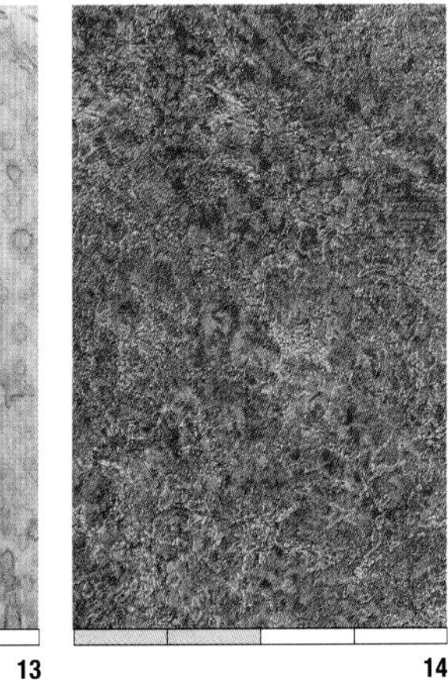

14

15

12 Crowson/Madre Color **80** Alternative colors **available** Width **5in/13cm** Length **11yd/10m** Repeat **–** Price ★

13 Maya Romanoff/Grecian Crystal MR-W54-482 Color **dusty lilac** Alternative colors **available** Width **30¼in/77cm** Length **3¾yd/3.5m** Repeat **–** Price ★★★★ T

14 Fine Decor/Caserta 20131 Color **dark green** Alternative colors **available** Width **20½in/52cm** Length **11yd/10m** Repeat **21in/53cm** Price ★

15 Jane Churchill/Feathers Color **dark green** Alternative colors **available** Width **20½in/ 52cm** Length **11yd/10m** Repeat **10¼in/26cm** Price ★

16 Jean Louis Seigner/La Perse Color **24** Alternative colors **available** Width **27½in/70cm** Length **11yd/10m** Repeat **10¼in/26cm** Price ★★

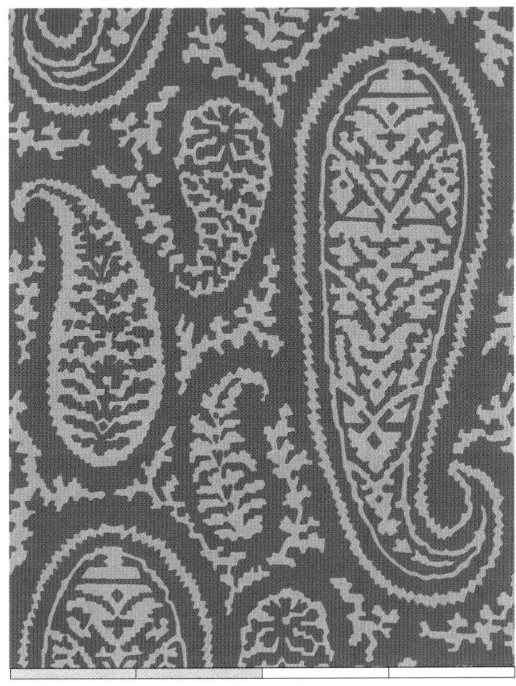

16

Overall Pattern: **Late 20th century**

Many of the plant-form patterns favored in the 1950s and 1960s (*see* pages 260-1) enjoyed a new lease on life during the late 20th century. This was largely as a result of manufacturers adapting them to suit more contemporary aesthetics. In the early 1970s, for example, some of these papers were reproduced in incandescent or muted colors on shiny or dull metallic grounds, a look that made them perfectly suited to what *Vogue* magazine described as "a Nickelodeon land of Art Deco with potted palms and mirrored halls."

Starting in the 1970s, metallic finishes also served as patterns in their own right. Most of these finishes showed random mottling that essentially replicated the appearance of tarnished metals and alloys–such as copper and bronze–in much the same way that some distressed paint finishes do. However, metallic finishes did not dominate late 20th-century wallpaper designs. Abstract doodles, wavelike patterns, snowflakes under the microscope, small repeats of fruits and berries, and imitations of limed wood were also much in evidence. In contrast, there was a resurgence of documentary patterns dating back to the 17th century.

Jane Churchill/Coral JY44W-02 Color **pink** Alternative colors **available** Width **20½in/52cm** Length **11yd/10m** Repeat **4in/10.5cm** Price ★

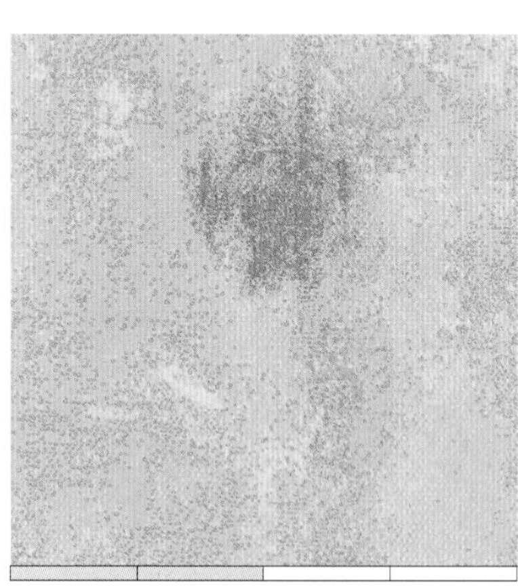

Anna French/Collioure Color **COLWP02** Alternative colors **available** Width **20½in/52cm** Length **11yd/10m** Repeat **20½in/52cm** Price ★

Harlequin/57012 Color **turquoise** Alternative colors **available** Width **20½in/52cm** Length **11yd/10m** Repeat **24in/61cm** Price ★

Jane Churchill/Esher JY66W-05 Color **blue** Alternative colors **available** Width **20½in/52cm** Length **11yd/10m** Repeat **10½in/27cm** Price ★

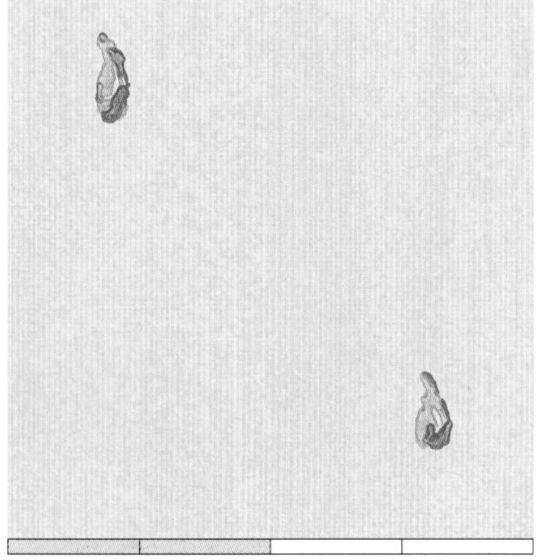

K and K Designs/96004 Color **sunshine yellow and blue** Alternative colors **available** Width **21in/53cm** Length **11yd/10m** Repeat **5in/13cm** Price ★

Jean Louis Seigner/Mai 68 Color **A1** Alternative colors **available** Width **27½in/70cm** Length **11yd/10m** Repeat **15¾in/40cm** Price ★ ♣

Jean Louis Seigner/Feuillage 23 Color **A2** Alternative colors **available** Width **27½in/70cm** Length **11yd/10m** Repeat **15¾in/40cm** Price ★ ♣

Graham & Brown/Marble 16533 Color **blue** Alternative colors **available** Width **32¼in/82cm** Length **11yd/10m** Repeat **25in/64cm** Price ★

Graham & Brown/Camphus Leaf 56126 Color **green** Alternative colors **available** Width **24¼in/62cm** Length **11yd/10m** Repeat **21in/53cm** Price ★

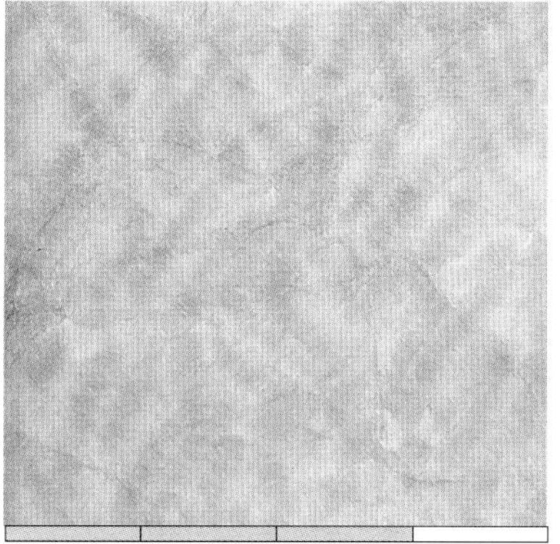

Maya Romanoff/Crushed Pearl MR-P50-971 Color **medium peach** Alternative colors **available** Width **31in/79cm** Length **4yd/3.6m** Repeat **27in/69cm** Price ★★★★ [T]

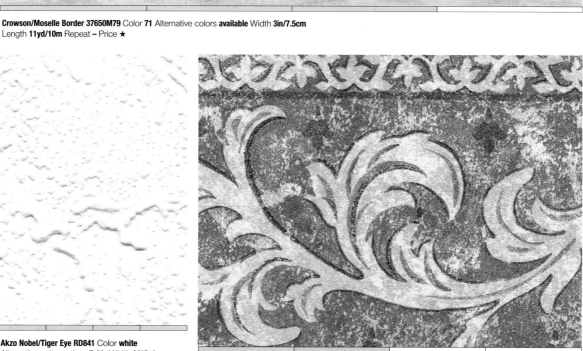

Crowson/Moselle Border 37650M79 Color **71** Alternative colors **available** Width **3in/7.5cm** Length **11yd/10m** Repeat **–** Price ★

Nobilis-Fontan/Papiers Bois Couleur PBC103 Color **yellow** Alternative colors **available** Width **49in/125cm** Length **to order** Repeat **–** Price ★★★★

Akzo Nobel/Tiger Eye RD841 Color **white** Alternative colors **not available** Width **20½in/52cm** Length **11yd/10m** Repeat **12½in/32cm** Price ★

Harlequin/1568 Border Color **green and neutral** Alternative colors **available** Width **5in/13cm** Length **5½yd/5m** Repeat **–** Price ★

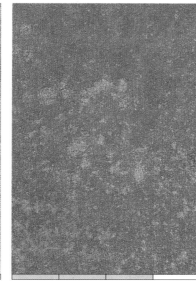

Graham & Brown/Paint Effect 56105 Color **antique gold** Alternative colors **available** Width **24¼in/62cm** Length **11yd/10m** Repeat **25in/64cm** Price ★

Anya Larkin/Moondust Teapaper Color **evergreen** Alternative colors **available** Width **40¼in/102cm** Length **3½yd/3m** Repeat **–** Price ★★★★

Crowson/Fiori Border 37650F26 Color **15** Alternative colors **available** Width **6¾in/17.5cm** Length **11yd/10m** Repeat **–** Price ★

Geometric Wallpapers

Geometric and linear patterns appeared on wallpapers as soon as they were introduced as an alternative to textile wall-hangings during the late 15th century. Most of the geometric designs that were fashionable before the 18th century have been revived, particularly during the second half of the 19th century when designers on both sides of the Atlantic produced patterns based entirely on geometric principles of ornament. The catalog of geometric patterns available to wallpaper designers has been extensive, having steadily increased since the Renaissance as Oriental, Islamic, African, and South American geometric imagery has been assimilated into Western culture. Favored designs have included vertical stripes; checks; powdered ornament (stars and other geometric shapes); diaper patterns (trelliswork, latticework, and strapwork); and, during the 20th century, mathematical and abstract shapes inspired by Cubist and Constructivist art. Some of these patterns have been augmented with, or provided the ground for, non-geometric imagery, such as stylized plant forms.

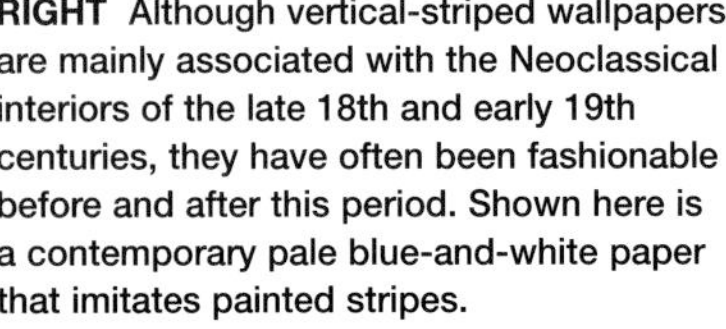

RIGHT Although vertical-striped wallpapers are mainly associated with the Neoclassical interiors of the late 18th and early 19th centuries, they have often been fashionable before and after this period. Shown here is a contemporary pale blue-and-white paper that imitates painted stripes.

ABOVE The geometric wallpaper on the walls of this bathroom in a French Mediterranean villa was designed to imitate blue-and-white gingham.

DIAPER PATTERNS

Trelliswork, latticework, and strapwork patterns, which are collectively known as diaper patterns, have appeared on fabrics since the Middle Ages, and on wallpapers since the 17th century. Diaper patterns, original to both European and Oriental decoration, often enclose small motifs. They also provide a ground for, and are often interlaced with, different types of plant-form imagery. Sometimes, however, these geometric patterns have been unembellished, as with the blue-on-yellow latticework paper in this partly updated, early 19th-century provincial English drawing room.

KEY DESIGNS

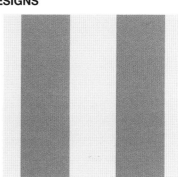

1 Diaper designs have been employed on wallpapers since the Renaissance. This flower-pea-and-leaf trelliswork pattern dates from the Classical Revival of the early years of the 20th century.

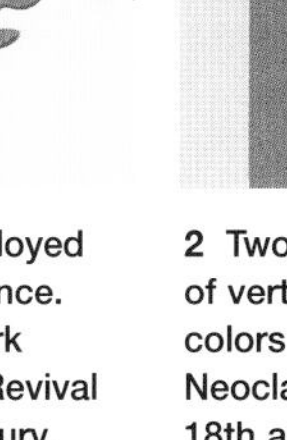

2 Two-tone striped papers made up of vertical bands of alternating solid colors were especially fashionable in Neoclassical interiors during the late 18th and early 19th centuries.

3 While many trelliswork patterns appear unembellished, others are either entwined with or, as here, enclose or provide a ground for other motifs, such as naturalistic or stylized plant forms.

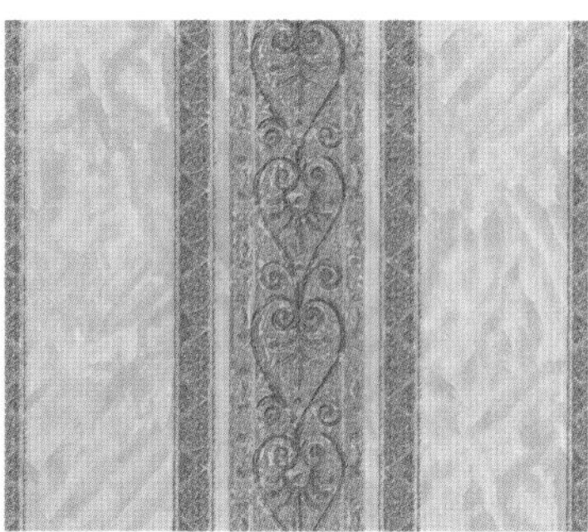

4 Many striped papers consist of vertical bands of alternating widths and colors. The bands are often embellished with small motifs, or show tonal configurations similar to that of moiré silk.

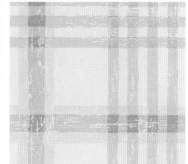

5 Striped papers produced in two colors have appeared since the late 18th century, some with alternating vertical bands slightly overlapped to create defining stripes in a third tone.

6 Checked-and-striped wallpapers produced in imitation of geometrically patterned fabrics, such as gingham and madras, became fashionable during the early years of the 20th century.

1 **Cole & Son/Audrey Trellis 12/067/PR** Color **green** Alternative colors **not available** Width **21in/53cm** Length **11yd/10m** Repeat **7in/18cm** Price ★

2 **Harlequin/95017** Color **forest green/taupe** Alternative colors **available** Width **20½in/52cm** Length **11yd/10m** Repeat **–** Price ★

3 **Hodsoll McKenzie/Flemish Flower 505/620** Color **green** Alternative colors **available** Width **20½in/52cm** Length **11yd/10m** Repeat **2½in/6.5cm** Price ★

4 **Coloroll/Japonica Stripe 527787** Color **green** Alternative colors **available** Width **20½in/52cm** Length **11yd/10m** Repeat **3½in/9cm** Price ★

5 **John Wilman/Traviata 170235** Color **red** Alternative colors **available** Width **20½in/52cm** Length **11yd/10m** Repeat **–** Price ★

6 **Osborne & Little/Parnasse W1120/02** Color **red** Alternative colors **available** Width **20½in/52cm** Length **11yd/10m** Repeat **10½in/27cm** Price ★

Geometrics: **Pre-19th century**

Some of the earliest woodcut-printed papers of the 16th century were patterned with simple repeats of spots or trelliswork, and many French papers of this period displayed rose motifs on vertical-striped grounds. Fashionable patterns of the 17th century included nailheads (small pyramid shapes); powdered ornament (sprinklings of stars or small flowers); trelliswork (often consisting of chevron-shaped pairs of leaves); strapwork (twisted and intertwined bands similar to ribbons or strips of leather); jeweled strapwork (in which the banding was augmented with imitations of faceted jewels); and *guilloche* (Islamic in origin and consisting of interlaced, curved bands, some forming circular shapes, embellished with floral motifs).

Diaper patterns–mostly trelliswork and latticework–were also featured in the Rococo and Gothick interiors of the 18th century. Some were flocked, and many provided the ground for, respectively, *chinoiserie* and heraldic imagery. However, the most prevalent geometric patterns in the Neoclassical interiors of the late 18th century were vertical stripes, consisting of either plain bands of alternating widths and colors, or made up of stacked chevrons, or classical motifs such as leaves, urns, or figures.

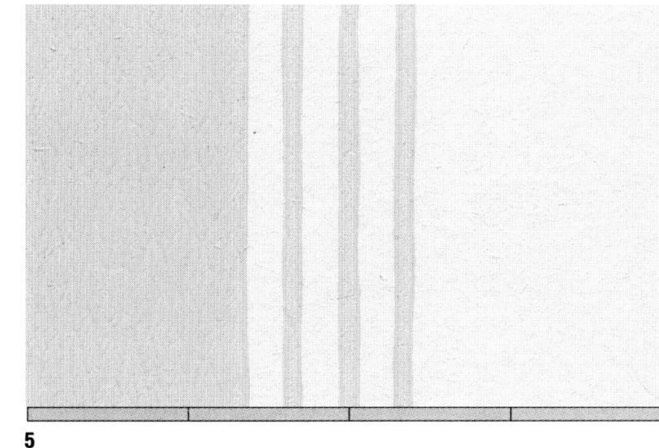

5

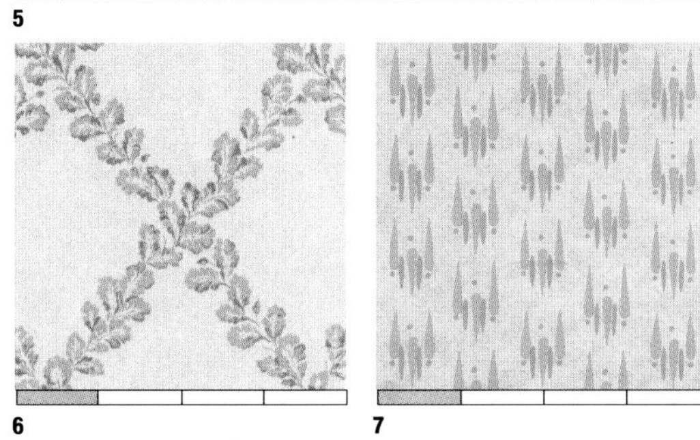

6 7

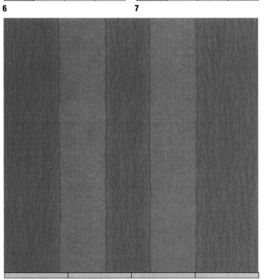

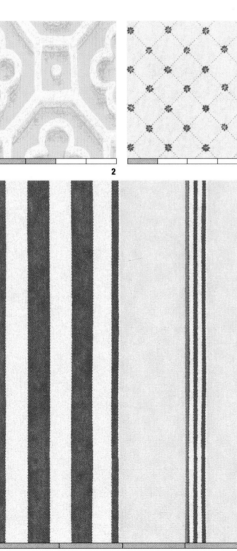

1 2 3

8

1 **Osborne & Little/Cordelova W1374/04** Color **blue** Alternative colors **available** Width **20½in/52cm** Length **11yd/10m** Repeat **10½in/27cm** Price ★

2 **Osborne & Little/Box Parterre W1126/03** Color **yellow** Alternative colors **available** Width **20½in/52cm** Length **11yd/10m** Repeat **4in/10cm** Price ★

3 **Zoffany/Welbeck Trellis** Color **gold, blue on beige** Alternative colors **available** Width **20½in/52cm** Length **11yd/10m** Repeat **1¾in/4.5cm** Price ★

4 **Zoffany/Ticking Stripe 36TK03** Color **03** Alternative colors **available** Width **20½in/52cm** Length **11yd/10m** Repeat **–** Price ★

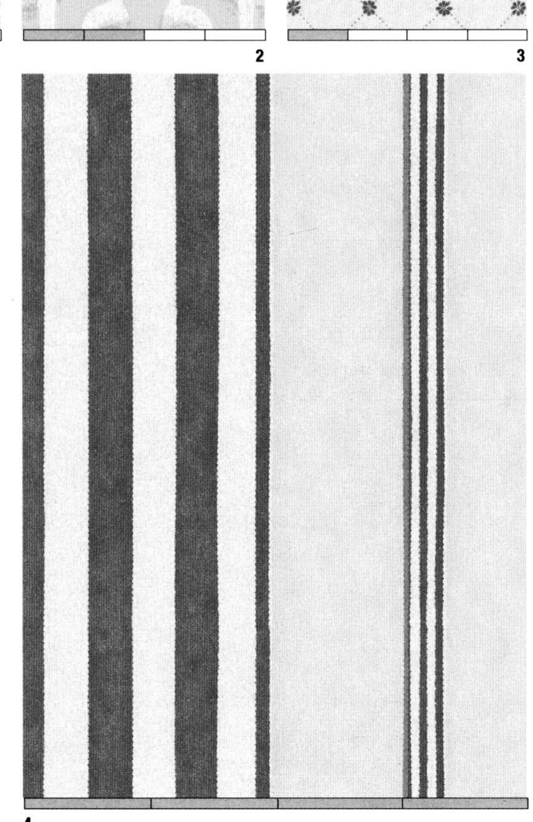

4

9

5 **Colefax and Fowler/Juliana 7405/02** Color **yellow** Alternative colors **available** Width **20½in/52cm** Length **11yd/10m** Repeat **–** Price ★

6 **Zoffany/Oak Garland Trellis 215602** Color **02** Alternative colors **available** Width **20½in/ 52cm** Length **11yd/10m** Repeat **5in/13cm** Price ★

7 **Hamilton Weston/Strand Teardrop** Color **8124** Alternative colors **available** Width **20½in/52cm** Length **11yd/10m** Repeat **1¼in/3cm** Price ★★ ♣

8 **Ornamenta/Beaufort Stripe STR205** Color **red** Alternative colors **available** Width **20½in/52cm** Length **11yd/10m** Repeat **–** Price ★

9 **Osborne & Little/Antwerp W1370/04** Color **blue** Alternative colors **available** Width **20½in/52cm** Length **11yd/10m** Repeat **2½in/6cm** Price ★

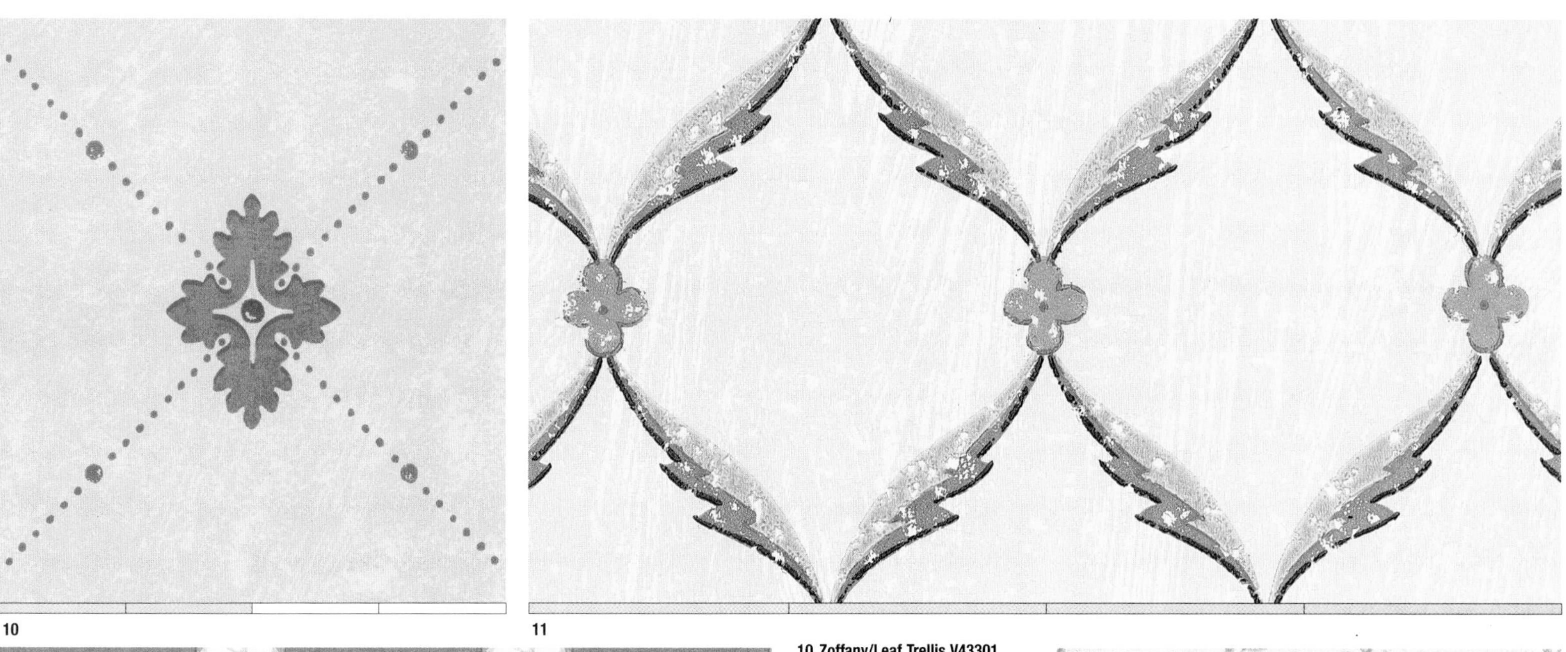

10 11

12

10 Zoffany/Leaf Trellis V43301 Color **01** Alternative colors **available** Width **20½in/52cm** Length **11yd/10m** Repeat **6¾in/17cm** Price ★

11 Osborne & Little/Pipori W1013/05 Color **beige/red** Alternative colors **available** Width **20½in/52cm** Length **11yd/10m** Repeat **3½in/9cm** Price ★

12 Zoffany/Venetian Grille V43405 Color **05** Alternative colors **available** Width **20½in/52cm** Length **11yd/10m** Repeat **3in/8cm** Price ★

13 Zoffany/Trellis V21502 Color **02** Alternative colors **available** Width **20½in/52cm** Length **11yd/10m** Repeat **20½in/52cm** Price ★

14 Osborne & Little/Domino W1378/02 Color **yellow** Alternative colors **available** Width **20½in/52cm** Length **11yd/10m** Repeat **1¾in/4.5cm** Price ★

15 Ramm, Son & Crocker/Treillage W1580 Color **gold** Alternative colors **available** Width **20½in/52cm** Length **11yd/10m** Repeat **20in/51cm** Price ★

16 Hamilton Weston/Bedford Stripe Color **303** Alternative colors **available** Width **20½in/52cm** Length **11yd/10m** Repeat **6in/15cm** Price ★

17 Ramm, Son & Crocker/Fern Trellis W1532 Color **blue** Alternative colors **available** Width **20½in/52cm** Length **11yd/10m** Repeat **5in/13cm** Price ★

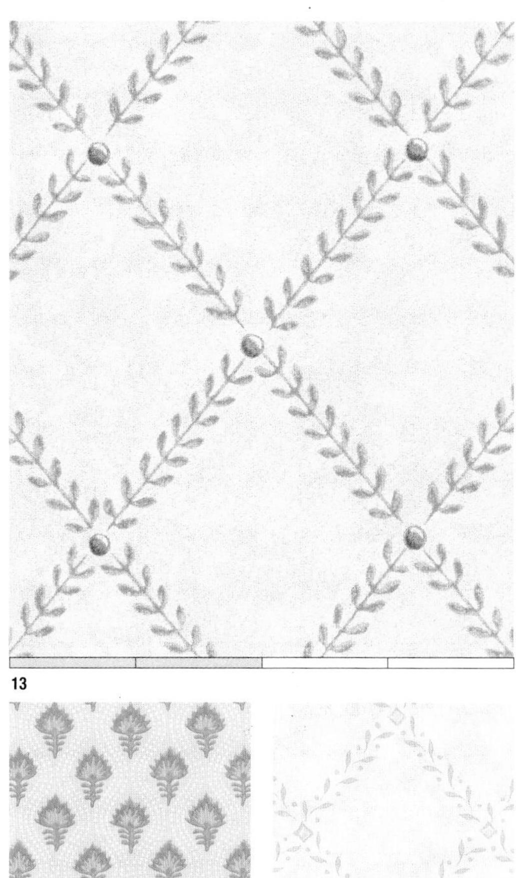

13

14 15

16

17

Geometrics: **Early 19th century**

Striped wallpapers inspired by contemporary textiles were highly fashionable in French Empire, English Regency, and American Federal interiors during the early 19th century. In many cases the striped pattern consisted of solid vertical bands of alternating widths and colors, while in others some of the bands were made up of stylized foliage patterns or were edged with thin stripes that were similar in appearance to the decorative trimmings used as edgings on curtains.

Other popular geometric wallpaper designs of the first half of the 19th century included Greek key borders; checker patterns, brightly colored in imitation of Indian ginghams and often embellished with small motifs; and Oriental diaper patterns. One of the most significant examples of the latter was the "three-dimensional" *chinoiserie*-latticework design. Set on a wave-pattern blue ground, this was devised by Robert Jones and J. G. Grace for the Royal Pavilion in Brighton, England. Medieval and Renaissance diaper patterns, especially jeweled strapwork, also came back into fashion in Gothic Revival interiors during the 1840s, as did powdered ornament (evenly spaced scatterings of small, stylized motifs).

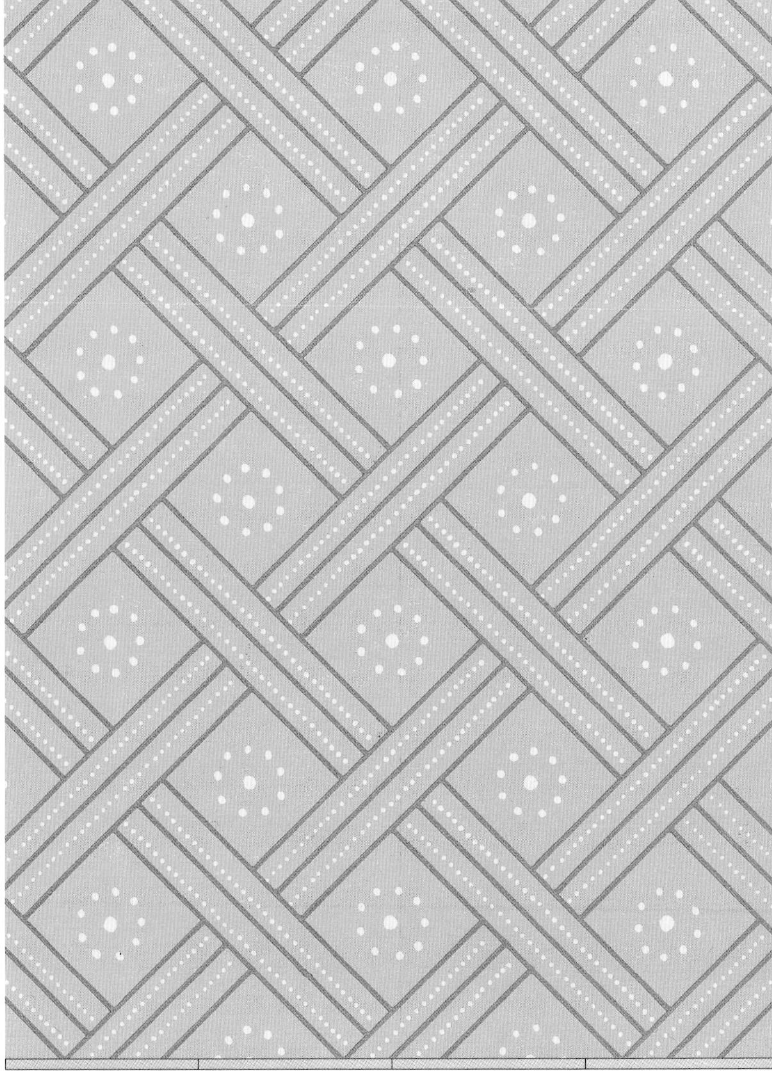

Hamilton Weston/Bloomsbury Square Color **501** Alternative colors **available** Width **20½in/52cm** Length **11yd/10m** Repeat **1½in/4cm** Price ★

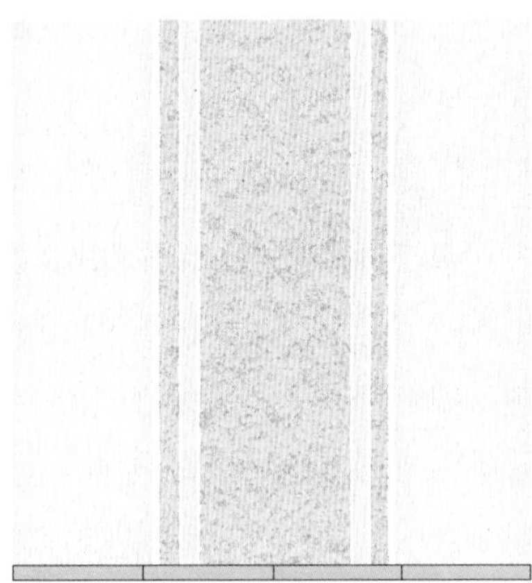

Cole & Son/Viscount Stripe 25/PK330/PR Color **cream** Alternative colors **available** Width **21in/53cm** Length **11yd/10m** Repeat **–** Price ★

G. P. & J. Baker/Thebes W0089-64 Color **64** Alternative colors **available** Width **20½in/52cm** Length **11yd/10m** Repeat **21in/53cm** Price ★

19th century

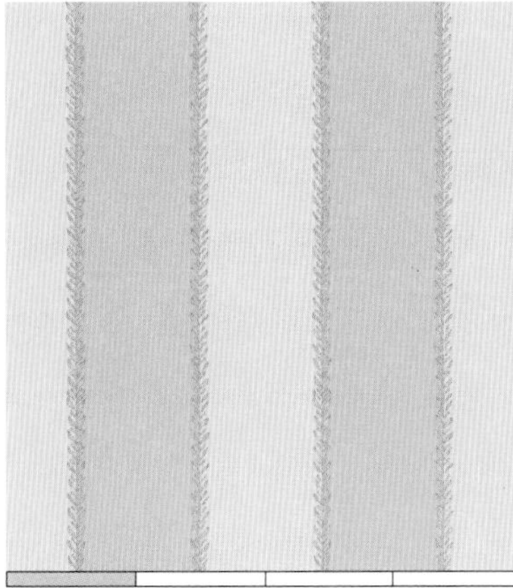

Coloroll/Hambledon 527848 Color **peach** Alternative colors **available** Width **20½in/52cm** Length **11yd/10m** Repeat **–** Price ★

Cole & Son/Georgian Rope Trellis 12-076/PR Color **beige** Alternative colors **available** Width **19in/48cm** Length **11yd/10m** Repeat **9¼in/23.5cm** Price ★

Hodsoll McKenzie/Scroll Stripe 615/601 Color **pink** Alternative colors **available** Width **20½in/52cm** Length **11yd/10m** Repeat **5¼in/13.5cm** Price ★

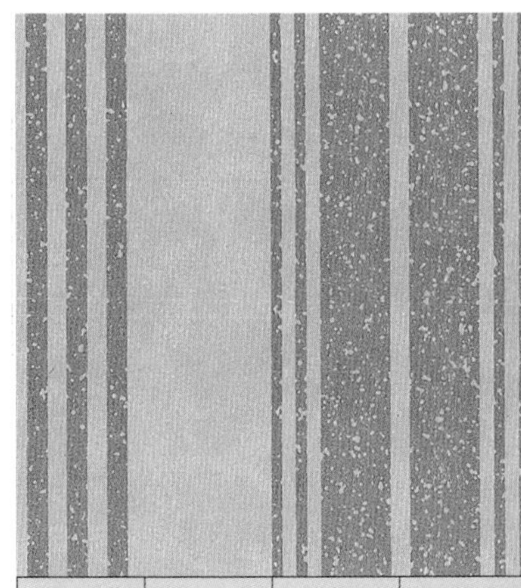

Hamilton Weston/Empire Stripe Color **701** Alternative colors **available** Width **20½in/52cm** Length **11yd/10m** Repeat **–** Price ★

Zoffany/Regency Trellis 36TR05 Color **05** Alternative colors **available** Width **20½in/52cm** Length **11yd/10m** Repeat **4in/10cm** Price ★

Baer & Ingram/Daisy Paper DSW04 Color **yellow** Alternative colors **available** Width **20½in/52cm** Length **11yd/10m** Repeat **1¾in/4.5cm** Price ★

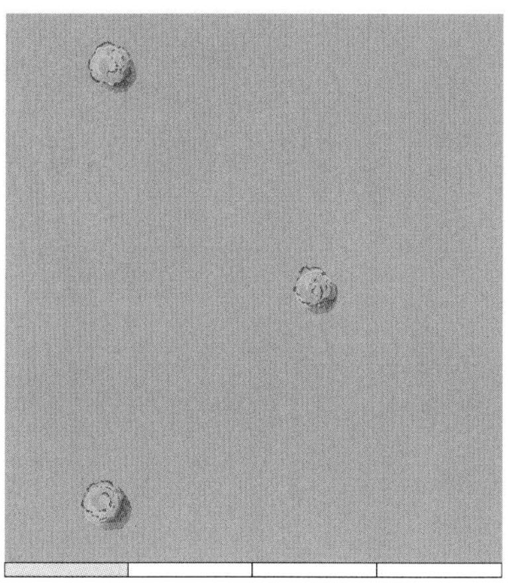

K and K Designs/16204 Color **orange** Alternative colors **available** Width **21in/53cm** Length **11yd/10m**Repeat **–** Price ★

Osborne & Little/Couronne B590/04 Color **beige** Alternative colors **available** Width **8½in/22cm** Length **11yd/10m** Repeat **–** Price ★

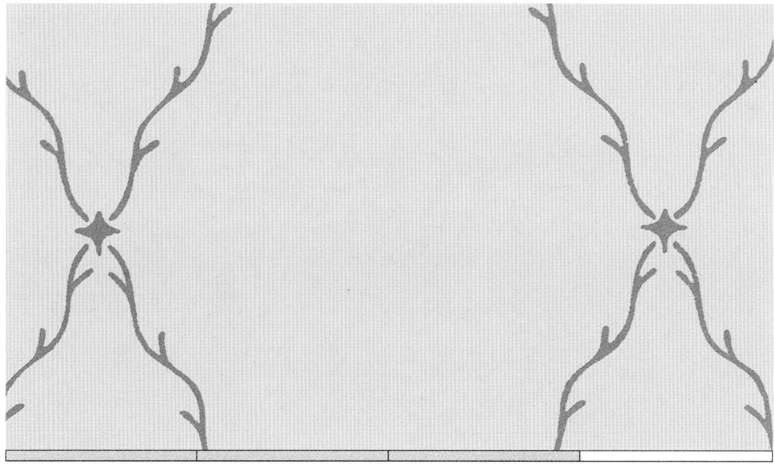

Cole & Son/Christopher Trellis 54/4632/PR Color **yellow** Alternative colors **available** Width **20½in/52cm** Length **11yd/10m** Repeat **7in/18cm** Price ★

Zuber/Rayures à Auge Color **190 jaune** Alternative colors **available** Width **18½in/47cm** Length **11yd/10m** Repeat **–** Price ★★

Cole & Son/Regency Stripe 54/4656/PR Color **red** Alternative colors **available** Width **20½in/52cm** Length **11yd/10m** Repeat **–** Price ★

Cole & Son/Edward Trellis 25/PK346/PR Color **green** Alternative colors **available** Width **21in/53cm** Length **11yd/10m** Repeat **5in/13cm** Price ★

Geometrics: **Mid-19th century**

Although geometric-patterned wallpapers had proved fashionable during the early part of the 19th century, they were produced in far greater numbers following the publication of Owen Jones's *Grammar of Ornament* in 1856, in which he stipulated that "all ornament should be based on geometric construction." Jones had reached this conclusion partly as a result of a distaste for European pictorial and overblown naturalistic decoration, but mainly through his extensive studies of Egyptian, Turkish, Spanish, Chinese, Persian, Indian, and Arabic styles of ornament. Jones's views, and the patterns he devised, proved highly influential with his design contemporaries. Among the numerous geometric patterns produced around the middle of the century were jeweled strapwork and trelliswork and latticework grounds embellished with stylized plant-form motifs. However, ogival patterns also became fashionable, and stripes and powdered ornament retained their popularity from earlier in the century.

1

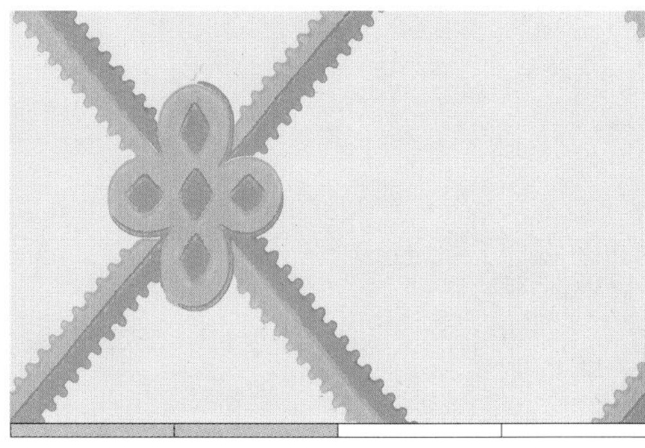

2

3

1 Watts of Westminster/Brandiles ZBR/J001 Color **khaki** Alternative colors **available** Width **18½in/47cm** Length **11yd/10m** Repeat **11½in/29cm** Price ★★

2 Ramm, Son & Crocker/Ludlow Trellis W1013 Color **green** Alternative colors **available** Width **20½in/52cm** Length **11yd/10m** Repeat **6in/15cm** Price ★

3 Hamilton Weston/Trellis Border BOR8161 Color **green and cream** Alternative colors **available** Width **6¾in/17.5cm** Length **11yd/10m** Repeat **20½in/52cm** Price ★★★

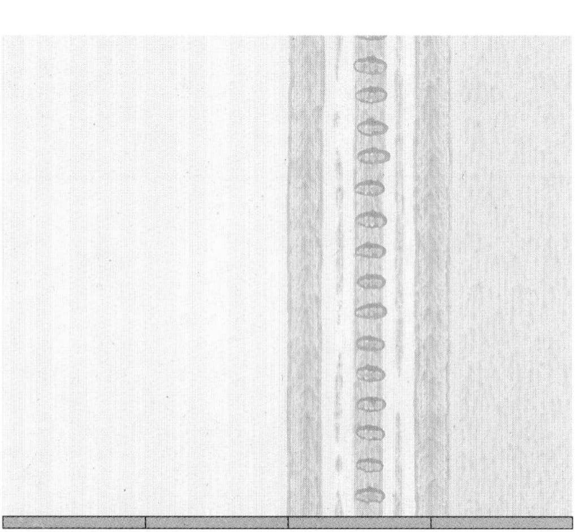

4

4 Ramm, Son & Crocker/Lynford W1148 Color **lettuce** Alternative colors **available** Width **20½in/52cm** Length **11yd/10m** Repeat – Price ★

5 John Wilman/Traviata 170259 Color **green** Alternative colors **available** Width **20½in/52cm** Length **11yd/10m** Repeat – Price ★

6 Malabar/Picota Cherimoya WCPI/10 Color **10** Alternative colors **available** Width **20½in/52cm** Length **11yd/10m** Repeat – Price ★

7 Osborne & Little/Gimp B1390/10 Color **green** Alternative colors **available** Width **2in/5cm** Length **11yd/10m** Repeat – Price ★

8 Schumacher/Baroque Stripe Color **green/gold** Alternative colors **available** Width **27in/68.5cm** Length **4½yd/4m** Repeat **38in/96.5cm** Price ★

6

5

7

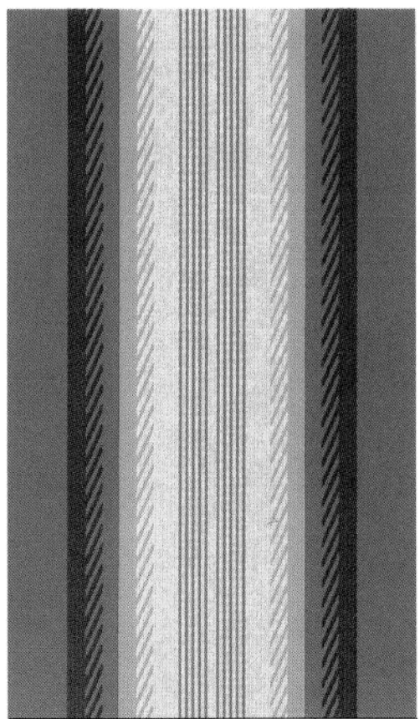

8

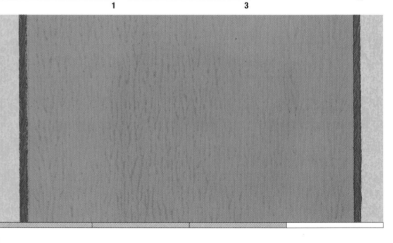

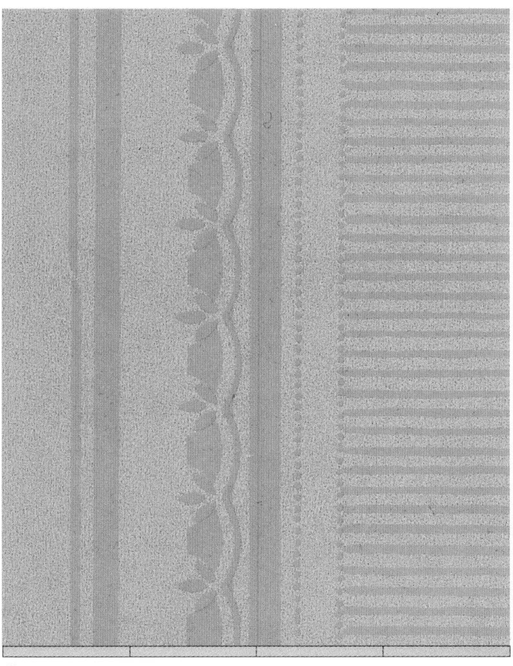

9

12

10

13

14

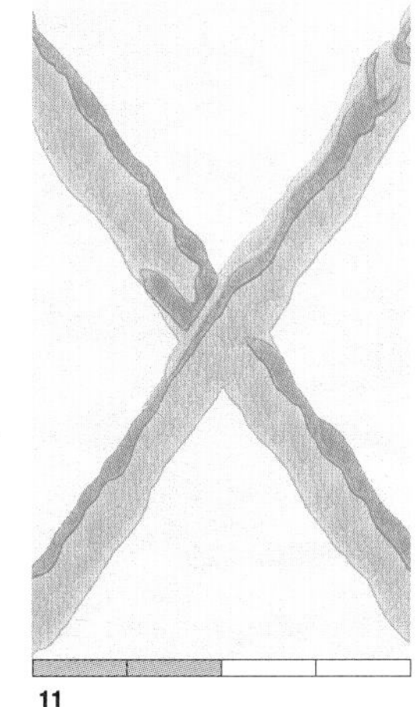

11

12 Joanna Wood/Classic Stripe LW35/53 Color **summer blue** Alternative colors **available** Width **20½in/52cm** Length **11yd/10m** Repeat **–** Price ★

13 Colefax and Fowler/Ditchley 7062/05 Color **green/beige** Alternative colors **available** Width **2in/5cm** Length **11yd/10m** Repeat **–** Price ★

14 Hamilton Weston/Richmond Trellis Color **8162** Alternative colors **available** Width **21in/53cm** Length **11yd/10m** Repeat **6¾in/17.5cm** Price ★

9 Hamilton Weston/French Stripe Color **peach/blue** Alternative colors **available** Width **20½in/52cm** Length **11yd/10m** Repeat **–** Price ★★

10 Sanderson/Durham WR7723/8 Color **8** Alternative colors **available** Width **21in/53cm** Length **11½yd/10.5m** Repeat **–** Price ★

11 G. P. & J. Baker/Bamboo W0077-02 Color **02** Alternative colors **available** Width **20½in/52cm** Length **11yd/10m** Repeat **21in/53cm** Price ★

BORDERS

Decorative paper borders were sometimes applied to the few inches of wall space between the top of wooden paneling and the edge of the ceiling in houses during the 16th century. This makes them one of the oldest types of wallpaper. But it was during the 19th century that the use of borders became widespread. Used as friezes, and as alternatives to the traditional dado and picture rails in fashionable tripartite divisions of walls, they appeared in numerous patterns. Among the most popular were the simple flat or *trompe l'oeil* geometric repeats, such as Greek keys, dots, pearls, and peas framed by horizontal parallel stripes.

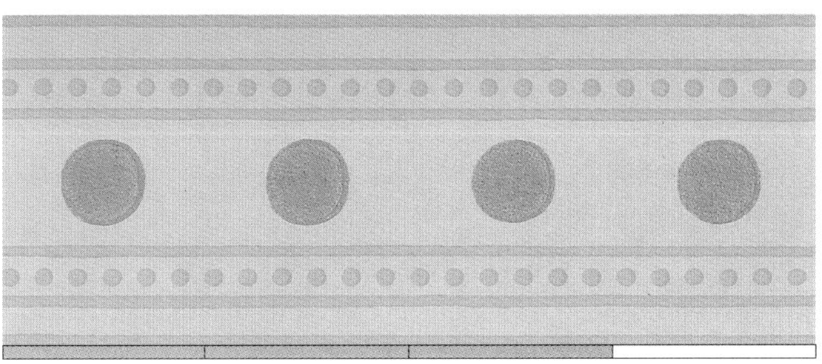

Cole & Son/Dot Border 56/4014/PR Color **4014** Alternative colors **available** Width **1½in/4cm** Length **11yd/10m** Repeat **–** Price ★

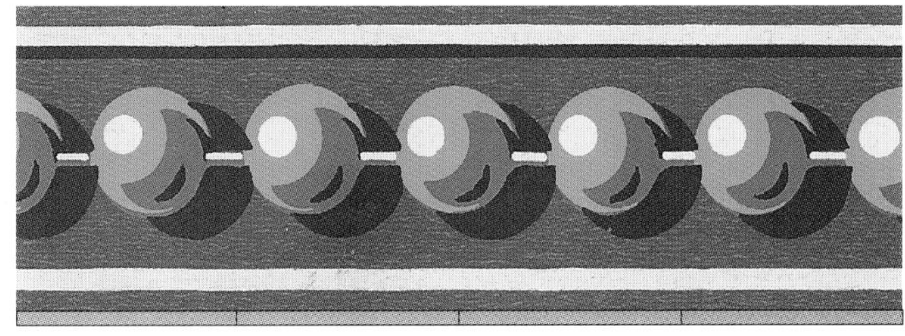

Hamilton Weston/Pearl BD31 Color **brown/green** Alternative colors **available** Width **1¼in/3cm** Length **11yd/10m** Repeat **–** Price ★

Geometrics: **Late 19th century**

Publications such as D. R. Hay's *Original Geometrical Diaper Designs* (1844), and, especially, Owen Jones's *Grammar of Ornament* (1856) continued to exert a tremendous influence on wallpaper designers during the last quarter of the 19th century. Their promotion of the view that geometry provided a fundamental basis for ornament was reflected not only in the striped, checked, chevron, and diaper-patterned papers produced during this period, but also underpinned the stylized organic patterns, devised by leading designers such as Christopher Dresser, in which considerable emphasis was placed on the hexagonal, octagonal, and elliptical shapes to be found in natural plant forms.

The original source material for many of these geometric patterns was medieval, and therefore they were widely employed (often in stenciled form) in fashionable Gothic and Romanesque Revival interiors on both sides of the Atlantic. However, Islamic, Minoan, South Pacific, and Celtic geometric ornament also figured large on numerous wallpapers, particularly borders. Typical designs incorporated abstract shapes, such as blocks, circles, dots, and, from Celtic decoration, triquetra (triangular motifs of interlaced crescents) and triskele (Y-shaped sun motifs).

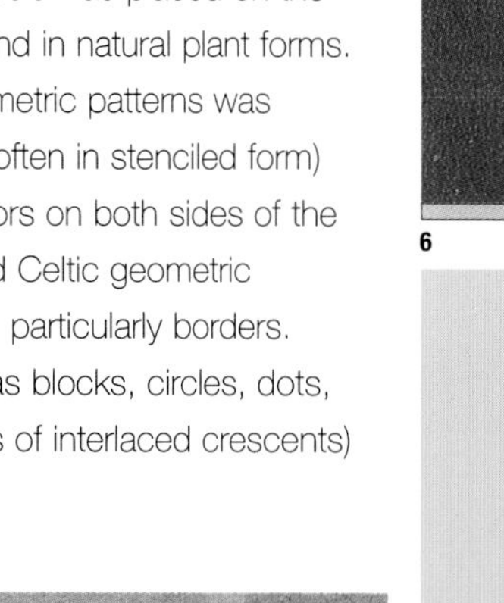

6

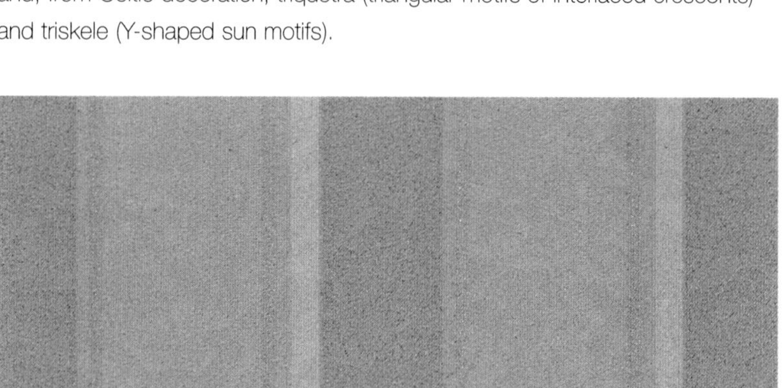

1

2

3

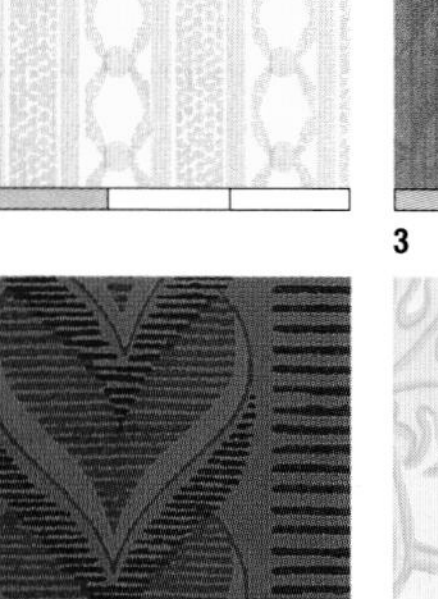

4

5

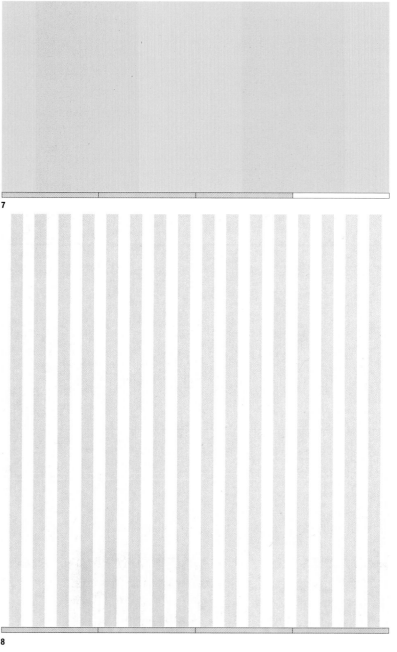

7

8

19th century

1 **Coloroll/Chevalier Stripe 703679** Color **dark green** Alternative colors **available** Width **20½in/52cm** Length **11yd/10m** Repeat **–** Price ★

2 **John Wilman/Aida 170549** Color **green** Alternative colors **available** Width **20½in/52cm** Length **11yd/10m** Repeat **½in/1.5cm** Price ★

3 **Nina Campbell/Chevron Stripe NCW301-02** Color **green** Alternative colors **available** Width **20½in/52cm** Length **11yd/10m** Repeat **–** Price ★

4 **Schumacher/Satin Leaf Stripe 519075** Color **red** Alternative colors **available** Width **27in/68.5cm** Length **3½yd/3m** Repeat **25in/64cm** Price ★

5 **Osborne & Little/Kalamkari** Color **yellow** Alternative colors **available** Width **20½in/52cm** Length **11yd/10m** Repeat **10½in/27cm** Price ★

6 **Crowson/Cheron 37550C52** Color **91** Alternative colors **available** Width **20½in/52cm** Length **11yd/10m** Repeat **–** Price ★

7 **Zoffany/Clarendon V21903** Color **03** Alternative colors **available** Width **20½in/52cm** Length **11yd/10m** Repeat **–** Price ★

8 **Harlequin/95002** Color **pastel** Alternative colors **available** Width **20½in/52cm** Length **11yd/10m** Repeat **–** Price ★

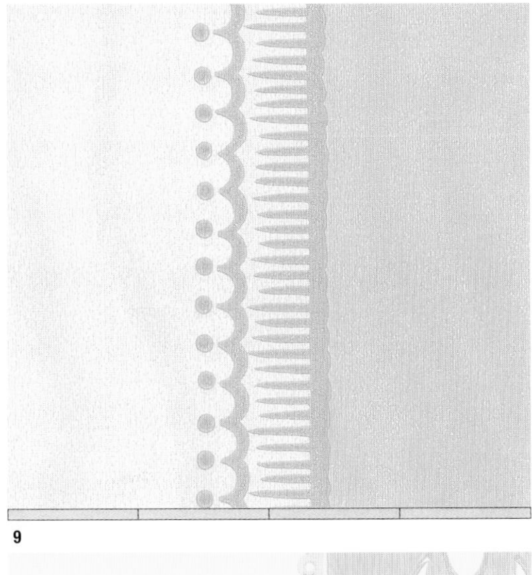

9

10

9 Nina Campbell/Sackville Stripe NCW510/01 Color **yellow** Alternative colors **available** Width **20½in/52cm** Length **11yd/10m** Repeat **–** Price ★

10 Colefax and Fowler/ Cordelia 7612/02 Color **yellow** Alternative colors **available** Width **20½in/52cm** Length **11yd/10m** Repeat **4½in/11.5cm** Price ★

11 Zoffany/Middle Hertford ZV0701 Color **01** Alternative colors **available** Width **20½in/52cm** Length **11yd/10m** Repeat **–** Price ★

12 Alexander Beauchamp/ Greek Key Border Color **brown, black, and green** Alternative colors **available** Width **7in/18cm** Length **11yd/10m** Repeat **22¼in/ 56.5cm** Price ★★★★★ ♣

13 Hamilton Weston/Uppark Trellis Color **document** Alternative colors **available** Width **21in/53cm** Length **11yd/10m** Repeat **4½in/ 11.5cm** Price ★★★ ♣

14

15

16

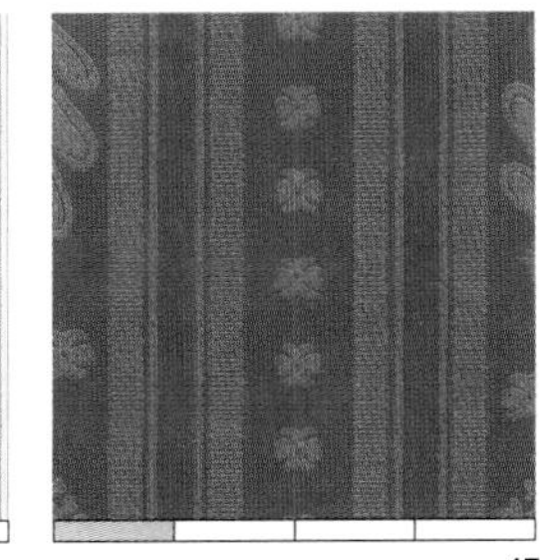

17

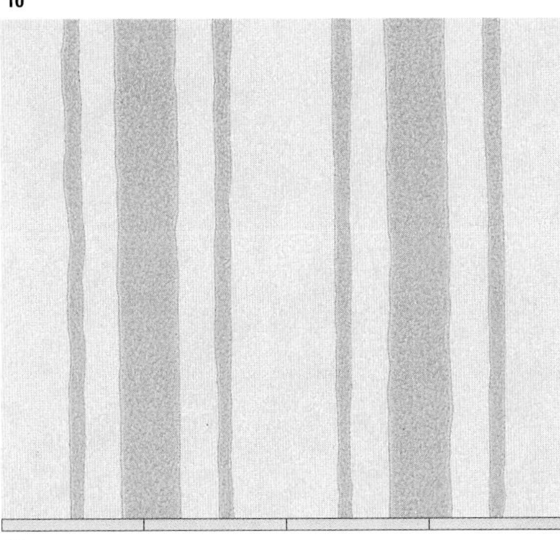

11

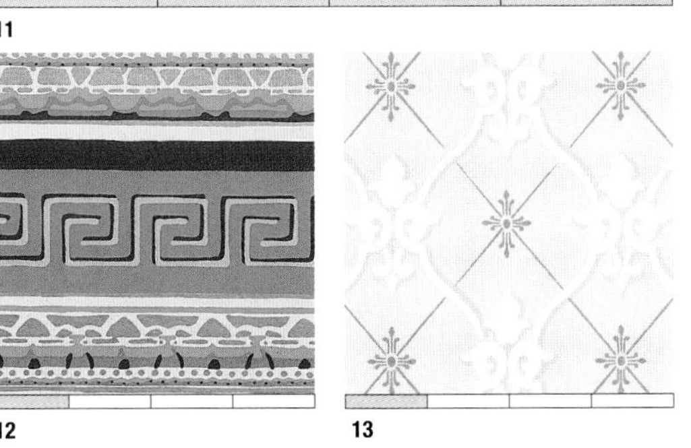

12

13

18

14 Cole & Son/Victorian Trellis 12/057/PR Color **peach** Alternative colors **available** Width **21in/53cm** Length **11yd/10m** Repeat **2½in/6cm** Price ★

15 Crowson/Latina 37550L24 Color **25** Alternative colors **available** Width **20½in/52cm** Length **11yd/10m** Repeat **–** Price ★

16 Jane Churchill/Langdale Stripe JY63W-08 Color **red** Alternative colors **available** Width **20½in/52cm** Length **11yd/10m** Repeat **–** Price ★

17 The Design Archives/Hugo Stripe 58033 Color **red** Alternative colors **available** Width **20½in/52cm** Length **11yd/10m** Repeat **18in/46cm** Price ★

18 Colefax & Fowler/Wickham 7610/02 Color **yellow** Alternative colors **available** Width **20½in/52cm** Length **11yd/10m** Repeat **–** Price ★

Geometrics: **Early 20th century**

Wallpapers that featured geometric patterns were much in evidence during the first half of the 20th century. Many Art Deco papers featured highly mathematical forms such as overlapping squares or oblongs derived from Cubist paintings, while some were inspired by Constructivist art–circles, triangles, or rectangles appearing with one side defined and the other merged into the background (*see* page 216). Striped papers also proved fashionable during the 1920s, the stripes either plain, hatched, or containing small, repeat motifs. Also widely seen in the mid-1920s were pastel-colored geometrics in which stripes, squares, and triangles were harmoniously presented in subtly balanced tones of a single color. In addition to a revival of Victorian striped and diaper-pattern designs, the 1930s witnessed the launch of the Bauhaus papers. Intended to encourage Modernist designers to use papered rather than painted finishes, they displayed shimmering cross-hatching, vertical, horizontal, or wavy lines, or delicate latticework in closely related pastel tones. Many of these designs, together with patterns of sparsely arranged arrows, mazes, and grids printed in bright colors on pale grounds, retained their popularity throughout the 1940s.

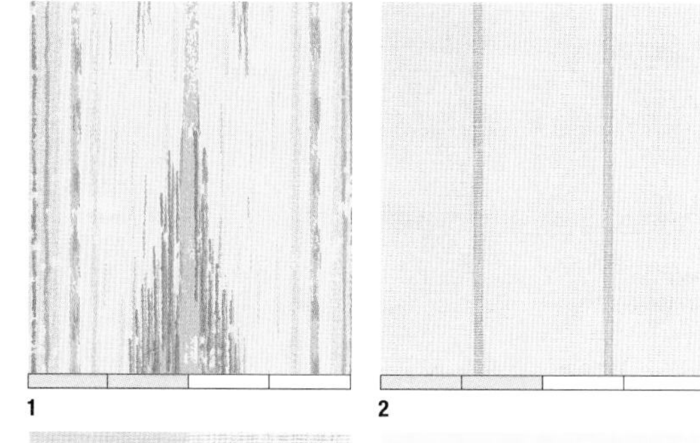

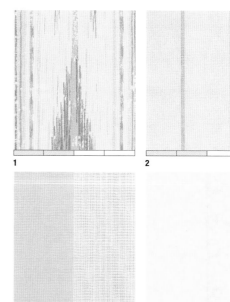

1 **Osborne & Little/Patola W1011/07** Color **blue** Alternative colors **available** Width **20½in/52cm** Length **11yd/10m** Repeat **10½in/ 27cm** Price ★

2 **Graham & Brown/Regal Stripe 26020** Color **gray** Alternative colors **available** Width **24¼in/62cm** Length **11yd/10m** Repeat – Price ★

3 **Cole & Son/Wide Moire Stripe 55/3100/PR** Color **off white** Alternative colors **available** Width **20½in/52cm** Length **11yd/10m** Repeat **2¾in/7cm** Price ★

4 **Osborne & Little/Shagreen Stripe VW784/09** Color **green** Alternative colors **available** Width **20½in/52cm** Length **11yd/10m** Repeat – Price ★

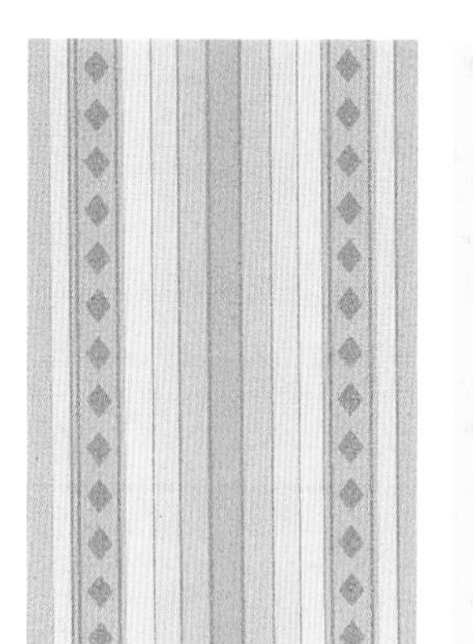

5

6

7

8

9

5 **Coloroll/Pageant Stripe 703556** Color **blue** Alternative colors **available** Width **20½in/52cm** Length **11yd/10m** Repeat – Price ★

6 **Jane Churchill/Fernhurst JY61W-05** Color **stone** Alternative colors **available** Width **20½in/ 52cm** Length **11yd/10m** Repeat **3in/7.5cm** Price ★

7 **Mauny/Grecque Frieze 506L** Color **multi** Alternative colors **available** Width **1½in/4cm** Length **11yd/10m** Repeat – Price ★ ♟

8 **Osborne & Little/Harlequin W840/ 06** Color **yellow** Alternative colors **available** Width **20½in/ 52cm** Length **11yd/10m** Repeat **2½in/6.5cm** Price ★

9 **Cole & Son/Pinstripe 55/3043/PR** Color **yellow** Alternative colors **available** Width **21in/53cm** Length **11yd/10m** Repeat – Price ★

10

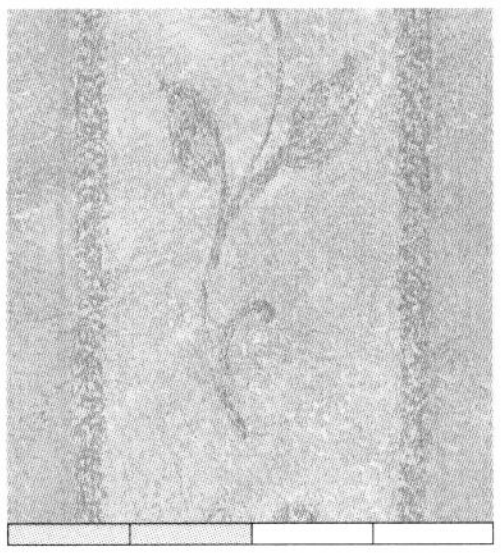

11

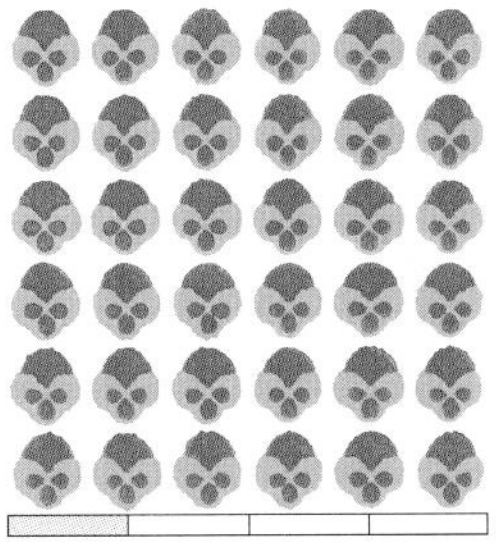

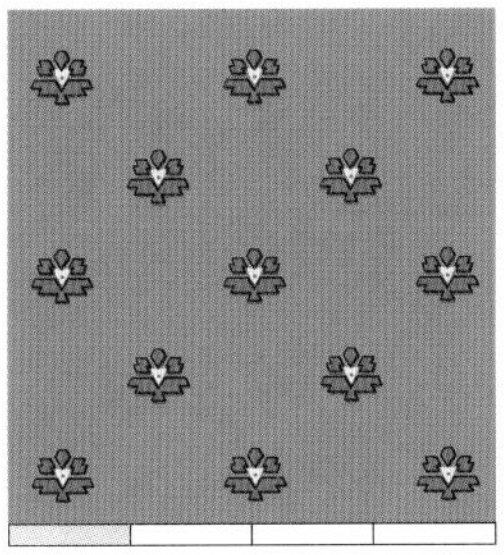

12

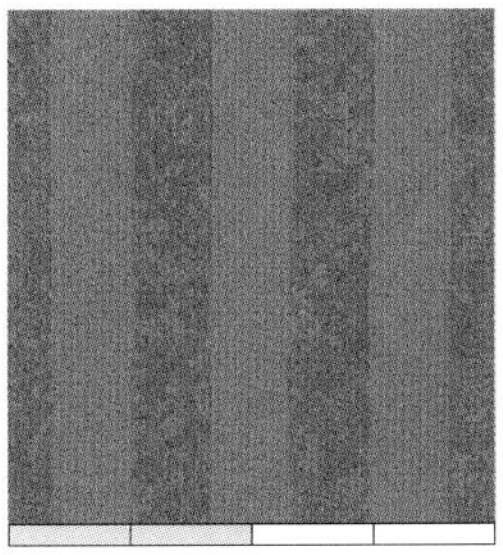

13

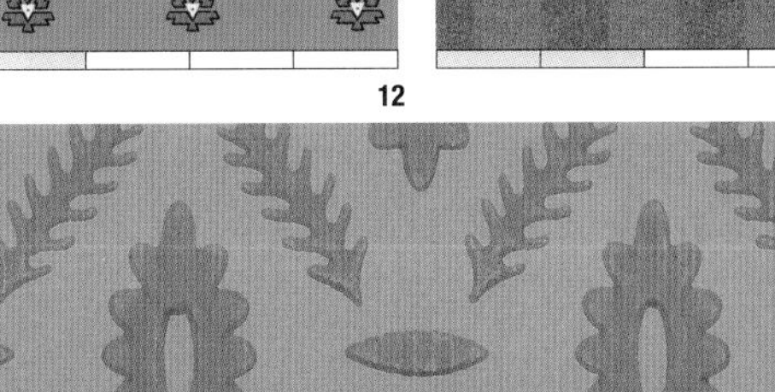

15

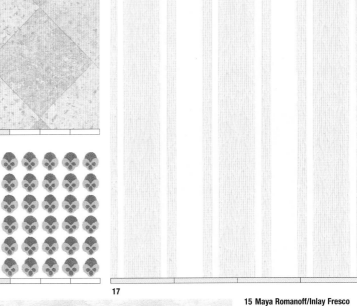

16

17

15 **Maya Romanoff/Inlay Fresco MR-D57-972/177-5** Color **multi** Alternative colors **available** Width **36½in/93cm** Length **22yd/20m** Repeat **–** Price ★★★★★ T

16 **Mauny/Pensée 5016** Color **multi** Alternative colors **available** Width **18½in/47cm** Length **11yd/10m** Repeat **–** Price ★★★ ♣

17 **Colefax and Fowler/Candy Stripe 7409/02** Color **pink** Alternative colors **available** Width **20½in/52cm** Length **11yd/10m** Repeat **–** Price ★

18 **Osborne & Little/Marguerite W1017/06** Color **green** Alternative colors **available** Width **20½in/52cm** Length **11yd/10m** Repeat **1¾in/4.5cm** Price ★

18

10 **Zoffany/Fresco Check V43604** Color **04** Alternative colors **available** Width **20½in/52cm** Length **11yd/10m** Repeat **4in/10.5cm** Price ★

11 **Crowson/Acacia 37550AA2** Color **65** Alternative colors **available** Width **20½in/52cm** Length **11yd/10m** Repeat **10¼in/26cm** Price ★

12 **Brunschwig & Fils/Aix 69222.06** Color **blue** Alternative colors **available** Width **27in/69cm** Length **5yd/4.5m** Repeat **2½in/6cm** Price ★★

13 **Harlequin/15067** Color **sage/dark green** Alternative colors **available** Width **20½in/52cm** Length **11yd/10m** Repeat **10¼in/26cm** Price ★

14 **Colefax and Fowler/Albemarle 7074/06** Color **red** Alternative colors **available** Width **20½in/52cm** Length **11yd/10m** Repeat **3¼in/8.5cm** Price ★

14

IMITATION SILK

Many manufacturers since the First World War have produced both patterned and plain wallpapers that are intended to simulate traditional fabric wall-hangings. Notable examples include linen, cotton, and, as shown here, silk. Various methods have been employed to achieve the desired effect, including flocking, screen-printing, and, more recently, photogravure printing, the latter building up the pattern and texture of the paper through a series of small colored dots of varying degrees of translucency and opacity.

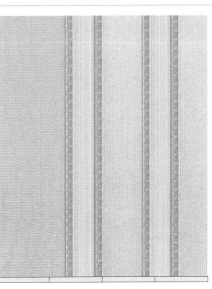

Coloroll/Avalon 401650 Color **green** Alternative colors **available** Width **20½in/52cm** Length **11yd/10m** Repeat **–** Price ★

Geometrics: **Late 20th century**

During the 1950s and 1960s, the link between wallpaper patterns and the designs employed in contemporary fine art that had been evident early in the 20th century was further consolidated by the appearance of the British designer Lucienne Day's geometric papers, featuring linear patterns and ovoid shapes. The abstract, geometric shapes that appeared on the "Corbusier papers" launched in the late 1950s also revealed the influence of contemporary architecture. Other "modern" or "futuristic" designs of note included, from Scandinavia, giant circles and waving vertical bands displayed on rectangular grids in strong tone-on-tone colors, and, in America, France, and Britain, patterns made up of small geometric motifs rendered in reds, yellows, grays, mauves, and black on dark backgrounds. For the more traditionally minded, striped-and-checked plaid patterns also proved popular during the 1950s and 1960s, while a mid-1960s and 1970s Art Deco revival provided nostalgia of more recent origin. However, apart from a substantial increase in the production of documentary geometric papers dating from as early as the 17th century, the latter years of the 20th century were most notable for the appearance of naturalistic photogravure papers produced in imitation of brick walls and blocks of stone.

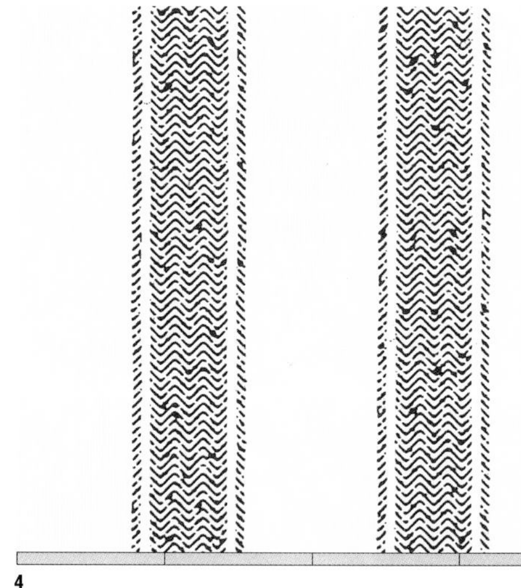

4

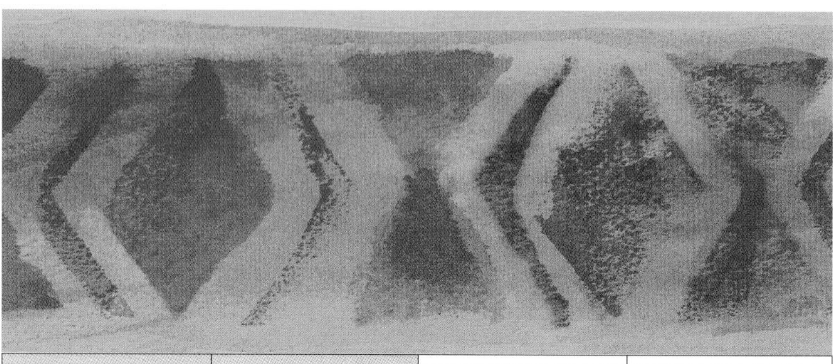

1

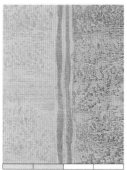

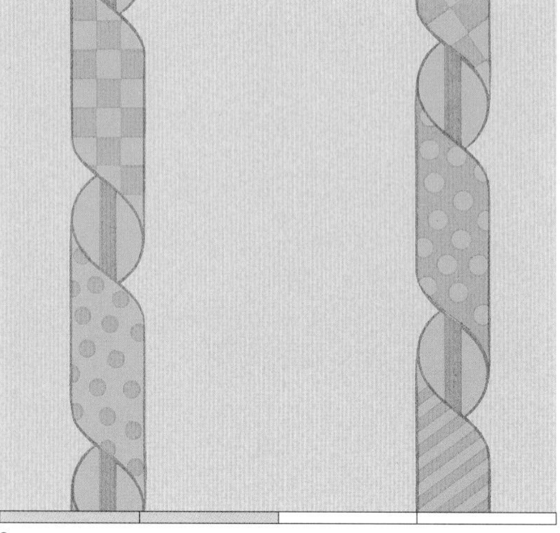

2

5

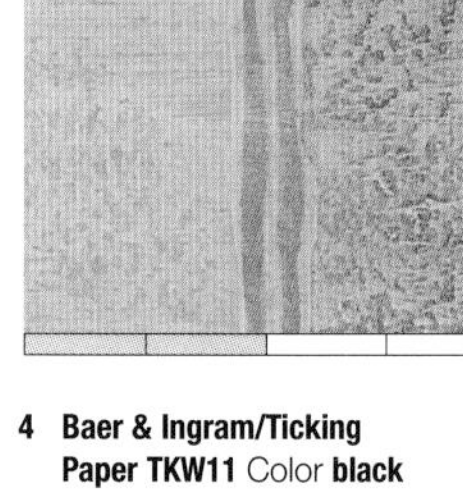

6

3

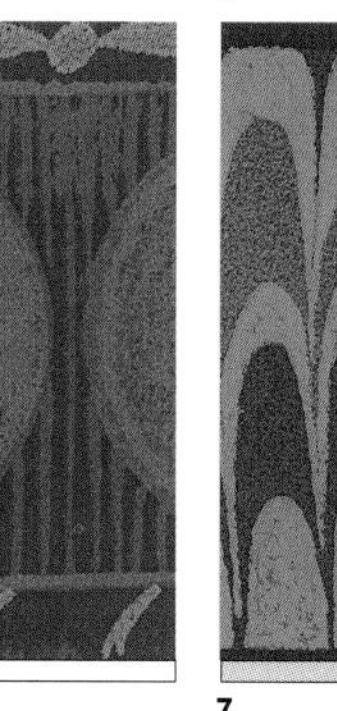

7

8

1 **Harlequin/5503 Border** Color **orange** Alternative colors **available** Width **6in/15cm** Length **5½yd/5m** Repeat **–** Price

2 **Jane Churchill/Banner JY14W-05** Color **dark red/ cream** Alternative colors **available** Width **20½in/52cm** Length **11yd/10m** Repeat **10¼in/26cm** Price

3 **Sandberg/Otto Border 995** Color **64** Alternative colors **available** Width **2½in/6cm** Length **11yd/10m** Repeat **–** Price

4 **Baer & Ingram/Ticking Paper TKW11** Color **black** Alternative colors **available** Width **20½in/52cm** Length **11yd/10m** Repeat **1¾in/ 4.5cm** Price ★★★★

5 **Harlequin/88016** Color **cream, yellow, and blue** Alternative colors **available** Width **20½in/52cm** Length **11yd/10m** Repeat **6¾in/ 17.5cm** Price ★★★

6 **Anna French/Bitter Stripe** Color **WP082BI** Alternative colors **available** Width **20½in/ 52cm** Length **11yd/10m** Repeat **26in/66cm** Price ★

7 **Osborne & Little/Carina Border B1071/01** Color **blue** Alternative colors **available** Width **4in/10.5cm** Length **11yd/10m** Repeat **–** Price ★

8 **Fine Decor/Latina 14161** Color **yellow** Alternative colors **available** Width **20½in/52cm** Length **11yd/10m** Repeat **5¼in/13.5cm** Price ★

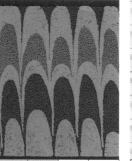

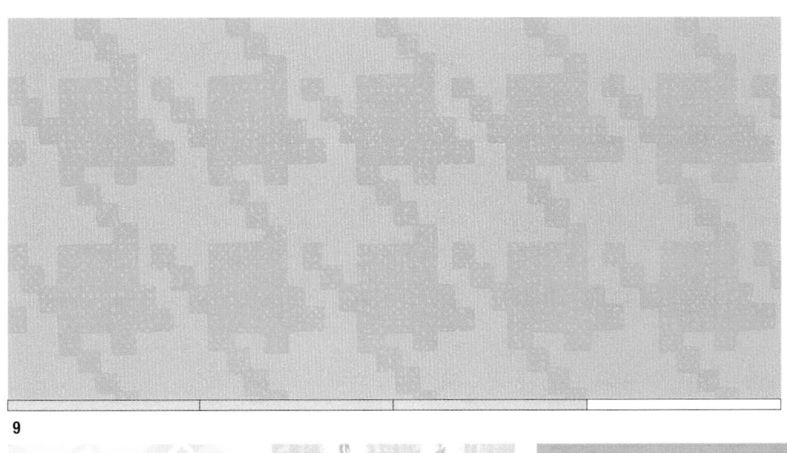

9

10

11 12 13 14 15 16

17

18

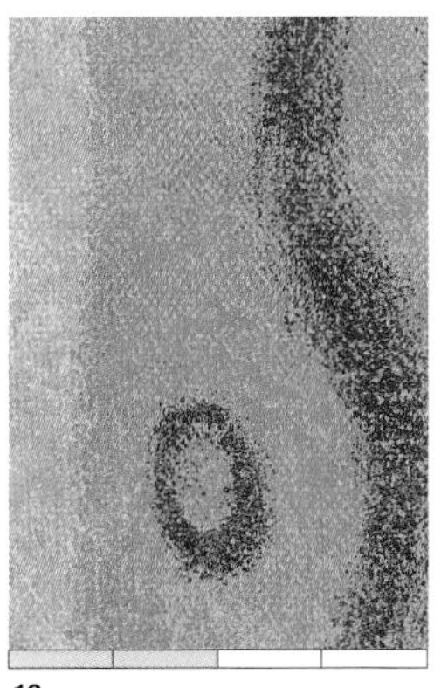

19

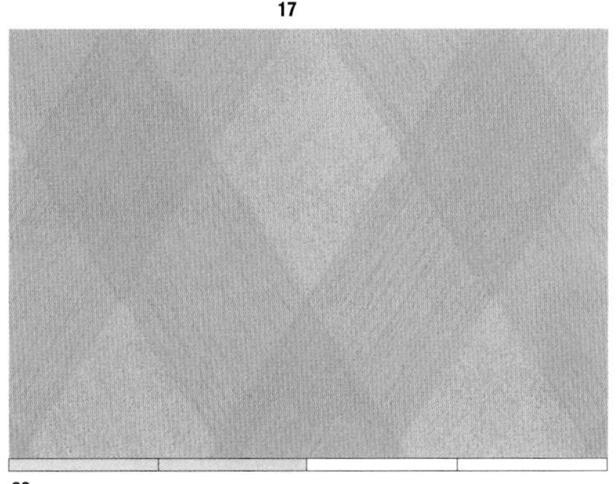

20

9 Ottilie Stevenson/Houndstooth V0035 Color **yellow** Alternative colors **available** Width **20½in/52cm** Length **11yd/10m** Repeat **1¼in/3cm** Price ★

10 Anya Larkin/Artemis AR1 Color **gray/blue on gold ingot** Alternative colors **available** Width **30in/76cm** Length **3½yd/3m** Repeat **9in/23cm** Price ★★★★★

11 Jane Churchill/Provence Check JY02W-05 Color **yellow** Alternative colors **available** Width **20½in/52cm** Length **11yd/10m** Repeat **4in/10.5cm** Price ★

12 Pippa & Hale/Mercury Stripe MIW063 Color **063** Alternative colors **available** Width **21in/53cm** Length **11yd/10m** Repeat **–** Price ★

13 Anna French/Knave Color **KNAWP014** Alternative colors **available** Width **20½in/52cm** Length **11yd/10m** Repeat **18in/46cm** Price ★

14 Fine Decor/Levanto 14131 Color **green** Alternative colors **available** Width **20½in/52cm** Length **11yd/10m** Repeat **7in/18cm** Price ★

15 Jean Louis Seigner/Patio 1992 Color **red and green** Alternative colors **available** Width **28¾in/73cm** Length **10yd/9m** Repeat **7¼in/18.5cm** Price ★★ ♣

16 Anna French/Tintagel Color **TINWP015** Alternative colors **available** Width **20½in/52cm** Length **11yd/10m** Repeat **20½in/52cm** Price ★

17 Nobilis-Fontan/Tenor Border BOR3604 Color **red, green, and yellow** Alternative colors **available** Width **5½in/14cm** Length **10yd/9m** Repeat **–** Price ★★ ♣

18 Coloroll/Blowder Stripe 402022 Color **lilac** Alternative colors **available** Width **20½in/52cm** Length **11yd/10m** Repeat **–** Price ★

19 Anna French/Tangier Color **TANWP026** Alternative colors **available** Width **20½in/52cm** Length **11yd/10m** Repeat **–** Price ★

20 Osborne & Little/Malacca W1123/07 Color **green** Alternative colors **available** Width **20½in/52cm** Length **11yd/10m** Repeat **10½in/27cm** Price ★

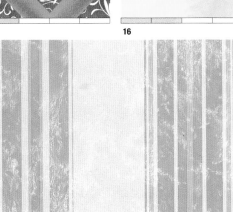

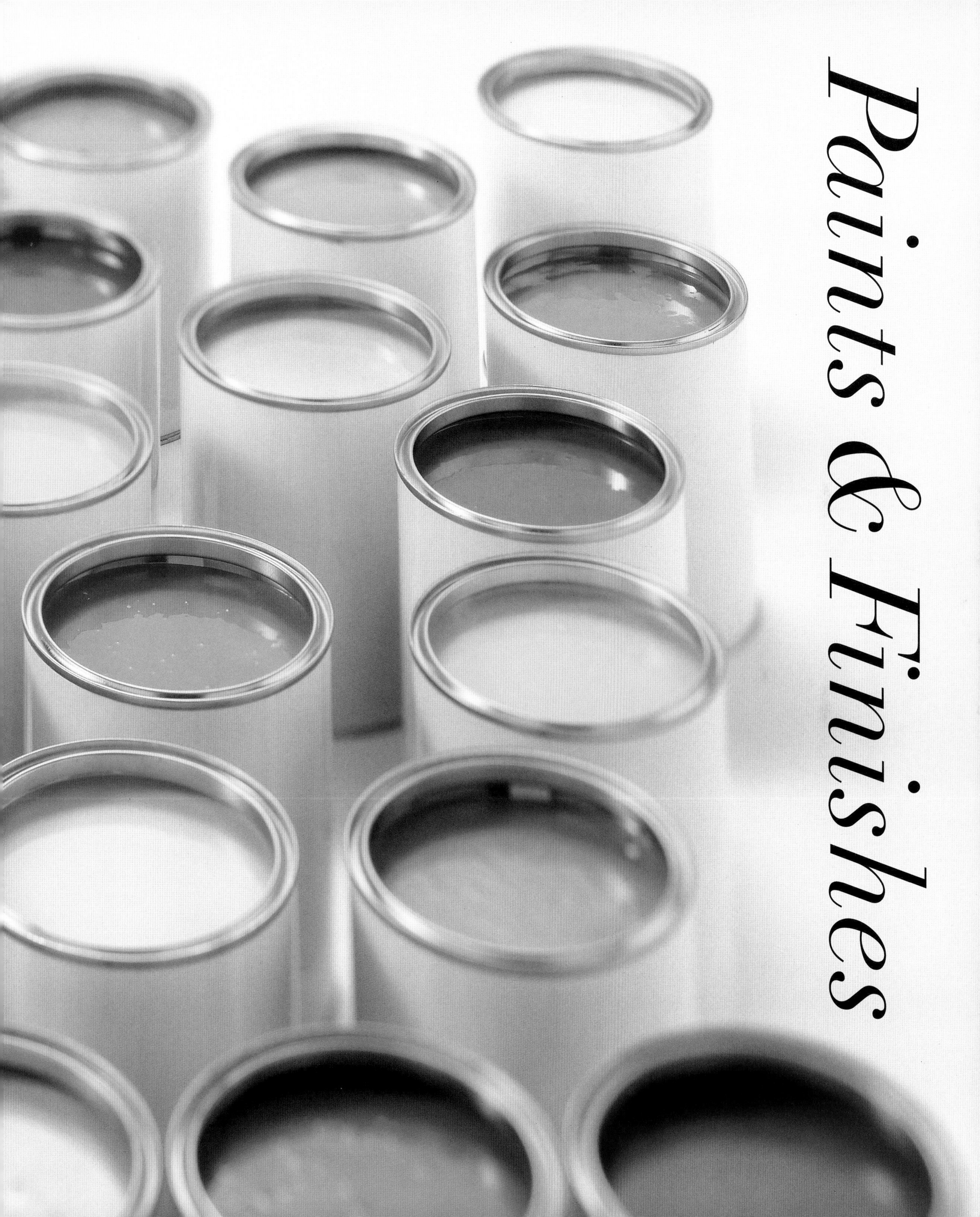

Paints & Finishes

Paints

Prior to the mid-19th century, most pigments were derived from clays, vegetable matter, and the by-products of the mining industry, such as cobalt, carbonate, copper, and iron and chrome oxides. Until drugstores began selling vials of premixed pigments at the end of the 19th century, most paints were prepared on-site by itinerant craftsmen. Although a diverse range of hues could be produced from these pigments, many proved unstable (fugitive) when they were exposed to moisture and sunlight, causing bright colors to fade and blotch.

The invention of aniline dyes in the 1850s, and, even more significantly, of various synthetic chemical pigments from the 1920s to 1960s, resulted in more stable, durable paints, and an expansion of the color palette. Mass production also gave rise to far greater uniformity of color. Since the 1980s, however, there has been a renewed appreciation of the decorative qualities of some of the earlier paints –notably limewash and milk paint–with formulas modified to ensure greater stability and longevity than before.

LEFT **The linear configuration of the color scheme in this late 20th-century bathroom echoes some of the Art Deco interiors of the 1920s and 1930s (and Art Deco Revival interiors of the 1960s). However, the pale yellow and lilac hues used here are lighter and cooler than the hot, saturated colors often employed in classic Art Deco rooms.**

ABOVE The ambience in this southern Mediterranean hallway is created by the open archway and the juxtaposition of the quarry-tiled floor and staircase with a cool blue colorwash on the walls.Blue is often used in Mediterranean kitchens and hallways because of its cooling effect.

LEFT This is a typical, 19th-century Shaker bedroom. The stone-colored painted walls and the Shaker blue, milk-painted woodwork provide a cool, understated backdrop that enhances the warm, natural wood finishes of the beautifully made Shaker furniture. Notable Shaker colors include yellow ocher, olive green, and earthy shades of terracotta and pink.

KEY COLORS

1 Oxblood, burgundy, and other dark red paints were a feature of decorative schemes from the Middle Ages to the early 18th century and enjoyed numerous revivals thereafter.

2 Vegetable- and mineral-pigmented dark green paints were often used on woodwork from the early 17th to the mid-18th centuries. Acid greens became very fashionable during the Victorian era.

3 Lighter, more muted greens have included gray-green "drab" during the 18th century; olive green ("greenery-yallery") in the late 19th century; and *eau de nil* during the 1930s and 1940s.

4 Terracotta-colored paints, tinted with clay pigments, have been produced for thousands of years, but stronger, more vivid mustard yellows only emerged with the invention of aniline dyes in the 1850s.

5 Pale blues, such as turquoise and Wedgwood blue, were fashionable from the 1750s until the 1840s, particularly on plasterwork. Light pastel blues have also proved popular since the 1930s.

6 Pale pinks were in vogue from the 1750s until the 1840s, while hotter, more vivid pinks (often combined with black) were a feature of Art Deco schemes of the 1920s and 1930s.

1 **Finnaren & Haley** Color **Mt. Vernon red 520315** Composition and finish *water-based:* **flat, semigloss** *oil-based:* **semigloss** Price ★★★ W

2 **Sanderson** Color **northern pine 56-1U** Composition and finish *water-based:* **flat, silk** *oil-based:* **eggshell, gloss** Price ★ W C

3 **Sigma Coatings/BS4800 Color Range** Color **Westmorland 12B21** Composition and finish *water-based:* **flat, satin** *oil-based:* **gloss, satin** Price ★ W

4 **Annie Sloan** Color **strong yellow 27** Composition and finish *water-based:* **flat** *oil-based:* **semigloss** Price ★★ W

5 **Brats/Mediterranean Palette 113** Color **Alexandria** Composition and finish *water-based:* **flat** Price ★ W

6 **Ace Royal** Color **forever sacred** Composition and finish *water-based:* **flat** *oil-based:* **satin, semigloss** Price ★★ W

Paints: **Pre-18th century**

Before the 18th century, limewash was the favored medium for decorating masonry and plaster surfaces (*see* page 283). Limewash was also sometimes applied to woodwork, although if it was mixed incorrectly it tended to rub off onto clothing if brushed against. Milk paint, however, provided a more stable medium for woodwork and furniture (*see* page 284), and was in widespread use, particularly in rural areas. By the beginning of the 17th century, durable oil paints were increasingly used on woodwork and furniture, while egg tempera (powder pigments mixed with linseed oil, water, and egg yolk) was used on furniture only. However, both were more costly to mix and apply and their use was confined to wealthier urban houses. Polychromatic color schemes were fashionable up until the end of the 17th century. Primary colors–rich reds, yellows, and blues–were much in evidence, as were various shades of green and brown. Pigments were mostly derived from earth, clays, and vegetable matter, although diverse materials such as ox blood, cattle urine, and beetle juice were also utilized by colorists who, since the Middle Ages, had belonged to specialist guilds that jealously guarded the secrets of pigment production.

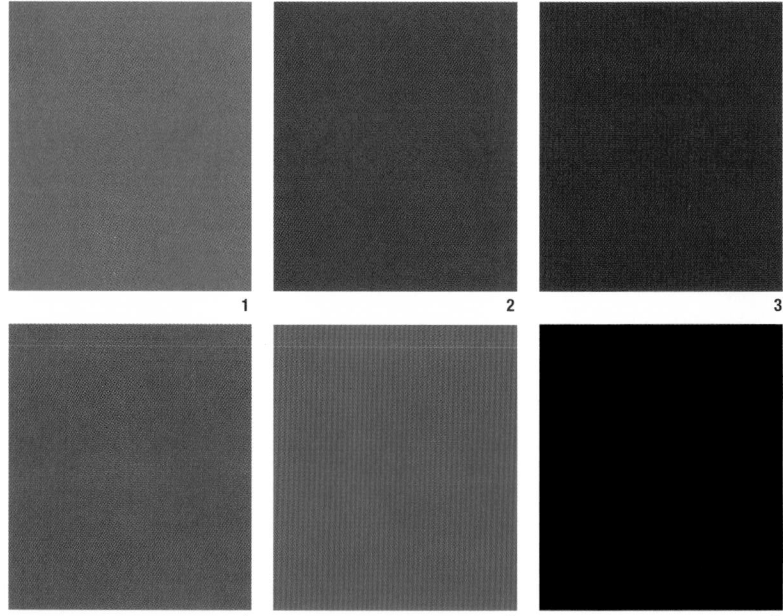

1 **Cole & Son** Color **pimento** Composition and finish *water-based:* **flat** Price ★★★ W C

2 **Paint Library** Color **Elizabethan Red** Composition and finish *water-based:* **flat, silk** *oil-based:* **dead flat, gloss** Price ★★★ W F

3 **Auro Organic Paints/Emulsion Paint** Color **cranberry/15D** Composition and finish *water-based:* **flat** Price ★★ W F

4 **Auro Organic Paints/Color Topcoat Gloss and Mixing Guide** Color **240-10(0)** Composition and finish *oil-based:* **eggshell, gloss** Price ★★★★

5 **Glidden/Heritage Colors** Color **90RR22/227** Composition and finish *water-based:* **flat, silk, soft sheen** *oil-based:* **dead flat, eggshell, gloss** Price ★ W C

6 **Paint Library** Color **lamp black** Composition and finish *water-based:* **flat, silk** *oil-based:* **dead flat, gloss** Price ★★★ W F

DARKER HUES

Prior to the 18th century, most softwood wall-paneling and other woodwork found in the reception rooms of houses was painted in dark colors. While milk paint was often used in rural areas and less affluent households, the favored medium in urban areas and grander homes was oil paint, mixed on site from boiled linseed oil, ground chalk (whiting), turpentine, and ground pigment. The latter was invariably in earth colors (mostly browns, reds, and greens) derived from clays, plants, and metal oxides.

J. W. Bollom/Bromel Color **earthenware 08C39 JWB421** Composition and finish *water-based:* **flat, silk** *oil-based:* **eggshell, gloss** Price ★★ W C

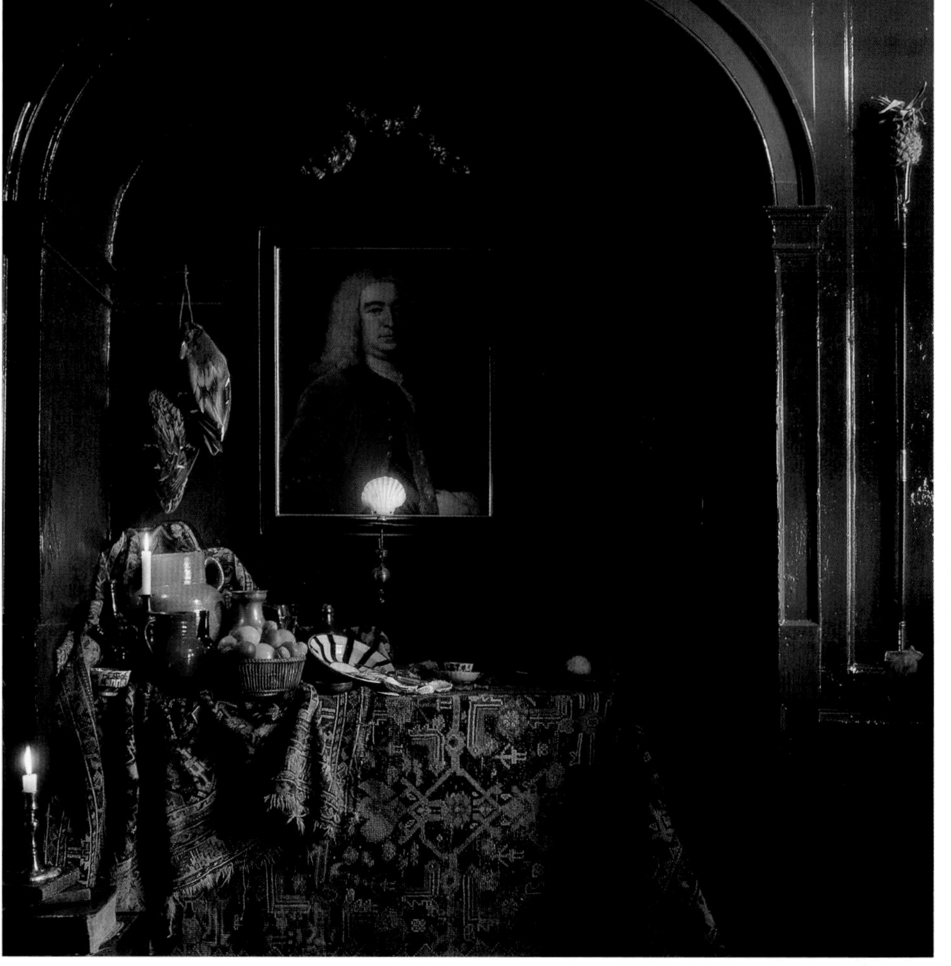

The plasterwork and wooden paneling and moldings in Dennis Severs' authentically restored 17th-century house in London, England, have been painted with a gloss finish–dark green oil paint typical of the period.

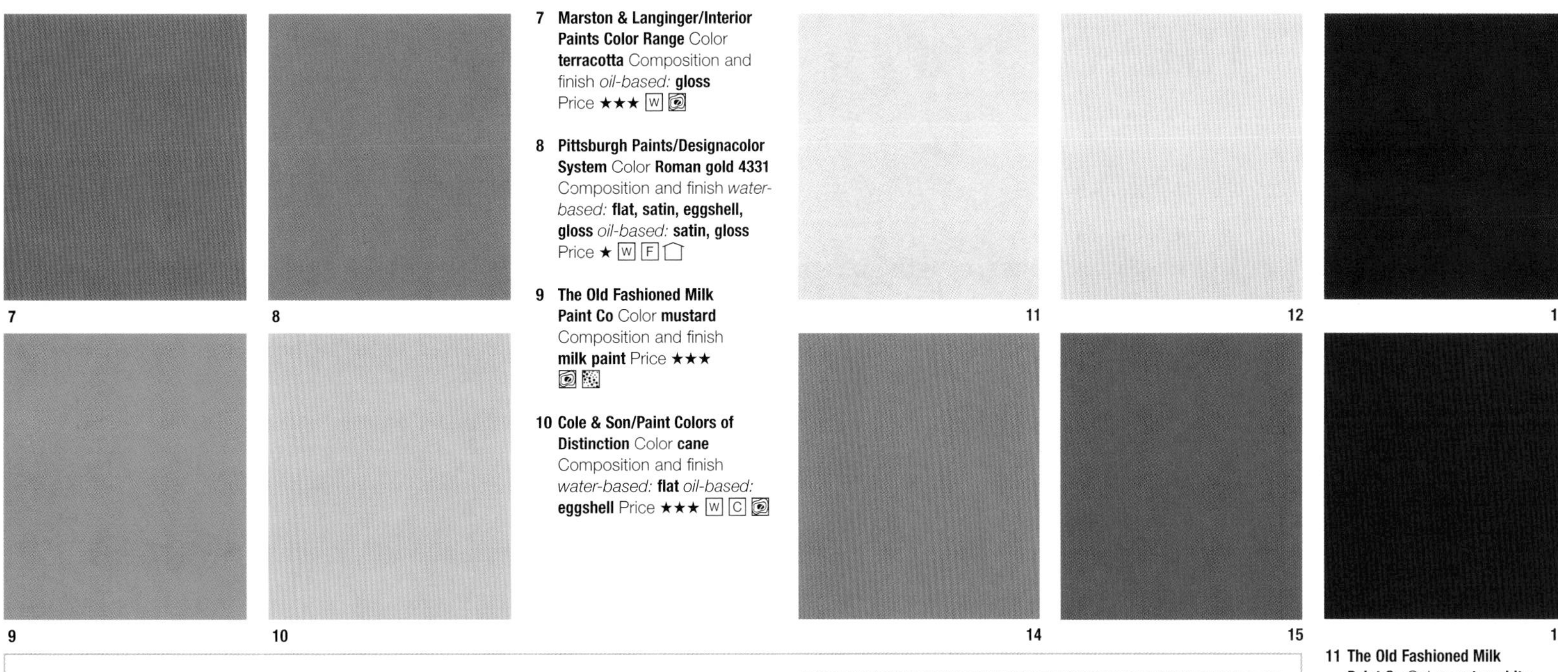

7 Marston & Langinger/Interior Paints Color Range Color **terracotta** Composition and finish *oil-based:* **gloss** Price ★★★ [W]

8 Pittsburgh Paints/Designacolor System Color **Roman gold 4331** Composition and finish *water-based:* **flat, satin, eggshell, gloss** *oil-based:* **satin, gloss** Price ★ [W] [F]

9 The Old Fashioned Milk Paint Co Color **mustard** Composition and finish **milk paint** Price ★★★

10 Cole & Son/Paint Colors of Distinction Color **cane** Composition and finish *water-based:* **flat** *oil-based:* **eggshell** Price ★★★ [W] [C]

11 The Old Fashioned Milk Paint Co Color **oyster white** Composition and finish **milk paint** Price ★★★

12 Sanderson/Spectrum Color **pheasant's feather 2-23M** Composition and finish *water-based:* **flat, silk** *oil-based:* **eggshell, gloss** Price ★★ [W]

13 Colorman Paints/Reproduction Colors Color **100** Composition and finish *water-based:* **flat** Price ★★ [W]

14 Paint Library Color **Medici** Composition and finish *water-based:* **flat, silk, gloss** *oil-based:* **dead flat** Price ★★★ [W] [F]

15 Colorman Paints/Reproduction Colors Color **115** Composition and finish *water-based:* **flat** Price ★★ [W]

16 Pittsburgh Paints/Designacolor System Color **deep marine 7090** Composition and finish *water-based:* **flat, satin, eggshell, gloss enamel** *oil-based:* **satin, gloss** Price ★ [W] [F]

LIMEWASH PAINTS

First employed ca. 8000 B.C., white limewash is made by mixing lime putty with water and raw linseed oil. Colored versions are created by adding earth or metallic pigments. Applied to stonework and lime plasters, limewash dries to an opaque "pure" white or color that appears bright and luminous under strong light and darker and matte under poor light. It also has the advantage of allowing moisture in the underlying surface to evaporate, thereby preventing structural deterioration.

1

2

1 Liz Induni Color **terracotta** Composition and finish **limewash, distemper** Price ★ [W] [F]

2 Liz Induni Color **pale pink** Composition and finish **limewash, distemper** Price ★ [W] [F]

3 Rose of Jericho Color **chromium oxide COC150** Composition and finish **limewash, distemper** Price ★ [W] [F]

4 Cy-Près Color **Alice Grace** Composition and finish **limewash, distemper** Price ★ [W] [F]

3

4

Paints: **18th century**

In the 18th century, limewash (*see* page 283) and milk paint (*see* below) remained in widespread use on plasterwork and woodwork respectively. However, as the century progressed, flat, mid-sheen, and gloss oil paints became the most frequently used finishes for plaster and wooden surfaces in more affluent households. As far as the choice of color was concerned, starting in the 1750s there was a general move from darker to lighter hues (*see* opposite), with bright, vivid colors such as citron, violet, turquoise, pea green, and cerise proving especially popular toward the end of the century.

Underpinning the new aesthetic was a growing understanding of color theory. An influential publication on the subject was the Englishman Moses Harris's *The Natural History of Colours* (1766), which explained how to mix over 300 tints from 15 basic colors. The consequences of this were that a wider choice of colors became available and decorators were able to use varying shades of the same basic color on adjacent flat and molded surfaces to subtly emphasize the architectural proportions and details of a room.

MILK PAINTS

Casein ("milk") paint was used on woodwork and furniture throughout Europe, Scandinavia, and North America fromthe 16th to 19th centuries, especially in rural areas. Cheap and durable, it was made by tinting buttermilk or skimmed milk with earth or vegetable pigments; a little lime was added to inhibit insect infestation and fungal growth. Milk paint dries to a subtle sheen and displays a clarity and opacity of color that is rarely matched by modern paints. It is available as a powder to be mixed with water from specialist paint manufacturers.

1

2

3

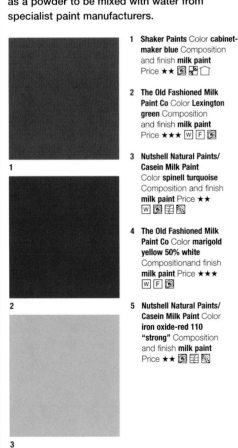

1 **Shaker Paints** Color **cabinet-maker blue** Composition and finish **milk paint** Price ★★

2 **The Old Fashioned Milk Paint Co** Color **Lexington green** Composition and finish **milk paint** Price ★★★ W F

3 **Nutshell Natural Paints/ Casein Milk Paint** Color **spinell turquoise** Composition and finish **milk paint** Price ★★ W

4 **The Old Fashioned Milk Paint Co** Color **marigold yellow 50% white** Compositionand finish **milk paint** Price ★★★ W F

5 **Nutshell Natural Paints/ Casein Milk Paint** Color **iron oxide-red 110 "strong"** Composition and finish **milk paint** Price ★★

4

5

1

2

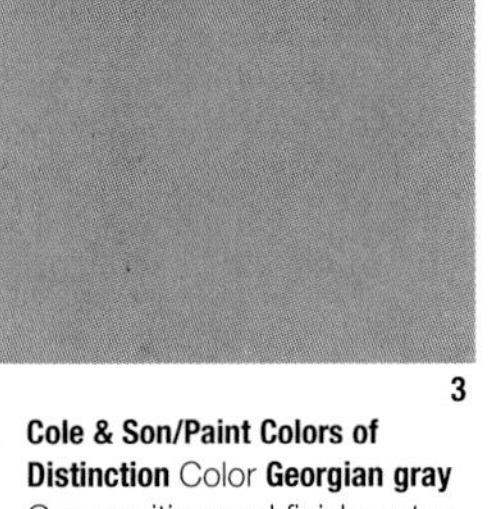

3

4

1 **Cole & Son/Paint Colors of Distinction** Color **Georgian gray** Composition and finish *water-based:* **flat** *oil-based:* **eggshell** Price ★★★ W C

2 **Ace Royal/Historical Colors** Color **castle rock** Composition and finish *water-based:* **flat, satin, semigloss** Price ★★★★ W

3 **Crown/Non-Drip and Liquid Gloss** Color **antique gray 117** Composition and finish *oil-based:* **gloss** Price ★★

4 **Sanderson/Spectrum** Color **almond cream/11-1P** Composition and finish *water-based:* **flat, silk** *oil-based:* **eggshell, gloss** Price ★★ W C

5 **Glidden/Heritage Colors** Color **DH White 51YY85117** Composition and finish *water-based:* **flat, silk, soft sheen** *oil-based:* **dead flat, eggshell, gloss** Price ★ W C

6 **Sanderson/Spectrum** Color **straw yellow 3-10M** Composition and finish *water-based:* **flat, silk** *oil-based:* **eggshell, gloss** Price ★★ W C

7 **Glidden/Heritage Colors** Color **DH lemon 1643 Y05R** Composition and finish *water-based:* **flat, silk, soft sheen** *oil-based:* **dead flat, eggshell, gloss** Price ★ W C

8 **Paint Magic/Color Collection** Color **haystack** Composition and finish *water-based:* **flat** Price ★★ W

5

6

7

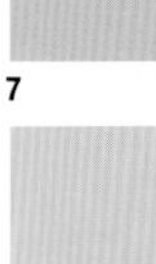

8

9 Glidden/Heritage Colors Color **pearl 34GY69077** Composition and finish *water-based:* **flat, silk, soft sheen** *oil-based:* **dead flat, eggshell, gloss** Price ★ [W] [C]

10 Farrow & Ball/National Trust Range Color **pea green 33** Composition and finish *water-based:* **distemper, flat** *oil-based:* **dead flat, eggshell** Price ★ [W]

11 Paint Magic/Color Collection Color **study green** Composition and finish *water-based:* **flat** Price ★★ [W]

12 Fired Earth/Victoria & Albert Museum Color **terre vert 16** Composition and finish *water-based:* **distemper, flat** *oil-based:* **dead flat, eggshell** Price ★★ [W] [C]

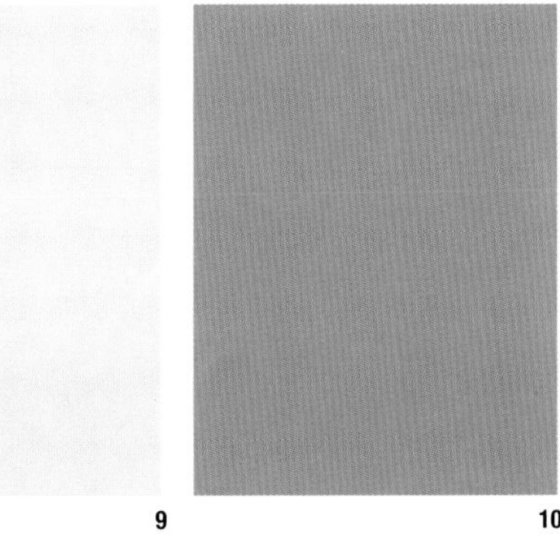

9 10

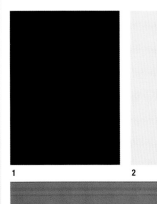

11 12

13

14

15 16

17 18

19

20

13 Colorman/Reproduction Colors Color **104** Composition and finish *water-based:* **flat** Price ★★ [W]

14 Crown/Non-Drip and Liquid Gloss Color **deep ivy** Composition and finish *oil-based:* **gloss** Price ★★

15 Pittsburgh Paints/Designacolor System Color **Naples 4035** Composition and finish *water-based:* **flat, satin, eggshell, gloss** *oil-based:* **satin, gloss** Price ★ [W] [F]

16 The Old Fashioned Milk Paint Co Color **Federal blue 90% white** Composition and finish **milk paint** Price ★★★ [F]

17 Pratt & Lambert/Interior Wall & Trim Color **princely blue 1148** Composition and finish *water-based:* **flat, satin, eggshell, semigloss, gloss** Price ★★ [W] [F]

18 Colorman/Reproduction Colors Color **126** Composition and finish *water-based:* **flat** Price ★★ [W]

19 Paint Library Color **Sophie Rose** Composition and finish *water-based:* **flat, silk** *oil-based:* **dead flat, eggshell, gloss** Price ★★★ [W] [F]

20 Paint Library Color **copper beech** Composition and finish *water-based:* **flat, silk** *oil-based:* **dead flat, gloss** Price ★★★ [W] [F]

FROM DARK TO LIGHT

Light-colored decorative schemes originated in the white-painted and gilded state rooms of French palaces during the late 17th century, but it took another 50 years for them to filter through to ordinary European, Scandinavian, and North American households. Consequently, for the first half of the 18th century, darker earth colors, such as muddy browns and greens ("drabs"), remained very much in evidence on walls and woodwork. Fashionable hues included pinks and light terracottas, pale greens and blues, and various yellows, such as "straw," "citron," and "Chinese."

1 2

1 Paint Magic Color Collection Color **Spitalfields green** Composition and finish *water-based:* **flat** Price ★★ [W]

2 Berger Color **pale lemon** Composition and finish *water-based:* **flat** Price ★★ [W] [C]

Subtly contrasting shades of pale lemon on the walls and ceiling complement the fine, mahogany furniture, accentuate natural light, and contribute to a general sense of spaciousness in this late 18th-century drawing room.

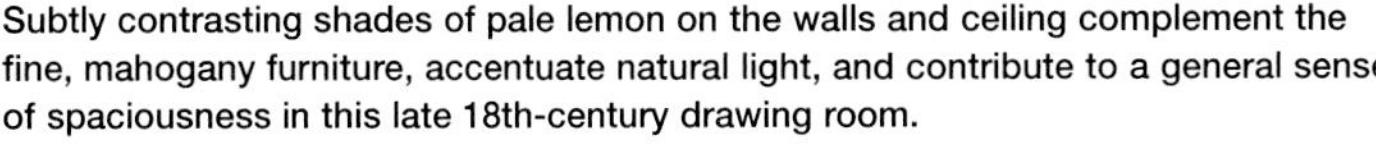

Paints: **19th century**

Until the 1840s, light colors, such as pearl white, pale pink, and lavender, were generally fashionable, although darker hues, notably crimson, were sometimes used in reception rooms. By the middle of the century, however, stronger colors were popular again, partly due to the invention of aniline dyes, which produced sharp yellows, deep blues, acid greens, and lurid purples and mustards with a new intensity. Traditional earthy reds and browns were also in evidence, but were these invariably brightened by the juxtaposition of gold or yellow.

While strong and vivid colors remained popular in many households until the end of the century, a reaction to their use soon began to set in. Favored Aesthetic Movement colors included ivory, pale gray, and olive green ("greenery-yallery"). The latter, along with burgundy, old rose, hyacinth blue, and ebony (for wood), also proved popular in Arts and Crafts houses. Meanwhile, Art Nouveau schemes featured off white, muted greens, lilacs, purples, and black.

1 2

3 4

1 **Glidden/Heritage Colors** Color **Brunswick green 48GY11249** Composition and finish *water-based:* **flat, silk, soft sheen** *oil-based:* **dead flat, eggshell, gloss** Price ★ [W] [C]

2 **Old Village Paints** Color **soldier blue 1208** Composition and finish *oil-based:* **satin** Price ★★★

3 **Pratt & Lambert/Interior Wall & Trim** Color **osprey 1292** Composition and finish *water-based:* **flat, satin, eggshell, semigloss, gloss** Price ★★ [W] [F]

4 **Grand Illusions/Traditional Paints** Color **duck egg blue** Composition and finish *water-based:* **flat** Price ★★ [W] [F]

5 **The Stulb Company** Color **Windsor chair pink 81.2000.2** Composition and finish **milk paint** Price ★★★ [W] [F]

6 **Farrow & Ball/National Trust Range** Color **eating room red 43/U/C 49** Composition and finish *water-based:* **distemper, flat** *oil-based:* **distemper, dead flat, eggshell, gloss** Price ★★ [W]

7 **Paint Library** Color **Galway blazer** Composition and finish *water-based:* **flat, silk, eggshell, gloss** *oil-based:* **dead flat** Price ★★★ [W] [F]

8 **Glidden/Trade Color Palette** Color **09YR 11/476** Composition and finish *water-based:* **flat, silk, soft sheen** *oil-based:* **dead flat, eggshell, gloss** Price ★ [W] [C]

9 **J. W. Bollom/Bromel** Color **RAL 4005** Composition and finish *water-based:* **flat, silk** *oil-based:* **eggshell, gloss** Price ★★ [W] [C]

10 **Sanderson/Spectrum** Color **imperial purple 54-18U** Composition and finish *water-based:* **flat, silk** *oil-based:* **gloss** Price ★★ [W] [C]

5

6

7

8

9

10

RESEARCHING AUTHENTIC COLORS

During the the 20th century, considerable research was undertaken on both sides of the Atlantic to establish authentic period color schemes, work pioneered during the first half of the century by the influential English restorers and decorators Nancy Lancaster and John Fowler. The paints shown here are from a palette of 18th- and 19th-century colors produced by the English company Fired Earth following a research and development program carried out in conjunction with the Victoria & Albert Museum in London, England.

1

1 **Fired Earth/Victoria & Albert Museum** Color **Morris green** Composition and finish *water-based:* **distemper, flat** *oil-based:* **dead flat, eggshell** Price ★★ [W] [C]

2 **Fired Earth/Victoria & Albert Museum** Color **aconite yellow** Composition and finish *water-based:* **distemper, flat** *oil-based:* **dead flat** Price ★★ [W] [C]

3 **Fired Earth/Victoria & Albert Museum** Color **periwinkle blue** Composition and finish *water-based:* **distemper, flat** *oil-based:* **dead flat, eggshell** Price ★★ [W] [C]

4 **Fired Earth/Victoria & Albert Museum** Color **madder red** Composition and finish *water-based:* **distemper, flat** *oil-based:* **dead flat, eggshell** Price ★★ [W] [C]

2

3

4

19th century

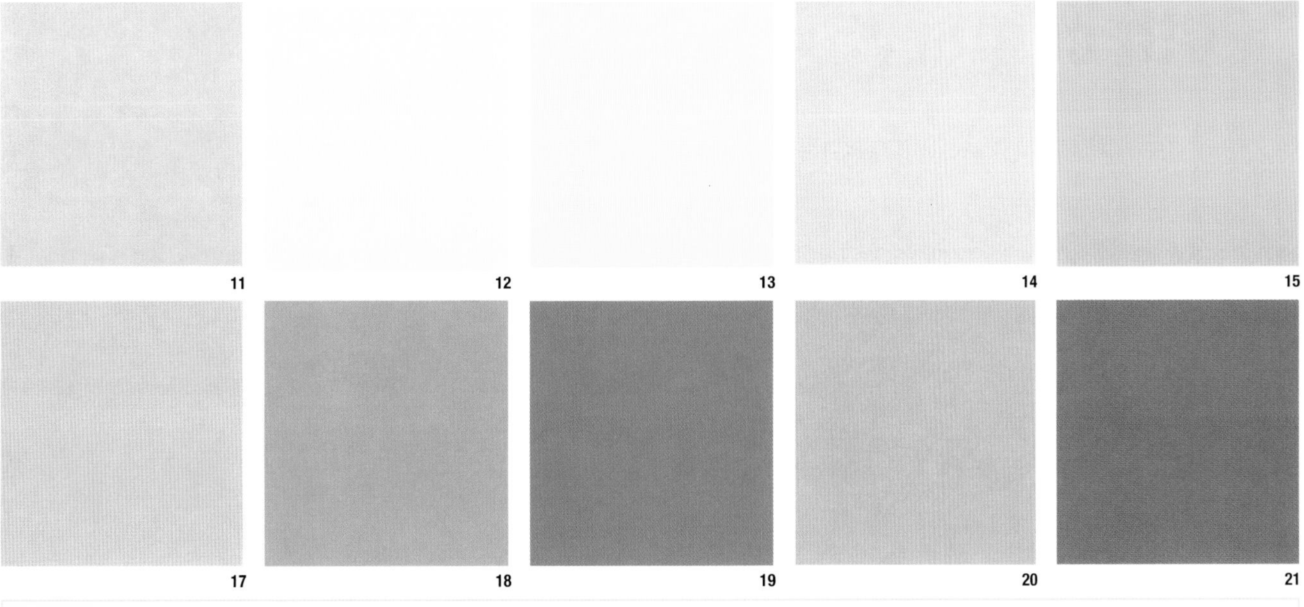

11 Glidden/Heritage Colors Color **French gray 16BB50066** Composition and finish *water-based:* **flat, silk, soft sheen** *oil-based:* **dead flat, eggshell, gloss** Price ★ W C

12 Finnaren & Haley/Shades of '76 Color **marblehead 520183** Composition and finish *water-based:* **flat, satin, semigloss, gloss** *oil-based:* **semigloss** Price ★ W

13 Pittsburgh Paints/Designacolor System Color **Boston creme 2514** Composition and finish *water-based:* **flat, satin, eggshell, gloss** *oil-based:* **satin, gloss** Price ★ W F

14 Sherwin Williams/Preservation Palette Color **Downing sand SW 2822** Composition and finish *water-based:* **flat, satin, semigloss** *oil-based:* **semigloss** Price ★★ W

15 The Stulb Company Color **fancy chair yellow 74.2000.1** Composition and finish **milk paint** Price ★★★ W F

16 Paint Library Color **Ming** Composition and finish *water-based:* **flat, silk, eggshell, gloss** *oil-based:* **dead flat** Price ★★★ W F

17 Sherwin Williams/Preservation Palette Color **Queen Anne lilac SW 0021** Composition and finish *water-based:* **flat, satin, semigloss** *oil-based:* **semigloss** Price ★★ W

18 Grand Illusions/Traditional Paints Color **fresco pink** Composition and finish *water-based:* **flat** Price ★★ W F

19 Finnaren & Haley/Shades of '76 Color **Saybrook ivory 520800** Composition and finish *water-based:* **flat, satin, semigloss, gloss** *oil-based:* **semigloss** Price ★★★ W

20 Farrow & Ball/National Trust Range Color **ointment pink** Composition and finish *water-based:* **distemper** *oil-based:* **distemper, dead flat, eggshell, gloss** Price ★★ W

21 Sherwin Williams/Preservation Palette Color **Rookwood clay SW2823** Composition and finish *water-based:* **flat, satin, semigloss** *oil-based:* **semigloss** Price ★★ W

THE FEDERAL PALETTE

During the 18th and 19th centuries, the colors used in North American interiors were strongly influenced by those that were fashionable in Britain and France. This was particularly evident in the southern states of America, where rich plantation owners vied with one another to decorate their mansions in the most up-to-date Continental styles. Consequently, during the first half of the 19th century, the "Colonial-Federal palette," which had combined earth colors such as almond, rust red, and red-brown with bright blues, greens, and yellows, was gradually superseded by a later "Federal palette" that favored terracottas, deep pinks, milky yellows, lavender, and various stone colors, including several shades of gray.

1

1 Ace Royal/Interior Wall Paint Color **bouquet yellow** Composition and finish *water-based:* **flat, eggshell, semigloss** Price ★★ W

2

2 Glidden/Trade Color Palette Color **MYR 13/558** Composition and finish *water-based:* **flat, silk, soft sheen** *oil-based:* **dead flat, eggshell, gloss** Price ★ W C

Walls painted milky yellow provide the backdrop to a late 1830s, flame-cut mahogany settee in the Old Merchant's House in New York. Yellow walls enlivened with gilt-framed paintings were particularly fashionable in the mid-19th century.

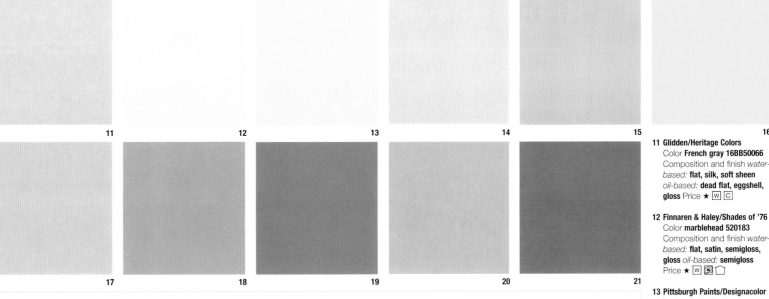

Paints: **20th century**

A significant development in the manufacture and use of paints during the 20th century was the general replacement of limewash as a decorative finish for plaster, initially with whitewash (in the first half of the century), and then with highly stable, water-based latex emulsions (in the second half of the century). Other advances included a dramatic increase in the number of colors available, primarily as a result of the development of new synthetic dyes and more sophisticated methods of manufacture.

Aesthetically, the most enduring trend was the widespread adoption of predominantly white and off white color schemes (*see* "Brilliant White" below), with pale colors such as buff, beige, coffee, pastel blues and pinks, and pale green (*eau de nil*) also proving popular starting in the 1930s.

Paralleling the fashion for light hues was a vogue for combining stronger, hotter colors, which began in the 1920s (*see* opposite), but was also particularly evident in the 1960s and 1990s. In the 1990s there was also a revival of period color schemes–particularly medieval and 18th and 19th centuries–and an accompanying increase in the production of authentic period colors.

1

2

3

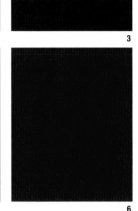

4

5

6

1 **Sherwin Williams/Preservation Palette** Color **Burma jade SW 2862** Composition and finish *water-based:* **flat, satin, semigloss** *oil-based:* **semigloss** Price ★★ [W] [C]

2 **Glidden/Heritage Colors** Color **eau de nil 15GY44268** Composition and finish *water-based:* **flat, silk, soft sheen** *oil-based:* **dead flat, eggshell, gloss** Price ★ [W] [C]

3 **Jane Churchill** Color **emerald green JCU4** Composition and finish *water-based:* **flat** *oil-based:* **eggshell** Price ★★ [W] [F]

4 **Sherwin Williams/Preservation Palette** Color **holiday turquoise SW0076** Composition and finish *water-based:* **flat, satin, semigloss** *oil-based:* **semigloss** Price ★★ [W] [C]

5 **Habitat/Household Paint** Color **real turquoise** Composition and finish *water-based:* **flat** Price ★★★ [W] [F]

6 **John Oliver** Color **Betty II blue** Composition and finish *water-based:* **flat** Price ★★ [W]

BRILLIANT WHITE

The fashion for all white color schemes, or predominantly white schemes offset with stone-colored surfaces (such as a single wall, fireplace, or floor), began early in the 20th century. For example, in 1904, Cowtan & Sons, an English decorating company, noted "We seem to have done everything flatted white or enamelled white paint," while in the late 1920s Syrie Maugham created the influential "All White Room" at her London home and Elsie de Wolfe produced similar interiors in the United States. This enthusiasm for white grew under the influence of the Modernist Movement, and as manufacturers produced increasingly "pure" brilliant whites (often by adding a little blue). However, it was also underpinned by practical considerations: White no longer dirtied as quickly following a general crackdown on fossil fuel-generated air pollution.

Paint Library Color **York stone** Composition and finish *water-based:* **flat, silk, eggshell, gloss** *oil-based:* **dead flat** Price ★★★ [W] [F]

Crown/Emulsion Color **pure brilliant white** Composition and finish *water-based:* **flat, silk** Price ★★ [W] [C]

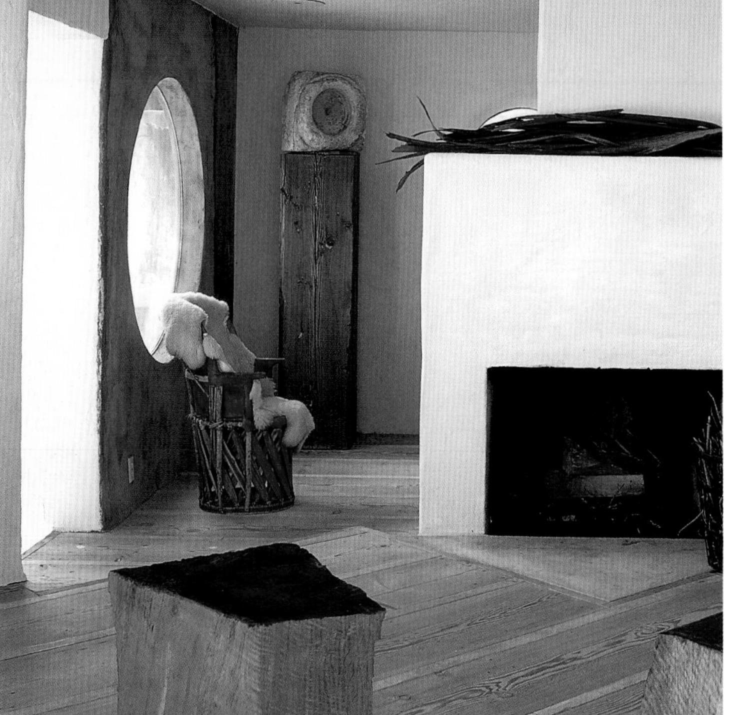

Walls and ceilings painted white provide an unobtrusive, neutral background for the natural colors and textures of a collection of functional and decorative wooden artifacts in designer Ivy Rosequist's 20th-century, cliffside home in California.

7 Crown/Emulsion for Walls and Ceilings Color **dusty rose** Composition and finish *water-based:* **flat, silk** Price ★★ [W] [C]

8 Aalto Country Colors Color **frock** Composition and finish *water-based:* **flat** Price ★★ [W] [C]

9 Sanderson/Spectrum Color **London gray** Composition and finish *water-based:* **flat, silk** *oil-based:* **eggshell, gloss** Price ★★ [W] [C]

10 Glidden/Heritage Colors Color **0710 Y10R** Composition and finish *water-based:* **flat, silk, soft sheen** *oil-based:* **dead flat, eggshell, gloss** Price ★ [W] [C]

11 Jane Churchill Color **primrose 12** Composition and finish *water-based:* **flat** Price ★★ [W] [F]

12 Aalto Country Colors Color **turmeric** Composition and finish *water-based:* **flat** Price ★★ [W] [C]

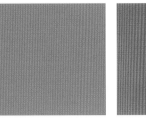

7

8

9

10

11

12

HOT COLORS

While predominantly white color schemes proved popular throughout the 20th century, there was also a significant and contrasting fashion for using combinations of hot, vivid colors. This can be traced back to the *Exposition des Arts Décoratifs*, held in Paris, France, in 1925, which launched the Art Deco Movement internationally. Colors on show at the exhibition included ultramarine, sea green, deep blue, turmeric yellow, black, crimson, burnt orange, and hot pink; these tints have remained in fashion ever since.

J. W. Bollom Color **mandarin 06E51 JWB74** Composition and finish *water-based:* **flat, silk** *oil-based:* **eggshell, gloss** Price ★★ [W] [C]

John Oliver Color **kinky pink** Composition and finish *water-based:* **flat** *oil-based:* **eggshell, gloss** Price ★★ [W]

This living room is painted and furnished in pink, beige, orange, and black. The scheme is 1990s, but the color combinations originated Art Deco interiors in the1920s.

13 Habitat/Household Paint Color **abstract green** Composition and finish *water-based:* **flat** Price ★★★ [W] [F]

14 Glidden/Trade Color Palette Color **72YY 47/743** Composition and finish *water-based:* **flat, silk, soft sheen** *oil-based:* **dead flat, eggshell, gloss** Price ★ [W] [C]

15 Brats/Mediterranean Palette Color **Tuscany (7) 107** Composition and finish *water-based:* **flat** Price ★ [W]

16 Sherwin Williams/Preservation Palette Color **pink flamingo SW0080** Composition and finish *water-based:* **flat, satin, semigloss** *oil-based:* **semigloss** Price ★★ [W] [C]

17 Ace Royal/Interior Wall Paint Color **laser red** Composition and finish *water-based:* **flat** *oil-based:* **satin, semigloss** Price ★★ [W]

18 Aalto Country Colors Color **highland red** Composition and finish *water-based:* **flat** Price ★★ [W] [C]

13

14

15

16

17

18

19

19 Aalto Country Colors Color **Bora Bora** Composition and finish *water-based:* **flat** Price ★★ [W] [C]

20 Crown/Solo Gloss for Wood and Metal Work Color **coffee** Composition and finish *oil-based:* **gloss** Price ★★

21 Ace Royal/Exterior Colors Color **maybe Monday** Composition and finish *water-based:* **flat** *oil-based:* **satin, semigloss** Price ★★ [W]

22 Paint Magic/Color Collection Color **Matisse blue** Composition and finish *water-based:* **flat** Price ★★ [W]

20

21

22

THANKFULLY,

INSPIRATION

IS OF

NO FIXED

ABODE.

Specialist Paints & Waxes

Whether hand-mixed by 18th-century itinerant craftsmen, or mass-produced in 20th-century factories, most paints have been designed to cover plaster, masonry, or wooden surfaces with a smooth, opaque film of color. The majority have simply been used to decorate and protect a surface, and even though they mask the underlying material they do not disguise what it is, nor are they intended to do so. But there are some specialist paints and waxes that are intended to visually transform plaster, masonry, or wood into a different material, or replicate another decorative medium. These include metallic paints and gilt creams, which simulate base or precious metals; liming pastes, which reproduce the bleaching effects of quicklime on wood; textured paints that mimic decorative plasterwork; multicolored paints that look like stonework or ceramics; and "broken color" applications that replicate the fugitive pigmentation of early paints, or simply confer an abstract pattern on a surface.

LEFT The built-in closet in the bathroom of this 19th-century town house in London, England, would originally have been painted or grained to match the woodwork. It now boasts a silver metallic paint finish that is more in keeping with the decorating style of 1990s. The silver paint also works harmoniously with the wall mirror, serving to brighten the room.

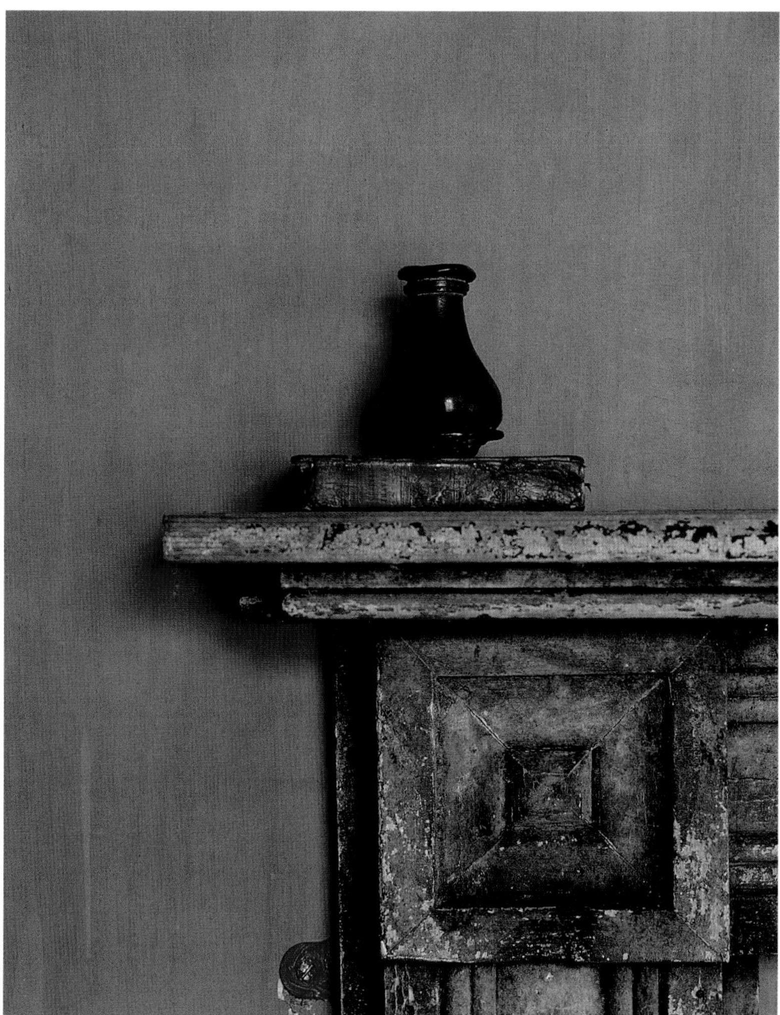

ABOVE Set against a dark, terracotta-colored, limewashed wall, this fire surround has been given a painted a faux marble finish. During the last quarter of the 20th century, many paint manufacturers produced paint kits (complete with specialist applicators) for producing faux marble, faux porphyry, and wood-grained finishes on plaster and wood.

ABSTRACT FINISHES

During the latter part of the 20th century, "broken color" techniques, such as ragging, sponging, stippling, spattering, dragging, and combing, proved very popular. Derived from fine art, these techniques involve applying paints and glazes over a contrasting colored base to produce subtle patterns and gradations of color. Manufacturers often put together kits with paints and application tools designed for this purpose. This example is an abstract pattern; others may simulate stone.

KEY PAINT EFFECTS

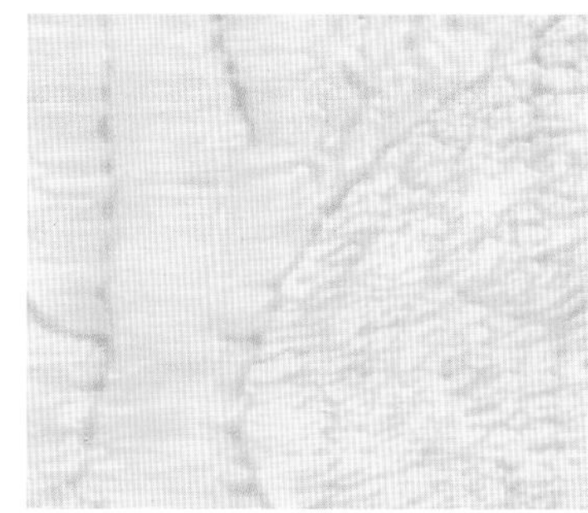

1 Many manufacturers supply paints designed to reproduce distressed finishes, such as ragging and rag-rolling, or to simulate materials such as porphyry.

2 Textured paints have been available since the early 20th century, and are mostly used to simulate the appearance of rustic plasterwork.

3 Gilt creams and waxes have been used since the Renaissance as an easy alternative to the traditional method of gilding wooden furniture and woodwork with metal leaf or metallic powders.

4 Paints that produce a coating that imitates beaten and hammered metal, available in a range of colors and finishes, became particularly popular in the late 20th century.

1 **Glidden/Duette** Color **coral cascade** Composition and finish *water-based:* **flat** Price ★★ [W] [C]

2 **Berger/Textures** Color **heavy texture with marble chips** Composition and finish *solvent-based:* **marble/stone** Price ★★★ [W] [C]

3 **Liberon Waxes** Color **Fontainebleau** Composition and finish *spirit-based:* **satin sheen** Price ★★★

4 **Trimite/Hammer Finishes** Color **stoving red 811** Composition and finish *water-based:* **metallic** Price ★★

ABOVE The *chinoiserie* decoration on this four-poster bed has been executed in shades of gold metallic paint on a black oil-painted background. The soft, flat finish was achieved by applying clear matte polyurethane varnish, lightly rubbed with fine-grade wire wool.

Specialist Paints & Waxes

Metallic paints can be used on metal, wood, and plaster and are available in a wide range of colors. They are also produced in a range of different textures, including smooth, hammered, and metallic cloth. Gilt creams and waxes, on the other hand, are always burnished smooth. When they are used on moldings, they replicate leaf- or powder-gilding. The colors include copper and shades of gold and silver.

Liming kits are sold as hard waxes and soft pastes: The former is used on open-grained hardwoods, such as oak, the latter on close-grained softwoods, such as pine. Some contain lime, which bleaches the wood a gray-white hue; others mimic this by depositing flecks of whiting (chalk powder) in the grain.

Textured paints are mainly used to disguise cracked plaster, and are patterned with a serrated tool in imitation of the random swirls of rustic plasterwork. Similarly, most paints that mimic the appearance of ceramics (notably earthenware) and decorative stones (such as porphyry), or simulate the breakdown of pigments seen in pre-20th-century paints, are distressed with a specialist tool, or a brush or rag (*see* opposite). A few are sold with an applicator that spatters colors randomly on top of one another.

1

2

3

4

5

6

1 **Craig & Rose/Metallic Finishes–Hammer** Color **steel** Composition and finish *oil-based:* **glossy metallic** Price ★★★

2 **Tor Coatings/Ardenbrite** Color **old penny bronze/35** Composition and finish *spirit-based:* **satin** Price ★★

3 **Paint Library/Metallic Paint** Color **westwood** Composition and finish *water-based:* **metallic** Price ★★★★

4 **Tor Coatings/Ardenbrite** Color **black enamel** Composition and finish *spirit-based:* **satin** Price ★★

5 **Liberon Waxes** Color **gilt cream chantilly** Composition and finish *spirit-based:* **satin sheen** Price ★★★★

6 **Paint Library/Metallic Paint** Color **ottolene** Composition and finish *water-based:* **metallic** Price ★★★★

7

8

9

FAUX STONE FINISHES

Since Greek and Roman times, "broken color" techniques, such as ragging, sponging, stippling, and spattering have been employed to simulate stones such as marble, limestone, sandstone, granite, and prophyry. Faux stone finishes have been used on architectural fixtures and fittings, and on furniture and decorative artifacts when the natural material has been unavailable, too expensive, or structurally unsuitable. In the past the authenticity of the finish has depended on the skills of the person applying it, but the specialist faux stone paint kits now available help guarantee effective results even for novices.

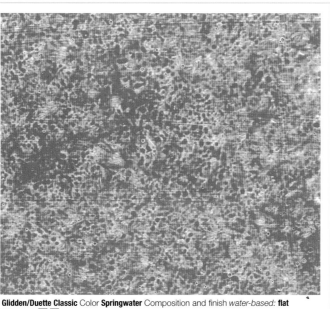

Glidden/Duette Classic Color **Springwater** Composition and finish *water-based:* **flat** Price ★★ W C

10

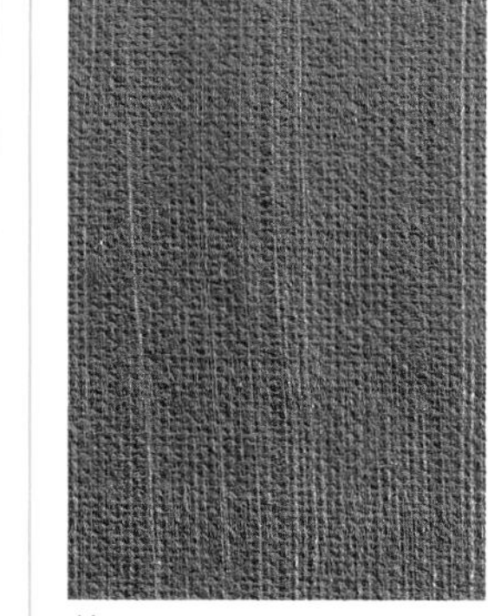

11

7 Berger/Luxatile Epoxy Polyurethane System Color **white** Composition and finish *solvent-based:* **high sheen, gloss** Price ★★ W C

8 Glidden/Sonata Color **pyjama blue** Composition and finish *water-based:* **flat** Price ★★ W C

9 Berger/Textures Color **stoneshield** Composition and finish *solvent-based:* **marble/stone** Price ★★★ W C

10 Trimite/Hammer Finishes Color **dark green/828** Composition and finish *water-based:* **metallic** Price ★★

11 Paint Library/Metallic Paint Color **Atlantic** Composition and finish *water-based:* **metallic** Price ★★★★ W

12 Artex/Decorative Textured Finishes Color **white** Composition and finish *water-based:* **textured** Price ★ W C

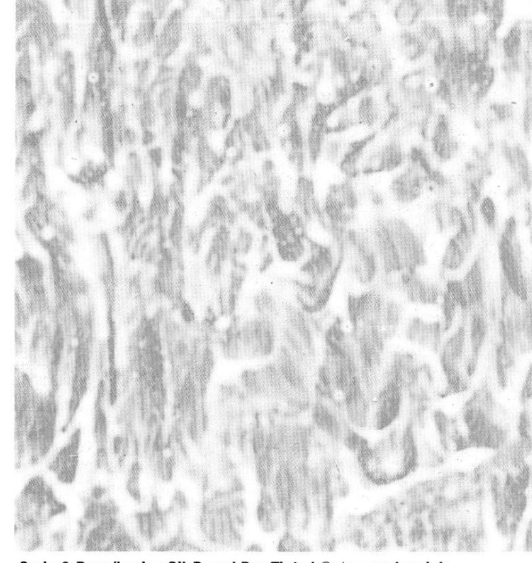

Craig & Rose/Luxine Oil-Based Pre-Tinted Color **smoke pink** Composition and finish *oil-based:* **flat** Price ★★ W

The Stencil Store/Paint Effects Color **earthenware pink** Composition and finish *water-based:* **flat** Price ★★★ W

12

Wood Finishes

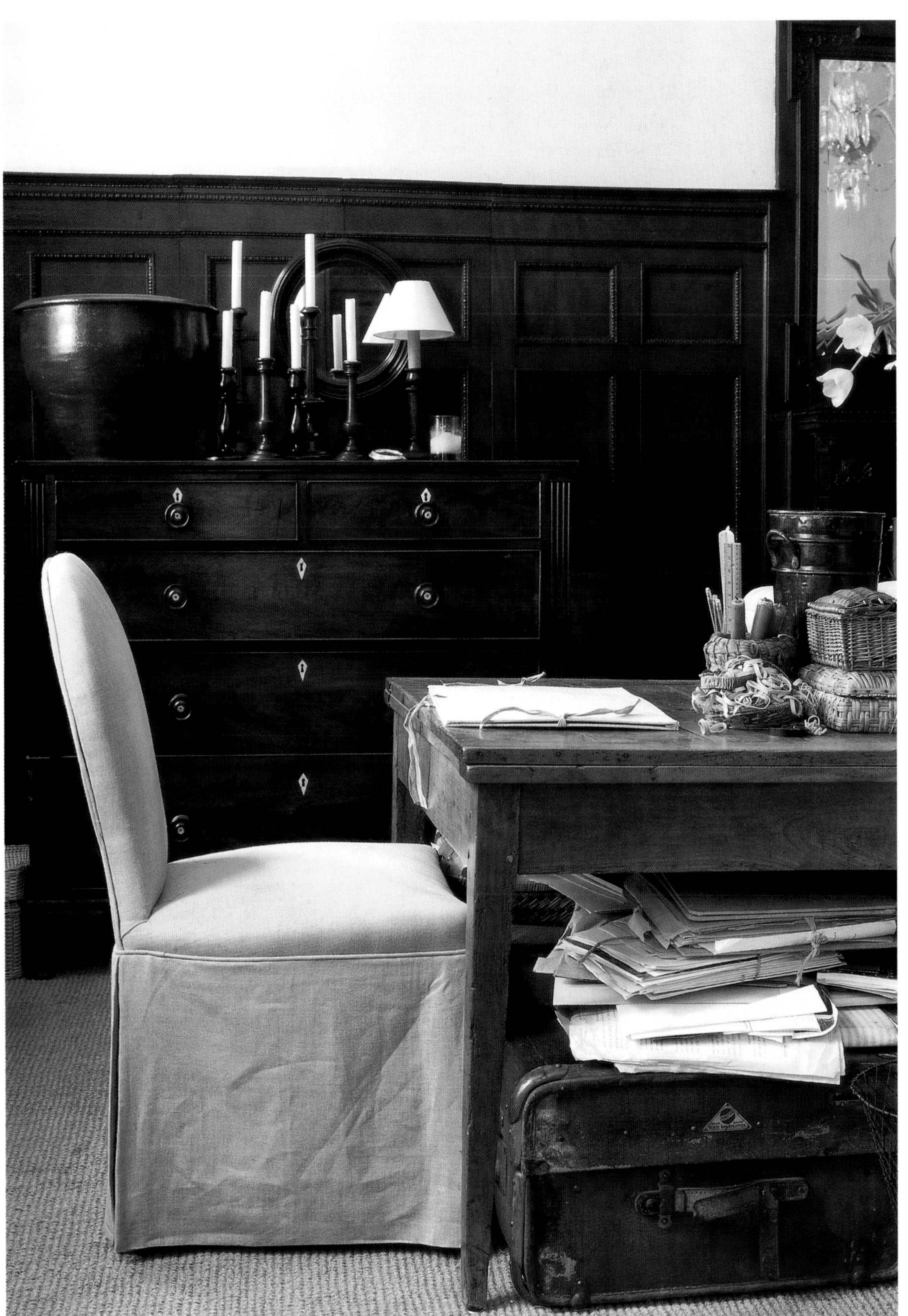

Unless heavily diluted, paints dry to an opaque finish and thus obliterate the natural appearance of any wooden surface. Therefore, they have traditionally been discarded in favor of translucent and semitranslucent stains and varnishes when the goal has been to highlight the figuring and grain of a particular wood. This is especially true in the case of hardwoods, such as walnut, mahogany, and oak, which display more attractive markings than their softwoods counterparts, such as pine and fir among others.

Wood stains are available in various formulations (*see* pages 296–7). Some are intended for external woodwork, others for internal wood and furniture. Some offer protection against moisture and general wear and tear in a single coat, while others require an additional application of varnish or shellac and wax. However, the real versatility of wood stains resides in the colors available, which range from "natural" hues, such as brown or red mahogany, ebony, and pine, to "non-naturalistic" tones, such as shades of blue, green, and gray.

LEFT This 18th-century mahogany chest has been restored using a dark brown, water-based mahogany stain which has then been shellacked and polished–the traditional finish. The half-height wall-paneling, typical of both Georgian and later Arts and Crafts interiors, has been treated in the same manner.

KEY FINISHES

1 Oil-based stains produce pure, transparent colors on wood, and since the 1970s have often been formulated to allow moisture to evaporate rather than remain trapped in the wood.

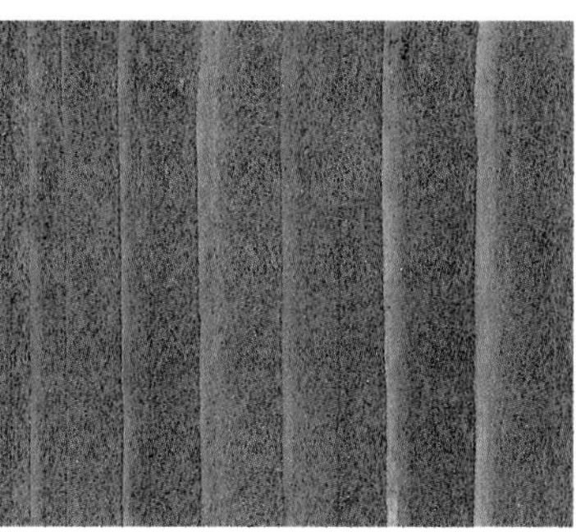

2 Many interior water-based stains require additional varnishing to make the wood waterproof. However, those designed for exterior use repel water and have antifungal properties.

3 Many chemical-based stains produce color by reacting with the tannic acid that is present in wood. This light oak stain is designed for exterior use and formulated to resist cracking, peeling, and flaking.

4 Nowadays manufacturers often incorporate pigments in solvent- or spirit-based stains that help to filter out ultraviolet rays, thereby reducing the fading of darker colors constantly exposed to sunlight.

1 **Auro Organic Paints/Woodstains** Color **ultramarinblau nr. 130-21** Composition and finish *oil-based:* **satin** Price ★★★★

2 **Protim Solignum/Fencetone** Color **golden cedar** Composition and finish *water-based:* **flat** Price ★★★

3 **Dacrylate/Nordac Wood Shades** Color **light oak** Composition and finish *chemical-based:* **natural** Price ★★

4 **Glidden/Weathershield Exterior Wood Stain** Color **ebony** Composition and finish *solvent-based:* **transparent satin** Price ★★★

ABOVE The cabinet, mirror frame, tongue-and-groove dado cladding and butt-jointed floorboards in this bathroom are made of pine. They have been coated with clear varnish to protect them against moisture. The contrasting wooden rim of the bath has been mahogany stained and clear varnished.

RIGHT This late 20th-century dining table stands on lightly limed, butt-jointed pine floorboards in the main living area of a restored 19th-century malt house in Somerset, England. The table is made of elm and has a clear, beeswax polish finish that allows the natural color and figuring of the wood to show through.

Wood Finishes

There are four basic types of wood stains: Water-, oil-, spirit-, and chemical-based. Water-based stains produce clear, vivid colors that are well suited to light, close-grained woods, such as beech and pine. Water-based stains raise the grain of the wood, which then needs sanding before varnishing, or shellacking and waxing.

Oil-based stains do not raise the grain nor do they have to be varnished or shellacked; also, they produce more even and transparent coloration on both hardwoods and softwoods. If the stains are spirit-based, the colors are muted and the grain is raised. Spirit-based stains are best suited to oily or hard, fine-grained woods, especially before French polishing.

Chemical stains are many and varied. Notable types include biochromate of potash, which turns beech a light tan and walnut a pale yellow, and blue copperas, which gives most woods a light gray hue. However, exact coloration is unpredictable since it is affected by the level of tannic acid in the wood.

1

1 **Ronseal/All-in-One Quick & Simple Woodstain** Color **walnut** Composition and finish *oil-based:* **satin, gloss** Price ★★★

2 **Cabot Stains/O.V.T. Solid Color Stains** Color **oracle sun** Composition and finish *oil-based:* **matte** Price ★★

3 **Cabot/O.V.T. Solid Color Stains** Color **Chesapeake** Composition and finish *oil-based:* **flat** Price ★★

4 **Auro Organic Paints/Woodstains** Color **grau Nr. 130-11** Composition and finish *oil-based:* **satin** Price ★★★★

5 **Protim Solignum/Timbertone** Color **petrol blue** Composition and finish *oil-based:* **translucent flat, translucent sheen** Price ★★★

6 **Paint Magic/Liming Paste** Color **natural** Composition and finish *water-based:* **matte** Price ★★★

7 **Glidden/Protective Woodstain** Color **elderberry** Composition and finish *solvent-based:* **transparent satin** Price ★★★

2

3

5

6

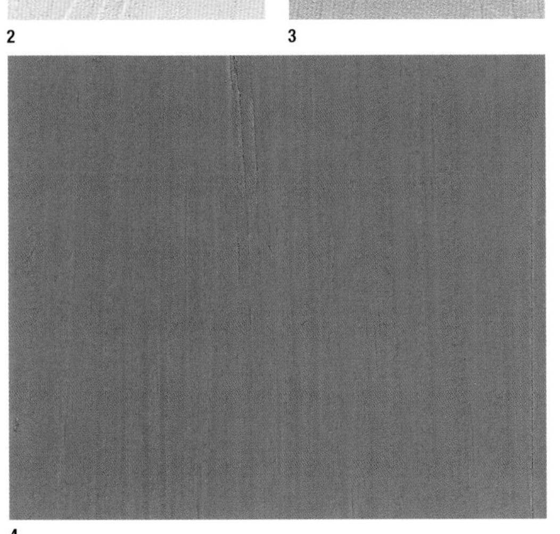
4

7

8

9

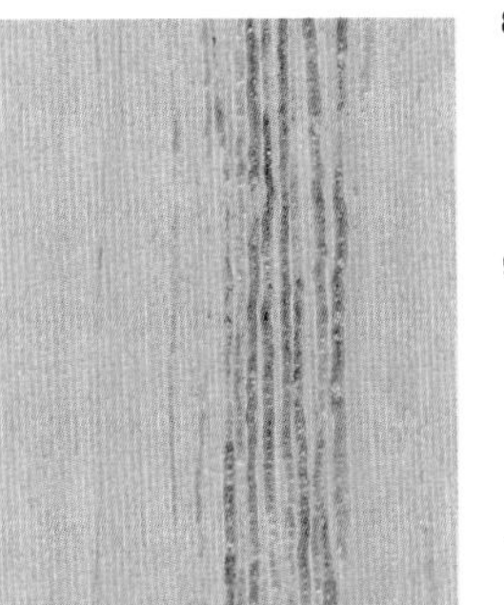

10

8 Auro Organic Paints/ Woodstains Color **orange Nr. 130-02** Composition and finish *oil-based:* **satin** Price ★★★

9 Cuprinol/Interior Quick Drying Woodstain Color **brown mahogany** Composition and finish *oil-based:* **semitransparent satin** Price ★★★

10 Cuprinol/Quick Drying Wood Dye Color **light oak** Composition and finish *oil-based:* **semitransparent satin** Price ★★★

11

11 Glidden/Weathershield Exterior Woodstain Color **antique pine** Composition and finish *solvent-based:* **flat** Price ★★★

12 Glidden/Protective Woodstain Color **watermelon** Composition and finish *solvent-based:* **transparent satin** Price ★★

13 Rustins/Colorglaze Transparent Satin Colors Color **gray** Composition and finish *oil-based:* **satin** Price ★★

14 Rustins/Colorglaze Color **yellow** Composition and finish *oil-based:* **satin** Price ★★

12

13

MICROPOROUS WOOD STAINS & VARNISHES

Anyone who wants to produce a durable, decorative finish on wooden surfaces has to contend with the fact that timber readily absorbs moisture in the atmosphere and from any material with which it is in contact. When it is warm and humidity levels drop, the moisture evaporates, causing traditional stains and varnishes that seal the surface to "bubble" and eventually lift off. However, manufacturers have recently formulated microporous stains and varnishes that allow moisture to evaporate through them without causing such damage.

Dacrylate Paints/Nordac Wood Shades Color **pine** Composition and finish *chemical-based:* **natural** Price ★★

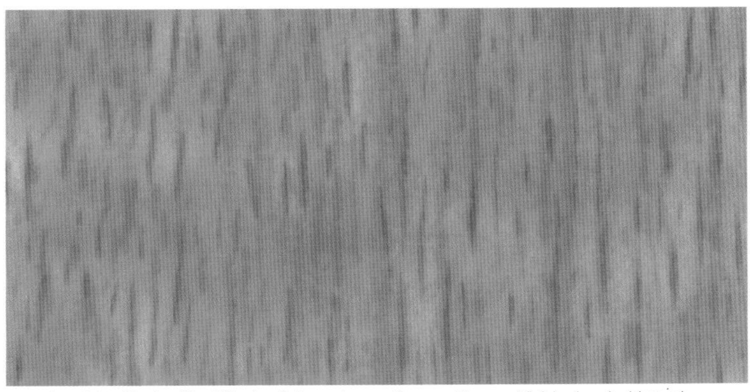

Dacrylate Paints/Nordac Wood Shades Color **mahogany** Composition and finish *chemical-based:* **natural** Price ★★

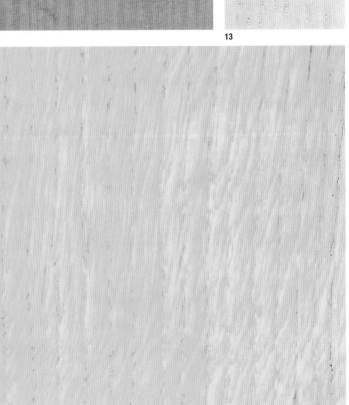

14

Tiles

Plain Tiles

ABOVE This bathroom in the Rockcliffe Mansion in Hannibal, Missouri, is typical of a luxury bathroom installation of the late 19th century. It features plain white tiles that have been laid in brick fashion with relief-molded capping. Similar arrangements of tiles were popular until the mid-1930s.

In the middle of the 12th century, plain tiles were used in large numbers on the floors of churches, cathedrals, and royal palaces throughout Europe. Most were made locally using red-firing clays, often with a honey-colored lead glaze to minimize wear. This was sometimes applied over a layer of white slip to produce yellow tiles, while the addition of a little copper to the glaze gave a range of greens.

Plain, unglazed quarry tiles were very popular during the 18th and early 19th centuries, but in the mid-19th century these were superseded by the flatter, smoother tiles that were produced by Herbert Minton using the dust-pressing technique invented by the Englishman Richard Prosser in 1840. Initially conceived as a method of making ceramic buttons from dried clay, Minton realized that this technique could also be used to form ceramic *tesserae* and larger tiles. Plain tiles have been popular ever since. In Art Nouveau schemes, pastel-shaded tiles were particularly popular, while red-and-black tiles were dominant in the Art Deco interiors of the late 1920s and the 1930s. In more recent years the plain, "rustic" tile has become fashionable once again.

LEIGHTON HOUSE

Early mosaics, made up of thousands of small, plain tiles, often featured Islamic-inspired patterns. The mosaic panel shown here, with a geometric floral pattern, is from the entrance hall of Leighton House in London, England. The artist Lord Leighton displayed his large collection of Islamic tiles in the "Arab Hall." The walls and ceilings were clad with original 16th- and 17th-century Iznik tiles, with the reproductions made by his friend William de Morgan to complete damaged panels.

RIGHT A simple but effective floor pattern has been achieved here by using just two colors of plain tile, laid alternately. This style of floor has its origins in medieval cathedrals across Europe and was often recreated during the Renaissance using black and white marble.

KEY DESIGNS

1 Natural stone has always been used for flooring. Recycled limestone tiles and ceramic tiles imitating natural materials are now in vogue.

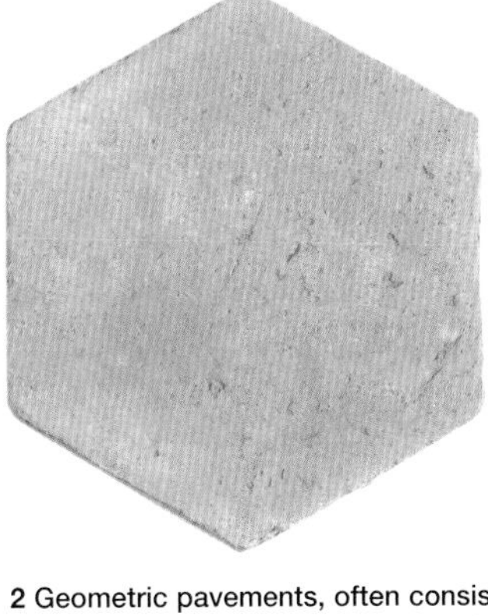

2 Geometric pavements, often consisting of triangular, hexagonal, or rectangular-shaped plain tiles, enjoyed a renaissance in the late 20th century.

3 The humble, unglazed quarry tile has been used for centuries as a hard and durable floor covering. Plain terracotta tiles have become very fashionable in homes in recent years.

4 Glazed tiles, with an uneven, slightly translucent appearance, were much liked in the mid-19th century. The Victorians favored this "handmade" look on their mass-produced tiles.

5 Light-reflective, easy-to-clean white tiles were widely seen during the mid-19th century, and have become almost universally in demand in recent years.

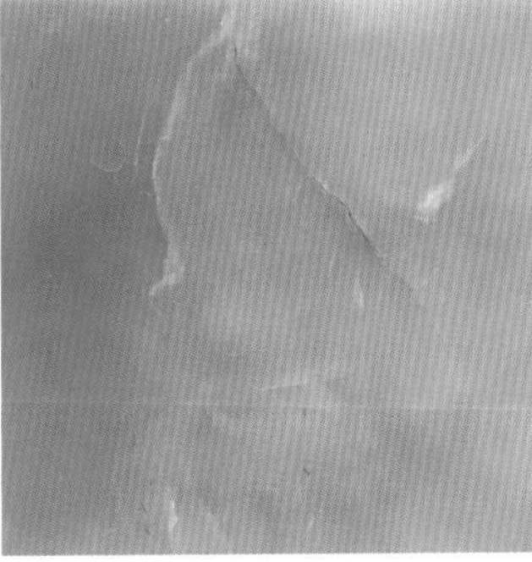

6 Marble, a durable crystalline limestone, is available in an array of colors and patterns. Decorative and practical, it has remained a popular floor covering.

1 **Stonell/Bamboo** Color **gray with rust streak** Alternative colors **available** Composition **slate** Size **4 x 4 x ½in/10 x 10 x 1.2cm** Price ★ [F] [+]

2 **Attica/Hexagono Terracotta** Color **yellow** Alternative colors **available** Composition **terracotta** Size **4 x 4 x ¾in/10 x 10 x 2cm** Price ★ [F]

3 **Elon/Saltillo Square** Color **terracotta** Alternative colors **not available** Composition **terracotta** Size **11¾ x 11¾ x ¾in/30 x 30 x 2cm** Price ★ [F] [+]

4 **Winchester Tile Co/Colors** Color **lime green** Alternative colors **available** Composition **ceramic** Size **4 x 4 x ¼in/ 10.5 x 10.5cm x 7mm** Price ★ [W] [+]

5 **Kenneth Clark Ceramics/Plain Colors G3** Color **crazed white** Alternative colors **available** Composition **ceramic** Size **6 x 6 x ¼in/15 x 15cm x 7mm** Price ★ [W] [+]

6 **Pisani/Onyx Green** Color **green** Alternative colors **available** Composition **marble** Size **12 x 12 x ⅜in/30.5 x 30.5 x 1cm** Price ★★★★★★ [F] [+]

Plains: **Pre-20th century**

Most early plain tiles were simple, single-colored handmade products, formed from the local clays. A glaze was often applied to make a more durable surface or to add to the limited range of colors available. These tiles were used in large quantities on the floors of abbeys, cathedrals, and parish churches throughout Europe.

In 1840, in England, the dust-pressing technique was invented by Richard Prosser. It used dry clay, which was ground into a fine powder, then moistened with water and pressed into shape in a tile press. International interest in this process stemmed from the fact that tiles could now be produced with smoother surfaces and more accurate dimensions. A greater range of colors was also made possible as pigments could be added much more easily to dry clay. Large quantities of dust-pressed tiles were produced for constructing geometric pavements, which relied on the many different colors now available for their decorative effect. The mid-19th century saw a large increase in the production of plain-glazed wall tiles. This was due to the construction of railway stations and new demands for hygiene in hospitals, which created a need for light-reflective, easy-to-clean, durable surfaces.

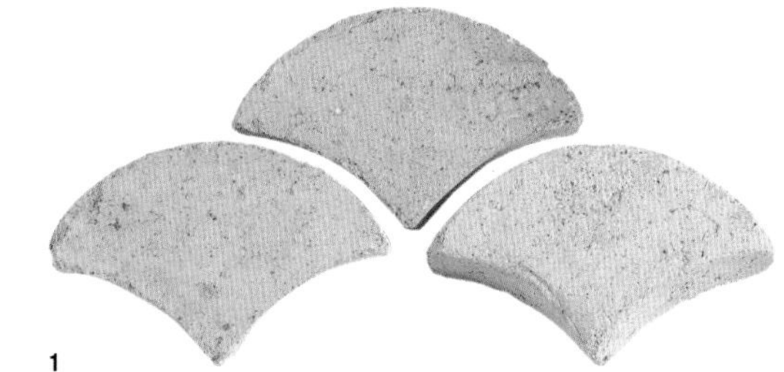
1

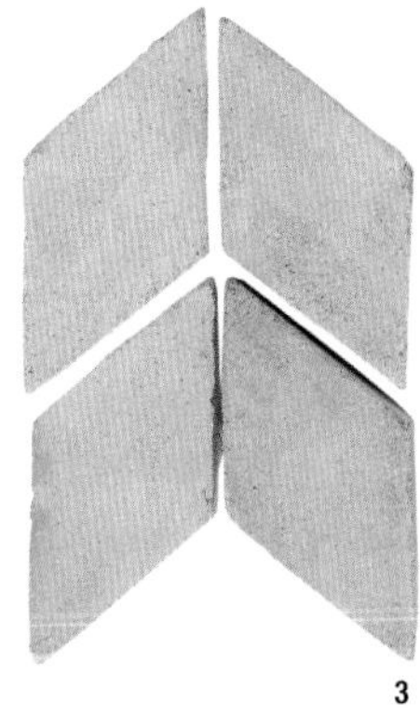
3

2

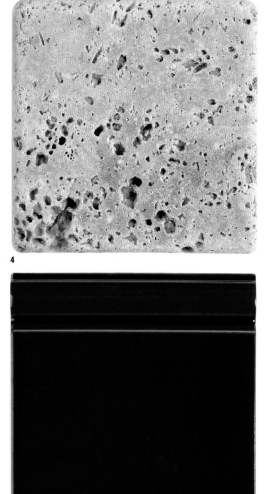

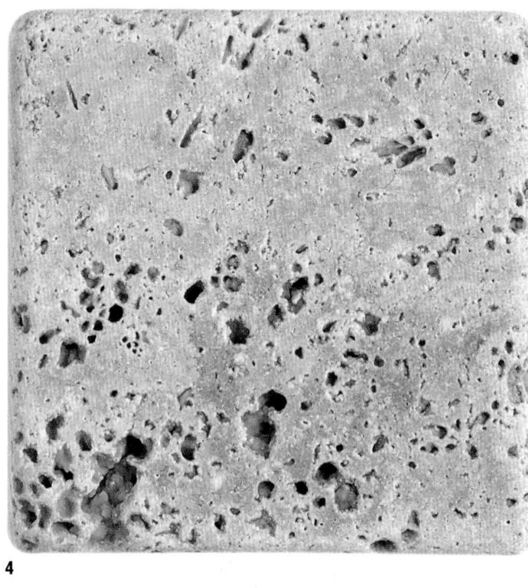
4

5

6

7

8

9

1 **Attica/Scallope** Color **terracotta** Alternative colors **available** Composition **terracotta** Size **2 x 2 x 1¼in/ 5 x 5 x 3cm** Price ★ [F]

2 **Kievel Stone/Fossil Stone** Color **cream** Alternative colors **not available** Composition **limestone** Size **15¾ x 8 x ¼in/40 x 20cm x 7mm** Price ★ [F] [+]

3 **Attica/Rombo** Color **light** Alternative colors **available** Composition **terracotta** Size **3 x 2 x 1¼in/8 x 5 x 3cm** Price ★ [F]

4 **Fired Earth/VM Travertino** Color **travertino** Alternative colors **available** Composition **Venetian marble** Size **4 x 4 x ¾in/10 x 10 x 2cm** Price ★ [F]

5 **Attica/Travertine Inset** Color **white** Alternative colors **available** Composition **terracotta** Size **2 x 2 x ½in/ 5 x 5 x 1.5cm** Price ★ [W] [F]

6 **Marble Flooring Specialists/ Labrador Blue Pearl** Color **blue pearl** Alternative colors **not available** Composition **granite** Size **11¾ x 11¾ x ⅜in/ 30 x 30 x 1cm** Price ★★ [F] [+]

7 **Attica/Quartzite Egyptian Gold** Color **Egyptian gold** Alternative colors **not available** Composition **quartzite** Size **11¾ x 11¾ x ¾in/30 x 30 x 2cm** Price ★ [F] [+]

8 **Original Style/Skirting Tile G9903** Color **royal blue** Alternative colors **available** Composition **ceramic** Size **4 x 4 x ¼in/10 x 10cm x 6mm** Price ★ [W]

9 **Stonell/Mountain Green Slate** Color **mountain green** Alternative colors **not available** Composition **slate** Size **11¾ x 11¾ x ½in/ 30 x 30cm x 9mm** Price ★ [F] [+]

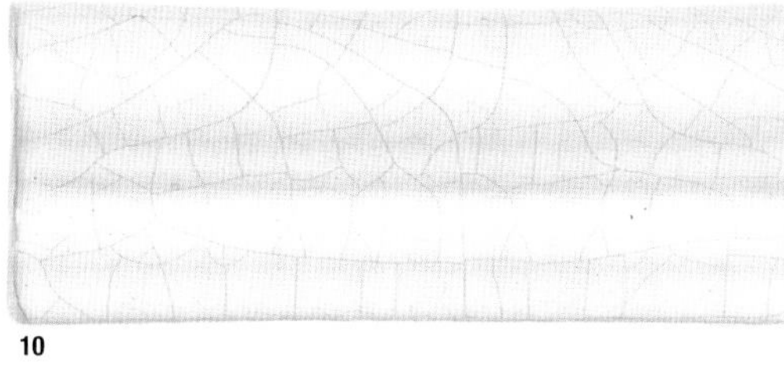
10

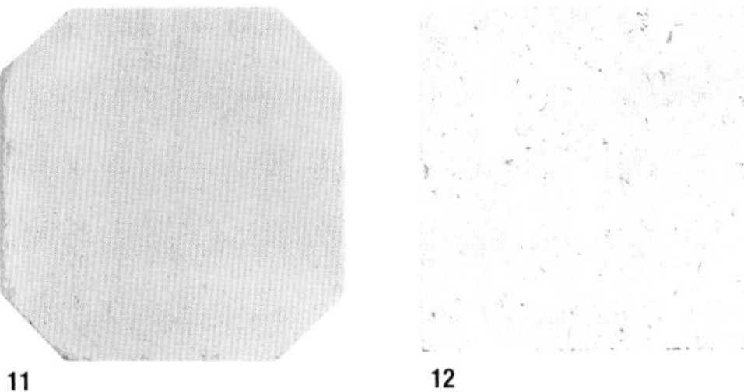
11

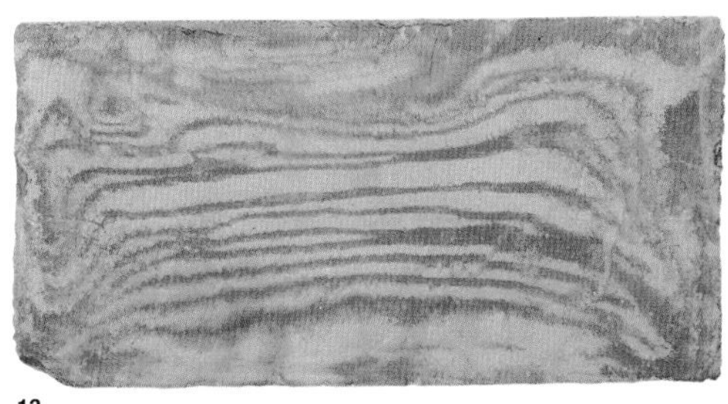
12

13

10 Fired Earth/Valencia Dado Color **crackle** Alternative colors **available** Composition **ceramic** Size **5 x 2 x ¾in/12.5 x 5 x 2cm** Price ★ W

11 Attica/Octagonal Terracotta Color **terracotta** Alternative colors **available** Composition **terracotta** Size **8 x 8 x ¾in/ 20 x 20 x 2cm** Price ★ F

12 Stonell/Firenze Color **white** Alternative colors **not available** Composition **limestone** Size **15¾ x 15¾ x ¾in/40 x 40 x 2cm** Price ★★ F ⊞

13 Attica/Michelato Terracotta Color **terracotta** Alternative colors **not available** Composition **terracotta** Size **14 x 7 x ¾in/36 x 18 x 2cm** Price ★★ F

14 Fired Earth/Roman Mosaic Natural Floor Color **white** Alternative colors **available** Composition **stone** Size **8 x 8 x ½in/20 x 20 x 1.2cm** Price ★★ F

14

NATURAL STONE AND MARBLE

The range of colors available to tilemakers was at one time limited to the natural materials that were available. These materials had an enormous wealth of subtle tones and natural patterning that is still appreciated today. Stone provided a rich variation of subtle hues according to the locality from which it was taken; these ranged from dark slate or granite to pale, warm sandstones. Marble, which has a distinctive, veined appearance, was a more costly alternative to stone. In the case of both stone and marble, most of the durable materials are of neutral, earthy tones.

Attica/Blue English Limestone Color **blue** Alternative colors **not available** Composition **limestone** Size **11¾ x 11¾ x ½in/ 30 x 30 x 1.5cm** Price ★★★ F ⊞

15

16

17

18

19

20

21

15 Fired Earth/Renaissance Inset Color **green** Alternative colors **available** Composition **ceramic** Size **1¼ x 1¼ x ½in/ 3 x 3 x 1.2cm** Price ★ F

16 Elon/Carrillo Plain Color **terracotta** Alternative colors **available** Composition **ceramic** Size **8 x 8 x ⅝in/20 x 20 x 1.5cm** Price ★ W F ⊞

17 Froyle Tiles/Vellum Color **vellum** Alternative colors **available** Composition **stoneware** Size **4 x 4 x ⅜in/ 10 x 10 x 1cm** Price ★ W F ⊞

18 Winchester Tile Co/Colors Color **yellow** Alternative colors **available** Composition **ceramic** Size **5 x 5 x ⅓in/ 12.5 x 12.5cm x 8mm** Price ★ W ⊞

19 Ceramiche Eurotiles/Triangolo Verde AT/5 Color **green** Alternative colors **available** Composition **ceramic** Size **6 x 4 x 4 x ½in/15 x 10 x 10 x 1.2cm** Price ★ W F

20 Original Style/KK5903 Color **foxglove** Alternative colors **available** Composition **ceramic** Size **5½ x 4 x 4 x ¼in/14 x 10 x 10cm x 6mm** Price ★ W

21 Attica/Moss Green Color **moss green** Alternative colors **available** Composition **ceramic** Size **7 x 5 x ½in/ 18 x 13 x 1.5cm** Price ★ W F ⊞

Plains: **20th century**

At the beginning of the 20th century, the Art Nouveau influence began to manifest itself in tile design. Most Art Nouveau tiles were individual designs that were intended to be set among plain tiles within a scheme. However, by the 1920s, plain tiles in pastel shades had become dominant and entire rooms were decorated with them, sometimes with a narrow row of simple black-and-white geometric border tiles set at dado height. Highly glazed tiles gradually became less popular and manufacturers responded by producing eggshell and matte-glazed plain tiles. Stronger colors, including red and black, were used in the late 1920s and early 1930s as Art Deco schemes became increasingly popular. Interest in strong colors on plain tiles was further enhanced as tilemakers employed chemists to develop new glaze colors and effects.

During the 1960s and 1970s, there was a move toward using not only strong colors but also textures and mottling in the decoration of tiles. In the latter part of the 20th century, "rustic" plain tiles, produced by hand or in imitation of hand-production, became popular; variations in shape and shade made them more visually pleasing than their predecessors.

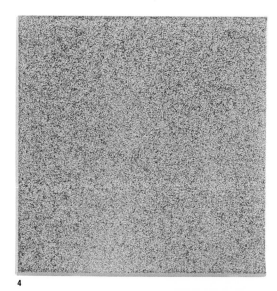

1

2

3

4

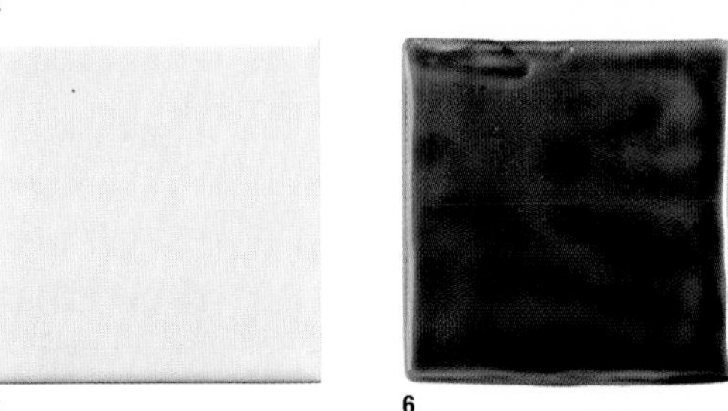

5

6

7

8

1 **Corres Mexican Tiles/Colors** Color **dark blue** Alternative colors **available** Composition **ceramic** Size **4 x 4 x ⅜in/10 x 10 x 1cm** Price ★ [W] [+]

2 **Elite Tiles/Porcelain Tile** Color **polish** Alternative colors **available** Composition **porcelain** Size **11¾ x 11¾ x ⅓in/30 x 30cm x 9mm** Price ★ [F]

3 **Corres Mexican Tiles/Colors** Color **Mexican white** Alternative colors **available** Composition **ceramic** Size **4 x 4 x ⅜in/10 x 10 x 1cm** Price ★ [W] [+]

4 **Kenneth Clark Ceramics/Plain Colors D6** Color **sienna** Alternative colors **available** Composition **ceramic** Size **4 x 4 x ¼in/10 x 10cm x 7mm** Price ★ [W] [+]

5 **Domus Tiles/Interni Ghiaccio** Color **white** Alternative colors **available** Composition **ceramic** Size **4 x 4 x ¼in/10.5 x 10.5cm x 7mm** Price ★ [F]

6 **Winchester Tile Co/Colors** Color **gray** Alternative colors **available** Composition **ceramic** Size **4 x 4 x ¼in/10.5 x 10.5cm x 7mm** Price ★ [W] [+]

7 **Elon/Carrillo Plain** Color **red** Alternative colors **available** Composition **ceramic** Size **4 x 4 x ¼in/10 x 10cm x 7mm** Price ★ [W] [F]

8 **Florida Tile Co/Hotspots** Color **yellow** Alternative colors **available** Composition **ceramic** Size **6 x ½ x ⅜in/15 x 1.2 x 1cm** Price ★ [W] [+]

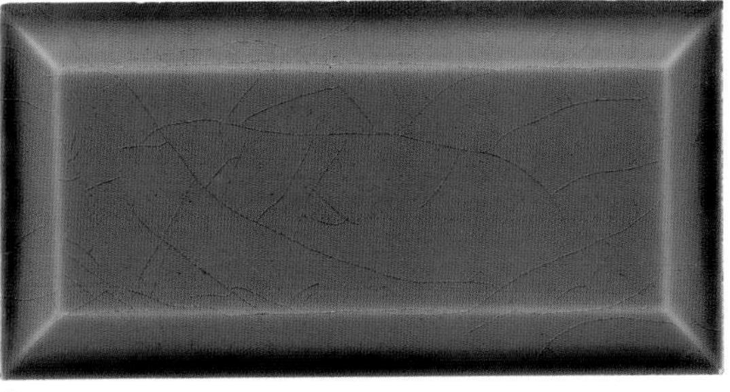

9

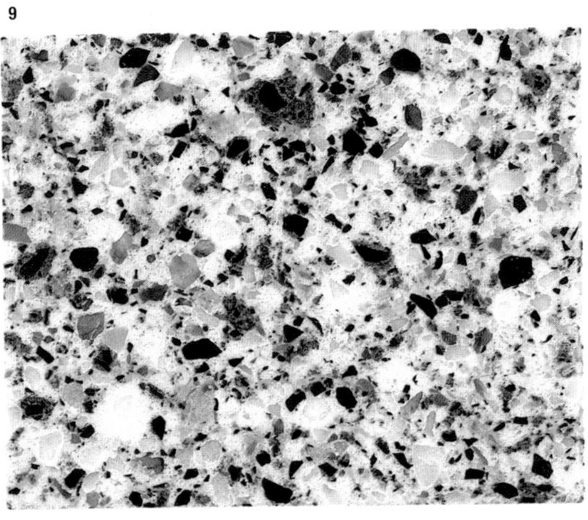

10

11

9 Carré/Carometro Color **green** Alternative colors **available** Composition **ceramic** Size **6 x 3 x ¼in/15 x 7.5cm x 6mm** Price ★ [W] [+]

10 Marble Flooring Specialists/ Marchestone Grigio Plata M234 Color **multi** Alternative colors **available** Composition **marble** Size **11¾ x 11¾ x ⅜in/ 30 x 30 x 1cm** Price ★ [F] [+]

11 Winchester Tile Co/Colors Color **turquoise** Alternative colors **available** Composition **ceramic** Size **4 x 4 x ¼in/ 10.5 x 10.5cm x 7mm** Price ★ [W] [+]

12

13

14

15

12 Winchester Tile Co/Colors Color **mauve** Alternative colors **available** Composition **ceramic** Size **4 x 4 x ¼in/ 10.5 x 10.5cm x 7mm** Price ★ [W] [+]

13 Carocim/Palette U15 Color **violet** Alternative colors **available** Composition **ceramic** Size **8 x 8 x ⅜in/ 20 x 20 x 1cm** Price ★ [W] [F] [+]

14 Imports Direct/Ice Blue Color **ice blue** Alternative colors **available** Composition **cement** Size **8 x 8 x ½in/ 20 x 20 x 1.5cm** Price ★ [F]

15 Daltile/Semigloss Color **Chinese red** Alternative colors **available** Composition **ceramic** Size **6 x 6 x ¼in/ 15 x 15cm x 7mm** Price ★ [W] [+]

16 Elon/Carrillo Plain Color **plum** Alternative colors **available** Composition **ceramic** Size **4 x 4 x ¼in/10 x 10cm x 7mm** Price ★ [W] [F]

17 H. & R. Johnson/ Provençale Rustic Color **brown** Alternative colors **available** Composition **ceramic** Size **12 x 8½ x ⅓in/31 x 22cm x 8mm** Price ★ [F]

16

17

Motif Tiles

ABOVE This view of the entrance hallway of Hall Place in London, England, indicates just how strong the Gothic Revival influence was on interior design during the middle of the 19th century. The inlaid tiles on the floor of the room enhance the Gothic look. They feature striking, Islamic-inspired medieval motifs.

Symbolism was an integral part of medieval art, and many contemporary tiles reflect this in the motifs used in inlaid patterns. Large numbers of motif tiles were employed in churches and featured the religious symbols familiar to the congregations. Arabesques were a common motif on delftware tiles from the late 16th century to the mid-17th century, but they gradually gave way to the more simply painted corner motifs that are a feature of later tiles.

In the 1770s, with the rise of interest in Neoclassicism, swags, drapes, and classic urns all appeared on tiles. The Gothic Revival of the 1830s and 1840s brought about a return to the symbolism of medieval tiles but in an updated form, while the Aesthetic Movement in the 1860s saw the use of prunus blossoms and Chinese *mons* on tiles. Military or musical symbols became popular images on tiles during the 1880s.

By the 1920s motifs were seldom used in tile design due to the influence of the Art Deco Movement, which relied on strong geometric images. The latter part of the 20th century saw a return to motif-decorated tiles with traditional designs being produced alongside "New Age" motifs such as the sun, the moon, and the stars.

TILED STOVES

In Eastern Europe and Scandinavia, tiled stoves, like this late 19th century one, were common from the 15th century onward. The tiles were functional as well as decorative, retaining heat and distributing it evenly around the room. Although such stoves were not common in England, A. W. N. Pugin designed one in 1850 for the Minton Company to display at the Great Exhibition in London. Afterward the stove was destroyed, leaving only a few remaining tiles and a contemporary engraving.

ABOVE The pressing of natural materials into an unfired clay tile has its origins in the animal footprints that are sometimes found on old Roman roof tiles. The example shown here is modern, although the technique was first used by J. & J. G. Lowe in America in the 1880s.

LEFT The floor tiles in this bathroom of a house in Suffolk, England, feature strongly Islamic-inspired motifs. They form the perfect foil for the plainer, Victorian-style sanitary ware and tiles.

KEY DESIGNS

1 In the 1830s and 1840s, architects were inspired by motifs on medieval tiles, such as those on this Gothic Revival design panel.

2 Corner motifs are a particular feature of tin-glazed and delft tiles. When placed together, the corner patterns join to form another design.

3 Neoclassical imagery, such as the urn, has been very popular on tiles since the 1770s. Swags, trophies, and drapes have also been frequently used.

4 The motifs of the Aesthetic Movement are characterized by the juxtaposition of Chinese and Japanese ornament with elements of early Egyptian design.

5 Complete coats of arms have long been used on tiles, as well as individual elements from heraldry, such as the lion, the unicorn, and the cross or chevron.

6 The fleur-de-lis or, more correctly, the Burgundian Lily, has been a popular motif on tiles since medieval times when it was a symbol of the Holy Trinity.

1 **Original Style/Gladstone 6260** Color **blue/brown** Alternative colors **available** Composition **ceramic** Size **6 x 6 x 2in/ 15 x 15 x 5cm (4-tile panel)** Price ★★★★ [F]

2 **Attica/Maillo** Color **multi** Alternative colors **available** Composition **ceramic** Size **6 x 6 x ⅜in/15 x 15 x 1cm** Price ★★★★★ [W] [F]

3 **Julie Arnall/Urn No. 2** Color **crackle graze** Alternative colors **available** Composition **ceramic** Size **5 x 5 x ⅜in/13 x 13 x 1cm** Price ★★★ [W] [+]

4 **Candy & Co/Pineapple Linking No. 1** Color **multi** Alternative colors **not available** Composition **ceramic** Size **6 x 6 x ¼in/ 15 x 15cm x 7mm** Price ★ [W]

5 **Fired Earth/Heraldic Inset No. 5** Color **blue and white** Alternative colors **not available** Composition **terracotta** Size **2¾ x 2¾ x ½in/ 7 x 7 x 1.5cm** Price ★ [F]

6 **Ceramiche Eurotiles/Giglio Lucido Dec ES/ I 44** Color **multi** Alternative colors **available** Composition **ceramic** Size **2¾ x 2¾ x ½in/ 7 x 7 x 1.5cm** Price ★ [W] [F]

Motifs: **Pre-19th century**

The use of motifs on tiles originated in the Middle Ages when symbolism was used as a way of educating the people and focusing their thoughts on God. Thus the motifs that adorned early tiles were strongly based on Christian beliefs and ideals. Typical motifs were the fish (a mystical symbol of the church), the fleur-de-lis (representing the Holy Trinity), and the circle (symbolizing eternity). Certain symbols also became associated with heraldry.

As Islamic influences spread across Europe via Spain, arabesques, which had originated as cloud scrolls on Chinese porcelain, became a popular motif on tiles. By the early 17th century these had been reduced to a simple corner motif on the delftware tiles produced in the Netherlands, Germany, England, and other European countries. There are a great many variations of these corner motifs, rejoicing in such names as spider's head, ox head, fleur-de-lis, and oak leaf. Delftware tiles, imported from the Netherlands, were equally popular in Colonial America.

The popularity of classical ornamentation in Europe during the late 18th century was also reflected in tile design. Numerous classical motifs, including urns and birds, were used as decorative designs on tiles.

1

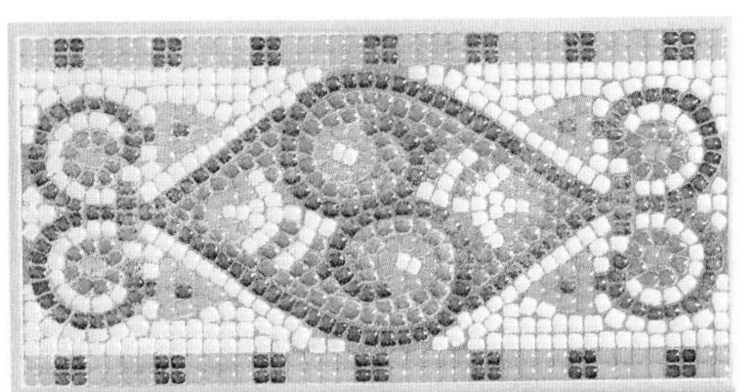
2

3

4

5

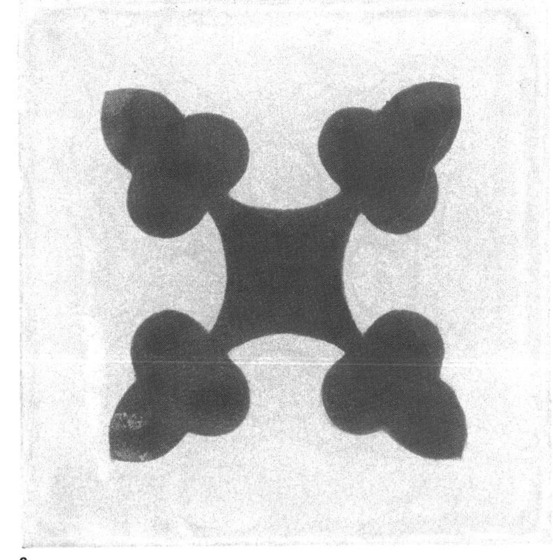
6

7

8

9

10

11

1 **Fired Earth/Stoneage Square No. 5** Color **rosso** Alternative colors **available** Composition **Venetian marble** Size **4 x 4 x ¾in/10 x 10 x 2cm** Price ★★ [F]

2 **Yorkshire Tile Co/Cella 1(III)** Color **multi** Alternative colors **not available** Composition **ceramic** Size **11¾ x 6 x ½in/30 x 15 x 1.2cm** Price ★ [F]

3 **Julie Arnall/Star** Color **crackle glaze** Alternative colors **available** Composition **ceramic** Size **5 x 5 x ⅜in/ 13 x 13 x 1cm** Price ★★★ [W] [+]

4 **Julie Arnall/Virgo** Color **cream** Alternative colors **available** Composition **ceramic** Size **5 x 5 x ⅜in/ 13 x 13 x 1cm** Price ★★★ [W] [+]

5 **Life Enhancing Tile Co/ Islamic Motif** Color **buff/ green** Alternative colors **available** Composition **encaustic** Size **2 x 2 x ½in/ 5 x 5 x 1.2cm** Price ★ [W] [F] [+]

6 **Carocim/Gothic** Color **red and blue** Alternative colors **available** Composition **ceramic** Size **8 x 8 x ⅜in/ 20 x 20 x 1cm** Price ★ [W] [F] [+]

7 **Life Enhancing Tile Co/Fish** Color **black** Alternative colors **available** Composition **encaustic** Size **2 x 2 x ½in/ 5 x 5 x 1.2cm** Price ★ [W] [F] [+]

8 **Ann Sacks/Batchelder Lion** Color **stoneware** Alternative colors **available** Composition **ceramic** Size **4 x 4 x ⅓in/ 10 x 10cm x 9mm** Price ★ [W]

9 **Florida Tile Co/Flores** Color **azul-clay** Alternative colors **available** Composition **ceramic** Size **4 x 4 x ⅓in/ 10 x 10cm x 8mm** Price ★ [W] [F] [🗑]

10 **Florida Tile Co/Escudo** Color **azul-rose** Alternative colors **available** Composition **ceramic** Size **4 x 4 x ⅓in/ 10 x 10cm x 8mm** Price ★ [W] [F] [🗑]

11 **Life Enhancing Tile Co/Fleur de Lys** Color **brown/buff** Alternative colors **available** Composition **encaustic** Size **2 x 2 x ½in/5 x 5 x 1.2cm** Price ★ [W] [F] [+]

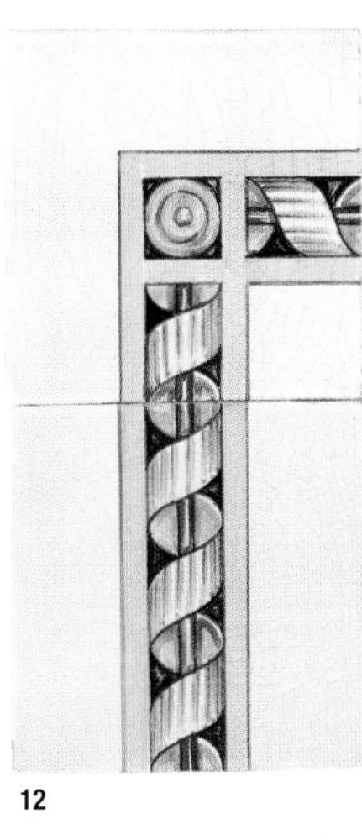
12

12 Attica/Ribbon Border Color **multi** Alternative colors **not available** Composition **ceramic** Size **6 x 6 x ⅜in/15 x 15 x 1cm** Price ★★★ [W]

13 Attica/Greek Lion Color **black and terracotta** Alternative colors **not available** Composition **ceramic** Size **6 x 6 x ⅜in/15 x 15 x 1cm** Price ★★★★★ [W]

14 Julie Arnall/Urn No. 1 Color **cream** Alternative colors **available** Composition **ceramic** Size **5 x 5 x ⅜in/ 13 x 13 x 1cm** Price ★★★ [W] [+]

15 Fired Earth/Heraldic Inset No. 4 Color **blue and white** Alternative colors **not available** Composition **terracotta** Size **2¾ x 2¾ x ½in/ 7 x 7 x 1.5cm** Price ★ [F]

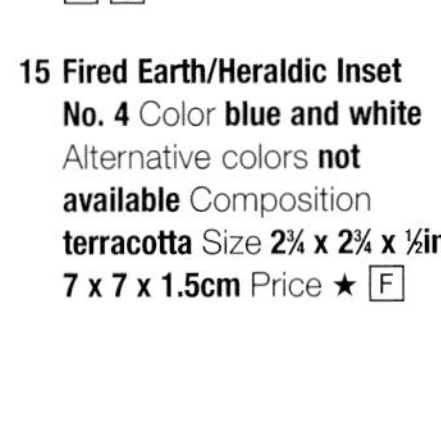
13

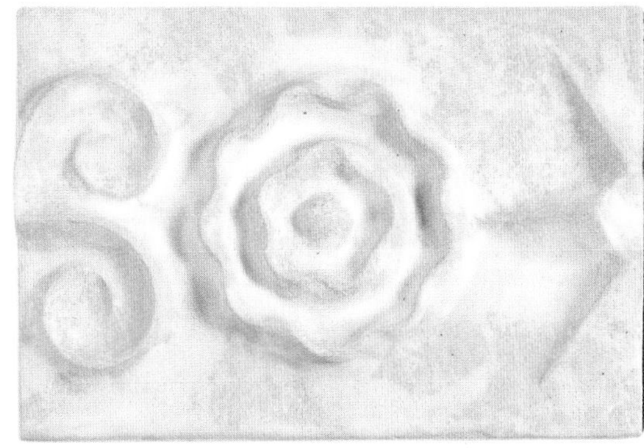

16

17

18

19

16 Lowitz & Co/Talisman Panel Beginnings Border Color **white** Alternative colors **available** Composition **ceramic** Size **6 x 4 x ¼in/ 15 x 10cm x 7mm** Price ★★★ [W] [⌂]

17 Attica/Ancient Rhythm Fresco Color **multi** Alternative colors **available** Composition **ceramic** Size **6 x 6 x ⅜in/15 x 15 x 1cm** Price ★★★★ [W]

18 Attica/Shell Border Color **multi** Alternative colors **not available** Composition **ceramic** Size **6 x 6 x ⅜in/15 x 15 x 1cm** Price ★★★ [W]

19 Walker Zanger/Tagina Visconti Decodot Color **multi** Alternative colors **not available** Composition **ceramic** Size **2 x 2 x ½in/ 5 x 5 x 1.5cm** Price ★ [W] [F]

20 Fired Earth/Gaelic Knot Color **black** Alternative colors **available** Composition **stone** Size **8 x 8 x ½in/20 x 20 x 1.2cm** Price ★★★★ [W] [F]

14

15

20

Motifs: **19th century**

By the mid-19th century, A. W. N. Pugin and other Gothic Revival architects were finding inspiration in the Christian and heraldic symbols used on medieval tiles. Such motifs became icons for these architects and they soon added new symbols of their own to the repertoire. These included the chalice and wafer, the Paschal Lamb, and the alpha and omega.

The opening up of trade routes to the Orient led to an influx of porcelain and metal goods from the Far East, which was to serve as a source of inspiration for the followers of the Aesthetic Movement later in the century. Tiles featuring motifs such as the prunus blossom, often as a background to Japanese *mons* or armorial seals, proved particularly popular. Also widely used as a motif in tile decoration was a highly stylized sunflower, which was to become one of the Aesthetic Movement's chief symbols (*see* page 320). The fan, too, was a favorite symbol on tiles, and inspired a variety of designs. Toward the end of the century, the use of very stylized military or musical motifs became popular throughout Europe and America. These were often combined with stylized swags or ribbons that served to unify the image and provided an extra, decorative element.

6

1

2

7

3

4

5

8

1 **Original Style/Victorian Border Tile 6034** Color **Colonial white** Alternative colors **not available** Composition **ceramic** Size **6 x 6 x ¼in/ 15 x 15cm x 7mm** Price ★ W

2 **Ceramiche Eurotiles/Listello Florence LS/21** Color **blue and white** Alternative colors **available** Composition **ceramic** Size **8 x 4 x ¼in/ 20 x 10cm x 7mm** Price ★★ W

3 **Minton Hollins/Assyrian Field Tile** Color **green** Alternative colors **available** Composition **ceramic** Size **6 x 6 x ⅓in/ 15 x 15cm x 8mm** Price ★ W

4 **Walker Zanger/Sol Deco** Color **cebolla** Alternative colors **available** Composition **ceramic** Size **4 x 4 x ½in/ 10 x 10 x 1.5cm** Price ★★ W

5 **Minton Hollins/Acanthus MA10** Color **black** Alternative colors **available** Composition **ceramic** Size **6 x 6 x ⅓in/ 15 x 15cm x 8mm** Price ★ W

6 **Yorkshire Tile Co/Latina 3B(V)** Color **multi** Alternative colors **not available** Composition **ceramic** Size **13 x 13 x ¼in/33 x 33cm x 7mm** Price ★ F

7 **Yorkshire Tile Co/Gothic Crema Listello** Color **crema** Alternative colors **available** Composition **ceramic** Size **8 x 3 x ¼in/20 x 8cm x 6mm** Price ★ W

8 **Candy & Co/Pineapple Linking No. 2** Color **multi** Alternative colors **not available** Composition **ceramic** Size **6 x 6 x ¼in/ 15 x 15cm x 7mm** Price ★ W

9

12

9 Walker Zanger/Seville 248-B Chantilly Color **white** Alternative colors **not available** Composition **terracotta** Size **11 x 5½ x ½in/28 x 14 x 1.2cm** Price ★★ W

10 Walker Zanger/Florentine Palladio No. 30A Deco Color **multi** Alternative colors **not available** Composition **terracotta** Size **6 x 6 x ½in/15 x 15 x 1.2cm** Price ★★★ W

10 Minton Hollins/Ivy Link UIL5 Color **multi** Alternative colors **available** Composition **ceramic** Size **6 x 6 x ½in/ 15 x 15 x 1.2cm** Price ★★★ W

10

13

14

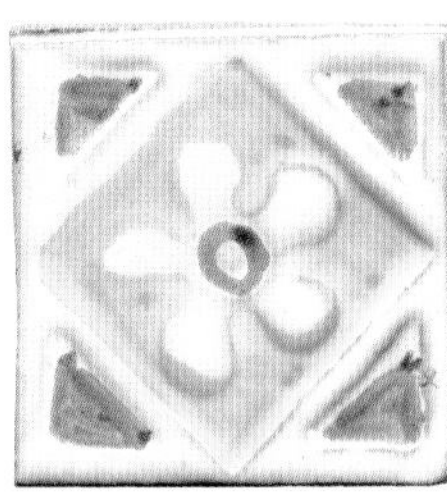

15

16

12 Original Style/Phoenix K9020A Color **Baltic blue** Alternative colors **available** Composition **ceramic** Size **6 x 6 x ¼in/15 x 15cm x 7mm (2-tile panel)** Price ★★ W

13 Ceramiche Eurotiles/Giglio Rete B Lucido EC/D34 Color **white** Alternative colors **available** Composition **ceramic** Size **6 x 6 x ⅝in/ 15 x 15 x 1.5cm** Price ★★ W

14 Imports Direct/7300 Color **green** Alternative colors **available** Composition **cement** Size **8 x 8 x ½in/ 20 x 20 x 1.5cm** Price ★ F

15 Ceramiche Eurotiles/Kler Lucido Dec Color **multi** Alternative colors **available** Composition **ceramic** Size **2¾ x 2¾ x ½in/7 x 7 x 1.5cm** Price ★★ W F

16 Original Style/Evening Reverie 6046 Color **multi** Alternative colors **not available** Composition **ceramic** Size **6 x 1½ x ¼in/ 15 x 4cm x 7mm** Price ★ W

ARTS AND CRAFTS DESIGNS

In 1860, when William Morris was looking for tiles for his new home, Red House, in Kent, England, he lamented the fact that there was no company in England that manufactured handmade tiles. He decided to buy handmade, white, glazed Dutch tiles and decorate them with the enamels he used for stained glass. Subsequently, many of Morris's artist friends designed tiles for his company. The tile shown below is based upon one of Morris's own designs, known as "Swan."

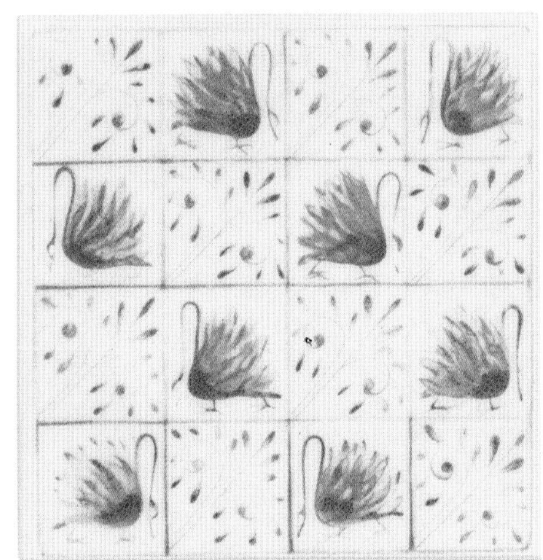

Candy & Co/Swan Repeat Color **blue** Alternative colors **available** Composition **ceramic** Size **6 x 6 x ¼in/ 15 x 15cm x 7mm** Price ★ W

11

The most beautiful places
always bear traces
of the hands that shape them

TALISMAN

TIMELESS DESIGN IN HANDMADE STONEWARE TILE

Please contact us for the name of your nearest Talisman showroom.
Distribution opportunities available internationally.
Lowitz & Company · 4401 N. Ravenswood Avenue · Chicago, Illinois 60640 USA
phone 773-784-2628 · fax 773-784-2656

Spiral Wave 4×4" and 2×6" with Combination Molding 2×6", Wavy Liner 1×6" and Rustic Half-Round 1×6"

Beginnings Square 6×6"

MICHELLE GRIFFOUL STUDIOS

Design & Manufacture Custom Ceramic Tile

CLASSICAL
CONTEMPORARY
TILE
Creating an environment to awaken the senses

Suitable for residential and commercial applications including floors and pools. Frostproof available.

Michelle Griffoul Studios
P.O. Box 1149
Buellton, CA 93427 USA
805-688-9631
805-688-9965 fax

Fallen Leaves

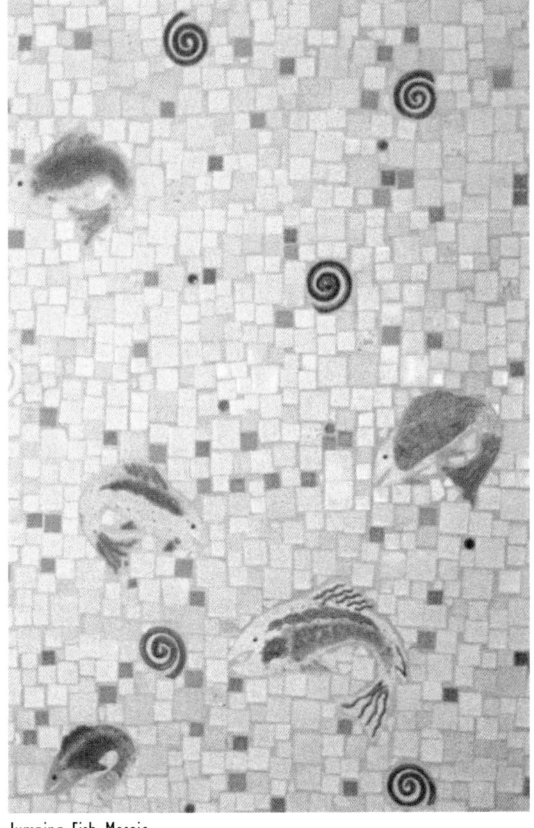

Jumping Fish Mosaic

Motifs: **Early 20th century**

Perhaps as a reaction to the designs of the Art Nouveau Movement, some tile manufacturers returned to Neoclassical imagery at the beginning of the 20th century. However, as labor costs rose, manufacturers sought methods of production that were cheaper and faster than the traditional printing and hand-coloring and this led to the development of machine-molded relief tiles. Tiles molded with drapes, wreaths, bowls or baskets of fruit, shells, and other still-life compositions were arranged as borders along the tops of walls, the remainder of the tiling being plain. Molded tiles were used in commercial buildings such as butchers and dairies as well as in domestic halls and on porches.

In the 1920s and 1930s, many companies such as Carter & Co in Dorset, England, produced tiles that featured small motifs to be used in conjunction with their pictorial tiles; these ranged from a clump of grass to a bunch of flowers. During this period in America, companies such as Malibu Tiles and Gladding McBean were producing tiles decorated with a range of boldly colored, Catalan-inspired motifs, designs that were frequently in relief. In addition, the influence of Art Deco in Europe and America inspired graphic, linear motifs based on objects such as fans and stylized flowers.

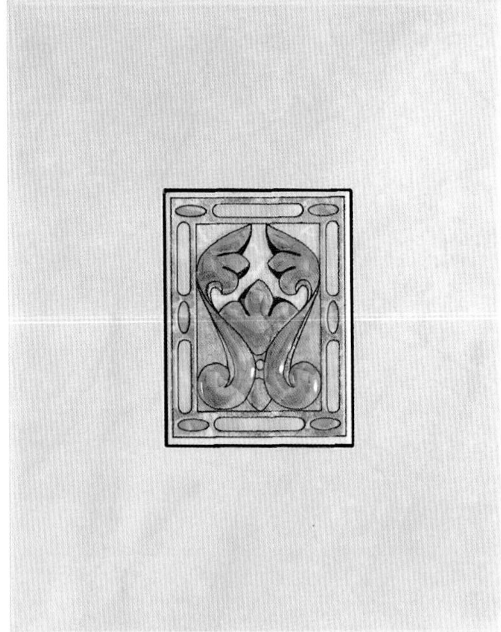

5

1

2

3

4

6

7

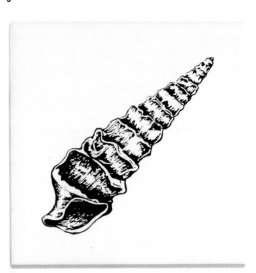

1 **Ann Sacks/Topiary Tree** Color **SW05** Alternative colors **available** Composition **ceramic** Size **6 x 3 x ⅓in/ 15 x 7.5cm x 8mm** Price ★★★ [W]

2 **Original Style/Shell Frieze 6991B** Color **multi** Alternative colors **not available** Composition **ceramic** Size **6 x 3 x ¼in/ 15 x 7.5cm x 7mm (2-tile set)** Price ★★ [W]

3 **Fired Earth/Cherry** Color **red, cream, and green** Alternative colors **not available** Composition **ceramic** Size **4¼ x 4¼ x ½in/11 x 11cm x 8mm** Price ★★★ [W] [bin]

4 **Ceramiche Eurotiles/Sirina Seminato SS/1** Color **blue** Alternative colors **available** Composition **ceramic** Size **6 x 6 x ¼in/15 x 15cm x 6mm** Price ★ [W]

5 **Yorkshire Tile Co/Nacar Cream Decor** Color **cream** Alternative colors **available** Composition **ceramic** Size **10 x 8 x ¼in/25 x 20cm x 6mm** Price ★ [W]

6 **Kenneth Clark Ceramics/ Shells S3** Color **black on white** Alternative colors **available** Composition **ceramic** Size **4 x 4 x ¼in/ 10 x 10cm x 7mm** Price ★ [W] [bin] [+]

7 **Winchester Tile Co/Hen** Color **white** Alternative colors **available** Composition **ceramic** Size **4 x 4 x ½in/ 10.5 x 10.5cm x 8mm** Price ★★ [W]

20th century

8

8 Fired Earth/Lyon Color **white on ivory** Alternative colors **not available** Composition **encaustic** Size **8 x 8 x ¾in/ 20 x 20 x 2cm (4-tile set)** Price ★ [F]

9 Winchester Tile Co/Cherry Border Color **off white** Alternative colors **available** Composition **ceramic** Size **4 x 4 x ⅓in/10.5 x 10.5cm x 8mm** Price ★★ [W]

10 Fired Earth/Anita B Color **blue** Alternative colors **available** Composition **ceramic** Size **4 x 4 x ⅜in/10 x 10 x 1cm** Price ★ [W] [F] [🗑]

11 Minton Hollins/Baroque ANFI Color **blue** Alternative colors **available** Composition **ceramic** Size **6 x 6 x ⅓in/ 15 x 15cm x 8mm** Price ★ [W]

12

9

10

11

12 Corres Mexican Tiles/ Pattern No. 21 Color **blue/red on buff** Alternative colors **not available** Composition **ceramic** Size **4 x 4 x ⅜in/ 10 x 10 x 1cm** Price ★ [W] [+]

13 Ann Sacks/Celtic Deer Color **springwheat** Alternative colors **available** Composition **ceramic** Size **4 x 4 x ⅓in/ 10 x 10cm x 8mm** Price ★★★ [W]

14 Kenneth Clark Ceramics/ Doves Relief Color **primrose yellow** Alternative colors **available** Composition **ceramic** Size **6 x 3 x ¼in/ 15 x 7.5cm x 6mm** Price ★★ [W]

13

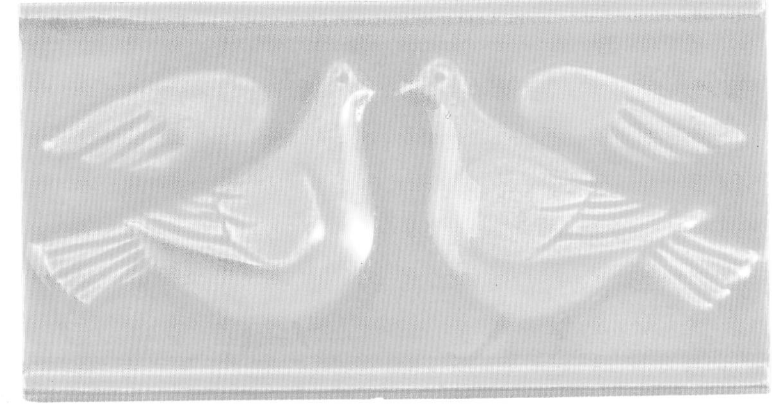

14

Motifs: **Late 20th century**

The years following the Second World War were a time of austerity, and very few tiles other than plain pastels and simple mottles were produced. However, by the mid-1950s, companies began to experiment with new techniques to meet the demand for decorated tiles. At that time, Carter & Co in England introduced the world's first automated screen-printing production line for tiles, enabling them to supply for kitchen and bathroom tiles with motifs such as fruits, kitchen utensils, seashells, fish, and the signs of the zodiac. These tiles were generally inset at random in a field of matching plain tiles. By the mid-1970s, tiles were being mass-produced with simple overall patterns, while the latter part of the 20th century saw a return to the use of motif-decorated tiles, with the tile industry becoming more craft oriented. As well as traditional tile motifs, many of these modern tiles featured motifs such as the sun, moon, and stars, which were popularized by the New Age Movement.

3

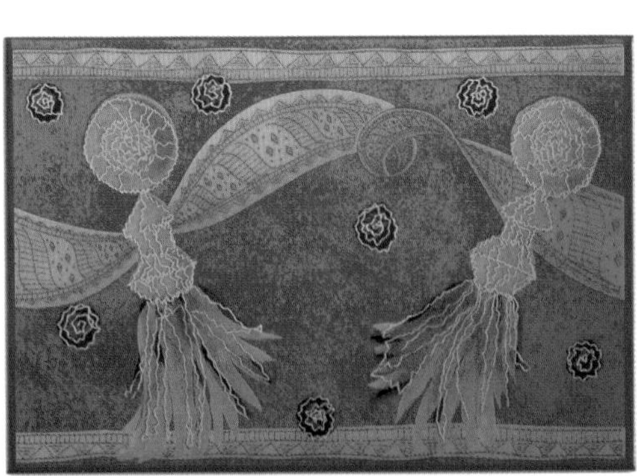
1

2

4

5 6

7

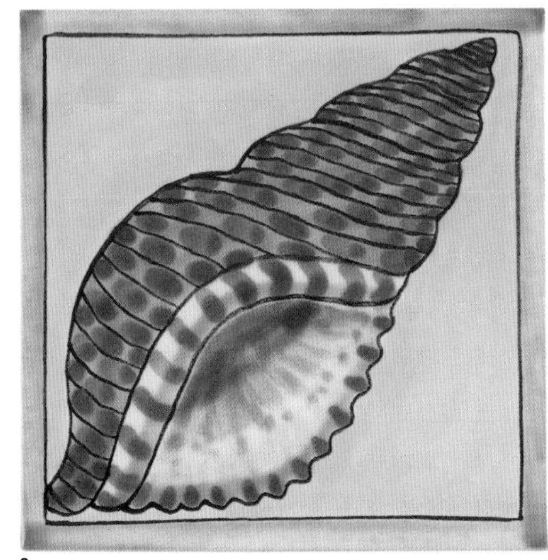
8

1 **Villeroy & Boch/Paloma Picasso Decor** Color **multi** Alternative colors **not available** Composition **ceramic** Size **11¾ x 8 x ¼in/ 30 x 20cm x 6mm** Price ★★★ [W]

2 **Carocim/Grenouille** Color **blue and green** Alternative colors **available** Composition **ceramic** Size **8 x 8 x ⅜in/ 20 x 20 x 1cm** Price ★ [W] [+]

3 **Kenneth Clark Ceramics/ Reverie: Bird** Color **night** Alternative colors **available** Composition **ceramic** Size **6 x 6 x ¼in/15 x 15cm x 7mm** Price ★★★ [W] [+]

4 **Elon/Romana Peacock** Color **white** Alternative colors **not available** Composition **ceramic** Size **6 x 6 x ⅜in/ 15 x 15 x 1cm** Price ★★ [W]

5 **Winchester Tile Co/Dragonfly** Color **white** Alternative colors **available** Composition **ceramic** Size **4 x 4 x ⅓in/ 10.5 x 10.5cm x 8mm** Price ★★ [W]

6 **Tiles of Stow/Heraldic S tar** Color **multi** Alternative colors **not available** Composition **ceramic** Size **4¼ x 4¼ x ¼in/11 x 11cm x 7mm** Price ★★ [W]

7 **Elon/Vegetable** Color **white** Alternative colors **not available** Composition **ceramic** Size **4 x 4 x ⅜in/ 10 x 10 x 1cm (7-tile set)** Price ★★★★★ [W]

8 **Reptile/Sealife No. 29** Color **multi** Alternative colors **available** Composition **ceramic** Size **6 x 6 x ⅓in/ 15 x 15cm x 8mm** Price ★★★ [W]

9

10

9 Kenneth Clark Ceramics/ Woodland Color **white and green** Alternative colors **not available** Composition **ceramic** Size **6 x 6 x ¼in/ 15 x 15cm x 7mm** Price ★ W +

10 Villeroy & Boch/Abadan Color **multi** Alternative colors **not available** Composition **ceramic** Size **8 x 6 x ¼in/20 x 15cm x 6mm** Price ★★ W

11 Winchester Tile Co/Grapes Color **off white** Alternative colors **available** Composition **ceramic** Size **4 x 4 x ⅓in/ 10.5 x 10.5cm x 8mm** Price ★★ W

12 Walker Zanger/Toltec Sol Color **clear** Alternative colors **not available** Composition **glass** Size **6 x 6 x ⅓in/15 x 15cm x 8mm** Price ★★★ W

11

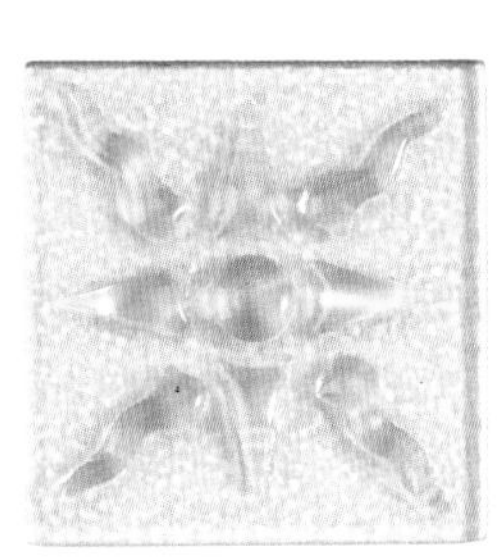

12

13

14

13 Fired Earth/Star Color **kitchen green** Alternative colors **available** Composition **ceramic** Size **4 x 4 x ⅜in/ 10 x 10 x 1cm** Price ★★ W

14 Original Style/Prawn Laurel Color **glazed green** Alternative colors **available** Composition **ceramic** Size **4 x 4 x ⅜in/10 x 10 x 1cm** Price ★★ W

15 Kenneth Clark Ceramics/ Magic Lantern ML10 Color **gray and blue** Alternative colors **not available** Composition **ceramic** Size **4 x 4 x ¼in/10 x 10cm x 7mm** Price ★★ W +

16 Corres Mexican Tiles/Fruit and Veg No. 76 Color **multi** Alternative colors **not available** Composition **ceramic** Size **4 x 4 x ¼in/ 10 x 10cm x 7mm** Price ★ W

15

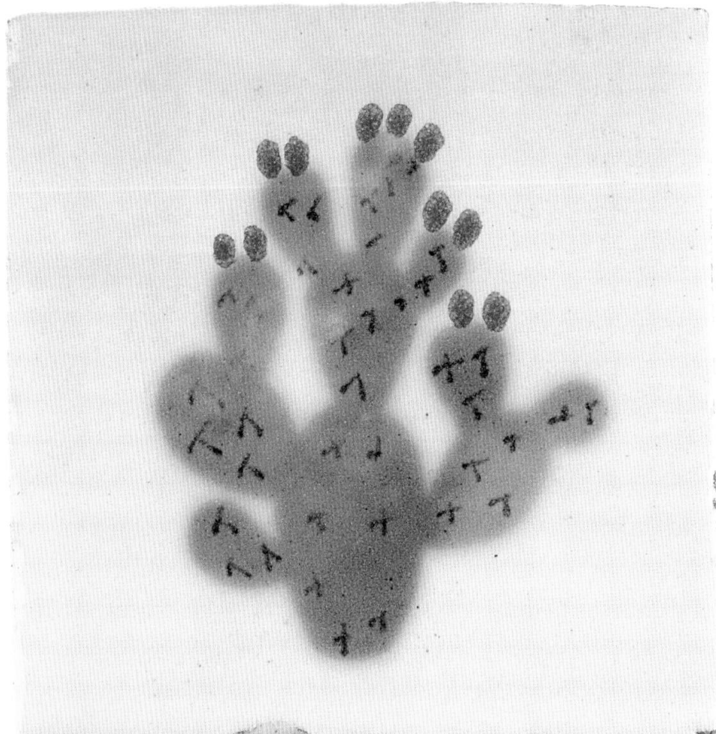

16

Floral Tiles

Floral designs have been a recurrent theme on tiles from earliest times. Styles have varied over the years, ranging from the simple lotus and daisy patterns of ancient Egypt to the elaborate flowers on Islamic tiles, which were echoed in the 19th century by the Arts and Crafts potter William de Morgan. Flowers have been featured as backgrounds in Islamic calligraphic tiles, as borders and corner ornaments and primary motifs on delftware tiles, and in vases or pots on large Dutch and Portuguese tile panels. They have also been seen as repeating designs on late 18th- and 19th-century tiles, in highly stylized form on Art Nouveau tiles, and in posies and bunches on mid-20th-century tiles.

Designs have been taken from a variety of sources including nature itself, herbals and florilegia in the late Middle Ages, and even from bulb growers' catalogs, a source used by the early 17th-century delftware painters. Flowers featured have ranged from the naturalistic to the highly stylized, where the original species is indeterminable.

LEFT The light, uncluttered style of this Swedish tiled stove was particularly popular in Scandinavia. While the tiles on most Eastern European stoves were decorated with darker, lead-based glazes, the Scandinavian stoves invariably featured tiles based on white tin-glazes, similar to those used on delft tiles.

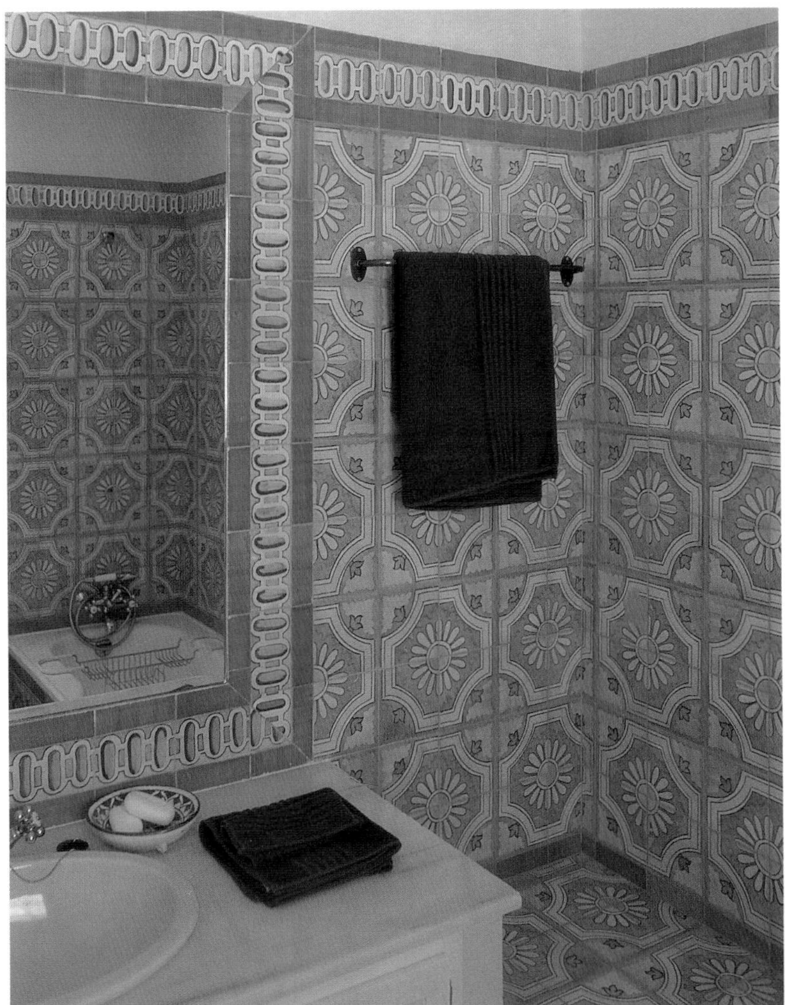

ABOVE A corner of a bathroom in La Heredia near Malaga in Spain that, although built in the late 20th century, captures the spirit of a 16th-century Spanish tiled interior. There is an almost unbroken history both in and around Seville of the manufacture of these richly glazed tiles, which are decorated with bold floral motifs.

BATHROOM TILING

In wealthier homes in the late 19th century, bathrooms frequently contained elaborate mahogany paneled baths decorated with insets of tiles. These tiles were sometimes arranged in large panels of naturalistic or stylized patterns. Sinks were often housed in matching mahogany cabinets, with tiled backsplashes echoing those on the bath. The example shown here also includes tiles set into the doors, and features a tip-up basin that is inverted to dispose of the water.

KEY DESIGNS

1 The image of a flower as a botanical specimen was popular on early delftware tiles, the inspiration for which was often taken from bulb growers' catalogs.

2 Abstract designs–where the flower is depicted as a geometric pattern–have been frequently used on tiles since the Victorian era.

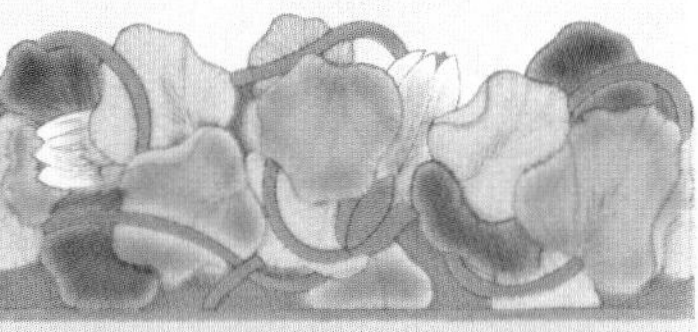

3 Floral designs in particular lend themselves to the imagination of the designer, with stylization reaching its height during the Art Nouveau period in the late 19th century.

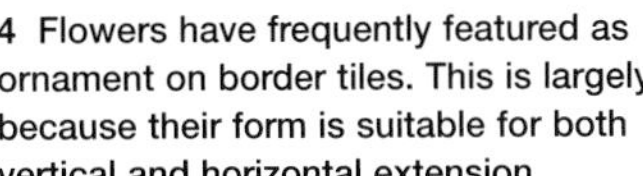

4 Flowers have frequently featured as ornament on border tiles. This is largely because their form is suitable for both vertical and horizontal extension.

5 Floral tile designs have been taken from nature and printed sources, with some naturalistic images covering a whole panel with an overall pattern.

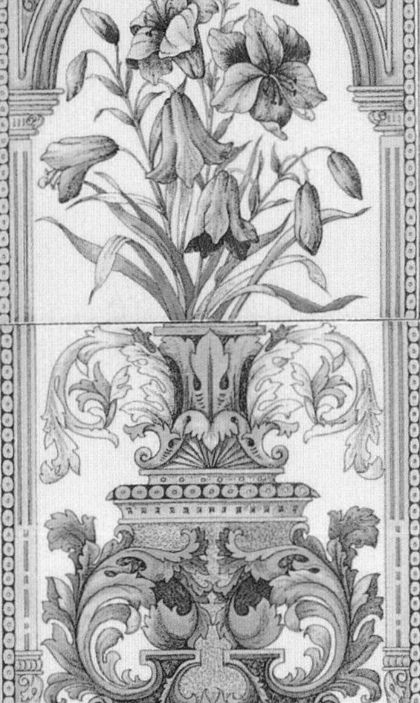

6 Magnificent arrangements of flowers in vases or pots either on a single tile or a large panel of tiles were popular in 17th-century Portugal and the Netherlands, as well as on some English delft tiles.

1 **Fired Earth/Tuscany Herb No. 6** Color **rustic white** Alternative colors **available** Composition **stoneware** Size **4 x 4 x ¼in/10 x 10cm x 7mm** Price ★★ [W] [🗑]

2 **Elon/Seville B** Color **B** Alternative colors **available** Composition **ceramic** Size **4 x 4 x ¼in/10 x 10cm x 7mm** Price ★ [W] [+]

3 **Tiles of Newport & London/Decoro Foglie Laguna** Color **multi** Alternative colors **not available** Composition **ceramic** Size **8 x 4 x ⅜in/20 x 10 x 1cm** Price ★★ [W]

4 **Winchester Tile Co/Small Border 4** Color **multi** Alternative colors **available** Composition **ceramic** Size **8 x 4 x ¼in/20 x 10cm x 7mm** Price ★★ [W]

5 **Tiles of Newport & London/Flowers of the Wood** Color **multi** Alternative colors **not available** Composition **ceramic** Size **6 x 6 x ½in/15 x 15 x 1.2cm** Price ★★★★ [W]

6 **Minton Hollins/Lilies TRP1** Color **ivory** Alternative colors **available** Composition **ceramic** Size **6 x 6 x ⅜in/15 x 15cm x 8mm (2-tile panel)** Price ★★★ [W]

Florals: **Pre-19th century**

The flower was an important element of early Egyptian culture, and fragments of tile bearing lotus blossom and daisy patterns dating from about 1370 B.C. have been excavated from Tell-el-Amarna (north of Thebes). Floral themes recur on Islamic tiles from about A.D. 1200, when they were used as a background for calligraphic inscriptions.

Tulips, carnations, daisies, and leaf shapes were predominant themes on Iznik pottery of the 15th to 17th centuries. Tulips also appear on early polychrome delftware tiles, but by 1625, the fashion for colored ceramics declined as the trade in Chinese blue-and-white porcelain brought about a change in taste. A few large tile panels featuring vases of flowers were made toward the end of the 17th century; some fine examples can still be seen in the kitchens at Rambouillet Palace, southwest of Paris, France. Small quantities of polychrome, purple or blue and white flower vase tiles were produced in Liverpool, Bristol, and London, England, as well as in some areas of Germany during the mid-18th century.

1

1 **Fired Earth/Margarite B/Y** Color **yellow and green** Alternative colors **available** Composition **ceramic** Size **4 x 4 x ⅜in/10 x 10 x 1cm** Price ★ W

2 **Ceramiche Eurotiles/Fantasy Rosa** Color **rosa** Alternative colors **available** Composition **ceramic** Size **8 x 8 x ¼in/ 20 x 20cm x 7mm** Price ★ W

3 **Minton Hollins/Delft DL111** Color **delft** Alternative colors **not available** Composition **ceramic** Size **6 x 6 x ⅓in/ 15 x 15cm x 8mm** Price ★ W

2

3

4

7

8

5

6

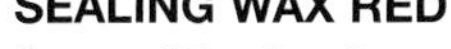

4 Ceramiche Eurotiles/Formella Lineare Chia Rosa CH/1 Color **rosa** Alternative colors **not available** Composition **ceramic** Size **6 x 6 x ½in/15 x 15 x 1.2cm** Price ★★★ [W]

5 H. & R. Johnson/DLB1 Color **delft** Alternative colors **not available** Composition **ceramic** Size **6 x 3 x ⅓in/15 x 7.5cm x 8mm** Price ★ [W]

6 Ceramiche Eurotiles/Midi Angolo Listello LA19 Color **blue and white** Alternative colors **not available** Composition **ceramic** Size **4 x 4 x ¼in/10 x 10cm x 7mm** Price ★★ [W]

7 Ceramiche Eurotiles/ Listello Gazebo Color **rosa** Alternative colors **not available** Composition **ceramic** Size **8 x 4 x ¼in/ 20 x 10cm x 7mm** Price ★★ [W]

8 Fired Earth/Cosmos Inset No. 10 Color **blue** Alternative colors **not available** Composition **terracotta** Size **3 x 3 x ¾in/8 x 8 x 2cm** Price ★ [F]

9 H. & R. Johnson/Rhian RHIA 6E Color **peach and blue** Alternative colors **available** Composition **ceramic** Size **8 x 8 x ¼in/20 x 20cm x 6mm** Price ★ [W]

SEALING WAX RED

Some of the finest examples of the tilemaker's art were the beautiful floral tiles produced in Iznik, the modern-day Turkish town of Nicea, between 1575 and 1600. One of their most striking features is the rich sealing wax red, which refers to the color of this glaze which is raised above the surface of the tile. The secret ingredients of this color elude modern potters, although contemporary glazes have achieved a good approximation to the distinctive rich red.

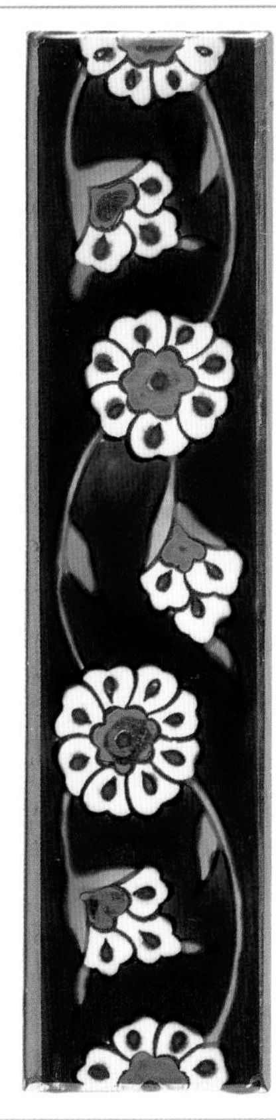

Fired Earth/Izmir Silk Border Color **multi** Alternative colors **not available** Composition **ceramic** Size **8 x 2 x ⅓in/ 20 x 5cm x 8mm** Price ★★ [W]

9

Florals: **19th century**

Floral designs were rarely used on tiles in the late 18th and early 19th centuries, but they experienced a renaissance in the 1860s as designers were inspired by the new Aesthetic Movement, which drew heavily upon Japanese and other Oriental designs and forms. William de Morgan, the English Arts and Crafts potter and friend of William Morris, revived interest in Islamic-inspired floral designs in the 1870s. It also became fashionable to make realistic drawings of flowers, such as sunflowers, and to create more abstract decorative motifs from them. This can be seen in the work of tile designers such as C. F. A. Voysey in England, J. & J. G. Low in America, and Rafael Bordallo Pinheiro in Portugal. Floral tiles were used as inserts in cast-iron fireplaces. Traditionally each side of the fireplace held a run of five tiles, and many panels depicting a pot or vase of flowers were created to suit this design. These tiles were usually transfer-printed, but hand-painted versions were available for wealthier clients. Toward the end of the century, relief-molded tiles gave a "three-dimensional" look to floral designs.

1

1 Candy & Co/Bedford Park Daisy Color **multi** Alternative colors **not available** Composition **ceramic** Size **6 x 6 x ¼in/15 x 15cm x 7mm** Price ★ W

2 Candy & Co/BBB Border Color **multi** Alternative colors **not available** Composition **ceramic** Size **6 x 6 x ¼in/15 x 15cm x 7mm** Price ★ W

3 Candy & Co/Bedford Park Anemone Color **multi** Alternative colors **not available** Composition **ceramic** Size **6 x 6 x ¼in/15 x 15cm x 7mm** Price ★ W

4 Fired Earth/English Rose Color **multi** Alternative colors **not available** Composition **ceramic** Size **6 x 6 x ⅓in/15 x 15cm x 8mm** Price ★★★ W

2

3

4

19th century

5

6

7

8

9

10

5 **Minton Hollins/Antonia FTR25** Color **multi** Alternative colors **not available** Composition **ceramic** Size **6 x 1 x ⅓in/ 15 x 2.5cm x 8mm** Price ★★★★ W

6 **Minton Hollins/Kew Border** Color **ivory** Alternative colors **available** Composition **ceramic** Size **6 x 3 x ⅓in/15 x 7.5cm x 8mm** Price ★ W

7 **Minton Hollins/Cleaves Field Tile CLE2A** Color **ivory** Alternative colors **available** Composition **ceramic** Size **6 x 6 x ⅓in/15 x 15cm x 8mm** Price ★ W

8 **Original Style/Blue Iris 6080A** Color **multi** Alternative colors **not available** Composition **ceramic** Size **6 x 6 x ¼in/ 15 x 15cm x 7mm (5-tile panel)** Price ★★★★ W

9 **Minton Hollins/Framed Flower UFF5** Color **burgundy** Alternative colors **available** Composition **ceramic** Size **6 x 6 x ⅓in/15 x 15cm x 8mm** Price ★ W

10 **Original Style/Rose & Trellis 6970A** Color **multi** Alternative colors **not available** Composition **ceramic** Size **6 x 6 x ¼in/ 15 x 15cm x 7mm** Price ★ W

Florals: **Early 20th century**

With the advent of the Art Nouveau Movement, the floral tile became increasingly abstract and stylized in its design. In Continental Europe, Art Nouveau–style tiled panels were used to create complete interiors, while in America and England such floral designs tended to be on individual tiles or arranged as small panels up to dado height. In the early 20th century, many tiles were produced by tube-lining. In this technique, the linear elements of a design are applied to stand out from the surface of the tile, allowing designers to create fluid, sinuous shapes with positive outlines separating the colored glazes.

In Portugal, Spain, Belgium, and the Netherlands, highly elaborate Art Nouveau floral panels were often used to cover the facades of buildings, while in Britain tiles were largely confined to interiors. By the 1920s, floral tiles became noticeably less stylized once again, with naturalistic flowers frequently shown in small posies or within larger arrangements. Many floral tiles in this style were made by Carter & Co in Dorset, England, closely echoing the brightly colored pots made at Poole Pottery, which is also in Dorset. Meanwhile, in America, the Rookwood Pottery in Cincinnati, Ohio, which was also well known for its pots, produced a wide range of spectacular floral tiles and tile panels.

1

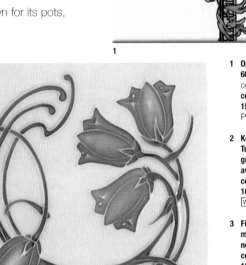

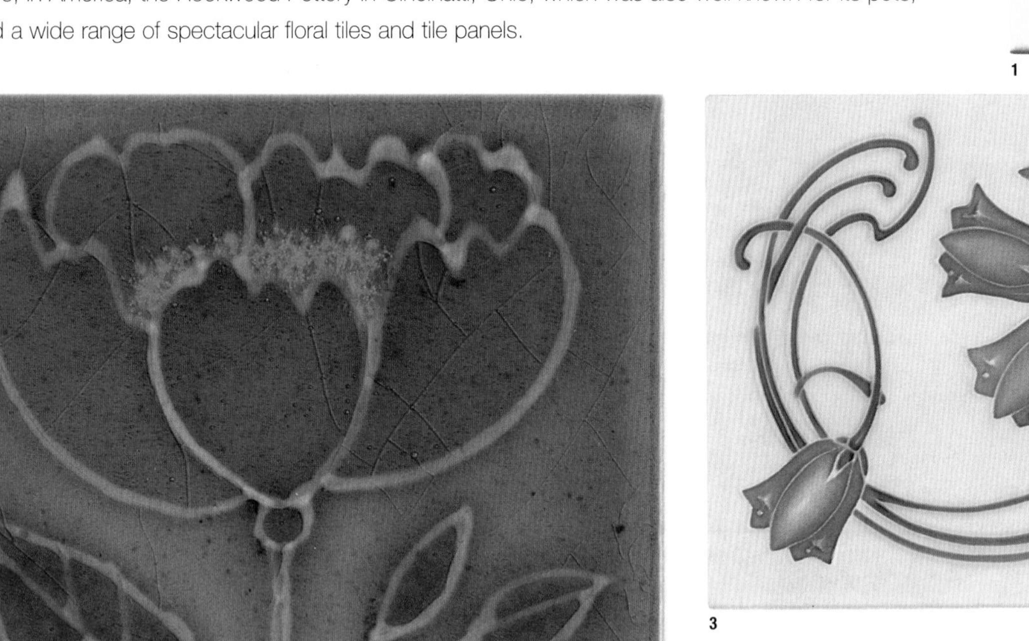

2

3

4

5

6

7

1 **Original Style/Spring Border 6062** Color **lilac** Alternative colors **available** Composition **ceramic** Size **6 x 6 x ¼in/ 15 x 15cm x 7mm** Price ★ W

2 **Kenneth Clark Ceramics/ Tubeline Flowers GTF1** Color **green** Alternative colors **available** Composition **ceramic** Size **4 x 4 x ¼in/ 10 x 10cm x 6mm** Price ★★ W ⊞

3 **Fired Earth/Bluebells** Color **multi** Alternative colors **not available** Composition **ceramic** Size **6 x 6 x ⅓in/ 15 x 15cm x 8mm** Price ★★★ W

4 **Fired Earth/Yellow Rose** Color **yellow** Alternative colors **available** Composition **ceramic** Size **4¼ x 4¼ x ⅓in/11 x 11cm x 8mm** Price ★★ W

5 **Minton Hollins/Fanfare AN11** Color **multi** Alternative colors **not available** Composition **ceramic** Size **6 x 6 x ⅓in/15 x 15cm x 8mm** Price ★ W

6 **Walker Zanger/Baleno 501 Florence Bianco** Color **white** Alternative colors **not available** Composition **terracotta** Size **11¾ x 4 x ⅝in/30 x 10 x 1.5cm** Price ★★★ W

7 **Tiles of Newport & London/ Decorated Tozzetto TNL414A** Color **multi** Alternative colors **not available** Composition **ceramic** Size **1½ x 1½ x ¼in/4 x 4cm x 7mm** Price ★ W

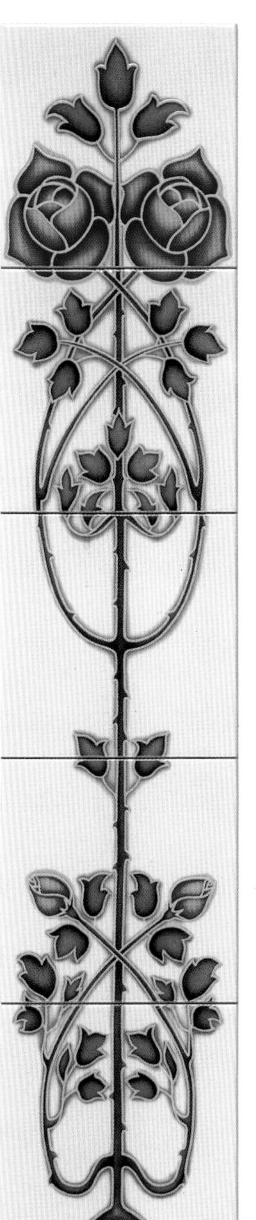

8

8 Original Style/Rose and Bud Color **Colonial white** Alternative colors **available** Composition **ceramic** Size **6 x 6 x ¼in/15 x 15cm x 7mm (5-tile panel)** Price ★★★★ W

9 H. & R. Johnson/Country Garland Inset COG 3D Color **soft cream** Alternative colors **available** Composition **ceramic** Size **8 x 8 x ¼in/ 20 x 20cm x 6mm** Price ★ W

10 Original Style/Sunflower Color **clematis** Alternative colors **available** Composition **ceramic** Size **4 x 4 x ¼in/ 10 x 10cm x 7mm** Price ★★★ W

11 Original Style/Orchid (Orchidée) 1902 6054 Color **multi** Alternative colors **not available** Composition **ceramic** Size **6 x 6 x ¼in/15 x 15cm x 7mm** Price ★ W

11

9

10

ART NOUVEAU

The opening of the shop L'Art Nouveau in Paris, France, in 1896 heralded the beginning of a new style movement that was to shape the decorative arts for the next 25 years. This was a period of highly stylized, curvilinear designs, which were often based on sinuous floral motifs and glamorous female figures. Such designs lent themselves particularly well to tube-lining, a technique similar to piping icing onto a cake. The raised lines give a "three-dimensional" appearance to the design on the tile.

Kenneth Clark Ceramics/Tubeline Tulip Border Color **green** Alternative colors **available** Composition **ceramic** Size **4 x 4 x ¼in/10 x 10cm x 6mm** Price ★★ W ⊞

Florals: **Late 20th century**

Government restrictions in Great Britain, and to some extent in Continental Europe, inhibited the production of decorative tiles in the years following the Second World War. At this time, most building construction was commissioned by the government, and plain tiles, rather than decorated ones, were considered a much better use of limited resources. In Europe, this restriction affected some countries more than others, but overall this period saw a temporary lull in the production of decorative tiles.

By the 1960s, tile production in Europe and America was increasing rapidly but was chiefly in the hands of a few large companies that specialized in mass production, such as Villeroy & Boch in Germany and H. & R. Johnson in England. Floral tiles tended to be simple, pastel-colored designs that could be produced quickly and easily by screen-printing or wax-resist techniques. Perhaps as a reaction to this, many small companies specializing in handmade and decorated tiles emerged during the 1980s and 1990s in both Europe and America . At the same time, the colorful tiles traditionally used in European countries such as Spain and Italy became more widely sought after, and were exported to other European countries and to America.

1

2

3

4

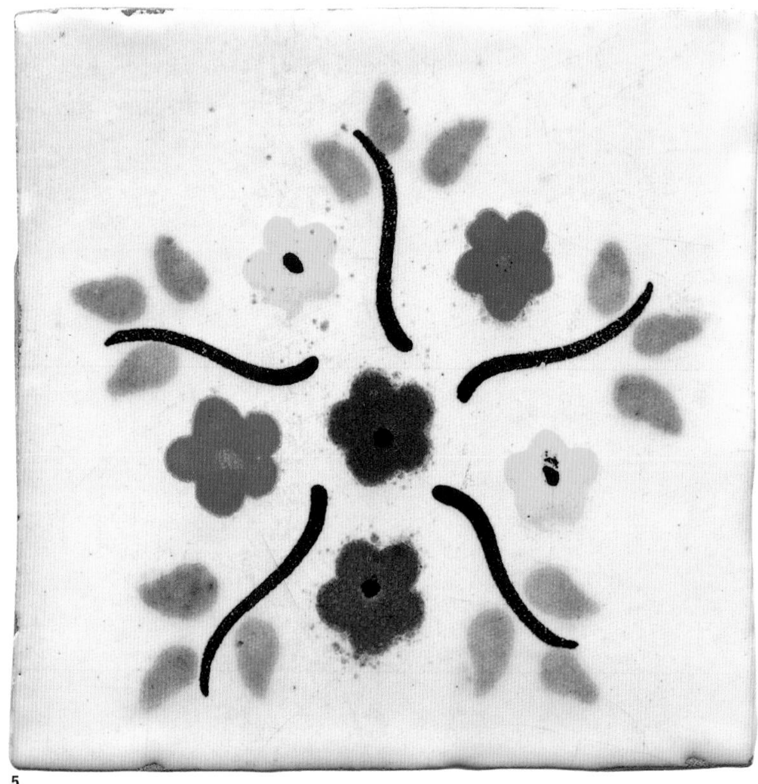

5

1 **Tiles of Stow/Summer Flowers Border** Color **multi** Alternative colors **not available** Composition **ceramic** Size **6 x 6 x ⅕in/15 x 15cm x 5mm** Price ★★ W

2 **Tiles of Stow/Summer Flowers** Color **multi** Alternative colors **not available** Composition **ceramic** Size **6 x 6 x ⅕in/ 15 x 15cm x 5mm** Price ★★★ W

3 **Tiles of Stow/Fleur Antique Border** Color **multi** Alternative colors **not available** Composition **ceramic** Size **4¼ x 4¼ x ¼in/11 x 11cm x 6mm** Price ★★★ W

4 **Wendy Wilbraham/Cornish Slate Tiles** Color **stone** Alternative colors **not available** Composition **stone and cement** Size **8 x 6 x ⅝in/ 20 x 15 x 1.5cm** Price ★★ W +

5 **Elon/Bouquet** Color **multi** Alternative colors **not available** Composition **ceramic** Size **4 x 4 x ¼in/ 10 x 10cm x 7mm** Price ★ W

6

7

6 Winchester Tile Co/Flower No. 6 Color **pure white** Alternative colors **available** Composition **ceramic** Size **4 x 4 x ¼in/10.5 x 10.5cm x 7mm** Price ★★ W

7 Original Style/Wild Rose Color **clematis** Alternative colors **available** Composition **ceramic** Size **4 x 4 x ¼in/ 10 x 10cm x 7mm** Price ★★★ W

8 Florida Tile Co/Crocus Border 438986D Color **multi** Alternative colors **not available** Composition **ceramic** Size **4 x 4 x ⅓in/ 10 x 10cm x 8mm** Price ★ W

9 Kenneth Clark Ceramics/ Magic Lantern: Tulip Color **ML6** Alternative colors **not available** Composition **ceramic** Size **4 x 4 x ¼in/ 10 x 10cm x 6mm** Price ★★ W ⊞

10 Villeroy & Boch/Kenzo Decor Color **orange** Alternative colors **available** Composition **ceramic** Size **15¾ x 11¾ x ¼in/40 x 30cm x 6mm** Price ★★★ W

9

8

10

20th century

Pictorial Tiles

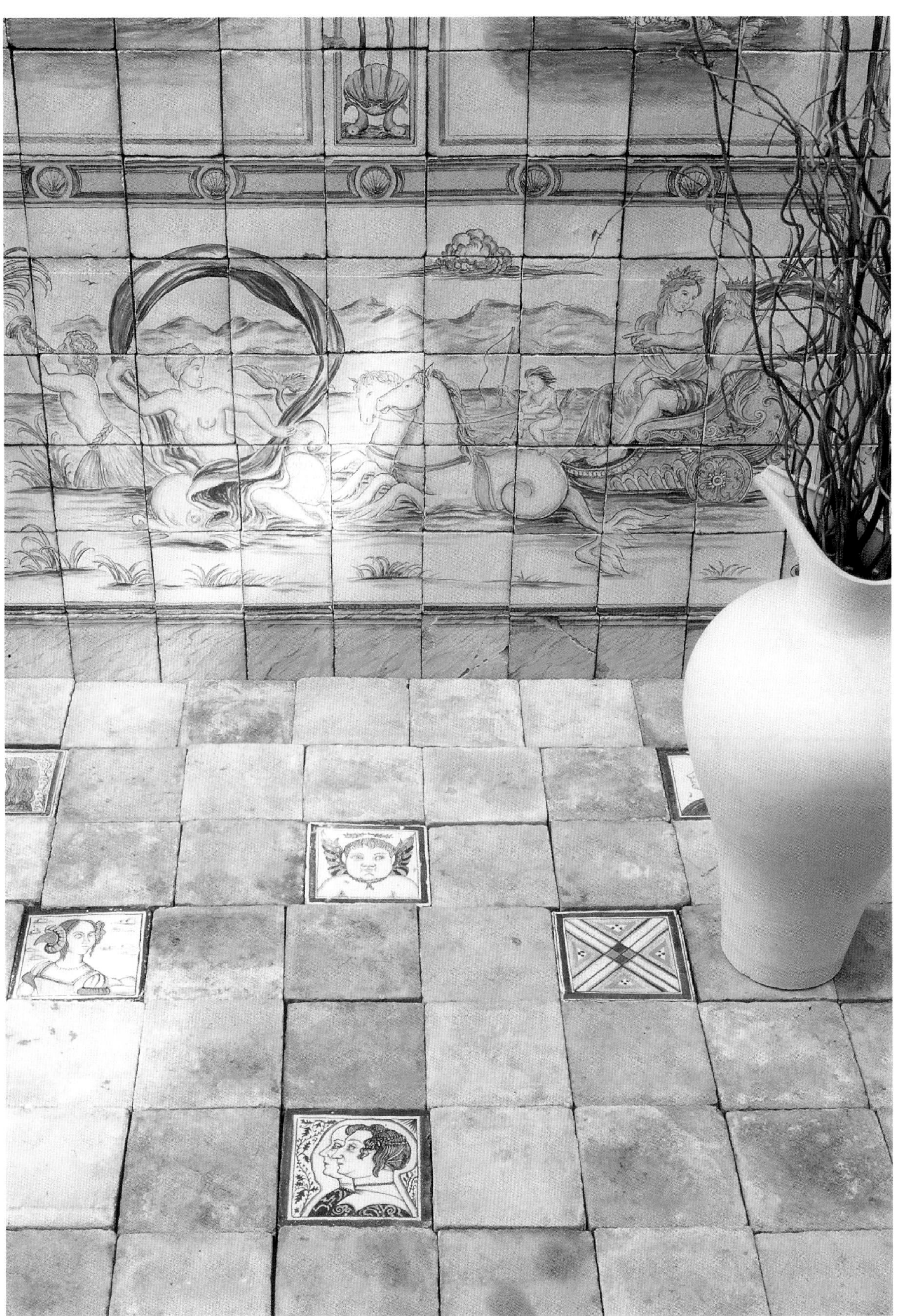

Since the earliest times, pictorial tiles have been a major feature of the tilemaker's repertoire. The mythical creatures and warriors depicted on the tilework on the walls of the city of Babylon, built in about 580 B.C., were intended to frighten potential invaders. The medieval romance and hunting scenes that occur on many 13th- and 14th-century tile installations reflect the lifestyle of the noblemen who were the tilemakers' patrons.

In the deeply religious countries of Spain and the Netherlands, tiles often depicted saints and Biblical scenes. The tilemakers of the Netherlands also produced maritime scenes on tiles, influenced by the nation's strong connections with the sea.

By the mid-19th century there was a great interest in literary subjects that is reflected in the numerous series of tiles depicting scenes from the works of writers and artists such as William Shakespeare and Albrecht Dürer. The advent of photography brought a new enthusiasm for in pictorial subjects, and many tile companies reproduced actual scenes on their tiles.

LEFT In Italy during the 15th and 16th centuries, tin-glazed tiles were commonly used on the floors as well as the walls of wealthy homes. On the floors, pictorial designs or motifs were often interspersed with areas of plain tiling. On the walls, pictorial panels, often featuring mythological subjects, were common.

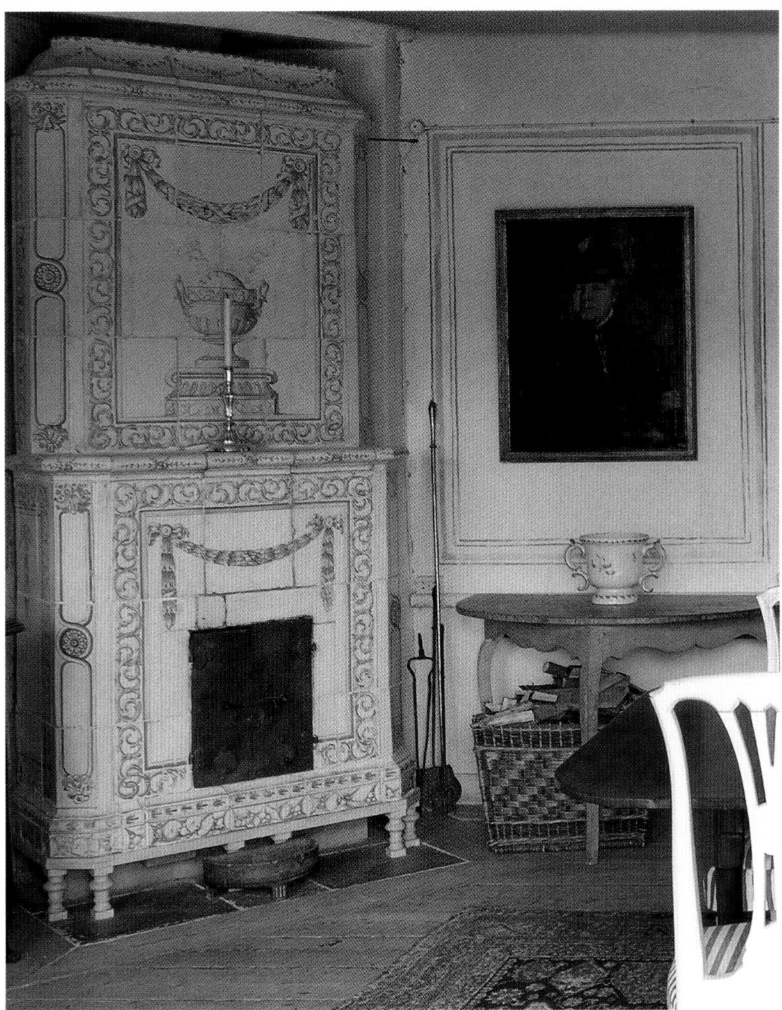

ABOVE An original 18th-century Swedish tiled stove sits in Lars Sjoberg's home at Odenslunda in Stockholm, Sweden. The individual tiles are quite large and combine to form an impressive pictorial design. Swags feature at the top and bottom of the stove, while the central image is that of a large urn.

POWDER GROUND

The English delft tiles shown here were made in London from 1730 to 1750. They surround a niche decorated in plain tiles and marble. The border on the octagonal tiles is known as a powder ground, and was produced by spattering pigment through a metal stencil. Most powder ground tiles have a purple border produced from manganese ore, but occasionally English delft tiles are found with red, green, or blue borders. These colors were never used on Dutch powder ground tiles.

KEY DESIGNS

1 Depictions of saints were often seen on early Spanish tiles, while the Dutch produced biblical scenes on delft tiles, as did the British in the late 18th century.

2 Marine-themed tiles were widely liked among the seafaring Dutch, and were a favorite subject for the Arts and Crafts potter William de Morgan.

3 Occupations, children's games, sports, and pastimes have been popular since the 17th century, especially on delftware. Allegorical and symbolic designs were much used in the 19th century.

4 Landscape tiles and tile panels (often featuring people) have been widely seen since the 17th century. In the Victorian era, imagery as well as naturalistic scenes were common.

5 Since the middle of the 19th century, tiles depicting scenes from literary works, such as this *Alice in Wonderland* design, have remained fashionable.

6 Animals have long been popular subjects for tile designers. This late 20th-century kitchen tile is typical of a modern, cartoonlike scene.

1 **Attica/Greek Figure Fresco** Color **black on terracotta** Alternative colors **not available** Composition **ceramic** Size **6 x 6 x ⅜in/ 15 x 15 x 1cm** Price ★★★★★ W

2 **Original Style/Viking Longship 6966B** Color **multi** Alternative colors **not available** Composition **ceramic** Size **6 x 6 x ¼in/ 15 x 15cm x 6mm** Price ★★ W

3 **Fired Earth/Musician No. 1** Color **multi** Alternative colors **not available** Composition **ceramic** Size **5 x 5 x ¼in/ 13 x 13cm x 7mm** Price ★★ W

4 **Original Style/Figures in a Landscape** Color **blue/white** Alternative colors **not available** Composition **ceramic** Size **/5 x 5 x ¼in/12.5 x 12.5cm x 7mm (6-tile set)** Price ★★★★ W

5 **Attica/Alice and Flamingo** Color **satin glaze** Alternative colors **not available** Composition **ceramic** Size **6 x 6 x ⅜in/15 x 15 x 1cm** Price ★★★ W

6 **Metropolitan Tile Co/Farmyard: Sheep** Color **multi** Alternative colors **not available** Composition **ceramic** Size **4¼ x 4¼ x ¼in/ 11 x 11cm x 6mm** Price ★★ W

Pictorials: **Pre-19th century**

In the 13th century, many inlaid floor tiles were produced with designs that depicted dogs, stags, and huntsmen. Although made as individual tiles, they were often laid in groups to give the effect of a chase. In about 1500, the potter Francesco Niculoso moved from Pisa in Italy to Seville in Spain, where he introduced the art of painting ceramics in tin-glaze. From Spain the art spread to Belgium and the Netherlands, and, by the 17th century, many fine picture tiles and tile panels were being produced in Antwerp, Rotterdam, and Delft. The tin-glaze technique gave the tilemaker a wider palette of color, allowing freer, more realistic designs. Large-scale panels consisting of four or five hundred tiles (such as those by the Dutch artist Cornelis Bouwmeester (1651-1733), best known for his shipping scenes), were expensive, but even the most humble of homes were decorated with single pictorial tiles. In 1756, in Liverpool, England, Sadler and Green perfected a method of transferring an image from a printing plate to a tile by means of a transfer tissue to allow consistent reproduction of very fine detail. The majority of of Sadler and Green's output was pictorial, with designs taken mainly from Rococo prints. In Colonial America, delftware tiles imported from the Netherlands were favored, particularly those depicting figures or moral or religious themes.

4

1

2

3

1 **Simmy Ceramics/Cherubs** Color **blue on white** Alternative colors **available** Composition **ceramic** Size **8 x 8 x ⅓in/20 x 20cm x 8mm (6-tile panel)** Price ★★★★★ [W] [+]

2 **Attica/Balloon** Color **satin glaze** Alternative colors **available** Composition **ceramic** Size **5 x 5 x ⅜in/13 x 13 x 1cm** Price ★★★★ [W]

3 **Attica/Delft Figure** Color **delft** Alternative colors **not available** Composition **ceramic** Size **5 x 5 x ⅜in/13 x 13 x 1cm** Price ★★★ [W]

4 **Attica/16th Century Italian Maiolica** Color **multi** Alternative colors **available** Composition **terracotta** Size **35½ x 35½ x ¾in/ 90 x 90 x 2cm (9-tile panel)** Price ★★★★★ [F]

DELFTWARE

These tiles usually feature a central picture framed by a decorative border and a small ornamental motif at each corner. The delft tile painter faces a task akin to painting a watercolor on blotting paper. After the tile has been biscuit-fired, it is dipped in a liquid tin-glaze; the tile absorbs the moisture, leaving a thin layer of powdered glaze. The outline is marked on this glaze by dabbing powdered charcoal through a pricked paper pattern, and the tile painter then follows this outline, using a very fine brush to apply the color.

1

2

1 **Fired Earth/Windmill 2** Color **delft** Alternative colors **not available** Composition **ceramic** Size **5 x 5 x ⅓in/13 x 13cm x 8mm** Price ★★ [W]

2 **Original Style/River Scenes 4423** Color **delft** Alternative colors **not available** Composition **ceramic** Size **5 x 5 x ¼in/12.5 x 12.5cm x 7mm** Price ★ [W]

5

5 **Corres Mexican Tiles/Coffee Bean** Color **multi** Alternative colors **not available** Composition **ceramic** Size **4 x 4 x ⅜in/10 x 10 x 1cm (2-tile panel)** Price ★★★ W

6 **Topps Tiles/Akiba Le Grazie** Color **multi** Alternative colors **not available** Composition **ceramic** Size **11¾ x 10 x ⅓in/ 30 x 25cm x 8mm** Price ★★★ W

6

7

7 **Winchester Tile Co/King of Diamonds** Color **multi** Alternative colors **not available** Composition **ceramic** Size **6 x 4 x ⅓in/ 15 x 10.5cm x 9mm (4-tile set)** Price ★★★ W

8 **Attica/Pavimenti Turtle** Color **multi** Alternative colors **available** Composition **terracotta** Size **6¼ x 6¼ x ½in/16 x 16 x 1.5cm** Price ★★★★ F

9 **Attica/Valencia Fresco** Color **ocher** Alternative colors **available** Composition **ceramic** Size **6 x 6 x ⅜in/15 x 15 x 1cm** Price ★★★★ W

10 **Fired Earth/Lemon Tree** Color **multi** Alternative colors **not available** Composition **ceramic** Size **6 x 6 x ¾in/15 x 15 x 2cm** Price ★★ W

11 **Reptile/Birds and Bees** Color **multi** Alternative colors **not available** Composition **ceramic** Size **6 x 6 x ¼in/15 x 15cm x 7mm** Price ★★★ W

12 **Attica/Midsummer Night's Dream** Color **multi** Alternative colors **available** Composition **ceramic** Size **6 x 6 x ¾in/15 x 15 x 2cm (16-tile panel)** Price ★★★★★ W

9

10

11

12

8

Pictorials: **19th century**

Comparatively few tiles were made in the first 40 years of the 19th century, but by 1845 the master British ceramicist Herbert Minton had introduced his first series of picture tiles, based on the romantic paintings of the French artist Jean-Antoine Watteau. These were so successful that they were still in production in the early 20th century. By the 1870s, his company, Minton China Works of Stoke-on-Trent, was one of the largest commercial potteries in the world.

In the 19th century, pictorial tiles were also produced in the style of the Aesthetic Movement, echoing the renewed interest in the Orient. These tiles were all mass-produced, which was an anathema to William Morris and the other leaders of the Arts and Crafts Movement in Britain and in America. Morris made tiles himself for a few years before turning to his friend William de Morgan to make and paint decorative tiles for his company. Galleons, and real and mythical animals–such as sea monsters–all appear on the de Morgan tiles, which were painted in monochrome, full color, and his own wonderful lusters. Meanwhile, in America, tilemakers such as Henry Chapman Mercer and William H. Grueby, who formed part of the American Arts and Crafts Movement, produced an interesting range of pictorial relief tiles, including the distinctive floor tiles made by Mercer for Wellington House in New York.

1

2

3

4

1 **Tiles of Newport & London/Grape Border Type B** Color **multi** Alternative colors **not available** Composition **ceramic** Size **8 x 4 x ⅜in/20 x 10 x 1cm** Price ★★ W

2 **Minton Hollins/Victorian Delight Plaque** Color **delft** Alternative colors **available** Composition **ceramic** Size **11¾ x 11¾ x ¾in/ 30 x 30 x 2cm** Price ★★★★★ W

3 **Candy & Co/Fish Stream** Color **Victorian blue** Alternative colors **not available** Composition **ceramic** Size **6 x 6 x ¼in/ 15 x 15cm x 7mm (8-tile panel)** Price ★★★★★ W

4 **Original Style/Boy on a Dolphin 6781A** Color **multi** Alternative colors **not available** Composition **ceramic** Size **6 x 6 x ¼in/15 x 15cm x 7mm (3-tile panel)** Price ★★★ W

5

6

7

5 Candy & Co/Scholar Color **multi** Alternative colors **not available** Composition **ceramic** Size **6 x 6 x ¼in/ 15 x 15cm x 7mm (2-tile panel)** Price ★★ W

6 Candy & Co/Philip Webb Birds Color **terracotta on delft crazed** Alternative colors **available** Composition **ceramic** Size **15 x 15cm x 7mm/6 x 6 x ¼in (3-tile set)** Price ★★★ W

7 Original Style/Nocturnal Slumber 6042 Color **multi** Alternative colors **not available** Composition **ceramic** Size **6 x 6 x ¼in/ 15 x 15cm x 7mm (3-tile panel)** Price ★★★ W

8 Welbeck Tiles/Victorian Jelly Color **cream crackle** Alternative colors **not available** Composition **ceramic** Size **5 x 5 x ⅓in/ 12.5 x 12.5cm x 8mm** Price ★★★ W

9 Candy & Co/Victorian Zebra Color **delft white** Alternative colors **available** Composition **ceramic** Size **6 x 6 x ⅓in/ 15 x 15cm x 8mm (6-tile set)** Price ★★★★ W

10 Original Style/Cameo Carousel 6006 Color **imperial ivory** Alternative colors **not available** Composition **ceramic** Size **6 x 6 x ¼in/ 15 x 15cm x 7mm (5-tile panel)** Price ★★★★ W

11 Original Style/Exotic Birds (Left) 6968A Color **multi** Alternative colors **not available** Composition **ceramic** Size **6 x 6 x ¼in/ 15 x 15cm x 7mm (3-tile panel)** Price ★★★ W

12 Original Style/Peacock Border 6960A Color **multi** Alternative colors **not available** Composition **ceramic** Size **6 x 3 x ¼in/ 15 x 7.5cm x 7mm (2-tile panel)** Price ★★ W

9

10

11

8

12

19th century

Pictorials: **20th century**

The Art Nouveau Movement produced a plethora of wonderful tiled interiors, particularly in Belgium and France, many in the style of the graphic illustrations by the Czech artist Alphonse Mucha. In England, few pictorial tiles were made until the 1920s and 1930s when Carter & Co produced several series of brightly colored, hand-painted picture tiles in the Art Deco style, covering subjects ranging from nursery rhymes to water birds. Packard and Ord, established in London in 1935, specialized in hand-painted pictorial sets.

In America, the influence of the Arts and Crafts Movement continued, and many small tilemakers produced striking relief landscapes and other pictorial tiles. Since the 1970s, tile murals, often in *trompe l'oeil* form, regained their popularity. There was also a trend for manufacturers to commission fashion designers such as Fendi and Kenzo to develop ideas for tiles, such as Fendi's white-on-white relief wall tile series "Astrologia."

1

2

1 **Fired Earth/Pea Green Boat** Color **multi** Alternative colors **not available** Composition **ceramic** Size **6 x 6 x ⅜in/ 15 x 15 x 1cm** Price ★★★ [W]

2 **Original Style/Laurel (Le Laurier) 6052** Color **multi** Alternative colors **not available** Composition **ceramic** Size **6 x 6 x ¼in/ 15 x 15cm x 7mm** Price ★★ [W]

3 **Fired Earth/Castle Window** Color **multi** Alternative colors **not available** Composition **ceramic** Size **6 x 6 x ⅜in/15 x 15 x 1cm** Price ★★★ [W]

4 **Minton Hollins/Elegance ELE2P** Color **peach** Alternative colors **available** Composition **ceramic** Size **6 x 6 x ⅓in/ 15 x 15cm x 8mm (3-tile panel)** Price ★★★ [W]

5 **Ann Sacks/Algonquin Tent** Color **earthenware** Alternative colors **available** Composition **ceramic** Size **4 x 4 x ⅜in/10 x 10 x 1cm** Price ★★★ [W]

6 **Reptile/4 Fishes No. 21** Color **multi** Alternative colors **not available** Composition **ceramic** Size **6 x 6 x ¼in/15 x 15cm x 7mm** Price ★★★ [W]

7 **Surving Studios/Vine Tree Frog Triptych** Color **green** Alternative colors **available** Composition **ceramic** Size **4 x 4 x ¼in/10 x 10cm x 7mm (3-tile panel)** Price ★★★★★ [W]

8 **Tiles of Stow/Sixpence Bird** Color **multi** Alternative colors **not available** Composition **ceramic** Size **6 x 6 x ¼in/ 15 x 15cm x 7mm** Price ★★★ [W]

3

4

5

6

7

8

9

9 Reptile/Seal No. 17 Color **multi** Alternative colors **available** Composition **ceramic** Size **6 x 6 x ¼in/15 x 15cm x 7mm** Price ★★★ [W]

10 H. & R. Johnson/Berries BER1D Color **beige** Alternative colors **not available** Composition **ceramic** Size **4¼ x 4¼ x ¼in/ 11 x 11cm x 6mm (6-tile set)** Price ★★ [W]

11 Kenneth Clark Ceramics/Magic Lantern Color **ML3** Alternative colors **not available** Composition **ceramic** Size **4 x 4 x ¼in/10 x 10cm x 7mm** Price ★★ [W] [+]

10

11

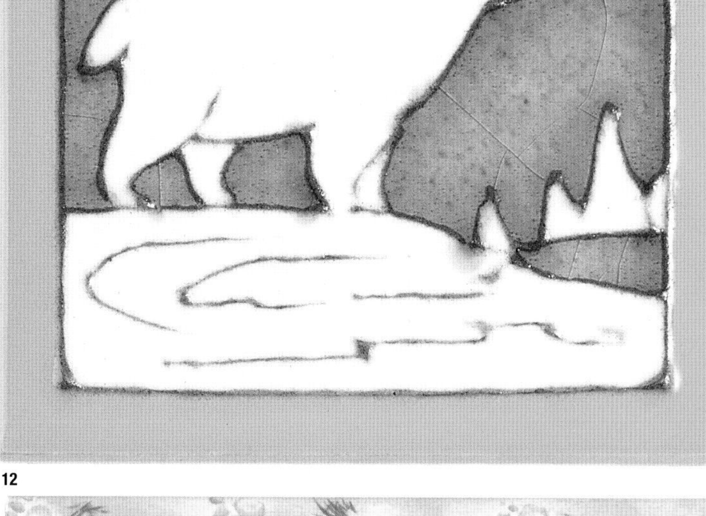

12

16

17

13

14

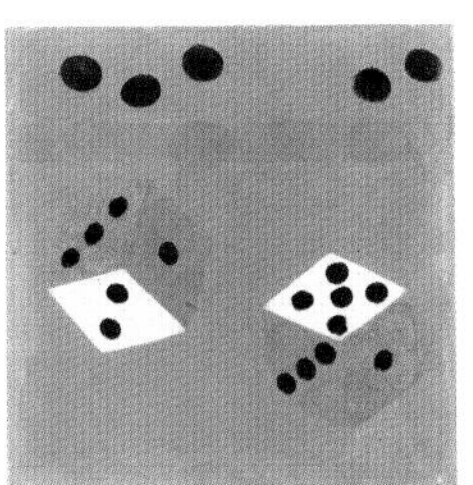

15

12 Kenneth Clark Ceramics/ Alphabet Pictures: Polar Bear Color **blue and white** Alternative colors **available** Composition **ceramic** Size **4 x 4 x ¼in/10 x 10cm x 7mm** Price ★★★ [W] [+]

13 Winchester Tile Co/Nuthatch Color **multi** Alternative colors **not available** Composition **ceramic** Size **4 x 4 x ⅜in/10.5 x 10.5 x 1cm** Price ★★ [W]

14 Simmy Ceramics/The International Restaurant Range Color **white** Alternative colors **not available** Composition **ceramic** Size **8 x 8 x ⅓in/ 20 x 20cm x 8mm** Price ★★★★ [W] [+]

15 Carocim/Dé Jeté H. M. C. 08 Color **green** Alternative colors **available** Composition **ceramic** Size **8 x 8 x ⅜in/20 x 20 x 1cm** Price ★ [W] [F] [+]

16 Villeroy & Boch/Safari 1429SH30 Color **multi** Alternative colors **not available** Composition **ceramic** Size **8 x ½ x ¼in/20 x 1.2cm x 7mm** Price ★ [W]

17 Villeroy & Boch/Safari SH31 Color **multi** Alternative colors **not available** Composition **ceramic** Size **8 x 2½ x ¼in/20 x 6.5cm x 7mm** Price ★★ [W]

18 Kenneth Clark Ceramics/ Magic Lantern Color **ML2** Alternative colors **not available** Composition **ceramic** Size **4 x 4 x ¼in/ 10 x 10cm x 7mm** Price ★★ [W] [+]

19 Tiles of Stow/Grasslands Tiger Color **white** Alternative colors **available** Composition **ceramic** Size **5 x 5 x ⅜in/13 x 13 x 1cm** Price ★★★ [W]

20 Winchester Tile Co/Sweetcorn and Mushroom Color **multi** Alternative colors **not available** Composition **ceramic** Size **4 x 4 x ¼in/ 10.5 x 10.5cm x 7mm** Price ★★ [W]

TILES & ADVERTISING

Because they are durable and easy to clean, tiles have often been used to advertise products and services. It was once very common to see butchers and dairies with tile panels depicting sheep, cattle, and poultry, although many of these have now disappeared behind modern laminated surfaces. During the 1920s and 1930s, W. H. Smith, the English stationer and bookseller, used a number of Carter & Co's tiles to advertise their products, while the Santa Fe Railroad in America used tiled logos on its principal stations.

Rye Tiles/Rooster Panel Color **multi** Alternative colors **available** Composition **ceramic** Size **4¼ x 4¼ x ¼in/11 x 11cm x 7mm (12-tile panel)** Price ★★★★★ [W]

18

19

20

20th century

Overall Pattern Tiles

By their very nature, tiles create an overall pattern when laid. Even when the design extends across a large number of tiles, the basic grid pattern is visible in the joints. Delft tile painters tried to conceal this by carrying their designs to adjacent tiles using various forms of corner ornament, but these corners themselves created a further element in the overall pattern.

Individual tiles have also been designed with an overall pattern. By covering the tile with a repeated pattern of small motifs, often organic and vegetal in nature, an effect approaching that of wallpaper is achieved. The application of printing techniques to tile manufacture in the 1750s enabled such overall designs to be produced accurately and cheaply. Marble effects were also very popular on tiles, particularly in the Netherlands, and subsequently reappeared in modified form during the 1920s and 1930s as the mottled tiles so beloved of fireplace manufacturers. The advent of Pop Art in the 1950s and 1960s inspired a wealth of tiles with simple designs that consisted of dots, squiggles, lines, and other patterns, many of which are today designed by computer.

ABOVE This modern fireplace incorporates tiles that are essentially based upon traditional designs and patterns. The inspiration is derived from the "Masters of Tabriz" from the dado of the Muradiye in Edirne, Turkey, which dates from the middle of the 15th century. The border tiles in the fireplace are based upon later Iznik tiles of the 17th century.

RIGHT The strong geometric shapes of Charles Jencks's Post Modernist home are characteristic of the Art Deco period. The patterns in which the simple, mottled tiles are laid in the bathroom reflect this style. Brightly colored tiles of this kind were a particular feature of Art Deco schemes. The stepped window surround is also in keeping with the distinctive feel of the room.

KEY DESIGNS

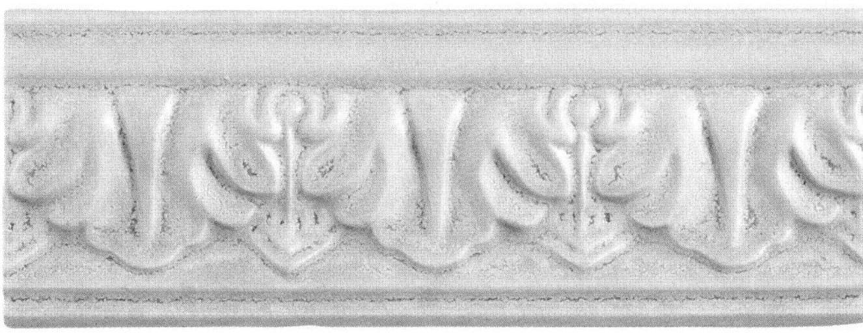

1 Tile designs have often imitated architectural features. This is particularly true of border tiles, where the overall pattern simulates plaster or stone moldings.

2 The repeated use of a small floret or other motif can create an overall effect that almost gives the impression of "ceramic wallpaper."

3 The reproduction of stone and granite effects first used in the Netherlands in the late 17th century is now used on porcelain floor tiles.

4 Dots, squiggles, and a variety of other small-scale decorations have often been used in the 20th century as backgrounds for a feature tile or tile panel, or as patterns in their own right.

---

1 **Walker Zanger/Acanthus Leaf** Color **Aegean Sea** Alternative colors **available** Composition **ceramic** Size **8 x 3 x ½in/20 x 8 x 1.5cm** Price ★★ [W]

2 **Elon/Terracotta Frieze** Color **terracotta** Alternative colors **available** Composition **ceramic** Size **4 x 4 x ¼in/10.5 x 10.5cm x 7mm** Price ★ [W]

3 **H. & R. Johnson/Gatsby Field GTY1A** Color **black** Alternative colors **available** Composition **ceramic** Size **6 x 6 x ¼in/15 x 15cm x 6mm** Price ★ [W]

4 **Carocim/Souleiado-Tortillon 5510** Color **blue** Alternative colors **available** Composition **ceramic** Size **8 x 8 x ⅜in/20 x 20 x 1cm** Price ★ [W] [F] [+]

Overall Pattern: **Pre-20th century**

Early ceramic tiles rarely featured overall patterns, largely because of the difficulty of producing regular patterns by hand-painting. Some medieval tiles did feature overall patterns, but the tiles were invariably divided up into panels of four, nine, or sixteen by additional lines of plain tiles.

In the Netherlands, a number of tiled rooms still exist that show how the corner ornaments on 17th- and 18th-century delft tiles created a cohesive pattern when used *en masse*. The marble patterns that appear on delft tiles from the end of the 17th century were produced before the tiles were fired, by splashing pigments onto the surface or by swirling color into the glaze with a comb. The printing technique developed by Sadler and Green in England during the 1750s loaned itself to the production of tiles with repeated small motifs and patterns, similar to those seen on wallpaper.

During the 19th century, more heavily patterned designs were used on tiles. Many of these designs were based on stylized, rhythmical, organic, and vegetal forms. This was particularly true of the second half of the 19th century, and reflected the generally busy, cluttered feel of Victorian interiors. Classical patterns such as scrollwork also remained popular.

1

2

3

4

5

6

7

1 **Fired Earth/Ironbridge Spinney** Color **Prussian blue** Alternative colors **available** Composition **ceramic** Size **6 x 3 x ⅜in/15 x 7.5cm x 9mm** Price ★★ W

2 **Fired Earth/Roman Mosaic Rope Border** Color **black** Alternative colors **available** Composition **stone** Size **15¾ x 4 x ½in/40 x 10 x 1.2cm** Price ★★★★ F

3 **Walker Zanger/Alhambra Algiers Border** Color **multi** Alternative colors **available** Composition **ceramic** Size **4 x 4 x ⅝in/10 x 10 x 1.5cm** Price ★★ W

4 **Carocim/Victoria** Color **black and white** Alternative colors **available** Composition **ceramic** Size **8 x 8 x ⅜in 20 x 20 x 1cm** Price ★ W F +

5 **Tiles of Stow/Tozetto Inset** Color **blue on white** Alternative colors **available** Composition **ceramic** Size **1½ x 1½ x ⅜in/4 x 4 x 1cm** Price ★★ W F

6 **Yorkshire Tile Co/D-717-M** Color **multi** Alternative colors **available** Composition **ceramic** Size **11 x 5½ x ¼in/28 x 14cm x 7mm** Price ★ W

7 **Candy & Co/Foliage Repeat** Color **green** Alternative colors **available** Composition **ceramic** Size **6 x 6 x ¼in/15 x 15cm x 7mm** Price ★ W

MEXICAN TILES

Although there had been an indigenous pottery industry in Mexico for many centuries, the Spanish conquistadores introduced the technique of painting on tin-glaze. During the 17th and 18th centuries colorful tiles combining Spanish and native Mexican designs were used to decorate the facades of churches. The traditional center for tilemaking was Puebla, where, in the late 20th century, there was a revival of the craft. Most of the Spanish influence has now disappeared and modern production has a more traditional feel.

Elon/Carrillo Arbor G Color **Mexican white and green** Alternative colors **not available** Composition **ceramic** Size **4 x 4 x ⅓in/10 x 10cm x 8mm** Price ★ W

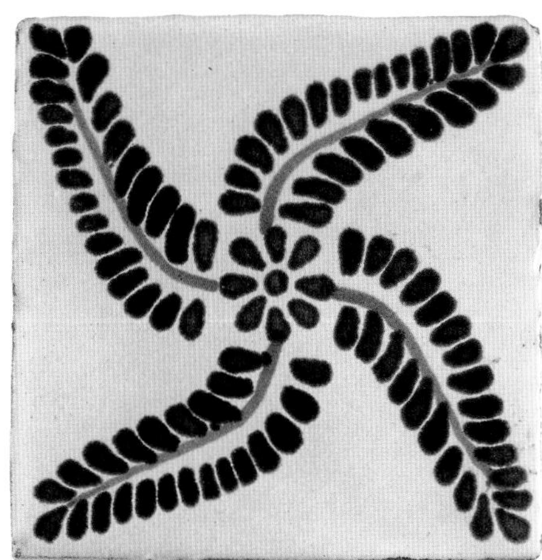

Corres Mexican Tiles/Patterns No. 10 Color **blue** Alternative colors **not available** Composition **ceramic** Size **4 x 4 x ⅜in/10 x 10 x 1cm** Price ★ W ⊞

12

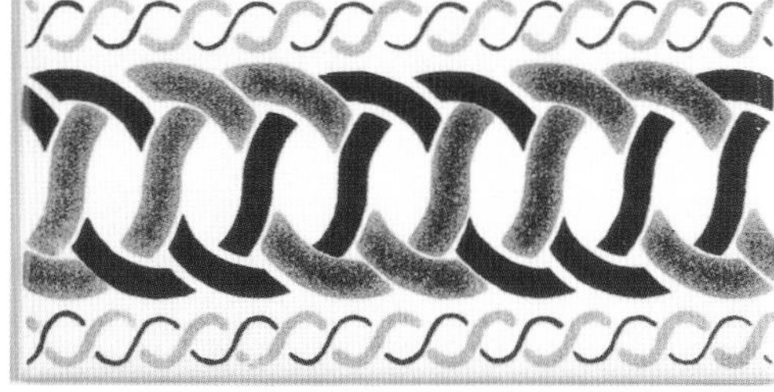

8

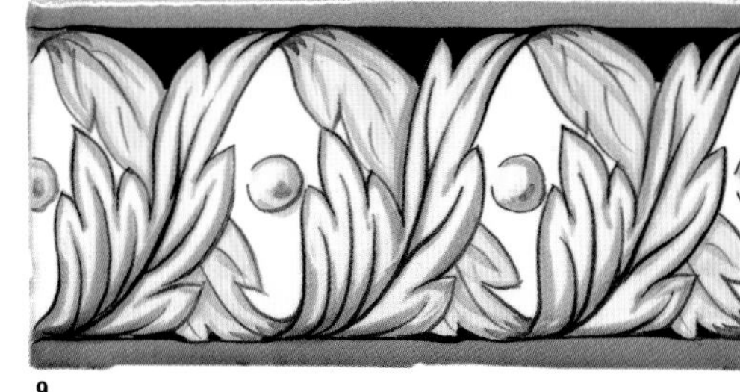

9

10

11

13

14

8 Kenneth Clark Ceramics/ Celtic Weave Color **multi** Alternative colors **not available** Composition **ceramic** Size **6 x 3 x ¼in/ 15 x 7.5cm x 7mm** Price ★ W

9 Walker Zanger/Palladio No. 30 Color **multi** Alternative colors **not available** Composition **ceramic** Size **6 x 3 x ½in/ 15 x 7.5 x 1.2cm** Price ★★★ W

10 Original Style/Cornice K9904 Color **Baltic blue** Alternative colors **available** Composition **ceramic** Size **6 x 3 x ¼in/15 x 7.5cm x 7mm** Price ★ W

11 Candy & Co/Willow Wand Color **burgundy** Alternative colors **available** Composition **ceramic** Size **6 x 3 x ¼in/15 x 7.5cm x 7mm** Price ★ W

12 Walker Zanger/Fresco Assisi Color **blue** Alternative colors **not available** Composition **ceramic** Size **8 x 4 x ½in/20 x 10 x 1.2cm** Price ★★★★ W

13 Fired Earth/Anatolia 2 Color **blue and white** Alternative colors **not available** Composition **ceramic** Size **6¾ x 6¾ x ⅜in/17.5 x 17.5 x 1cm** Price ★★ W

14 Candy & Co/Chelsea Square Color **floral blue** Alternative colors **available** Composition **ceramic** Size **6 x 6 x ¼in/ 15 x 15cm x 7mm** Price ★ W

Overall Pattern: **20th century**

The use of overall tile patterns declined markedly at the beginning of the 20th century, largely as a result of the Art Nouveau Movement sweeping across Europe, and, to some extent, America. In keeping with this movement, plain tiles were used predominantly for room schemes, while patterned tiles were restricted to a dado-height row or a random insert.

By the 1920s, plain tiles gave way to mottles, often produced in the newly developed matte or eggshell glazes. At this time, tilemakers began to investigate the chemistry of glazes and to develop new and varied ones, many with small, random crackle or star-burst effects. These and the mottled tiles were a popular choice for decorating fireplaces, but they were also used to cover entire walls, especially in bathrooms and kitchens.

Increased mechanization in the 1950s and 1960s led to the simplification of tile design and the subsequent introduction of the many bland and repetitive patterns that swamped the market during the 1970s. Overall pattern designs featuring small floral motifs, in the style of Laura Ashley, were produced during the late 1970s and early 1980s, while in the late 1980s and early 1990s computer-generated tile designs became commonplace, although handmade tiles also remained popular.

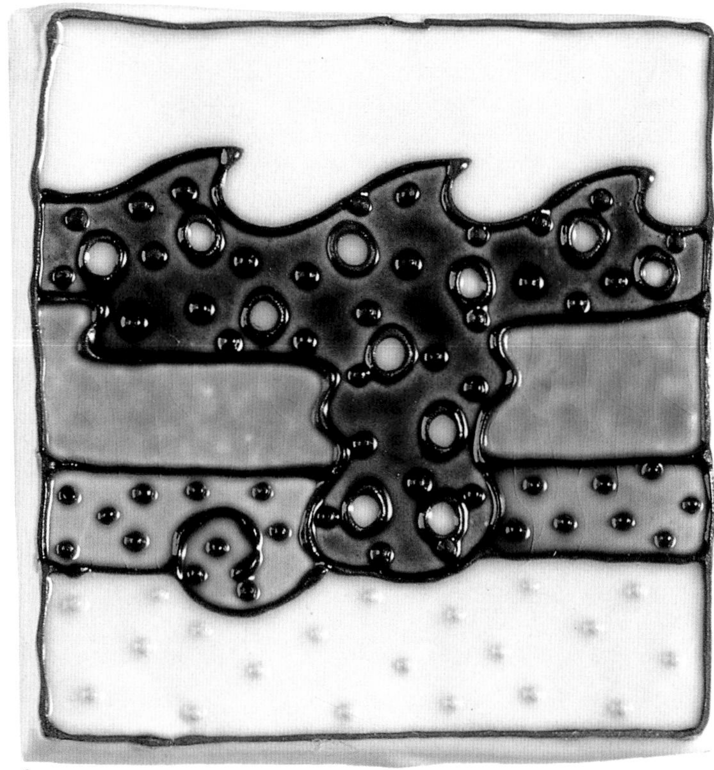
3

1

2

1 **Kenneth Clark Ceramics/ Waves** Color **emerald** Alternative colors **available** Composition **ceramic** Size **4 x 4 x ¼in/10 x 10cm x 7mm** Price ★★ [W]

2 **Original Style/Laurel Quarter Tile** Color **multi** Alternative colors **not available** Composition **ceramic** Size **6 x 1½ x ¼in/15 x 4cm x 7mm** Price ★ [W]

3 **Metropolitan Tile Co/ Wave Border** Color **multi** Alternative colors **not available** Composition **ceramic** Size **4¼ x 4¼ x ¼in/11 x 11cm x 6mm** Price ★★★ [W]

4 **Walker Zanger/Coronado Santa Fe LR** Color **multi** Alternative colors **not available** Composition **terracotta** Size **6 x 3 x ¼in/15 x 7.5cm x 7mm** Price ★★ [W]

5 **Corres Mexican Tiles/ Laurel Border** Color **laurel** Alternative colors **not available** Composition **ceramic** Size **4 x 4 x ⅜in/ 10 x 10 x 1cm** Price ★ [W] [+]

4

5

6 Daltile/Keystones Color **royal rose** Alternative colors **available** Composition **ceramic** Size **2 x 2 x ¼in/5 x 5cm x 7mm** Price ★ W F C

7 Surving Studios/Pebbles Color **browntone** Alternative colors **available** Composition **ceramic** Size **4 x 4 x ¼in/10 x 10cm x 7mm** Price ★★★ W F

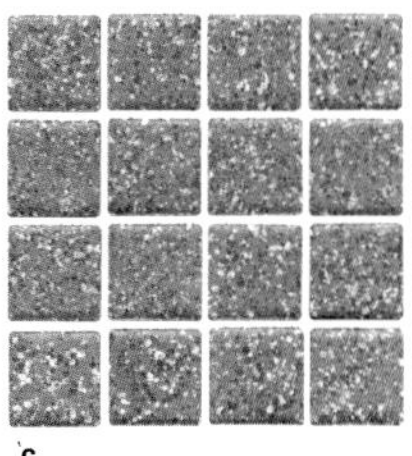

6

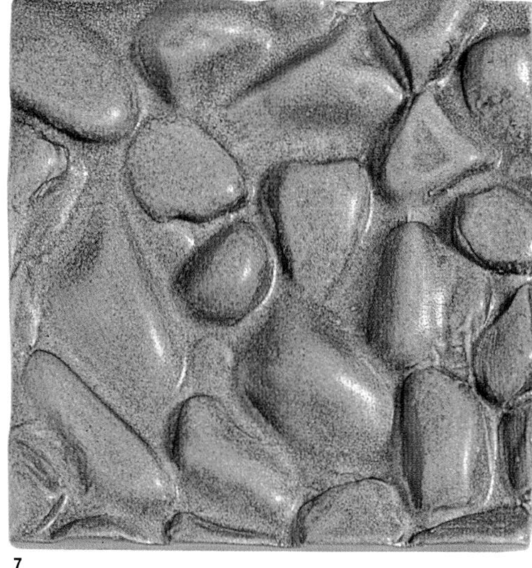

7

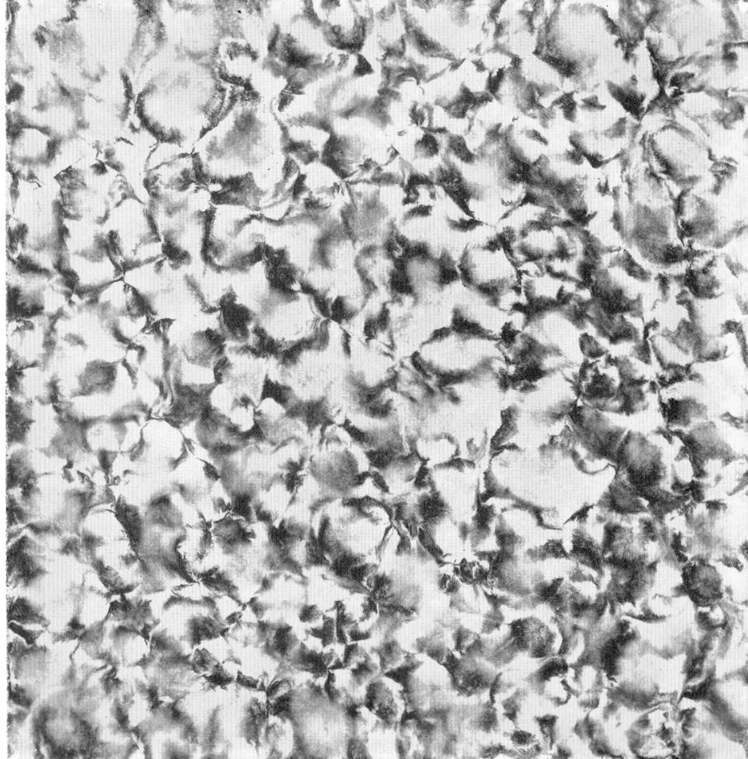

11

8 Winchester Tile Co/Leaf Border Color **white** Alternative colors **available** Composition **ceramic** Size **4 x 4 x ¼in/10.5 x 10.5cm x 7mm** Price ★★ W

8

9 H. & R. Johnson/Holst HOLS1P Color **multi** Alternative colors **not available** Composition **ceramic** Size **8 x 8 x ¼in/20 x 20cm x 6mm (6-tile panel)** Price ★★★★★ W

9

10 Walker Zanger/Florentino Bolzano No. 20 liner Color **multi** Alternative colors **not available** Composition **terracotta** Size **6 x 3 x ⅜in/15 x 7.5 x 1cm** Price ★★★ W

11 Carocim/Music Color **yellow/black** Alternative colors **available** Composition **ceramic** Size **8 x 8 x ⅜in/20 x 20 x 1cm** Price ★ W F

12 Fired Earth/Sunflower Leaves Color **green** Alternative colors **not available** Composition **ceramic** Size **4¼ x 4¼ x ⅓in/11 x 11cm x 8mm** Price ★★★ W

13 Minton Hollins/Fanfare ANS1 Color **ivory** Alternative colors **not available** Composition **ceramic** Size **6 x 1 x ⅓in/15 x 2.5cm x 8mm** Price ★ W

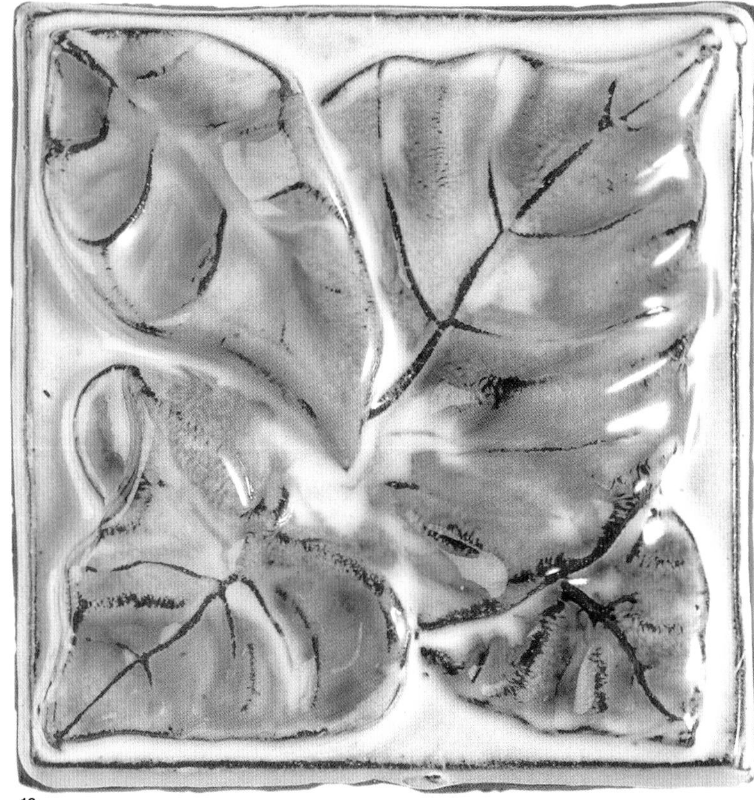

12

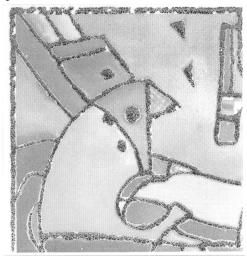

10

13

20th century

Geometric Tiles

Tiles are essentially geometric in form, and, even when the design extends across a number of tiles, the geometric pattern of the tiling is still evident.

Since the Middle Ages, geometry has also been a basis for tile decoration, often in the form of checks, trellises, and overlapping circles.Designs of this nature are fundamental to Islamic culture, and this is reflected in the tiles and mosaics of Spain, North Africa, and the Middle East.

In 18th-century Portugal, so-called "pombaline" tiles, which have a diagonal pattern of foliage, were placed together to form a trellis pattern. The geometric patterns were also very popular on the tin-glazed tiles produced in France, and to a lesser extent in the Netherlands toward the end of the 19th century. At the same time, pavements composed of geometrically- shaped tiles in various colors were very popular for use in hallways, porches, and public buildings throughout Europe. The 20th century has seen movements such as Pop Art enhance the popularity of geometrically-patterned tile's.

RIGHT **Designs composed of overlapping circles have been used on tiles since medieval times, and relieve the square effect of the tile itself, as is effectively demonstrated in this 18th-century-style Spanish kitchen. Such geometric patterns have appeared in many eras, notably in Art Deco interiors of the early 20th century.**

ABOVE The tiles positioned around the Aga stove in the Scottish home of Annie and Lachlan Stewart were all handmade and hand-painted. The ever-popular plaid pattern, here in various shades of green, fits in perfectly with the style of this farmhouse kitchen, with its traditional stove and painted woodwork.

ZILLIJ MOSAIC DESIGNS

Zillij is the name given to traditional North African cut mosaic tilework. Originally, large square tiles were cut after firing into the individually shaped pieces required to make up these elaborate patterns. However, nowadays the pieces are shaped before firing and glazing. The shapes of the pieces and the arrangements of the colors are traditional and have varied surprisingly little over the last 500 years.

KEY DESIGNS

1 The use of interlocking shapes dates back to the medieval period, but it reached its height in Moorish Spain when very simple geometric shapes were used to produce extremely complex patterns.

2 Some tiles give the illusion of having interlocking components, such as this geometric *trompe l'oeil* design. The visual effect is heightened when several tiles are placed together.

3 Perhaps the simplest and most popular of geometric shapes is the square arranged in alternating colors, either straight or diagonally as a diamond pattern.

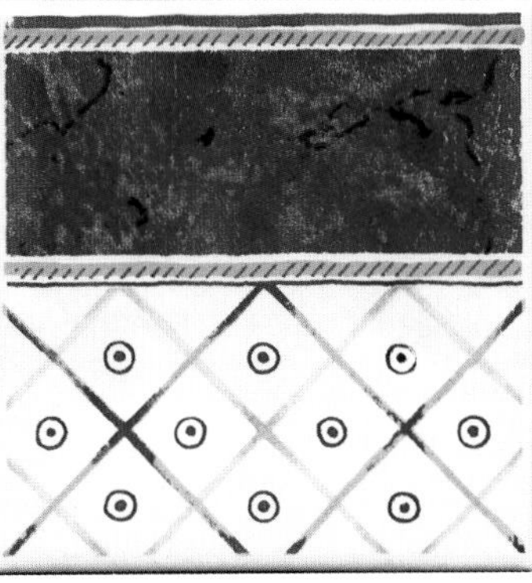

4 Tiles that feature an integral border, like this modern geometric design, have long been used as a way of giving the illusion of a separate border panel. This tile also features a trellis pattern.

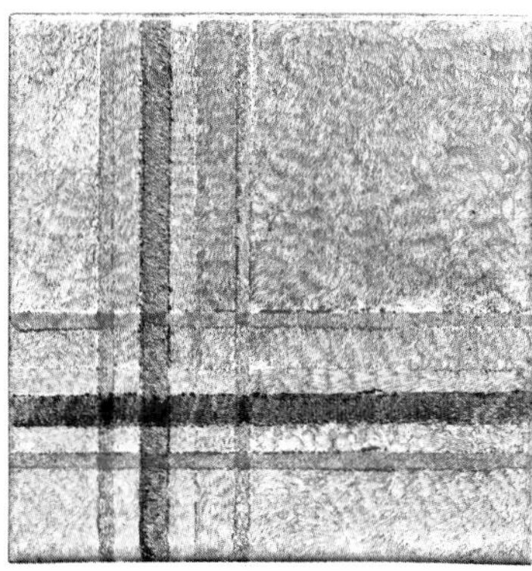

5 Plaid designs have been popular since the 19th century, and were still employed by tile designers in the late 20th century, often updated with new color combinations.

---

1 **Metropolitan Tile Co/Series 700 Border** Color **winter** Alternative colors **available** Composition **Venetian marble** Size **12 x 7 x ¼in/31 x 18cm x 7mm** Price ★★ [F]

2 **Attica/Trompe l'Oeil Large Step** Color **multi** Alternative colors **available** Composition **stone** Size **8 x 8 x ¾in/20 x 20 x 2cm** Price ★ [F]

3 **Kenneth Clark Ceramics/Greenwich Yellow** Color **yellow** Alternative colors **available** Composition **ceramic** Size **6 x 6 x ¼in/15 x 15cm x 7mm** Price ★ [W]

4 **Villeroy & Boch/Camargue ART3247** Color **multi** Alternative colors **not available** Composition **ceramic** Size **4 x 4 x ¼in/10 x 10cm x 6mm** Price ★ [W]

5 **Tiles of Stow/Check** Color **green and purple** Alternative colors **available** Composition **ceramic** Size **4 x 4 x ⅛in/10 x 10cm x 5mm** Price ★★★ [W]

Geometrics: **Pre-19th century**

During the Roman Empire, geometric mosaic floors were laid in domestic buildings as well as in public ones, particularly in Great Britain and Italy. The use of cut geometric mosaics was brought to Spain by the Moors from North Africa in the 8th century A.D. and who remained there until the 15th century. This style still survives in buildings such as the 14th-century Alhambra in Granada. In the early 13th century, a number of abbeys in the north of England were tiled with elaborate pavements of geometrically-shaped interlocking tiles. By the end of the 13th century, however, these had been superseded by inlaid tiles, often with intricate geometric patterns. These were used in abbeys and churches across Europe.

Due to the difficulty in producing cut geometric mosaics, these designs were soon reproduced on tiles. Painted geometric tiles were used on walls in many Portuguese interiors during the 14th and 15th centuries, often creating a *trompe l'oeil* "three-dimensional" box effect. By the 17th century, the Portuguese were also applying tiles to the exteriors of buildings, often resembling ornate trelliswork.

1

2

3

4

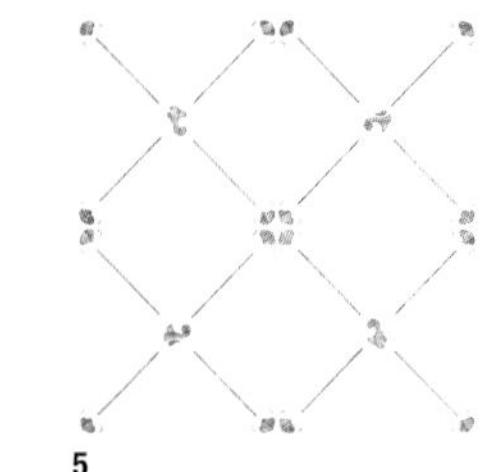
5

1 **Attica/Mosaic Terracotta** Color **multi** Alternative colors **available** Composition **terracotta** Size **4 x 4 x ⅜in/10 x 10 x 1cm** Price ★ W F

2 **Elon/Corinth Border** Color **gray** Alternative colors **available** Composition **ceramic** Size **12½ x 6¼ x ⅜in/32 x 16 x 1cm** Price ★ W F

3 **Attica/Therastar Fresco** Color **multi** Alternative colors **available** Composition **ceramic** Size **6 x 6 x ⅜in/15 x 15 x 1cm** Price ★★★ W

4 **Saloni Ceramica/Ocana Blanco** Color **multi** Alternative colors **not available** Composition **ceramic** Size **10 x 2 x ¼in/25 x 5cm x 7mm** Price ★ W

5 **Yorkshire Tile Co/Isadora 4** Color **blue and white** Alternative colors **not available** Composition **ceramic** Size **11¾ x 11¾ x ⅓in/30 x 30cm x 8mm** Price ★ W

THE SAN MARCO PAVEMENT

The floor of the Basilica of San Marco in Venice, Italy, is one of the most stunning examples of the use of geometric patterns. Probably dating from the 12th century, the floor has a large number of geometric *trompe l'oeil* designs, ranging from simple boxes to elaborate vortices, all executed in different colored marbles. George Maw, founder of the English tile-making firm of Maw and Co, visited San Marco in 1861, made a number of tracings of this remarkable pavement, and used the designs to create some of the earliest Victorian geometric tile pavements.

Attica/San Marco Pavement Color **multi** Alternative colors **available** Composition **terracotta, slate, and stone** Size **6 x 6 x ¾in/15 x 15 x 2cm** Price ★★ F

6

7

8

9

10

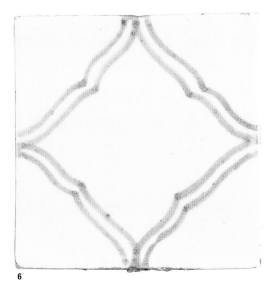

6 Elon/Trellis G Color **green and cream** Alternative colors **available** Composition **ceramic** Size **4 x 4 x ¼in/10 x 10cm x 7mm** Price ★ [W]

7 Tiles of Newport & London/ Vecchia American Decorated Tozetto Color **414B/AV** Alternative colors **available** Composition **ceramic** Size **1½ x 1½ x ¼in/4 x 4cm x 7mm** Price ★ [W] [+]

8 Winchester Tile Co/Painted Edge Lines Color **red** Alternative colors **available** Composition **ceramic** Size **4 x 4 x ¼in/10.5 x 10.5cm x 7mm** Price ★ [W] [+]

9 Attica/Ancient Rhythm Fresco Color **multi** Alternative colors **available** Composition **ceramic** Size **6 x 6 x ⅜in/15 x 15 x 1cm** Price ★★★★ [W]

10 Elon/Daisy May II G Color **green** Alternative colors **available** Composition **ceramic** Size **4 x 4 x ¼in/ 10 x 10cm x 7mm** Price ★ [W]

11 Carocim/Grec Color **brown and white** Alternative colors **available** Composition **ceramic** Size **8 x 8 x ⅜in/ 20 x 20 x 1cm** Price ★ [W] [F] [+]

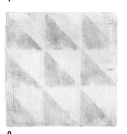

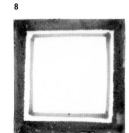

11

12

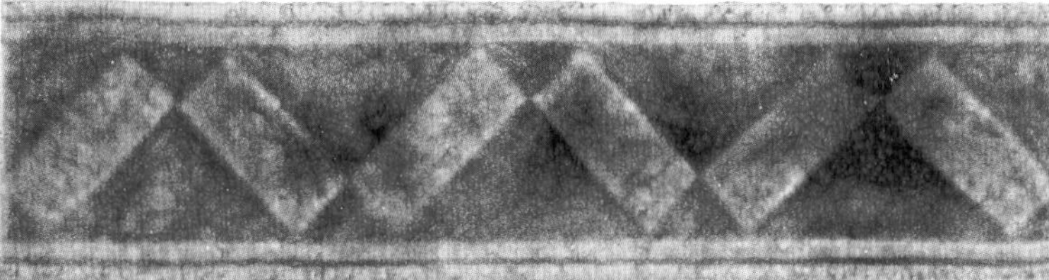

13

14

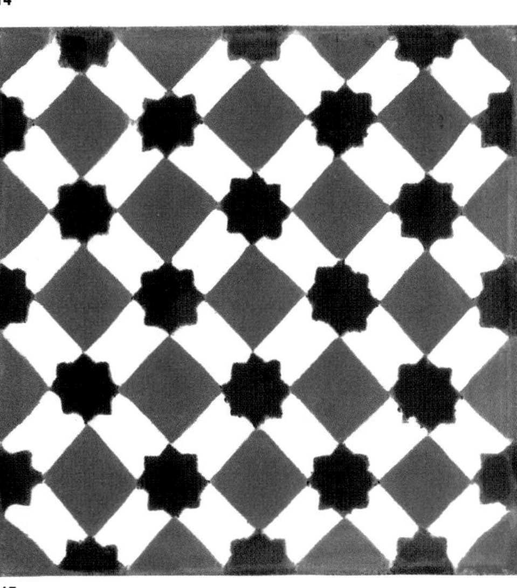

15

12 Carocim/Tanger Alternative colors **multi** Alternative colors **available** Composition **ceramic** Size **8 x 8 x ⅜in/ 20 x 20 x 1cm** Price ★★ [W] [F] [+]

13 Tiles of Newport & London/ Maurizio B2 LC2 Color **turquoise** Alternative colors **available** Composition **ceramic** Size **10¼ x 2½ x ¼in/26 x 6.5cm x 7mm** Price ★★ [W]

14 Saloni Ceramica/Navas Siena 788460 Color **siena** Alternative colors **available** Composition **ceramic** Size **10 x 4 x ¼in/25 x 10cm x 7mm** Price ★★ [W]

15 Carocim/Petit Latti M172 Color **blue and black** Alternative colors **available** Composition **ceramic** Size **8 x 8 x ⅜in/20 x 20 x 1cm** Price ★ [W] [F] [+]

Geometrics: **19th century**

When the Gothic Revival took place in the early 19th century, architects in England and elsewhere in Europe rediscovered the geometric designs of the Middle Ages. Chief among these in England was A. W. N. Pugin who collaborated with the potter Herbert Minton to create a range of encaustic tiles based on Gothic designs. Many of these were strongly geometric in form. In 1840, Herbert Minton purchased the rights to Richard Prosser's patent for dust-pressing clay products and realized that the process could be used to form ceramic *tesserae* and tiles. He was soon able to produce hundreds of geometric shapes based on fractions of a 6-inch (15-centimeter) square. The technique also made it easier to stain the clay different colors, and the tiles were used to create elaborate and colorful geometric pavements suitable for public buildings and residential houses. In France, intricate geometric patterns were stenciled onto tin-glazed tiles, particularly in the Pas de Calais region toward the end of the century.

3

3 **Fired Earth/Circulaire** Color **black and white** Alternative colors **available** Composition **encaustic** Size **8 x 8 x ¾in/20 x 20 x 2cm** Price ★ F

4

4 **Original Style/Culloden Stirling Tartan (Plaid) Border 6791S** Color **multi** Alternative colors **not available** Composition **ceramic** Size **6 x 3 x ¼in/ 15 x 7.5cm x 7mm** Price ★ W

5 **Ceramiche Eurotiles/Canossa Bordura BA/1** Color **blue and white** Alternative colors **not available** Composition **ceramic** Size **6 x 6 x ¼in/15 x 15cm x 6mm** Price ★ W

1

1 **Original Style/Royal Stewart Tartan (Plaid) Border 6795A** Color **multi** Alternative colors **not available** Composition **ceramic** Size **6 x 3 x ¼in/15 x 7.5cm x 7mm** Price ★ W

2 **Kenneth Clark Ceramics/ Gingham** Color **black and white** Alternative colors **available** Composition ceramic Size **6 x 3 x ¼in/ 15 x 7.5cm x 7mm** Price ★ W

2

5

6

7

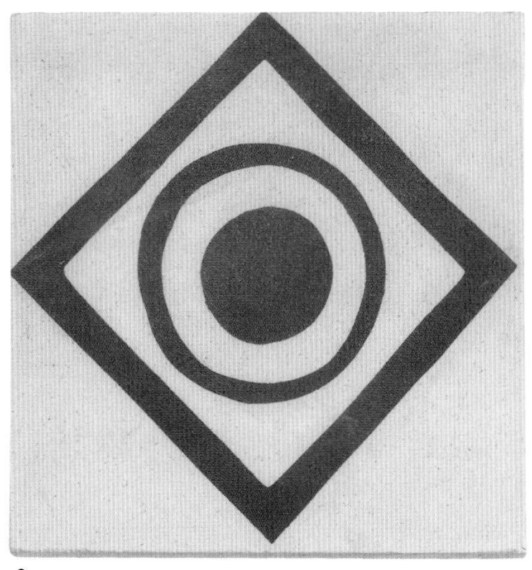
8

9

6 Tiles of Stow/English Lattice Color **blue** Alternative colors **not available** Composition **ceramic** Size **6 x 6 x ¼in/15 x 15cm x 6mm** Price ★ [W]

7 Original Style/Melbourne Border Color **black spot** Alternative colors **available** Composition **ceramic** Size **6 x 1 x ¼in/15 x 2.5cm x 7mm** Price ★ [F]

8 Life Enhancing Tile Co/ Encaustic Inset 52(S) Color **green and buff** Alternative colors **available** Composition **encaustic** Size **3 x 3 x ½in/ 7.5 x 7.5 x 1.2cm** Price ★★ [W] [F] [+]

9 Imports Direct/7880 Color **multi** Alternative colors **not available** Composition **cement** Size **8 x 4 x ½in/ 20 x 10 x 1.5cm** Price ★ [F]

10 Carocim/Petit Carré M201 Color **red and yellow** Alternative colors **available** Composition **ceramic** Size **8 x 8 x ⅜in/ 20 x 20 x 1cm** Price ★ [W] [F] [+]

10

11

11 Kenneth Clark Ceramics/San Marco Small Color **multi** Alternative colors **available** Composition **ceramic** Size **4 x 4 x ¼in/10 x 10cm x 7mm** Price ★ [W] [+]

12 Kenneth Clark Ceramics/ Marquee Color **green** Alternative colors **available** Composition **ceramic** Size **4 x 4 x ¼in/10 x 10cm x 7mm** Price ★ [W] [+]

13 Yorkshire Tile Co/Victoria Azul Color **azul** Alternative colors **not available** Composition **ceramic** Size **8 x 8 x ¼in/20 x 20cm x 6mm** Price ★ [W]

14 Imports Direct/7820 Color **multi** Alternative colors **not available** Composition **cement** Size **8 x 8 x ½in/ 20 x 20 x 1.5cm** Price ★ [F]

12

13

14

Geometrics: **20th century**

Perhaps as a reaction to the excesses of Victorian design, early 20th-century tiles were often plain or simply molded with a geometric effect that resembled bricks in a wall. During the 1920s and 1930s, bold, geometric shapes in tile work were often applied to Art Deco buildings. This style was particularly popular in America, and was also used to decorate a number of buildings in England, for example, the Hoover Building in Perivale, designed by the architects Wallis, Gilbert & Partners and opened in 1933. Not only did tiles form bold designs on the exteriors of such buildings, but they were also used on the inside.

On a smaller scale, some geometric tube-lined tiles were produced for domestic use in fireplaces by, for example, the English firm of Maw & Co. Geometric designs became increasingly popular during the 1950s and 1960s with the advent of Pop Art, whose designs featured squares, circles, and triangles that were often overlaid and printed in bright colors. The technique of screen-printing on tiles, which was developed from the 1940s to 1960s, loaned itself particularly well to this style of decoration. In the latter part of the 20th century, geometric tiles often featured a single design element, such as a diagonal line or a quadrant, which was combined in different ways to create a wide range of patterns.

1

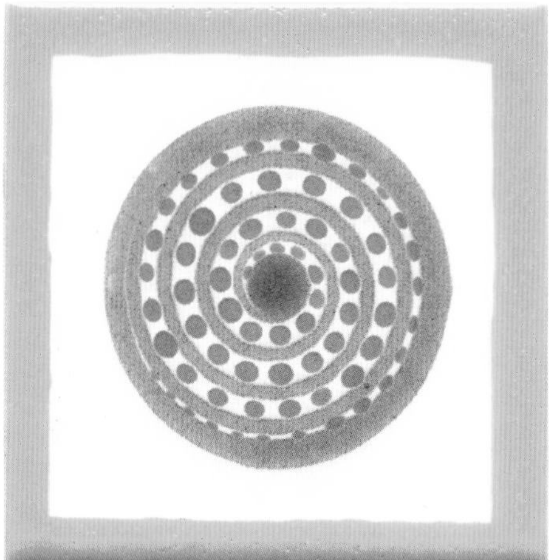

2

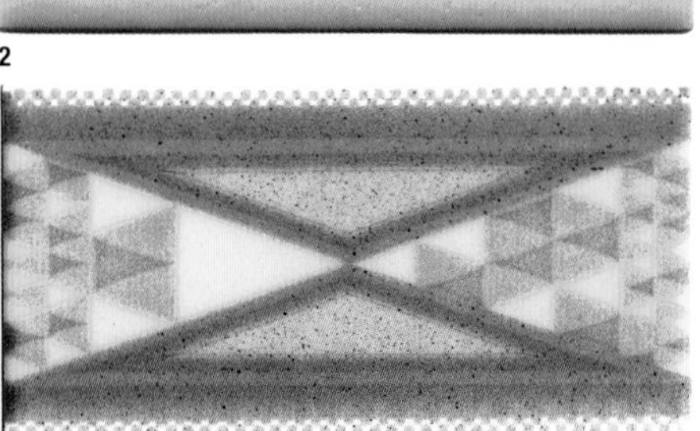

3

4

5

1 **Carocim/Horta** Color **purple and white** Alternative colors **available** Composition **ceramic** Size **8 x 8 x ⅜in/20 x 20 x 1cm** Price ★ W F +

2 **Kenneth Clark Ceramics/Midi No. 6** Color **multi** Alternative colors **available** Composition **ceramic** Size **4 x 4 x ¼in/ 10 x 10cm x 7mm** Price ★★ W +

3 **Kenneth Clark Ceramics/ Mardi Gras** Color **multi** Alternative colors **not available** Composition **ceramic** Size **8 x 4 x ¼in/ 20 x 10cm x 7mm** Price ★ W

4 **Mosquito/Dichroic Sparkle Tile** Color **turquoise** Alternative colors **available** Composition **ceramic/glass** Size **8 x 8 x ½in/20 x 20 x 1.5cm** Price ★★★★ W

5 **Carocim/Casson M221** Color **multi** Alternative colors **available** Composition **ceramic** Size **8 x 8 x ⅜in/ 20 x 20 x 1cm** Price ★ W F +

6

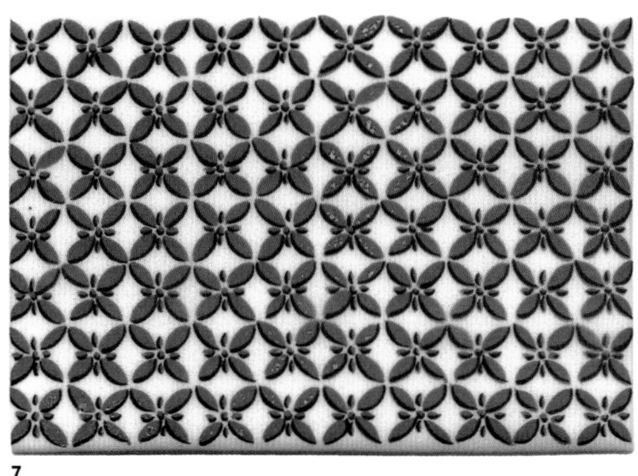

7

6 **Kenneth Clark Ceramics/ Peppercorn Sands** Color **multi** Alternative colors **available** Composition **ceramic** Size **6 x 6 x ¼in/ 15 x 15cm x 7mm** Price ★ W

7 **Winchester Tile Co/Osborne & Little Snap Patterned Field Tile** Color **blue and white** Alternative colors **not available** Composition **ceramic** Size **6 x 4 x ⅓in/ 15 x 10.5cm x 8mm** Price ★ W

8 **H. & R. Johnson/CTMR4** Color **aquamarine** Alternative colors **available** Composition **ceramic** Size **8 x 8 x ⅓in/ 20 x 20cm x 8mm** Price ★ [W] [⌂]

9 **H. & R. Johnson/Sigma** Color **multi** Alternative colors **not available** Composition **ceramic** Size **8 x 3 x ¼in/ 20 x 7.5cm x 7mm** Price ★ [W]

10 **Original Style/Manhattan Border 6490** Color **multi** Alternative colors **not available** Composition **ceramic** Size **6 x 2 x ¼in/ 15 x 5cm x 7mm** Price ★ [W]

11 **Mosquito/Sparkle Tile** Color **cobalt blue** Alternative colors **available** Composition **ceramic/glass** Size **8 x 8 x ½in/20 x 20 x 1.5cm** Price ★★★★★ [W]

8

9

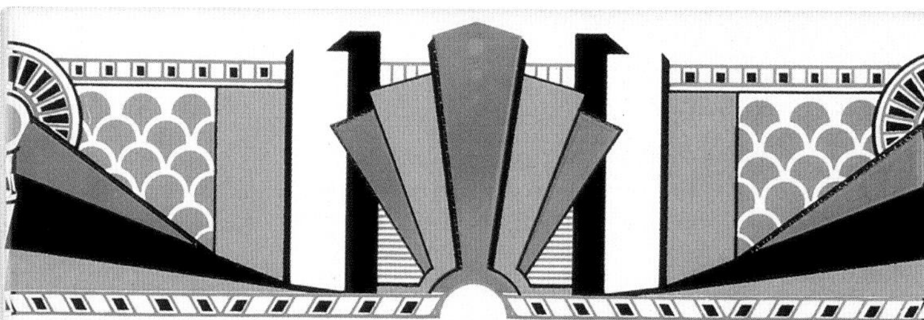

10

11

12

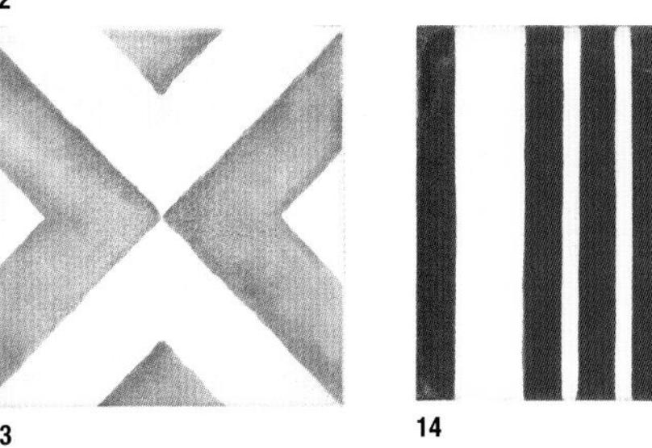

13

14

15

16

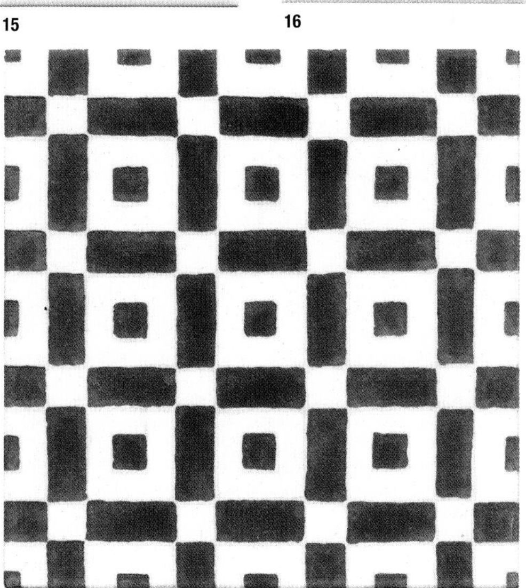

17

12 **Yorkshire Tile Co/Cameo Gris Border** Color **gray** Alternative colors **available** Composition **ceramic** Size **8 x 3 x ¼in/20 x 7.5cm x 6mm** Price ★ [W]

13 **Ceramiche Eurotiles/Midi Decorato MI/2** Color **blue and white** Alternative colors **not available** Composition **ceramic** Size **8 x 8 x ¼in/20 x 20cm x 6mm** Price ★ [W]

14 **Carocim/Souleiado– Madras S505** Color **multi** Alternative colors **available** Composition **ceramic** Size **8 x 8 x ⅜in/20 x 20 x 1cm** Price ★ [W] [F] [+]

15 **Tiles of Stow/Kingham Border** Color **blue** Alternative colors **available** Composition **ceramic** Size **6 x 6 x ¼in/ 15 x 15cm x 6mm** Price ★ [W]

16 **Tiles of Newport & London/ Check** Color **yellow** Alternative colors **available** Composition **ceramic** Size **8 x 8 x ¼in/20 x 20cm x 6mm** Price ★ [W]

17 **Ceramiche Eurotiles/ Stresa Nero Decorato SD/2** Color **black** Alternative colors **not available** Composition **ceramic** Size **8 x 8 x ¼in/20 x 20cm x 6mm** Price ★ [W]

ART DECO DESIGNS

The Art Deco Movement was particularly influential in Germany, Austria, and America, where it was a major source of inspiration in the architecture of the day. Tiles were designed with bold geometric patterns, often based on objects such as fans, bows, and flowers. The origin of the pattern is not always apparent at first glance, especially if the tiles are viewed *en masse*. The tile shown here is based on a fan, but when it is placed with other tiles, a zigzag effect is produced.

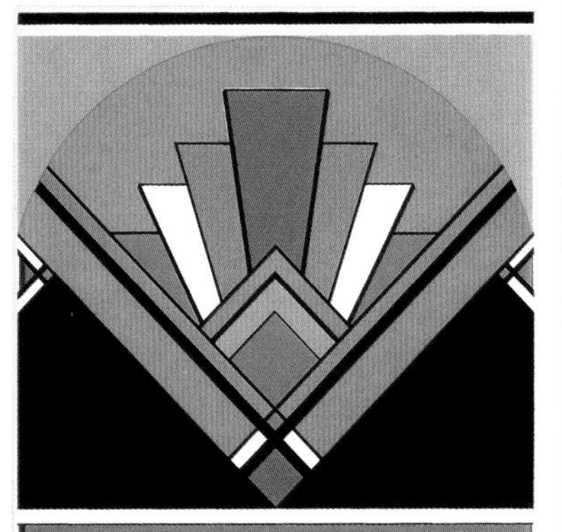

Original Style/Salmon Color **multi** Alternative colors **not available** Composition **ceramic** Size **6 x 6 x ¼in/15 x 15cm x 7mm** Price ★★ [W]

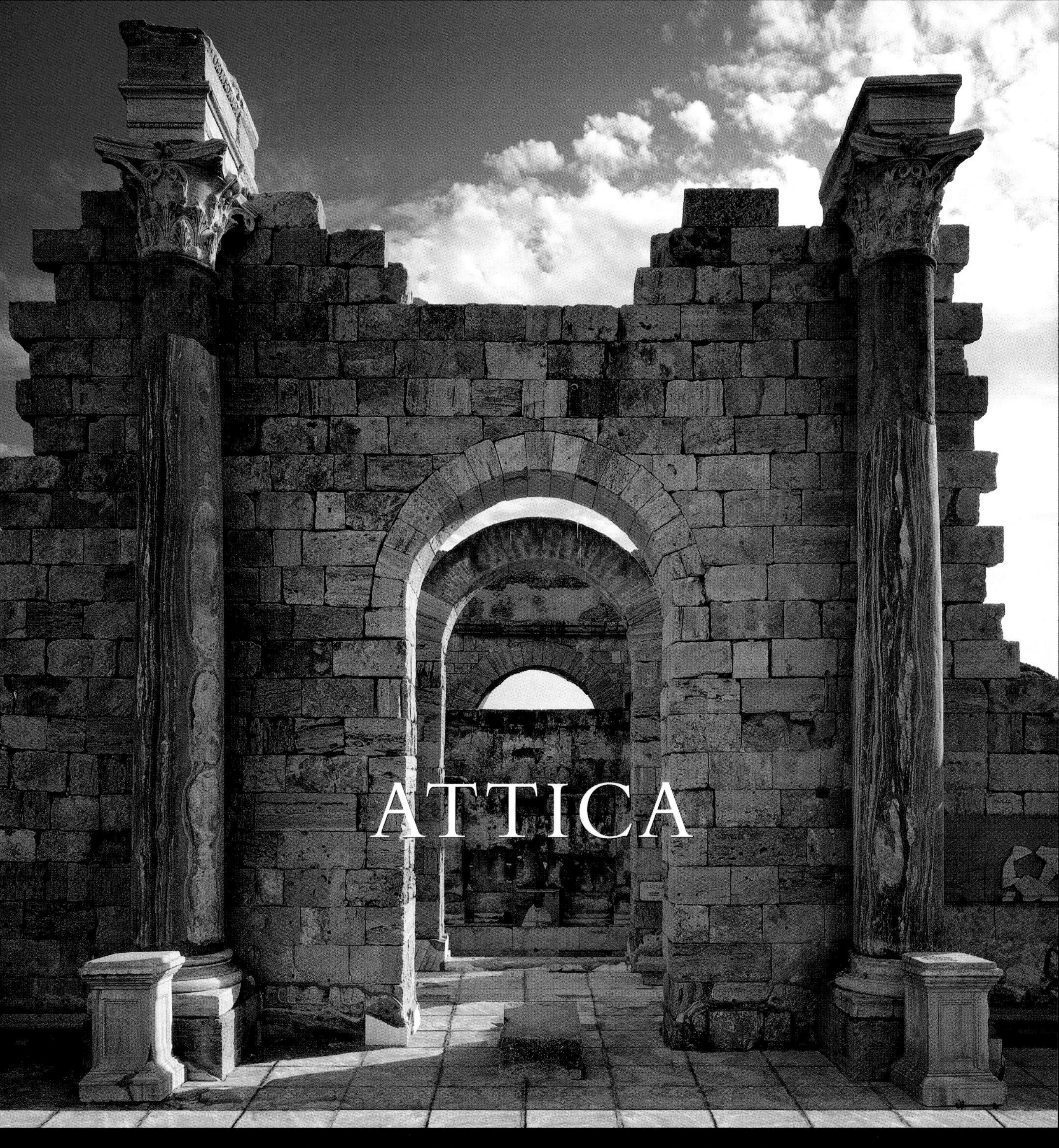

Flooring

Wooden Flooring

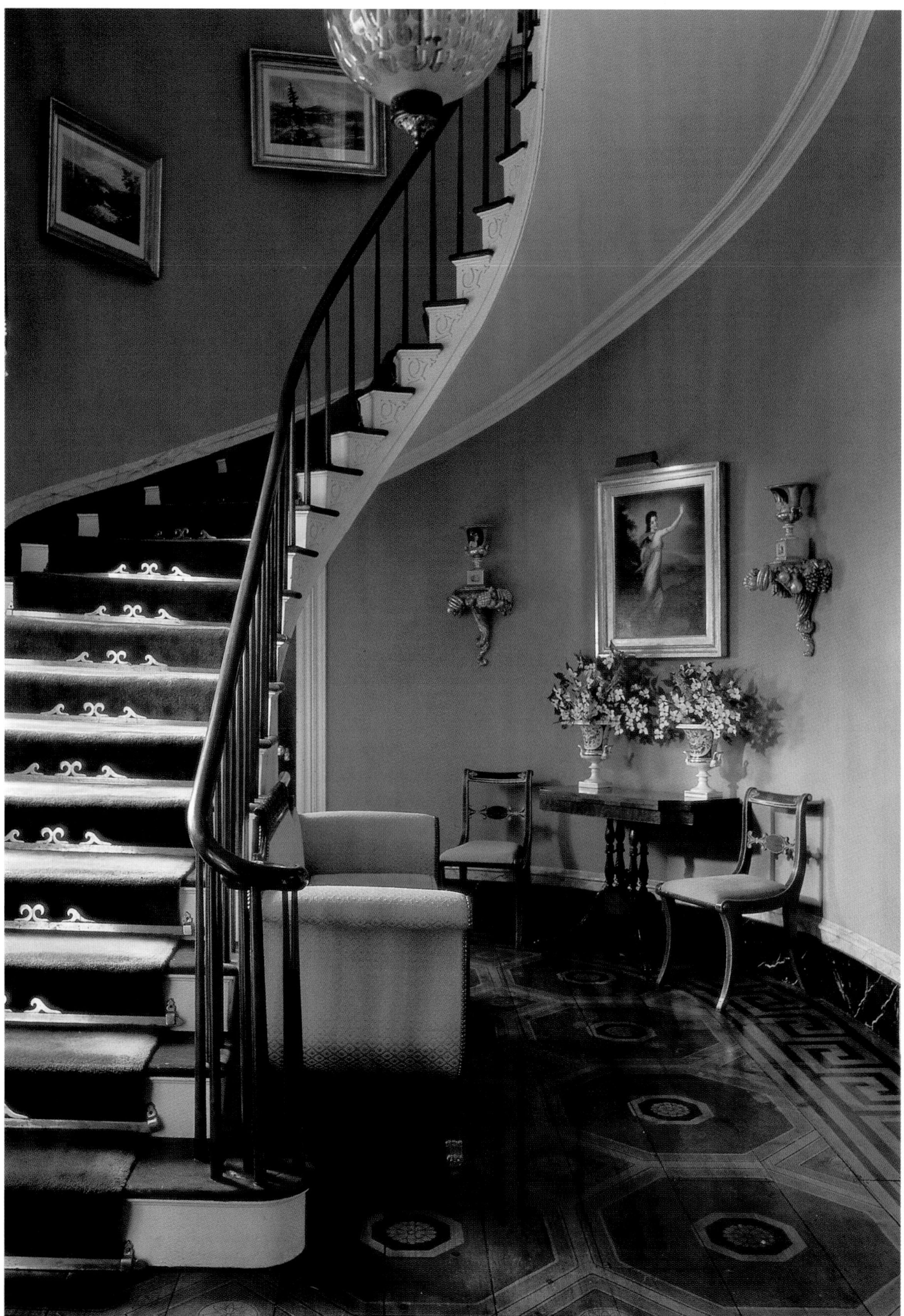

The use of wood as a flooring material predates the classical civilizations of Ancient Greece and Rome. However, before the late 17th century, wooden boards were usually confined to the upper stories of a house; thereafter they were also increasingly employed at the first floor. Until the 16th century, the wood used was generally restricted to local trees, but subsequently the expansion of international trade allowed house builders to use imported wood.

Fashionable alternatives to plain, solid boards have included marquetry (*see* 357), which originated in Persia and was brought to Europe in the 14th century, and parquetry (*see* opposite), a cheaper and more practical alternative. Favored patterns included lozenges and diamonds. Stenciled patterns have also been much in evidence, especially during the 18th and 19th centuries. In the 20th century, hardwood and softwood laminates provided more affordable alternatives to solid wooden flooring, although older floorboards that are stripped and polished are now much sought after.

LEFT The hallway of Richard Jenrette's house in New York State is dominated by a sweeping staircase and an inlaid wooden floor copied from a floor in the Tsar's Palace in St. Petersburg, Russia. The design features large octagonal motifs and an Islamic-inspired geometric border. The furniture and color scheme complete the early 19th-century look.

ABOVE The wide, uneven oak floorboards in this American kitchen typify the rustic simplicity of the Colonial look. Usually, boards of varying widths were laid, with the widest in the middle and the narrowest at the edges. Simple and practical, these boards were neatly tacked down using headless nails.

PARQUET FLOORS

Parquetry originated in France in the 17th century, and was first applied to small areas such as half-landings and stair treads. It involves the use of hardwood blocks arranged in geometric patterns, echoing the "three-dimensional" and *trompe l'oeil* effects of inlaid and paved stone. The parquet floor in this 18th-century French house consists of a basic geometric pattern, although lozenge arrangements were also very popular at this time. Other parquetry patterns include stars, diamonds, and latticework.

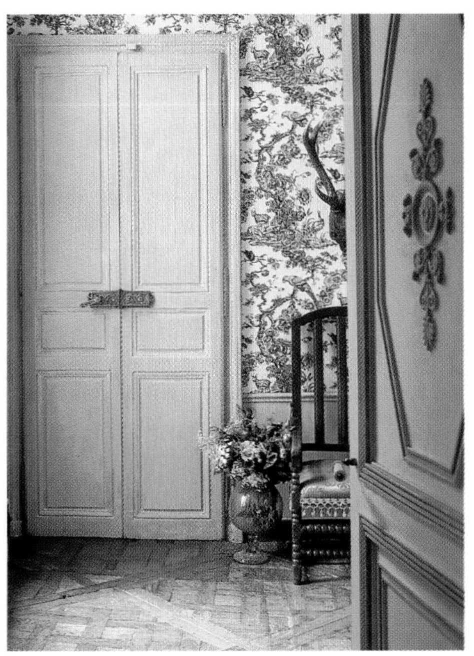

KEY DESIGNS

1 Cut from 400-year-old oak, these boards are of varying widths. Restored traditional wood has become popular as much for its appearance as for environmental reasons.

2 Basic geometric parquetry patterns have been popular since the early 17th century. The latticework arrangement is possibly the most enduring of all the parquet patterns.

3 Marquetry patterns inlaid in wooden floors can consist of many different types of wood as well as other materials such as ivory and pewter, offering decorators a choice of designs.

4 By the early 20th century, floorboards of the same width were usually laid in each room. A more recent alternative consists of a thin top layer of laminated hardwood glued to a plank of softwood.

5 The chevron or herringbone pattern is a popular parquet design. In Europe, Rhodesian teak was used extensively for this at the end of the 19th and beginning of the 20th centuries.

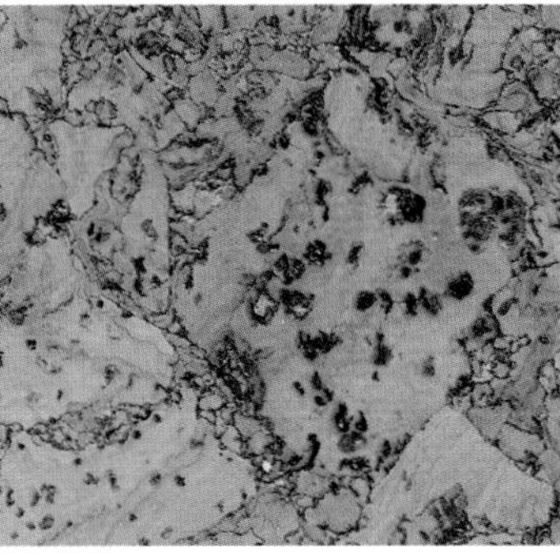

6 Cork tiles, first developed in the 1920s, are made from the bark of the cork oak. The bark is stripped every nine years, granulated, then made into blocks from which the tiles are cut.

1 **Victorian Wood Works/400 Year Old Oak Boards** Color **natural** Alternative colors **available** Composition **oak** Width **8in/20cm** Repeat – Price ★★★★

2 **Victorian Wood Works/Chantilly** Color **AA** Alternative colors **available** Composition **oak** Width **to order** Repeat – Price ★★★★

3 **Historic Floors of Oshkosh/Border 129** Color **natural** Alternative colors **available** Composition **Santos mahogany, maple, and American cherry** Width **8in/20cm** Repeat – Price ★★

4 **Boen Parkett/Ash Sheet** Color **natural** Alternative colors **available** Composition **ash** Width **5½in/14cm** Repeat – Price ★

5 **Lassco/Herringbone** Color **natural** Alternative colors **available** Composition **Rhodesian teak** Width **to order** Repeat – Price ★★

6 **Siesta Cork Tiles/Harlequin** Color **green** Alternative colors **available** Composition **cork** Width **12 x 12in/30.5 x 30.5cm (tile)** Repeat – Price ★

Wooden Flooring: **Pre-19th century**

The choice of wood as a flooring material was due as much to its availability as its intrinsic beauty. Initially, wide boards were used, although they were often covered by matting or loose rushes. It was not until the 17th century that ornate designs in wood became common in Europe. Parquet flooring (*see* page 351) was popular in grander houses in the mid-17th century, particularly in France. This brought about the use of more unusual woods, and resulted in an increase of exotic woods–such as mahogany from the West Indies–being imported to Europe. In the early 18th century, floorboards were sometimes decorated by painting or stenciling, a practice thought to have originated in the Netherlands. More elaborate designs often imitated the patterns and *trompe l'oeil* effects of marble, stone paving, or garden parterres.

In America during the 17th and 18th centuries, floors were considered to be strictly functional, and floorboards were invariably left bare. Pine was laid in broad planks, and was scrubbed, not waxed or polished. Occasionally, the boards were painted or stenciled with floral patterns, animals, or folk art motifs. At this time in both Europe and America, fine parquet floors were still considered the preserve of the wealthy.

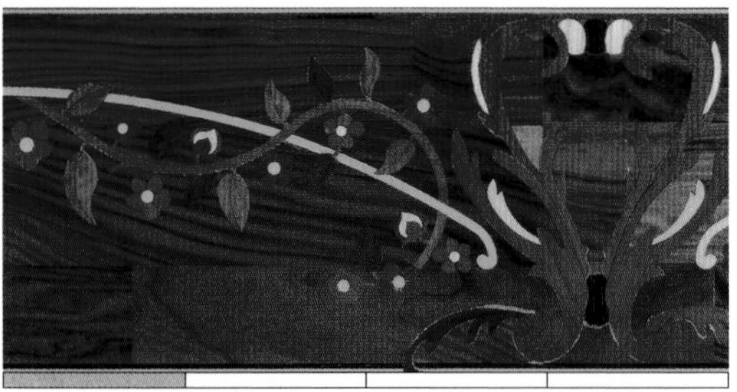

1

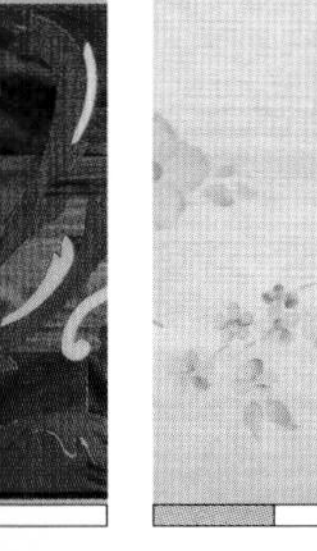

2

3

1 **Berti Pavimenti Legno/Mod Trissino Border** Color **natural** Alternative colors **not available** Composition **French walnut, sycamore, oak, wenge, ipe, and mahogany** Width **to order** Repeat **–** Price ★★★★★

2 **Perstorp/Flower Design P7250** Color **white** Alternative colors **not available** Composition **pine** Width **8in/20cm** Repeat **–** Price ★★

3 **Historic Floors of Oshkosh/ Marseille 145** Color **natural** Alternative colors **available** Composition **American cherry** Width **to order** Repeat **–** Price ★★★★★

4

4 **Sinclair Till/Greek Key Border** Color **natural** Alternative colors **available** Composition **walnut and maple** Width **11¼in/28.5cm** Repeat **–** Price ★★

5 **Historic Floors of Oshkosh/ Medallion 306** Color **natural** Alternative colors **available** Composition **walnut, American cherry, red oak, and mahogany** Width **to order** Repeat **–** Price ★★★★

6 **Berti Pavimenti Legno/ Bonfadini Border** Color **natural** Alternative colors **not available** Composition **jatoba and maple** Width **to order** Repeat **–** Price ★★★★★

5

6

7

8

7 Historic Floors of Oshkosh/ Rose Border 130 Color **natural** Alternative colors **available** Composition **maple, mahogany, bubinga, walnut, and green poplar** Width **to order** Repeat **4in/10.5cm** Price ★★★

8 Historic Floors of Oshkosh/ Château 152 Color **natural** Alternative colors **available** Composition **ipe** Width **to order** Repeat – Price ★★★

9 Berti Pavimenti Legno/ Giustinian Intarsio Color **natural** Alternative colors **not available** Composition **walnut, ipe, maple, and oak** Width **to order** Repeat – Price ★★★★★

10 Berti Pavimenti Legno/ Todeschini Border Color **natural** Alternative colors **not available** Composition **doussie, wenge, gatambu, and walnut** Width **to order** Repeat – Price ★★★★★

11 Historic Floors of Oshkosh/ Louve 154 Color **natural** Alternative colors **available** Composition **white oak** Width **to order** Repeat – Price ★★★

12 Victorian Wood Works/Jacobean Oak Stain Plank Color **Jacobean oak** Alternative colors **available** Composition **oak** Width **8in/ 20cm** Repeat – Price ★★⊞

13 Historic Floors of Oshkosh/ Fontainebleau Color **natural** Alternative colors **available** Composition **red and white oak** Width **to order** Repeat – Price ★★★

9

10

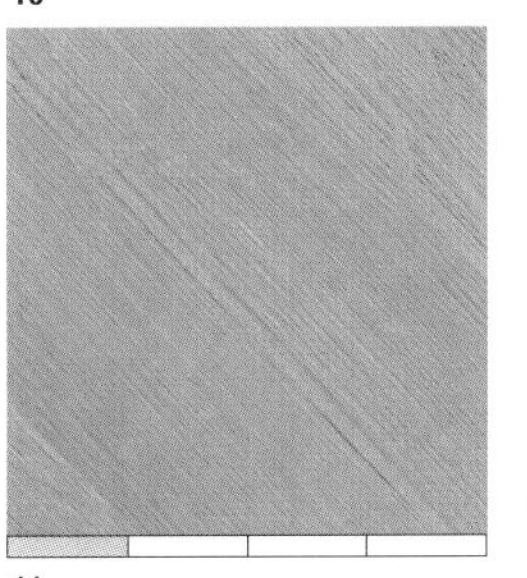

11

12

SECURING BOARDS

Methods for securing floorboards have changed little over the years. In medieval times, they were loosely laid over supporting joists on upper stories. From the late 16th century, headed nails were used to secure the boards, although headless nails soon became popular. Another method (as shown here) is Alpine fashion, where wooden butterfly clips are hammered into the adjacent boards. In the 20th century, this technique is employed for aesthetic reasons. Modern methods include securing boards with glue and wooden pins.

Perstorp/Walnut Intarsia P7224 Color **natural** Alternative colors **not available** Composition **walnut** Width **8in/20cm** Repeat – Price ★★

13

Wooden Flooring: **19th century**

During the 19th century in Europe and America, narrower floorboards came into use, especially in wealthier homes. Such floorboards were often only 4in (10cm) in width, in contrast to the 9in- (23cm-) wide floorboards used in poorer homes. In the 1820s, tongue and groove wooden boards were introduced. As the century progressed, these were increasingly prepared by machine, and, as a result, became more even in width.

In America, the practice of painting wooden floors developed into a popular craft, although plain colored versions were as well liked as stenciled ones. In Europe, the tradition of floor painting continued, as did the fashion for staining wood with different oils. However, as carpets became more common, floors were generally painted or glazed in a single color, and the designs for parquet floors became simpler. At the same time, it was discovered that thin boards could be glued, nailed, or screwed down onto a solid backing to produce a good imitation of a floor composed of solid wood blocks. This was the forerunner of the modern parquet floor. By the end of the 19th century, American manufacturers began to offer intricate, ready-made examples consisting of oak blocks glued to cloth or softwood in a closely woven pattern.

Historic Floors of Oshkosh/Border 125 Color **natural** Alternative colors **available** Composition **red oak and Santos mahogany** Width **to order** Repeat **–** Price ★★★

Prestige Enterprise/New Jeffersonian Color **sable** Alternative colors **available** Composition **oak** Width **12in/30.5cm (panel)** Repeat **–** Price ★

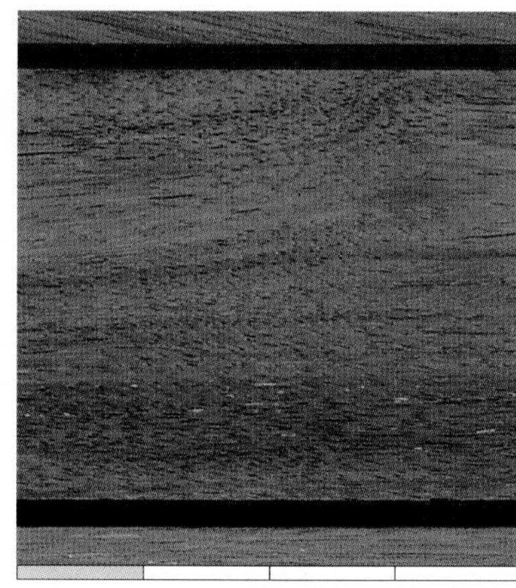

Boen Parkett/Ship's Deck Color **natural** Alternative colors **available** Composition **merbau** Width **5½in/14cm** Repeat **–** Price ★

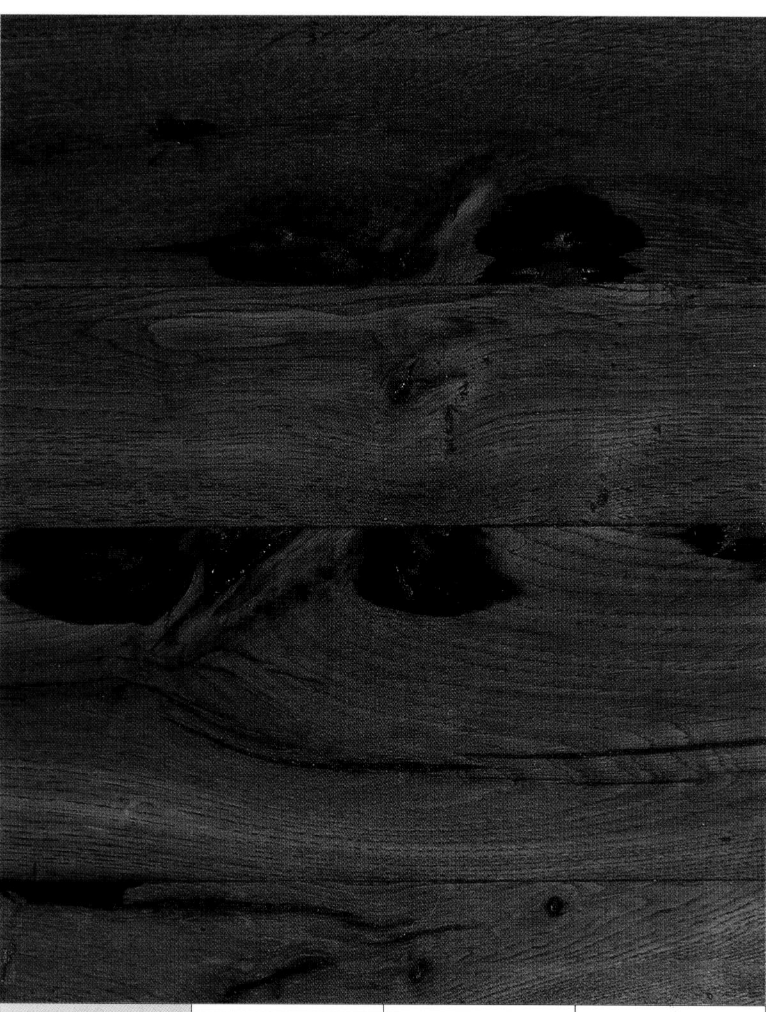

Victorian Wood Works/Oil-Stained Oak Color **oil stain** Alternative colors **available** Composition **oak** Width **8in/20cm** Repeat **–** Price ★★ ⊞

Kentucky Wood Floors/Trinity Color **natural** Alternative colors **available** Composition **oak** Width **to order** Repeat **–** Price ★★★★★

19th century

Historic Floors of Oshkosh/Border 137 Color **natural** Alternative colors **available** Composition **Santos mahogany, maple, and red oak** Width **to order** Repeat **–** Price ★★★

Victorian Wood Works/Somerset Oak Color **natural** Alternative colors **available** Composition **oak** Width **8in/20cm** Repeat **–** Price ★★⊞

Historic Floors of Oshkosh/Border 135 Color **natural** Alternative colors **available** Composition **ash, mahogany, bubinga, and walnut** Width **to order** Repeat **–** Price ★★★

Victorian Wood Works/Inlaid Border Color **natural** Alternative colors **available** Composition **wenge** Width **11¼in/28.5cm** Repeat **–** Price ★★★⊞

The Hardwood Flooring People/Antiqued English Oak Color **antiqued** Alternative colors **available** Composition **oak** Width **to order** Repeat **–** Price ★★★

19th century

Victorian Wood Works/Chantilly Color **rustic** Alternative colors **available** Composition **oak** Width **to order** Repeat **–** Price ★★★

Kentucky Wood Floors/Florentine Color **natural** Alternative colors **available** Composition **Brazilian cherry, walnut, bird's-eye maple, and brass** Width **to order** Repeat **–** Price ★★★★★

Wooden Flooring: **20th century**

Although parquet borders were popular in the early 20th century as an accompaniment to larger rugs and nonfitted carpets, it was not until the 1930s that complete parquet floors enjoyed a resurgence in Europe that was to last until the 1950s. The designs were extremely basic, with the polished hardwood blocks or strips being laid in clear, simple patterns.

By the 1970s, a revival in appreciation for the qualities of wood led to a fashion for revealing and restoring old wooden floorboards, as well as for laying new ones. This led to the development of new types of wooden flooring systems that catered to a growing international market. By the 1990s, there were many different options to choose from, including prefinished floors of oiled wood planks and floors with a wooden laminate surface over a high-density fiberboard or chipboard base. The popularity of wood-laminate flooring arose because it is easy to lay, as it is glued at the tongue and groove and does not need to be secured to the subfloor. In addition, tongue and groove parquets were available in many different woods of various colors, grades, and thicknesses. Marquetry designs also remained popular, and replicas of old parquet floors, made by gluing thin panels of oak, beech, or birch to a solid backing, also became widely available.

7

1

2

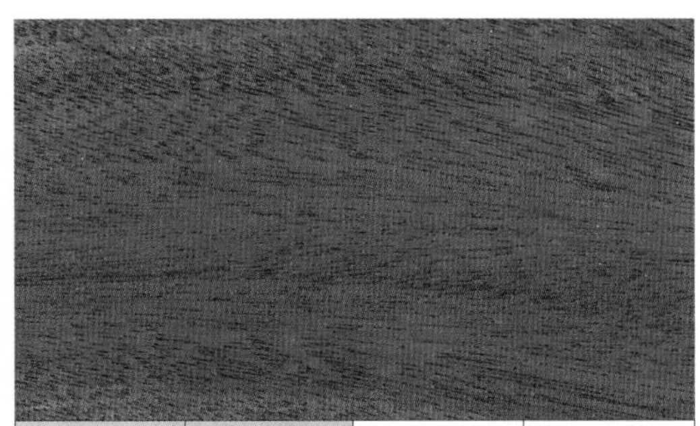

3

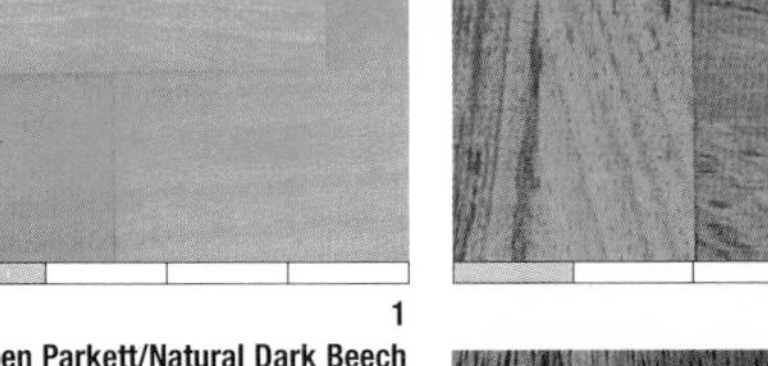

1 Boen Parkett/Natural Dark Beech Color **dark** Alternative colors **available** Composition **beech** Width **5½in/14cm** Repeat – Price ★

2 Westco/C480012 Color **natural** Alternative colors **not available** Composition **Rhodesian teak** Width **18¾ x 18¾in/47.5 x 47.5cm (panel)** Repeat – Price ★

3 Natural Wood Floor Co/African Walnut Planks Color **natural** Alternative colors **available** Composition **African walnut** Width **3½in/9cm** Repeat – Price ★ ⊞

4 Junckers/Merbau Plank 065300-189 Color **natural** Alternative colors **available** Composition **merbau** Width **4¾in/12cm** Repeat – Price ★

5 LBC/Solid Elm Planks Color **natural** Alternative colors **available** Composition **elm** Width **to order** Repeat – Price ★★

6 Historic Floors of Oshkosh/Oxford 150 Color **natural** Alternative colors **available** Composition **Santos mahogany, ipe, American cherry, and maple** Width **to order** Repeat – Price ★★★

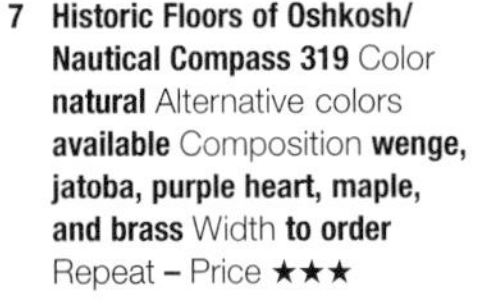

7 Historic Floors of Oshkosh/Nautical Compass 319 Color **natural** Alternative colors **available** Composition **wenge, jatoba, purple heart, maple, and brass** Width **to order** Repeat – Price ★★★

8 LBC/Pitch Pine Boards Color **natural** Alternative colors **not available** Composition **pine** Width **5in/13cm** Repeat – Price ★★⊞

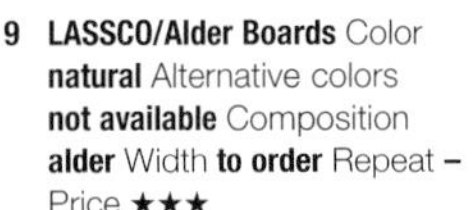

9 LASSCO/Alder Boards Color **natural** Alternative colors **not available** Composition **alder** Width **to order** Repeat – Price ★★★

10 Kahrs/Rotterdam Diagonal Pattern 3215 OB 50 Color **natural** Alternative colors **available** Composition **birch and oak** Width **6in/15cm** Repeat – Price ★

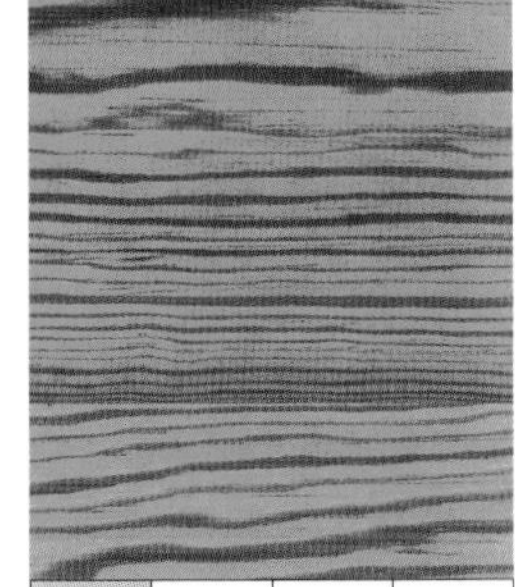

8

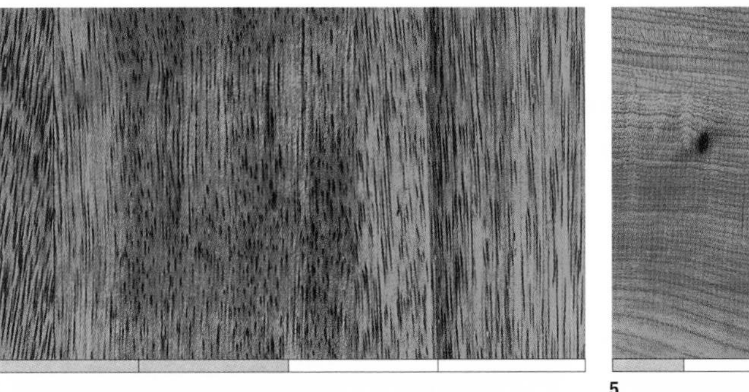

4

5

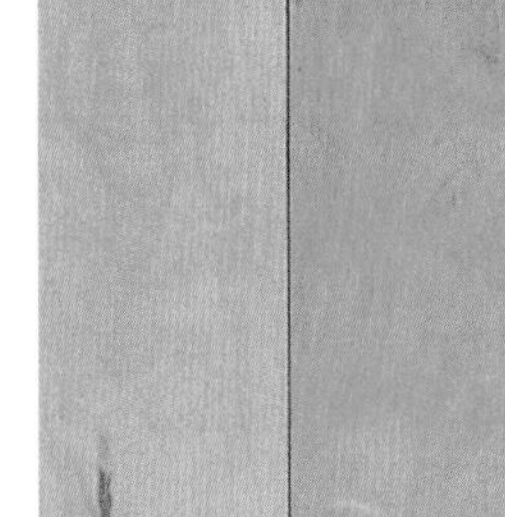

9

6

10

11 **Bruce Hardwood/Dakota Plank E-153** Color **harvest** Alternative colors **available** Composition **oak** Width **3in/7.5cm** Repeat – Price ★★

12 **Bruce Hardwood/Dakota Plank E150** Color **toast** Alternative colors **available** Composition **oak** Width **3in/7.5cm** Repeat – Price ★★

13 **Wicanders/Terracotta and River Cork LS05 & LS09** Color **terracotta and river** Alternative colors **available** Composition **cork** Width **12 x 12in/30.5 x 30.5cm (tile)** Repeat – Price ★

14 **Perstorp/Prisma P214** Color **indigo** Alternative colors **available** Composition **beech** Width **8in/20cm** Repeat – Price ★★

11

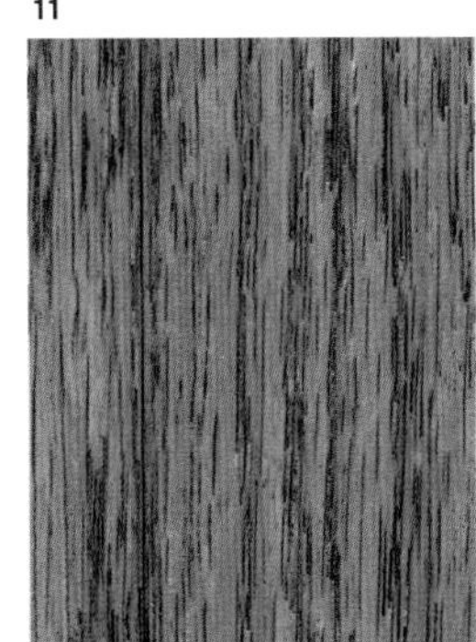

12

MARQUETRY

The art of marquetry is the inlaying of wood with pieces of different colored wood or other materials, such as ivory and metal, to form mosaics, arabesques, or pictures. First seen in Italy in the 14th century, marquetry was mainly used on furniture. By the early 17th century, it was often used in France, and it soon spread to the rest of Europe. Today, many marquetry firms use a laser beam to cut all of the shapes, thus ensuring a precision only previously attained through the time-consuming cutting by hand.

Historic Floors of Oshkosh/Medallion 340 Color **natural** Alternative colors **available** Composition **maple and ipe** Width **to order** Repeat – Price ★★★★★

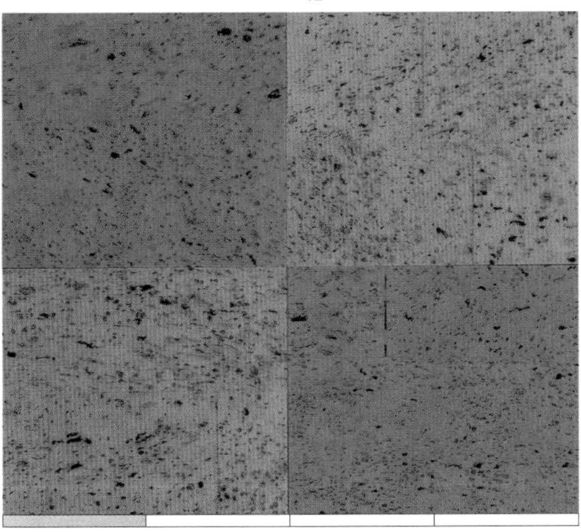

13

14

15

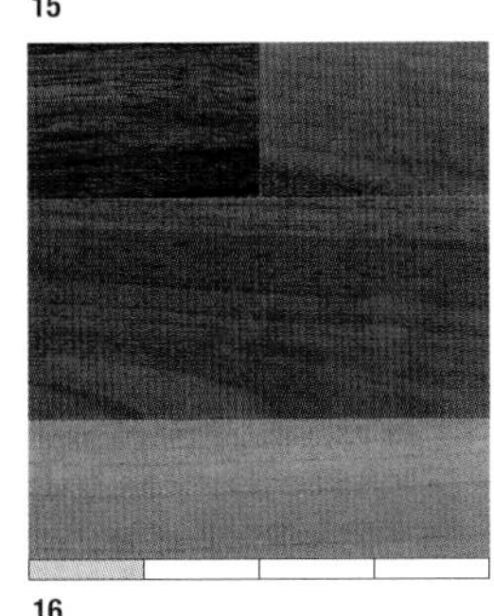

16

17

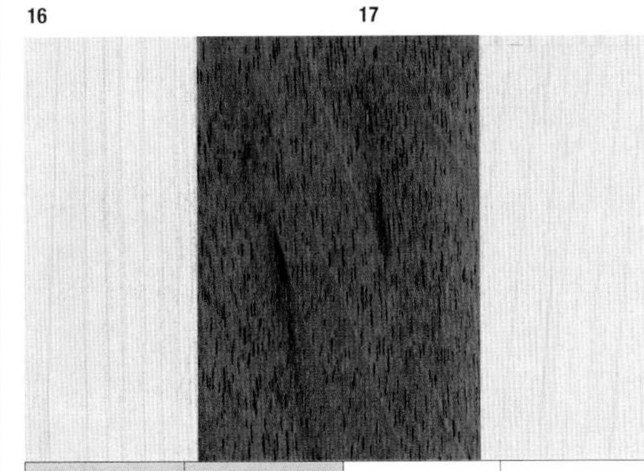

18

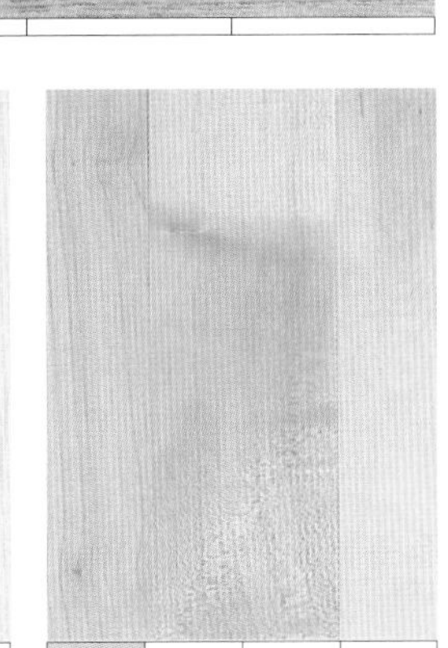

19

15 **Junckers/Sylvaket Plank** Color **natural** Alternative colors **available** Composition **sylvaket** Width **5in/13cm** Repeat – Price ★

16 **Wicanders/Walnut 3 Strip PT57** Color **natural** Alternative colors **available** Composition **walnut** Width **5in/13cm** Repeat – Price ★

17 **Boen Parkett/Oak Dutch Pattern** Color **natural** Alternative colors **available** Composition **oak** Width **5½in/14cm** Repeat – Price ★

18 **Seri Parquet/Duo** Color **natural** Alternative colors **available** Composition **maple and merbau** Width **7in/18cm** Repeat – Price ★

19 **LASSCO/Sycamore Boards** Color **natural** Alternative colors **not available** Composition **sycamore** Width **to order** Repeat – Price ★★★

Matting

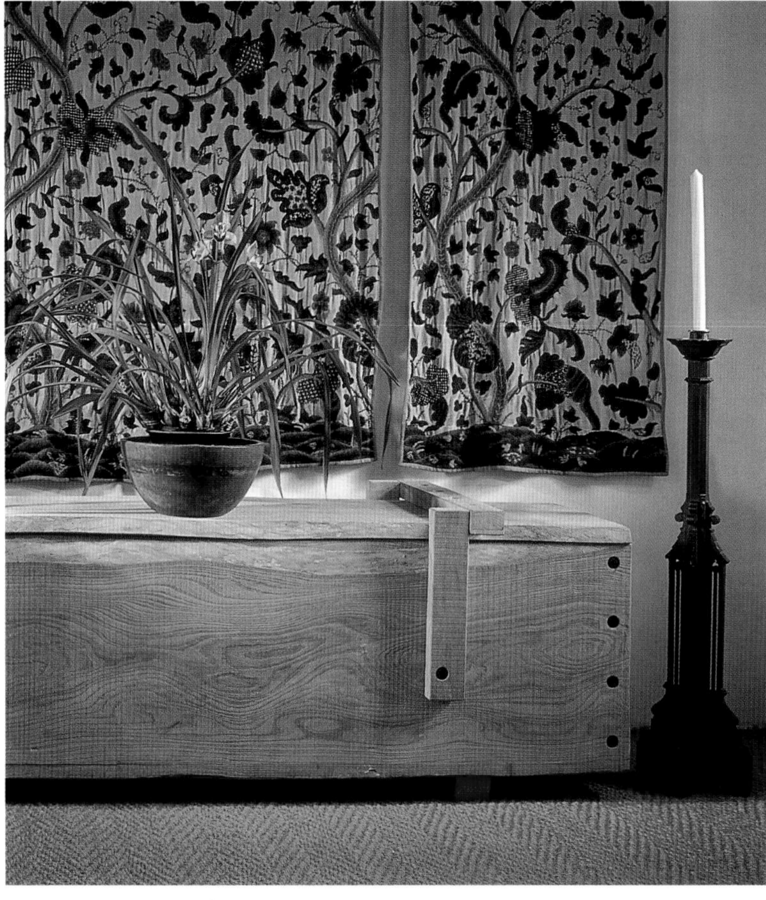

ABOVE This medieval-style room features an elegant coir matting floor covering. Coir is harvested in two main seasons: the freshwater season, when fiber lying in the lagoons is washed daily, and the saltwater season. The fiber is then beaten from the coconut husks before being spun and woven into patterns such as this herringbone design.

Matting evolved from the spreading of rushes, straw, and herbs over floors for both insulation and comfort. By the 17th century in Europe, braided rush strips sewn together to cover the whole floor were common in wealthier houses, although the matting was often covered by Oriental carpets. As trade with North Africa opened up in the 17th century, more lightweight mattings–made from narrow strips of braided rushes–became popular. These finely woven and delicately patterned floor coverings were known as Africa, Barbary, or Portugal mats and largely superseded the traditional European rush matting, which was heavy and needed replacing every few years. The introduction of mass-produced carpets led to a decline in the use of matting, although it was still used in informal areas of houses. In America, matting was popular in the early 19th century, as importers brought in mats from India and Africa.

Contemporary production techniques allow matting to be machine-woven and to be given a latex backing. This has increased its durability and made it reasonably stain-resistant.

GRASSES

The different grasses used in matting depend upon where they are produced. Sisal is a fiber taken from the leaf of the Mexican agave plant, coir is produced from the husks of coconuts, while jute is derived from the stalk of an herb of an Indian *Tiliaceae* family. With the expansion of maritime trade, these fibers gradually replaced the rush (shown here) as the traditional component of matting in Europe. All can be woven into a variety of patterns and are particularly suitable for early period homes.

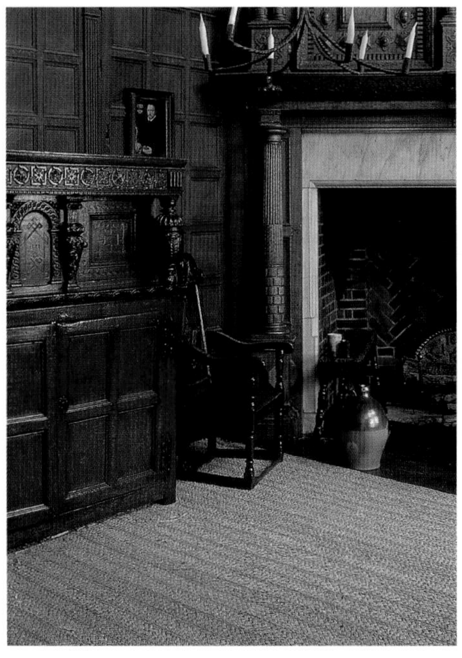

RIGHT Forms of rush matting have been woven for centuries and methods have changed very little. The ancient Egyptians used bullrushes from the Nile to weave floor coverings; today, rush matting is equally suited to contemporary interiors.

KEY DESIGNS

1 Jute has been used as a floor covering since the 18th century. Once harvested, it is tied together, soaked in water, then pounded with wooden mallets. This provides a very soft matting.

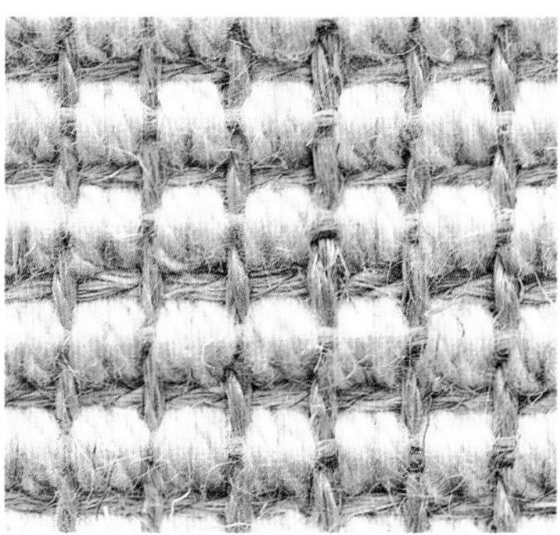

2 Wool is often mixed with plant fibers to produce a combination of the durability of matting with a relatively soft texture. This example has a pure wool warp within sisal weft threads.

3 As well as a wide variety of weaves, sisal is available in numerous color combinations. Deep reds, blues, and greens proved particularly popular in the late 20th century.

4 Over the years, matting has been decorated with different patterns–such as this medieval design–using either paints or dyes, and it can be printed, stenciled, or hand-painted.

5 Modern techniques make it easier for different materials and colors to be combined. This is a mixture of coir and a dyed sisal weave that provides an appealing splash of color.

6 Coir matting, produced from coconut fiber and then spun and woven, varies in color depending upon the time at which it is harvested. It became extremely fashionable in the late 20th century.

1 **The Alternative Flooring Co/Panama AFC 612** Color **bleached** Alternative colors **available** Composition **100% jute** Width **4½yd/4m** Repeat – Price ★

2 **Fired Earth/Hungerford Ribbed** Color **cream** Alternative colors **available** Composition **80% wool, 20% sisal** Width **4½yd/4m** Repeat – Price ★

3 **The Alternative Flooring Co/Sisal Bouclé AFC 222** Color **Brookfield** Alternative colors **available** Composition **100% sisal** Width **4½yd/4m** Repeat – Price ★

4 **Sinclair Till/Wrought Iron** Color **black** Alternative colors **available** Composition **100% sisal** Width **to order** Repeat – Price ★★★

5 **Crucial Trading/Bouclé Weft BCS1** Color **red** Alternative colors **available** Composition **70% coir, 30% sisal** Width **4½yd/4m** Repeat – Price ★

6 **Natural Flooring Direct/Herringbone** Color **natural** Alternative colors **available** Composition **100% coir** Width **4½yd/4m** Repeat – Price ★

Matting

Thick rush matting (*see* opposite), common in Europe in the 16th century, was largely replaced during the 17th century by imported North African matting. Consisting of narrow strips of braided bullrushes sewn together with rush, the imported variety was lightweight, decorative, and often brightly colored. In the late 18th and early 19th centuries, Indian matting was particularly popular. Made of natural reeds or grass, it was often woven into yard-wide strips and bound with linen twill. In the latter part of the 19th century, mats from China and Japan were fashionable. They were made from grass and had a jute warp, and invariably featured tight chevron patterns in bright colors, with the ends bound with oilcloth.

In the early part of the 20th century, popular colors for matting included natural, white, olive, and red-and-white checks. In the last decade of the century, there was a renewed interest in plain-colored plant-fiber matting, including varieties made from sisal and coir (*see* pages 358-9).

3

1

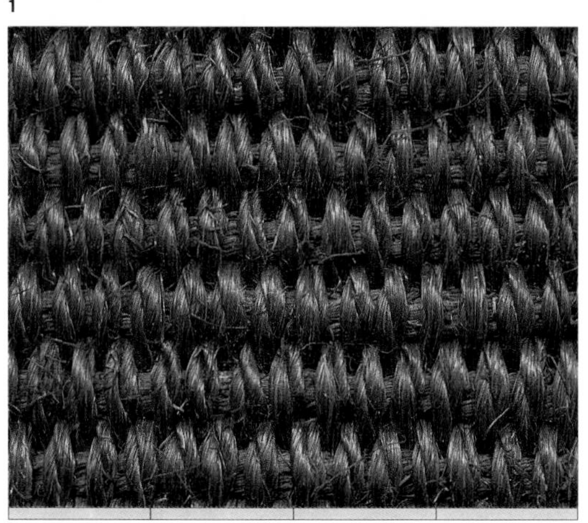

2

4

5

6

1 **Crucial Trading/Herringbone Contrast HBC** Color **natural** Alternative colors **not available** Composition **100% coir** Width **4½yd/4m** Repeat **–** Price ★

2 **Crucial Trading/Silk E667** Color **Burmese red** Alternative colors **available** Composition **100% sisal** Width **4½yd/4m** Repeat **–** Price ★★

3 **Afia/Step** Color **726** Alternative colors **available** Composition **100% sisal** Width **2⅛yd/2m** Repeat **–** Price ★★★

4 **Afia/Matto** Color **235** Alternative colors **not available** Composition **100% paper** Width **2⅛yd/2m** Repeat **–** Price ★★★★

5 **Three Shires/Panama Bleached J07** Color **bleached** Alternative colors **available** Composition **100% jute** Width **4½yd/4m** Repeat **–** Price ★

6 **Three Shires/Sisal Bouclé SI21** Color **light honey** Alternative colors **available** Composition **100% sisal** Width **4½yd/4m** Repeat **–** Price ★

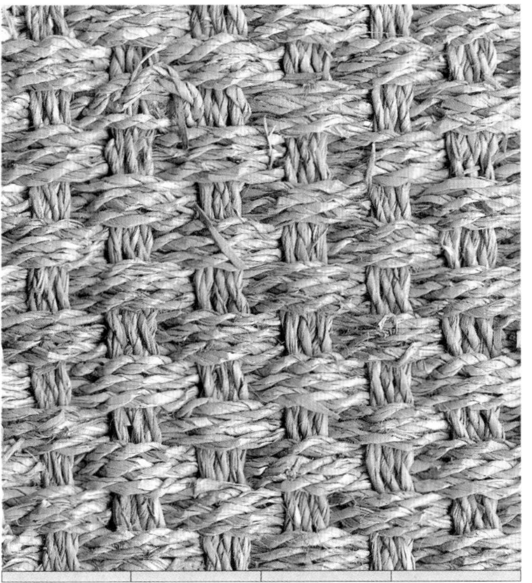
7

7 **The Alternative Flooring Co/ Buckingham Basketweave AFC 102** Color **natural** Alternative colors **not available** Composition **100% Indian grass** Width **4½yd/4m** Repeat – Price ★

8 **The Alternative Flooring Co/Sisal Bouclé AFC 221** Color **Bampton** Alternative colors **available** Composition **100% sisal** Width **4½yd/4m** Repeat – Price ★★

9 **Sinclair Till/Giraffe** Color **giraffe** Alternative colors **available** Composition **100% sisal** Width **to order** Repeat – Price ★★★

10 **Crucial Trading/Tortoiseshell E924** Color **green** Alternative colors **available** Composition **100% sisal** Width **4½yd/4m** Repeat – Price ★★

8

9

10

11

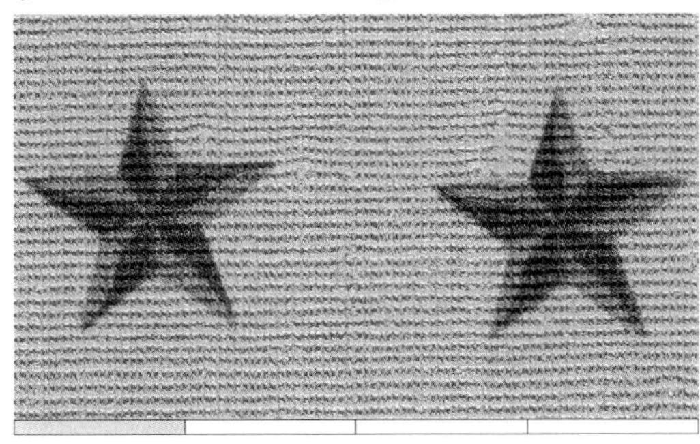
12

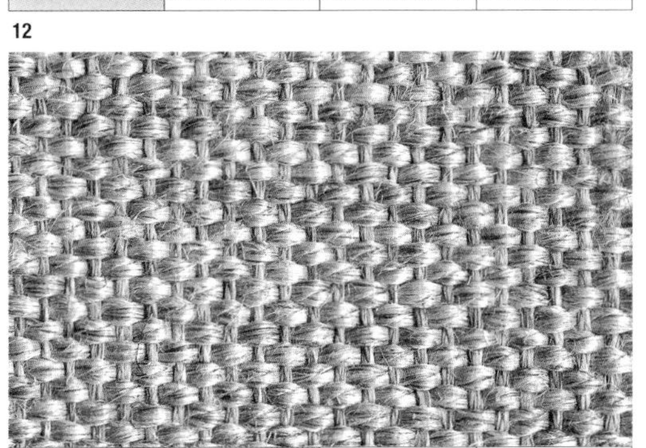
13

11 **Fired Earth/Rousham Diagonal RDN** Color **natural** Alternative colors **not available** Composition **100% inland grass** Width **4½yd/4m** Repeat – Price ★

12 **Sinclair Till/Stars** Color **black/blue** Alternative colors **available** Composition **100% sisal** Width **to order** Repeat – Price ★★★

13 **The Alternative Flooring Co/ Sisal Panama AFC 503** Color **Donegal** Alternative colors **available** Composition **100% sisal** Width **4½yd/4m** Repeat – Price ★★

14 **Three Shires/Pava SI01** Color **pava** Alternative colors **not available** Composition **100% sisal** Width **4½yd/4m** Repeat – Price ★★

TRADITIONAL RUSH MATTING

Rush matting is still made almost entirely using the traditional method of the Middle Ages. The rushes are soaked in cold water to make them pliable, squeezed dry, then plaited into strips, each consisting of 9 strands. These strips used to be sewn together with rush but they are now sewn with string, the only deviation from the traditional method. The matting is then edged with a finer 11-ply strip. Those who use rush matting in their homes must sprinkle it with water every 6–8 weeks to keep it supple.

Waveney Apple Growers/Rush Medieval Matting Color **natural** Alternative colors **not available** Composition **100% rush** Width **to order** Repeat – Price ★★★

14

Carpets

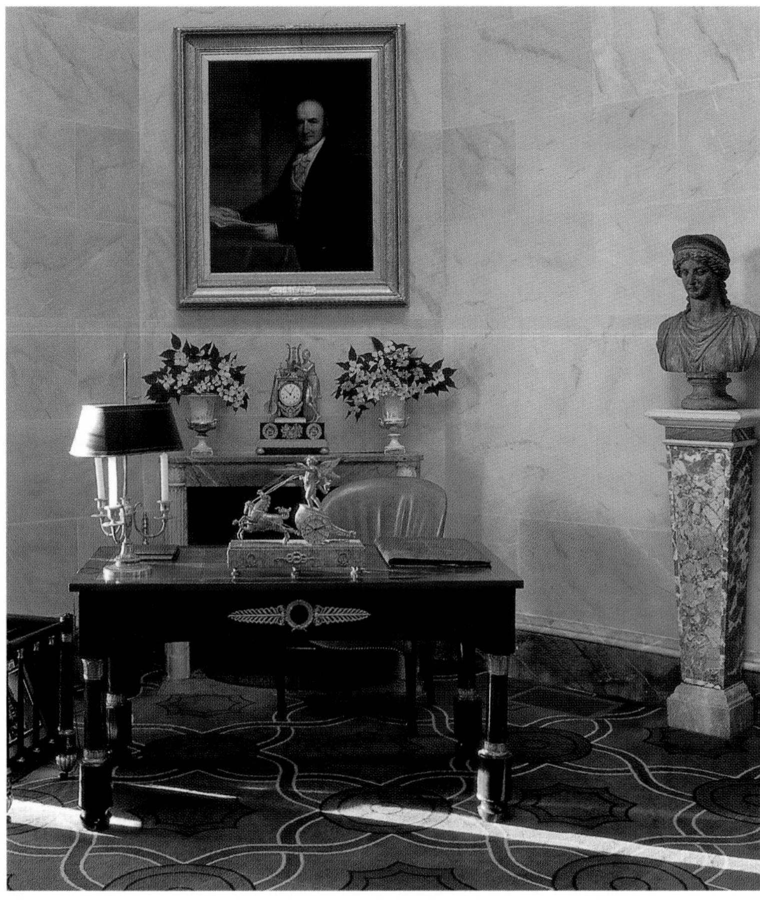

ABOVE This carpet in Richard Jenrette's New York State house combines strong, symmetrical lines with simple motifs that epitomize the American Empire style. This style mirrors the French Empire and English Regency styles, but lacks the opulence and elaboration that characterize European and British carpets of the period.

Carpets are a highly decorative textile that are produced on a horizontal or vertical loom. A knotting technique is used to create an artificial pile that hides the supporting grid of horizontal and vertical strands. The yarns and fibers used range from wool, silk, and cotton to modern synthetics such as nylon and viscose.

The earliest known knotted carpet, the Altai carpet, was found preserved in the ice of Siberia and dates from approximately 500 B.C. From the 11th century, carpets were used to cover walls, chairs, and tables, but it was only in the late 17th century that they began to be used regularly as a floor covering. During the 1500s, European imitations of Oriental carpets, such as turkeywork (*see* page 364), emerged, but it was the development of European and American looms in the 19th century that made carpets available to everyone. By the mid-20th century, wall-to-wall carpets were widespread.

Designs and decorative motifs have varied enormously throughout the centuries, although abstract or stylized geometric designs have remained consistently popular.

WILTON CARPET

Developed from Brussels carpet (*see* page 366), Wilton has a velvetlike surface that is formed by cutting the looped pile to give it a more luxurious feel. It was first produced in the mid-18th century in Wilton, England, but the method soon spread to Europe and America. It was traditionally woven in 27in (69cm) wide strips, with repeating patterns so they could be laid wall-to-wall. The introduction of the Jacquard loom in 1805 meant that Wilton became cheaper than hand-knotted carpets, and, as such, extremely popular.

RIGHT The principal staircase in Sir John Soane's house in London, England, is covered by a sumptuous, deep red and gold stair runner. The scrolling leaf border in gold and the red moiré-effect pile reflect the influence of the French Neoclassical Movement.

KEY DESIGNS

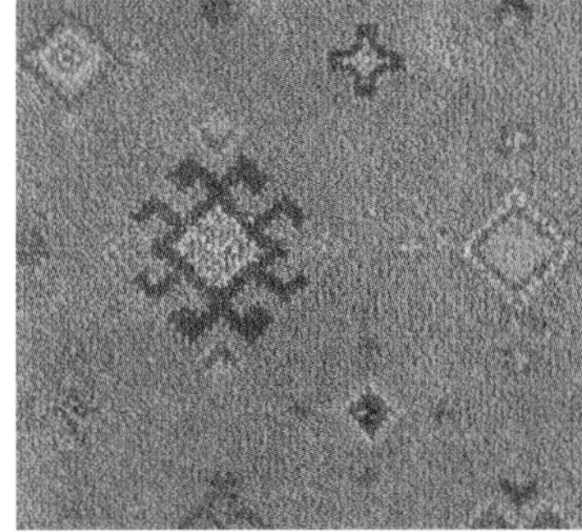

1 Small, symmetrical motif designs are typical of North African carpets, woven by nomadic tribes such as the Berbers. Their popular motifs often originated from ancient tribal and religious emblems.

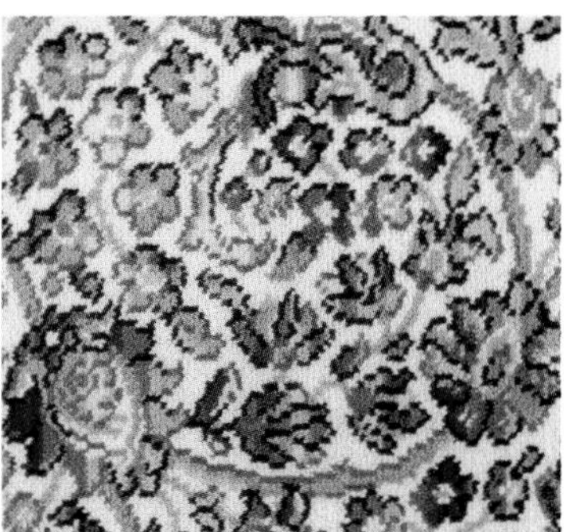

2 Stylized and naturalistic floral designs originated in Persia and India in the 16th century and have been fashionable ever since. This example features scrolling patterns with a floral and leaf ornament.

3 Geometric diaper patterns are a recurring design on carpets. The patterns trelliswork, latticework, and strapwork, and, like this design, often enclose floral motifs or plant-form imagery.

4 Carpets are available in a variety of colors. Bright colors are normally produced by chemical dyes, which were introduced in the 1860s and quickly replaced natural dyes.

5 The pile in this monochromatic tufted carpet consists of long strands of wool stitched into a prewoven backing. Carpets with a deep pile were especially in demand in the 20th century.

6 The mottled coloring of this woolen carpet is typical of the late 20th century. In this example, synthetic fibers are woven in a loop effect and provide a similar texture wool.

---

1 **Tomkinsons Carpets/Caraway 90/2706** Color **90** Alternative colors **available** Composition **80% wool, 20% nylon** Width **4yd/3.66m** Repeat **13½in/34.5cm** Price ★★ ⊞

2 **Brintons/Persian Garden 2/543** Color **2** Alternative colors **not available** Composition **80% wool, 20% nylon** Width **4yd/3.66m** Repeat **–** Price ★★ ⊞

3 **Stoddard Templeton/Midnight Embroidery 4/4540** Color **4** Alternative colors **not available** Composition **80% wool, 20% nylon** Width **4yd/3.66m** Repeat **30in/76cm** Price ★★ ⊞

4 **Ulster Carpets/Velvet W9205** Color **seascape** Alternative colors **available** Composition **80% wool, 20% nylon** Width **4yd/3.66m** Repeat **–** Price ★ ⊞

5 **Ollerton Hall/Shag Pile** Color **pink** Alternative colors **available** Composition **100% wool** Width **4yd/3.66m** Repeat **–** Price ★

6 **Louis de Poortere/Basalt TR** Color **crushed rose** Alternative colors **available** Composition **100% polyamide** Width **4½yd/4m** Repeat **–** Price ★ ⊡

Carpets: **Pre-19th century**

In Europe during the Middle Ages, Oriental carpets were the preserve of the wealthy. However, during the 15th and 16th centuries, English workshops began producing "turkeywork," a less expensive hand-knotted pile cloth used for chair upholstery and table coverings. Some of these cloths were later introduced into America by European settlers. Embroidered carpets commissioned in America, featuring heraldic motifs and floral patterns.

By the middle of the 18th century, the carpet industry was thriving in Europe, the two main centers for production being Britain and France. In Britain, the Earl of Pembroke gave his patronage to the Wilton factory in 1740; the carpet weavers Thomas Whitty and Thomas Moore started working in Axminster and London respectively; and there was great carpet-making activity in Scotland, the north of England, and Kidderminster. In France, Henry IV supported Pierre Dupont in establishing a workshop in the Louvre to produce carpets in "the manner of the Orient." The workshop later moved to the Savonnerie site. At Aubusson, the long-established tapestry weavers turned their skills to producing tapestry carpets, which were less costly than Savonneries. With their delicate floral patterning, these carpets became extremely popular during the reigns of Louis XV and Louis XVI of France.

5

1

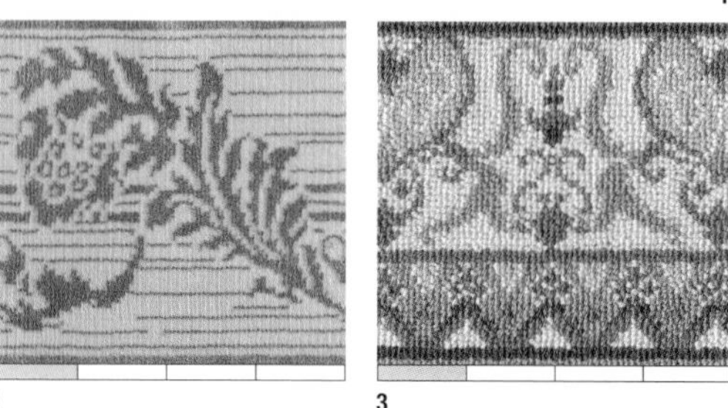

2 3

6

4

7

1 **Stark/Dartmouth** Color **multi** Alternative colors **not available** Composition **100% wool** Width **27in/68.5cm** Repeat **13¾in/35cm** Price ★★★★

2 **Stark/Brissac Border** Color **white and gold** Alternative colors **available** Composition **80% wool, 20% viscose** Width **9in/23cm** Repeat **8⅝in/22cm** Price ★★★

3 **Stark/Czardis Border** Color **spice** Alternative colors **not available** Composition **100% wool** Width **6¾in/17cm** Repeat **6¼in/16cm** Price ★★

4 **Stark/Czardis** Color **spice** Alternative colors **not available** Composition **100% wool** Width **4yd/3.72m** Repeat **12in/30.5cm** Price ★★★★

5 **Axminster Carpets/Turkish Splendor 380/01803** Color **Oriental gold** Alternative colors **available** Composition **100% wool** Width **4yd/3.66m** Repeat **35¾in/91cm** Price ★★ ⊞

6 **Stark/Dover** Color **stock** Alternative colors **available** Composition **100% wool** Width **4yd/3.66m** Repeat **12in/30.5cm** Price ★★★★

7 **Hugh Mackay/Ribbon 100089-910953** Color **multi** Alternative colors **available** Composition **100% wool** Width **27in/69cm** Repeat **4¼in/11cm** Price ★★

8 **Ulster Carpet Mills/ Turkestan 10/2381** Color **red** Alternative colors **not available** Composition **80% wool, 20% nylon** Width **4yd/3.66m** Repeat **37in/94cm** Price ★★ ⊞

9 **Brintons/Flake 1/2455** Color **1** Alternative colors **available** Composition **80% wool, 20% nylon** Width **4½yd/4m** Repeat **19¾in/50cm** Price ★★★ ⊞

10 **Hugh Mackay/Fleur de Lys 126893-910063** Color **multi** Alternative colors **available** Composition **80% wool, 20% nylon** Width **27in/ 69cm** Repeat **3½in/9cm** Price ★★★ ⊞

11 **Brintons/Abbotsford 8/5536** Color **8** Alternative colors **available** Composition **80% wool, 20% nylon** Width **2¼yd/2m** Repeat **10in/25cm** Price ★★

12 **Hugh Mackay/Balmoral 99956-910984** Color **multi** Alternative colors **available** Composition **100% wool** Width **27in/69cm** Repeat **17in/43cm** Price ★★

13 **Stark/Brissac** Color **white/gold** Alternative colors **available** Composition **80% wool, 20% viscose** Width **27in/ 68.5cm** Repeat **21in/53cm** Price ★★★★

8

CLASSICAL WREATHS

Used in Ancient Greece and Rome to laud the achievements of emperors, heroes, poets, and athletes, the wreath symbolizes eternity, sovereignty, honor, and glory. It consists of a garland of leaves (usually laurel, but oak or olive are also seen), often bound with ribbon. Wreaths became popular in carpet designs in the mid-18th century as the Neoclassical style spread throughout Europe.

Brintons/Wreath 9/13710 Color **9** Alternative colors **available** Composition **80% wool, 20% nylon** Width **4½yd/4m** Repeat **19¾in/50cm** Price ★★★ ⊞

17th century

18th century

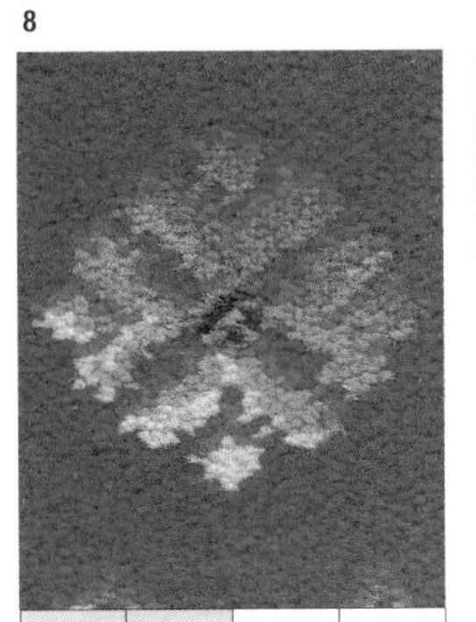

9

10

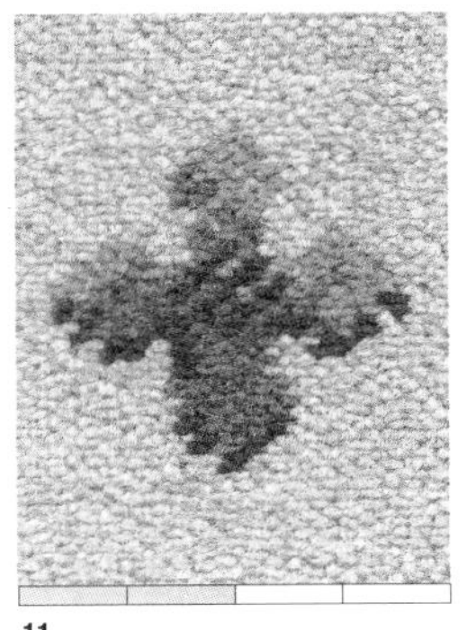

11

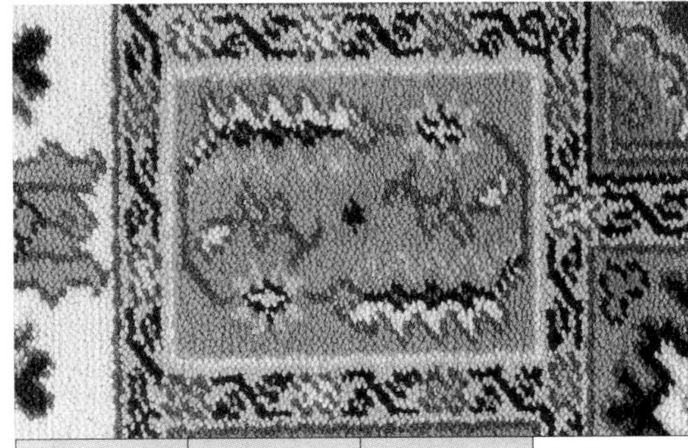

14

12

13

15

14 **Axminster Carpets/Persian Panel 34/01397** Color **slate blue** Alternative colors **available** Composition **100% wool** Width **4yd/3.66m** Repeat **33½in/85cm** Price ★★ ⊞

15 **Stark/Filigrane et Fleurs** Color **pastel** Alternative colors **available** Composition **100% wool** Width **39¾in/ 101cm** Repeat **51½in/131cm** Price ★★★★★

Carpets: **Early 19th century**

The early 19th century saw the Jacquard loom largely supplanting the old hand looms, thereby greatly increasing carpet production. In Britain, Kidderminster remained a major center for carpet manufacture, with at least 1,000 carpet looms in operation. Brussels carpets, where a worsted warp is brought to the surface to form a pile, and Wilton, where the looped pile is cut to create a more velvetlike surface, were particularly popular at this time, both of them being versatile and inexpensive. In America, non-pile, reversible carpets, such as Ingrain and Scotch, were being produced in large numbers. These were made in strips and laid to cover the whole floor in a room.

Designs that were fashionable in America and Europe at this time included those based on architectural panels, as well as paisley and Indian motifs, naturalistic floral designs, and *verdure* patterns of ferns, foliage, and palms. Heraldic motifs were also popular. In France, delicate floral carpets in soft colors were in vogue.

5

5 **Chatsworth/Buckingham** Color **constitution gold** Alternative colors **available** Composition **100% wool** Width **4½yd/4m** Repeat **35½in/90cm** Price ★★★

6 **Stark/Houles** Color **floral black** Alternative colors **available** Composition **100% wool** Width **4yd/3.66m** Repeat **39in/99cm** Price ★★★★

7 **Stark/Fontainebleau Ribbon Border** Color **creme** Alternative colors **available** Composition **100% wool** Width **13½in/34.75cm** Repeat **17¼in/44cm** Price ★★★

8 **Stark/Clichy** Color **yellow** Alternative colors **available** Composition **100% wool** Width **39¾in/101cm** Repeat **10in/25cm** Price ★★★★

9 **Hugh Mackay/142974/7282** Color **multi** Alternative colors **available** Composition **100% wool** Width **35¾in/91cm** Repeat **33½in/86cm** Price ★★ ⊞

1

2

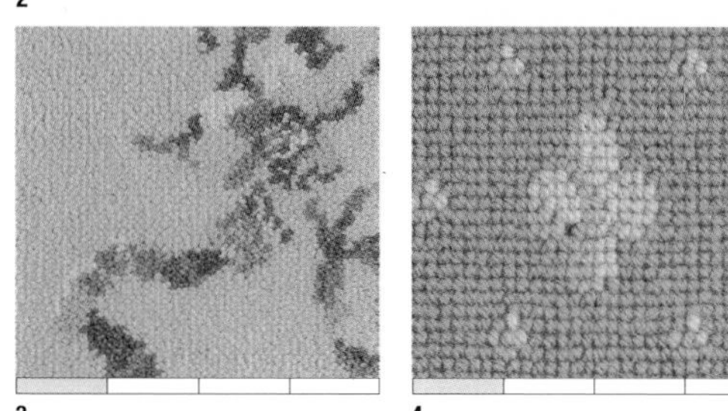

3

4

1 **Stark/Summer Flowers Border** Color **yellow** Alternative colors **not available** Composition **100% wool** Width **9in/23cm** Repeat **2½in/6cm** Price ★★★★★

2 **Stark/Kingston Border** Color **blue** Alternative colors **available** Composition **100% wool** Width **6¾in/17cm** Repeat **7in/18cm** Price ★★

3 **Brintons/Golden Serenade 116/4700** Color **116** Alternative colors **available** Composition **80% wool, 20% nylon** Width **4½yd/4m** Repeat **39¼in/100cm** Price ★★ ⊞

4 **Woodward Grosvenor/Emblem 36/5681** Color **36** Alternative colors **available** Composition **100% wool** Width **4½yd/4m** Repeat **5in/13cm** Price ★★★

6

7

8

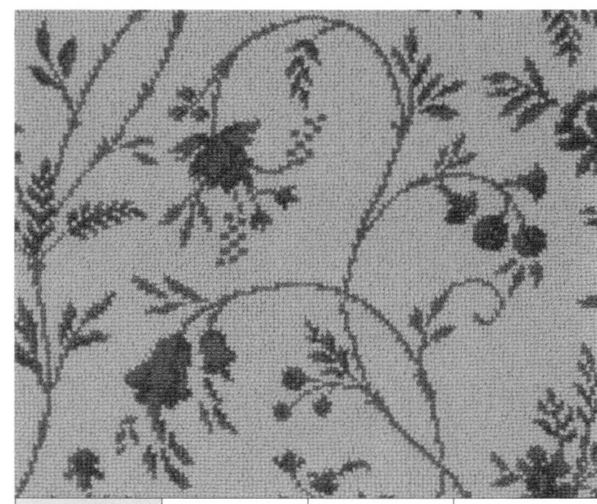

9

10

10 Stark/Pandora Floral Color **white** Alternative colors **available** Composition **100% wool** Width **4yd/3.66m** Repeat **36in/91cm** Price ★★★★

11 Brintons/Rochester 44/10551 Color **green** Alternative colors **available** Composition **80% wool, 20% nylon** Width **4yd/3.66m** Repeat **9in/23cm** Price ★★

12 Brintons/93/10833 Color **93** Alternative colors **available** Composition **80% wool, 20% nylon** Width **4yd/3.66m** Repeat **3in/8cm** Price ★★ ⊞

13 Stark/Navarre Border Color **olive** Alternative colors **not available** Composition **100% wool** Width **6¾in/17cm** Repeat **6¾in/17cm** Price ★★

12

11

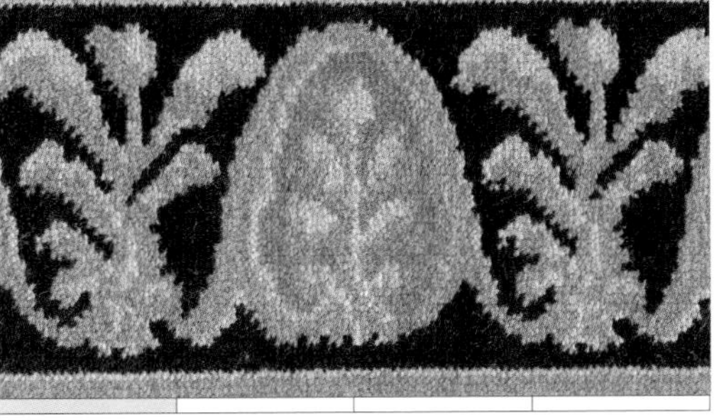
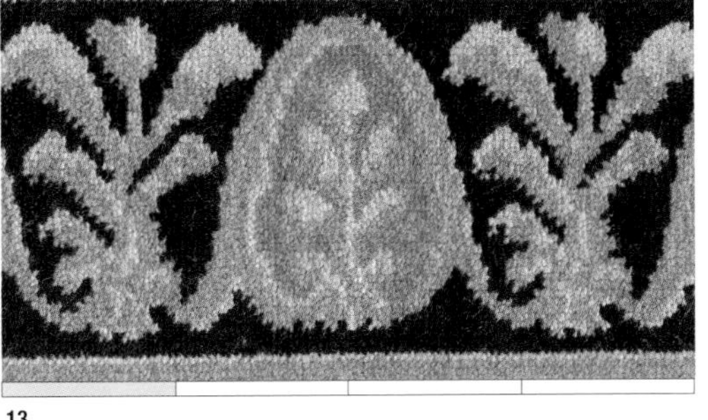

13

14

14 Tomkinsons Carpets/Sheik 51/3009 Color **jade** Alternative colors **available** Composition **80% wool, 20% nylon** Width **4yd/3.66m** Repeat **33in/84cm** Price ★★ ⊞

15 Stark/Small Star Color **cobalt blue** Alternative colors **available** Composition **100% wool** Width **4yd/3.66m** Repeat **6in/15cm** Price ★★★

16 Stark/Small Star Border Color **cobalt blue** Alternative colors **available** Composition **100% wool** Width **6¾in/17cm** Repeat **11¼in/29.5cm** Price ★★

17 Bosanquet Ives/Icicles Color **01** Alternative colors **available** Composition **80% wool, 20% nylon** Width **27in/69cm** Repeat **–** Price ★★

18 Stark/Kingston Color **blue** Alternative colors **available** Composition **100% wool** Width **4yd/3.72m** Repeat **3in/8cm** Price ★★★★

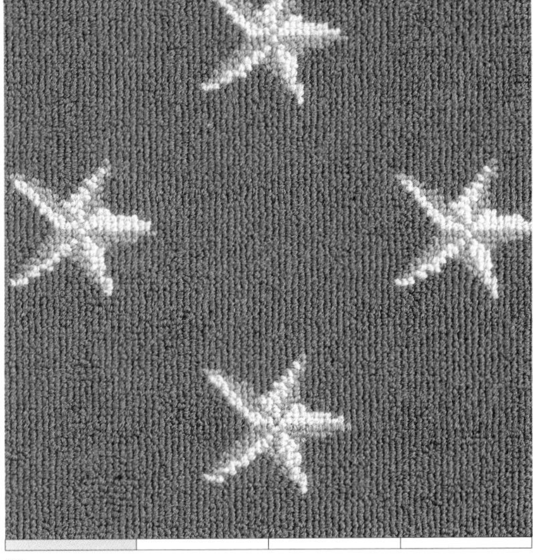

15

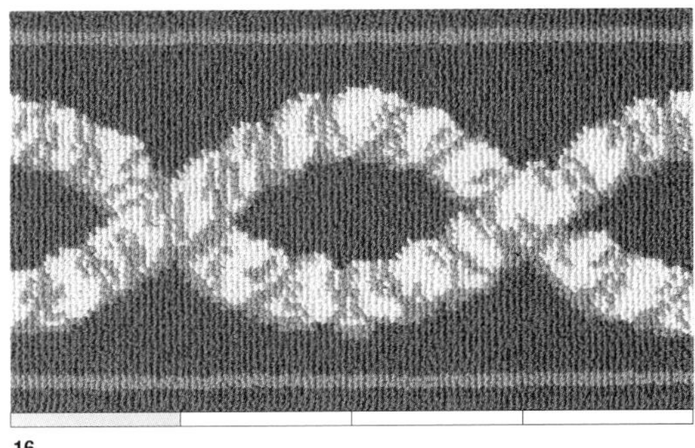

16

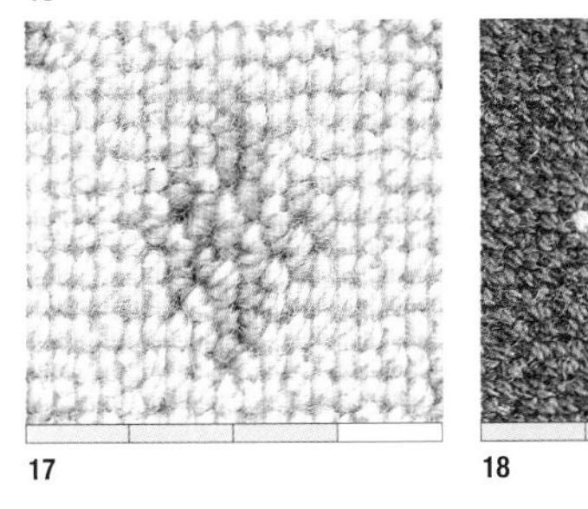

17

18

Carpets: **Late 19th century**

Factors such as the development of synthetic dyes and the power loom, along with the increased wealth of the middle class, gave great impetus to the British and American carpet industries. Engineers in America developed the Axminster loom in 1876, and Brintons in Kidderminster, England, introduced the Gripper version in 1890. The Kleitos Axminster Broadloom, brought from America and patented by Tomkinson Ltd. in Kidderminster in 1896, enabled the production of large carpets with unlimited color, giving full rein to the floral chintz that became a hallmark of the British industry. The mid-19th-century exhibition of Oriental carpets in Berlin triggered a revival in Persian and Indian designs. Many carpets were based on Baroque themes using blues and crimsons. Other influences on design were Owen Jones's *Dictionary of Ornament* (1856) and Christopher Dresser's *Principles of Design* (1879). The Great Exhibition of 1851 in Britain inspired the carpet designs by Morris and Company, C. F. A. Voysey, and other members of the Arts and Crafts Movement. For example, William Morris's floral designs, such as the acanthus and poppy Axminsters of the 1870s, were reinterpretations of Persian designs, while in America, the Arts and Crafts designs of Frank Lloyd Wright and Greene & Greene were more restrained.

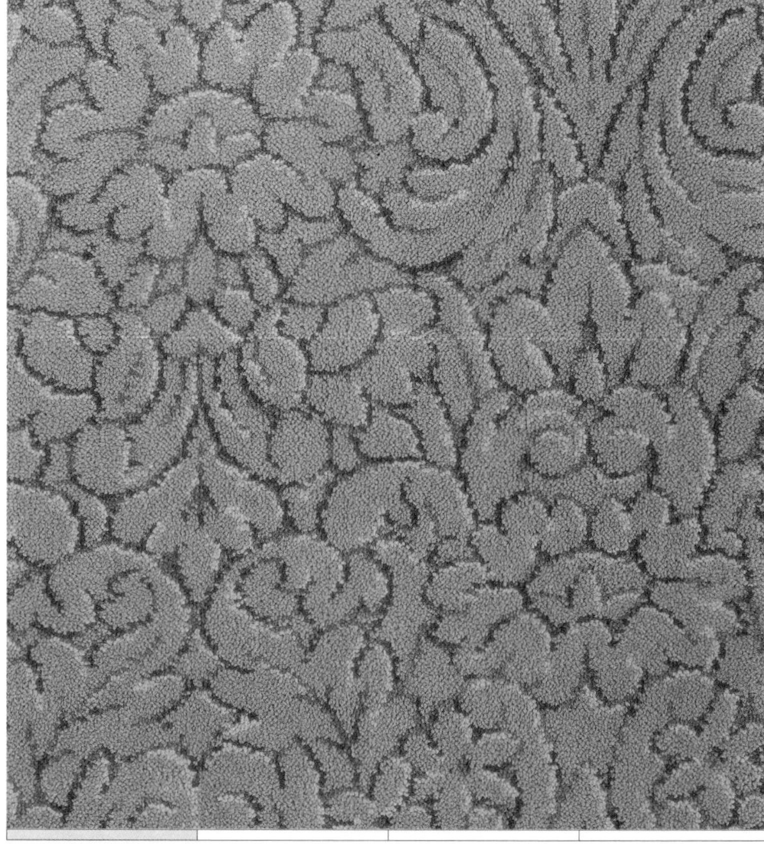
5

1

2

6

7

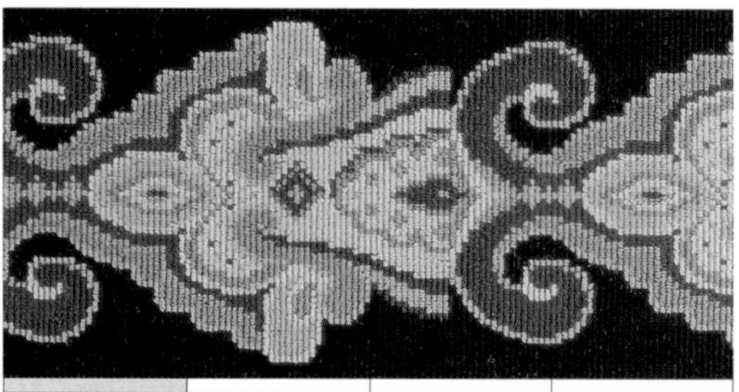
3

4

8

1 **Stark/Winford Rose Border** Color **yellow** Alternative colors **not available** Composition **100% wool** Width **9in/23cm** Repeat **24in/61cm** Price ★★★★★

2 **Woodward Grosvenor/Pearl Damask 26/5687** Color **26** Alternative colors **available** Composition **100% wool** Width **4½yd/4m** Repeat **29¼in/74.5cm** Price ★★★

3 **Stark/Chambone Border** Color **stock** Alternative colors **not available** Composition **100% wool** Width **9in/23cm** Repeat **18½in/47cm** Price ★★★

4 **Stark/Flanders Border** Color **stock** Alternative colors **not available** Composition **100% wool** Width **9in/23cm** Repeat – Price ★★★

5 **Ryalux/Crown Damask** Color **gold** Alternative colors **available** Composition **80% wool, 20% nylon** Width **to order** Repeat **19¾in/50cm** Price ★★

6 **Stark/Buisson des Roses** Color **stock** Alternative colors **not available** Composition **100% wool** Width **39¾in/101cm** Repeat **4½in/11.5cm** Price ★★★★

7 **Afia/Carlotta** Color **black and white** Alternative colors **not available** Composition **100% wool** Width **27in/69cm** Repeat **33½in/85cm** Price ★★★★

8 **Axminster Carpets/Flowers and Ribbons 152/80235** Color **shadow green** Alternative colors **available** Composition **100% wool** Width **4yd/3.66m** Repeat **35¾in/91cm** Price ★★★ ⊞

19th century

9 **Bosanquet Ives/Wool Linen** Color **multi** Alternative colors **available** Composition **80% wool, 20% linen** Width **4½yd/4m** Repeat – Price ★

10 **Stark/Villandry** Color **green and peach** Alternative colors **available** Composition **100% wool** Width **27in/69cm** Repeat **30in/76cm** Price ★★★★★

11 **Stark/Kenshire** Color **gold/green** Alternative colors **available** Composition **100% wool** Width **27in/68.5cm** Repeat **7in/18cm** Price ★★★★

12 **Stark/Petite Diagonal Border** Color **navy blue** Alternative colors **available** Composition **100% wool** Width **9in/23cm** Repeat **21½in/55cm** Price ★★★★

13 **Stark/Polo** Color **stock** Alternative colors **not available** Composition **100% wool** Width **27in/68.5cm** Repeat **7in/18cm** Price ★★★★

14 **Stark/Chambone** Color **stock** Alternative colors **not available** Composition **100% wool** Width **39¾in/101cm** Repeat **41¼in/105cm** Price ★★★★★

15 **Woodward Grosvenor/21/7051** Color **red** Alternative colors **available** Composition **100% wool** Width **27in/69cm** Repeat – Price ★★

16 **Woodward Grosvenor/19/7050** Color **green** Alternative colors **available** Composition **100% wool** Width **27in/69cm** Repeat **11½in/29.5cm** Price ★★★

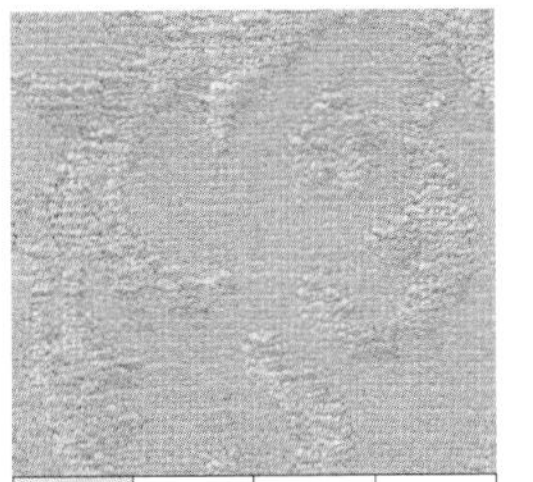
9

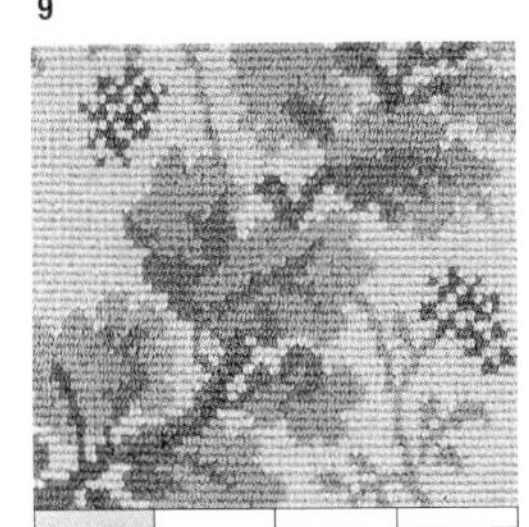
10

11

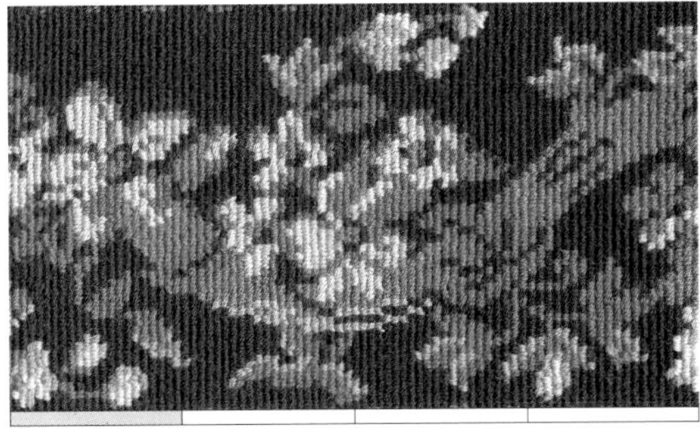
12

13

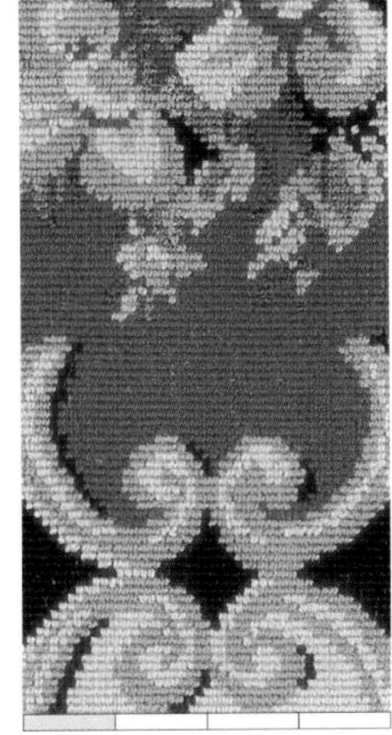
14

15

16

DESIGN PAPERS

Carpets have traditionally been designed using "point paper." Point paper is divided into inch squares, with each square then redivided to represent one tuft. The transferring of the design to the paper has to be precise, and applied in a semitransparent form so that each square can be counted–this is necessary to calculate the exact amount of yarn for each color. In spite of computerization, which is now universal, many companies still retain the services of a designer who understands these techniques.

The design paper shown above was used to produce the carpet seen below, which is an interpretation of a historic Persian design.

Stoddard Templeton/Antiquarian 1/8312 Color **multi** Alternative colors **not available** Composition **80% wool, 20% nylon** Width **54in/137cm** Repeat **36½in/93cm** Price ★★ ⊞

19th century

Carpets: **Early 20th century**

In Britain, the transition from Art Nouveau to Art Deco was most clearly seen in the work of Charles Rennie Mackintosh, who stripped away gratuitous ornament and pointed the way to cleaner, simpler lines. This simplicity was reflected in the carpet designs of the early 20th century. Geometric patterns, reflecting the Modernist preoccupation with the machine, were particularly favored, as were plain, wall-to-wall carpets. In Britain, Scotland, and America, brilliantly colored abstracts were woven for the new movie theaters and department stores. Large hotels and ocean liners were treated to soft, muted designs with large repeats, intended to create a mood of calm. In France, highly formal, stylized floral carpets were in demand.

Other inspirations for designs on both sides of the Atlantic came from the Ballet Russe, the discovery of the tomb of Tutankhamun, and the popularity of African art. At the same time, the tradition of Persian, Turkish, and chintz designs also remained an important part of carpet ranges (*see* opposite).

1

2

1 Stark/Navarre Color **olive** Alternative colors **not available** Composition **100% wool** Width **4yd/3.72m** Repeat **4in/10cm** Price ★★★★

2 Bosanquet Ives/Trellis Color **olive and khaki** Alternative colors **available** Composition **100% wool** Width **27in/69cm** Repeat **–** Price ★★★

3 Stark/Laseine Color **cocoa** Alternative colors **not available** Composition **100% wool** Width **4yd/3.72m** Repeat **36½in/93cm** Price ★★★★

4 Axminster Carpets/Honeycomb 40/2505 Color **champagne** Alternative colors **available** Composition **100% wool** Width **4yd/3.66m** Repeat **9in/23cm** Price ★★ ⊞

3

4

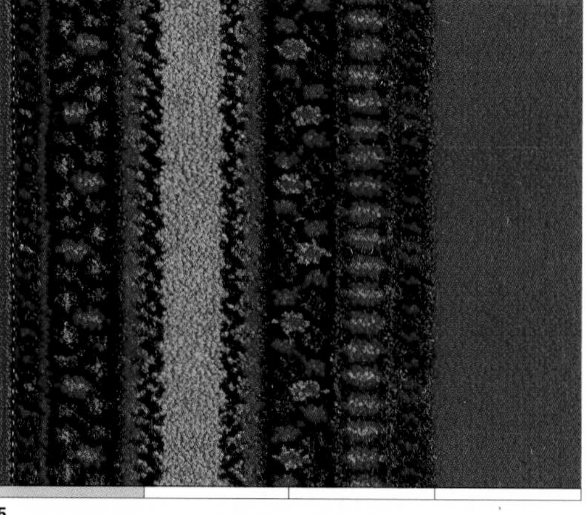

5

5 Tomkinsons Carpets/Saraband Border 3/2315 Color **cochineal** Alternative colors **available** Composition **80% wool, 20% nylon** Width **12in/30.5cm** Repeat **2½in/6.5cm** Price ★★

6 Stoddard Templeton/Samarkand 23/3110 Color **multi** Alternative colors **available** Composition **80% wool, 20% polypropylene** Width **4yd/3.66m** Repeat **18in/46cm** Price ★★ ⊞

7 Tomkinsons Carpets/Tatton Park 71/2501 Color **multi** Alternative colors **not available** Composition **80% wool, 20% nylon** Width **4yd/3.66m** Repeat **33in/84cm** Price ★★ ⊞

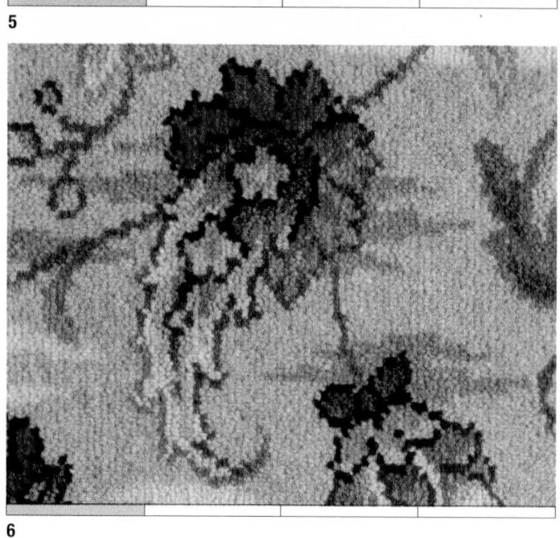

6

7

8

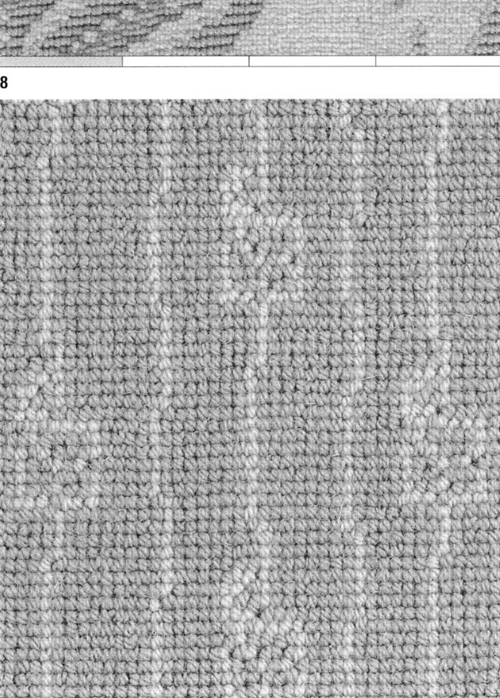
9

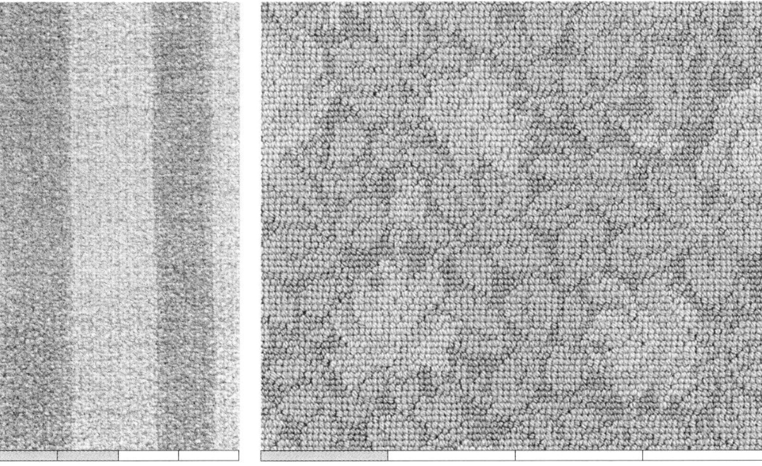
10

11

8 Bosanquet Ives/Woodlands Color **multi** Alternative colors **available** Composition **100% wool** Width **27in/69cm** Repeat – Price ★★★

9 Woodward Grosvenor/Strata 26/5677 Color **26** Alternative colors **available** Composition **100% wool** Width **4½yd/4m** Repeat **4in/10cm** Price ★★★

10 Stark/Bristol Border Color **sienna gold** Alternative colors **available** Composition **100% wool** Width **6¾in/17cm** Repeat – Price ★★★

11 Woodward Grosvenor/Rambling Rose 16/5684 Color **16** Alternative colors **available** Composition **100% wool** Width **4½yd/4m** Repeat **17in/43cm** Price ★★★

12 Brintons/Trinity 4/11106 Color **4** Alternative colors **not available** Composition **80% wool, 20% nylon** Width **27in/69cm** Repeat **27in/69cm** Price ★★ [T]

13 Afia/Havorford Color **black and white** Alternative colors **not available** Composition **100% wool** Width **4yd/3.66m** Repeat **11¾in/30cm** Price ★★★★★ [+]

14 Stark/Neuvel Color **stock** Alternative colors **not available** Composition **100% wool** Width **27in/68.5cm** Repeat **4½in/11.5cm** Price ★★★★

15 Afia/Lys et Aruns 14959 Color **red** Alternative colors **not available** Composition **100% wool** Width **27in/69cm** Repeat **33½in/85cm** Price ★★★★

12

13

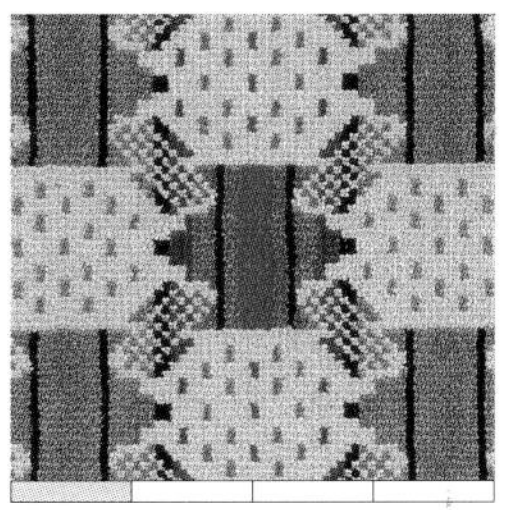
14

15

PERSIAN INFLUENCE

The influence of Persian carpets, with their rich coloring and complex patterns, on contemporary European and American designs has been profound. Although Art Deco and Modernist schemes largely eschewed them, such carpets were arguably more popular in the early 20th century than ever before. Carpets from Sarouk in Persia, salmon pink in color and featuring geometric or floral decoration, were much in demand in America.

Brintons/Trinity 5/11078 Color **5** Alternative colors **not available** Composition **80% wool, 20% nylon** Width **27in/69cm** Repeat **27in/69cm** Price ★★ [T]

Carpets: **Mid-20th century**

From the mid-20th century onward, there was a great increase in the use of synthetic fibers for carpets. Although the traditional fiber was always wool because of its natural resilience and ability to absorb dye, it is comparatively more expensive than synthetic fibers. To improve carpet durability, wool is often blended with nylon in a ratio of 80:20 percent, and synthetic fibers are also blended in various combinations.

In terms of patterning, there was a new range of influences on carpet design during this time. In 1951, the Festival of Britain had a profound impact on the carpet industry, which produced delicate, linear "spot" designs for the first time. In the late 1950s and 1960s, there was a noticeable response to the leading painters and designers with, for example, the American painter Jackson Pollock greatly influencing domestic Axminster and Gripper ranges. Carpets with Middle Eastern and African ornament–including animal-print patterns–were fashionable in Europe and America. Plain carpets were also popular.

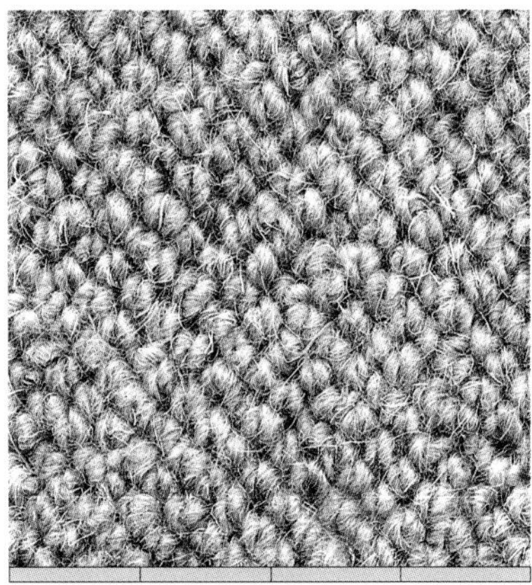

Ollerton Hall/Grain Color **sea green** Alternative colors **available** Composition **100% wool** Width **4½yd/4m** Repeat **–** Price ★

Louis de Poortere/Capella TR Color **440** Alternative colors **available** Composition **100% polyamide** Width **4½yd/4m** Repeat **–** Price ★

Brintons/Bell Twist 9582 Color **dianthus** Alternative colors **available** Composition **80% wool, 20% nylon** Width **4yd/3.66m** Repeat **–** Price ★★ ⊞

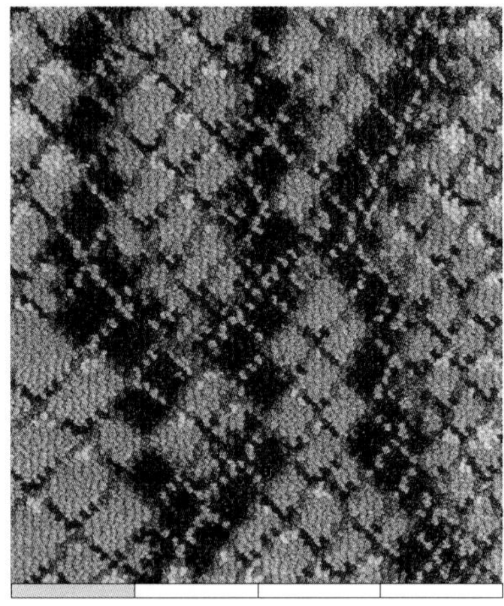

Hugh Mackay/Indian River Snake 1377/7152 Color **multi** Alternative colors **available** Composition **80% wool, 20% nylon** Width **27in/69cm** Repeat **11¾in/30cm** Price ★★★

Afia/Paintbox Border Color **sable with porridge** Alternative colors **available** Composition **80% wool, 20% Woolbond** Width **4¾in/12cm** Repeat **–** Price ★

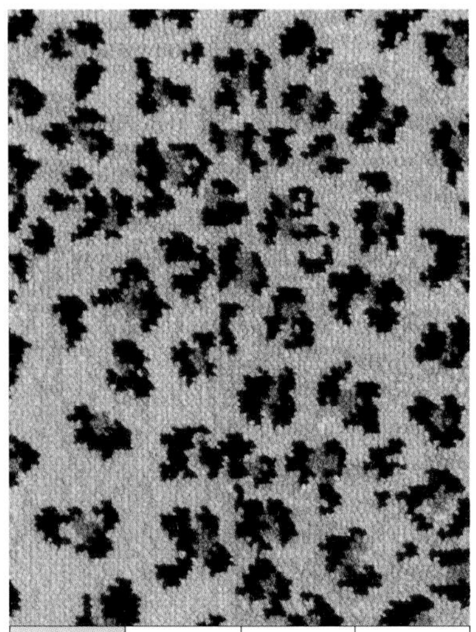

Afia/Somali Panther Color **stock** Alternative colors **not available** Composition **100% wool** Width **4yd/3.66m** Repeat **2yd/1.87m** Price ★★★★★

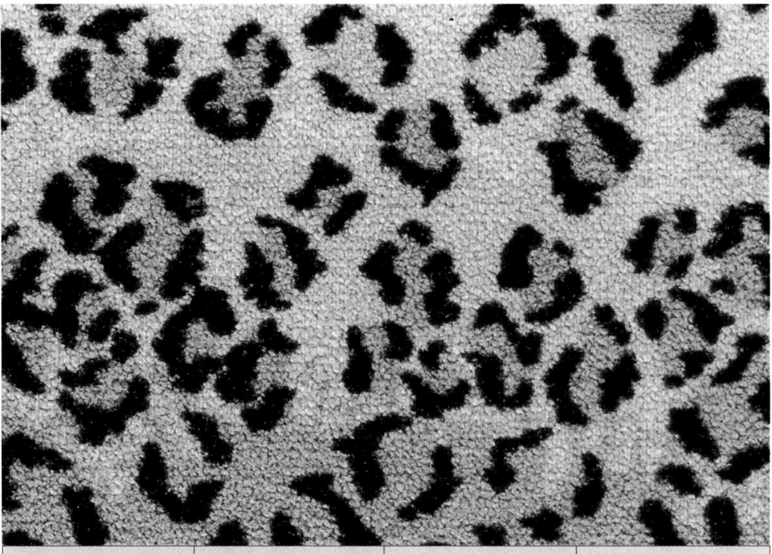

Chatsworth/Leopard Skin Color **multi** Alternative colors **not available** Composition **100% nylon** Width **4yd/3.66m** Repeat **35½in/90cm** Price ★★

Chatsworth/White Tiger Color **black and white** Alternative colors **not available** Composition **100% nylon** Width **4yd/3.66m** Repeat **35½in/90cm** Price ★★

Ollerton Hall/Woolrich Color **brown** Alternative colors **available** Composition **100% wool** Width **4yd/3.66m** Repeat **4in/10cm** Price ★

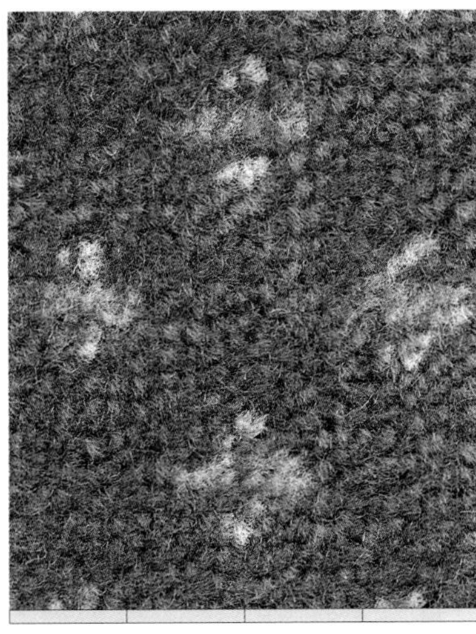

Ollerton Hall/Saturn Color **red** Alternative colors **available** Composition **100% polypropylene** Width **to order** Repeat **1½in/4cm** Price ★

Ollerton Hall/Graphics Color **dark blue** Alternative colors **available** Composition **100% polypropylene** Width **4½yd/4m** Repeat **–** Price ★

Mannington Carpets/Sorata RERI Color **red river** Alternative colors **available** Composition **100% nylon** Width **4yd/3.66m** Repeat **–** Price ★ ⊞

Hugh Mackay/Macbeth Tartan 1389-7104 Color **multi** Alternative colors **available** Composition **80% wool, 20% nylon** Width **27in/69cm** Repeat **27in/69cm** Price ★★★

Brintons/Trinity 3/12740 Color **multi** Alternative colors **not available** Composition **80% wool, 20% nylon** Width **27in/69cm** Repeat **27in/69cm** Price ★★ T

Stoddard Templeton/New England 3/8334 Color **multi** Alternative colors **not available** Composition **80% wool, 20% nylon** Width **4yd/3.66m** Repeat **25½in/65cm** Price ★★ ⊞

Ollerton Hall/Princess 6TCP Color **burgundy** Alternative colors **available** Composition **80% wool, 20% nylon** Width **4½yd/4m** Repeat **–** Price ★ ⊞

Tomkinsons Carpets/Caress 937/139 Color **cashew** Alternative colors **available** Composition **100% polypropylene** Width **4½yd/4m** Repeat **–** Price ★ ⊞

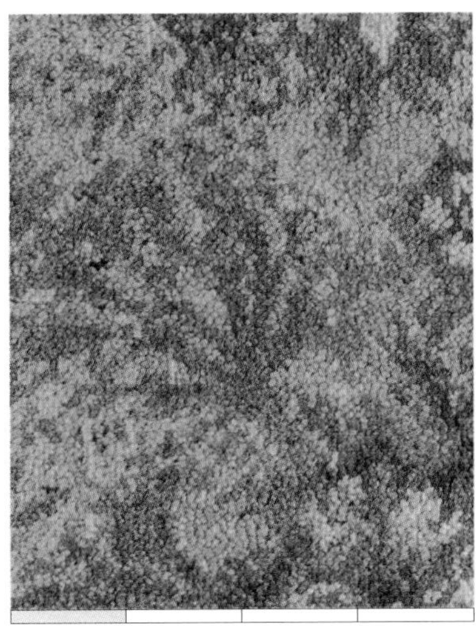

Axminster Carpets/French Impressions 232/15020 Color **Erica pink** Alternative colors **available** Composition **100% wool** Width **4yd/3.66m** Repeat **35¾in/91cm** Price ★★ ⊞

Hugh Mackay/127864-942416 Color **multi** Alternative colors **available** Composition **80% wool, 20% nylon** Width **27in/69cm** Repeat **–** Price ★★ ⊞

Carpets: **Late 20th century**

The development of synthetic fibers, computerization, and an expanding range of textures resulted in the majority of carpets in the late 20th century being mass-produced using a tufting process. Unlike woven carpet, where the backing is an integral part of the cloth, tufted yarn is machine-sewn to a ready-woven backing that is then covered with latex. The machines used to produce such carpets resemble gigantic sewing machines with hundreds of needles. These tufted carpets were often produced in soft modulated colors, which was achieved with space-dyed yarns or screen-printing. There was also experimentation with injection dyeing, which involved each tuft receiving its own jet of dye, providing complete freedom for designers and producing highly colorful product ranges.

The last decade of the century saw the revival of the loose carpet square–available in sizes as large as 1 square yard or meter; this provided designers with new pattern opportunities. Contemporary designers in Europe and America continued drawing inspiration for the patterning of carpets from the bold influences of Africa, India, and South America and a wide range of styles from the past, as well as creating exciting new designs and experimenting with colors and patterning.

1

2

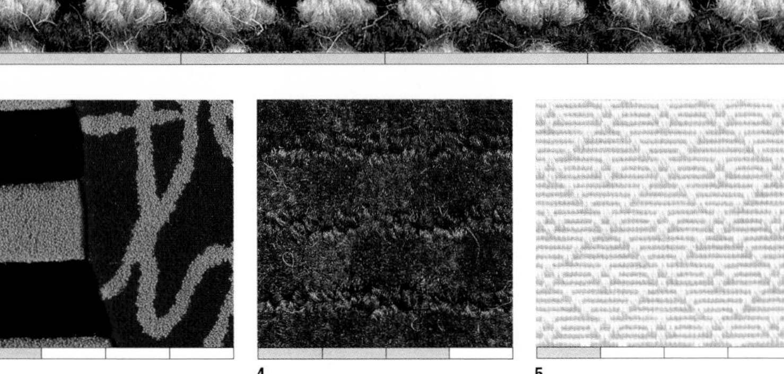

3 4 5

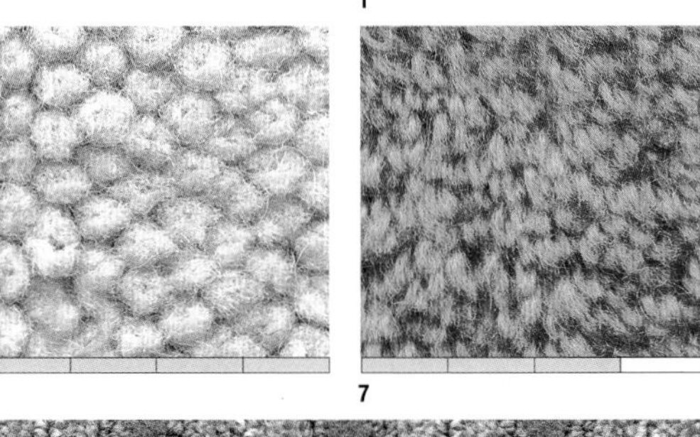

6 7

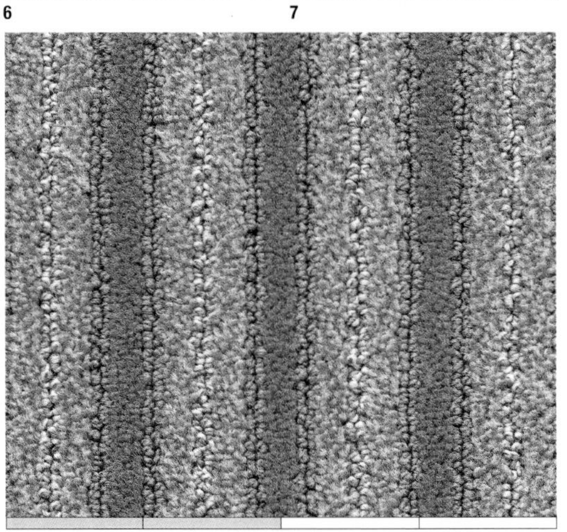

8

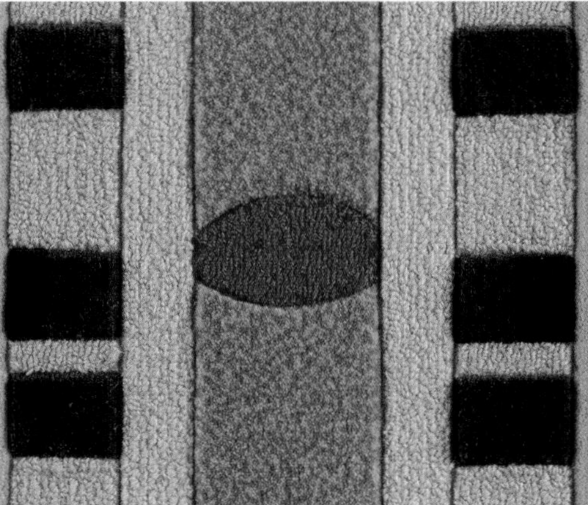

9

1 **Chatsworth/Pebbles** Color **silver gray** Alternative colors **available** Composition **100% wool** Width **4½yd/4m** Repeat – Price ★★★★★ ⊞

2 **Afia/Broadway** Color **ocean** Alternative colors **available** Composition **80% wool, 20% nylon** Width **4½yd/4m** Repeat – Price ★★★

3 **Chatsworth/Keyboard** Color **multi** Alternative colors **available** Composition **100% wool** Width **to order** Repeat – Price ★★★★★

4 **Mannington Carpets/Grayson** Color **sterling** Alternative colors **available** Composition **100% nylon** Width **4yd/3.66m** Repeat – Price ★★

5 **Afia/Pastiche** Color **spin drift** Alternative colors **available** Composition **100% wool** Width **4½yd/4m** Repeat **2in/5cm** Price ★★

6 **Bosanquet Ives/Sinfonie** Color **54** Alternative colors **available** Composition **100% wool** Width **4½yd/4m** Repeat – Price ★★★★

7 **Ollerton Hall/Ultimate Shag Pile** Color **pink** Alternative colors **available** Composition **100% wool** Width **to order** Repeat – Price ★★

8 **Atlas Carpet Mills/Tintoretto TT01** Color **Danube** Alternative colors **available** Composition **100% nylon** Width **4yd/3.66m** Repeat **1½in/4cm** Price ★★

9 **Chatsworth/Dakee SP121** Color **multi** Alternative colors **available** Composition **100% wool** Width **to order** Repeat – Price ★★★★★

10 Chatsworth/Link Border (carved) Color **blue and green** Alternative colors **available** Composition **100% wool** Width **to order** Repeat **–** Price ★★★★

11 Bosanquet Ives/Woolen Chord Color **multi** Alternative colors **available** Composition **100% wool** Width **to order** Repeat **–** Price ★★★

12 Louis de Poortere/Byzance 330 Color **yellow** Alternative colors **available** Composition **100% polyamide** Width **4½yd/4m** Repeat **–** Price ★

13 Chatsworth/Foresta 8520 Color **white** Alternative colors **available** Composition **100% wool** Width **to order** Repeat **–** Price ★★★★

10

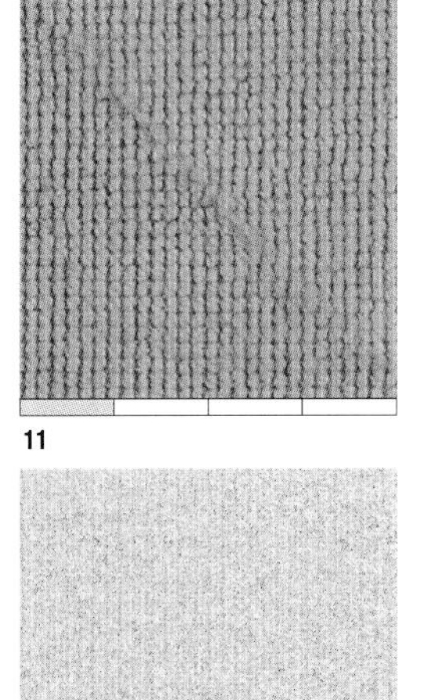

11

12

13

14

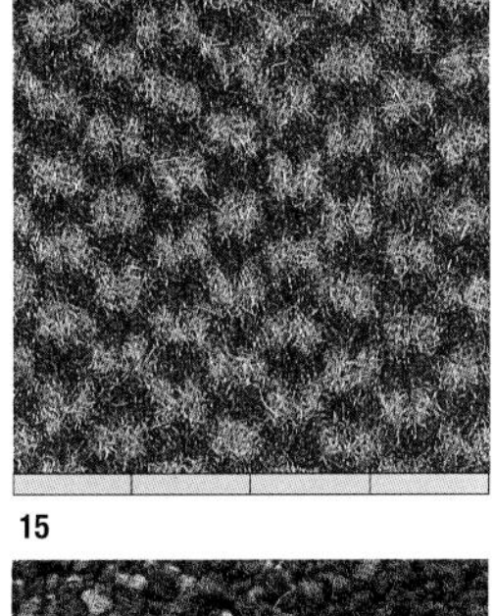

15

16

17

18

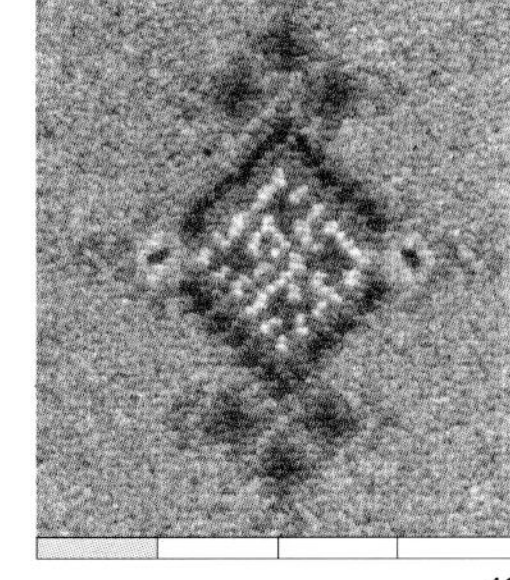

19

14 Atlas Carpet Mills/Cipriani 35 Color **R947 Lapis** Alternative colors **available** Composition **100% nylon** Width **4yd/3.66m** Repeat **¾in/2cm** Price ★★

15 Louis de Poortere/Adriana II Color **241** Alternative colors **available** Composition **100% polyamide** Width **4½yd/4m** Repeat **–** Price ★

16 Westbond/8L Color **curry, Bastille gray, and white Russia** Alternative colors **available** Composition **100% nylon** Width **19¾ x 19¾in/50 x 50cm (tile)** Repeat **–** Price ★★ ⊞

17 Mannington Carpets/Strategies ZENI Color **zenith** Alternative colors **available** Composition **100% nylon** Width **4⅛yd/3.8m** Repeat **18½in/47cm** Price ★★

18 Chatsworth/Greek Key Border Color **black and beige** Alternative colors **available** Composition **100% wool** Width **to order** Repeat **–** Price ★★★★★

19 Brintons/Marrakesh 22/11894 Color **22** Alternative colors **available** Composition **80% wool, 20% nylon** Width **4yd/3.66m** Repeat **7in/18cm** Price ★★ ⊞

COMBINATION WEAVES

Owing to the ever increasing sophistication of looms and tufting machines, a great range of textures is now available in carpets. For example, high and low pile, cut and uncut loops, and "carved" effects can all be employed in a single carpet, thereby giving it a mixture of several different textures. New yarns can also provide "pebble" surfaces, while space-dyed yarns provide a speckled appearance. There are also no limits to the number of colors that can be used in high-quality tufted carpets.

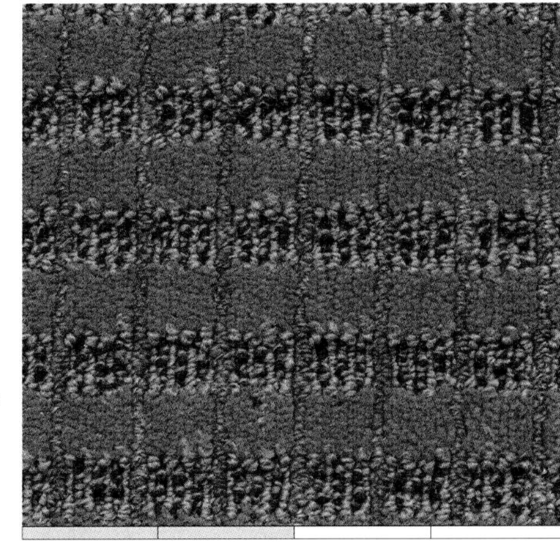

Monterey/Presidio 602-384 Color **general** Alternative colors **available** Composition **100% nylon** Width **4yd/3.66m** Repeat **–** Price ★★

Patrick/Straw Market P803 Color **barley** Alternative colors **available** Composition **100% nylon** Width **4yd/3.66m** Repeat **–** Price ★

Sheet Flooring

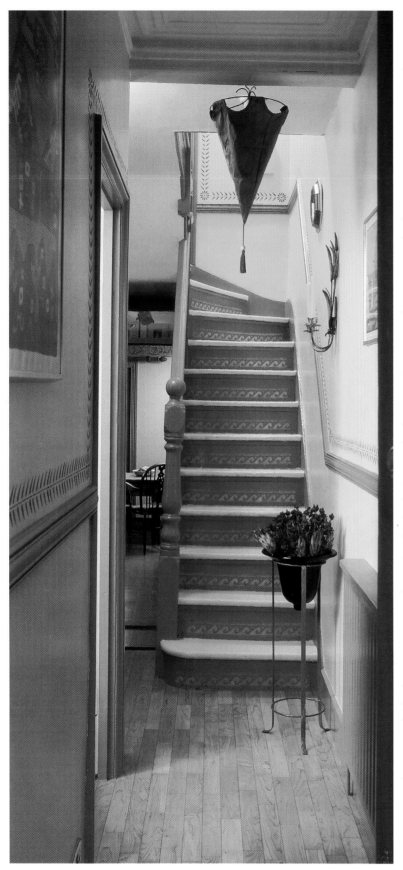

Sheet flooring is the collective term for a range of practical floor coverings that include floorcloths, vinyl, linoleum, and rubber.

Floorcloths first appeared in the late 17th century as groundsheets for marquees, but they were soon used in interiors as an economical and decorative means of covering floors. Often made from oilcloth, they came into use as a result of the availability of large amounts of sailcloth from the shipbuilding industry. Stemming from the older practice of painting floorboards, floorcloth patterns often simulated stone and marble pavings.

The rapid growth of industrial mass production in Britain in the 19th century brought with it the invention of linoleum (see page 379). Made from relatively cheap materials, it remained the most popular form of sheet flooring for domestic use until the mid-20th century. The social changes since then have brought an increased demand for easy-to-clean, mass-produced flooring. By the 1950s, developments in the plastics industry led to the introduction of vinyl and resin floorings that could imitate wood, stone, and terracotta. The late 20th century saw the beginning of a move into the domestic market of contract flooring materials such as rubber and metal flooring.

ABOVE Today, vinyl flooring can duplicate even the most intricate designs found on traditional floor coverings, and can be colored to complement any interior. This bold geometric design on a bathroom floor is based on a classical pattern.

LEFT The white vinyl floor tiles in this modern interpretation of a 17th-century interior give the appearance of a polished marble floor, yet provide a surface that is easy to clean and warm to the touch.

FAR LEFT Cushion vinyl, invented in the United States in 1963, cleverly simulates a wood finish in this modern interior. It is now produced in many different designs and textures. It also has the advantage of being warm underfoot and is especially suitable for use in apartments as it is much more sound absorbent than wood.

KEY DESIGNS

1 Popular since the middle of the 19th century, linoleum is available in a wide range of colors. However, the traditional colors–browns, reds, and yellows–are still very fashionable.

2 Rubber is a highly durable 20th-century floor covering, used especially in public areas and airports. With new technology it can now be produced in a variety of colors and textures.

3 Traditional terracotta slates are one of the styles imitated by vinyl flooring. Made in rolls and tiles, vinyl patterns can simulate stone, ceramic and wood, and sometimes feature modern abstract designs.

4 Resin laminates that imitate wood are a durable, easy to care for, and cheaper alternative to natural wood boards. A wide range of different grains, colors and board sizes is available.

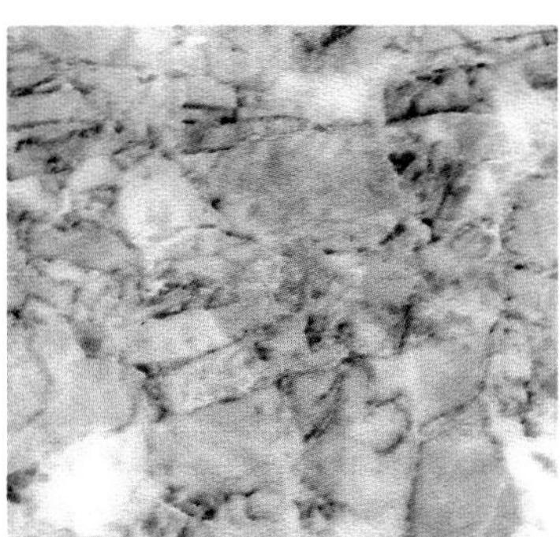

5 Modern techniques can reproduce the look of natural stone to a highly accurate degree, as seen on this imitation marble. The benefits of this include the ease of installation and lower cost.

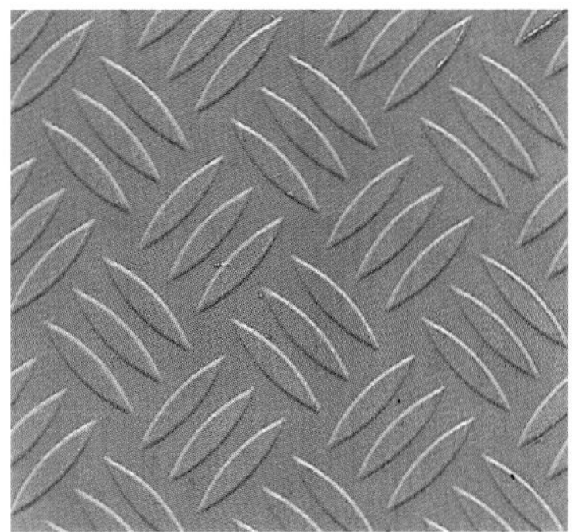

6 Metal sheet flooring became increasingly popular in the late 20th century. Durable and stylish, this type of flooring was often found in domestic as well as commercial settings.

1 **DLW/Marmorette 121-18** Color **18** Alternative colors **available** Composition **100% linoleum** Width **2⅛yd/2m** Repeat – Price ★

2 **Dalsouple/Uni** Color **pêche** Alternative colors **available** Composition **100% rubber** Width **13¼ x 13¼in/34 x 34cm (tile)** Repeat – Price ★★

3 **Westco/Cobble Gold Embossed** Color **cobble gold** Alternative colors **available** Composition **100% PVC** Width **12 x 12in/30.5 x 30.5cm (tile)** Repeat – Price ★

4 **Formica/Sylva 1069** Color **olive wood** Alternative colors **available** Composition **100% resin laminate** Width **12 x 4¾in/30.5 x 12cm (tile)** Repeat – Price ★

5 **Amtico/Napoleon Marble NL41** Color **tan** Alternative colors **not available** Composition **100% vinyl** Width **12 x 12in/30.5 x 30.5cm (tile)** Repeat – Price ★★★

6 **Deralam/Footplate AD866** Color **pewter tone** Alternative colors **not available** Composition **100% aluminum laminate** Width **48in/122cm** Repeat – Price ★

Sheet Flooring: **Pre-20th century**

In the 18th century, floors were often covered by painted, stenciled, or printed floorcloths. Canvas was stretched and nailed down so that it would hold its shape. It was then soaked with water, and primed and painted several times on each side with finely ground ochers or leads and linseed oil to give it a base coat before decorating. Floorcloths, often employed in imposing Neoclassical entrance halls, were either painted one color or decorated, much as painted floorboards were to resemble stone, marble paving, or mosaic. Other patterns popular in the 18th century included the simulation of elaborate Roman floors. The patterns of Eastern carpets were also copied, while in America geometric checker patterns were very common.

In Britain, painted floorcloths were being mass-produced in factories by the late 18th century. The introduction of a printing process in about 1770, as well as improvements in coloring pigments, made more elaborate designs possible. Though waterproof, painted floorcloths were very fragile and could not withstand a great deal of wear and tear. However, in spite of the advent of harder-wearing linoleum in 1860 (*see* opposite), the production of floorcloths continued until after the First World War.

1

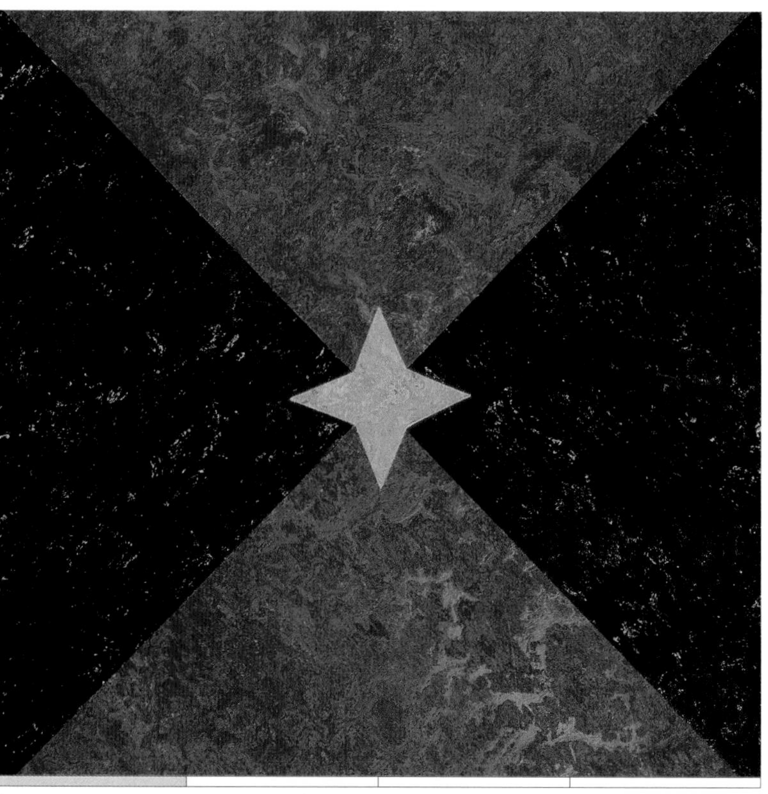

2

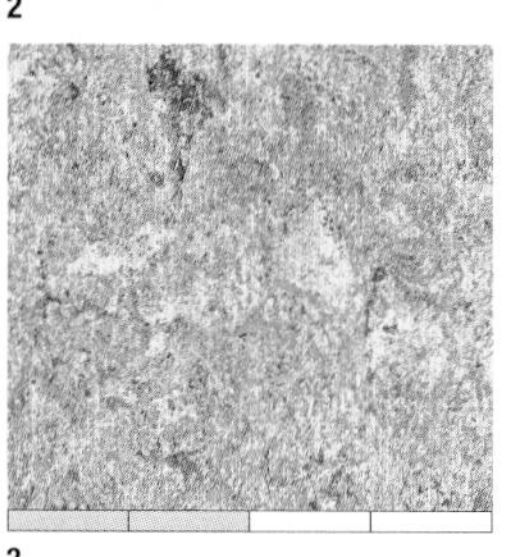

3

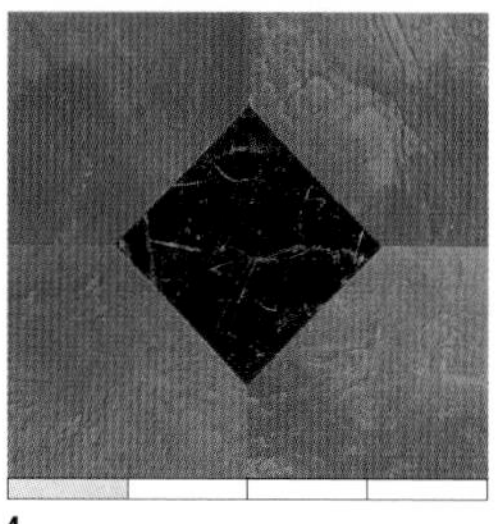

4

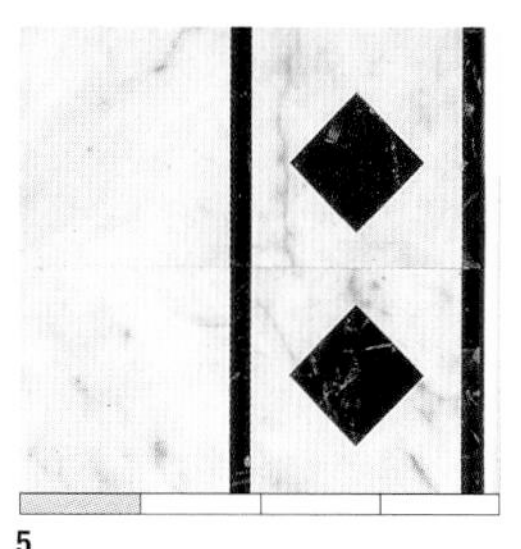

5

1 **Sinclair Till/Tartan** Color **multi** Alternative colors **available** Composition **100% linoleum** Width **to order** Repeat **–** Price ★★

2 **Sinclair Till/Checkerboard with Inlaid Stars** Color **multi** Alternative colors **available** Composition **100% linoleum** Width **to order** Repeat **–** Price ★★

3 **DLW/Marmorette 121-70** Color **70** Alternative colors **available** Composition **100% linoleum** Width **2⅛yd/2m** Repeat **–** Price ★

4 **Karndean/Desert Clay Terracotta & Midnight Black Marble TC42 & T74** Color **red and black** Alternative colors **available** Composition **100% vinyl** Width **12 x 12in/30.5 x 30.5cm (tile)** Repeat **–** Price ★

5 **Karndean/Carrara Marble & Diamond T90 & B300 Border** Color **white and black** Alternative colors **available** Composition **100% vinyl** Width **12 x 12in/30.5 x 30.5cm (tile)** Repeat **–** Price ★

6 **Natalie Woolf/Forbidden Fruit** Color **all yellows** Alternative colors **available** Composition **100% paint on canvas** Width **to order** Repeat **–** Price ★★★★★

7 **Sinclair Till/Inlaid Curlicue and Star Border** Color **multi** Alternative colors **available** Composition **100% linoleum** Width **to order** Repeat **–** Price ★★

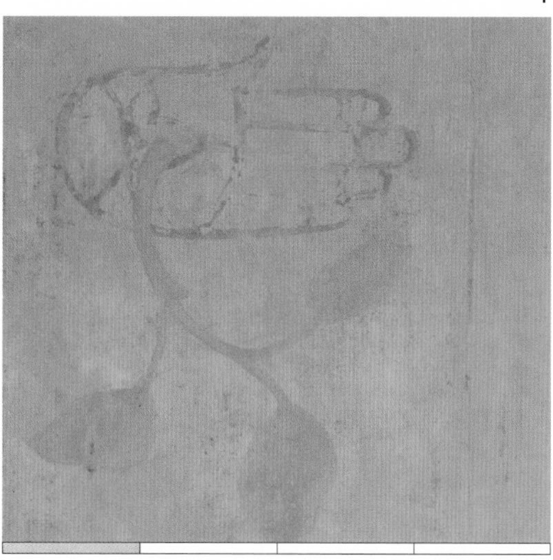

6

7

18th century

19th century

8

9

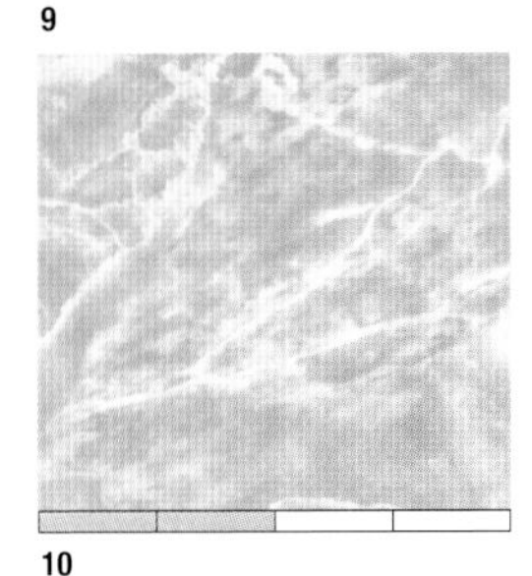

10

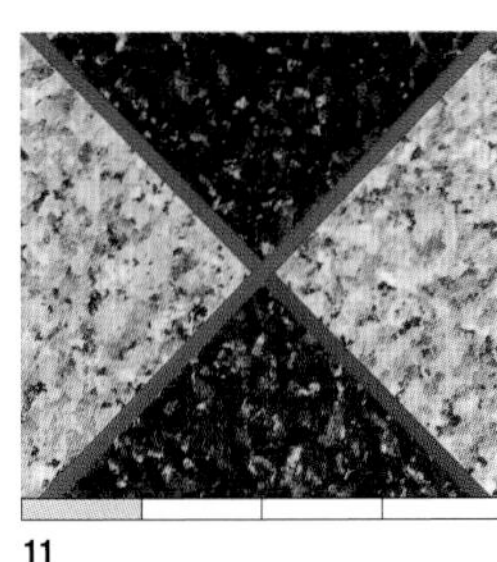

11

12

8 Jane Knapp/Fossil Stone Marble Floorcloth Color **multi** Alternative colors **available** Composition **100% paint on canvas** Width **to order** Repeat **–** Price ★★★★★

9 Amtico/Norwegian Slate SN36 Color **silver** Alternative colors **not available** Composition **100% vinyl** Width **12 x 12in/30.5 x 30.5cm (tile)** Repeat **–** Price ★★★ ⊞

10 Formica/Italian Marble 3002 Color **white** Alternative colors **not available** Composition **100% resin laminate** Width **12 x 5in/30.5 x 13cm (tile)** Repeat **–** Price ★ ⊞

11 Karndean/Granite Dove & Raven D202/D203 Color **gray and black** Alternative colors **available** Composition **100% vinyl** Width **12 x 12in/30.5 x 30.5cm (tile)** Repeat **–** Price ★

12 Marley/Leaf Border Color **MBF4MPC** Alternative colors **available** Composition **100% vinyl** Width **6in/15cm** Repeat **35½in/90cm** Price ★

LINOLEUM

Cheap and easy to produce, linoleum was first patented by Frederick Walton in Scotland in 1860, and was originally the trade name for a canvas floorcloth covered in solidified linseed oil, resin, and kauri gum. The ingredients were pressed through heated rollers onto the canvas or jute backing, then hung and left to dry for several days. Today, linoleum is made in much the same way, apart from slight changes in the composition to incorporate hard-wearing, synthetic fibers and a wider selection of color pigments. The demand for eco-friendly products means that linoleum is now reclaiming some of the market that it lost to vinyl starting in the 1950s.

DLW/Marmorette 121-78 Color **78** Alternative colors **available** Composition **100% linoleum** Width **2⅛yd/2m** Repeat **–** Price ★

Sheet Flooring: **20th century**

The first half of the 20th century saw little change in the sheet flooring market. Floorcloths were produced in factories until after the First World War, while linoleum continued to dominate the market until the introduction of vinyl-based products in the 1950s. The Art Deco and Modernist movements influenced linoleum design in the 1940s and early 1950s and soon inspired designs on vinyl. Imitation brick, tile, wood, and even carpet designs were all possible on vinyl, and this resulted in a reduction in the sales of linoleum. The new vinyl sheet flooring was sound and shock absorbent, slip resistant, gave good heat insulation, and was easy to clean. In the late 20th century, a small, specialist market for floorcloths appeared, with designs based on traditional as well as modern patterns. There was also a renewed interest in linoleum–its use of natural materials making it fashionable again in the environmentally conscious 1990s. Other types of sheet flooring emerged. Traditional industrial flooring, such as rubber, was adapted slightly and offered with designs suited to domestic use. Such flooring became the keynote of the high-tech style of the late 1970s and early 1980s (*see* page 383). Metal sheet flooring in a variety of finishes also became fashionable in the last decade of the century.

1

2

3

5

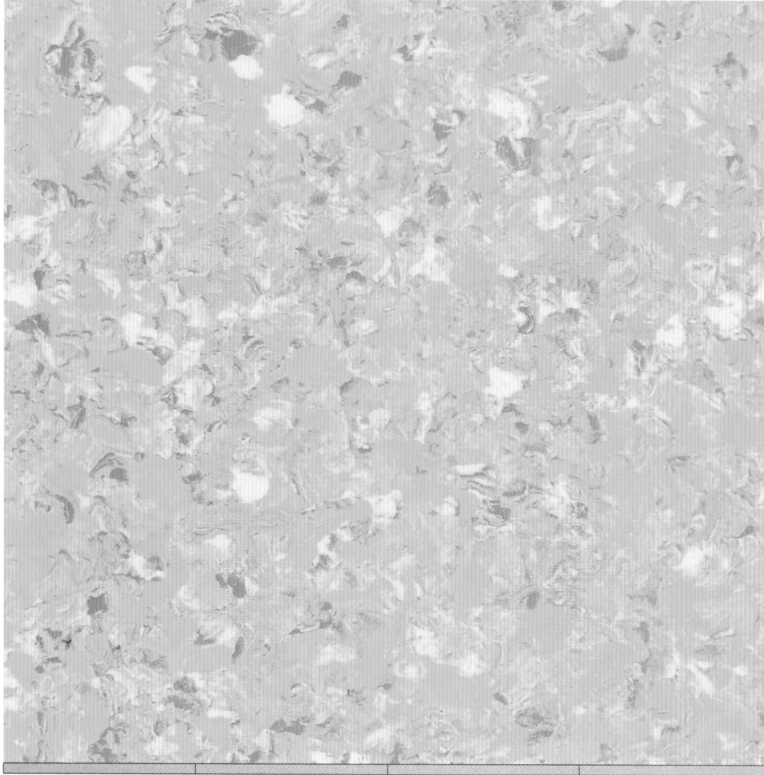
4

6

1 **Formica/Laques Metallisees 0877** Color **clio** Alternative colors **available** Composition **100% resin laminate** Width **12 x 4¾in/30.5 x 12cm (tile)** Repeat – Price ★

2 **Westco/Aristocrat** Color **London brick** Alternative colors **available** Composition **100% PVC** Width **12 x 12in/30.5 x 30.5cm (tile)** Repeat – Price ★

3 **Jaymart/Hovi Kimara M602** Color **1132** Alternative colors **available** Composition **100% quartz vinyl** Width **11¾ x 11¾in/30 x 30cm (tile)** Repeat – Price ★

4 **Marley/Eclipse BEF528** Color **sunflower** Alternative colors **available** Composition **100% vinyl** Width **2⅙yd/2m** Repeat – Price ★ ⊞

5 **Formica/Peat Burl** Color **peat** Alternative colors **available** Composition **100% resin laminate** Width **12 x 5in/30.5 x 13cm (tile)** Repeat – Price ★ ⊞

6 **Karndean/Knight Plank D101-4** Color **pinewood** Alternative colors **available** Composition **100% vinyl** Width **36 x 4in/ 91.5 x 10.5cm (tile)** Repeat – Price ★

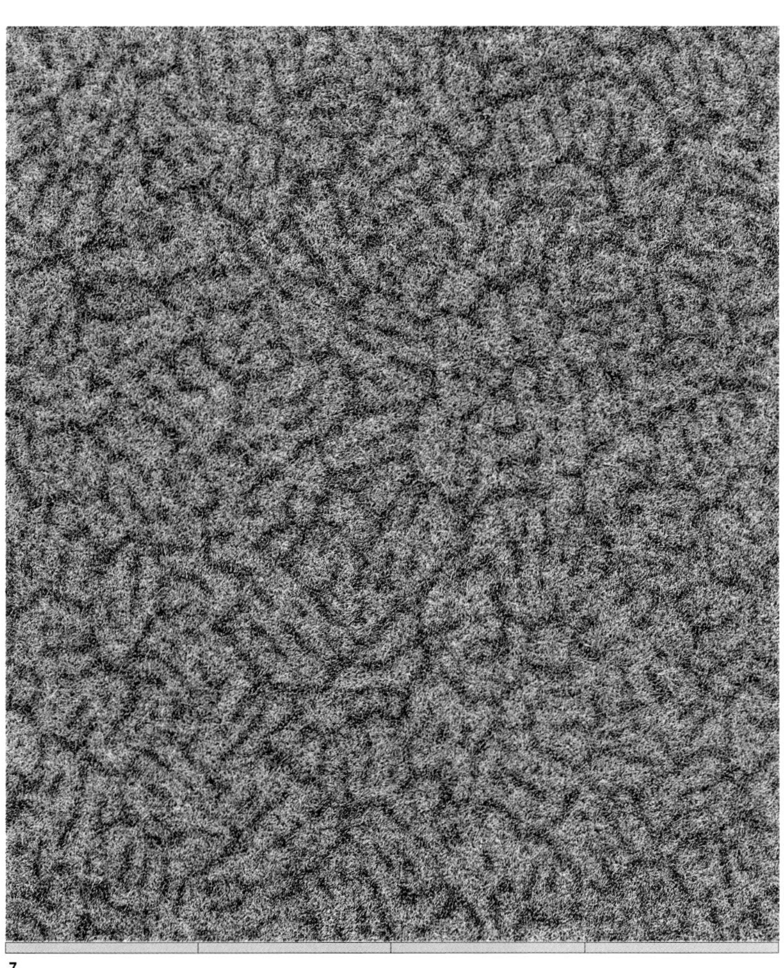

7

7 Bonar & Flotex/Tivoli 11-027036 Color **watermint** Alternative colors **available** Composition **100% nylon** Width **19¾ x 19¾in/50 x 50cm (tile)** Repeat – Price ★

8 Bill Amberg/Leather Floor (Tile) Color **light tan** Alternative colors **available** Composition **100% leather** Width **to order** Repeat – Price ★★★★★

9 Bill Amberg/Leather Floor (Stitch) Color **tan** Alternative colors **available** Composition **100% leather** Width **to order** Repeat – Price ★★★★★

10 Westco/Floral Color **multi** Alternative colors **not available** Composition **100% PVC** Width **12 x 12in/30.5 x 30.5cm (tile)** Repeat – Price ★

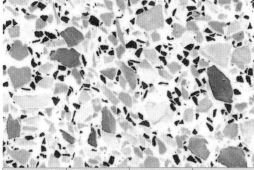

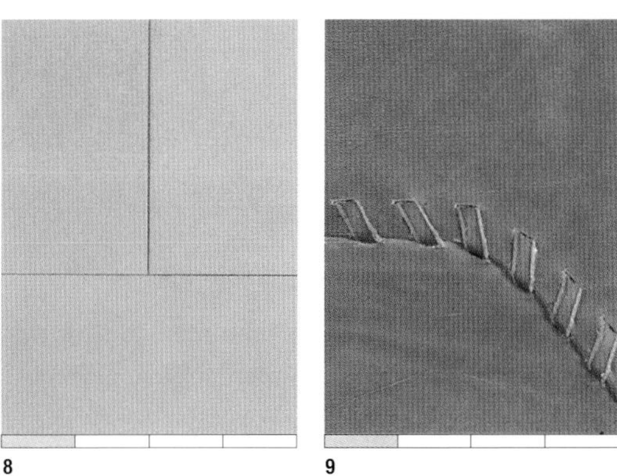

8 9

10

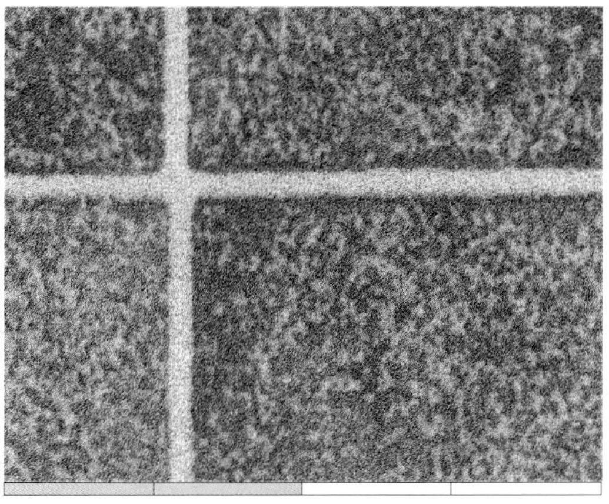

11

11 Bonar & Flotex/China Slate 01-064005 Color **oyster** Alternative colors **available** Composition **100% nylon** Width **2⅛yd/2m** Repeat **14in/35.5cm** Price ★★

12 Formica/Terrazzo 4323 Color **blue** Alternative colors **available** Composition **100% resin laminate** Width **12 x 5in/30.5 x 13cm (tile)** Repeat – Price ★

13 Marley/Pegasus Algarve Color **FPG4922** Alternative colors **available** Composition **100% vinyl** Width **4½yd/4m** Repeat **39¼in/100cm** Price ★

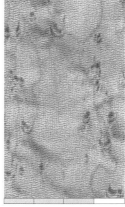

14 Amtico/Tilewood TW 714 Color **warm maple** Alternative colors **available** Composition **100% vinyl** Width **12 x 12in/30.5 x 30.5cm (tile)** Repeat – Price ★★★

15 Domco/Crystal Walk 74563 Color **green** Alternative colors **available** Composition **100% vinyl** Width **4yd/3.66m** Repeat – Price ★★

16 Westco/Diamond Black Embossed Color **diamond black** Alternative colors **available** Composition **100% PVC** Width **12 x 12in/30.5 x 30.5cm (tile)** Repeat – Price ★

12

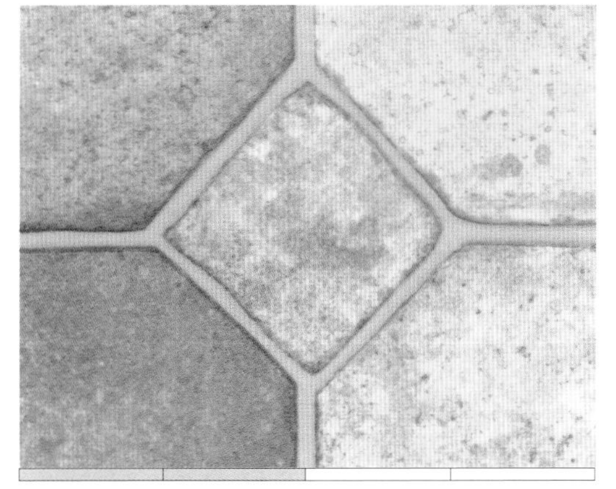

13

14

15

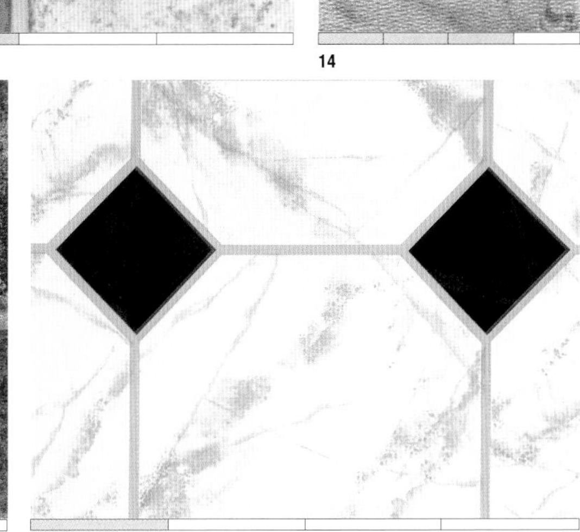

16

20th century

Sheet Flooring: **20th century**

During the late 20th century, patterns on sheet flooring were often derived from classical designs, such as the Ancient Greek key pattern. Some manufacturers provided the components, including borders and key squares, for constructing formal classical patterns. Recent designs also included the café-revivalist flooring of the 1950s, semiflexible PVC tiles in different colors incorporating sparkling silica quartz, and sheet flooring consisting of colored vinyl chips suspended in clear vinyl to produce a "three-dimensional" effect.

The art of mimicking other, rather more costly materials in synthetic flooring became increasingly sophisticated in the late 20th century. Imitation wood was produced using a material with a fiber-board core that was laminated with a wood-textured photoprint overlay and bonded with melamine resin. Marble, granite, and terracotta were still extremely popular effects, as they were on floorcloths, and offer the look of the original material but with the added advantages of being hard-wearing and washable.

1

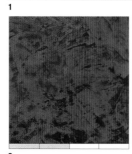

2

4

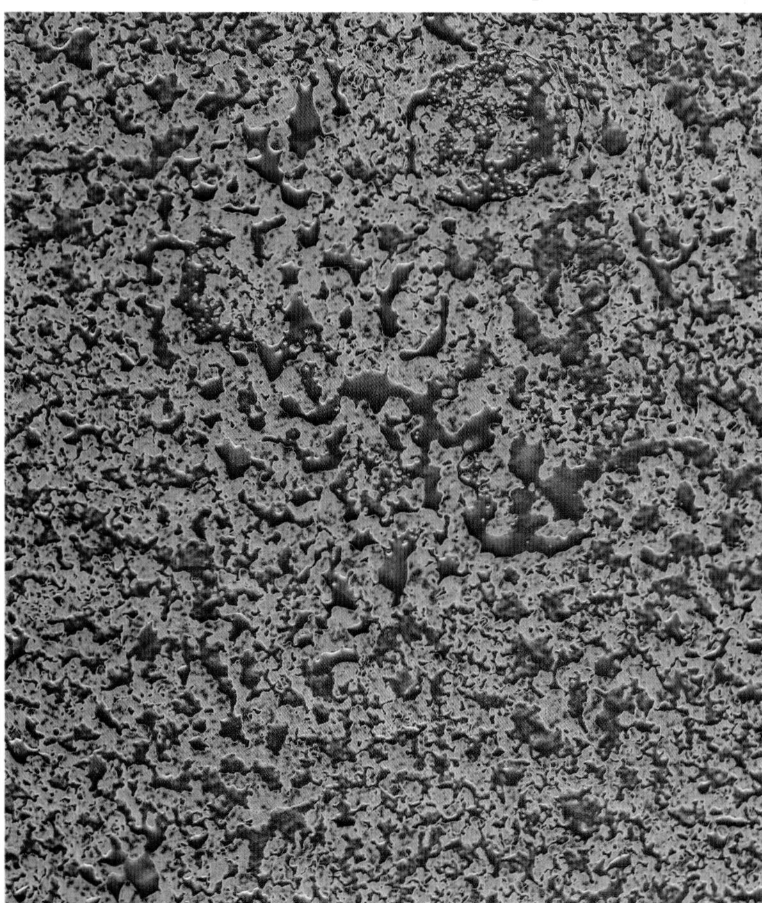

3

1 **Dalsouple/Martelé** Color **rose indien** Alternative colors **available** Composition **100% rubber** Width **26¾in/68cm** Repeat – Price ★★

2 **Deralam/Antique Copper CD490** Color **copper** Alternative colors **not available** Composition **100% copper laminate** Width **48in/122cm** Repeat – Price ★★

3 **Deralam/Copper Relief CD710** Color **green/black** Alternative colors **not available** Composition **100% copper laminate** Width **48in/122cm** Repeat – Price ★★

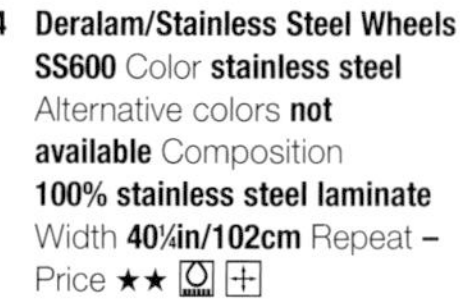

4 **Deralam/Stainless Steel Wheels SS600** Color **stainless steel** Alternative colors **not available** Composition **100% stainless steel laminate** Width **40⅛in/102cm** Repeat – Price ★★

5 **Formica/Rock 2253-72** Color **black** Alternative colors **available** Composition **100% resin laminate** Width **12 x 4¾in/30.5 x 12cm (tile)** Repeat – Price ★

6 **Formica/Cheetah 4327** Color **black, gray, and white** Alternative colors **not available** Composition **100% resin laminate** Width **12 x 4¾in/30.5 x 12cm (tile)** Repeat – Price ★

7 **Natalie Woolf/Stone** Color **multi** Alternative colors **available** Composition **100% paint on canvas** Width **to order** Repeat – Price ★★★★★

5

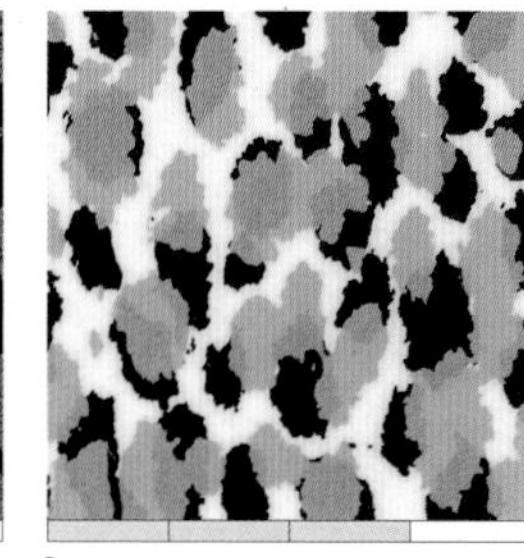

6

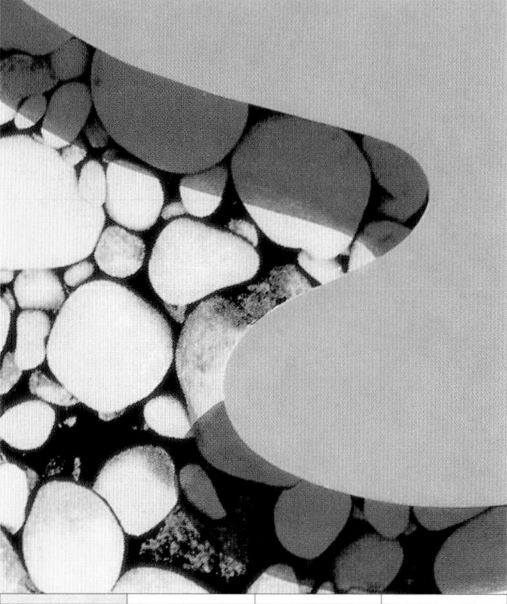

7

8 **Jaymart/Fishface** Color **black** Alternative colors **not available** Composition **100% rubber** Width **39¼in/100cm** Repeat – Price ★

9 **Natalie Woolf/Tropical Fruit Salad Series 3** Color **hot earth** Alternative colors **available** Composition **100% paint on canvas** Width **to order** Repeat – Price ★★★★★

10 **Amtico/Treadplate** Color **silver** Alternative colors **available** Composition **100% vinyl** Width **12 x 12in/30.5 x 30.5cm (tile)** Repeat – Price ★★★

11 **Formica/Ligna 4423** Color **metallic green** Alternative colors **available** Composition **100% resin laminate** Width **12 x 5in/30.5 x 13cm (tile)** Repeat – Price ★

12 **Jaymart/Astroturf M44** Color **classic green** Alternative colors **available** Composition **100% vinyl** Width **35¾in/91cm** Repeat – Price ★

8

RUBBER FLOORING

First produced in the 1930s, sheet rubber flooring has been regularly used in the industrial market. It is tough, hard-wearing, and easy to clean, and, because of developments in the 1990s, available in virtually any color. Popular designs include terrazzo effects as well as a variety of studded surfaces. The high-tech style of the late 1970s and early 1980s first introduced rubber into a domestic setting. Eco-friendly rubber flooring has also been produced using recycled car tyres.

Dalsouple/Metro Color **vert pomme** Alternative colors **available** Composition **100% rubber** Width **26¾ x 26¾in/68 x 68cm (tile)** Repeat – Price ★★

9

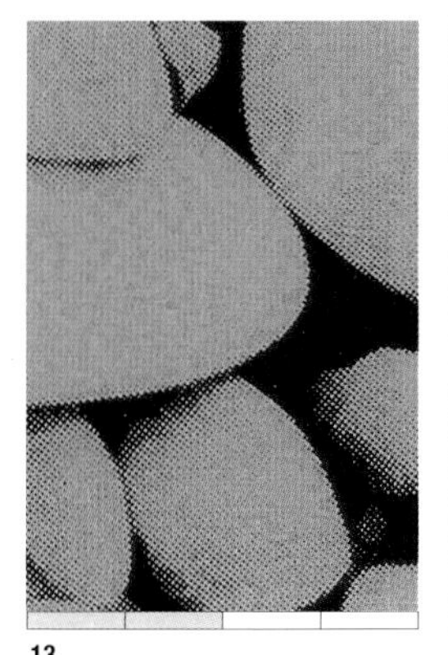

13

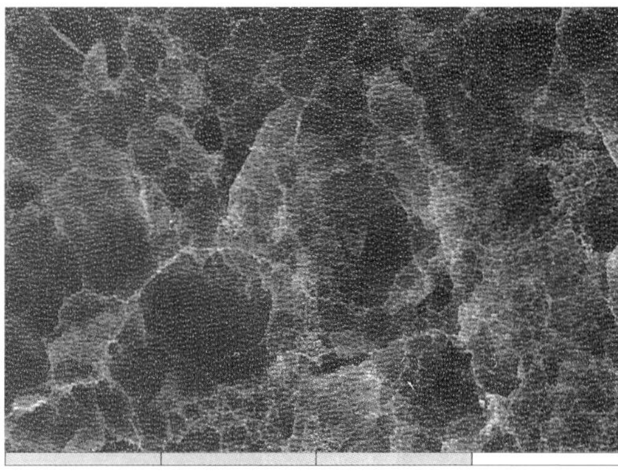

14

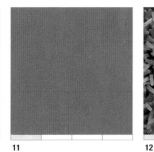

13 **Natalie Woolf/Pebble Design** Color **blue** Alternative colors **available** Composition **100% vinyl** Width **12 x 12in/30.5 x 30.5cm (tile)** Repeat – Price ★★★★

14 **Amtico/Florentine NM-97** Color **blue** Alternative colors **available** Composition **100% vinyl** Width **12 x 12in/30.5 x 30.5cm (tile)** Repeat – Price ★★★

15 **Formica/Copper Leaves 2113** Color **copper** Alternative colors **not available** Composition **100% resin laminate** Width **9½ x 4¾in/24 x 12cm (tile)** Repeat – Price ★

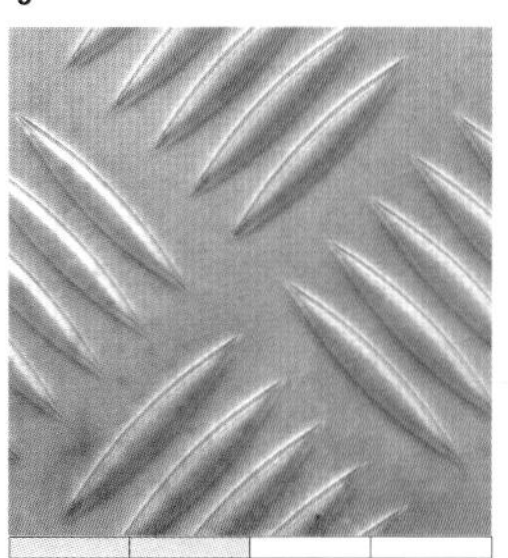

10

11

12

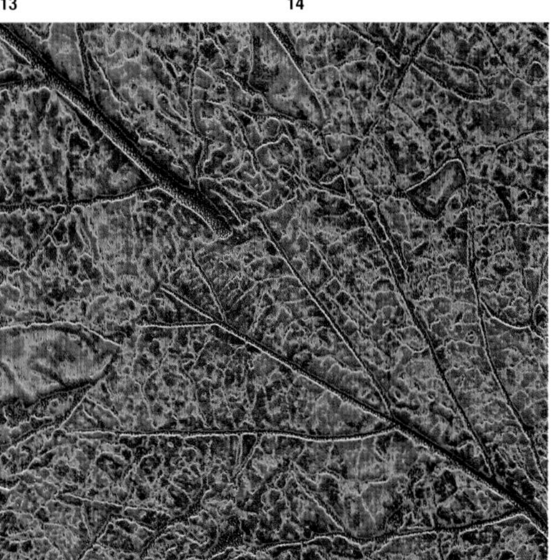

15

zeyko®
kitchens
PERFECT BY NATURE
MAIN UK DESIGN CENTRE
The Business Design Centre
52 Upper Street
Islington Green
London N1 OQH
Tel: 0171 288 6123
Fax: 0171 288 6122

Glossary

★ Asterisked terms have a separate entry

A

acanthus Foliage ornament based on the serrated leaves of the *Acanthus spinosus* plant. Similar to thistle, parsley, and poppy leaves and sometimes used for *scrolling foliage. Originally used in *Classical Greek and Roman architecture and ornament.

Adam style A *Neoclassical style pioneered by the English Adam brothers during the late 18th century, inspired by Classical Greek and Roman (*see* *Classical style) and *Renaissance ornament. Characterized by motifs such as *swags, *guilloches*, *friezes, *anthemia, and *palmettes.

Aesthetic Movement *See* page 43.

aniline dyes Synthetic dyes made from coal tar. Formulated in the late 1820s, but not developed for general use until the 1850s.

anthemion A floral motif similar to the *palmette and primarily associated with the Classical vocabulary of ornament. Based on either the flower of the *acanthus, the flower and leaf of the honeysuckle, or the Egyptian lotus.

appliqué Technique of applying cutout patterns of fabric onto a ground cloth using either plain or embroidery stitches.

arabesque A stylized, interlaced foliage pattern of Near Eastern origin, probably based on laurel leaves. In Western ornament it is often combined with *bandwork or *strapwork. In the 18th century, French designers used the term to describe panels of *grotesque designs incorporating figures, bandwork, and *scrolling foliage.

Art Deco *See* pages 49-51.

Art Nouveau *See* page 46.

Arts and Crafts Movement *See* pages 42-8.

Aubusson French town where, in the "Royal Manufactury," flat-weave tapestries were made from ca. 1665, and thick- and short-pile carpets were made from ca. 1742.

Axminster English town where Thomas Whitty established a carpet factory in 1755 (the factory moved to Wilton in 1835). Before 1860 it made hand-woven, woolen pile carpets (called Axminsters); later, machine-woven equivalents were also produced.

B

bandwork An 18th-century term for *strapwork.

Baronial style Mock-*Gothic style of architecture and decoration inspired by the castles and manor houses of barons, the medieval feudal overlords. Popular during the late 19th and early 20th centuries.

Baroque Style of architecture and ornament prevalent during the 17th century. A *Classical style that was characterized by elaborate sculptural forms, painted decoration, marble inlays, carved gilding, and architectural elements applied purely ornamentally. Typical motifs included *swags, urns, and flaming torches.

batik *See* Indonesian style, page 126.

Bauhaus School of arts and crafts founded at Weimar in Germany in 1906. Moved to Berlin in 1932; closed by the German Nazi party in 1933. Initially inspired by the *Arts and Crafts Movement, but from the 1920s focused on industrial designs characterized by a stark, cubic simplicity.

bed-hangings Collective term for fabrics draped above or around beds. Includes canopies, valances, drapes, and coronas.

Biedermeier *See* page 29.

"black stitch" *Embroidery worked in black thread on a white or ivory-colored ground fabric. Also known as "blackwork."

block-printing *See* *hand-blocking.

braid Decorative woven ribbon made of almost any fiber. Used for trimming and edging seams, especially on upholstered furniture.

brocade Heavy fabric with elaborately figured patterns that are raised against a ground cloth by the addition of supplementary *wefts.

brocatelle A variant of *damask, with raised areas of pattern.

Brussels carpet A flat-weave carpet woven from *linen and *worsted with a looped, uncut pile. Typically decorated with bold patterns in two or three colors (but sometimes more).

bullion fringe *See* page 191.

buttonhole stitch A looped outline stitch used to finish the raw edges of fabric, and to create straight or curved lines in embroidery patterns.

C

calico A *plain-weave cotton fabric, originally from India but also produced in the West from the 17th century. Naturally cream-colored, but can also be bleached white, dyed, and printed with motifs and patterns.

cambric A fine, slightly stiff, plain-weave cotton fabric.

campaign fringe *See* page 185.

canvas A coarse, hardwearing fabric woven from fibers of hemp or flax. It can be unbleached, bleached white, or dyed.

cartouche A decorative panel consisting of a scroll-shaped frame with a plain, decorated, or inscribed center. Much used in *Renaissance, *Baroque, and *Rococo decoration.

casein paint *See* *milk paint.

chenille "Caterpillar" in French. A velvetlike fabric woven from a soft, fuzzy-textured woven yarn of natural or synthetic fiber.

checker A geometric pattern consisting of regularly spaced squares of alternating color.

chevrons V-shaped motifs, traditionally symbolizing water and lightning. Either stacked singly in a vertical series or strung together horizontally to form a zigzag.

chiaroscuro Originally a fine art technique employing shades of black, gray, and white to introduce areas of light and shade (and therefore a sense of depth and perspective) into a painting. Since the 17th century it has also been used on fabrics and wallpapers.

chiffonier A wooden cupboard with twin doors, surmounted by drawers and a flat top sometimes supporting one or two shelves.

chimera A fire-breathing creature from classical mythology with the head, mane, and legs of a lion, the body of a goat, the tail of a dragon, and the wings of an eagle.

chinoiserie Western adaptations of traditional Chinese artifacts and styles of ornament.

Classical style Revivals of the principles and forms of Ancient Greek and Roman architecture and ornament. There have been numerous revivals and reinterpretations, beginning with *Renaissance in the late 14th- to late 16th-century, when illustrated treatises, engravings, and pattern books of the monuments and ruins of the Roman Empire first become widely available. Notable and influential 17th-century examples include the architecture of Perrault and Mansart in France, and Inigo Jones in England–the latter inspired by the work of Palladio (*see* *Palladianism). During the 18th century the Classical vocabulary was expanded (and better understood) following excavations at Pompeii and Herculaneum. This resulted in the *Neoclassicism of *Adam style, *Empire style, *Federal style, and the *Greek Revival. Late 19th- and early 20th-century classicism took the form of various *Renaissance, *Baroque, and *Empire Revivals, while 20th-century *Modernism was also partly inspired by Classical forms.

coir Fiber made from coconut husks and woven into matting.

Colonial style The styles of architecture and decoration prevalent in the American colonies during the 17th and 18th centuries. The primary sources of inspiration were contemporary or recent English, and, to a lesser extent, European designs (*see* pages 14-21).

combing A *distressed paint finish that involves dragging a comb through a wet *glaze to produce vertical, horizontal, or wavy stripes that allow a contrasting-colored ground coat to ghost through. Sometimes employed in wood-graining.

Constructivism An early 20th-century Russian style of architecture and design, based on the principles of utilitarian simplicity and logical use of materials, notably glass and metal, in construction and decoration.

cord A form of rope, of various thicknesses, made from twisted threads (of any fiber). Primarily used for *tiebacks and as a trimming on upholstered seating.

corduroy A pile fabric (*see* pages 66-71) with regularly spaced, parallel ridges (or wales or ribs).

cornice A decorative molding used to cover the join between the walls and the ceiling.

cotton Lightweight fabric woven from spun fibers from the boll (the fruit) of the cotton plant.

cotton duck *See* page 59.

crewelwork *See* page 109.

Cubism Abstract art movement of the early 20th century that analyzed the interrelation of forms. In practice, several views of the subject were combined and superimposed onto one another to provide an account of the entire structure of the subject, rather than simply one view of it.

cypher *See* page 89.

D

dado Lower section of a wall, running from the floor to waist height, the latter often defined by a wooden or plaster dado rail. Also *see* *tripartite division.

damask *See* pages 72-81.

damascening A decorative technique, originally applied to metalwork, in which gold, silver, and copper are inlaid in *arabesque patterns into base metal. Developed in the Near East, it was brought in the 15th century to Europe where the patterns were also applied to other decorative mediums.

deal Collective term for softwoods (pine and fir) used in the construction of furniture and architectural fixtures and fittings.

delftware Pottery made in England from the late 17th century, in imitation of the Dutch tin-glazed earthenwares named after the town of Delft, the principal center of production. Typical decoration included *chinoiserie* and European (mostly Dutch) landscapes.

dentils *Classical ornament consisting of a row of small, regularly spaced blocks. Originally applied along a *cornice, but from the early 17th century it was also applied to furniture.

Deutscher Werkbund An association of manufacturers, architects, artists, and designers founded in Munich, Germany, in 1907. Its purpose was to create a national style of art, architecture, and design without any stylistic imitation and based on sound principles of construction. Their ideas were taken over by the *Bauhaus during the 1920s.

diaper patterns Collective term for patterns incorporating a geometric framework, such as *latticework or *trelliswork.

distemper Alternative English term for whitewash: a water-based paint made from whiting (ground chalk) and animal glue. Forerunner of modern latex emulsion paints.

distressed finishes Collective term for paint finishes, mostly derived from fine art, in which semitranslucent paints or *glazes are applied over a contrasting-colored, opaque ground coat, and then distressed while wet to produce patterns and subtle gradations of color. *See:* *combing, *dragging, *ragging, *spattering, *sponging, and *stippling.

dobby A mechanical attachment for a loom that facilitated the production of patterns made up of small, regularly repeated motifs, particularly geometric shapes. Invented in the early 19th century.

documentary fabrics *See* page 113.

dogtooth A star-shaped motif, developed from the *nailhead, applied in regular repeats and popular in *Gothic and *Renaissance decoration.

dragging A *distressed paint finish that involves dragging a brush through a wet glaze in parallel sweeps to produce a striped finish in simulation of the figuring and grain of wood.

drawboy Type of loom, named after the weaver's assistant (a young boy) who operated the harness that raised the *warp threads when weaving patterns. Introduced into Europe from the Near East during the *Middle Ages, and a forerunner of the *Jacquard loom.

E

earthenware Porous pottery (unless glazed) produced by firing earth or clays at low temperatures.

egg-and-dart A decorative molding consisting of alternating egg and V shapes. Originated in *Classical Greek architecture.

egg tempera A paint made by mixing powder pigments with linseed oil, water, and egg yolk. Primarily used on furniture.

embroidery Decorative stitching applied to the surface of a fabric.

Empire style *See* pages 29-33.

encaustic tiles *Earthenware tiles patterned with inlays of colored clay *slips.

enfield A *heraldic beast, with the body of a dog, the head, hind-quarters, and tail of a fox, and the claws of an eagle.

F

Federal style The predominant style of architecture and decoration in America between 1776, following the Declaration of Independence, and ca. 1830. Initially based on *Adam style, but superseded by the adoption of *Empire style–in turn, gradually supplanted by the *Greek Revival.

felt A dense cloth made from compressed wool or animal fur.

fêtes galantes Pictorial decoration showing fashionably dressed men and women in romantic landscapes. Originated in mid-18th-century France, and widely used in *Rococo style.

field The section of a wall that extends down from the *cornice or *frieze to the top of the *dado. Also *see* *tripartite division.

flame stitch *See* page 151.

fleur-de-lis A stylized three- or five-petal lily. Originally a symbol of purity, the motif has been used since the early *Middle Ages, notably in *heraldic ornament.

flock Wallpaper with a raised, textured pattern formed by sprinkling fine particles of *wool (or other fibers) over the paper. These stick to an adhesive applied to the paper in the shape of the pattern.

floorcloth A floor covering made from *canvas stiffened with linseed oil, and then either painted or *stenciled (often to resemble more expensive floor coverings such as carpet, *parquet, or tiles).

formalized *See* *stylized.

French knots Decorative embroidery knots worked on the show side of a fabric to create textured dots of color.

frieze Section of wall extending from the ceiling or *cornice down to the top of the *field. Also *see* *tripartite division.

fringe A trimming for upholstery and curtains. Consists of threads, or decorative shapes made from materials such as fabric, wood, glass, or metal, hung from a heading (such as *braid).

fustian Collective term for a group of coarse, usually patterned fabrics woven from *wool, *worsted, or *cotton and *wool.

gaufrage French for stamping, and a method of embossing patterns onto the surface of fabrics with heated metal rollers. Often applied to velvets.

galloon A decorative tape or ribbon primarily used to disguise the stitched or glued seams between joined sections of fabric.

gimp A type of *braid traditionally made from strands of *silk, *worsted, or *cotton, braided or twisted around a cord or wire.

gingham A lightweight *cotton fabric with a geometric check pattern of two alternating colors on a white or off white ground.

glaze In ceramics, a clear or colored vitreous coating fired over the body of the object. In painting, a semitranslucent paint applied over an opaque ground. (Also *see* *distressed finishes.)

Gothic The predominant style of architecture and ornament during the *Middle Ages. Also *see* page 13.

Gothic Revival A late 18th- and 19th-century revival of *Gothic architectural forms and ornament.

Gothick *See* page 19.

grass cloth *See* page 201.

Greek key pattern A regular repeat of interlocking right-angle and vertical lines. Used as a border ornament in *Classical architecture and decoration.

Greek Revival *See* page 57.

grisaille A **trompe l'oeil* technique in which figures and patterns are rendered in shades of black, gray, and white to produce a "three-dimensional" effect.

grotesques Decorations based on Ancient Roman wall paintings (*grottesche*) discovered in buried ruins in Rome in the late 15th century. Subsequently also applied to ceramics, fabrics, and wallpapers. Typical motifs included animals, birds, and fishes. Grotesques provided the inspiration for 18th-century, Neoclassical *arabesques.

grotto ornament Decorative elements, including stalactite- and shell-encrusted ceilings and walls, water cascades, and pools of ornamental fishes, frogs, lizards, and snakes. Originally used in Ancient Roman grottoes. Revived in the 17th and 18th centuries.

guilloche A decorative repeat of interlacing curved bands, sometimes forming circles embellished with floral motifs. Used in *Classical ornament.

H

hand-blocking *See* page 229.

half-tester A bed with an overhead canopy extending from the headboard to partway along the bed.

hemp Coarse fabric woven from fibers of plants such as *Cannabis sativa*. The fibers can also be twisted and braided into rope.

heraldic motifs *See* page 91.

herbals Illustrated accounts of botanical forms. Circulated in Europe during the late *Middle Ages and the *Renaissance.

herringbone Geometric pattern consisting of alternating diagonal lines similar in appearance to the spine and ribs of a herring fish.

hieroglyphics Picture characters developed by the Ancient Egyptians and accommodated within *Classical Roman ornament.

holland Generic term for fine-woven linen cloth, available unbleached, bleached white, dyed, or patterned (usually with stripes) and glazed or unglazed. Produced since the 16th century, notably for upholstery and window shades.

ikat Indonesian fine cotton or silk fabric decorated with blocks, circles, or stripes and softened by a vegetable-dyeing process that blends the edges of the colors into one another.

indiennes *See* page 128.

Iznik pottery *Earthenware of Turkish origin. Either *tin-glazed or coated with white *slip. Decorated with brightly colored designs.

Jacquard loom A mechanical loom, invented in the early 19th century. Did away with the need for a *drawboy by employing a system of punch cards (similar to a piano roll) to control the harness mechanism that raised the *warp threads during weaving. Now often computer controlled.

japonaiserie English, European, and American furniture, ceramics, metalwares, wallpapers, and fabrics decorated in the style of imported Japanese equivalents. Typical motifs include blossoms, chrysanthemums, bamboo, exotic birds and animals, and *diaper patterns. Especially fashionable during the last quarter of the 19th century.

jeweled strapwork *See* *strapwork.

jute Fiber derived from Asian plants. Woven into a floor matting.

L

lacquerware *Oriental furniture and wooden artifacts coated with numerous polished layers of sap of the lacquer tree. Untreated, the lacquer dries to a lustrous black color. However, it can also be dyed various colors, notably red, and inlaid with shells or decorative powders. European and American pieces have also been produced, in imitation of the Oriental originals.

lambrequin A stiff, shaped *pelmet similar in shape to a horse's harness. First used in the 17th century; in the 18th and 19th centuries often extended over half-way down the sides of the window.

latticework A gridlike design made up of open diamond shapes. The pattern for leading in late 16th-century glazed windows. Also worked in stone or wood as an architectural and furniture embellishment, and used as a pattern on ceramics, fabrics, wallpapers, and metalwares.

limewash *See* page 283.

linen Strong fabric woven from fibers of flax plant stalks. Mostly used for bedsheets, pillowcases, tablecloths, and upholstery.

linenfold paneling Wooden paneling in which the individual panels are carved to resemble the vertical folds of draped linen.

lit-en-bateau French term meaning "boat bed." A bed with outwardly curving wooden head-boards and footboards (of equal height), their shape approximating to the bow and stern of a boat.

lusterware Ceramics or glass-wares with a metallic sheen, produced by firing them with a thin coating of metallic *glaze.

madras Brightly colored checked and *plaid *cotton or *silk cloth from Madras in India.

Manchester velvet A *cotton velvet with a pile that simulated the sheen of expensive silk velvets. Made in a wide range of colors and patterns (woven or *gaufrage*). Manufactured in Manchester, England, during the late 18th century and for most of the 19th century. Popular in Britain, Europe, and America.

marquetry *See* page 357.

matelassé *See* page 81.

Medieval style *See* pages 12-13.

Middle Ages Historical period extending from the fall of the Roman Empire (5th century AD) to the beginning of the Renaissance (late 14th century).

milk paint *See* page 284.

millefleurs French for a thousand flowers. A flower-studded pattern originally used on medieval pictorial tapestries. Favored flowers, naturalistically depicted, include roses, anemones, pinks, and violas.

Modernism *See* pages 49-52.

moiré *See* page 65.

monochrome One color (or shades of one color).

moquette A woolen velvet, either plain or patterned, the patterns either woven or *gaufrage*. Used for upholstery and carpeting.

moresques Alternative name for *arabesque patterns from the late 16th to the early 17th centuries.

mosaic A pattern constructed from small pieces of colored stone, ceramic, or glass. Originally used in Roman architecture.

mottled tiles Tiles decorated with spots of varying shades of color. Introduced in the 1920s.

mullions Vertical bars used to divide windows into sections.

muslin A lightweight, *plain-weave cotton gauze. Either plain or patterned with motifs.

N, O

nailheads Small, pyramid-shaped motifs, often regularly repeated to create an overall pattern.

naturalistic Realistic depictions of organic or inorganic forms.

Neoclassical style *See* page 22.

noile *Silk fabric with a shimmery surface created by the presence of tiny balls made from the waste products of spun silk mixed with *cotton or *wool.

ogival Pointed arch formed by pairs of serpentine-shaped curves.

oilcloth *See* *floorcloth.

Op Art A 20th-century style of art and decoration in which geometric forms are precisely arranged so that the movement of the observer's eye, or loss of focus, creates an illusion of movement in the painting or pattern.

organza A fine, *plain-weave, sheer *cotton fabric. Produced either plain or printed with motifs.

Oriental Collective term used in the West for Eastern artifacts and styles of decoration and ornament. Includes Arabian, Chinese, Indian, Japanese, Persian, and Turkish styles.

P, Q

paisley *See* page 150.

Palladianism *See* pages 18-23.

palmette Foliate motif loosely based on a formalized palm leaf. Often indistinguishable from the *anthemion and much used in *Classical decoration.

parquetry *See* page 351.

passementerie Collective term for decorative trimmings applied to soft furnishings. Includes, ribbons, bows, braids, tassels, and fringes.

pastoral Romanticized imagery of life in the countryside. Also *see* *Picturesque.

paterae Oval- or circular-shaped form or motif based on dishes or wine holders used in religious ceremonies. Usually decorated with a stylized flower and/or fluting. In Neoclassical ornament often designed as *rosettes.

pelmet Fabric-covered wooden fitting, or a stiffened section of fabric, fixed above a window and designed to conceal the curtain pole and the top of the curtains.

petit point Form of *embroidery using very fine, small stitches.

photogravure A method of machine-printing wallpaper using metal rollers photochemically engraved with tiny cells or dots that together make up the design. Colored inks are scraped into the cells and the paper is then forced between the rollers and a rubber cylinder, which forces the surface of the paper into the cells to take up the inks.

picot A decorative furnishing trim that is made up of small loops of thread.

Picturesque Late 18th- and early 19th-centuries taste for *pastoral imagery combined with theatrical architectural forms (especially *Gothick).

plaid A *plain- or *twill-weave cloth, such as Scottish tartan, with a pattern of intersecting stripes in both the *warp and the *weft.

plain weave A simple weave in which the *warp and the *weft yarns cross at right angles to each other, are spaced at roughly equal intervals, and the wefts are passed alternately over and under the warps in one direction and vice versa in the other direction. Also known as "tabby" weave.

plush A velvetlike fabric, but with a longer, less dense pile. Mostly used for upholstery.

point-paper Paper used for designing carpets. Divided into small squares, these being further divided into tiny blocks, with each block representing one tuft in the pile of the carpet.

Pointillism Style of painting, developed in France during the late 19th century, in which images are gradually built up through the application of small dots of color. In the 20th century, it was also applied to fabrics and wallpapers.

polychromatic Multicolored.

polyester Durable, crease-resistant, synthetic fiber.

pombaline A form of tile decoration prevalent in Portugal during the 18th century, in which individual tiles are decorated with a diagonal band of foliage so that a *trellis pattern is formed when the tiles are placed together.

Pop Art An art movement of the 1960s, producing graphic images of everyday figures and objects using techniques employed in film, television, and advertising.

poplin Lightweight fabric traditionally woven with fine *silk *warps covering coarser *worsted *wefts to produce a ribbed effect.

portiere A curtain designed to be hung over an archway or door.

Post-Modernism An architectural and design movement that began in the mid-1960s as a reaction to the plain, unadorned forms of *Modernism, and revived traditional *Classical forms of ornament.

powder ground Tile decoration created by *spattering fine sprays of pigment through a stencil.

powdered ornament Patterns consisting of evenly spaced scatterings of small motifs such as flower sprigs and stars. Originated in *heraldic ornament.

print room *See* page 239.

putti Images of children based on cherubs and the infant attendants of Cupid or Eros (gods of classical mythology).

quarries Small panes of glass, usually diamond shaped, supported by *latticework leading in 16th-century glazed windows.

quarry tile An unglazed floor tile made from fired clay.

R

ragging A *distressed paint finish that involves brushing a semi-translucent glaze over an opaque, contrasting-colored ground coat and dabbing it with a rag to remove random patches of glaze.

Regency *See* pages 29-35.

relief tiles Tiles decorated with a molded pattern that is raised above the surface.

Renaissance Historical period and a term used to describe the movement in art, architecture, design, and ornament that originated in Italy in the late 14th century and spread across Europe during the course of the next 200 years. At its heart lay a revival of the architecture and ornament of Ancient Greece and Rome (*see* *Classical style).

rep *Plain-weave, ribbed fabric mainly used for upholstery. Made from *silk, *wool, or *silk and *wool, and sometimes *cotton.

rocaille A form of ornament prevalent in *Rococo style. Based on asymmetrical rock and shell forms found in *grotto decoration.

Rococo *See* page 19.

rosette A circular, formalized floral ornament of Mesopotamian and Ancient Greek origin, widely employed in *Classical decoration since the Renaissance. Also used to describe any circular ornament with decorative elements, such as fluting, radiating from its center.

rush Grasslike, marshland plant, the dried stalks of which are braided into strips and sewn together to form floor matting.

S

sanitary papers *See* page 257.

sash window A window made of glazed wooden frames (sashes) that slide up and down in vertical grooves by means of counter-balanced weights.

saturated color Dense, opaque colour, as opposed to thin, semi-transparent color.

screen printing A method of transferring a design onto fabric or paper by squeezing dyes or inks through a mesh screen placed on the surface. The screen is masked in those areas where a color is not required for the design.

scrolling foliage Naturalistic plant forms presented in abstract, curving lines (*See* page 143).

seersucker Originally an Indian striped fabric of mixed *silk and *cotton, but from the 17th century also manufactured in the West. Characterized by a rippled or puckered texture formed by weaving the cotton *warps at a looser tension than the silk *wefts.

shellac A transparent varnish with a red-brown tint, made from a resin secreted on the twigs of trees by Asian lac insects.

silk Luxury cloth woven from the shiny, smooth filaments spun from the cocoons of the silkworm.

singerie French for monkey, and a style of pictorial decoration showing monkey figures engaged in human activities (often set within *scrolling foliage or *bandwork). Popular in *Rococo interiors.

sisal A fiber produced from the leaf of the Mexican agave plant. Woven into rope or floor matting.

slip A creamy mixture of clay and water used to decorate pottery. Also a fascia, usually of marble or glazed tiles, set into a fireplace.

slub silk Raw silk fabric with a textured surface produced by incorporating small flecks of the silkworm cocoon in the weave.

Spanish stitch Embroidery characterized by naturalistic floral, fruit, and insect patterns.

spattering A *distressed paint finish that involves flicking flecks of wet *glaze from the bristles of a brush over an opaque, contrasting-colored ground coat to create a pattern of random specks of color. Used to simulate stones such as porphyry and granite.

sponging *Distressed paint finish that involves dabbing a sponge over a *wet glaze applied to a contrasting colored ground coat. The resulting pattern of random specks and gradations of color is often incorporated in faux marble and stone finishes.

stem stitch An overlapping embroidery stitch particularly suited to producing curving lines, and thus often employed for plant-form patterns (especially florals).

stenciling A technique for applying motifs and patterns to a surface by dabbing paints, glazes, or dyes through cutouts made in a stencil–a thin card usually made of oiled paper, but sometimes wood, metal, or plastic.

stippling *Distressed paint finish that involves tapping the bristle tips of a brush over wet glazes applied to an opaque, contrasting colored ground coat. Used to blend different colored glazes and create subtle shading and gradations of color.

strapwork Form of ornament consisting of twisted and intertwined bands (similar in appearance to strips of leather or ribbons). Sometimes combined with *arabesques or serving as the framework for *grotesques. Also often studded with *rosettes, *nailheads, or faceted jewellike forms–the latter known as *jeweled strapwork.

strié A mottled effect produced on the surface of a fabric by dyeing the yarns with two different colors before weaving.

stucco A fine cement or plaster made from sand, slaked lime, and gypsum. Applied to the surface of walls, moldings, and other architectural ornaments. By the 19th century, it was generally used as a term for exterior plastering.

stylized Non-*naturalistic depictions of organic or inorganic forms, the original subject matter merely providing inspiration for the final design.

swag Both a loop of drapery and a pendant garland made up of, or depicting, flowers, fruit, vegetable, leaves, or shells

swag-and-tail A style of hanging curtains in which the main body of the fabric is looped horizontally along the top of a window or door, and the ends, or tails, are allowed to hang down at the sides.

Swedish style In the 20th-century, a simple style of interior decoration characterized by the use of muted colors such as cobalt blue, gray, and white, restrained ornamentation, and the extensive use of natural materials, notably wood and glass. However, in the 18th century, Swedish "Gustavian" style based on *Rococo was far more elaborate.

T

taffeta A firm, closely woven *silk or *linen fabric with an identical glossy surface on both sides.

tassel *See* pages 186-9.

terracotta A red-colored *earthenware, usually unglazed.

terazzo A decorative finish for walls and floors, made of chips of marble or other stones set into mortar and then polished smooth.

tesserae The small cubes of colored stone, ceramic, or glass used to make *mosaic patterns.

ticking *See* page 157.

tieback A length of rope, *cord, or fabric used to secure a curtain to one side of a window.

tin-glaze A glassy white *glaze made by adding tin oxide to lead glaze. Used to decorate pottery such as *delftware.

toile de Jouy *See* page 131.

tongue and groove A method of jointing boards, in which the edge of one board has a tongue, or lip, that fits into a groove cut into the edge of the next board.

tours de cheminées Plain or decorative lengths of fabric hung from the leading edge of the mantelshelf of a fireplace.

transfer printing A method of printing designs onto ceramics by first printing an engraved design onto paper, using an oil-based ink. The paper is then laid over the body of the ceramic and burned off during firing, to leave an outline design that can be colored in by hand.

"Tree of Life" An English pattern developed during the late 16th century, possibly from ancient Persian or Indian ornament, and symbolizing the life force. Much used on fabrics, it usually consisted of a central trunk, branches, sinuous stems and tendrils, fantastical flowers and exotic fruits, all woven around exotic birds and insects.

trelliswork A crisscross wooden support for plants, and a decorative pattern devised in imitation of. Notably popular in *Medieval, *Regency, and *Arts and Crafts decoration.

tripartite division The horizontal division of a wall into three sections –*frieze, *field, and *dado–for the purposes of decoration.

triquetra A three-lobed, triangular motif made up of interlaced crescent shapes. Of Celtic origin.

triskele A Y-shaped sun motif, originally used in Ancient Greek and Celtic ornament.

trompe l'oeil French for "trick of the eye." A decorative technique in which paints or dyes are applied to stone, plaster, wood, fabric, or paper to create the appearance, form, and often texture of "three-dimensional" scenes or objects. Typical examples included marbling, wood-graining, *grisaille*, and architectural components or vistas rendered in perspective.

tube-lining A method of decorating tiles in which raised lines of *slip are piped onto the surface through a thin tube. The lines define the pattern by separating subsequently applied colored glazes.

tufting A technique used in the mass production of carpets, in which a pile is created by sewing tufted yarn onto a ready-woven backing fabric; the backing is then coated in latex to secure the yarn.

tulle Fine *muslinlike material made of silk. First produced in France during the 18th century.

turkeywork An inexpensive woolen pile fabric produced in imitation of expensive Turkish and Persian carpets. Used for upholstery and table and floor coverings during the 17th century.

tweed A coarse-textured, *twill-weave cloth made from different colored woolen yarns.

twill weave A variation of a *plain weave. Has a diagonal grain produced by floating the *weft threads diagonally over and under groups of, rather than alternating, *warps.

V, W, Y, Z

valance A short, soft curtain, either used at the top of a window to hide the curtain pole and the top of the main curtains, or hung from the canopy or base of a bed.

velour Heavy, velvetlike fabric with a thick pile that lies in one direction. Woven from *wool, *cotton, or synthetic fibers.

verdure French for "greenness," and for tapestry with a green color cast and displaying plant form-imagery.

vinyl A synthetic polymer used in resin form to produce sheet flooring. Also used for vinyl wallpapers (*see* page 237).

voile A fine, crisp, sheer fabric woven from *cotton, *silk, *wool, or synthetic fibers.

warp The threads that run lengthways in a piece of cloth. They are set and spaced on a loom and the *wefts are woven through them from side to side.

waterleaf A motif consisting of a broad, blade-shaped leaf with crimped edges and curling tip. Probably based on the water lily leaf and widely used in *Gothic and *Neoclassical ornament.

weft The threads in a piece of cloth that are woven from side to side through the *warps.

Wiener Werkstätte A studio founded in Vienna, Austria, in 1907. Specialized in handmade fabrics, furniture, and metalwork in the *Art Nouveau style.

Wilton Generic name for a type of carpet first produced in Wilton, England, in the mid-18th century. Similar to *Brussels carpet, but with a cut pile.

wool A yarn spun from the fibrous coat of an animal, such as a sheep or a goat.

worsted Smooth, strong woolen cloth made from carded and combed wool yarn.

ypotryll A *heraldic beast with the head of a boar, the body of an antelope, and the tail of a lion.

zillij Traditional North African *mosaic tilework.

Directory

All items featured in the book are available either via a distributor or a store, or by mail order. If a stockist in your area is not listed, please contact the head office address (shown first beneath the company name) for details of a local supplier. Before visiting suppliers, please telephone first since not all outlets are open to the public.

A

Aalto Country Colors
8 Railway Street
Newmarket, Auckland
New Zealand
Tel. 9 522 2019
and
29 Leslie Hills Drive
Christchurch, Auckland
New Zealand
Tel. 3 348 8015
(Distributor of Farrow & Ball)

Abbott & Boyd
Chelsea Harbour
Design Centre
London SW10 0XE
UK
Tel. 0171 351 9985
(See also Brunschwig & Fils)

Ace (Royal) Hardware Corporation Paint Division
21901 South Central Avenue
Matteson
Illinois 60443
USA
Tel. (708) 720 0600

Afia Carpet Limited
Chelsea Harbour
Design Centre
London SW10 0XE
UK
Tel. 0171 351 5858
(Distributor of Stark Carpet Corp.)

Akzo Nobel Decorative Coatings Limited
PO Box 37
Crown House
Hollins Road
Darwen
Lancs BB3 0BG
UK
Tel. 01254 704951
and
Bentley Brothers
2709 South Park Road
Louisville
Kentucky 40219
USA
Tel. (502) 969 1464
and
Decorlux
7733 Bordeaux
Ville La Salle, Quebec
Canada
Tel. (514) 367 4522
and
Decoroll Homewares
121 Wetherhill Street
PO Box 6005
Silverwater, NSW 2128
Australia
Tel. 9 748 7799
and
Pacific Wallcoverings Ltd
Private Bag 50-907
Porirua
New Zealand
Tel. 4 237 8029
and
Waly Interior Products Ltd
1F Decca Centre
21 Cheung Lee Street
Chaiwan
Hong Kong
Tel. 2 898 8191

Alexander Beauchamp
2/12 2nd Floor
Chelsea Harbour
Design Centre
London SW10 0XE
UK
Tel. 0171 376 4556
and
Fonthill Ltd
D & D Building
979 Third Avenue
New York, NY 10022
USA
Tel: (212) 755 6700

The Alternative Flooring Co
14 Anton Trading Estate
Andover, Hants SP10 2NJ
UK
Tel. 01264 335111

Altfield Ltd
Chelsea Harbour
Design Centre
London SW10 0XE
UK
Tel. 0171 351 5893
(Distributor of Maya Romanoff and Scalamandré)
and
942 Third Avenue
New York, NY 10022
USA
Tel. (212) 980 3888
and
Passementeries Ltd
131 Wilson Street
Newton NSW
Australia
Tel. 2 550 5510
and
Matsumoto Designers Ltd
7-7-15 Rappongi
Minato-Ku, Tokyo
Japan
Tel. 3 3401 1801
and
Aftex Fabrics Pte Ltd
9 Penang Road
Unit 06-01 Park Mall
Singapore 0923
Tel. 3 388 655

The Amtico Company Ltd
Kingfield Road,
Coventry CV6 5PL
UK
Tel. 01203 861400
and
Amtico Studio
200 Lexington Avenue
32nd Street
Suite 809
New York, NY 10016
USA
Tel. (212) 545 1127
and
86-88 Dickson Avenue
Artarmon, Sydney
NSW 2064
Australia
Tel. 2 9901 4199
and
Irvine International Floors Ltd
48 Kingsley Street
PO Box 7545, Christchurch
New Zealand
Tel. 3 377 7537
and
Electric Plus Ltd
G/F 158 Lockhart Road
Wanchai
Hong Kong
Tel. 5 111 115
and
Kagawa & Co Ltd
8-17, 5 Chome
Nishiawaji
Higashiyodogawa-ku
GPO Box 871, Osaka
Japan
Tel. 7 8841 1826
and
Deco Expression Pte Ltd
74/74a Neil Road
Singapore 0408
Tel. 2 258 433
and
Taaf Hamman Trading Ltd
22 Dublin Road
Bramley View Ext 6 2090
Johannesburg
South Africa
Tel. 11 882 1000
and
Floors Carpet Contracts
PO Box 8762, Dubai
UAE
Tel. 4 213 958

Andrew Martin International Ltd
200 Walton Street
London SW3 2JL
UK
Tel. 0171 584 4290
and
Kravet Fabrics Inc
225 Central Avenue South
Bethpage
Long Island, NY 11714
USA
Tel. (516) 293 2000
and
Unique Fabrics Ltd
19 Garfield Street
PO Box 37692
Parnell, Auckland
New Zealand
Tel. 9 377 8444
and
Caroline Harper Interiors Ltd
402 Yu Yuet Lai Building
43-55 Wyndham Street
Central
Hong Kong
Tel. 5 238 226
and
Marquis Furniture Gallery Ltd
134 Joo Seng Road
Nobel Design House
Singapore 368359
Tel. 3 830 120
and
Halogen International Ltd
PO Box 52599
Saxonwold 2132
Johannesburg
South Africa
Tel. 11 448 2060
and
The Gallery
PO Box 1003
Prince Turki Street
Block 820
Al-Khobar 31952
Saudi Arabia
Tel. 3 896 1469

Ann Sacks Tile and Stone
5 East 16th Street
New York, NY 10003
USA
Tel. (212) 463 8400
(Distributor of Lowitz & Co)
and
Yaletown Tileworks
1017 Cambie Street
Vancouver, BC
Canada
Tel. (604) 682 3060
and
Orbit
Adham St, Al-Hambra Area
Jeddah 21424, KSA
Saudi Arabia
Tel. 1 667 3618

Anna French
343 Kings Road
London SW3 5ES
UK
Tel. 0171 351 1126
and
Classic Revivals Inc
Suite 534
5th Floor
1 Design Center Place
Boston
Massachussetts 02210
USA
Tel. (617) 574 9030

Anne and Robert Swaffer
Bakewell Road
Orton Southgate
Peterborough
Cambs PE2 6WQ
UK
Tel. 01733 371727

Annie Sloan
Relics UK
35 Bridge Street
Witney
Oxon 0X8 6DA
UK
Tel. 01993 704611

Anta Scotland Ltd
Fearn, Tain
Ross-shire IV20 1XW
UK
Tel. 01862 8324775

Antico Setificio Fiorentino
Via L Bartolini 4
50124 Firenze
Italy
Tel. 55 21 38 61

Anya Larkin
8th Floor
39 West 28th Street
New York, NY 10001
USA
Tel. (212) 532 3263
(See also Donghia)

Apenn
33 Kensington Park Road
London W11 2EU
UK
Tel. 0171 792 2457

Artex-Bluhawk Ltd
Artex Avenue
Newhaven
East Sussex BN9 9DD
UK
Tel. 01273 513100

Atlas Carpet Mills
2200 Saybrook Avenue
Los Angeles
California 90040
USA
Tel. (800) 372 6274
(See also Christy Trading)

Attica
543 Battersea Park Road
London SW11 3BL
UK
Tel. 0171 736 1234
http://www.attica.co.uk

Auro Organic Paints
Unit 1
Goldstones Farm
Ashdon, Saffron Walden
Essex CB10 2LZ
UK
Tel. 01799 584888
and
Sinan Company
PO Box 857
2202 Muir Woods Place
Davis, California 95617
USA
Tel. (916) 753 3104
and
Imui Corporation
No 2-5, 2 Chome
Doshio-Machi, Chuo-Ku
Osaka 541
Japan
Tel. 6 231 2971

Axminster Carpets Ltd
Axminster
Devon EX13 5PQ
UK
Tel. 01297 32244
and
919 3rd Avenue
New York
NY 10022
Tel. (212) 421 1051

B

Baer & Ingram
273 Wandsworth Bridge Road
London SW6 2TX
UK
Tel. 0171 736 6111
and
Davan Industries
144 Main Street
Port Washington, NY 11000
USA
Tel. (516) 9446498

Baumann Fabrics
41/42 Berners Street
London W1P 3AA
UK
Tel. 0171 637 0253
and
114 North Center Avenue
Rockville
Rockville Center, NY 11570
USA
Tel. (516) 764 7431

Beaumont & Fletcher
261 Fulham Road
London SW3 6HY
UK
Tel. 0171 352 5594
and
Travers
D & D Building
979 Third Avenue
New York, NY 10002
USA
Tel. (212) 888 7900

Belinda Coote Tapestries
Chelsea Harbour
Design Centre
London SW10 0XE
UK
Tel: 0171 351 0404

Bennett Silks
Crown Royal Park
Higher Hillgate
Stockport SK1 3HB
UK
Tel. 0161 477 5979
and
44 Dartford Road
Sevenoaks, Kent TN13 3TQ
UK
Tel. 01732 464810

Bennison Fabrics
16 Holbein Place,
London SW1W 8NL
UK
Tel. 0171 730 8076
and
76 Greene Street
New York, NY 10012
USA
Tel. (212) 941 1212

Bentley & Spens
1 Mornington Street
London NW1 7QD
UK
Tel. 0171 387 7374
and
Christopher Hyland Inc
D & D Building
979 Third Avenue
Suite 1714
New York, NY 10022
USA
Tel. (212) 688 6121

and
Designers International
77a Parnell Road
Auckland
New Zealand
Tel. 9 309 1589
and
E & Y Co Ltd
Milles Roches B1
5-3-5 Minami-Aoyama
Minato-Ku
Tokyo 107
Japan
Tel. 3 5485 8461

Berger International Ltd
PO Box 27524
Dubai
UAE
Tel. 4 391 000
and
22 Benoi Sector
Singapore 629854
Tel. 2 615 224
and
Room 601
Shiu Fung Hong Building
239-41 Wing Lok Street
Hong Kong
Tel. 5 443 768

Bernard Thorp & Co
53 Chelsea Manor Street
London SW3 3ST
UK
Tel: 0171 352 5745
(See also Stark Carpet Corp.)

Berti Pavimenti Legno
Via Rettilineo 83
35010 Villa del Conte
Padova
Italy
Tel. 49 93 25 011
and
PM Hardwoods
5 Nelson Street
Southend-on-Sea
Essex SS1 1ES
UK
Tel. 01702 348877
and
David Gunton Hardwood Floors (supplier)
Grange Lane
Whitegate, nr. Winsford
Cheshire
CW7 2PS
UK
Tel. 01606 861 442

Bill Amberg
The Shop
10 Chepstow Road
London W2 5BD
UK
Tel. 0171 727 3560

and
The Workshops
23 Theatre Street
London SW11 5ND
UK
Tel. 0171 924 4296

Boen Parkett
4740 Tveit
Norway
Tel. 38 06 30 11

Bonar & Flotex
High Holborn Road
Ripley
Derbs DE5 3NT
UK
Tel. 01773 744121

Borderline
1 Munro Terrace
London SW10 0DL
UK
Tel. 0171 823 3567
and
Chawton House
3/50 Bayswater House
Kings Cross
Sydney NSW 2011
Australia
Tel. 2 9331 5022

Bosanquet Ives
3 Court Lodge
48 Sloane Square
London SW1 8AT
UK
Tel. 0171 730 6241

Bradbury & Bradbury
PO Box 155
Benicia
California 94510
USA
Tel. (707) 746 1900
http://www.bradbury.com
(See also Hamilton Weston)

Brats
Brats Paints
281 Kings Road
London SW3 5EW
UK
Tel. 0171 351 7674
and
624c Fulham Road
London SW6 5RS
UK
Tel. 0171 731 6915

Brian Yates
Riverside Park
Caton Road, Lancs LA1 3PE
UK
Tel. 01524 381161
(Distributor of Sheila Coombes)

Brintons Ltd
PO Box 16
Exchange Street
Kidderminster
Worcs DY10 1AG
UK
Tel. 01562 820000
and
Brintons Carpets (USA) Ltd
E-210 Route 4
Paramus, New Jersey 07652
USA
Tel. (201) 368 0080

Bruce Hardwood
185 Milton Park
Abingdon, Oxon OX14 4SR
UK
Tel. 01235 862222

Bruno Triplet
Chelsea Harbour
Design Centre
London SW10 0XE
UK
Tel. 0171 795 0395

Brunschwig & Fils
10 The Chambers
Chelsea Harbour
Design Centre
London SW10 0XF
UK
Tel. 0171 351 5797
and
D & D Building
979 Third Avenue
New York, NY 10022-1234
USA
Tel. 212 838 7878
(Distributor of Abbott & Boyd)
and
St James Furnishings Pty Ltd
164 Burwood Road
Hawthorn
Victoria 3122
Australia
Tel. 3 9819 1569
and
St James Furnishings (NZ) Ltd
The Foundation
8 George Street
Parnell, Auckland
New Zealand
Tel. 9 303 3915
and
Source Interiors Ltd
205 Wilson House
13 Wyndham Street
Central
Hong Kong
Tel. 5 216 214
also
Textile Lida Co Ltd
1-1 Motoyoyogi-Cho
Shibuya-Ku, Tokyo 151
Japan
Tel. 3 3465 5001

and
Halogen International Ltd
PO Box 52599
Saxonwold 2132
Johannesburg
South Africa
Tel. 11 448 2060

Buckland Books
Holly Tree House
18 Woodlands Road
Littlehampton
W Sussex BN17 5PP
UK
International mail order book service (ceramics etc.)

Busby & Busby
The Old Stables
Winterborne Whitechurch
Dorset DT11 9AW
UK
Tel. 01258 881211

C

Cabot Stains
Samuel Cabot Inc
100 Hale Street
Newburyport
Massachusetts 01950
USA
Tel. (508) 465 1900

Candy & Co
Heathfield
Newton Abbot
Devon TQ12 6RF
UK
Tel. 01626 832641

Carocim
BP 10,1515 Route du Puy
Sainte Réparade
13540 Puyricard
France
Tel. 4 42 92 20 39

Carré
91 Quai de Valmy
75010 Paris
France
Tel. 1 53 35 83 50
(See also Reed Harris)

Cath Kidston
8 Clarendon Cross
London W11 4AP
UK
Tel. 0171 221 4000

Celia Birtwell
71 Westbourne Park Road
London W2 5QH
UK
Tel. 0171 221 0877

Ceramiche Eurotiles
Via del Commercio 25/27
41404 Spezzano di Fiorano
Modena
Italy
Tel. 5 36 84 47 58
and
Alba Corporation
Dai 5 Inose Building 2-9-12
Kita-Aoyama Minato-Ku
Tokyo 107
Japan
Tel. 3 5411 0661
and
Country Floors
15 East 16th Street
New York, NY 10003
USA
Tel. (212) 627 8300
and
Intersell Ltd
PO Box 32043
61320 Tel-Aviv
Israel
Tel. 546 5570
and
Elames Trading & Contracting
PO Box 26095
Bahrain
UAE
Tel. 73 701 166

Chatsworth Carpets
227 Brompton Road
London SW3 2EP
UK
Tel. 0171 584 1386

Chelsea Textiles
7 Walton Street
London SW3 2JD
UK
Tel. 0171 584 1165
and
1125 Globe Avenue
Mountainside
New Jersey
07092
USA
Tel. (908) 233 5645

Christy Trading
17 Darin Court
Crownhill
Milton Keynes
MK8 0AD
UK
Tel. 01908 265222
(Distributor of Atlas, Monterey and Patrick)

Ciel Decor
187 New Kings Road
London SW6 4SW
UK
Tel. 0171 731 0444
(Distributor of Les Olivades)

Claremont (Furnishings Fabrics Co Ltd)
29 Elystan Street
London SW3 3NT
UK
Tel. 0171 581 9575

Claremont Fabrics
Wren Nest Road
Glossop
Derbs SK13 8HB
UK
Tel. 01457 866927

Cole & Son
142-144 Offord Road
London N1 1NS
UK
Tel. 0171 607 4288
and
Whittaker & Woods
5100 Highlands Parkway
Smyrna
Georgia 30082
USA
Tel. (800) 395 8760
and
St James Furnishings Pty Ltd
164 Burwood Road
Hawthorn
Victoria 3122
Australia
Tel. 3 9819 1569

Colefax and Fowler Group plc
19–23 Grosvenor Hill
London W1X 9HG
UK
Tel. 0181 874 6484
(Distributor of Jane Churchill fabrics and wallpaper)
and
110 Fulham Road
London SW3 6RL
UK
Tel. 0171 244 7427

Coloroll
(See John Wilman Ltd)

Colorman Paints
Coton Clanford
Stafford
Staffs ST18 9PB
UK
Tel. 01785 282799

Contract Flooring Sales Ltd
Unit 1
Goldsworth Park Trading Estate
Woking
Surrey GU21 3AT
UK
Tel. 01483 720202

Corres Mexican Tiles
Unit 1A, Station Road
Hampton Wick
Kingston-upon-Thames
Surrey KT1 4HG
UK
Tel. 0181 943 4142
and
Regio Associated Manufacturers Inc
127 Apollo Drive
Donna
Texas 78537
USA
Tel. (800) 327 7281

Craig & Rose
172 Leith Walk
Edinburgh EH6 5EP
UK
Tel. 0131 554 1131
and
Unit 5
Lissue Industrial Estate
Moira Road
Lisburn
County Antrim
UK
BT28 2RS
Tel. 01846 622273

Crown Berger Ltd
Crown House
PO Box 37
Hollins Road
Darwen
Lancs BB3 0BG
UK
Tel. 01254 704951
and
Crown Corporation
3012 Huron Street
Suite 101
Denver
Colorado 80202
USA
Tel. (303) 292 1313
and
Pacific Wallcoverings Ltd
Private Bag 50-907
Porirua
New Zealand
Tel. 4 237 8029
and
Waly Interior Products Ltd
1F Decca Centre
21 Cheung Lee Street
Chaiwan
Hong Kong
Tel. 2 898 8191
and
Zaidan Decor Materials Trading Est
PO Box 6359
Sharjah
UAE
Tel. 1 654 3859

Crowson
Crowson House
Bellbrook Park
Uckfield
East Sussex TN22 1QZ
UK
Tel. 01825 761044

Crucial Trading
PO Box 11
Duke Place, Kidderminster
Worcs DY10 2JR
UK
Tel. 01588 673666
and
Hamilton Carpet
D & D Building
979 Third Avenue
New York, NY 10022
USA
Tel. (212) 752 3022
and
Shipwright Agencies Ltd
PO Box 37741
Parnell, Auckland
New Zealand
Tel. 9 524 8639
and
Altfield Interiors
Suite 617
45 Princes Buildings
10 Charter Road
Hong Kong
Tel. 5 244 8647
and
Fine Craft Co
2-6-12 Ebisu Minami
Shirbuya-Ku
Tokyo 150
Japan
Tel. 3 3792 3571
and
Décor Expression Private Ltd
74 & 74A Neil Road
Singapore
Tel. 2 258 433
and
Halogen International Ltd
PO Box 52599
Saxonwold 2132
Johannesburg
South Africa
Tel. 11 448 2060
and
Al-Saad Contracting & Trading
Interior Design Division
PO Box 13028
Jeddah 21493
Saudi Arabia
Tel. 2 683 0306

Cuprinol
Adderwell
Frome
Somerset BA11 1NL
UK
Tel. 01373 465151

Cy-Près
14 Bells Close
Brigstock
Kettering
Northants NN14 3JG
UK
Tel. 01536 373431

D

DLW
Centurion Court
Milton Park
Abingdon
Oxon OX14 4RY
UK
Tel 01235 831296

Dacrylate Paints
Lime Street
Kirkby in Ashfield
Nottingham NG17 8AL
UK
Tel. 01623 753845

Dalsouple Direct Ltd
PO Box 140
Bridgwater
Somerset TA5 1HT
UK
Tel. 01984 667233

Daltile
7834 Hawn Freeway
Dallas
Texas 75217
USA
Tel. (214) 398 1411
and
Toronto
Ontario
Canada
Tel. (905) 660 9588

David Bonk
(See Donghia)

De Gournay
11 Hyde Park Gate
London SW7 5DG
UK
Tel. 0171 823 7316
and
Sloan Miyasato
2 Henry Adams Street
Suite 207
San Francisco
California 94103
USA
Tel. (415) 431 1465

De Le Cuona Designs
1 Trinity Place
Windsor
Berks SL4 3AP
UK
Tel. 01753 830301
and
General Trading Company
144 Sloane Street
London SW1X 9BL
UK
Tel. 0171 730 0411

Dedar
(See Mary Fox Linton)

Deralam
Unit 461/4, Walton Summit
Bamber Bridge
Preston, Lancs PR5 8AR
UK
Tel. 01772 315888

The Design Archives
PO Box 1464
Bournemouth
Dorset BH4 9YO
UK
Tel. 01202 753248
(See also Lee Jofa)

Designers Guild
3 Olaf Street
London W11 4BE
UK
Tel. 0171 243 7300
(See also Osborne & Little)

Domco
6150 Grand Prairie
Boulevard, St Leonard,
Quebec H3B 1P9
Canada
Tel (514) 322 7934

Domus Tiles
33 Parkgate Road
London SW11 4NP
UK
Tel. 0171 223 5555

Donghia
Chelsea Harbour
Design Centre
London SW10 0XE
UK
Tel. 0171 823 3456
(Distributor of Anya Larkin and David Bonk)
and
485 Broadway
New York
NY 10013
USA
Tel. (212) 925 2777

Dovedale
(See Hill & Knowles)

Dulux
Wexham Road
Slough
Berks SL2 5DS
UK
Tel. 01753 550000

E

Elite Tiles
Elite House, The Broadway
London NW9 7BP
UK
Tel. 0181 202 1806

Elizabeth Eaton
85 Bourne Street
London SW1W 8HF
UK
Tel. 0171 730 2262

Elon
66 Fulham Road
London SW3 6HH
UK
Tel. 0171 460 4600
and
12 Silver Road
London W12 7SG
UK
Tel. 0181 932 3000

Fardis
(See G. P. & J. Baker)

Farrow & Ball
Uddens Trading Estate
Wimborne
Dorset BH21 7NL
UK
Tel. 01202 876 141
(See also Aalto Country Colors; distributor of Jane Churchill paints and Aalto Country Colors)

Fine Decor
Victoria Mill
Macclesfield Road
Holmes Chapel, Crewe
Cheshire CW4 7PA
UK
Tel. 01477 544000

Finnaren & Haley
901 Washington Street
Conshohocken
Pennsylvania 19428
USA
Tel. (610) 825 1900

Fired Earth plc
Twyford Mill
Oxford Road
Adderbury
Oxon OX17 3HP
UK
Tel. 01295 812088
and
117-119 Fulham Road
London SW3 6RL
UK
Tel. 0171 589 0489
(Distributor of Froyle Tiles)
and
2404 Dominion Centre
43-59 Queens Road East
Hong Kong
Tel. 2 861 3864

Firifiss Contemporary Textiles
PO Box 1464
Bournemouth
Dorset BH4 9YQ
UK
Tel. 01202 753251
(See also Lee Jofa)

Florida Tile Industries Inc.
PO Box 447
Lakeland
Florida 33802
USA
Tel. (941) 284 4048
and
Centura
53 Apex Road
Toronto, Ontario M6A 2V6
Canada
Tel. (416) 785-5165
and
PAMAS Est
Baladeyyah Street,
Riyadh 11484
Saudi Arabia
Tel. 1 465 3349

Formica Ltd
Coast Road
North Shields
Tyne & Wear NE29 8RE
UK
Tel. 0191 259 3000
and
Formica Corporation
North America Product
Design Group
10155 Reading Road
Cincinnati
Ohio 45241
USA
Tel. (513) 786-3457

Froyle Tiles
Froyle Pottery
Lower Froyle
Alton, Hants GU34 4LL
UK
Tel. 01420 23693
(See also Fired Earth)

G

G. P. & J. Baker
PO Box 30
West End Road
High Wycombe
Bucks HP11 2QD
UK
Tel. 01494 467400
(Distributor of Fardis)

Gainsborough Silk Weaving
Alexandra Road
Sudbury
Suffolk CO10 6XH
UK
Tel. 01787 372081

Galliards
(See Hill & Knowles)

Garin
First Textile Ltd
1 Carlton Crescent
Luton
Beds AU3 1EN
UK
Tel. 01582 737400

George Spencer Decorations
4 West Halkin Street
London SW1 8JA
UK
Tel. 0171 235 1501
and
Christopher Norman Inc
41 West 25th Street
10th Floor
New York, NY 10010
USA
Tel. (212) 647 0303

Glant
(See Mary Fox Linton)

Graham & Brown
Harwood Street
Blackburn
Lancs BB1 3BR
UK
Tel. 01254 661122

Grand Illusions
2/4 Crown Road
St. Margaret's
Twickenham
TW1 3EE
UK
Tel. 0181 892 2151

Guy Evans
96 Great Titchfield Street
London W1P 7AG
UK
Tel. 0171 436 7914
(Distributor of Mauny)

H

H. & R. Johnson
Highgate Tile Works
High Street, Turnstall
Stoke on Trent
Staffs ST6 4JX
UK
Tel. 01782 575575
(Distributor of Minton Hollins)
and
Johnson USA Inc
PO Box 2335
Farmingdale
New Jersey 07727
USA
Tel. (908) 280 7900
and
PO Box 50518
Dubai
UAE
Tel. 4 453 004

Habitat
196 Tottenham Court Road
London W1
UK
Tel. 0171 255 2545

Hamilton Weston Wallpapers
18 St Mary's Grove
Richmond, Surrey TW9 1UY
UK
Tel. 0181 940 4850
(Distributor of Bradbury & Bradbury)
and
Classic Revivals Inc
1 Design Center Place
Suite 545, Boston
Massachusetts 02210
USA
Tel. (617) 574 9030

The Hardwood Flooring People
Fisherton Mill
108 Fisherton Street
Salisbury
Wilts SP2 7QY
UK
Tel. 01722 415000

Harlequin
Cossington Road
Sileby, Loughborough
Leics LE12 7RU
UK
Tel. 01509 816575
and
Saletex
4716 Thimens Boulevard
Montreal H4R 2B2
Canada
Tel. (514) 334 7533
and
Wilson Fabrics & Wallcoverings
46-56 Kippax Street
Surry Hills, NSW 2010
Australia
Tel. 2 9699 1288
and
Pacific Wallcoverings Ltd
Private Bag 50-907
Porirua
New Zealand
Tel. 4 237 8029
and

Waly Interior Products Ltd
1F Decca Centre
21 Cheung Lee Street
Chaiwan
Hong Kong
Tel. 2 898 8191
and
Phoenix International
Nihon Seimei Building 4F
1-21-1 Jinan
Shibuya-Ku, Tokyo 150
Japan
Tel. 3 3496 5811

Henderson Woven Designs
35 Wendover Road
Ettingshall Park
Wolverhampton
West Midlands WV4 6ND
UK
Tel. 01902 680844

Henry Newbery & Co
18 Newman Street
London W1P 4AB
UK
Tel. 0171 636 5970

Hill & Knowles
13 Mount Road
Feltham, Middx TW13 6AR
UK
Tel. 0181 893 4222
(Distributor of Galliards)

Historic Floors of Oshkosh
911 East Main Street
Winneconne
Wisconsin 45986
USA
Tel. (920) 582 9977

Hodsoll McKenzie
52 Pimlico Road
London SW1W 8LP
UK
Tel. 0171 730 2877
and
Clarence House
111 8th Avenue
New York
NY 10011
USA
Tel. (212) 752 2890
and
Charles Radford
Furnishings
8-18 Glass Street
Burnley
Victoria
Australia
Tel. 3 9429 6122
and
St Leger & Viney Pty Ltd
PO Box 55508
Northlands 2116
Gauteng
South Africa
Tel. 11 444 6722

Hugh Mackay
PO Box 1
Durham City DH1 2RX
UK
Tel. 0191 386 4444
and
Roman House
Wood Street
London EC2Y 5BU
UK
Tel. 0171 606 8491

I

Ian Mankin
109 Regents Park Road
London NW1 8UR
UK
Tel. 0171 722 0997
and
271 Wandsworth Bridge Road
London SW6 2TX
UK
Tel. 0171 371 8825
and
Coconut Company
129-131 Greene Street
New York, NY 10012
USA
Tel. (212) 539 1940
and
The Natural Textile Company Inc
2571 West Broadway
Vancouver
BC V6K 2E9
Canada
Tel. (604) 736 2101
and
Tobu Department Co Ltd
1-1-25 Nishi Ikebukuro
Toshima-Ku
Tokyo 171
Japan
Tel. 3 5951 5415

Ian Sanderson
PO Box 148
Newbury
Berks RG15 9DW
UK
Tel. 01635 33188

Imports Direct
182 Battersea Park Road
London SW11 4ND
UK
Tel. 0171 627 4646

Interdesign UK Ltd
Chelsea Harbour
Design Centre
London SW10 0XE
UK
Tel. 0171 376 5272
and
Lebanon
Tel. 9 218 712

The Isle Mill Ltd
12 West Moulin Road
Pitlochry PH16 5AF
UK
Tel. 01796 472390

Ivo Prints
3 Trident Way
International Trading Estate
Southall
Middx UB2 5JX
UK
Tel. 0181 574 7943
and
Lowsuma Pty Ltd
10/39 Wunulla Road
Point Piper
Sydney, NSW 2027
Australia
Tel. 2 9328 1080
and
Interior Asia (Decor) Ltd
15F Radio City
505-511
Hennessy Road
Causeway Bay
GPO Box 4244
Hong Kong
Tel. 280 22320

J

J. W. Bollom
PO Box 78
Croydon Road
Beckenham
Kent BR3 4BL
UK
Tel. 0181 658 2299

Jab International Furnishings Ltd
Chelsea Harbour
Design Centre
London SW10 0XE
UK
Tel. 0171 349 9323
(Distributor of Stroheim & Romann)
and
155 East 56th Street
New York
NY 10022
USA
Tel. (212) 486 1500
and
326 Davenport Road
Toronto
Ontario M5R 1K6
Canada
Tel. (416) 927 9192
and
Seneca Textiles Ltd
10-12 Adolph Street
Richmond
Victoria 3121
Australia
Tel. 3 428 5021
and
14 Heather Street
PO Box 37-702
Parnell
Aucklan
New Zealand
Tel. 9 309 6411
and
Tai Ping Carpets Ltd
Rm 3708
Bank of America Tower
12 Harcourt Road
Hong Kong
Tel. 2 521 6281
and
National Trading Inc
5-2 Minami-Azab 4-Chome
Minato-ku
Tokyo 106
Japan
Tel. 3 3442 4791
and
Aftex Fabrics Pte Ltd
9 Penang Road
Unit 06-01 Park Mall
Singapore 0923
Tel. 3 388 655
and
The Fabric Library
Stand 61 Old Pretoria Road
PO Box 912
Halfway House 1685
South Africa
Tel. 11 805 4211

Jack Lenor Larsen
Larsens
233 Spring Street
New York, NY 10013
USA
Tel: (212) 462 1300
and
232 East 59th Street
New York, NY 10022
USA
Tel. (212) 462 1300

Jane Churchill
151 Sloane Street
London SW1X 9BX
UK
Tel. 0171 730 9847
(See also Colefax & Fowler for fabrics and wallpapers, and Farrow & Ball for paints)

Jane Knapp
6 Chatham Row
Walcot, Bath
Avon BA1 5BS
UK
Tel. 01225 463468

Jason D'Souza
Chelsea Harbour
Design Centre
London SW10 0XE
UK
Tel. 0171 351 4440

Jaymart Rubber & Plastics Ltd
Woodlands Trading Estate
Eden Vale Road
Westbury
Wilts BA13 3QS
UK
Tel. 01985 215408

Jean Louis Seigner
3 rue Coëtlogon
75006 Paris
France
Tel. 1 45 49 91 20

Jim Thompson
(See Mary Fox Linton)

Joanna Wood
Lewis & Wood
48A Pimlico Road
London SW1W 8LP
UK
Tel. 0171 730 5064

John Boyd Textiles
Higher Flax Mills
Castle Cary
Somerset
BA7 7DY
UK
Tel. 01963 350451
and
Lee Jofa Inc
201 Central Avenue South
Bethpage
New York
NY 11714
USA
Tel. (516) 752 7600
and
William Switzer & Associates
6-611 Alexander Street
Vancouver
BC V6A 1E1
Canada
Tel. (604) 255 5911
and
Ascraft Fabrics
19a Boundary Road
Rushcutters Bay
NSW
Australia
Tel. 2 9360 2311
and
Rata
44 Ghuznee Street
Wellington
New Zealand
Tel. 4 801 9589
and
Waly Interior Products Ltd
1F Decca Centre
21 Cheung Lee Street
Chaiwan
Hong Kong
Tel. 2 898 8191
and
Textile Lida Co Ltd
1-1 Motoyoyogi-Cho
Shibuya-Ku
Tokyo 151
Japan
Tel. 3 3465 5001

John Oliver Ltd
33 Pembridge Road
London W11 3HG
UK
Tel. 0171 221 6466

John Wilman
Culshaw Street
Burnley, Lancs BB12 4PQ
UK
Tel. 01282 830300
(Distributor of Coloroll)
and
Maxwell Fabrics
188 Victoria Drive
Vancouver, BC V5L 4C3
Canada
Tel. (604) 253 7744
and
John Kaldor
110 McEvoy Street
PO Box 395
Alexandria 2015
Australia
Tel. 2 9698 7700
and
James Dunlop
PO Box 1632
Duncora House
39 Peterborough Street
Christchurch
New Zealand
Tel. 3 366 8681
and
Sunray
11F Wah Ming Building
34 Wong Chuk Hang Road
Hong Kong
Tel. 2 555 7323
and
Taiyo
5/11 3 Chome
Nakanoshima Kita-Ku
Osaka
Japan
Tel 6 443 5585
and
Verton
161 Kallang Way 03-14
Kolam Ayer Industrial Park
Singapore 349247
Tel. 3 921 848
and
Fabric Lines
PO Box 4261
Halfway House, 1685 Midrand
Johannesburg
South Africa
Tel. 11 314 1711
and
Sulaiman, Al Suwailem
PO Box 25309, Riyadh 11466
Saudi Arabia
Tel. 1 466 3111

Julie Arnall
26 Woodwaye
Watford, Herts WD1 4NW
UK
Tel. 01923 228465

Junckers
Wheaton Court
Commercial Centre
Wheaton Road
Witham, Essex CM8 3UJ
UK
Tel. 01376 517512
and
4920 East Landon Drive
Anaheim, California 92807
USA
Tel. (714) 777 6430
and
Hussey Seating Co Ltd
#6, 3700 – 19 Street NF
Calgary, Alberta T2E 6V2
Canada
Tel. (403) 291 3166
and
G. P. Embelton & Co Pty Ltd
147-149 Bakers Road
PO 207 Coburg,
Victoria 3058
Australia
Tel. 3 9350 2811
and
Hardwood Technology Ltd
17 Greenmount Drive
PO Box 58771
East Tamaki, Auckland
New Zealand
Tel. 9 274 8568
and
Bermian Ltd
10-20 Tai Wo Street
1/F Fook Wo Building
Wanchai
Hong Kong
Tel. 2 893 3133
and
Dai-ichi Nishiwaki Building
5th Floor
1-58-10 Yoyogi Shibuya
Tokyo 151
Japan
Tel. 3 5354 7538
and
Prospect (Far East) Pte Ltd
No 28F Penjuru Road 01-01
Singapore 609134
Tel. 7 777 888
and
CE Westergaard (Pty) Ltd
Titaco House, 4th Floor
CNR Joia & Bertha Streets
2001 Dtaamtontein
PO Box 62114
Marshalltown 2107
South Africa
Tel. 11 403 3805

K

K and K Designs International
Unit 1D
Reydon Business Park
Lowestoft Road
Reydon, Suffolk IP18 6SZ
UK
Tel. 01502 724040

Kahrs UK Ltd
Timberlaine Estate
Quarry Lane
Chichester
West Sussex PO19 2FJ
UK
Tel. 01243 778747
and
Hardwood Flooring Co
146/152 West End Lane
West Hampstead
London NW6 1SD
UK
Tel. 0171 328 8481
and
951 Mariner's Island Blvd.
Suite 630
San Mateo, California 94404
USA
Tel. (650) 341 8400
and
Europlex International
307C-1546 Derwent Way
Delta BC, V3M 6M4
Canada
Tel. (604) 525 1135
and
c/o Swedish Trade Council
25th Floor, 44 Market Street
Sydney, NSW 2000
Australia
Tel. 2 9262 1070
and
Wooden Floors Ltd
70 Sale Street
Auckland
New Zealand
Tel. 9 307 5241
and
ABC Trading Co Ltd
12–14 2-Chome
Nagata-Cho, Chiyoda-Ku
Tokyo
Japan
Tel. 3 350 7707
and
Jocels Marketing Pte Ltd
Blk 6003 #1-556
Ang Mo Kio Industrial Park 3
Singapore 569455
Tel. 4 818 801

Karndean Ltd
Ferry Lane
Offenham, Evesham
Worcs WR11 5RT
UK
Tel. 01386 49902
and
Karndean North America
37 Shulman Avenue
Stoughton
Massachussetts 02072
USA
Tel. (888) 266 4343
and
Karndean International Pty Ltd
Unit 1, 4 Samantha Court
PO Box 15
Knoxfield, Victoria 3180
Australia
Tel. 3 9764 9466
and
Unit A
73 Greenmount Drive
East Tamaki, Auckland
New Zealand
Tel. 9 273 5430

Kenneth Clark Ceramics
The North Wing
Southover Grange
Southover Road
Lewes, E Sussex BN7 1TP
UK
Tel. 01273 476761

Kentucky Wood Floors
PO Box 33276
Louisville, Kentucky 40232
USA
Tel. (502) 451 6024

Kievel Stone
Lower Farm
Lower Farm Lane
Ampfield, Hants S051 9BP
UK
Tel. 01794 368865

Knowles & Christou
Unit 44
110 Kingsgate Road
London NW6 2JG
UK
Tel. 0171 372 3807
and
Davan Industries
144 Main Street
Port Washington, NY 11050
USA
Tel. (516) 944 6498

L

LASSCO Flooring
101-108 Britannia Walk
London N1 7LU
UK
Tel. 0171 251 5157

LBC Hardwood Flooring
100 Weston Grove
Upton Chester
Cheshire CH2 1QN
UK
Tel. 01244 377811

Lee Jofa
Chelsea Harbour
Design Centre
London SW10 0XE
UK
Tel. 0171 351 7760
and
201 Central Avenue South
Bethpage
NY 11714
USA
Tel. (516) 752 7600
(Distributor of The Design Archives, Firifiss, Monkwell and Mulberry)

Lelièvre
101 Cleveland Street
London W1P 5PN
UK
Tel. 0171 636 3461
and
Telio & Cie
1407 rue de la Montagne
Montreal H3G 1Z3
Canada
Tel: (514) 842 9116
and
Order Imports Ltd
11A Boundary Street
Rushcutter Bay, NSW 2011
Australia
Tel: 2 9360 3565
and
Source Interiors Ltd
19-27 Wyndham Street
Central, Hong Kong
Tel. 2 521 6214
and
Manas Trading Inc
5F Nissan Building
4-21 Himon'ya-Megoru Ku
Tokyo 152
Japan
Tel: 3 3792 7111
and
Aftex Fabrics Pte Ltd
9 Penang Road
Unit 06-01
Park Mall
Singapore 0923
Tel. 3 388 655
and
Macromac
PO Box 76178
12D Kramer Road
Wendywood 2144
Johannesburg
South Africa
Tel: 11 444 1584

Lennox Money Antiques
93 Pimlico Road
London SW1W 8PH
UK
Tel. 0171 730 3070
and
Classic Revivals Inc
1 Design Center Place
Suite 534
Boston
Massachusetts 02210
USA
Tel. (617) 574 9030
and
Boyac Decorative Furnishings
234 Auburn Road
Melbourne
Victoria 3122
Australia
Tel. 3 9818 5300
and
St Leger & Viney Pty Ltd
PO Box 55508
Northlands 2116, Gauteng
South Africa
Tel. 11 444 6722

Liberon Waxes
Mountfield Industrial Estate
Learoyd Road
New Romney. Kent TN28 8XU
UK
Tel. 01797 367555

Liberty & Co
Regent Street
London W1
UK
Tel: 0171 734 1234
(See also Osborne & Little)

Life Enhancing Tile Co
31 Bath Buildings
Montpelier
Bristol
Avon BS6 5PT
UK
Tel. 0117 907 7673

Liz Induni
11 Park Road
Swanage, Dorset BH19 2AA
UK
Tel. 01929 423 776

Louis de Poortere
Rue de la Royenne 45
B-7700 Mouscron
Belgium
Tel. 56 39 31 11
and
136 Cass Street
Adairsville, Georgia 30103
USA
Tel. (770) 773 7934

Lowitz & Company
1776 West Winnemac
Avenue
Chicago, Illinois 60640
USA
Tel. (473) 784 2628
(See also Ann Sacks Tile & Stone)

M

The Malabar Cotton Company Ltd
31-33 The South Bank
Business Centre
Ponton Road
London SW8 5BL
UK
Tel. 0171 501 4221
and
Davan Industries
144 Main Street
Port Washington
NY 11050
USA
Tel. (516) 944 6498
and
W H Bilbrough & Co Ltd
Designers Walk
326 Davenport Road
Toronto, Ontario M5R 1K6
Canada
Tel. (416) 960 1611
and
103-105 Regent Street
Chippendale NSW 2008
Australia
Tel. 2 9699 3193
and
Fabric Fair Ltd
4/F Ho Lee Commercial
Building
38-42 D'Aguilar Street
Central
Hong Kong
Tel. 2 810 7618
and
The Penny Wise
2-31-6 Ebisu Shibuya-Ku
Tokyo 150
Japan
Tel. 3 3443 4311
and
Cottons & Linens
19 Tanglin Road
2-3 Tanglin Shopping Centre
247909 Singapore
Tel. 7 341 178
and
Halogen International Ltd
PO Box 52599
Saxonwold 2132
Johannesburg
South Africa
Tel. 11 448 2060
and
American Homes Furniture
Madina Plaza
11 Madina Road
Jeddah 21431
Saudi Arabia
Tel. 2 682 4091
and
Areeca Furniture
PO Box 5165
Abu Dhabi, UAE
Tel. 2 782 000

Mannington Carpets International
Unit 19 Leafield Trading
Estate
Corsham, Wilts SN13 9SW
UK
Tel. 01225 811476

Manuel Canovas Ltd
2 North Terrace
Brompton Road
London SW3 2BA
UK
Tel. 0171 225 2298
and
136 East 57th Street
New York, NY 10022
USA
Tel. (212) 486 9230
and
Telio & Cie
1407 Rue de la Montagne
Montreal, Quebec H3G 1Z3
Canada
Tel. (514) 842 9116
and
Order Imports Ltd
11A Boundary Street
Rushcutter Bay, NSW 2011
Australia
Tel: 2 9360 3565
and
Caroline Harper Interiors Ltd
402 Yu Yuet Building
43-55 Wyndham Street
Central
Hong Kong
Tel. 2 523 8226
and
Tomita Textiles Co
3-16 Kyobashi
2 Chome, Chuo-ku
Tokyo 104
Japan
Tel. 3 3275 0225
and
Aftex Fabrics Pte Ltd
9 Penang Road
Unit 06-01 Park Mall
Singapore 0923
Tel. 3 388 655
and
Mavromac
PO Box 76178
Wendywood 2144
South Africa
Tel. 11 444 1584
and
Sofrace Dubai
PO Box 28119
Dubai, UAE
Tel. 4 696 800

Marble Flooring Specialists
110 Ashley Down Road
Bristol, Avon BS7 9JR
UK
Tel. 0117 942 0221

Marley Floors and Waterproofing
Dickley Lane
Lenham
Maidstone
Kent ME17 2DE
UK
Tel. 01622 854000

Marston & Langinger
192 Ebury Street
London SW1W 8UP
UK
Tel. 0171 823 6829

Marthe Armitage
1 Strand-on-the-Green
London W4 3PQ
UK
Tel. 0181 994 0160

Marvic Textiles
1 Westpoint Trading Estates
Alliance Road
London W3 0RA
UK
Tel. 0181 993 0191
and
Roger Arlington Inc
D & D Building
Suite 1411
979 Third Avenue
New York, NY 10022
USA
Tel. (212) 752 5288

Mary Fox Linton
Chelsea Harbour
Design Centre
London SW10 0XE
UK
Tel. 0171 351 9908
(Distributor of Dedar, Glant, and Jim Thompson)

Mauny
(See Guy Evans)

The Maya Romanoff Corporation
1730 West Greenleaf
Chicago, Illinois 60626
USA
Tel. (312) 465 6909
(See also Altfield)

Metropolitan Tile Co
Lower Audley Centre
Kent Street
Blackburn, Lancs BB1 1DE
UK
Tel. 01254 695 111

Michael Szell
Tel. 0171 262 4578

Minton Hollins
(See H. & R. Johnson)

Monkwell
10-12 Wharfdale Road
Bournemouth
Dorset BH4 9BT
UK
Tel. 01202 752944 *(See also Lee Jofa; distributor of Design Archives and Firifiss)*

Monterey Carpet Mills
3201 South Susan Street
Santa Anna, California 92704
USA
Tel. (800) 678 4640
(See also Christy Trading)

Montgomery Tomlinson Ltd
Broughton Mill Road
Bretton
Chester CH4 0BY
UK
Tel. 01244 661363

Mosquito Ltd
62 Lower Ham Road
Kingston upon Thames
Surrey KT2 5AW
UK
Tel. 0181 715 5611

Mulberry
Kilver Court
Shepton Mallet
Somerset BA4 5NF
UK
Tel. 01749 340 500
(See also Lee Jofa)

N

Natalie Woolf Surface Design
3rd Floor Studios
10 Wharfedale Street
Leeds LS7 2LF
UK
Tel. 0113 262 7704

Natural Flooring Direct
Unit A02
Tower Bridge Business Complex
Clements Road
London SE16 4DG
UK
Tel. 0800 454721

Natural Wood Floor Co
20 Smugglers Way
London SW18 1EQ
UK
Tel. 0181 871 9771

Nice Irma's
46 Goodge Street
London W1P 1FJ
UK
Tel. 0171 580 6921

Nina Campbell
(See Osborne & Little)

Nobilis-Fontan
1/2 Cedar Studios
45 Glebe Place
London SW3 5JE
UK
Tel. 0171 351 7878
and
57a Industrial Road
Berkeley Heights
New Jersey 07922
USA
Tel. (908) 464 1177
and
Crown Wallpapers
88 Ronson Drive
Rexdale, Ontario M9W 1B9
Canada
Tel. (416) 245 2900
and
Redelman & Son Pty Ltd
96 Dalmeny Avenue
Roseberry 2018 NSW
Australia
Tel. 2 313 6811
and
Vivace
Studio 6, 125 The Strand
PO Box 90664
Parnell, Auckland
New Zealand
Tel. 9 309 6271
and
Source Interiors Ltd
205 Wilson House
13 Wyndham Street
Central
Hong Kong
Tel. 2 5216214
and
Inter Fabrics Corp
3.17.12 Sendagaya
Shibuya-Ku
Tokyo 151
Japan
Tel. 3 3479 4552
and
Aftex Fabrics Pte Ltd
9 Penang Road
Unit 06-01 Park Mall
0923 Singapore
Tel. 3 388655
and
Macromac
PO Box 76178
12D Kramer Road
Wendywood 2144
Johannesburg
South Africa
Tel: 11 444 1584
and
Patrick Feildel
Dubai
UAE
Tel. 4 836 913

Northwood Designs
Trinity Gask
Auchterarer
Perthshire PH3 1LG
UK
Tel. 01764 683334

Nutshell Natural Paints
10 High Street
Totnes, Devon
UK
Tel. 01364 642892

O

The Old Fashioned Milk Paint Co
436 Main Street
PO Box 222
Groton
Massachussetts 01450
USA
Tel. (978) 448 6336
http://www.milkpaint.com
and
Nitty Gritty Reproductions
163 Queen St East
Toronto
Ontario M5A 1S1
Canada
Tel. (416) 364 1393
and
Coating Media Service Company Ltd
1-19 Ichigaya-Tumachi
Shinjuku-ku
Tokyo 162
Japan
Tel. 3 326 6028
and
Pendorosa Pine Design
Kooiweg-West G
4107 LR Culemborg
Netherlands
Tel. 345 520 393

Old Village Paints
PO Box 1030
Fort Washington
Pennsylvania 19034-1030
USA
Tel. (215) 654 1770

Old World Weavers
D & D Building
979 Third Avenue
New York
NY 10022
USA
Tel. (212) 752 9000

Olicana Textiles
Brook Mills
Crimble, Slaithwaite
Huddersfield
West Yorks HD7 5BQ
UK
Tel. 01484 847666
and
Domus
1919 Piedmont Road
Atlanta
Georgia 30324-4116
USA
Tel. (404) 872 1050

Les Olivades
(See Ciel Decor)

Ollerton Decor
Ollerton Hall
Ollerton
Knutsford
Cheshire WA16 8SF
UK
Tel. 01565 650222

Original Style
Falcon Road
Sowton Industrial Estate
Exeter
Devon EX2 7LF
UK
Tel. 01392 474058

Ornamenta
Old Chelsea Mews
Danvers Street
London SW3 5AN
UK
Tel. 0171 352 1824

Osborne & Little plc
49 Temperley Road
London SW12 8QE, UK
Tel. 0181 675 2255
(Distributor of Liberty and Nina Campbell)
and
90 Commerce Road
Stamford
Connecticut 06902
USA
Tel. 203 359 1500
(Distributor of Designers Guild and Liberty)

Ottilie Stevenson
4 Charlotte Road
London EC2A 3DH
UK
Tel. 0171 729 8508

P

Paint Library
5 Elystan Place
London SW3 3NT
UK
Tel. 0171 823 7755

Paint Magic
79 Shepperton Road
London N1 3DF
UK
Tel. 0171 354 9696
and
Other UK branches:
Arundel Tel. 01903 883653
Bath Tel. 01225 469966
Belfast Tel. 01232 421881
Brighton Tel. 01273 747980
Guildford Tel. 01483 306072
Harrogate Tel. 01423 568020
Islington Tel. 0171 359 4441
Marlow Tel. 01628 477707
Notting Hill Tel. 0171 792 8012
Richmond Tel. 0181 940 9799
Shrewsbury Tel. 01743 341682
and
30 Watten Rise
Singapore 1128
Tel. 463 1982
and
255 Dizengoff (406) Street
Tel-Aviv 63117
Israel
Tel. 3 605 0045

Patrick
716 Bill Myles Drive
Mobile
Alabama 36671
USA
Tel. (800) 421 1846
See also Christy Trading

Percheron
Chelsea Harbour
Design Centre
London SW10 OXE
UK
Tel. 0171 580 5156

Perstorp
18-19 Cromwell Park
Chipping Norton
Oxon OX7 5SR
Tel. 01608 646200
http://www.pergo.com

Pierre Frey
253 Fulham Road
London SW3 6HY
UK
Tel. 0171 376 5599
and
D & D Building
979 Third Avenue
New York, NY 10022
USA
Tel.
and
12 East 33rd Street
8th Floor
New York, NY 10016
USA
Tel. (212) 213 3099

Pippa & Hale
(See Today Interiors Ltd)

Pisani Ltd
Unit 12
Transport Avenue
Great Western Road
Brentford TW8 9HF
UK
Tel. 0181 568 5001

Pittsburgh Paints
PPG Industries
1 PPG Place
Pittsburgh
Pennsylvania 15272
USA
Tel. (888) 774 1010

Pratt & Lambert
PO Box 22
Buffalo
NY 14240
USA
Tel. (800) 289 7728

Prestige Enterprise Inc
4785 Eastern Avenue
Cincinnati
Ohio 45226
USA
Tel. (513) 871 8510
and
Toptech Co Ltd
Toom 2408-2412
8 Commercial Tower
8 Sun Yip Street
Chai Wan
Hong Kong
Tel. 2 8284488
and
Robbins Tokyo Office
Ishii Building 3F
8-5 Monzennaka-Cho
1-Chome, Koto-Ku
Tokyo 135
Japan
Tel. 3 3643 6991

Protim Solignum
Fieldhouse Lane
Marlow
Bucks SL7 1LS
UK
Tel. 01628 486644

R

Ramm, Son & Crocker
Chiltern House
The Valley Centre
Gordon Road
High Wycombe
Bucks HP13 6EQ
UK
Tel. 01494 603555
and
200 Clearbrook Road
Elmsford
NY 10623
USA
Tel. (914) 592 3311

RBI International Ltd
Chelsea Harbour
Design Centre
London SW10 0XE
UK
Tel. 0171 376 3766

Reed Harris & Company Ltd
Riverside House
27 Carnworth Road
London SW6 3HR
UK
Tel. 0171 736 7511
(Distributor of Carré)

Reptile
Gwaith Meyn
Llanglydwen
Whitland, Dyfed SA34 0XP
UK
Tel. 01994 419402

Ronseal Ltd
Thorncliffe Park
Chapeltown
Sheffield S35 2YP
UK
Tel. 0114 246 7171

Rose of Jericho
West Hill Barn
Evershot
Dorchester
Dorset DT2 OLD
UK
Tel. 01935 83676

Rustins
Waterloo Road
London NW2 7TX
UK
Tel. 0181 450 4666
and
The Woodsmith Pty Ltd
1 Burgess Road
North Bayswater
Victoria 3153
Australia
Tel. 3 761 4622
and
Latimer Marketing Ltd
5a Victoria Park Road
Christchurch
New Zealand
Tel. 3 337 0445
and
Hardware Centre
PO Box 3760
Johannesburg 2000
South Africa
Tel. 11 791 0850

Ryalux Carpets Ltd
Rochdale
Lancs OL11 2NU
UK
Tel. 0800 163 632

Rye Tiles
Rye, East Sussex TN31 7DH
UK
Tel. 01797 223038
and
12 Connaught Street
London W2 2AF
UK
Tel. 0171 723 7278

S

Sahco Hesslein
Chelsea Harbour
Design Centre
London SW10 0XE
UK
Tel. 0171 352 6168
and
Bergamo Fabrics
37-20 34th Street,
Long Island City
NY 11101
USA
Tel. (718) 392 5000

Saloni Ceramica
Carretera Alcora km.17
12130 san Juan de Moro
Apart. 550
12080 Castellon
Spain
Tel. 9 64 34 34 34

Sandberg Tapeter AB
Box 69
SE-523 22
Ulricehamn
Sweden
Tel. 321 12115
and
Sandberg Tapeter, UK
Tel. 0800 967 222
and
Atelier Textiles, New Zealand
Tel. 9 378 1415
and
Kinsan, Hong Kong
Tel. 2 5262309
and
Cottons & Linens, Singapore
Tel. 734 1178

Sanderson
100 Acres
Sanderson Road
Uxbridge
Middlesex UB8 19H
UK
Tel. 01895 238244
and
3 Patriot Centre
285 Grand Avenue
Englewood
New Jersey 07631
USA
Tel. (201) 894 8400
(Distributor of Brian Yates and Sheila Coombes)

Scalamandré Silks
300 Trade Zone Drive,
Ronkonkoma
NY 11779-7381
USA
Tel. (516) 467 8800
(See also Altfield)

Schumacher & Co
939 Third Avenue
New York
NY 10022
USA
Tel. (212) 415 3900
(See Turnell & Gigon)
and
Wardlaw Pty Ltd
230-232 Auburn Road
Hawthorn 3122
Victoria
Australia
Tel. 3 9819 4233
and
Tai Ping Interiors Ltd
Bank of America Tower,
32nd Floor
12 Harcourt Road
Hong Kong
Tel. 2 5216281
and
Tomita Textiles Co
3-16 Kyobashi
2 Chome
Chuo-ku
Tokyo 104
Japan
Tel. 3 3275 0225
and
Interiors Showplace
211 Henderson Road
02-04 Henderson Ind Park
Singapore 0315
Tel. 270 1355
and
The Fabric Library
Stand 61
Old Pretoria Road
PO Box 912
Halfway House 1685
South Africa
Tel. 11 805 4211

Seamoor Fabrics
2 Seamoor Road
Westbourne
Bournemouth
Dorset BH4 9AJ
UK
Tel. 01202 768768

Seri Parquet
BP60
ZI du Centre
12300 Deccazeville
Belgium
Tel. 65 43 39 72

Dennis Severs' House
18 Folgate Street
London E1 6BX
UK
Tel. 0171 247 4013
Unique 18th-19th-century house tours; booking essential

Shaker Ltd
25 Harcourt Street
London W1H 1DT
UK
Tel: 0171 724 7672
and
322 Kings Road
London SW3 5DU
UK
Tel: 0171 352 3918

Sheila Coombes
(See also Brian Yates (UK) and Sanderson (US)

Sherwin Williams
101 Prospect Street
Cleveland, Ohio 44115
USA
Tel. (216) 566 3140

Siesta Cork Tile Co
Unit 21, Tate Road
Gloucester Road
Croydon CR0 2DP
UK
Tel. 0181 683 4055

Sigma Coatings Ltd
Tingewick Road
Buckingham MK18 1ED
UK
Tel: 01280 812 081

The Silk Gallery
Chelsea Harbour
Design Centre
London SW10 0XE
UK
Tel. 0171 351 1790

Simmy Ceramics
Sayer House, Oxgate Lane
London NW2 7JN
UK
Tel: 0181 208 0416

Sinclair Till
793 Wandsworth Road
London SW8 3JQ
UK
Tel. 0171 720 0031

Stark Carpet Corporation
D & D Building
979 Third Avenue,
New York, NY 10022
USA
Tel. (212) 752 9000
(See also Afia Carpets)

The Stencil Store
20/21 Heronsgate Road
Chorleywood
Herts WD3 5BN
UK
Tel. 01923 285 577

Stoddard Templeton Carpets Ltd
Glenpatrick Road
Elderslie, Johnstone
Renfrewshire PA5 9UJ
UK
Tel. 01505 577000

Stonell
Bockingfold
Ladham Road
Goudhurst, Kent TN17 1LY
UK
Tel. 01580 211 167

Stroheim & Romann
155 East 56th Street
New York, NY 10022
USA
Tel. (212) 486 1500
(See also JAB)

Stuart Interiors
Barrington Court
Illminster
Somerset TA19 0NQ
UK
Tel: 01460 240349

The Stulb Company
PO Box 597
Allentown
Pennsylvania 18105
USA

Surving Studios
RD 4 Box 449
Middletown, NY 10940
USA
Tel. (914) 355 1430

T

Thomas Dare
341 Kings Road
London SW3 5ES
UK
Tel. 0171 351 7991
and
Fonthill
D & D Building
979 Third Avenue
New York, NY 10022
USA
Tel. (212) 755 6700
and
The Silk Company
PO Box 1738
Parkland 2121
South Africa
Tel. 11 4 828073

Three Shires
2 Eastboro Court
Alliance Business Park
Attleborough Fields
Nuneaton, Warks CV11 6SD
UK
Tel. 01203 370365

Tiles of Newport & London
The Taling Centre
Unit 3
Bagleys Lane
London SW6 2BW
UK
Tel. 0171 736 9323

Tiles of Stow
Langston Priory Workshops
Station Road
Kingham, Oxon OX7 6UP
UK
Tel. 01608 658951

Timney Fowler
388 Kings Road
London SW3 5UZ
UK
Tel. 0171 352 2263
and
W H Bilbrough & Co Ltd
326 Davenport Road
Toronto, Ontario M5R 1K6
Canada
Tel. (416) 960 1611
and
Cheshire Pty Ltd
100 Auburn Road
Hawthorn 3122, Victoria
Australia
Tel. 3 9818 8799
and
Atelier Textiles
27 Crummer Road
PO Box 5017
Wellesley Street, Auckland
New Zealand
Tel. 9 378 1415
and
Kinsan Collections
56 D'Aquilar Street
Central
Hong Kong
Tel. 2 5262309
and
St Leger & Viney Pty Ltd
PO Box 55508
Northlands 2116
Gauteng
South Africa
Tel. 11 444 6722
and
Aati
PO Box 2623
Dubai
UAE
Tel. 14 377825

Tissunique Ltd
Chelsea Harbour
Design Centre
London SW10 0XE
UK
Tel: 0171 349 0096
and
Quadrille
D & D Building
979 Third Avenue
New York
NY 10022
USA
Tel. (212) 753 2995

Today Interiors
Hollis Road
Grantham
Lincs NG31 7QH
UK
Tel. 01476 574401
(Distributor of Pippa & Hale)
and
Stroheim & Romann
31-41 Thompson Avenue
Long Island City
NY 11101
USA
Tel. (718) 706 7000
and
Metropolitan Weave
275 Swan Street
Richmond 3121
Melbourne
Australia
Tel. 3 428 1800
and
Robert Malcolm Ltd
PO Box 914
348 Manchester Street
Christchurch
New Zealand
Tel. 3 366 9839
and
CETEC Ltd
29 Wellington Street
Hong Kong
Tel. 5 211325
and
Interiors Showplace
300 Orchard Road
03-14/15 The Promenade
Singapore 0923
Tel. 734 4510
and
St Leger & Viney Pty Ltd
PO Box 55508
Northlands 2116
Gauteng
South Africa
Tel. 11 444 6722
and
Al Hazeem Furniture
PO Box 5945
Sharjah
UAE
Tel. 16 330668

Tomkinsons Carpets Ltd
PO Box 11
Worcs DY10 2JR
UK
Tel. 01562 820006
and
Carpet Resource Ltd
701 Connaught Commerce Building
185 Wanchai Road
Hong Kong
Tel. 2 8382988
and
Decor Marwell KK
1-1 Minatoshima-Nakamachi
5-Chome
Chuo-Ku
Kobe
Japan
Tel. 7 8302 5221
and
Middle Curtain & Carpet Pte Ltd
237 Upper Thomson Road
Singapore 574368
Tel. 4 535155
and
Walltracts (LLC)
PO Box 25163
Dubai
Tel. 14 827200
and
Euro Diwan Furnishing Centre
26650 Safat
13127 Kuwait
Tel. 54 722835

Topps Tiles
Mortimer Road Industrial Estate
Narborough
Leicester LE9 5GA
UK
Tel: 0116 284855

Tor Coatings Group
Portobello Industrial Estate
Birtley
Chester le Street
Co. Durham DH3 2 RE
UK
Tel. 0191 410 6611

Trimite Ltd
Arundel Road
Uxbridge, Middx UB8 2SD
UK
Tel. 01895 251234

Turnell & Gigon Ltd
Chelsea Harbour
Design Centre
London SW10 0XE
UK
Tel. 0171 351 5142
(Distributor of Schumacher)

U

Ulster Carpet Mills
Castleisland Mill, Portadown
Northern Ireland BT62 1EE
UK
Tel. 01762 334433
and
Ulster Carpet Mills
North America Inc
212 Church Street
Marietta, Georgia 30060
USA
Tel: (770) 514 0707
and
Ulster Carpet Mills
Pty Ltd
PO Box 72253
Mobemni 4060
South Africa
Tel: 31 912 1310

V. V. Rouleaux
10 Symons Street
London SW3 2TJ
UK
Tel. 0171 730 3125

Victorian Wood Works
International House
London International Freight
Terminal
Temple Mills Lane
London E15 2ES
UK
Tel. 0181 534 1000

Villeroy & Boch (UK) Ltd
Building Ceramic Division
267 Merton Road
London SW18 5JS
UK
Tel. 0181 871 4028
and
Villeroy& Boch (USA) Inc.
350 Littlefield Avenue
South San Francisco
California 94080
USA
Tel. (415) 873 8453
and
2230 LBJ Freeway No. 100
Dallas, Texas 75234
USA
Tel. (972) 488 3393
and
1600 Cottontail Lane
Somerset, New Jerseay
08873
USA
Tel. (908) 302 0987
and
Villeroy & Boch AG
PO Box 1130
D-66688 Mettlach
Germany
Tel. 6864 810

Vymura
PO Box 15, Talbot Road
Hyde, Cheshire SK14 4EJ
UK
Tel. 0161 3688321

W

Walker Zanger
8901 Bradley Avenue
Sun Valley, California 91352
USA
Tel. (818) 504 0235
and
World Mosaic Ltd
1665 West 7th Avenue
Vancouver, BC V6J 1S4
Canada
Tel. (604) 736 8158

Warner Fabrics plc
Bradbourne Drive
Tilbrook, Milton Keynes
Bucks MK7 8BE
UK
Tel. 01908 366900
and
Chelsea Harbour
Design Centre
London SW10 0XE
UK
Tel. 0171 376 7578
and
Whittaker & Woods
51000 Highlands Parkways
Smyrna, Georgia 30082
USA
Tel. (770) 435 9720
and
Anne Starr Agencies
Suite 100, 611 Alexander Street
Vancouver, BC V6A 1E1
Canada
Tel. (604) 254 3336
and
Wardlaw Pty Ltd
230-232 Auburn Road
Hawthorn, Victoria 3122
Australia
Tel. 3 9819 4233
and
Robert Malcolm Ltd
PO Box 914
348 Manchester Street
Christchurch, New Zealand
Tel. 3 366 9839
and
Adair (HK) Ltd
Rm 1528-32, 15th Floor
Willy Commercial Building
28-36 Wing Kut St
Hong Kong
Tel. 5 455132
and
Centre Studio Corporation
6-21 Tamagawa-Denenchofu
2-Chome, Setagaya-Ku
Tokyo 158 Japan
Tel. 3 3442 4501

and
St Leger & Viney Pty Ltd
PO Box 55508
Northlands 2116, Gauteng
South Africa
Tel. 11 444 6722
and
Euro Diwan Furnishings
Centre
PO Box 26650, Safat 13127
Kuwait
Tel. 5 472 2835

Warwick Fabrics UK Ltd
Hackling House
Bourton Industrial Park
Bourton-on-the-Water
Gloucs GL54 2EN
UK
Tel: 01451 822383

Watts of Westminster
Chelsea Harbour
Design Centre
London SW10 0XE
UK
Tel. 0171 376 4486
and
Christopher Norman Inc
41 West 25th Street
10th Floor
New York, NY 10010
USA
Tel. (212) 647 0303
and
Hazelton House
234 Davenport Road
Toronto, Ontario M5R 1J6
Canada
Tel. (416) 925 4779
and
Boyac Decorative
Furnishings
234 Auburn Road
Melbourne, Victoria 3122
Australia
Tel. 3 9818 5300
and
Caroline Harper Interiors Ltd
402 Yu Yuet Lai Building
43-55 Wyndham Street
Central
Hong Kong
Tel. 2 5238226

Waveney Apple Growers Ltd
Common Road, Aldeby
Beccles, Suffolk NR34 0BL
UK
Tel. 01502 677345

Welbeck Tiles
Unit 3, Tan Gallop
The Welbeck Estate
Worksop, Notts S80 3LW
UK
Tel. 01909 476539

Wemyss Houlès
40 Newman Street
London W1P 3PA
UK
Tel. 0171 255 3305

Wendy Cushing Trimmings
8/9 Orient Industrial Park
Simonds Road
Leyton
London E10 7DE
UK
Tel. 0181 556 3555
and
Chelsea Harbour
Design Centre
London SW10 0XE
UK
Tel. 0171 351 5796
and
Robert Malcolm Ltd
PO Box 914
348 Manchester Street
Christchurch
New Zealand
Tel. 3 366 9839
and
Caroline Harper Interiors Ltd
402 Yu Yet Lai Building
43-45 Wyndham Street
Central
Hong Kong
Tel. 5 238226
and
Tomita Textiles Có
3-16 Kyobashi
2 Chome, Chuo-ku
Tokyo 104
Japan
Tel. 3 3275 0225
and
Aftex Fabrics Pte Ltd
9 Penang Road
Unit 06-0
Park Mall
Singapore 0923
Tel. 3 388655

Wendy Wilbraham
Mulberry & Tomlinson
11 Croxted Road
West Dulwich
London SE21 8FZ
UK
Tel. 0181 670 1022

Westbond
1 Home Farm
Luton Hoo
Beds LU1 3TD
UK
Tel. 01582 876161

Westco
Penarth Road
Cardiff CF1 7YN
UK
Tel. 01222 233926

and
Western Cork Australia
PO Box 54
Newpor
NSW 2106
Australia
Tel. 9 997 1888
and
Eden Distributors Ltd
Kaiapoi
Christchurch
New Zealand
Tel. 3 327 6642

Wicanders
Star Road
Partridge Green
West Sussex RH13 8RA
UK
Tel. 01403 710001

Winchester Tile Co
Unit C1
Pegasus Court, Ardglen Road
Whitchurch
Hants RG28 7BP
UK
Tel. 01256 896922
and
Sintra Design
PO Box 5403
Vail, Colorado 81658
USA
Tel: (970) 827 4211

Woodward Grosvenor
Green Street
Kidderminster DY10 1AT
UK
Tel. 01562 820020

Y, Z

Yorkshire Tile Co
Hill Street, Bramall Lane
Sheffield S2 4SP
UK
Tel: 0114 273 1133

Zimmer & Rohde
Chelsea Harbour
Design Centre
London SW10 0XE
UK
Tel. 0171 351 7115
and
D & D Building
979 Third Avenue
Suite 1616
New York, NY 10022
USA
Tel. (212) 758 5357
and
Primavera Interior
Accessories Ltd
160 Pears Avenue
Suite 210
Toronto, Ontario M5R 1T2
Canada
Tel. (416) 921 3334

and
Mokum Textiles Ltd
Suite 1
15-19 Boundary Street
Rushcutters Bay
Sydney
NSW 2011
Australia
Tel. 2 9380 6188
and
Mokum Textiles Ltd
11 Cheshire Street
Parnell, Auckland
New Zealand
Tel. 9 379 3041
and
CETEC Ltd
29 Wellington Street
Hong Kong
Tel. 2 5211325
and
Fujia Textile Co Ltd
7-12, 4 Chome
Sendagaya-Shibuyaku
Tokyo 151
Japan
Tel. 3 3405 1312
and
CETEC Pte Ltd
34/35 Duxton Road
Singapore 0208
Tel. 227 7118
and
Home Fabrics
PO Box 5207
Halfway House
Midrand 1685
South Africa
Tel. 11 805 0300

Zoë Barlow Passementerie
1 Ravenwood Drive
Hale Barnes
Altrincham
Cheshire WA15 OJA
UK
Tel. 0467 815010

Zoffany
Talbot House
17 Church Street
Rickmansworth
Herts WD3 1DE
UK
Tel. 01923 710680
and
63 South Audley Street
London W1Y 5BF
UK
Tel. 0171 495 2505

and
Whittaker & Woods
5100 Highlands Parkway
Smyrna
Georgia 30082
USA
Tel. (800) 395 8760

Zuber & Cie
42 Pimlico Road
London SW1W 8LP
UK
Tel. 0171 824 8265
and
D & D Building
979 Third Avenue
New York, NY 10022
USA
Tel. (212) 486 9226

Telephone numbers are supplied by the listed companies and are current at the time of publication. Neither the publisher nor the companies can be held responsible for errors or subsequent changes.

Index

Companies in *italic* appear in the Directory

A

Aalto Country Colors, 289
Abbott & Boyd, 62, 63, 64, 80, 100, 103, 109, 111, 127, 130, 134, 135, 136, 168, 175, 179, 185, 187, 189, 192, 194
Ace Royal, 281, 284, 287, 289
acorn motifs, 101
Adam, James, 23
Adam, Robert, 23
Adam style:
  damask and brocade, 76
  motif fabrics, 92
advertisements, tiled, 333
Aesthetic Movement, 43-5, 134, 136, 192
  floral fabrics, 118
  floral tiles, 320
  floral wallpapers, 232
  geometric fabrics, 166
  motif fabrics, 98
  motif tiles, 306, 307, 310
  motif wallpapers, 214
  overall pattern fabrics, 150
  overall pattern wallpapers, 251, 256
  paints, 286
  pictorial tiles, 330
Afia, 360, 368, 371, 372, 374
African style:
  carpets, 372
  geometric fabrics, 172
  pictorial fabrics, 36, 134
  pictorial wallpapers, 244, 246
Akzo Nobel, 216, 233, 259, 263
Alexander Beauchamp, 210, 216, 217, 224, 225, 227, 233, 241, 243, 245, 252, 253, 256, 273
Alhambra, Granada, Spain, 342
Altai carpet, 362
Alternative Flooring Co., 359, 361
Altfield, 187
American Empire style, carpets, 362
American Federal style, 53
  damask and brocade, 78
  geometric wallpapers, 268
  motif wallpapers, 210
  paints, 287
Amtico, 377, 379, 381, 383
Anaglypta, 233, 259
Andrew Low House, Savannah, Georgia, 156
Andrew Martin, 70, 76, 91, 102, 103, 141, 201, 217
aniline dyes, 62, 116, 280
animal motifs:
  patterned pile fabrics, 70
  pictorial tiles, 327, 328
  wallpapers, 207
animal skin patterns:
  carpets, 372
  fabrics, 143, 155
Ann Sacks, 308, 309, 312, 313, 332
Anna French, 104, 105, 122, 172, 175, 178, 180, 204, 220, 221, 223, 236, 237, 239, 249, 260, 262, 276, 277
Anne and Robert Swaffer, 113, 149
Annie Sloan, 281
Anta, 159
Antico Setificio Fiorentino, 64, 74, 163, 166, 167
antiquing lace, 175
Anya Larkin, 201, 263, 277
Apenn, 93, 101, 113, 125, 147
arabesques:
  fabrics, 73, 145
  tiles, 306
  wallpapers, 241
Art Deco, 48-9, 53, 138
  carpets, 370
  floral fabrics, 107, 120
  floral wallpapers, 234
  fringes, 192
  geometric fabrics, 168
  geometric tiles, 340, 346, 347
  geometric wallpapers, 274, 276
  motif fabrics, 100
  motif tiles, 306, 312
  motif wallpapers, 216, 217
  overall pattern fabrics, 152
  overall pattern tiles, 334
  overall pattern wallpapers, 258
  paints, 280, 281, 289
  pictorial tiles, 332
  plain tiles, 300, 301
  sheet flooring, 380
  tassels, 188
Art Nouveau, 45, 53, 338
  carpets, 370
  floral fabrics, 107, 118
  floral tiles, 316, 317, 322, 323
  floral wallpapers, 232, 234, 236
  motif fabrics, 89, 98, 100, 102
  motif wallpapers, 214, 216, 218
  overall pattern fabrics, 150, 152, 154
  overall pattern wallpapers, 251, 256, 258, 260
  paints, 286
  pictorial fabrics, 136
  pictorial tiles, 332
  plain tiles, 300, 304
  tapestry, 87
Artex, 293
Arthur H. Lee, 101
Arts and Crafts Movement, 43-5, 134
  carpets, 368
  floral fabrics, 107, 118, 119, 120
  floral tiles, 316
  floral wallpapers, 232, 234
  geometric fabrics, 166
  motif fabrics, 89, 98, 100, 104
Arts and Crafts Movement (continued):
  motif tiles, 311
  motif wallpapers, 214, 216
  overall pattern fabrics, 150, 152, 154
  overall pattern wallpapers, 251, 258, 260
  paints, 286
  pictorial fabrics, 136, 138
  pictorial tiles, 327, 330, 332
  pictorial wallpapers, 246
  tapestry, 83
Ashley, Laura, 338
Atlas Carpet Mills, 374, 375
Attica, 301, 302, 303, 307, 309, 327, 328, 329, 341, 342, 343
Attwell, Mabel, 247
Aubusson:
  carpets, 23, 30-1, 364
  tapestries, 84, 86
Audubon, John James, 239
Auro Organic Paints, 282, 296, 297
Axminster Carpets, 364, 365, 368, 370, 372, 373

B

Babylon, 326
Baer & Ingram, 90, 164, 203, 207, 209, 236, 269, 276
Ballets Russes, 370
bandwork, fabrics, 160
Banks-Pye, Roger, 106
Baronial style tapestries, 86
Baroque Revival, 37, 96, 212
Baroque style, 14
  carpets, 368
  fabrics, 90, 126
bathroom tiles, 317
batiks, 124, 126
Bauhaus, 153, 274
Baumann Fabrics, 61, 142, 171, 181
Beaumont & Fletcher, 68, 76, 109, 110, 116, 118, 144
Beauvais tapestries, 84
bee motifs, fabrics, 89
Belinda Coote Tapestries, 83, 84, 86, 149
Bennett Silks, 107, 175, 177, 179
Bennison Fabrics, 93, 96, 98, 112, 113, 115, 117, 125, 143, 147, 151, 168
Bentley & Spens, 70, 81, 135, 140, 172, 179, 182, 183
Berger, 285, 291, 293
Bernard Thorp & Co., 91, 109, 144, 177
Berti Pavimenti Legno, 352, 353
Biedermeier style, 29, 89
Bill Amberg, 381
bird motifs, damask and brocade, 74
block-printing, 142
bobbin lace, 174, 175, 176
Bodley, G. F., 207
Boen Parkett, 351, 354, 356, 357
Bonar & Flotex, 381
Borderline, 96, 115, 116, 118, 137, 151
borders:
  tiles, 317, 335
  wallpapers, 221, 271
Bosanquet Ives, 367, 369, 370, 371, 374, 375
Boulgard, 238
Bourdichon, Jean, 238
Bouwmeester, Cornelis, 328
Bradbury & Bradbury, 207, 215, 216, 233, 234, 235, 244, 245, 257
braids, 184, 185, 194-5
Brats, 281, 289
Brighton Pavilion, Brighton, England, 133, 268
Brintons, 363, 365, 366, 367, 368, 371, 372, 373, 375
brocade, 72-81
brocatelles, 72, 74, 78, 80
"broken color" paints, 290, 291
Bruce Hardwood, 357
Bruno Triplet, 141, 155
Brunschwig & Fils, 61, 71, 87, 92, 94, 101, 112, 113, 114, 118, 121, 123, 126, 128, 129, 131, 132, 133, 136, 147, 148, 149, 151, 152, 153, 165, 170, 192, 193, 194, 195, 223, 225, 226, 232, 236, 242, 244, 245, 275
Brussels carpets, 29, 366
bullion fringe, 185, 191
burlap wallpapers, 201
Busby & Busby, 92, 103, 129, 135, 149

C

Cabot Stains, 296
Calhoun Mansion, Charleston, South Carolina, 42, 43, 184
calico, 58, 60
calicoes (*indiennes*), 106, 108, 110, 128
cambric, 58, 60
"campaign" fringes, 185
Candy & Co, 307, 310, 311, 320, 330, 331, 336, 337
canvas, 58
  flooring, 378
Carocim, 305, 308, 314, 333, 335, 336, 339, 343, 345, 346, 347
carpets, 17, 362-75
Carré, 305
Carter & Co., 312, 314, 322, 332, 333
casein paint *see* milk paint
Cath Kidston, 235, 247, 260
Cedar Grove, 37
ceilings, 23
  papers for, 245
  tented, 59
Celia Birtwell, 101, 127, 139, 181
Celtic motifs, wallpapers, 272
Ceramiche Eurotiles, 303, 307, 310, 311, 312, 318, 319, 344, 347
Charleston, South Carolina, 72

Château de Compiègne, France, 23
Château de Morsan, France, 20, 106
Chatsworth, 366, 372, 374, 375
checks:
  fabrics, 156, 158, 160, 164
  wallpapers, 264, 265
Chelsea Textiles, 108, 111
chemical-based wood stains, 295, 296
chenille, 66, 67, 68, 70
chevrons:
  fabrics, 158, 166, 168
  wooden floors, 351
chiaroscuro wallpapers, 240, 242, 252
Chilperic I, King of the Franks, 95
chinoiserie, 23
  damasks, 76
  floral fabrics, 106, 107, 110
  floral wallpapers, 224, 226, 236
  geometric fabrics, 162
  geometric wallpapers, 268
  motif fabrics, 90
  motif wallpapers, 23, 206
  pictorial fabrics, 128, 130, 132, 134, 136
  pictorial wallpapers, 239, 240, 243, 244, 246
  tapestries, 84
chintzes:
  faded, 117
  floral, 107, 110, 112, 120, 122
  motifs, 102
  pictorial, 138
Chippendale, Thomas, 128, 239
Christian symbols, tiles, 310
Church of England, 207
Ciel Decor, 218, 225, 237, 252
Claremont, 188, 189, 190, 191, 194, 195
Claremont Fabrics, 74, 93, 123, 126, 141, 176, 177
Classical Revival:
  ceiling papers, 245
  motif fabrics, 94, 96
  pictorial wallpapers, 244
  tapestry, 83
Classical style, 14
  carpets, 365
  motif fabrics, 90, 92
  motif tiles, 308
  motif wallpapers, 206, 207, 208, 210, 212, 214
  Palladianism, 19
  pictorial fabrics, 140
  sheet flooring, 382
  see also Neoclassical style
coal tar dyes, 116
coats-of-arms, tiles, 307
coir matting, 358, 359, 360
Cole & Son, 204, 208, 209, 211, 212, 213, 215, 217, 225, 227, 229, 230, 232, 235, 239, 246, 254, 255, 256, 257, 258, 265, 268, 269, 271, 273, 274, 282, 283, 284
Colefax, Sybil, 122
Colefax and Fowler, 92, 111, 116, 136,
Colefax and Fowler (continued):
  163, 211, 223, 227, 228, 230, 231, 232, 234, 246, 251, 254, 255, 266, 271, 273, 275
Collier, Susan, 169
Colonial style, 53
Coloroll, 202, 204, 216, 218, 219, 221, 233, 235, 237, 249, 255, 261, 265, 268, 272, 274, 275, 277
Colorman Paints, 283, 285
colors:
  carpets, 363
  "color and weave," 173
  color theory, 284
  plain fabrics, 62
  paints, 281-93
Comoglio, 88
Constructivism:
  geometric wallpapers, 264, 274
  motif wallpapers, 206, 216
Le Corbusier, 49, 276
corduroy, 66
cork tiles, 351
corner motifs, tiles, 307, 308, 334, 336
Corres Mexican Tiles, 304, 313, 315, 329, 337, 338
cotton duck, 59
cottons:
  damask and brocade, 72, 80
  plain-weave, 59
Cowson, 258
Cowtan, 288
Craig & Rose, 292, 293
Crane, Walter, 118, 247
crewelwork, 109, 139
Crown, 284, 285, 288, 289
Crowson, 75, 79, 121, 170, 176, 181, 203, 205, 221, 236, 249, 261, 263, 272, 273, 275
Crucial Trading, 359, 360, 361
Cubism, 49, 153
  geometric fabrics, 156, 170
  geometric wallpapers, 264, 274
  motif wallpapers, 206, 216, 218
Cuprinol, 297
cushion vinyl flooring, 377
Cy-Près, 283
cyphers, motif fabrics, 89

D

Dacrylate, 295, 297
dado rails, 23
Dalsouple, 377, 382, 383
Daltile, 305, 339
damask, 72-81
David Bonk, 201
Day, L. F., 152
Day, Lucienne, 276
da Vinci, Leonardo, 163
De Gournay, 202, 241, 243
De Le Cuona Designs, 59, 60, 61
de Morgan, William, 300, 316, 320, 327, 330
de Wolfe, Elsie, 288
Dearle, J.H., 260
Dedar, 167
deep-pile carpets, 363
Delaunay, Sonia, 168, 169
delftware tiles, 306, 307, 308, 327, 328, 334, 336
Della Robbia earthenware, 134
Denon, Baron, 94
Deralam, 377, 382
The Design Archives, 80, 92, 96, 128, 130, 131, 162, 207, 209, 210, 240, 273
Designers Guild, 64, 65, 81, 105, 173, 183, 220, 236
Deutscher Werkbund, 49, 216, 234, 258
diaper patterns:
  carpets, 363
  damask, 73
  fabrics, 157, 158, 160, 166
  wallpapers, 264, 265, 266
distressed finishes, paints, 291, 292
DLW, 377, 378, 379
"dobby" looms, 78
documentary designs, floral fabrics, 113
Domco, 381
Domus Tiles, 304
Donghia, 63, 70, 76, 92, 101, 103, 126, 141, 152, 168, 169, 170, 181, 199, 201, 260
Dovedale, 77, 80
Dralon, 70
Dresser, Christopher, 150, 207, 256, 272, 368
Ducerceau, P. A., 108
Dufour, Joseph, 238
Dufy, Raoul, 168
Dupont, Pierre, 364
Duppa, James, 253
Dürer, Albrecht, 326
dust-pressed tiles, 302, 344
dyes:
  aniline, 62, 116, 280
  vegetable, 64

E

Eastlake, Charles, 43, 180, 232
egg tempera, 282
Egyptian style, 46
  fabrics, 94, 100
  tiles, 318
  wallpapers, 206, 210, 217, 246
Elite Tiles, 304
Elizabeth I, Queen of England, 14
Elizabeth Eaton, 90, 173, 178, 179, 182, 208, 224, 226, 227, 229, 231, 233
Elizabethan Revival, fabrics, 168
Elon, 301, 303, 304, 305, 314, 317, 324, 335, 337, 342, 343
embossed wallpapers, 204
embroidery:
  crewelwork, 109, 139
  flame stitch, 151
Empire style *see also* American Empire style and French Empire style
emulsion paints, 288
encaustic tiles, 344
English delft tiles, 327
Etruscan style:
  fabrics, 94, 162
  wallpapers, 210
Eugénie, Empress, 93
Exposition des Arts Décoratifs, Paris, France (1925), 49, 289
Expressionism, 49

F

fabric-effect wallpapers, 204, 226, 275
fabrics:
  braids and trimmings, 184-95
  damask and brocade, 72-81
  floral, 106-23
  geometric patterns, 156-73
  lace and sheers, 174-83
  motifs, 88-105
  overall patterns, 142-55
  patterned pile, 66-71
  pictorial, 124-41
  plain, 58-65
  tapestry, 82-7
Fardis, 204, 259
Farrow & Ball, 285, 286, 287
Fauvism, 49
faux stone finishes, paints, 291, 293
Federal style:
  damask and brocade, 78
  motif fabrics, 92, 94
Fendi, 332
Festival of Britain, London, England (1951), 372
fêtes galantes, 130
Fine Decor, 154, 202, 204, 205, 221, 237, 261, 276, 277
Finnaren & Haley, 281, 287
Fired Earth, 84, 85, 285, 286, 302, 303, 307, 308, 309, 312, 313, 315, 317, 318, 319, 320, 322, 327, 328, 329, 332, 336, 337, 339, 344, 359, 361
fireplaces, tiles, 320, 334, 346
Firifiss, 153, 169, 177
flame stitch, 151
fleur-de-lis:
  fabrics, 89
  tiles, 307
  wallpapers, 207
flocked wallpapers, 204, 224
floorboards, 23, 37-40, 350, 351, 352, 354, 356
  securing, 353
floorcloths, 376, 378, 380
flooring:
  carpets, 362-75
  matting, 358-61

flooring (continued):
sheet flooring, 376-83
wooden, 350-7
floral motifs:
carpets, 363, 370
fabrics, 72, 73, 106-23, 175
tiles, 316-25
wallpapers, 222-37
Florida Tile Co., 301, 304, 308, 325
Fontaine, Pierre, 94
Formica, 377, 379, 380, 381, 382, 383
Fowler, John, 122, 286
French Empire style, 23, 28-9
damask and brocade, 78
motif fabrics, 88, 89, 94
wallpapers, 210, 268
fringes, 184, 190-3
bullion fringe, 185, 191
"campaign" fringes, 185
Froyle Tiles, 303
fruit motifs, fabrics, 89
Furber, Robert, 114
fustian, 110
Futurism, 49

G

Gainsborough Silk Weaving, 73, 74, 81
Galliards, 96, 120
galloons, 184, 189, 194
Garin, 79, 87, 97, 105, 111, 114, 120, 122, 123, 143, 169, 181, 183
Garner, Thomas, 207
Garth Woodside Mansion, Hannibal, Missouri, 43
gaufrage velvet, 66, 67, 68, 70
Geffrye Museum, London, England, 49
Genoa velvet, 66, 67, 68, 70
geometric patterns:
carpets, 363, 370
fabrics, 156-73
tiles, 301, 340-7
wallpapers, 264-77
George IV, King of England, 133, 165
George Spencer Decorations, 64, 91, 96, 114, 116, 122, 128, 130, 146, 160, 194
Ghirlandaio, Domenico, 74
Glant, 71
gilt creams, 290, 291, 292
gingham, 157, 164, 166, 170
Gladding McBean, 312
glazed tiles, 301, 302, 338
Glidden, 282, 284, 285, 286, 287, 288, 289, 291, 293, 295, 296, 297
Gobelins tapestries, 84
Godwin, E. W., 150, 232, 256
Gollut, Christophe, 67
Gothic Revival, 37, 41
geometric fabrics, 164
geometric tiles, 344
geometric wallpapers, 268, 272
motif fabrics, 89, 96, 98
Gothic Revival (continued):
motif tiles, 306, 310
motif wallpapers, 206, 207, 212, 213, 214
pictorial fabrics, 134, 136
pictorial wallpapers, 244
tapestry, 83
Gothic style, 13, 14
damask and brocade, 80
motif fabrics, 89
Gothick style, 19, 23
fabrics, 76, 92, 146, 160
wallpapers, 266
Gozzoli, Benozzo, 74
G. P. & J. Baker, 81, 85, 87, 114, 118, 123, 133, 141, 155, 157, 168, 200, 205, 210, 211, 214, 224, 225, 235, 249, 253, 268, 271
Grace, J. G., 268
Graham & Brown, 203, 216, 217, 232, 234, 235, 237, 257, 259, 262, 263, 274
Grand Illusions, 286, 287
granite effects:
sheet flooring, 382
tiles, 335
grass cloth, 199, 201
grass matting, 358
Great Exhibition, London, England (1851), 116, 306, 368
Greek Revival, 29, 37, 162
Greenaway, Kate, 247
Greene & Greene, 368
grisaille wallpapers, 242, 252
Grueby, William H., 330
G. S. Fabrics, 143
guilloche:
fabrics, 146, 156, 158
wallpapers, 266
Guy Evans, 78, 94, 114, 130, 131, 132, 133, 138, 154

H

H. & R. Johnson, 305, 319, 323, 324, 333, 335, 339, 347
Habitat, 288, 289
Hamilton Weston, 115, 208, 209, 210, 211, 213, 214, 225, 226, 228, 229, 231, 239, 241, 252, 254, 255, 266, 267, 268, 270, 271, 273
hand-blocked wallpapers, 229
hardwood effects, wallpapers, 202, 250
Hardwood Flooring People, 355
hardwoods:
finishes, 294
paneling, 14
Harlequin, 104, 123, 143, 154, 172, 173, 199, 200, 203, 217, 220, 237, 259, 260, 262, 263, 265, 272, 275, 276
Harris, Moses, 284
Hay, D. R., 272
Henderson Woven Designs, 157, 173
Henry IV, King of France, 364
Henry Newbery & Co., 185, 186, 187, 188, 189, 190, 191, 192, 193
Hepplewhite, George, 26
heraldic style, 13, 14
fabrics, 90, 91
tiles, 307, 310
wallpapers, 206, 207, 208
Herculaneum, 23, 132, 208
herringbone patterns:
fabrics, 58, 59, 168
wooden floors, 351
Heywood, Higginbottom & Smith, 257
Hill & Knowles, 67, 100, 139, 148, 149, 157, 158, 170, 177, 178, 180, 182, 183
Historic Floors of Oshkosh, 351, 352, 353, 354, 355, 356, 357
Hodsoll McKenzie, 61, 67, 68, 69, 77, 92, 96, 99, 108, 110, 111, 113, 115, 117, 138, 148, 149, 165, 166, 212, 230, 231, 251, 257, 265, 268
Holland, 60
Hoover Building, Perivale, London, England, 346
horsehair fabrics, 60
hot colors, paints, 289
Hubbard, Elbert, 256
Hugh Mackay, 364, 365, 366, 372, 373
Huguenots, 74, 184
Huquier, J. G., 146

I

Ian Mankin, 59, 61, 157, 164, 168
Ian Sanderson, 60, 61, 63, 68, 70, 74, 77, 87, 133, 161, 162, 163, 170, 172, 176
ikats, 170
Imports Direct, 305, 311, 345
Indian style:
fabrics, 128, 130, 134, 136, 162
wallpapers, 244
indiennes (calicoes), 106, 108, 110, 128
Ingrain carpets, 366
Interdesign, 122, 176, 178, 179, 180, 183
International Modernism, 153
Iribe, Paul, 100
Islamic motifs, tiles, 308, 316, 318, 320, 340
The Isle Mill, 93, 157, 161, 164, 167, 169, 171
Ivo Prints, 140
Iznik tiles, 318, 319, 334

J

Jab, 59, 60, 61, 62, 63, 65, 71, 83, 84, 85, 100, 101, 102, 105, 110, 112, 120, 141, 152, 162, 170, 171, 172, 175, 180
Jack Lenor Larsen, 71, 182, 183
Jackson, John Baptist, 226, 238
Jacobean Revival:
floral fabrics, 107
geometric fabrics, 168
Jacobean Revival (continued):
motif fabrics, 100
overall pattern fabrics, 152
pictorial fabrics, 138, 139
pictorial wallpapers, 246
tapestry, 83, 86
Jacquard looms, 78, 362, 366
Jane Churchill, 117, 135, 139, 141, 199, 204, 211, 234, 239, 247, 249, 255, 258, 259, 261, 262, 273, 274, 276, 277, 288, 289
Jane Knapp, 379
japonaiserie:
fabrics, 107, 136
wallpapers, 244
Jason D'Souza, 90, 107, 109, 111, 144, 158
Jaymart, 380, 383
Jean Louis Seigner, 236, 237, 248, 249, 260, 261, 262, 277
Jencks, Charles, 52, 334
Jenrette, Richard, 350, 362
jeweled strapwork *see* strapwork patterns
Jim Thompson, 117, 119, 136, 137, 155, 165, 172
Joanna Wood, 239, 256, 271
John Boyd Textiles, 60, 166, 167, 171
John Oliver, 288, 289
John Wilman, 73, 77, 100, 104, 125, 131, 141, 159, 160, 161, 258, 265, 270, 272
Jones, Owen, 37
carpets, 368
fabrics, 146, 166
wallpapers, 212, 214, 230, 256, 270, 272
Jones, Robert, 268
Josephine, Empress of France, 95
Julie Arnall, 307, 308, 309
Jumel Mansion, New York, 28-9, 223
Junckers, 356, 357
jute matting, 358, 359, 360
J. W. Bollom, 205, 282, 286, 289

K

K and K Designs, 202, 220, 254, 262, 269
Kahrs, 356
Karndean, 378, 379, 380
Kenneth Clark Ceramics, 301, 304, 312, 313, 314, 315, 322, 323, 325, 333, 337, 338, 341, 344, 345, 346
Kentucky Wood Floors, 354, 355
Kenzo, 332
Kidderminster carpets, 364, 366
Kievel Stone, 302
Klee, Paul, 153
Knowles & Christou, 102, 154, 155, 173, 176

L

La Heredia, Malaga, Spain, 317
lace, 174-83
Lafon, Françoise, 46

Lancaster, Nancy, 286
landscape tiles, 327
LASSCO, 351, 356, 357
latticework:
fabrics, 162, 166
wallpapers, 264, 265
wooden floors, 351
LBC, 356
Le Moyne de Morgues, Jacques, 106
Lee Jofa, 89, 101, 109, 111, 115, 116, 118, 119, 121, 127, 139, 153, 169
Leeds Castle, Kent, England, 12, 13
Leighton, Lord, 300
Leighton House, London, England, 300
Lelièvre, 68, 73, 75, 81, 94, 95, 107, 119, 122
Lennox Money, 112, 113, 148, 150
leno, 174, 176
Liberon Waxes, 291, 292
Liberty, 54, 73, 87, 89, 94, 101, 103, 107, 109, 119, 120, 126, 135, 138, 143, 151, 153, 169
Life Enhancing Tile Co., 308, 345
limestone tiles, 301
limewash, 12, 14, 280, 282, 283, 284, 288
liming pastes, 290, 292
Lincrusta, 216, 233, 259
linen, damask and brocade, 72, 74, 76, 80
linoleum, 376, 377, 379, 380
Liz Induni, 283
looms:
"dobby", 78
Jacquard, 78, 362, 366
power looms, 116
Louis, King of France:
XI, 89, 238
XIV, 184, 195
XV, 364
XVI, 364
Louis XIV-style fabrics, 98
Louis de Poortere, 363, 372, 375
Lowe, J. & J. G., 307, 320
Lurçat, Jean, 86
lyre motifs, wallpapers, 207

M

Mackintosh, Charles Rennie, 370
madras fabrics, 156, 164, 166, 170
Malabar, 205, 215, 270
Malibu Tiles, 312
Manchester velvet, 66, 68
Mannington Carpets, 373, 374, 375
Manuel Canovas, 105, 121, 123, 125, 129, 154, 168, 215, 233, 240, 241
marble effects:
sheet flooring, 382
tiles, 334, 336
Marble Flooring Specialists, 302, 305
marble floors, 14, 37, 303
Marie Antoinette, Queen of France, 93, 112
marine themes, tiles, 327
Marley, 379, 380, 381
marquetry floors, 14, 350, 351, 356, 357
Marston & Langinger, 283
Marthe Armitage, 247, 248, 259, 260
Marvic Textiles, 61, 64, 77, 86, 87, 93, 100, 110, 119, 125, 131, 132, 134, 139, 164, 165, 171
Mary, Queen of Scots, 14, 108
Mary Fox Linton, 78, 79, 94, 97, 165, 166
matelassé, 81
Matisse, Henri, 236, 246
matting, 358-61
Maugham, Syrie, 288
Mauny, 205, 234, 235, 246, 247, 274, 275
Maw, George, 342
Maw and Co., 342, 346
Maya Romanoff, 199, 200, 201, 260, 261, 263, 275
Medieval style, 13, 14
carpets, 364
floral fabrics, 107
geometric fabrics, 160
motif fabrics, 89, 90
motif tiles, 307, 308, 310
overall pattern fabrics, 144
overall pattern tiles, 336
pictorial tiles, 326
tapestry, 83, 84
wallpapers, 251
Mercer, Henry Chapman, 330
metal sheet flooring, 377, 380
metallic finishes, wallpapers, 262
metallic paints, 290, 291, 292
Metropolitan Tile Co., 327, 338, 341
Mexican tiles, 337
Michael Szell, 122, 173
Mickey Mouse™, 247, 248
microporous woodstains, 297
Middle Ages *see* Medieval style
milk paint, 280, 282, 284
Miller, Philip, 146
Milner, Janet, 125
Minimalism, 53
Minton, Herbert, 300, 330, 344
Minton China Works, 330
Minton Company, 306
Minton Hollins, 310, 311, 313, 317, 318, 321, 322, 330, 332, 339
Miró, Jean, 246
Modernism, 49, 53, 138, 222
all white schemes, 288
geometric fabrics, 170
plain wallpapers, 198, 200, 202
sheet flooring, 380
tassels, 188
moirés, 58, 65
Monet, Claude, 236
Monkwell, 60, 62, 84, 91, 95, 105, 126, 127, 130, 131, 137, 145, 153, 170, 221
Monmouth House, Natchez, Mississippi, 38
monograms, 12, 13
Montagu, Lady Mary Wortley, 128
Monterey, 375
Montgomery, 113, 123, 155
Moore, Thomas, 364
Moorish motifs, fabrics, 96
moquette, 66, 68
"moresque" fabrics, 145
Morris, William, 43, 64
carpets, 368
fabrics, 104, 118, 119, 120, 122
tiles, 311, 330
wallpapers, 214, 232, 256, 260
Morris and Company, 368
Mortlake tapestries, 84
mosaic tiles, 341, 342
Mosquito, 346, 347
motifs:
carpets, 363
fabrics, 88-105
tiles, 306-15
wallpapers, 206-21
mottled tiles, 334, 338
Mucha, Alphonse, 332
Mulberry, 69, 127, 137
multicolored paints, 290
Muradiye, Edirne, 334
mural wallpapers, 248
muslin, 174, 175, 176, 178, 180, 182

N

nailheads, 158, 266
Napoleon I, Emperor of France, 29, 39, 88, 89, 94, 95, 132, 165, 192, 206, 210, 217
Napoleonic-style fabrics, 80, 95, 164
Natalie Woolf, 378, 382, 383
Nathaniel Russell House, South Carolina, 58
Natural Flooring Direct, 359
Natural Wood Floor Co., 356
needle lace, 174, 176
Neoclassical style, 23-6, 29
carpets, 362
damask and brocade, 76
furniture, 32
geometric fabrics, 161, 164
geometric wallpapers, 265
motif fabrics, 89, 92, 93
motif tiles, 306, 307, 312
motif wallpapers, 216, 217
overall pattern fabrics, 146, 148
overall pattern wallpapers, 254
pictorial fabrics, 130, 132, 140
neutral fabrics, 60-1
New Age motif tiles, 314
Nice Irma's, 65, 109, 175, 177, 186, 190, 195
Niculoso, Francisco, 328
Nieuhof, J., 90
Nina Campbell, 115, 131, 134, 143, 146, 164, 169, 200, 219, 243, 251, 254, 255, 272, 273
Nobilis-Fontan, 83, 157, 189, 194, 202, 226, 230, 240, 246, 247, 263, 277
noiles, 58, 60
Northwood Designs, 79, 81, 97, 115, 152, 168, 199, 204
Nottingham lace, 174, 178
nursery motifs, wallpapers, 239, 247, 248
Nutshell Natural Paints, 284
nylon carpets, 372

O

oak floors, 351, 354
oak-leaf motifs, fabrics, 89, 101
Oberkampf brothers, 125
oil-based wood stains, 295, 296
oil paints, 282, 284
The Old Fashioned Milk Paint Co., 283, 284, 285
Old Merchant's House, New York, 287
Old Village Paints, 286
Old World Weavers, 67, 68, 69, 71, 85, 86, 107, 111, 118, 129, 163, 166, 167, 178
Olicana, 62, 65
Les Olivades, 90
Ollerton Hall, 363, 372, 373, 374
Op Art, 54, 248
Organic Modernism, 102
organza, 174, 180, 182
Oriental carpets, 17, 368
Original Style, 302, 303, 307, 310, 311, 312, 315, 321, 322, 323, 325, 327, 328, 330, 331, 332, 337, 338, 344, 345, 347
Ornamenta, 200, 201, 202, 203, 204, 205, 209, 223, 266
Osborne & Little, 62, 63, 66, 71, 78, 103, 104, 105, 121, 123, 125, 140, 199, 203, 210, 211, 217, 218, 219, 220, 221, 228, 246, 247, 248, 251, 256, 258, 261, 265, 266, 267, 269, 270, 272, 274, 275, 276, 277
Ottilie Stevenson, 171, 277
overall patterns:
fabrics, 142-55
tiles, 334-9
wallpapers, 250-63

P

Packard and Ord, 332
paint-effect wallpapers, 199
Paint Library, 282, 283, 285, 286, 287, 288, 292, 293
Paint Magic, 284, 285, 289, 296
painted floors, 350, 352, 354
paints, 278-93
specialist, 290-3
paisley patterns, 46, 96, 143, 150
Palladianism, 19, 23, 76, 92
Palladio, Andrea, 19
Palmer, Thomas, 233
paneling, wood, 14
panels, tiled, 317, 318, 322, 328

panoramic wallpapers, 39, 240, 242, 243
papiers marbres, 226
Parham House, Sussex, England 14, 15, 82
Parkertex Fabrics, 175
parquet floors, 14, 350, 351, 352, 354, 356
passements, 184
Patrick, 375
Pembroke, Earl of, 364
Percheron, 63, 64, 67, 76, 79, 84, 89, 93, 95, 112, 120, 129, 135, 140, 145, 147, 170, 171, 185, 190, 191, 192
Percier, Charles, 94
Persian carpets, 371
Perstorp, 352, 353, 357
petit point, 124
Phyfe, Duncan, 32
pictorial motifs:
  fabrics, 124-41
  tiles, 326-33
  wallpapers, 238-49
Picturesque fabrics, 92
Pierre Frey, 71, 95, 104
pigments, paints, 280, 282
pile fabrics, 59, 66-71
Pillement, Jean, 128
pine floors, 352
Pinheiro, Rafael Bordallo, 320
Pippa & Hale, 59, 65, 123, 167, 220, 277
Pittsburgh Paints, 283, 285, 287
plaids:
  fabrics, 156, 157, 159, 164, 166, 168, 172
  tiles, 341
  wallpapers, 276
plain fabrics, 58-65
plain tiles, 300-5
plain wallpapers, 198-205
plant motifs, wallpapers, 207, 208, 218, 250-63
  see also floral motifs
plush, 66, 68
point-paper, carpet design, 369
Pointillist-style, fabrics, 154
Poiret, Paul, 168
Pollock, Jackson, 372
"pombaline" tiles, 340
Pompeii, Italy, 23, 132, 208, 214
Pompeiian-style fabrics, 98
Poole Pottery, 322
Pop Art, 54
  fabrics, 102
  tiles, 334, 340, 346
  wallpapers, 206, 248
poplin, 58
Post-Modernism, 52
  tiles, 334
  wallpapers, 200
Potter, Beatrix, 247, 248
powder-ground tiles, 327
powdered ornament:
  fabrics, 158, 164, 166
  wallpapers, 264, 266, 268
power looms, 116
Pratt & Lambert, 285, 286
Prestige Enterprise, 354
Prestwould Plantation, Clarksville, Virginia, 253
print rooms, 200, 239
printing:
  batik, 126
  block-printing, 142
  floral fabrics, 115
  pictorial fabrics, 132
  tiles, 328, 334
Prosser, Richard, 300, 302, 344
Protim Solignum, 295, 296
Puebla tiles, 337
Pugin, A. W. N.:
  fabrics, 96, 146, 190
  tiles, 306, 310, 344
  wallpapers, 207, 212, 213, 214, 230
PVC tiles, 382

Q

quarry tiles, 300, 301

R

raised relief designs, wallpapers, 259
Rambouillet Palace, France, 318
Ramm, Son & Crocker, 116, 117, 148, 149, 217, 224, 230, 231, 233, 234, 254, 256, 267, 270
Raphael, 246
RBI International, 67, 69, 108
red, sealing-wax red tiles, 319
Red House, Kent, England, 311
"Regency stripes," fabrics, 165
Regency style, 29
  fabrics, 78, 89, 94
  wallpapers, 210, 268
relief-molded tiles, 320
Renaissance Revival, 37
  fabrics, 96, 134
  wallpapers, 212
Renaissance style:
  damask and brocade, 74
  floral fabrics, 108
  floral wallpapers, 236
  geometric fabrics, 158, 160
  motif fabrics, 88, 89, 90, 92
  motif wallpapers, 206, 207
  overall pattern fabrics, 144
  overall pattern wallpapers, 252
  patterned pile fabrics, 68
  pictorial fabrics, 126
  tapestry, 83
  trimmings, 186
rep, 58
Reptile, 314, 329, 332, 333
resin laminate floorings, 376, 377
Réveillon, Jean-Baptiste, 226, 238
ribbed fabrics, 58
ribbons, 184, 185, 189, 194-5
Rococo Revival, 37
Rococo style, 18, 19, 20, 23, 24-5
  damask and brocade, 76
  floral fabrics, 110, 116
  geometric fabrics, 160, 161
  geometric wallpapers, 266
  motif fabrics, 92, 98
  motif wallpapers, 216
  overall pattern fabrics, 146
  pictorial fabrics, 128, 130
  pictorial tiles, 328
  pictorial wallpapers, 240
Roman shades, 157
Roman Empire, mosaics, 342
Roman style:
  fabrics, 89, 92, 94
  wallpapers, 210
  see also Classical style and Neoclassical style
Romanesque style, 13, 272
Ronseal, 296
Rookwood Pottery, 322
Rosalie, Natchez, Mississippi, 72
Rose of Jericho, 283
rose motifs, fabrics, 107
Rosequist, Ivy, 288
rosettes, trimmings, 187
rubber flooring, 376, 377, 380, 383
rush matting, 12, 358, 360, 361
"rustic" tiles, 300, 304
Rustins, 297
Ryalux, 368
Rye Tiles, 333

S

Sadler and Green, 328, 336
Sahco Hesslein, 63, 69, 70, 75, 102, 103, 154, 162, 163, 167, 169, 173, 178, 179, 181, 182, 183
St Mary's, Sussex, England, 14
saints, pictorial tiles, 327
Saloni Ceramica, 342, 343
San Marco, Venice, Italy, 342
Sandberg, 276
Sanderson, 118, 166, 178, 181, 230, 231, 235, 241, 244, 251, 271, 281, 283, 284, 286, 289
sanitary papers, 257
Santa Fe Railroad, 333
"satin" papers, 230
Savonnerie carpets, 23, 32, 364
Scalamandré 62, 67, 73, 74, 75, 76, 80, 89, 93, 95, 98, 99, 110, 114, 119, 133, 134, 138, 139, 156, 160, 163, 165, 180, 185, 188, 190, 192, 193, 194, 195, 226, 229, 239, 240, 242, 246, 253
Schumacher, 107, 113, 114, 130, 132, 134, 223, 227, 228, 229, 240, 241, 243, 245, 248, 252, 253, 270, 272
Scotch carpets, 366
Scott, Gilbert, the Younger, 207
screen-printing, tiles, 346
sealing-wax red tiles, 319
Seamoor Fabrics, 59, 159
Second Empire style, 37
seersuckers, 58
Séguy, E. A., 118, 120
"self-patterned" fabrics, 58, 59, 67
semi-sheer fabrics, 182
Seri Parquet, 357
Severs, Dennis, 282
shades, Roman, 157
Shaker, 284
Shaker paints, 281
Shakespeare, William, 326
sheers, 174-83
  colored, 181
  semi-sheers, 182
sheet flooring, 376-83
Sheila Coombes, 205, 225, 259
shellac, 294
Sheraton, Thomas, 26
Sherwin Williams, 287, 288, 289
Siesta Cork Tiles, 351
Sigma Coatings, 281
silk-effect wallpapers, 275
The Silk Gallery, 68, 69, 74, 77, 90, 91, 94, 146, 165
silks:
  damask and brocade, 72, 74, 76, 78
  plain-weave, 59
  slub silks, 58, 60
  Tussah silk, 60
Silver Studio, 256
Simmy Ceramics, 328, 333
Sinclair Till, 352, 359, 361, 378
sisal matting, 19, 358, 359, 360
Sjöberg, Lars, 327
Skipworth, Lady Jean, 253
slub silks, 58, 60
Smith, W.H., 333
Soane, Sir John, 362
softwood paneling, 14
South America, geometric fabrics, 172
spirit-based wood stains, 296
stains, wood, 294, 295
stair runners, 40
Stark, 364, 365, 366, 367, 368, 369, 370, 371
The Stencil Store, 293
stenciling:
  stencil-effect wallpapers, 221, 258
  wooden floors, 350, 352, 354
Stewart, Annie and Lachlan, 341
Stoddard Templeton, 363, 369, 370, 373
Stölzl, Gunta, 153
stone effects:
  paints, 291, 292, 293
  sheet flooring, 377, 382
  tiles, 335
  wallpapers, 202, 251, 276
stone floors, 301, 303
Stonell, 301, 302, 303
stoves, tiled, 306, 316, 327

strapwork patterns:
fabrics, 158, 160, 164, 166, 168
wallpapers, 264, 265, 266, 268
striped fabrics, 157, 160, 162, 164, 165
damask, 73
ticking, 157, 162, 168
velvets, 67
striped wallpapers, 264, 265, 266, 268, 274
Stroheim & Romann, 86, 99, 108
Stuart Interiors, 74, 75, 84, 89, 90, 108, 145
The Stulb Company, 286, 287
sunflower motif tiles, 310, 320
Surving Studios, 332, 339
swan motifs, fabrics, 89, 95
Swiss lace, 174
symbolism, motif tiles, 306
Sympson, Samuel, 89
synthetic fibers, carpets, 372, 374

T

"tabby" weave, 58
taffeta, 58
tapestry, 82-7
carpets, 364
pictorial fabrics, 124, 126, 138
tassels, 184, 185, 186-9
tempera, 282
Temple Newsam, Leeds, England, 250
tented ceilings, 59
textured paints, 290, 291, 292
Thomas Dare, 158, 176
Three Shires, 360, 361
ticking, 157, 162, 168
tiebacks, 186, 189, 194
tiles, 298-347
cork, 351
floral, 316-25
geometric, 340-7
motif, 306-15
overall patterns, 334-9
pictorial, 326-33
plain, 300-5
Tiles of Newport & London, 317, 322, 330, 343, 347
Tiles of Stow, 314, 324, 332, 333, 336, 341, 345, 347
Timney Fowler, 93, 104, 128, 131, 133, 137, 140, 146, 162, 240
tin-glazed tiles, 307, 326, 328, 337, 340, 344
Tissunique, 91, 93, 102, 112, 116, 121, 128, 132, 145, 150, 151, 162, 170
Today Interiors, 65, 79, 135, 243
toiles de Jouy:
fabrics, 124, 125, 131, 140
wallpapers, 223
Tomkinsons Carpets, 363, 367, 370, 373
tongue and groove floorboards, 354
Topps Tiles, 329
Tor Coatings, 292
Toulouze, Guillaume, 144
transfer-printing, tiles, 328
"Tree of Life," 13, 139
trelliswork:
fabrics, 161, 166
tiles, 340
wallpapers, 264, 265
Trimite, 291, 293
trimmings, 184-95
trompe l'oeil:
ceiling papers, 245
tiles, 341, 342
wallpapers, 239, 242, 244, 251
wooden floors, 351, 352
tube-lining, tiles, 322, 323
Tudor Revival:
fabrics, 100, 152
wallpapers, 216, 246
tufted carpets, 374, 375
tulle, 175
turkeywork carpets, 19, 362, 364
Turnell & Gigon, 133
Tutankhamun, Pharaoh, 370
tweeds, 58

U

Ulster Carpets, 363
upholstery, introduction of, 17
Utrecht velvet, 66, 68

Vallet, Pierre, 108
varnishes, 295
vegetable dyes, 64
velour, 59, 66, 68, 70
velvets, 59, 66, 67
verdure tapestries, 84, 86
Versailles, France, 112
Victoria, Queen of England, 166
Victoria & Albert Museum, London, England, 286
Victorian Wood Works, 351, 353, 354, 355
Villeroy & Boch, 314, 315, 324, 325, 333, 341
vinyl:
flooring, 376, 377, 380, 382
wallcoverings, 237
Virgin Mary, 107
voiles, 174, 175, 182
Voysey, C. F. A., 256, 320, 368
V. V. Rouleaux, 185, 186, 187, 189, 191, 193, 194, 195
Vymura, 249

wainscoting, 14
Walker Zanger, 309, 310, 311, 315, 322, 335, 336, 337, 338, 339
Wallis, Gilbert & Partners, 346
wallpapers, 40, 196-277
ceiling papers, 245
floral, 222-37
geometric, 264-77
motifs, 206-21
overall patterns, 250-63
pictorial, 238-49
plain, 198-205
Walton, Frederick, 233, 379
Warner Fabrics, 77, 78, 81, 94, 99, 110, 115, 117, 121, 137, 138, 147, 151, 153, 164, 244, 254
Warwick, 144, 158, 159, 163, 204, 219, 221, 230
washable wallpapers, 257
water-based wood stains, 295, 296
Watteau, Jean-Antoine, 128, 330
Watts of Westminster, 69, 74, 75, 78, 79, 80, 81, 84, 86, 97, 98, 99, 100, 108, 112, 146, 150, 151, 207, 212, 213, 215, 216, 231, 232, 244, 245, 252, 255, 257, 259, 270
Waveney Apple Growers, 361
waxes, 290, 292
weaving:
carpets, 362
"color and weave", 173
"dobby" looms, 78
Jacquard looms, 78
power looms, 116
tapestry, 82
Welbeck Tiles, 331
Wellington House, New York, 330
Wemyss Houlès, 190, 191, 192, 194
Wendy Cushing Trimmings, 186, 187, 188, 190, 191, 193, 194
Wendy Wilbraham, 324
Westbond, 375
Westco, 356, 377, 380, 381
Wharton, Edith, 180
white paint, 288
whitewash, 288
Whitty, Thomas, 364
Wicanders, 357
Wiener Werkstätte, 49, 234
Wilton carpets, 23, 362, 364, 366
Winchester Tile Co., 301, 303, 304, 305, 312, 313, 314, 315, 317, 325, 329, 333, 339, 343, 346
wood:
finishes, 294-7
flooring, 350-7
paneling, 14
wood effects:
sheet flooring, 382
wallpapers, 202, 250
wood-laminate flooring, 356
Woodward Grosvenor, 366, 368, 369, 371
wool:
carpets, 372
damask, 72
wool (continued):
matting, 359
Worcester tapestries, 84
wreath motifs:
carpets, 365
fabrics, 89
Wright, Frank Lloyd, 368

Yorkshire Tile Co., 308, 310, 312, 336, 342, 345, 347

zillij designs, tiles, 341
Zimmer & Rohde, 62, 63, 64, 65, 69, 70, 73, 75, 100, 101, 109, 111, 153, 158, 159, 160, 161, 162, 163, 171, 173
Zoë Barlow Passementerie, 187, 189
Zoffany, 69, 75, 91, 94, 97, 131, 133, 135, 147, 161, 167, 200, 209, 211, 213, 214, 215, 218, 219, 228, 229, 240, 241, 242, 258, 266, 267, 269, 272, 273, 275
Zuber, 39, 97, 150, 152, 207, 210, 212, 214, 217, 238, 241, 242, 253, 255, 256, 258, 269

Acknowledgments

I would very much like to thank the design, editorial, and production team at Mitchell Beazley for all the long hours, dedication, and skill they have committed to this book: Emma Boys, Kenny Grant, and Estelle Bayliss for tackling a vast array of source material and turning it into a comprehensive and informative visual treat; Penelope Cream for her efficiency in successfully running this large and complex project from beginning to end; Julia North for the intelligence of her editing, and, especially, for her unflagging sensitivity, patience, and encouragement in her dealings with this author; Claire Musters, Anna Nicholas, and Patrick Evans for liaising with manufacturers and eliciting from them information vital to the project; Arlene Sobel for translating the text for our American publisher; Steve Tanner for his photography; and Judith More and Janis Utton for knowledgeably overseeing the text and design. Thanks also to Samantha Gray, Jane Royston, Hilary Bird, Jo Wood and Glen Wilkins for their help in the production of the book.

I would also like to offer heartfelt thanks to the following for kindly allowing location photography: Lee Anderson; Andrew Lowe House; Sue Andrews; Roger Banks-Pye; Cornelia Bayley; Alison & Kip Bertram; Calhoun Mansion; Cedar Grove; Château de Compiègne; Comoglio Showroom; Colline Covington; Clifford Ellison; John Evert; Ruth Fane; Garth Woodside Mansion; Geffrye Museum; Christophe Gollut; Jacques Granges; Richard Gray; Paul & Lisa Grist; Richard Hampton Jenrette; Amelia Handegan; Michael Harris; Thierry & Agnès Hart; La Heredia; Jonathon Hudson; Charles Jencks; Mr. & Mrs. Michael Keehan; Wendy Kidd; Lyn von Kirsting; Leeds Castle; Ian Lieber; Linley Sambourne House; Lord & Lady McAlpine; The Malt House; Marshall Schule Associates; Justin Meath Baker; Jim & Debbie Millis; Janet Milner; Issey Miyake; Morris Jumel Mansion; Monmouth Mansion; Françoise Lafon; Nathaniel Russell House; The Old Merchant's House; Eileen O'Neill; Jaime & Janetta Parlade; Parham House; Tom Parr; Jack & Tasha Polizzi; Rockliffe Mansion; Rosalie Mansion; Ivy Rosequist; Jackl Sadoun; Dennis Severs; Shaker Museum; Lars Sjöberg; Keith Skeel; Sir John Soane Museum; Annie & Lachlan Stewart; Eric & Gloria Stewart; St. Mary's, Bramber; Temple Newsam House; Maryse and Michel Trama; David Warbeck; West Green House; Louis de Wet; Lillian Williams.

Picture Credits

Andrew Martin International (70 bc, p91 br); Attica (37, 326); Baumann (142–3); Bradbury & Bradbury (44-5 [Jeremy Samuelson], 206 [Ron Mitchell], 245 box br [Douglas Keister]); Tommy Candler (7); De Gournay (243 box); Dulux (280 l, 289, 291 bl, 358-9); Fired Earth (306-7 t, 334); James Merrell (316, 327 tl); Osborne & Little (1, 54, 66, 174, 250 tl, 327 b); Naim (376, 377 t); Reed Consumer Books Limited/Bill Batten (125)/Paul Bricknell (216)/Geoff Dann (250 bl)/Peter Marshall (198, 199 b)/James Merrell (2, 4, 12, 13 t/b, 14 t/b, 15, 16, 17, 18, 19, 20, 21, 22, 23 t/b, 24, 26 l, 28, 29 t/b, 30-1, 32 l, 33, 34-5, 36, 37 t, 38, 39, 40, 41 t/b, 42, 43 t/b, 46 l/r, 47, 48, 49, 50, 51, 52, 53 t/b, 58, 59 t/b, 67 t/b, 72 t/b, 73 l, 82, 83 bl/br/tl, 88 t/b, 89, 106 t/b, 107 t/b, 124, 125, 142 t/b, 155, 156, 157 t/b, 175 bl/tl, 184, 185 t/b, 199 t, 207 t/b, 222, 223, 238, 239 b/t, 250 tr/bl, 265 t/b, 280 t/b, 282, 285, 287, 288, 291 t, 294, 295 br, 300 t/b, 301, 306 bl/tl/b, 317 t/b, 334, 340, 341 t/b, 350, 351 t/b, 358 t/b, 362 b, 363, 376-7 b)/Kim Sayer (362 t)/Steve Tanner (10-11, 56-7, 196-7, 208-9, 278-9, 298-9, 348-9)/Andrew Twort (291 r)/Simon Upton (55, 264, 290, 295); Sanderson (27, 54); Vymura (249 Barbie™ © 1997 Mattel, Inc.; Thomas The Tank Engine™ © Britt Allcroft [Thomas] Limited 1997).

Style Guide

Fabrics

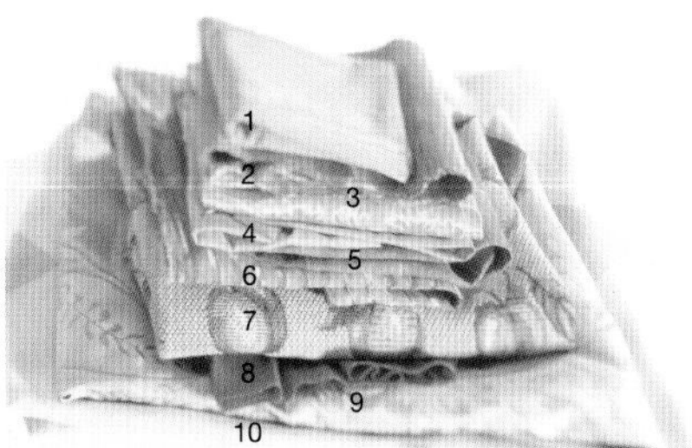

Wallpapers

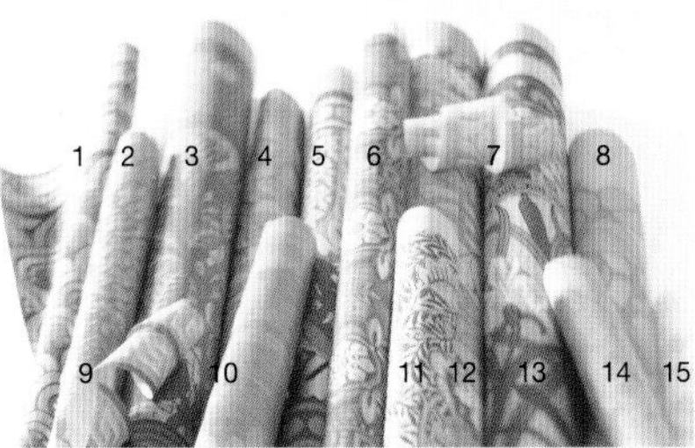

Paints & Finishes

Tiles

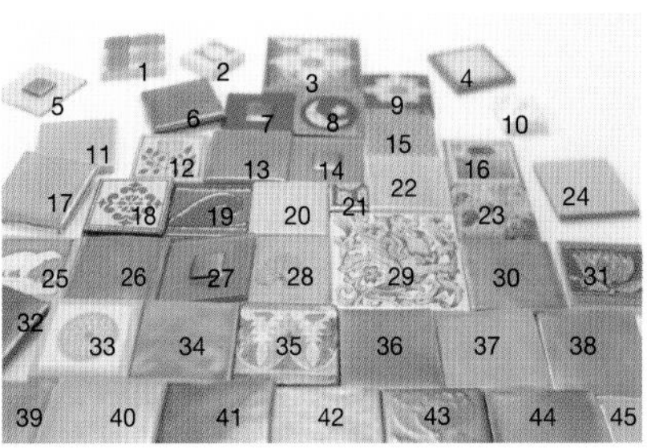

Flooring

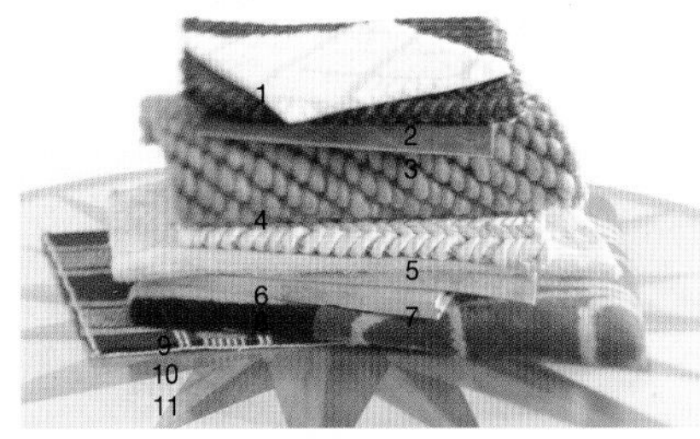

Guide To Chapter Opener Samples

Style Guide

1 Carillo Terracotta on White, Elon; **2** Honey, Winchester Tile Co; **3** Inlaid Wenge Border, Victorian Wood Works; **4** Beta, Henry Newbery & Co; **5** Vaison, Brunschwig & Fils; **6** Clarendon, Zoffany; **7** Peacock Border, Original Style; **8** Pompeiian Red, Weld Yellow, and Half Indigo, Fired Earth; **9** Les Abeilles, Percheron; **10** Middle Hertford, Zoffany.

Fabrics

1 Marvic Moiré, Marvic Textiles; **2** Spinato, Antico Setificio Florentino; **3** Crevelli, Watts of Westminster; **4** Adriatic Antique Taffeta, Scalamandré; **5** Matour, Warwick; **6** Luminescence, Jack Lenor Larsen; **7** Taranto, Sahco Hesslein; **8** Idris, Zimmer & Rohde; **9** Newport Damask, Scalamandré; **10** Amberley, G. P. & J. Baker.

Wallpapers

1 Eastlake Dado, Bradbury & Bradbury; **2** Pineapple Seton, Watts of Westminster; **3** Pomegranate Panel, Bradbury & Bradbury; **4** Cerises, Jean Louis Seigner; **5** Victory Frieze, Bradbury & Bradbury; **6** Algernon, Bradbury & Bradbury; **7** Egg-and-Dart Border, Zoffany; **8** Glasgow Panel, Bradbury & Bradbury; **9** Grècque Frieze, Mauny; **10** Venice Damas Or, Zuber; **11** Clementina, Bradbury & Bradbury; **12** Alcove Chambre de la Reine, Zuber; **13** Iris Frieze, Bradbury & Bradbury; **14** Triad, Watts of Westminster; **15** Kensington Ceiling, Bradbury & Bradbury.

Paints & Finishes

Supplied by The Paint Library. **1** Ming; **2** Sophia Rose; **3** Deep Water Green; **4** Blixel Coral; **5** Chelsea Green; **6** Lilac; **7** Blue Venom; **8** Galway Blazer; **9** Lullaby; **10** Hathaway.

Tiles

1 Blue Checks, Anta; **2** Enbluefish, Fired Earth; **3** English Rose, Fired Earth; **4** Trellis G, Elon; **5** Lilac Dichroic Sparkle, Mosquito; **6** Blue/Green, Winchester Tile Co; **7** Cobalt Blue Dichroic Sparkle, Mosquito; **8** Magic Lantern, Kenneth Clark Ceramics; **9** Pattern 21, Corres Mexican Tiles; **10** Gothic Fleur de Lys Corner, Fired Earth; **11** Candyfloss Pink, Winchester Tile Co; **12** Tulip, Kenneth Clark Ceramics; **13** Turquoise, Winchester Tile Co; **14** Green Dichroic Sparkle, Mosquito; **15** Multi, Imports Direct; **16** Elephant, Kenneth Clark Ceramics; **17** Gray/Blue, Winchester Tile Co; **18** Panita B, Fired Earth; **19** Waves, Kenneth Clark Ceramics; **20** 502, Tiles of Newport & London; **21** Izmir Corner 4, Fired Earth; **22** Sky Blue, Winchester Tile Co; **23** Verde Alpi Marble 188, Tiles of Newport & London; **24** Carillo Yellow, Elon; **25** Polar Bear, Kenneth Clark Ceramics; **26** Periwinkle, Winchester Tile Co; **27** Aqua Dichroic Sparkle, Mosquito; **28** Fossil Aquamarine Leaf, Fired Earth; **29** Assyrian Left Field Tile, H. & R. Johnson; **30** Blue, Winchester Tile Co; **31** Tubeline Tulip Border, Kenneth Clark Ceramics; **32** Azure Blue, Winchester Tile Co; **33** Midi, Kenneth Clark Ceramics; **34** Provence Pink, Fired Earth; **35** Ceramica Alhambra, Walker Zanger; **36** Gray, Winchester Tile Co; **37** Provence Yellow, Fired Earth; 38 Pale Turquoise, Winchester Tile Co; **39** Turquoise, Winchester Tile Co; **40** Pink, Winchester Tile Co; **41** Leaf Green, Elon; **42** Carrillo Intense Yellow, Elon; **43** Tubeline Flowers, Kenneth Clark Ceramics; **44** Provence Blanc Ancien, Fired Earth; **45** Celadon, Winchester Tile Co.

Flooring

1 Pastiche, Afia; **2** Loop, Chatsworth; **3** NM-97, Amtico; **4** Bubble, Chatsworth; **5** Natural Matting, Chatsworth; **6** Brissac Border, Stark; **7** Slate T84, Karndean; **8** Sylvaket, Junckers; **9** Keyboard, Chatsworth; **10** Havorford, Afia; **11** Medallion No. 319, Historic Floors of Oshkosh.